KT-562-814

THE MARK TWAIN PAPERS

THE MARK TWAIN PAPERS

Of the projected fifteen volumes of this edition of Mark Twain's previously unpublished works the following have been issued to date:

MARK TWAIN'S LETTERS TO HIS PUBLISHERS, 1867–1894
edited by Hamlin Hill

MARK TWAIN'S SATIRES & BURLESQUES
edited by Franklin R. Rogers

MARK TWAIN'S WHICH WAS THE DREAM?
edited by John S. Tuckey

MARK TWAIN'S HANNIBAL, HUCK & TOM
edited by Walter Blair

MARK TWAIN'S MYSTERIOUS STRANGER MANUSCRIPTS
edited by William M. Gibson

MARK TWAIN'S CORRESPONDENCE WITH HENRY HUTTLESTON ROGERS
edited by Lewis Leary

MARK TWAIN'S FABLES OF MAN
edited by John S. Tuckey
text established by Kenneth M. Sanderson
and Bernard L. Stein

MARK TWAIN'S NOTEBOOKS & JOURNALS, VOLUME I
edited by Frederick Anderson
Michael B. Frank
and Kenneth M. Sanderson

MARK TWAIN'S NOTEBOOKS & JOURNALS, VOLUME II
edited by Frederick Anderson
Lin Salamo
and Bernard L. Stein

MARK TWAIN'S NOTEBOOKS & JOURNALS

VOLUME I
(1855–1873)

Edited by Frederick Anderson
Michael B. Frank
and Kenneth M. Sanderson

Mark Twain

UNIVERSITY OF CALIFORNIA PRESS
Berkeley, Los Angeles, London 1975

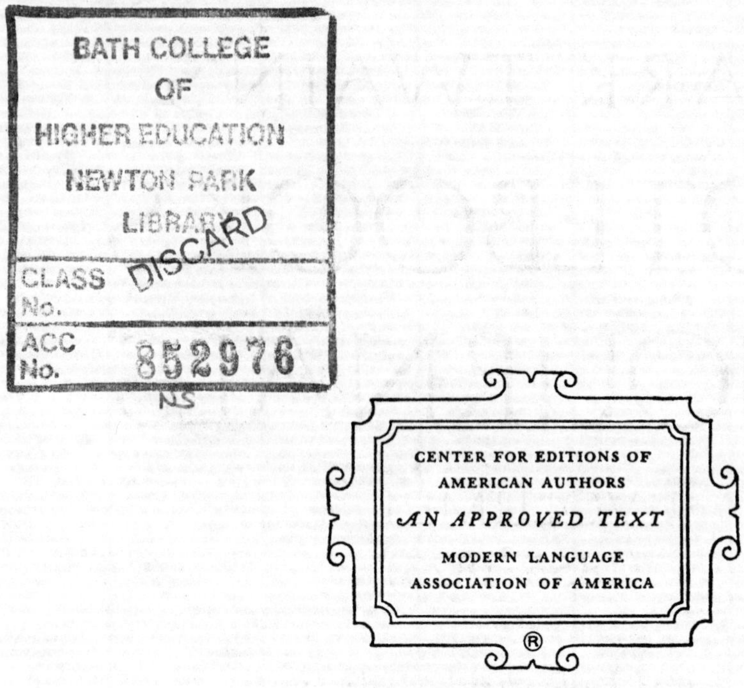

Editorial expenses for this volume have been in large part supported by grants from the National Endowment for the Humanities of the National Foundation on the Arts and Humanities administered through the Center for Editions of American Authors of the Modern Language Association.

UNIVERSITY OF CALIFORNIA PRESS
Berkeley and Los Angeles, California

UNIVERSITY OF CALIFORNIA PRESS, LTD.
London, England

Library of Congress Catalog Card Number: 72–87199
ISBN: 0–520–02326–9

Designed by Adrian Wilson
in collaboration with James Mennick

Manufactured in the United States of America

Preface

For twenty-five years after Samuel Clemens' death his designated biographer and editor, Albert Bigelow Paine, collected and edited his letters, his hitherto unpublished literary works, his Autobiographical Dictations, and finally, in 1935, a volume called *Mark Twain's Notebook*. In the *Notebook* Paine presented less than one-quarter of Clemens' journal entries, randomly selected and reordered to suit the editor's preferences. Now, on the occasion of the full publication of the complex documents from which Paine drew his earlier version, it seems appropriate to evaluate Paine's editorial labors against current standards of textual scholarship.

As Mark Twain's biographer, Paine was industrious, comprehensive, and, by the test of sixty years, surprisingly fair. Despite the absence of citations to sources for his information, despite his disregard for the dates of events, and even in spite of his preoccupation with the social figure rather than the creative man, Paine's biography is still the Mark Twain scholar's central reference. Those who followed him have in many instances corrected errors and introduced new evidence, but they have not substantially altered Paine's portrait. As Mark Twain's biographer, Paine served his subject, his readers, and subsequent generations very well in most respects.

Paine was also energetic in editing Mark Twain's work for posthumous publication, but here the value of his service to the reading public is less clear. In the year the author died Paine published a volume of Mark Twain's speeches, which he revised and reprinted fourteen years later. Seven years after Clemens' death, Paine, having completed and published the massive biography, presented a two-volume collection of letters. This is an interesting although arbitrary selection, and the reader is virtually unwarned that many letters have been silently censored, rearranged, and conflated.

In 1916 Paine contrived a version of Mark Twain's "Mysterious Stranger" manuscripts, deliberately pruning, amplifying, and reordering the original material in a manner which departed significantly from the author's intention. His literary decisions were so persuasive that the book was looked upon as an example of Mark Twain's major writing and its text remained virtually unchallenged for nearly five decades. Scholars with access to the Mark Twain Papers were aware that the book in print had been drastically revised from the surviving manuscripts, but the extent of Paine's editorial liberties became generally known only with the publication of *Mark Twain's Mysterious Stranger Manuscripts* in 1969.

Paine presented *Europe and Elsewhere* as a collection of loosely related shorter writings in 1923. No text of any of these pieces stands up under collation with its manuscript. *Mark Twain's Autobiography,* which Paine printed in two volumes a year later, contains less than one-half of the original document. Since the published portion is drawn from the first part of the manuscript, it is reasonable to suppose that the editor was deflected from a more ambitious undertaking either by other interests or by the publisher's lack of enthusiasm, perhaps as a result of disappointing sales. In the portion he selected Paine acted on Mark Twain's instructions in excluding parts of the autobiography, but he also deleted unfavorable references to living persons and suppressed those distortions of truth which reveal the imaginative reshaping of supposedly factual narrative.

To exploit the centenary of Mark Twain's birth, in 1935 Albert Bigelow Paine performed his final and most perfunctory editorial chore, *Mark Twain's Notebook*, supplying only casual documentation. With a misleading appearance of candor, the editor asserted in his introduction to that volume:

> A good while ago I wrote a biography of Mark Twain. In that book I drew briefly here and there upon the set of journals, diaries, or commonplace books which through a period of nearly fifty years he had kept and, what is still more remarkable, preserved. These little books are now offered in full. A man in his diary, if anywhere, can have his say. He is talking to himself—his thought and his language are strictly his own. Some of the things that Mark Twain set down in that privacy were hardly suited to the unadorned cheek of polite society in that purer pre-war day. Now all is changed. (*MTN*, pp. x–xi)

This editorial approach sounds promising, but the statement is dishonest. "Now offered in full" is contradicted by a comparison of the number of words in Paine's 1935 selection (120,000, including interspersed remarks by Paine) with the full text of roughly 450,000 words exclusive of editorial commentary. Among the words available in the present edition are a number which Paine apparently did not consider appropriate even for the no longer "unadorned cheek" of his society.

Yet there is no intention of claiming that this complete text of the notebooks offers shocking revelations about Mark Twain, since the documents have long been available to biographers and critics who have put on the record the facts Paine chose to ignore. The reader will likewise be disappointed if he expects to find here a writer's literary journals. To be sure, there are literary references throughout, and even occasional passages of sustained prose narrative. Primarily, however, the notebooks are those of a man actively engaged in society, in public affairs, in all of the time-wasting business enterprises which so appealed to Clemens but which were of such little real benefit to him. Still, the very nature of the random miscellany of reminder and comment has literary value. As Mark Twain in his Autobiographical Dictations felt he could most effectively present the truth of his life by allowing current interests and events to stimulate his rambling commentary on the past, so his notebooks provide the context of the distracting daily business and social activities within which the enormous quantity of his literary work was produced. The wide variety of comments on his world, its affairs, and his associates who populated it allows us to move with the author through place and time and experience. Perhaps here more than anywhere else we have the definitive autobiography of Mark Twain.

F. A.

Acknowledgments

THROUGHOUT the many years of preparation of *Mark Twain's Notebooks & Journals* almost every scholar concerned with Mark Twain—and innumerable others outside that restricted field—has supplied in person or through his published works information and advice which makes this edition possible. Recognition of specific indebtedness appears throughout the editorial material. A full list of the names of all the contributors would be impossible to reconstruct, but gratitude to each of them is no less great for their anonymity.

Among the research and editorial assistants employed in the Mark Twain Papers at early stages in the preparation of the notebooks in this volume, Evan Alderson, Rob Haeseler, Stuart Kiang, Linda Mullen, Susan Severin, Susan Sheffield, and John Reid performed outstanding work. Jill Youn and Wendy Won patiently typed the various stages of text, tables, footnotes, and headnotes.

The project has been supported by the financial aid of the University of California and of the Samuel Charles Webster Memorial Fund, made available through the generous bequest of Mrs. Webster. The Center for Editions of American Authors, under the directorships of William M. Gibson and Matthew J. Bruccoli, has supplied necessary grants in support of the preparation of texts for this volume.

Professor Henry Nash Smith by instruction and by example has been an editorial guide throughout. There is no way to express the acknowledgment properly due to him.

F. A.

Contents

Abbreviations

The following abbreviations have been used for citations in this volume. Unless otherwise indicated, all materials quoted in the documentation are transcribed from originals in the Mark Twain Papers, The Bancroft Library, University of California, Berkeley.

AD	Samuel L. Clemens' Autobiographical Dictation(s) (typed manuscript in MTP).
CCD	"Quaker City" Journal of Captain Charles C. Duncan, MS in Patten Free Library, Bath, Maine.
DV	Prefix designating literary manuscripts in the Mark Twain Papers.
MS	Manuscript
MT	Mark Twain
MTP	Mark Twain Papers, The Bancroft Library, University of California, Berkeley.
PH	Photocopy
SLC	Samuel L. Clemens
TS	Typescript

Published Works Cited

CG — *Contributions to "The Galaxy" 1868–1871 by Mark Twain*, ed. Bruce R. McElderry, Jr. (Gainesville, Florida: Scholars' Facsimiles & Reprints, 1961).

FM — *Mark Twain's Fables of Man*, ed. John S. Tuckey (Berkeley, Los Angeles, London: University of California Press, 1972).

HH&T — *Mark Twain's Hannibal, Huck & Tom*, ed. Walter Blair (Berkeley and Los Angeles: University of California Press, 1969).

JLS — *Journal Letters of Emily A. Severance* (Cleveland: Gates Press, 1938).

LAMT — Edgar M. Branch, *The Literary Apprenticeship of Mark Twain* (Urbana: University of Illinois Press, 1950).

LE — *Letters from the Earth*, ed. Bernard DeVoto (New York: Harper & Row, 1962).

MTA — *Mark Twain's Autobiography*, ed. Albert Bigelow Paine (New York: Harper & Brothers, 1924).

MTAb — Dewey Ganzel, *Mark Twain Abroad* (Chicago: The University of Chicago Press, 1968).

MTB — Albert Bigelow Paine, *Mark Twain: A Biography* (New York: Harper & Brothers, 1912).

MTBus — *Mark Twain, Business Man*, ed. Samuel C. Webster (Boston: Little, Brown and Co., 1946).

MTE — *Mark Twain in Eruption*, ed. Bernard DeVoto (New York: Harper & Brothers, 1940).

MTH — Walter Francis Frear, *Mark Twain and Hawaii* (Chicago: Lakeside Press, 1947).

MTHL — *Mark Twain-Howells Letters*, ed. Henry Nash Smith and William M. Gibson (Cambridge: Harvard University Press, Belknap Press, 1960).

MTL	*Mark Twain's Letters,* ed. Albert Bigelow Paine (New York: Harper & Brothers, 1917).
MTLBowen	*Mark Twain's Letters to Will Bowen* (Austin: University of Texas, 1941).
MTLP	*Mark Twain's Letters to His Publishers,* ed. Hamlin Hill (Berkeley and Los Angeles: University of California Press, 1967).
MTMF	*Mark Twain to Mrs. Fairbanks,* ed. Dixon Wecter (San Marino, California: Huntington Library, 1949).
MTN	*Mark Twain's Notebook,* ed. Albert Bigelow Paine (New York: Harper & Brothers Publishers, 1935).
MTS (1910)	*Mark Twain's Speeches,* ed. Albert Bigelow Paine (New York: Harper & Brothers, 1910).
MTSF	*Mark Twain's San Francisco,* ed. Bernard Taper (New York: McGraw-Hill Book Co., 1963).
MTTB	*Mark Twain's Travels with Mr. Brown,* ed. Franklin Walker and G. Ezra Dane (New York: Alfred A. Knopf, 1940).
PRI	*The Pattern for Mark Twain's "Roughing It,"* ed. Franklin R. Rogers (Berkeley and Los Angeles: University of California Press, 1961).
S&B	*Mark Twain's Satires & Burlesques,* ed. Franklin R. Rogers (Berkeley and Los Angeles: University of California Press, 1967).
SCH	Dixon Wecter, *Sam Clemens of Hannibal* (Boston: Houghton Mifflin Co., 1952).
SSix	*Sketches of the Sixties* (San Francisco: John Howell, 1927).
TIA	*Traveling with the Innocents Abroad,* ed. D. M. McKeithan (Norman: University of Oklahoma Press, 1958).
WG	*The Washoe Giant in San Francisco,* ed. Franklin Walker (San Francisco: George Fields, 1938).

Calendar

IN AN EFFORT to clarify the numbering of the notebooks, a new sequence has been substituted for that originally used for the typescripts in the files of the Mark Twain Papers. Since the typescript numbers have been frequently cited in print, this calendar lists both the previous and the present numbering systems.

The calendar also contains the inclusive dates for each of the notebooks published in this volume and provisional dates, in brackets, for notebooks to be published in forthcoming volumes. The dating comes from references made by Clemens and from internal evidence when there was no specific notation of a beginning or a terminal date. While many of the notebooks begin or end on specified days, the dating for many is so vague that only the month that Clemens started or finished an individual notebook is known. Therefore, only the month and year that a notebook covers have been listed here. The headnote for each notebook discusses the period of its use.

Notebooks in Volume I

No.	Former No.	Date	Location
1	1A	June–July 1855	Missouri, Iowa
2	1	April–July 1857	Mississippi River
3	2	November 1860–March 1861	Mississippi River

4	3	January–February 1865	California
5	4	March, June–September 1866	San Francisco, Sandwich Islands
6	5	March–April 1866	San Francisco, Sandwich Islands
7	6	December 1866–January 1867	San Francisco to New York City
8	7	May–July 1867	New York City, *Quaker City*
9	8	August–October 1867	*Quaker City*
10	9	August–December 1867	*Quaker City*, Washington, D.C.
11	10	July 1868	San Francisco to New York City
12	10A	June–July 1873	England, Belgium

Forthcoming Notebooks

No.	Former No.	Date
13	11	[May–July 1877]
14	12	[November 1877–July 1878]
15	12A	[July–August 1878]
16	12B	[August–October 1878]
17	13	[October 1878–February 1879]
18	14	[February–September 1879]
19	15	[July 1880–January 1882]
20	16	[January 1882–January 1883]
21	16A	[April–May 1882]
22	17	[May 1883–September 1884]
23	18	[October 1884–April 1885]
24	19	[April–August 1885]
25	20	[August 1885–January 1886]
26	21	[May 1886–May 1887]
27	22	[September 1887–July 1888]
28	23	[July 1888–September 1889]

29	24	[May 1889–December 1890]
30	25	[October 1890–June 1891]
31	26	[August 1891–July 1892]
32	26A	[May 1892–January 1893]
33	27	[March 1893–July 1894]
34	28	[March–December 1895]
35	28A	[May–October 1895]
36	28B	[December 1895–March 1896]
37	29	[January–April 1896]
38	30	[May–July 1896]
39	31	[September 1896–January 1897]
40	32	[January 1897–July 1899]
41	32A	[January–July 1897]
42	32B	[June 1897–March 1900]
43	33	[1900]
44	34	[1901]
45	35	[1902]
46	36	[1903–1904]
47	37	[1904]
48	38	[1905–1908]
49	39	[1910]

Introduction

IN THE summer of 1855, when the nineteen-year-old Sam Clemens traveled from Saint Louis to Hannibal, Paris, and Florida, Missouri, and then to Keokuk, Iowa, he carried with him a notebook in which he entered French lessons, phrenological information, miscellaneous observations, and reminders about errands to be performed. This first notebook thus took the random form which would characterize most of those to follow.

Two years later, according to his account in chapter 6 of *Life on the Mississippi,* Sam Clemens apprenticed himself to Horace Bixby, pilot of the *Paul Jones,* to learn "the Mississippi River from New Orleans to St. Louis for five hundred dollars." During his second four-hour watch Clemens was questioned by Bixby about the "points" they had passed during the preceding watch. When it became clear his apprentice had not learned "enough to pilot a cow down a lane," Bixby told him "in the gentlest way":

> "My boy, you must get a little memorandum-book, and every time I tell you a thing, put it down right away. There's only one way to be a pilot, and that is to get this entire river by heart." . . . By the time we had gone seven or eight hundred miles up the river, I had learned to be a tolerably plucky upstream steersman, in daylight, and before we

> reached St. Louis I had made a trifle of progress in night-work, but only a trifle. I had a note-book that fairly bristled with the names of towns, "points," bars, islands, bends, reaches, etc.; but the information was to be found only in the note-book—none of it was in my head.

Notebooks 2 and 3, as a result, consist largely of entries almost unintelligible to contemporary readers; their interest is confined to technical documentation of Mark Twain's account of his piloting apprenticeship as given in *Life on the Mississippi*. Extracts consisting of approximately one-fourth of the total text and extending even to the inclusion of a laundry list provide a full and honest sense of the original documents. Presentation of further material to fulfill some principle of completeness could only needlessly try the reader's patience.

Perhaps because of his wanderings and perhaps because of the lack of commitment to a career, no notebooks survive—if any were kept—to record Clemens' brief Civil War experience, his excursion to the West, or most of the years he was a reporter in Virginia City and San Francisco. Nevertheless, in a column which appeared in the 3 February 1863 Virginia City *Territorial Enterprise*—the first which he is known to have signed "Mark Twain"—the author commented, "I have the various items of his supper here in my note-book." At the end of a letter to the *Enterprise* on 13 September of the same year, Clemens made another tantalizing reference to an unknown journal. "I have got a note-book full of interesting hieroglyphics, but I am afraid that by the time I am ready to write them out, I shall have forgotten what they mean." It is probable the notes were in shorthand, and it is likely the information was incorporated in letters to the newspaper. Clemens' uncertainty about his capacity to decipher the notes suggests that he was not accustomed to carrying a notebook with him; nevertheless, there is little doubt that an effort was made, at least in 1863, to use notebooks and that they are lost. Early in 1865 Mark Twain had a notebook when he heard a version of the yarn he would publish as "The Celebrated Jumping Frog of Calaveras County" and when he recorded anecdotes which would enrich *Roughing It*. Notebook 4 is the first notebook intended for literary purposes that survives.

Upon receiving a commission to go to the Sandwich Islands in the spring of 1866 to report on conditions there for the Sacramento *Union*, the developing writer took at least three notebooks along. The two that survive are crammed with accounts of the people and the history of the islands, as well as facts about the current economy. He was now compiling the records and establishing the habits which would so shortly—within four years—transform him from an itinerant journalist into an author of national reputation.

Events of a single month's voyage from San Francisco to New York (with an overland crossing of the isthmus at Nicaragua) occupy one entire journal. The journey from 15 December 1866 to 12 January 1867 allowed Mark Twain to expand his notes into more finished form than had been characteristic of the six preceding notebooks. In contrast, the notebook entries compiled during the early summer of 1867 in New York City are feverish, as Mark Twain hastily recorded information for his letters as traveling correspondent of the San Francisco *Alta California* before embarking on the trip described in *The Innocents Abroad.*

Unlike those kept by many of his fellow passengers on that *Quaker City* cruise, Mark Twain's journals record systematically all but the most uneventful stretches of the voyage and the intermittent overland treks. The one interruption results from the loss of a notebook which contained his accounts of travel from Marseilles to Paris and through France, Switzerland, and Italy. The next surviving notebook resumes with the ship's departure from Naples on 11 August 1867.

Upon his return to New York and during a short stay in Washington, his use of notebooks subsided temporarily, since he was no longer committed to regular newspaper correspondence. Notebook 11 gives an account of a trip from New York to San Francisco in 1868 and contains two long fictional narratives written during that voyage.

No notebooks record the hectic years from 1869 through 1872, during which Clemens was courting Olivia Langdon, accumulating money by grueling lecture tours, seeing his first major book into print, and setting himself up, with his father-in-law's substantial aid, as a newspaper publisher and prominent citizen of Buffalo. There are indications that Clemens continued to keep notebooks during that period, although none have been found. On 17 December 1869, while on a lecture tour, he wrote a letter from Boston to his sister Pamela on three sheets of paper which are indisputably pages torn from a notebook. A further indication of this use of a notebook appears in a letter written on 6 January 1870 to Mrs. Fairbanks: "I always write to Livy in this way—in my note-book, after I go to bed." A letter to his fiancée dated 30–31 October 1869 (on twenty-one leaves from a ruled notebook) documents this practice. If the notebooks were consistently used for letters, as well as for ephemeral notes about his lecturing schedule, their disappearance is explained and even their real status as journals becomes doubtful.

When Clemens traveled to England in May 1873 he was accompanied by his wife, his two-year-old daughter Susy, a nursemaid, Livy's friend Clara Spaulding, and a young theological student, S. C. Thompson, who was to be Clemens' secretary. Thompson transcribed, largely in shorthand, a number of comments dictated by Clemens which are presented here as Notebook 12. The arrangement between Thompson and Clemens proved unsatisfactory, however, and Thompson was discharged after about two months. A tantalizing, if facetious, reference indicates that Clemens himself may also have kept a notebook during this period, although there is no other record of it. In an account of the visit of the shah of Persia to England, titled "O'Shah," dated 19 June 1873 Mark Twain wrote:

> When we first sailed away from Ostend I found myself in a dilemma; I had no notebook. But "any port in a storm," as the sailors say. I found a fair, full pack of playing cards in my overcoat pocket—one always likes to have something along to amuse children with—and really they proved excellent to take notes on, . . . I made all the notes I needed. The aces and low "spot" cards are very good indeed to write memoranda on, but I will not recommend the Kings and Jacks.

Many of Thompson's notes concern themselves with the arrival of the shah, and there is no conclusive evidence that Clemens was maintaining a concurrent notebook of his own, although he would do so nine years later when he again employed a stenographer, Roswell Phelps, to accompany him down the Mississippi.

No notebooks have been found for the span of four years after 1873. Mark Twain moved to Hartford where he built a house and became engaged in an established family life and the social and professional commitments of an author whose career was flourishing. It is possible these activities did not require the use of notebooks.

The next journal records an excursion to Bermuda in 1877, and it may be that Clemens needed the stimulus of travel to revive his habit of maintaining a portable record of his activities. Once revived, the habit was firmly fixed, and from 1877 to the year of his death, we have a scarcely broken sequence of notebooks. (A calendar of all forty-nine notebooks and their dates precedes this Introduction.) It is readily apparent from the customary interruption of notebook entries in early summer and their regular resumption about the first of October that Mark Twain did not make use of notebooks while at Quarry Farm, the Clemens family's summer residence. Life there was tranquil and secluded and the author's orderly days were each devoted to extending the previous day's work in the study where he wrote his major books.

Mark Twain's Use of His Notebooks

Mark Twain's evolving practice of maintaining his journals and converting them to literary use was most forthrightly expressed in an interview printed in the Bombay *Gazette* on 23 January 1896:

> It is a troublesome thing for a lazy man to take notes, and so I used to try in my young days to pack my impressions in my head. But that can't be done satisfactorily, and so I went from that to another stage—that of making notes in a note-book. But I jotted them down in so skeleton a form that they did not bring back to me what it was I wanted them to furnish. Having discovered that defect, I have mended my ways a good deal in this respect, but still my notes are inadequate. However, there may be some advantage to the reader in this, since in the absence of notes imagination has often to supply the place of facts.

In curious contrast to the actual use of notebook entries to stimulate and guide his writing, Mark Twain occasionally employed "quotation" from his journals as a literary device. Perhaps to suggest a sense of immediacy in his travel writings, Mark Twain would pretend to quote passages from his journals when little or no literal relationship exists between the supposed extract and the equivalent notebook passage. Lengthy accounts of life in the Sandwich Islands printed in *Roughing It* are preceded by such statements as

> In my diary of our third day in Honolulu, I find this . . .
>
> I still quote from my journal . . .
>
> I resume my journal at the point where . . .

The quoted passages were actually taken from the travel letters sent by the author to the Sacramento *Union.* A more puzzling pretense about material taken from notes pervades "My Platonic Sweetheart" (written in 1898), where the author purportedly refers to his journals for records of dreams which he describes in detail. But no related information appears in any of the notebooks we have, although at least one quite different dream is recorded in Notebook 40.

Although Clemens manufactured references to notebooks, he did in fact make literary use of information in the notebooks and upon occasion read back through his file of journals, as is indicated by retrospective comments in them often dated many years after the original entry was made. The Autobiographical Dictations provided a final impulse to examine the record of his earlier years. For example, he commented on 6 February 1906 regarding his daughter Susy's biography of him, written in 1885: "Yesterday while I was rummaging in a pile of ancient note-books of mine which I have not seen for years, I came across a reference to that biography."

Although Clemens himself was their intended reader, his private journals exhibit indications that he anticipated they might be seen by other eyes as well. Evidence of this, and of his own instinctive sense of propriety, is the habitual omission, abbreviation, or deletion of profane or indecent words and anecdotes. Perhaps he feared the notebooks might be read by members of his family. Quoting a passage from Notebook 13 to Howells on 27 June 1878 (the notes described Captain Ned Wakeman's entrance into heaven), Clemens mentioned that "Mrs. Clemens, who even reads note-books in her hunger for culture, was rather startled to run across this paragraph in mine, last night." Yet his practice of obscuring indelicate allusions preceded Clemens' marriage and persisted after his wife's death.

There are signs that Clemens was sensitive to the style of expression which emerged from hasty and haphazard notations in his journals. More than once he ridiculed a monotonous series of his notebook jottings. Very near the end of *The Innocents Abroad* Mark Twain illustrated a comment on "what a stupid thing a note-book gets to be at sea, anyway" by quoting a lengthy excerpt. This led the author to reminisce about a journal he pretended he kept as a boy, in which his record of each day's events consisted of "Got up, washed, went to bed." Mark Twain claimed he was so discouraged by the uneventfulness of his youthful days that "That journal finished me. I never had the courage to keep one since." Nevertheless, notebooks accompanied Clemens through most of his life, and it is fortunate they did. For a writer whose creative work thrived best when drawn from his own experience and direct observation, his spontaneous and immediate record of that experience provides an invaluable opportunity to examine the fact behind fiction.

The first significant alteration in the format that the notebooks had maintained for over four decades occurred, almost symbolically, at the turn of the century. In 1900 Clemens put aside the notebooks that measured approximately 4 by 6½ inches in favor of appointment books whose dimensions were about 2 by 3¼ inches. Although he continued to inscribe ideas for literary work, the entries focus on social and business affairs and present an almost oppressive repetition of tag lines for anecdotes and expurgated dirty jokes which must have become excessively familiar to the companions to whom they were told.

A single notebook reverting to the larger size contains entries which range from 1905 through 1908. Only approximately one-eighth of the pages were used, and the trivial entries they contain bear dates out of chronological order. It was during these four years that Mark Twain turned his attention to his Autobiographical Dictations which frequently record opinions that might earlier have found their way into pocket journals. It was also during this period that Mark Twain was most dependent upon a full-time secretary to attend to his daily affairs. The household journals Isabel Lyon had been keeping since 1903 began in 1906 to assume the tone of first-person remarks made by her employer. These journals too infrequently reflect Mark Twain's own language, however, to qualify as amanuensis notebooks.

The last notebook in Clemens' hand was kept during the physically and emotionally painful weeks in Bermuda shortly before he died. It reflects the sad, often querulous, responses of a man whose interests have contracted to immediate and inconsequential matters. The notebook was labeled by Albert Bigelow Paine: "This book is a private record made by Mark Twain, and must not be sold or given out in any way for fifty years following his death."

Sources for the Texts

Forty-five of the forty-nine notebooks known to exist are in the Mark Twain Papers. Most of them have accompanied the Papers throughout their moves from Redding, Connecticut, to the Widener Library at Harvard University to the Henry E. Huntington Library in San Marino to the University of California in Berkeley, where they are now one of the permanent collections in The Bancroft Library. Two of the notebooks—those kept for the "tramp abroad" in 1878 with the Reverend Joseph Twichell—were given to Twichell by Mark Twain after his account of their travels, *A Tramp Abroad*, was written. They are now in the American Literature Collections, Beinecke Library at Yale University, which freely made them available for this edition. One notebook kept between May 1892 and January 1893 appeared for sale at an auction in London in 1959 and was purchased for the Rare Book Collections at the University of Texas, Austin, through whose courtesy its text appears here. The first notebook Clemens is known to have kept came into the custody of his sister Pamela Moffett, whose daughter Annie gave it in turn to her son Samuel Charles Webster. It was among the manuscripts owned by Mr. and Mrs. Webster in 1954, when they had a photographic copy made for deposit in the Mark Twain Papers. No Mark Twain manuscripts owned by the Websters were in Mrs. Webster's possession at the time of her death in 1967, and their location is not yet known. Consequently the text for this notebook had to be established from the photocopy without reference to the original. The texts of all other notebooks have been prepared from the original documents.

The Text of the Notebooks

In order to avoid editorial misrepresentation and to preserve the texture of autograph documents, the entries are presented in their original, often unfinished, form with most of Clemens' irregularities, inconsistencies, errors, and cancellations unchanged. Clemens' cancellations are included in the text enclosed in angle brackets, thus <word>; editorially-supplied conjectural readings are in square brackets, thus [word]; hyphens within square brackets stand for unreadable letters, thus [--]; and editorial remarks are italicized and enclosed in square brackets, thus [*blank page*]. A slash separates alternative readings which Clemens left unresolved, thus word/word. The separation of entries is indicated on the printed page by extra space between lines; when the end of a manuscript entry coincides with the end of a page of the printed text, the symbol [#] follows the entry. A full discussion of textual procedures accompanies the tables of emendation and details of inscription in the Textual Apparatus at the end of each volume; specific textual problems are explained in headnotes or footnotes when unusual situations warrant.

Annotation of the Notebooks

A series of documents encompassing Mark Twain's adult life, a life which ranged from Missouri villages to European capitals, must contain many references so obscure they cannot be annotated, or so well known their explanation would offend the reader's intelligence. Every effort has been made to recover the obscure and to strike a balance in anticipating the reader's need for information not available in standard books of reference.

The erratic nature of the notebooks, with their diverse and often almost compulsive record of minute matters, allows us access far closer than more formal documents to the movements of a man's mind at a distant time. In order to guide the reader through this cryptic record of activities and observations, the documentation often is necessarily longer than the original entry. Since so much of the information in the notes has been assembled from a variety of sources, themselves often unpublished or otherwise very nearly inaccessible, citation to these is customarily confined to material directly quoted, with a bibliography of the most useful related material in the headnote where that seems appropriate.

Apart from the general discussion in headnotes concerning published material which derives from each notebook, no attempt has been made to collate notebook entries with their development in literary form except when such reference is necessary for an understanding of an entry. Occasional references to specific literary themes or topics which are not readily identifiable are made when it seems likely they might otherwise escape the reader's notice. Even these are selective and do not pretend to identify each instance in which ideas for characters or episodes are reworked in the various phases of the author's writing. What appear to be tag lines for jokes persist throughout the notebooks. Variant repetitions when assembled sometimes provide the substance of the anecdote, but since the form and language of these stories were doubtless adjusted for the raconteur's audience, their full versions have been left to each reader's imagination.

When no useful information can be assembled to document a troublesome entry, there is no statement of editorial failure. Mark Twain's comments on persons, events, or other subjects out of any recoverable context may result from spontaneous recall or anticipation, proposed literary projects, pure association, or his diverse reading. On one occasion Clemens himself remarked: "One often finds notes in his book which no longer convey a meaning—they were texts, but you forget what you were going to say under them" (Notebook 17). Later editors can seldom be more successful than the original inscriber in recovering the intention behind such entries.

I

"What I Was at 19-20"

(June–July 1855)

Samuel Clemens' forty-nine surviving notebooks had their genesis in a small account ledger which originally was intended to serve as a French lesson copybook. This first notebook presents evidence that the nineteen-year-old printer was learning chess as well as French, reading a book on phrenology, examining a theological controversy, and assisting in his family's business affairs. Although intrigued by feminine traits, he was surprisingly reticent about romantic emotions, observing and describing a young lady's personal characteristics with the same detachment with which he made out a laundry list. The impartial manner in which Clemens juxtaposed the ephemeral and trivial with matters of larger significance provides an index to his multiple interests, influences, and experiences in the summer of 1855. Entries in this notebook appear to have been made first in Saint Louis, then in Keokuk, Iowa, and afterwards during an excursion to three villages in Marion and Monroe counties, Missouri—Hannibal, Florida, and Paris.

Saint Louis in 1855 provided ample excitement and diversions even for a young man who had just returned from a *Wanderjahr* in New York City, Philadelphia, and Washington, D.C. Its population was nearly 125,000, and it was growing rapidly, although it still had characteristics of a frontier trading post. At midcentury Saint Louis was the thriving commercial center for all trade in the Upper Mississippi region, a point of exchange for raw material from the West and finished products from the East, for lumber and furs from the northern territories, and for hordes of emigrants coming up the river from New Orleans.

The site of major activity and the source of the city's prosperity and importance was the Mississippi levee. Nearly 3,500 steamboat arrivals were recorded at the Saint Louis wharves during the navigable season in 1855. There is evidence in this notebook and in a surviving letter of the period that even as early as 1855 Sam Clemens was trying without success to enter the respected profession of the riverboat pilot. In the spring of that year he appealed to a distant relative in Saint Louis, James Clemens, Jr., for an introduction to one of the veteran pilots with whom the businessman was acquainted, but the elder Clemens discouraged him from pursuing this ambition.

Another, more sympathetic relative residing in Saint Louis was William A. Moffett, who had married Pamela Clemens in 1851. Mark Twain would recall him many years later in an Autobiographical Dictation (29 March 1906) as "a fine man in every way." Moffett was prospering as a commission merchant and in 1853 had served on the Committee of Arbitration for the Saint Louis Chamber of Commerce. It was he who would advance Sam Clemens the down payment of $100 to begin his training as a pilot in 1857.

For the time being, however, Clemens was compelled to support himself by working as a printer, as he had during his recent travels. Opportunities in that trade were numerous in Saint Louis: 858 printers were employed by twenty-one newspapers and twelve magazines in the city, and additional jobs were available in eight book and job printing offices. There is an indication in this notebook that Sam Clemens hoped to find employment on the *Daily Evening News*, a Whig paper founded in 1852.

Some idea of the way Clemens felt about the city itself may be gathered from a letter which he would send to the San Francisco *Alta California* when he revisited Saint Louis in 1867. "I found it . . . the same happy, cheerful, contented old town—a town where the people are kind and polite, even to strangers—where you can go into a business house you never saw before and speak to a man you never heard of before, and get a perfectly civil answer" (*MTTB*, pp. 133, 141).

But his feelings toward Saint Louis were ambivalent. In 1868 he commented somewhat cryptically to Mrs. Fairbanks that "there is something in my deep hatred of St. Louis that will hardly let me appear cheery even at my mother's own fireside. Nobody knows what a ghastly infliction it is on me to visit St. Louis. I am afraid I do not always disguise it, either" (*MTMF*, p. 38). His earlier enthusiasm had ignored the civil disorders which resulted from antagonism between adherents of the Know-Nothing party and the German and Irish populations. Clemens may have witnessed the worst episode, the "election riots" of August 1854, when belligerent mobs invaded the Irish section of town, looting homes and exchanging occasional gunfire with residents who tried to block their way. Mark Twain mentions these riots in chapter 51 of *Life on the Mississippi,* where he recalls his decision to desert from a hastily formed militia of young men mustered to control the rampaging mobs.

Which of the Saint Louis disorders in the mid-fifties Clemens witnessed cannot be determined now because the meager evidence blurs his dates of residence in that city. It is known that he lived there in the summer of 1853, when he first left Hannibal on his way to see the Crystal Palace Exhibition in New York City. But statements regarding his return from this eastern excursion are speculative. Albert Bigelow Paine believed that Clemens returned "late in the summer of 1854" and then visited his family in Muscatine, Iowa, before returning to work on the Saint Louis *Evening News* (*MTB*, pp. 102, 103). A later historian, Fred W. Lorch ("Mark Twain in Iowa," *Iowa Journal of History and Politics* 27 [July 1929]: 414–417), was unable to find anything conclusive about Clemens' movements except a few indications that Clemens stayed in Muscatine longer than Paine suggests, perhaps for several months, before leaving that town for Saint Louis.

In any event, it is clear that he was again a resident of Saint Louis by 16 February 1855, when he wrote the first of two letters from there that were published in his brother Orion's Muscatine *Journal*. His second letter, written on 5 March 1855, reveals Clemens' acute interest in affairs along the river levee, and both letters document his regular attendance at lectures and theatrical productions. Moreover, the 24 February 1855 issue of the Saint Louis *Missouri Republican* includes Clemens in a list of persons having letters held for them at the Saint Louis Post Office.

Entries in the notebook show that during the month of July 1855 Clemens visited at least three towns in Missouri on business for his family.

He began his errands with a visit to Erasmus Moffett, William Moffett's brother, and Erasmus' wife, Sarah, in Hannibal. From Hannibal Clemens went to Florida and Paris, probably traveling part of the way on the plank road whose construction his uncle John A. Quarles had championed. Clemens may have worked for awhile in Saint Louis after he returned from this trip, but it is more likely that he went directly to Keokuk, 214 miles up the river, to join his younger brother Henry as a typesetter in Orion's never prosperous Ben Franklin Book and Job Office.

The town of Keokuk was in the midst of a boom during 1855 and 1856. Contemporary handbooks for the encouragement of Iowa immigration emphasized the geographic advantages of Keokuk: it merited its title, "The Gate City," because it was situated at the foot of the eleven-mile-long "Lower Rapids" on the Mississippi, which made it a transfer point for steamboat traffic during a great part of the year; it lay near the mouth of the Des Moines River, which carried trade into the fertile Des Moines Valley; moreover, at least three railroads were constructing lines toward the town. Clemens would mention the arrival of the first railroad locomotive in Keokuk in a letter to Henry Clemens on 5 August 1856. Ironically, it was these railroads that later nullified the advantages of Keokuk's location on the river. A canal that circumvented the river rapids, described by Mark Twain in chapter 57 of *Life on the Mississippi* as "a mighty work which was in progress there in my day," also led to its subsequent decline. But in 1855 and 1856 Keokuk could fairly claim advantages over most other cities along the Mississippi.

Because of its flourishing commerce, Keokuk's civic improvements were greater than might be expected in a western city incorporated as recently as 1847. Its Main Street was macadamized, the city had been connected to trunk telegraph wires for several years, and on 4 January 1856 it would be illuminated by gas street lamps. In 1857 Orion Clemens reported in his *Directory and Business Mirror* that there were three daily papers and three weeklies. Orion owned the only book and job printing shop in the town, but at least three of the newspapers also competed for this trade.

As in Saint Louis, the Know-Nothings swept into public office in the years of Clemens' residence in Keokuk, demonstrating the growing "Native American" sentiments among inhabitants of a town that had expanded from 620 persons in 1847 to more than 6,000 in 1855. By 1856 the population had soared to 11,000, and a year later, in 1857, it had reached 15,000. There was also another, even more heated national controversy which was engaging Keokuk citizens: the border location of Lee County, Iowa, insured vigorous, continuing debate on slavery and the actions of abolitionists in the years preceding the Civil War.

The scantiness of surviving data makes it difficult to determine how deeply "Native American" and slavery issues affected Clemens at the time. It is a matter of record, however, that he later expressed adult disdain for the views he held as a youth. On 1 November 1876 he wrote a slashing self-criticism to J. H. Burrough, with whom he had roomed in a Saint Louis boarding house:

> I can picture myself as I was, 22 years ago. . . . You think I have grown some; upon my word there was room for it. You have described a callow fool, a self-sufficient ass, a mere human tumble-bug, stern in air, heaving at his bit of dung & imagining he is re-modeling the world & is entirely capable of doing it right. Ignorance, intolerance, egotism, self-assertion, opaque perception, dense & pitiful chuckle-headedness—& an almost pathetic unconsciousness of it all. That is what I was at 19–20. (Kent Library, Southeast Missouri State College, Cape Girardeau)

The present location of Notebook 1 is not now known; consequently, the text has been taken from photostats of the original supplied to the Mark Twain Papers in 1954 by Mrs. Samuel Charles Webster, when the notebook was in her possession. Her husband published extracts from the notebook in chapter 3 of *Mark Twain, Business Man* in 1946.

The photocopy shows 36 pages, 4 of them blank. Pairs of facing blank pages were evidently not photographed. The photostats of the pages measure 5¹⁵⁄₁₆ by 3¹¹⁄₁₆ inches (15.1 by 9.4 centimeters). The pages are ruled with twenty-one horizontal lines and have a wide top margin that appears, except in a sequence of four pages, at the bottom of Clemens' page. The pages are divided by vertical lines into four unequal columns in account ledger fashion. The photographed cover appears to be paper and to be only loosely attached to the pages.

Variations in Clemens' writing materials cannot be determined from the photocopy. His handwriting in this notebook, while beginning to show the characteristics of his mature hand, is small, neat, and in accord with the conventional penmanship of the period.

Since the pages were not numbered when the photocopy was made, their sequence has been established from content and such physical evidence as tears along the spine and bent corners. The interruption of the phrenology passages and their erratic sequence, the inversion of the notebook to inscribe four pages, and the cramped appearance of some entries may indicate that Clemens wrote part of the notebook in an order other than that which appears here. However, in the absence of firm evidence, the physical sequence established from the photocopy has been followed throughout, except that Clemens' running titles for his French lessons (such as "Leçon 11") have been removed where he did not use the pages on which they appear for his language studies. Omitted headings are recorded as emendations.

Bibliography of Related Materials

In addition to the local newspapers of the period and the city and business directories for Saint Louis and Keokuk from 1853 until 1859, the following sources provided historical and genealogical descriptions relevant to Notebook 1:

History of Lee County, Iowa. Chicago: Western Historical Co., 1879.

Hyde, William and Conard, Howard L., eds. *Encyclopedia of the History of St. Louis.* 6 vols. New York: Southern History Co., 1917–1918.

Lorch, Fred W. "Mark Twain in Iowa," *Iowa Journal of History and Politics* 27 (July 1929): 408–456.

Saint Louis: The Missouri Historical Society. Mary C. Clemens Collection. Contains biographical information about James Clemens, Jr., of Saint Louis.

Scharf, John Thomas. *History of Saint Louis City and County.* 2 vols. Philadelphia: Louis H. Everts & Co., 1883.

Varble, Rachel M. *Jane Clemens: The Story of Mark Twain's Mother.* Garden City, New York: Doubleday & Co., 1964.

Webster, Samuel C., ed. *Mark Twain, Business Man.* Boston: Little, Brown, and Company, 1946.

Three individuals were especially helpful in assisting with research on Notebook 1. Ralph Gregory, curator of the Mark Twain Birthplace Memorial Shrine at Florida, Missouri, supplied valuable facts about Clemens' 1855 visit to that region; Mrs. Goldena Howard of the Reference Library and Mrs. Alma Vaughan of the Newspaper Library in the State Historical

Society of Missouri, Columbia, rendered repeated services in locating important information.

Samuel L. Clemens[1]

10 o'clock Saturday night on board steamer Westerner[2]

Carr Place[3]

[*unrecoverable words*]

Lesson 1.

Sur la langue Francaise
On the French language.
Les jours de la semaine.

---

[1] Both the front and back notebook covers are embellished with examples of Clemens' youthful signature, which vary in calligraphy as well as in form. The young man experimented with signing himself "Samuel L. Clemens," "S. L. Clemens," and simply "Clemens." Other writing on the covers, perhaps including additional signatures, is discernible but not recoverable from the photocopy.

[2] The *Westerner* was one of six steamboats operated by the St. Louis & Keokuk Packet Line. In 1855 the red-and-buff-painted steamers left Saint Louis daily at 5:00 P.M. for points upriver. Built in 1853, the sidewheel *Westerner* was praised by the Hannibal *Missouri Courier* as "perhaps the finest and most agreeable boat for travel, on the Western waters" (11 May 1854). The steamboat sank without loss of life on 3 January 1855 but was recovered in February and restored to operation during the spring of that year (Saint Louis *Daily Missouri Democrat*, 7 April 1855). She resumed her place in the regular schedule of Keokuk packets on 6 June, according to the Saint Louis *Missouri Republican*.

[3] Carr Place was a "delightful suburban resort" operated by Horatio Wood, where Saint Louis residents were invited to enjoy "an elysium of the beautiful and enjoyable things of Earth" (Saint Louis *Daily Missouri Democrat*, 7 May 1855). In addition to the "flowers and roses, and trees and music, and fair women" as well as "delicious ice creams," praised by one newspaper columnist (*Democrat*, 9 June 1855), the Carr Place pleasure ground offered such occasional attractions as balloon ascensions (with free admission for clergy and Sunday school classes), spiritualist performances, cotillion parties, exhibitions of exotic animals, and spectacular fireworks.

The days of the week.

Lundi,	Monday.
Mardi,	Tuesday.
Mercredi,	Wednesday.
Jeudi,	Thursday.
Vendredi,	Friday.
Samedi,	Saturday.
Dimanche	Sunday.
Son père	His father.
Sa mère	Her mother.

Cigars .... [.]25
Fare to H. .... 2[.]00[4]

Lesson 2.

Ton frère	Thy brother.
Ta soeur	Thy sister
Ma tante	My aunt.
Mon oncle	My uncle.
Moi mem,	Myself.
Ah, mon Dieu!	O, my God!
Cher papa,	Dear papa.
Oui <mamma> mamam,	Yes, mamma
Amitie	Friendship
Bon citoyen	Patriot.
Untre nous	Between ourselves.
Je suis Americain,	I am Americ[an]
Bontè	Goodness.

Lesson 3.

Gateau,	Cake.
Danser,	To dance.
Bouton de rose	Bud of rose.
Allumette	Match.

[4] Presumably, this was deck passage fare from Saint Louis to Hannibal. Clemens may have taken the *Westerner* for this fourteen-hour voyage upstream.

Aimer	To love.
Garçon	Boy.
Baisser	Kiss
Nè libre	Free born.
Pètit	Small.
Ma patrie	My native land.
Je pari	I bet.
Billet doux	Love letter
C’est just	That is right.
A votre service	At your service

Leçon 4.

Les mois de l’annèe.

The <seasons> months of the year.

Janvier,	January.
Fevrier,	February.
Mars,	March.
Avril,	April.
Mai,	May.
Juin,	June.
Juillet	July.
Aou,	August.
Septembre	September.
Octubre	October.
Novembre,	November.
Decembre,	December.

Leçon 5.

Les saisons de l’annèe.

The seasons of the year.

Le printemps.	The spring.
L’Etè,	The summer.
L’Automne	The autumn
L’Hiver,	The winter.
L’Europe,	Europe.
L’<Asiè>Asié,	Asia.

L'Afrique	Africa
L'Amerique	America
Canif,	Penknife.
Crayon,	Pencil.
Dormer,	Sleep.
Allons.	Let us go.

Lecon 6.

Bonjour, Monsieur,
Good morning, sir.
Bonsoir, Mademoiselle
Good evening, Miss.
Bonne nuit, Madame.
Good night, Madam.
Adieu, Messieurs.
Good-bye, Gentlemen.
Apprenez vous, le Francais?
Do you learn French?
Parlez vous Espagnol?
Do you speak Spanish?
Restez tranquille!
Stay still.
C'est moi, le Docteur Ricard
It is I, Doctor Ricards.

Leçon 7.

Feu de joie,	Bonfire.
Montrè le moi	Show it to me
Arretez.	Stop.
Pas plus.	No more.
Encore	Again
Assez.	Enough.
Je ne veut pas	I won't
Ca ira	That will do.
Debout	Standing

Ça et la	Up and down.
J'ai peur	I am afraid
Lentement,	Slowly.
Je n'aimie pas ça.	I don't like it.[5]

Uncle John[6] tells of one Ross—a very lazy man, who would cut down enough brush to make a respectable pile, then lay down and go to sleep near it. One day a neighbor caught him napping—crept up behind the brush pile, and called out "Ross! Ross! Ross!' Ross raised up and glanced

The Sanguine Temperament[7]

The third temperament is the "*Sanguine*," named from the blood. And as the blood is the furnace of the body, and carries the fire and flame by which the whole is warmed, it is but natural to suppose that this is the warming temperament. We read about "hot bloods." They are the people in whom this temperament predominates. It is the burning, flaming, flashing temperament.

---

[5] Although Clemens prepared headings through "Leçon 11," other interests intruded, and there are no additional language exercises until the last manuscript page of this notebook. He was making these notes either from oral lectures or an unidentified French grammar. The more advanced French entries in Notebook 3 suggest that he continued his study during the intervening years. Clemens' misplaced accents and other foreign language solecisms would persist throughout his life.

[6] Perhaps Clemens' uncle, John Quarles; perhaps fictional. Ross will appear again nineteen pages further on in the original notebook (p. 31 in the present text), but this anecdote remains obscure.

[7] A large proportion of the following entries records Clemens' introduction to an auxiliary theory of phrenology, the division of mankind into four predominating "temperaments." Phrenologists believed that bodily constitutions conformed with psychological dispositions. Clemens copied these classifications of human appearance almost verbatim from a handbook on character analysis written by a Saint Louis clergyman, the Reverend George Sumner Weaver's *Lectures on Mental Science According to the Philosophy of Phrenology* (New York: Fowlers and Wells, 1852), pp. 74–80. The exception to exact transcription occurs in the account of the sanguine temperament, where Clemens modified Weaver's descriptions to correspond to his own characteristics. Weaver had asserted that those dominated by the sanguine temperament generally possessed blue eyes; at that point Clemens added "or gray," to accord with his own eye color, described variously as blue or gray. He

Hence, it hangs out its signs of fire in its red, blazing hair and countenance, its florid or sandy skin. It has blue eyes or gray round full features; pliable, yielding muscles; full ample chest; generally, a thick, stout build; sometimes, chestnut hair. It gives activity, quickness, suppleness to all the motions of body and mind; great elasticity and buoyancy of spirit; readiness, and even fondness for change; suddenness and intensity to the feelings; impulsiveness, and hastiness of character; great warmth of both anger and love; it works fast and tires soon; runs its short race and gives over. It is fond of change; light, easy, active labor; fond of avocations that require but little hard labor, and much of out-of-door jollity (*not always*). It loves excitement, noise, bluster, fun, frolic, high times, great days, mass meetings, camp meetings, <c>big crowds, whether for religious, political, or social purposes. It is always predominant in those active, stirring, noisy characters that are found in every community. It is very sensitive and is first deeply hurt at a slight, the next emotion is violent rage, and in a few moments the cause and the result are both forgotten for the time being. It often forgives, but never entirely forgets an injury. It loves with a wild intensity, but gets over it soon, when deprived of the stimulus afforded by the *presence* of its object. It feels grief and sorrow most bitterly, but soon becomes calm, and forgets it all. It confers

---

similarly qualified Weaver's statement that people of sanguine temperament are fond of "out-of-door jollity" with the laconic remark "(*not always*)." Clemens entirely composed two sentences, inserted into Weaver's description of the sanguine temperament, which claim that: "It is very sensitive and is first deeply hurt at a slight, the next emotion is violent rage, and in a few moments the cause and the result are both forgotten for the time being. It often forgives, but never entirely forgets an injury." Equally revealing is the fact that Clemens moved the sanguine temperament from third position in Weaver's list to first in his own. The "notes" that follow and summarize each of the four temperaments were entirely devised by Clemens; Weaver does not include such synopses in his book. George Sumner Weaver (1818–1908) appears in the 1854/55 Saint Louis city directory as pastor of the Universalist church. These and other facts concerning Clemens' lifelong curiosity about phrenological character detection are discussed by Alan Gribben in "Mark Twain, Phrenology and the 'Temperaments': A Study of Pseudoscientific Influence," *American Quarterly* 24 (March 1972): 45–68.

the most perfect elasticity to the mind, and the sprightliest buoyancy to the spirit. It makes warm friends and fiery enemies, and they may be both friends and enemies in the same day, and be perfectly sincere. It has a ready tongue; is quick and sharp of speech; is full of eloquent flights and passionate appeals; is ardent, pathetic and tender, <the> to the last degree: can cry and laugh, swear and pray, in as short a time as it would take some people to think once.

Notes.—Sandy hair; light gray eyes—flash and glitter under excitement <; not very>. Also, *light or red hair*, florid or sandy skin; *blue eyes*; round, full features; full, ample chest; thick, stout build; sometimes chestnut hair. Quick action, quick speech & quick decision; when under no compulsion, is restless, & will not sit long in one place; constantly casts his eye from one place to another.

Bilious.

Four temperaments, viz:—The Osseous, or Bony; the <c>Circulatory or Sanguineous; the Digestive or Nutritious; and the Nervous. No. 1, Bilious. No. 2, Sanguine. No. 3, Lymphatic. No. 4, Nervous.

The first is called the "*bilious*" temperament, and is named from the osseous system. This is the skeleton, or framework of the body. Much of the strength and durability of the body depends upon the excellence of this system. It is this which sustains the weight of the body and bears its numerous burdens. X[8] When this temperament is properly developed, it gives a full, fair-sized, well-formed, and well-proportioned frame. The bones are neither too large nor small, nor the joints too clumsy, nor the frame too heavy, nor light. When it is strongly developed, so as to give its peculiar marks, it gives a dark, heavy, lowering aspect to the countenance, by its large arched eyebrows; large nose; high and prominent cheekbones; coarse black hair; large, black eyes; rough, bony forehead; and heavy chin. The

---

[8] This X is apparently for emphasis, since it does not have any counterpart in Weaver's text.

bones are large and angular; the joints large and rough; the whole framework strong and coarse. The complexion is dark, and the skin exhibits a somewhat coarse organization. It gives slow, heavy, awkward motions to the body, and confers strength and powers of endurance. It is slow to move, slow to work, and slow to get tired.—It is always best on a long race, and in the afternoon. It is the all-day temperament. It is powerful, but slow. It gives to the mental actions the same peculiarities that it does to the bodily.—coarseness, awkness, slowness, and power. It is often found in some of the greatest and most powerful of men, united with *good* sanguine and nervous temperaments. Daniel Webster and Thomas Corwin[9] are perhaps its two best living examples. Men of this temperament are seldom found in the higher ranks of literature, art or science. They are formed for power, but not for those nice, fine, keen perceptions which are necessary for the highest walks of life. If they are men of power, they are generally found in the field of political or military strife. Men of this tem. can bear burdens, losses, misfortunes, opposition, well; because they do not feel so acutely and sensitively as those of a different organization. Still, when anything does affect them, it affects them strongly, and they have not that elasticity of spirit which others often have, to throw off a load of oppression or despondency. They fail in buoyancy and elasticity of mind. They are permanent, firm, and enduring in power and feeling.

Note.—Dark complexion; large arched eyebrows; large nose; high cheek bones; coarse black hair; large black eyes; rough, bony forehead, heavy chin; coarse skin.[10] [#]

---

[9] Weaver had delivered the lectures on which he based his book in 1851 at the Western Liberal Institute of Marietta, Ohio, a denominational academy operated by Weaver's brother-in-law and sister. Thomas Corwin's name would have been familiar to any audience of Ohio students, as Corwin was a former Ohio governor and U.S. senator, then serving President Fillmore as secretary of the treasury.

[10] The notebook was inverted at this point, and four pages were used for the following notes, which interrupt the description of the temperaments. Since it is not now possible to determine the sequence of writing, the entries are printed in the order in which they physically appear.

Hopson's[11] notion of hell—between <Heav> the sun and earth—Manford's[12] reply—<Sodom & Gomorrah> Says "Hell *is* there, for it sprung a leak and <[bu]> the drippings set fire to Sodom and Gomorrah and burnt them up."

"Little red Rocking Chair; the Maps; Press—and everything that is mine—also, the books at Miller's[13] store, and rocking <[-]> chair at Sally Moffett's."[14] "Send up our secretary, table, press, &c."[15]

Let some of the rent (about $3) go for paint for the window sills.[16]

A thousand years from now this race may have passed away, and in its stead, a people sprung up, wearing the skins of animals for

---

[11] Winthrop Hartly Hopson (1823–1889) entered the ministry of the Christian Church in 1841 and in 1843 received an M.D. degree from McDowell College in Saint Louis. He continued evangelical work, made many converts, and was instrumental in founding schools and colleges. Hopson's espousal of a fundamentalist doctrine of eternal damnation and inexorable suffering made inevitable his disagreement with Erasmus Manford (1815–1884), a Saint Louis Universalist minister. Universalist ministers at the time were frequently debated by the more orthodox clergy because of the Universalists' belief in the eventual salvation of all souls.

[12] Evidently, Manford had ridiculed Hopson's concept of Hell in a way which also mocked the biblical account of Sodom and Gomorrah. Although Clemens' tone is noncommittal, here is evidence of an early encounter with conflicting doctrines which he would long examine. See page 33 for John Quarles' reaction to the controversy. Clemens may have been reading *The Golden Era*, a Universalist magazine published in Saint Louis at this time by Manford, assisted by George Sumner Weaver. Both Manford and his wife, Hannah Webster Bryant Manford, lectured and debated in Hannibal and the surrounding communities in the 1850s. Manford's controversial views included the belief that certain biblical stories should be regarded as figurative parables, rather than as literal truth.

[13] Thomas S. Miller and George B. Pogue had been partners in a wholesale grocery and general commission firm in Hannibal since 1852.

[14] Sarah M. Moffett, Pamela's sister-in-law, was the wife of Erasmus M. Moffett, wholesale grocer and commission merchant in Hannibal. Their two children had died in the early summer of 1853 (see Hannibal *Missouri Courier*, 9 June 1853).

[15] The quotation marks which enclose the instructions about furniture indicate that Clemens was recording dictated directions about distribution of family possessions which had been left in Hannibal.

[16] Orion Clemens is evidently giving his brother directions about repairs for the Clemens house at 206 Hill Street in Hannibal, which had been rented since Orion and his wife moved to Keokuk and Jane Clemens joined Pamela and William Moffett in Saint Louis.

raiment, and for food eating the berries that may grow where now stand the prouder buildings of this town. And this people will dig up with their rude instruments some memorial of the forgotten race—a steam boiler, perhaps—and gaze with <wonder> astonishment upon it, and wonder who <wh> made it; what they made it for; whence they came, and whither they are gone.[17]

Jas. Clemens must write to O that all back rents are paid,[18] and send this writing to Mr. Green, so that purchasers may see that there is no encumbrance in this respect—or, if back rents are due, O must pay them immediately, or get Mr. Clemens to consent that Mr. Moffet or O assume the debt, or that the purchaser pay to Mr. Clemens what is due on back rents out of his purchase money

Orion—will send me Ja^s Clemens Jr. written consent to the assignment of the lease and his acknowledgment in writing that all ground rent is paid up to this *date*

And that he is willing that you may assign the lease to another with all the rights therein contained—and that he claims no forfeitures for failures heretofore to pay the ground rent—

---

[17] Clemens had already published a similar reflection on the transitory nature of human affairs in the 8 May 1852 Philadelphia *American Courier*. The vocabulary and thought closely parallel much popular writing of the period.

[18] When John Marshall Clemens' Hannibal property was auctioned for debt in 1843, his distant cousin James Clemens, Jr., a prosperous Saint Louis merchant and real estate investor, bought one of the lots on Hill Street for $330. Samuel Clemens' parents subsequently leased the lot from their relative and built a two-story frame house on it (Hannibal *Courier-Post*, 19 April 1947; *SCH*, pp. 102–103, 121, 290 note 2). After John Marshall Clemens died in 1847, Orion was appointed administrator of his father's estate, and he entered into a new ground lease, written for twenty-five years. In 1855 the yearly rental was thirty-five dollars, in addition to payment of all taxes (Marion County Deed Records).

On 6 August 1855 James Clemens, Jr., would write Orion verifying that no back rents were due. He also approved the sale of the house: "By this same mail I write to your mother and without the least doubt as to her consent to the sale prefer that my consent should pass through her hands and therefore enclose it to her to give or withhold as she may please. . . . I have charged rent and interest up to the 16th October next which ends a year—when you sell you can add rent from that time to 16 Octo. next."

If you will do this I will have but little dificulty in selling the property[19] at your limit & may get more

Your friend
M. P. Green[20]

I will send to Palmyra[21] & get the original lease if it is there—If you have it send it to me—

The Lymphatic.

The second is the "*Lymphatic*" temp. named from the digestive or nutritious system. Every one knows that digesting is the enemy of thinking, and feeling, that the mental processes are in a great measure paralysed by the digestive processes. Hence the Lymphat. temp. cannot be considered a mental temp; it is rather a physical one; and when it predominates we can seldom look for great mentality. Its outward signs are fullness and rotundity of form and limbs, wide, thick, leaden, inexpressive features, thick lips; round, blunt chin; light, complexion, thin, soft, straight, rayless hair; light gray eyes; soft muscles; coarse, soft skin; with a relaxed, unstrung, loose appearance to the whole system. It is the office of this temp. to supply the waste occasiond by the mental. Hence, instead of working, it proposes resting; instead of thinking, it prefers sleeping; instead of excitement, it loves calmness. Instead of anything severe, intense, or active, it chooses a lazy, lubberly laugh. It is the slip-shod and go-easy temp., the eating and sleeping temp., the feeding and fattening temp. It is dangerous to predict intensity, activity, mentality, spirituality, when we find this temperament strongly preponderant. It makes good-natured, easy, quiet, harmless, people. Yet there are sometimes strong minds connected with this temper., but they never hurt themselves with work. They go to bed early, sleep

---

19 Only the house could be sold; the land would have to be leased from James Clemens, Jr. County deed records show that he owned the lot until 1866.

20 Moses P. Green was a Hannibal lawyer who was also serving as city attorney in 1855 (Return Ira Holcombe, *History of Marion County, Missouri* [Saint Louis: E. F. Perkins, 1884], p. 941). This passage, not in Clemens' hand, presumably was inscribed by Green.

21 Palmyra, Missouri, twelve miles northwest of Hannibal, was the county seat of Marion County.

soundly, and rise reluctantly to a late breakfast, which to such good feeders is the strongest temptation to seduce them from their slumbers. Their mental percep are gen'ly dull & cloudy, and actions all sluggish.

Note.—Fullness and rotundity of form and limbs; wide, thick, leaden, inexpressive features; thick lips, round *blunt* chin; light complexion; thin, straight, light hair; *light gray eyes.*

4. The Nervous. (Orion.)

The fourth temp. is the "*Nervous,*" and is just what its name indicates. It is given by the nervous system, & is emphatically the *mental temp*. It is this, and this alone, that gives mind. The others affect the manifestations of mind only as they modify the actions of this. As the nervous system is connected with, and related to the other systems of the body in the most intimate manner, it must be affected more or less by them: But it should be remembered that they affect mind only as they modify the actions of this temp. The nervous system is the mental medium. X[22] When this system is strongly predominant it gives the countenance a strong expression of intellectuality, a deep, clear, serene thoughtfulness, a brilliant dawning of mentality. It generally is shown in light, fragile, active forms; narrow, flat chests; tall stature; large head in proportion to the body, the upper part of the head being the larger; light complexions; thin, fine, glossy hair, usually quite light in color; blue, or hazel eyes; thin lips; sharp nose, narrow chin, or a sharpening of the lower part of the face; a clear, transparent skin; small neck; small, yeielding, flexible muscles; often a stooping posture; and a general lightness and gracefulness of motion. It gives clearness, precision and activity to all the mental perceptions; seeks mental pursuits rather than physical; thinks, loves, aspires, with great ardency and devotion. Its joys, pleasures, griefs, sorrows,—all its feelings are indescribably intense. It enters heart and soul into all it does; is permanent in its mental states, always the same ardent[,] devoted, intense intellectuality. It is the poetic temp., and fills the

[22] This X is apparently Clemens' mark of emphasis.

mind with the flames of poetic fire. It sees and feels every thing under a poetic aspect and character. Its feelings are all ardent passions, and they burn within it like deep, subterraneans fires; yet they are generally of an elevated character. It is the temp. which makes angels on earth, which gives us an idea of angelic feelings, aspirations and affections. The states of mentality to which it will elevate its possessor are altogether indescribable. It is the temper. which makes geniuses, precocious children, people of purely intellectual habits and tastes. In one word, it is the *Mental Temperament*.

Note.—*Thoughtful countenance*: light, fragile, active form; narrow, flat chest; *tall*; large head; at the top; light complexion; thin, fine, *light hair*, glossy; *blue* or *hazel eyes*, thin lips, sharp nose; narrow chin or lower face; clear, transparent skin; small neck; stooping

1—K.P. 2 sq
2—K.B.P. 2 sq
3—K.Kt. to K.B. 3^{d} sq
4—K.B. to Q.B. 4th sq
5 <th> K.Kt. takes K.Kt.P.
6 Q. Checks
7 Q. to K.B. 7th sq checking.
8 Q to her 5th sq, checking.
9 Q. to K. 5th sq checkmating

1—K.P. 2 sq
2—P. takes P.
3—K.Kt. P. 2 sq
4 K.B.P. 1 sq
5. P. takes Kt
6 K. to his 2^{d} sq
7 K to Q. 3^{d} sq
8 K. to his 2^{d} sq[23] [#]

---

[23] Clemens probably recorded this particular chess game for the sake of its abrupt checkmate. Technically the game is a rather amateurish defense against the king's gambit. Black loses with his fourth move, and Black's fifth move insures forced mate in four moves.

Received of Marion Biggs,—commissioner appointed by the Monroe Circuit Court to sell the real estate of Benjamin Lampton and Diana Lampton—the sum of Ninety 15/100 dollars, in part of her distributive share. Paid per Order, this, the 16th of July, 1855.

Jane Clemens,
Per Sam[l] L. Clemens.[24]

$146.35 due to be divided amongst the heirs of Benj. Lampton—due June 14, 1856.

<[--]> 2 plaster figures
8 pictures
2 maps Mo & U.S.
2 spittoons
3 windows
1 stove
1 looking-glass
2 bureaus
8 unpainted split-bottomed chairs.
<r> Rag carpet.[25] [#]

---

[24] Clemens had been sent to the county seat of Monroe County—Paris, Missouri—to collect his mother's share of an estate settlement. Benjamin Lampton was Jane Clemens' father, who had died in 1837; Diana Lampton was her aunt, the wife of Wharton Schooler Lampton. Benjamin Lampton had sold his farms south of Florida, Missouri (comprising 320 acres), to Diana, the wife of his younger brother, in 1836 for use by her and her children. The promissory note on the real estate was never paid in full, however, and the amount of $200 and interest was still owed to Benjamin Lampton's heirs at the time of Diana's death in 1851 and Wharton's in 1853. Diana Lampton's heirs entered a civil suit against the heirs of Benjamin Lampton in 1854 in order to clear title to the farms: the circuit court then sold the land and from the proceeds of the sale paid the remaining balance of the purchase money to the heirs of Benjamin Lampton; the rest of the amount was divided among the heirs of Diana Lampton. Jane Clemens evidently collected money from both actions of the partition suit proceedings, since she was an heir of both Benjamin and Diana Lampton (Ralph Gregory, "Mark Twain's Last Visit to Florida," Paris, Missouri *Monroe County Appeal*, 3 January 1962; Paris, Missouri *Mercury*, 7 March 1854).

[25] This may be an inventory of the Lampton farmhouse effects, but the omission of tables and beds is curious.

Robt. T. & Clarissa Abell (Catholics) married ([Boy] of 15, he)[26] (she married at 15, he at 20. Jolly, fat old lady.—girl 18 and boy 10

Old log hut without roof—yankee Clock—right hand road

Ross: Ross? [*three? words*][27]

Dr. Bibee, of Santa Fe,[28] says Pa bought a lot from him a long time ago, <and p> at $5, and a man wants to buy it from the D^{r} now for $10; but he don't know whether Pa ever paid him for it—or not—thinks if he did, we must have a deed for it somewhere. Look for it.

1 Press
3 Maps. [#]

---

[26] Clemens' scrawled handwriting is nearly illegible here. Robert Thadeus Abell (1805–1858) and Clarissa Spalding were married on 17 January 1826, when he was twenty-one and she was fifteen. They moved to Ralls County, Missouri, from Kentucky in the early 1830s with four infants; family records and U.S. census rolls reveal that by 1855 they had fifteen children. One of their seven sons was fifteen-year-old Robert J. Abell, to whom Clemens refers parenthetically; Isabelle Abell is the girl and Madison B. Abell is the boy mentioned at the conclusion of this entry. Forty-nine-year-old Abell and his forty-five-year-old wife lived on an eighty-acre farm in the predominantly Catholic settlement of Brush Creek, where community activities centered around Saint Peter's Church. Clemens' acceptance of prevailing anti-Catholic prejudice is documented by a comment in his 16 February 1855 letter from Saint Louis to Orion's Muscatine *Journal*: "A new Catholic paper (bad luck to it) is also soon to be established, for the purpose of keeping the Know Nothing organ straight" (*Mark Twain's Letters in the Muscatine "Journal,"* ed. Edgar M. Branch [Chicago: The Mark Twain Association of America, 1942], p. 24).

[27] Clemens' handwriting again deteriorated to near-illegibility with these words,

conceivably from an attempt to write while on a moving vehicle. They may be read as anything from "Die by g—" to "Dirty xg— —." Ross is the subject of an uncompleted anecdote recorded previously in this notebook.

[28] Dr. John S. Bybee, a Kentuckian, was an original settler of Santa Fe, a village in Monroe County about twelve miles southeast of Paris, Missouri. At one time Bybee owned several hundred acres of land in that vicinity and was referred to as the "proprietor" of the little town (*History of Monroe and Shelby Counties, Missouri* [Saint Louis: National Historical Co., 1884], p. 181).

$502.50—City Attor.[29]
2117 dogs killed.[30]

<Tell Mr. Green>
Get letter of int from Uncle John[31] to Sheriff
Am't. in Geoge's hands $107.71.[32]

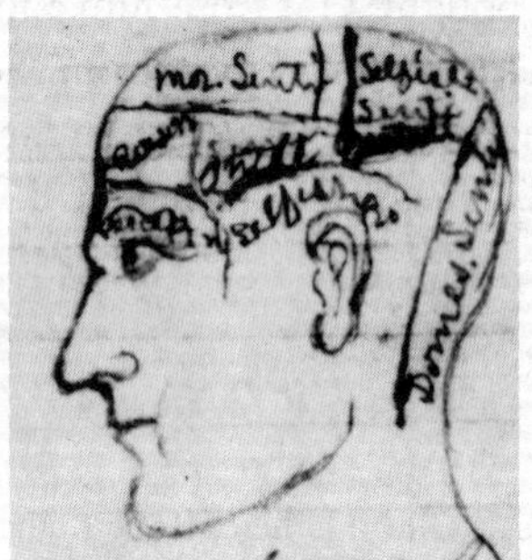
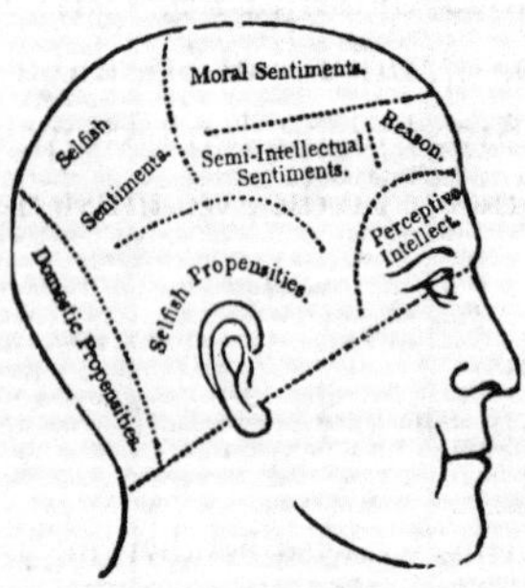

[*Clemens' sketch and the diagram he copied.*][33]

Adhesiveness loves friends; Veneration loves God; Self-Esteem loves self; Conscientiousness loves truth, right, holiness; Hope loves a glorious future; <Benevolent>Benevolence loves an object of

---

[29] Although Moses P. Green was the Hannibal city attorney at this time, there is no available explanation for his association with the amount of money cited.

[30] On 8 June 1855 the Keokuk *Gate City* had noted with approval a published report by the Saint Louis city marshal that 889 stray dogs had so far been slain during "the present season." The Keokuk newspaper added, editorially, "we should be pleased to record similar deeds of blood by the hands of our city officers."

[31] John A. Quarles undoubtedly still had considerable legal influence in the Florida, Missouri, vicinity, where he had been appointed a county court judge in 1850, although he resigned the office in 1852 (*History of Monroe and Shelby Counties, Missouri,* p. 195; Ralph Gregory, "John A. Quarles: Mark Twain's Ideal Man," *Bulletin of the Missouri Historical Society* 25 [April 1969]: 233).

[32] George Glenn was the Monroe County circuit court clerk and was involved in the settlement of Benjamin and Diana Lampton's estates, but there is no clear evidence which connects him with this entry.

[33] Clemens copied the skull diagram which charts the conventional "mental groups" of organs from Weaver's *Lectures on Mental Science* (p. 85). A comparison with the original illustration shows Clemens' painstaking attempts to duplicate the picture in reverse image. He extracted the following description of the "loving power" each phrenological faculty feels toward its particular object from page 95 of Weaver's book.

need; Ideality loves beauty; Comparison loves analogies; Wit loves differences, incongruities. Causality loves the relations of cause and effect; Acquisitiveness loves money; Constructiveness loves mechanics; Tune loves music; Man's whole active nature is expressed by the word *Love.*

Sam Bowen
Sam Clemens
Ray Moss
Wm Smith
Snowden Samuel
Geo. Davis
T. W. <Davis> Priest
Jim Collins
Billy Jackson[34]

Turn that book paper at the Office.[35]

U. J. says—"If Mr. Hopson should speak to me, I would just camly and quietly say to him: 'Now, sir, do you just go home and get down on your knees and pray to God[36] [#]

---

34 The names Samuel L. Clemens, Snoden P. Samuel, George Davis, and Jas. H. Collins appear on the roster of the Hannibal Cadets of Temperance (compiled about 1850). Sam Bowen and his brother Will were Clemens' close friends in Hannibal. Ray Moss was one of the sons of Russell Moss, the wealthy owner of a pork packing firm (see "Villagers of 1840–3," *HH&T*, p. 360). William Smith, T. W. Priest, and Billy Jackson were also presumably Hannibal contemporaries, but there is no explanation for the presence of this list of nine names here.

35 *Book paper* may well refer to a supply of sheets which Orion Clemens eventually would use for printing his *Keokuk City Directory*, to be published in July 1856. The paper would need to be turned occasionally to prevent warping. Orion had taken over the Ben Franklin Book and Job Office in Keokuk on 11 June 1855, and Clemens worked for him from late in the summer of 1855 until the early autumn of 1856. Orion finally sold his shop on the third floor of 52 Main Street in June 1857.

36 According to a writer who visited Florida, Missouri, in 1912 and talked with old-time residents, John Quarles was known to have held unorthodox religious beliefs: "The question of human destiny, the why, the whence, the whither, was always with him. Unable to reconcile it with the accepted dogmas of his people, and driven by the promptings of a vigorous mind and kindly heart, he became a 'Universalist.' What that meant during the days following the revival of Paulinian teaching

Florida, Mo., 16th July, 55.—Introduced to Miss Jule Violett, Miss Em Tandy, and Miss Em Young.[37]

Tall, slender, rather regular features medium sized <fo>hand, small foot, oblong face, dark hair, pug or turned-up nose, small ears, light, pencilled eyebrows, brilliant brown or black eyes; walks with a slow, languishing, and slightly graceful step. If adroitly put forward, she will listen attentively to the most absurd flattery, and by every means in her power continue to call it forth.—<Rig> She has scarcely enough pride, and an overwhelming amount of vanity; not very intelligent; is a quick observer of small things; apt to learn, <but rather more apt to forget what she does learn.> She can, or at least will try, to conceal her motives, but her emotions she cannot hide. But a slight argument will change her opinion generally. She is lazy and indolent She will give her confidence to any one, worthy or unworthy the trust—*especially* one whom she loves. She is as fickle as the wind, and a coquette. She is affectionate, and firm in her friendships, but in her loves, never. She will go any length to add an admirer to her list, and likes to be complimented on the number of her conquests. She has no "airs." She is kind to all, and nurses the sick with tenderness and attention. Is fond of fine clothes, and likes to display herself. She is very careless in minor matters, though <very> generally neat in her dress and the arrangement

---

in the valley country, begun by Campbell, Stone and Raccoon John Smith in the early '30s and '40s, we of today cannot appreciate. It was even worse than being an 'infidel,' and often converted a man into a social pariah, though Judge Quarles did not suffer this fate, his natural kindness and his usefulness as a man and citizen saving him from the common penalty" ([Thomas V. Bodine], "A Journey to the Home of Twain," Kansas City *Star*, 19 May 1912, p. 1B).

[37] The trip to Florida, Missouri, to settle the Lampton estate afforded Clemens the opportunity to make new social acquaintances. All three of these young women were Florida residents. Juliet E. Violett was the sixteen-year-old daughter of M. A. Violett, a saddle and harness maker. Emily S. Tandy was seventeen; she was the daughter of a pioneer Florida resident, Dr. William M. Tandy. Nineteen-year-old Emily G. Young's father, the Reverend John F. Young, was the Methodist minister at Florida. Her older sister, Sarah E. Young, married Benjamin Quarles, the oldest son of Clemens' uncle John A. Quarles (Ralph Gregory, "Sam Clemens and the Florida Girls," Perry, Missouri *Enterprise*, 1 July 1971).

of the parlor. Is always sorry when she hurts any ones feelings, and will not intentionally wound any one. She will despise you for your mean dress, yet listen to your compliments with eagerness, and weep at your recital of comparatively small misfortunes. There is an ocean <behind her black eyes> of passion behind her black eyes which <is terrible> will stop at nothing when lashed to <fury> fury. She is jealous and ambitious; a dreamer, and <pines> sighs for wealth and power; yet she will fall in love with a poor man about as quick as a rich one, adore either or both—until another catches her eye. She does not remember an injury long, but a kindness forever. <True worth in rags, <in>with her, is easily overbalanced by stupidity in broadcloth.>[38]

Wednesday, June 27th sent out to wash the following:[39]

1 pair heavy Pants;
1 " <">light do;
4 white Shirts;
4 " Collars;
2 pair white cotton Socks;
1 summer cravat;
2 white Handkerchiefs
1 pair twilled Drawers;
1 linen summer Coat;
———
17
6
———
102

Small, turned up, or pug, denotes vanity, susceptibility to flattery, &c. [#]

---

[38] Clemens' numerous deletions seem to indicate that he was not copying this passage from a book, but there are no clues to the identity of the young woman he is describing. Perhaps she is one of the three he met in Florida, Missouri.

[39] Probably made in Saint Louis, this laundry list notation supplies one of three dates mentioned by Clemens in Notebook 1 entries: the 27th of June occurred on Wednesday only in 1855 during the mid-fifties. If the seventeen clothing items were charged at 6¢ a unit, this would explain his total figure at the bottom of the column—his laundry cost $1.02.

2 shirts

2 collars,

1 hdkf

1 vest

1 coat

1 pants

See washerwoman.

See Mr. Clemens, 5 o'clock.[40]

See Pamela, 2 o'clock.[41]

See Mrs. Sexton.[42]

Go down to "News"[43] Office.*

<G[-t]> <mon <L>Français leçon.>

---

[40] These errands to be performed in Saint Louis could have been listed before or after his short trip to Hannibal, Florida, and Paris, Missouri. James Clemens, Jr., lived in Saint Louis, and the appointment recorded here may have been one of Samuel Clemens' applications to his wealthy relative for assistance in becoming a pilot. The 6 August 1855 letter James Clemens wrote to Orion about the Hannibal property (see note 18) mentions a conference with Samuel Clemens: "Your Brother who handed me an introductory letter from you was desirous to go on board a Boat to learn to become a Pilot—a friend of mine who is Pilot on one of the large boats I intended to speak to on the subject but when the Boat was in Port I was sick and did not see him—but I was then and am now of the opinion your brother should stick to his present trade or art."

[41] Clemens' sister was now a mother: Annie Moffett had been born in 1852. The Moffetts were still renting a house on Pine Street in Saint Louis in 1855, although William was becoming moderately prosperous as a commission merchant in the firm of Moffett, Stillwell, & Company. Jane Lampton Clemens had been living with Pamela and William since shortly before Orion's marriage on 19 December 1854. Clemens later would board with the Moffett family during part of his years as a river pilot, when they resided on Locust Street.

[42] A former boarder with the Clemens family in Hannibal, Mrs. Sexton was described in "Villagers of 1840–3" as a "nice, kind-hearted, smirky, smily dear Christian creature—Methodist" who pronounced her name "*Saxton* to make it finer." She also "talked much of N-Yorliuns; and hints and sighs of better days there, departed never to return" (*HH&T*, p. 34). She moved to Saint Louis with her daughter, Margaret, perhaps as early as 1854. Margaret is mentioned in letters Clemens wrote from Carson City on 8 February 1862 and Virginia City on 16 February 1863.

[43] The establishment of the Saint Louis *Daily Evening News*, "of large size, handsomely printed, and Whig in politics," had been noted in the Hannibal *Missouri Courier*, 22 April 1852. Possibly Clemens was looking for employment other than that available in Orion Clemens' shop. In American printers' jargon, the

See John Hamilton.[44]
*Sell my "string."
Go to Christian Church.
Pay Mrs. Pavey.[45]
Write to John Shoot.[46]

"Reading Room" on door of Hotel, Paris (no name)—reading variety consists of Jayne's Med. Almanac and pamphlet copy of Lives of Beaumont & Fletcher.[47] Paris, 16th July, 12 o'clock. [#]

---

term *string* referred to the aggregate proofs of type set by a compositor, pasted on a strip of paper. In effect, the *string* indicated the speed with which a typesetter worked.

44 John Hamilton's occupation at this time is not known for certain, but by 1857 he was a pilot. In a letter to Sam, Orion, and Mollie, Jane Clemens wrote on 28 September 1864 from Saint Louis about a pilots' wage dispute in which Hamilton was involved: "The pilots up to Keokuk are contrary. They want their salary raised. It was raised to $250—and they wanted 270. John Hamilton was at the head of it. They were all dismissed and new ones put on, that don't know the river good. I don't know how it will end" (*MTBus*, p. 82). In 1882, when he was planning his return visit to the Mississippi River, Clemens again made a notebook entry reminding himself to "See John Hamilton."

45 Quite likely this was one of the Paveys from Hannibal. Napoleon "Pole" W. Pavey is listed as a steamboat engineer, "Second Class," in the 1854/55 and 1857 Saint Louis city directories. Clemens stated that he lodged with the Paveys in 1853 when he lived in Saint Louis briefly before his trip to New York City, Philadelphia, and Washington, D.C. In a letter (15 December 1900) addressed to Frank E. Burrough, the son of a fellow boarder at the Pavey house, Clemens recalled: "I should say it was 1852 or 1853. I remember, at any rate, that the Know-Nothing disturbances were brisk at the time. Your father [J. H. Burrough] & I boarded & lodged with the Paveys, corner of 4th & Wash streets. It was a large, cheap place, & had in it a good many young fellows who were students at a Commercial College. I was a journeyman printer, freshly fledged, your father was a journeyman chair-maker. . . . He & I were comrades & close friends" (Kent Library, Southeast Missouri State College, Cape Girardeau, Missouri).

46 John A. Shoot was a former fellow member of the Hannibal Cadets of Temperance. He was probably a son of William Shoot, who had taken possession of the Brady House (renamed the Monroe House) in Hannibal in 1853 and who was also a joint owner of the Shoot, Jordan & Davis Livery Stable.

47 The condescension of this entry concerning the paltry literary collection available in the one hotel in Paris, Missouri, is understandable in a young man who had often spent his evenings in the free printers' libraries in New York City (SLC to Jane Lampton Clemens, 31 August 1853), one of which contained four thousand volumes (SLC to Pamela Clemens, [summer 1853]) and whose own father and older brother had been stockholders in a town library which owned "between four

Ask Moses Green if he took a copy of the ages of the children from the old family Bible in the box of books at Miller & Pogue's,—and if he took the deposition to prove the ages.

Toi<[-]>—Thou, thee.
Sans—Without
Inutile—Fruitless useless
Tout—All, everything
Il est tout malade
He is very sick
Tout à l'hure—Presently
Tout beau! Softly! gently! Not so fast!
Tout du long—From the beginning to the end
Tout d'un temps—At the same time

Argent! argent! sans toi tout est sterile
La vertu sans Argent, n'est qu'un meuble inutile![48]

La loup dans la bergerie

Go to Mont,[49] demain—[voici] [M. Bury], s.b. B. Campbell[50]—stay

---

and five hundred volumes" (Hannibal *Missouri Courier*, 22 June 1854). David Jayne (1799–1866) was a wealthy Philadelphia drug manufacturer, reported to be the first businessman to publish almanacs as a means of advertising. *Jayne's Medical Almanac and Guide to Health* was published annually and distributed free of charge to potential consumers of Jayne's expectorants, tonics, vermifuges, balsams, pills, and liniments. The other volume Clemens discovered in the meagerly appointed "Reading Room" may have been a separate pamphlet reprint of George Darley's essay, "Lives of Beaumont and Fletcher," originally published by Carey & Hart in *Lives of British Dramatists* (Philadelphia, 1846).

[48] This epigram is adapted from Epître V (lines 85–86) of the *Epîtres* of Nicolas Boileau-Despréaux. Taken out of context and altered slightly, the couplet here becomes an apostrophe to money; Clemens (or Clemens' source) has inverted the author's attack on materialism.

[49] Montrose, Iowa, was twelve miles above Keokuk on the Mississippi. Its location at the head of the dangerous Des Moines, or "Lower," Rapids, which terminated near Keokuk, made it the site of a great deal of transportation activity. Steamboats did not attempt to operate over this stretch of water during most stages of the river, so cargo was unloaded at Montrose and Keokuk and ferried by lighters between the two towns.

[50] The steamboat *Ben Campbell,* a sidewheel packet built in 1852, was operating above the Des Moines Rapids during the summer of 1855 (George Byron Merrick, *Old Times on the Upper Mississippi* [Cleveland, Ohio: Arthur H. Clark Co., 1909], p. 260; Saint Louis *Missouri Republican,* 11 August 1855). The boat left Montrose

till Saturday eve.—Ivins[51] directly after breakfast.

John O. Boyes, 33 Third st.
Between 2 & 7 PM.

boots
coat
pants
cap
vest
cravat
shirt[52]

---

at 12 o'clock nightly, carrying Chicago-bound passengers to points along the Illinois shore (Keokuk *Gate City*, 10, 11 May 1855).

Clemens may have been seeking an experienced river pilot to teach him the craft. The name "Bury" does not appear in contemporary records, but William T. and David Berry were listed as pilots in the 1854/1855 Saint Louis city directory. According to *Lloyd's Steamboat Directory* (Cincinnati: James T. Lloyd & Co., 1856), p. 300, David Berry was piloting only on the Upper Mississippi during 1855.

[51] Clemens boarded at the Ivins House, First and Johnson streets, while he worked for Orion in Keokuk; his brother Henry boarded with Orion and Mollie; and both boys slept at the printing office (*Keokuk City Directory for 1856–7*; also Fred W. Lorch, "Mark Twain in Iowa," *Iowa Journal of History and Politics* 27 [July 1929]: 418–419). It was at the Ivins House on 17 January 1856 that Clemens gave his first after-dinner speech, "replete with wit and humor," during a Keokuk printers' banquet, held in honor of the 150th anniversary of Benjamin Franklin's birth (reported by Orion Clemens, secretary of the Printers of Keokuk, in the Keokuk *Gate City*, 19 January 1856).

[52] Clemens covered the following back endpaper of this notebook with chaotically jotted arithmetical calculations. A few are legible, and others are discernible but not readable on the photocopy. Although the numbers resist identification and transcription, the recurrence of 32 and 35 in the jumble may link them to the rates paid to newspaper compositors in Saint Louis. In 1854 it was noted that "printers' wages are low, only 25 cents per 1000 ems" in Keokuk (William Rees, *Description of the City of Keokuk, Lee County, Iowa* [Keokuk: Keokuk Dispatch Print, 1854], p. 15), and a higher rate might well have prevailed in a larger city a year later. On 31 August 1853 Clemens had written to his mother from New York City about the pay scale for compositors: "The printers here are badly organized, and therefore have to work for various prices. These prices are 23, 25, 28, 30, 32, and 35 cents per 1,000 ems. The price I get is 23 cents; but I did very well to get a place at all" (Minnie M. Brashear, *Mark Twain, Son of Missouri* [Chapel Hill: University of North Carolina Press, 1934], p. 155).

II

"Get a Little Memorandum-Book"

(April–July 1857)

THE FIRST of the two memorandum books which survive from Clemens' piloting career served specifically as a river guide rather than as a record of literary and biographical events. It came into being out of the necessity of coping with the bars, snags, shallows, and other navigational hazards on the Mississippi, and Clemens allowed none of his personal life to invade its complex technical content. He developed a system of notation which today is often undecipherable without knowledge of the geography of the area and familiarity with the language peculiar to piloting. Because of the abbreviated words, the frequent illegibility of penciled entries, the difficulty of identifying many of the now-vanished river points, but above all because of the technical subject matter, the full text of these notes is not printed here. The representative selections which follow illustrate the techniques Clemens used to record information for safely retracing his route on the changing river course.

As described in the Introduction, Clemens obtained the first notebook after he was already on board a steamboat—presumably the *Paul Jones*—while it was near New Orleans. The thin book is ruled for use as a ledger, and a steamboat clerk's cargo records are scattered through its pages: the number of barrels shipped by "H & E," the weight of kegs dispatched by "J. B. Boyles," lengthy accounts of rates for boxes belonging to "K," "I & Mayer," "M K & M," and "S & Bro," and shipments of casks for "S. Glick" and "W & S." Clemens simply crossed out these penciled figures where they interfered with his own entries and left the others. Obliged to acquire a memorandum book on short notice, he had evidently persuaded one of the clerks on the *Paul Jones* to relinquish his ledger. This evidence corroborates Mark Twain's account in chapter 6 of *Life on the Mississippi,* where he recalled Horace Bixby's vexation when he realized that his pupil was failing to record his comments as their boat steamed northward from New Orleans. "My boy," Bixby said after his indignation subsided, "you must get a little memorandum-book, and every time I tell you a thing, put it down right away. There's only one way to be a pilot, and that is to get this entire river by heart."

The frequency with which the author reshaped his river experiences in *Life on the Mississippi* is amply demonstrated by Allan C. Bates in his dissertation "Mark Twain and the Mississippi River" (University of Chicago, 1968). The accuracy of Clemens' reminiscences about "the little memorandum-book," however, is documented by the entries in this notebook. The first entries describe river points for a boat heading north from New Orleans. Writing at Bixby's direction, Clemens began to set down piloting information in short, unorganized paragraphs, beginning with landmarks near the city wharf from which the boat departed. He copied the Louisiana portion of Bixby's directions on the endpaper at the back of the inverted notebook:

St[o--] Ladg—When stock ldg lights come out fm behind rope walk blow for McGill's brick warehouse[1]—300 G

Abreast thick bch is flat pt stand out [100] & go in 200 above—flat pt shows sharp & treeless. Leave shore abreast Carrolt[on][2]

Went through Covington bar—20 foot bank—go that way till dd lo water.

3 fath in Prophet when wilows out on Manchac. B. Sara nearly same. R. h. shore above Bat. Rouge—1st part, up to lo place, 3 or 400 above sng.

---

[1] McGill, Jackson & Company were salt dealers in New Orleans.

[2] Carrollton, Louisiana, long since a district of New Orleans, was then a few miles north of the city boundary.

These notes continue to a point near Morganza, Louisiana.

During this trip Clemens may have established the final form of his notebook: a series of distinctive blue pencil headings which label the major river points between Cairo, Illinois, and Natchez, Mississippi. These headings begin on the first page of the memorandum book and list the landmarks—islands, bends, and towns—probably from Bixby's dictation. This new system of note-taking allotted only one or two place names to each blank page, in order to allow for a fairly full description of navigational conditions under each heading. His notes thus became promptly accessible for reference on return voyages, and they could be read easily even in the poor light of the pilothouse at night.

Either Clemens decided that the ledger book did not contain enough pages to accommodate additional landmarks beyond the Cairo–Natchez run, or else Bixby wanted him to concentrate on that central portion of the river. At any rate his arrangement of headings proved disproportionate to the inscriptions he actually entered: the sections reserved for many regions remain blank or nearly blank. And because he had elected to set aside most of his space in the memorandum book for the Cairo–Natchez headings, Clemens was compelled to squeeze his records of voyages above and below this area into the four last pages of the notebook, adjacent to the back endpaper, on which he had previously noted his initial departure from New Orleans. These passages extend onto pages originally designated for "Hole-in the wall to Natchez I," "Natchez II," and "Below Natchez II" and are in part written directly over the blue pencil headings. Made with the notebook inverted, these additional notes begin on the notebook's last page and read toward the front of the notebook. They differ from Clemens' first, chaotic Louisiana entries in that each new paragraph begins with a key landmark name. This portion of the notebook is also more succinct than preceding notes. The first part of these faint, minutely-inscribed entries concerns a voyage from Cairo, Illinois, to Saint Louis. Although the order in which the towns are mentioned reveals that his boat was headed upstream, Clemens sometimes begins entries with "D. S." instructions—presumably in anticipation of the return trip downstream.

Cairo—D. S.—Com clear past ft of towh—Then, S on same h t or cor. of bar in ½ h on green clear Bnk ft big willows, till abr. old Bird's house, then S near ft Bird's fld, h about on or bel. 2 white houses ¼ m under pt.—bel. 2 sngs—1 in mid, tother in water line—

¼ l 2. Ft of towh. is abr mid of O. City.[3] 3 fath out fm Bd in h of Il toward ft of Il.

Bird's Il.—Hd towh br, & 250 under hd of Il—9 ft. D. S.—faint circle fm pt to hd towh, S open on pt.

As the boat approached Saint Louis, Clemens' records expand enough to convey some sense of the piloting experience, although the information is minimal:

Hoss-Tail—s on upper h. t (just bel. 2 dd t) h on work house, (open on cor of w bar—go far in toward where 3[d] towhead was, round s[ervn]t. Then shape up to pt, 150 out.

In Vide Poch Bd. fm Ill to bel. Lime Kiln, flat rock.

St. L.—St fm mid Kiho fld, wear till s high on hill, h opn on cor Il, (or on Bullard Church)—till full abr. hd of Il.—Then S on Ill cor. of Il, h opn on Ms pt.—go outside 2 sngs in neighborhood of wrecks mk 2 at h of Il.—<D>Went in to shore abov where pt begins to round off.

Saint Louis was generally the stopping place for steamboats engaged in the Lower Mississippi trade; at this point Clemens drew a heavy pencil line horizontally across his page, below which he recorded steering data on the return voyage from Saint Louis to Cairo. During the departure he assembled further instructions for the same stretch of the river:

St. L.—Toward Ill. cor. of Quai Il, till S on Ct House[4] h on ptch-roof house, op on ft of dry bar, up on upper jog Ill. hills, takes you shap of upper bar, 150 or 200 out—till abr. Sombart, ¼ 2—Then shap Quai. Il, 300 out, S at first bet. 2 pts, h about ft of blffs—shap <r>l.h. boi[-s], S will finally fall on ft Bloody Il, go in just bel. ft Kiho.

---

[3] Ohio City, Missouri, was across the river from Cairo. In the following entries Clemens began to use *Il* to refer to all islands.

[4] It is interesting to compare this actual notation for the Saint Louis vicinity with the fictionalized version Mark Twain would provide in "Old Times on the Mississippi," *Atlantic Monthly* 35 (June 1875): 727, later reprinted in chapter 15 of *Life on the Mississippi*: "St. Louis. Nine and a half (feet). Stern on court-house, head on dead cottonwood above wood-yard, until you raise the first reef, then pull up square."

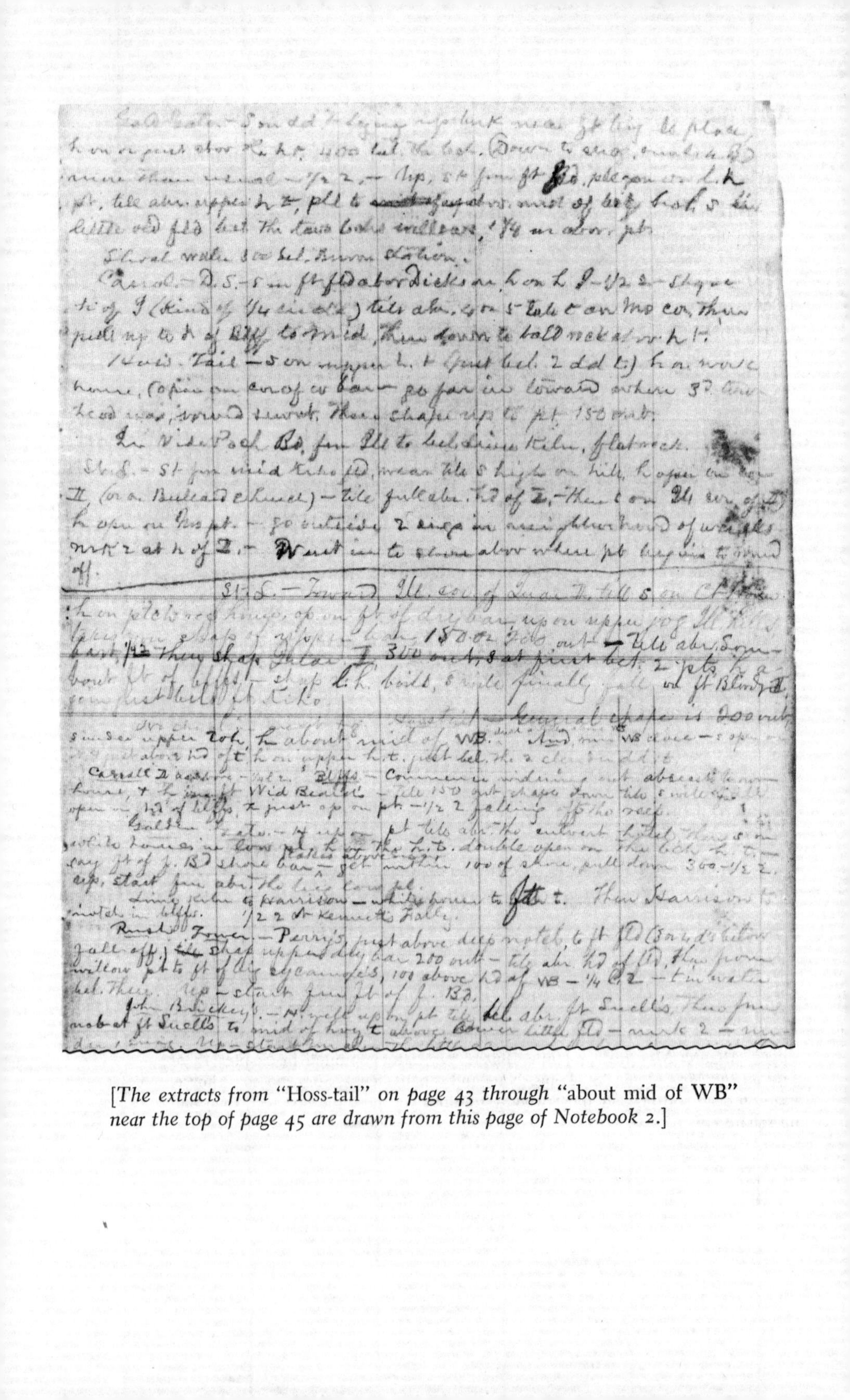

[*The extracts from* "Hoss-tail" *on page* 43 *through* "about mid of WB" *near the top of page* 45 *are drawn from this page of Notebook* 2.]

No chanl in next xg.

Hosstail—General shape is 200 out, S under upper toh, h about mid of WB.

Further downstream Clemens wrote:

Tower. II.—S. on 2d house bel. blff. h in sawmill fld ¼ l 2 <fath>—then S *down* on white bank, h on l.h. pt till abr. cottons on ft of II, pull up on fall-off of blff. S touching h of II. Up—start fm lowest houses.

Young Ship.—Inside of snag. (S. Shape shore, h 250 under h of Dev.—then S under h of blff, h. on h t. 700 bel. h of II. Down to houses—till can see into Bd under shoul of Dev. Then S on Shoul, h. in h of low. pl. upper bayou, big Sycamores—till <p>within 150 of shore, pull down to lower bayous, S on pt of dry bar.

Ft. of Dev.—Go close down around pt till can see the whole shap of Bd under it, then 2 r. h. pts open.—will take close to r. of logs ½ way bet. the 2 pts.

This succession of notes ends with the arrival of the steamboat at Cairo. There Clemens returned to his blue pencil headings, filling in information about each area as the boat reached it. Some entries under the headings begin with instructions for downstream navigation; probably Clemens had not been on watch when these points were passed during the initial trip upstream. Below his first heading ("Cairo Bend") Clemens many years later recorded his rediscovery of this early notebook:

(Notes made by me when I was learning to be a Mississippi River pilot, in 1856–7.)—

Found this book among some old rubbish to-day, Dec. 8, 1880.

S. L. Clemens

Hartford, Conn.

It is intriguing that Clemens entered his inscription in 1880 near the entry for Cairo Bend, the landmark that Huck and Jim miss because of their inexperience and inattentiveness. He was slightly mistaken in the date he assigned to the notebook, since his training as a pilot began in the spring of 1857.

There is another note, in Charles L. Webster's hand, further down the first page: "This book was found in an old box of rubbish in Chas. L. Webster's attic at Fredonia." The notebook had been left with Jane Clemens and the William Moffett family in Saint Louis when Clemens' career as a pilot came to an end. It was probably among the belongings which Jane Clemens brought with her when she moved to Fredonia, New York, in 1870 with her daughter and granddaughter, Annie Moffett, who married Charles L. Webster in 1875.

The notebook demonstrates on its remaining pages Clemens' increased proficiency in cataloguing information he needed under the orderly headings:

Cairo Bend.

Down inside the wreck <&> just shape of shore—down around pt & h above bch s on A. G. & Co. lower wharfboat. Up—go up shore till naturaly head some distance above wharfboat.

The notebook clearly was not intended as a log of his river trips, but merely as a working record of essential landmarks. Clemens occasionally made a note referring to specific dates and steamboats. The entry for Island No. 10, for example, places at least some of these entries in midsummer of 1857:

Island N°. 10

July 11th—no bottom around it. Go in at ft of t—take mid fm bel. ft of fld. & keep out fm l. h. shore till—S on ft of I. h on Harris ugly dd t.

Clemens made at least one of the trips recorded here on a boat other than the *Paul Jones*, for the entry under the Helena, Arkansas, heading begins, "*Up trip. Lackland, July.*" The *R. J. Lackland* was a sidewheel steamboat which operated on the Lower Mississippi from 1857 until 1863. There is no evidence that Clemens actually served aboard this ship; he may merely have made this one "up trip" as an observer in the pilothouse.

Many of the entries seem to be exact transcriptions of Bixby's speech, occasionally even capturing his verbal ellipses and colloquialisms. His great respect for Bixby, his precocious interest in and ear for language, or both, may have motivated Clemens to set down the veteran pilot's words this fully. This tendency is discernible in some explicit notes about navigating several troublesome areas below Helena:

Delta to head 62–3.

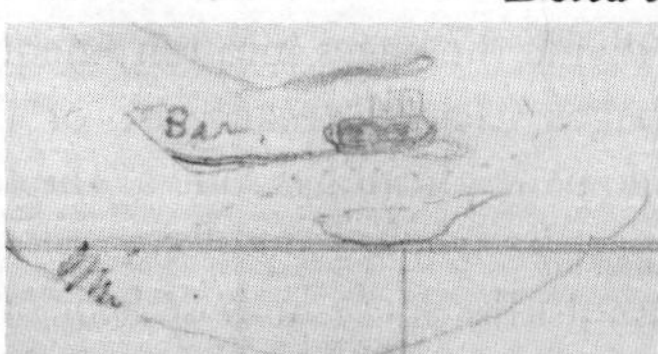

Coming up, when all the bar is covered, there is ¼ less 2 in chute of Montezuma. Shape bar till head of towhead & main point open—then hold open to right of high trees on towhead till get get close enough to go up shore of towhead. Channel out past head of towhead.

Outside of Montezuma.—6 or 8 feet more water. Shape bar till high timber on towhead gets nearly even with low willows do. do., then hold a little open on right of low willows—run 'em close if you want to, but come out 100 yards, when you get nearly to head of T. H.

These sample entries illustrate the two methods by which Clemens organized his notations about the entire reach of the Lower Mississippi—a prefabricated chart of the main (Cairo–Natchez) stretch, supplemented by a makeshift listing of river points on the lower (Louisiana) and upper (Cairo–Saint Louis) segments of the river. This notebook became his guide to the river, but it is only a rudimentary outline of landmarks. Most of the headings are followed by two brief entries, an upstream and a downstream description; very few places receive repeated treatment. The main work had to be done by what Mark Twain would call "about the most wonderful thing in the world"—the pilot's memory, which enabled him "to know every trivial detail of twelve hundred miles of river and know it with absolute exactness" (*Life on the Mississippi*, chapter 13). "Give a man a tolerably fair memory to start with," Mark Twain would write, "and piloting will develop it into a very colossus of capability. . . . Astonishing things can be done with the human memory if you will devote it faithfully to one particular line of business."

Notebook 2 now contains 70 pages, all inscribed, although the sole entries on some are Clemens' blue pencil headings, which name major points on the river. The pages measure 7$^{13}/_{16}$ by 4¾ inches (19.8 by 12 centimeters). They are divided approximately in half by a rust-colored double rule and are ruled with fifteen pale green horizontal lines above and seventeen such lines below this division. There are two rust-colored horizontal double rules at the top of each half-page, forming a band intended for column headings; rust-colored vertical lines divide the pages into ten unequal columns in ledger fashion. On many pages Clemens made use of the double-page format to enter two of his blue pencil headings, one at the top and one in the center; but for the most part he ignored the design of the page, often squeezing two lines of writing into the space intended for one. The endpapers are gray. The notebook was originally bound in a stiff cover of black fabric; the back and the spine were long ago recovered with black, grained oilcloth. The cover has come loose from the pages. With the exception of his 1880 inscription in blue ink on the first page and his blue pencil headings, all of Clemens' entries are in black pencil.

III

"A Pilot Now, Full Fledged"

(November 1860–March 1861)

IN CHAPTER 21 of *Life on the Mississippi* Mark Twain would summarize the sequel to his piloting apprenticeship: "In due course I got my license. I was a pilot now, full fledged. I dropped into casual employments; no misfortunes resulting, intermittent work gave place to steady and protracted engagements. Time drifted smoothly and prosperously on, and I supposed—and hoped—that I was going to follow the river the rest of my days, and die at the wheel when my mission was ended." Since the only surviving pilot's certificate issued to Samuel Clemens is dated 9 April 1859 and is identified as the "Original"—as opposed to a renewal—it is apparent he spent two years as a "cub" before becoming a licensed pilot. An additional year and a half as a pilot preceded the first dated entries in Notebook 3, which document all except the last month of Clemens' remaining career on the river.

The second of the two surviving river notebooks is far smaller than the earlier book. It was designed to fit in a pocket and thus more closely resembles the memorandum books that Clemens would carry throughout his later years. Nor did the now-experienced pilot limit its contents solely to river topics as the cub pilot had with Notebook 2. Here Clemens returned to the French studies which had been interrupted by a sudden fascination with phrenology in Notebook 1. The effects of his layover weeks in New Orleans are everywhere evident, not only in his resumption of French grammar lessons, but also in the names and addresses and errands he added to this book. When he did write about the river, usually it was to record the conditions he found on an unusual trip or aboard a strange boat—the type of informative report he once parodied for a Saint Louis newspaper.[1] Elementary reminders about routine boat channels and landmarks were not recorded; now he was concerned simply with observing altered phenomena. He sometimes remarked that things were still "same stage as last trip."

All of the entries with any biographical or historical significance are printed in their original sequence, although the excerpts, which contain somewhat less than half of Clemens' inscription, are not necessarily contiguous in the notebook itself. Interpolated editorial comments account for missing material and provide a context for the entries selected.

The notebook opens with snatches of French dialogue, a reminder of an errand, fragments of anecdotes, and a long extract from Voltaire:

> Je crois que vous le savez mieu que moi

> Inquire at Charity Hospital, in Common st., if an Englishman named Conlin died there of Yellow fever in 1853–4. He boarded with a Mrs. Reed in Tchoupitoulas street.[2]

> <"Keeping me here in exp[ense] all this time."> <[Hain]>
> "I'm small, old—punched 40 ye[ars]—but d—d if I can't whip man & [b--] in house
> What you done—Murder—<rape>—Theft—worse 'n that.
> Hold my coat Bro—I've found th man sht in [-h, <--->]
> <What's yr name?>
> Quel est votre nom?

---

[1] See Allan Bates, "Sam Clemens, Pilot-Humorist of a Tramp Steamboat," *American Literature* 39 (March 1967): 102–109. This article reprints Clemens' "Pilot's Memoranda," which was published in the 30 August 1860 issue of the Saint Louis *Missouri Republican*.

[2] According to the New Orleans city directories for 1855, 1858, and 1859, a Mrs. G. Reed did live at the corner of Tchoupitoulas and Notre Dame streets. The light Xs through this entry are unlike Clemens' customary cancellation marks and may indicate that he completed the errand.

"6 days"
Combien des jours avez vous travaillez?
"Pat Murphy<?>.
"Alez vouz à la bureau et prenez votre argent'
"I'll be <d–d> if I do—I'll [run] the boat first

Il est convalescent

Watch!—Venez vous <away> fm cette chaise!

<"Diable!> <S[-----] pourquoi> ne vous allai dans ce batteau? Parce que vous <s>ne sont accoup—

<Pat, Bridget a un enfant, et> que pensez-vous il ist?
C'ist un garcon?
Non.—C'ist un veiles niègre

From "Voltaire's Dialogues."

"Pladeur et Avocat."[3]

Le Pladeur

Eh, bien monsier, le procès de cès pauvre orphelines?

L'Avocat.

Comment! il n'y a que dix-huit ans que leur bien est aux saisies rèelles. On n'a mangè encore en frais de justice que le tiers de leur fortune; et vous vous plaignez!

Le Pladeur.

Je ne me plains point de cette bagatelle. Je connais l'usage; je le respecte; mais, pourquoi depuis trois mois que vous demandez audience n'avez-vous pu l'obtenir qu'aujourd'hui?

L'avocat.

C'est que vous ne l'avez pas demandèe vous-mème pour vos pupilles. Il fallait <alla>aller[4] plusieurs fois chez votre juge pour le supplier de vous juger.

[3] These are the opening passages (with occasional misspellings) of Voltaire's *"Dialogue Entre un Plaideur et un Avocat"* (1751). Clemens, who would declare that "to succeed in the other trades, capacity must be shown; in the law, concealment of it will do," evidently was impressed with Voltaire's cynical commentary on the imbecility of French litigation.

[4] Clemens wrote *er* over *a*.

Le Plaideur.

Son devoir est de rendre justice sans qu'on l'en prie. Il est bien grand<e> de dècider des fortunes des hommes sur son tribunal; il est bien petit de vouloir avoir des <malheureuz>malheureux[5] dans son antichambre. Je ne vais point à l'audience de mon curè le prier de chanter sa grand'messe (high mass.); pourquoi faut-il que j'aille supplier mon juge (supplicate) de remplir les (fulfill) fonctions de sa charge? Enfin donce après tant de delais (Finally, then, after many delays,) nous allons être juges aujourd'hui?

L'avocat.

Oui; il y a (there is) grande apparence que vous gagnerez un chef de votre procès; car vous avez pour vous un article dècisif dans Charondas.

Le Plaideur.

Ce Charondas est apparemment quelque chancelier (some) de nos premiers rois, qui fit une lois en (made a law) faveur des orphelines?

L'avocat.

Point du tout; (not at all,) c'est un particulier qui a dit son avis (opinion, advice,) dans un gros livre qu'on ne le point; (which is never read,) mais un avocat le cite (cites) les juges le croient (believes) et on gagne (gains) sa cause.

Le Plaideur.

Quoi! l'opinion d'un Charondas tient (taken instead) lieu de loi?

(*L'avocat.*)

Ce qu'il y a de triste (it is sad) c'est que vous contre (against) vous Turnet et Brodeau.

Le Plaideur.

Autres lègislateurs de la mème force, san doute?

L'avocat.

Oui. Le droit romain n'ayant pu être suffisamment expliqué

---

[5] Clemens wrote *x* over *z*.

(not having been sufficiently explicit in the case in point,) dans le cas dont'il s'agit, on se partage (divides) en plusieurs opinions diffèrentes.

Le Plaideur.

Que parlez-vous ici du droit romain? est-ce que nous vivons sous (live under) Justinien ou sous Thèodose?

L'avocat.

Non pas (no-no.)

Clemens ceased copying Voltaire's dialogue in midpage, and on the next notebook page he began his record of a specific voyage on the *Alonzo Child*. It is difficult to account for the apparent lapse of three years between his pilot memorandum books; perhaps he kept others during the interim which have not survived, or possibly he found that he could steer successfully by relying on the current reports of the Pilots' Benevolent Association, which are discussed in chapter 15 of *Life on the Mississippi*.

November 1860

1st. high water trip of "Child"

Ext. end of rudder on wreck above Tunica II, 1 ft out—top of rudder-post 3 feet out.—None of the main bar above covered—when it is, go up shore.

Strip of bar 100 long tailing across ft of slough at ft Desheroon's middle-bar 3 ft. out.

Bridge of bar across ft of shore slough opp ft Big Blk 3 ft out—½ 2 in ft Big Blk, & mrk 2 in hd—(should have been ½ 2. When that "bridge" is covered, go in at ft of t or <t[--]> else down bet. bars at Hurrican for <8 or> 9 ft—or when ft of H. II bar is covered pretty much—

With river as above, had 7 ft in hd of 103—more there, perhaps —had mark 3 in 98.

(Night—could not go thro' 93)

This account of river conditions is significant because it was during a trip from New Orleans to Saint Louis, begun on 10 November 1860, that Clemens ran the *Alonzo Child* aground about seventy miles above New

Orleans. One of the shallow places described here may have caused the delay about which he wrote to Orion on 20 November: "Running in the fog, on the coast, in order to beat another boat, I grounded the 'Child' on the bank, at nearly flood-tide, where we had to stay until the 'great' tide ebbed and flowed again (24 hours,) before she floated off. And that dry bank spell so warped and twisted the packet, and caused her to leak at such a rate, that she had to enter protest and go on the dock, here [Saint Louis], which delays us until Friday morning" (TS in MTP).

This was the last upriver trip made by the *Alonzo Child* in November. It next left New Orleans on 3 December, but Clemens' notes skip to the 29 January 1861 departure from that city.

2^{d} highwater trip—Jan <1860>1861[6]—Alonzo Child.—rising fast

Perhaps water enough opp. Bayou Goula—don't know

Manchac Bar covered—logs aground. Up Luda bar shore—no lead.

Up shore bel. Bat. Rouge

Had no bottom in <r[-]> Prophet's Island.

Up l. h. shore all the way in Bayou Sara chute

Up shore opp "Como".

" " Ft. Adams Reach

Was a good deal of water inside Dead Man. Was probably 6 or 7 ft in Glasscocks—night—didn't try.

This is one of the fullest reports of a run in Clemens' river memorandum books; here the twenty-five-year-old pilot, despite more than three years' experience, privately acknowledged a degree of professional timidity:

Was probably water enough bet. bars at head Hurricane—had to go after woodboat—didn't try.

Was about 3 or ½ 3 up Race Track shore—night—didn't.

Had ½ 3 in 102,—was about <¼—>½ 2 <or [-]>in 100—night—didn't.

Water through slough bel. 97. 6 ft. bank in 96–7—had 3 fath to l. of 96.

---

6 Clemens wrote 1 over 0.

Further on in his report Clemens became even more forthright:

Afraid of 82—had 3 fath in Gaines.

8 ft bank at fld sort [of] under pt ft Choctaw Bd—Went over—got close to cor of Choctaw—up a little & ran out—on 2 casts 9 ft—never more than 175 from I, fm shoul. to head.

Night—didn't run either 77 or 76 towheads

8 ft bank on Main shore, Ozark chute—can go up shore when 4 or 5 ft. bank.

Went up round wil. pt above Napoleon till [S] came open on it, or on the bch big t's, l. derrick on Beulah—3 fath—then went up over the big bar on 9 ft abr. hd 74.

Was probably 6 ft in Mid Grounds—(forgot to run it!)—*more* in 70–1.

His inclination toward caution is also evident in subsequent entries on the same trip:

Could have run Montezuma (either side,)—slough above Prairie Pt & shore opp Sterling—night—didn't.[7]

4 to 6 ft bank on pt bel. ft of Buck <I>II

Could have run Buck <I>II tohead—night—didn't.

The *Alonzo Child* left New Orleans again on 18 February, and Clemens made a detailed report:

Next Trip—February, '61—river same stage exactly as last up trip.

<Water> 10 to 15 foot banks on coast. Had ¼ l 4 behind Bayou Goula.

Would take 4 or 5 ft to put water in chute in Consort Pt. 7 ft bank at Jackson's house—10 or 12 bank higher up, (in the field. Ranged from 2½ to 4 ft bank up willows bel. Deadman bar—was 6 ft in it, <[*two words*]> sure—night—didn't.

---

[7] A bracket drawn in black ink in the margin beside this entry suggests that Clemens inspected Notebook 3 at a later period and that he found his Montezuma entry significant.

Even though the water at New Orleans was standing at the same level as on his preceding voyage, Clemens found sufficient change to fill twelve pages of his notebook with cryptic jottings. His last entry during the journey noted, "We've been on a smart rise since above Horse-Shoe [Bend]."

His fourth trip during March 1861 began at New Orleans on the twenty-eighth:

4th March Trip.

River just same stage as last trip, but falling.

Water in slough in Black Hawk Point, (night,)—had 8 at ft & Mark 2 in head of Dead Man—<p[---]n> Deep 4 in Glas 1 or 2 ft running down through Cowpen slough, & 2 ft or 3 in head Rifle—had 6½ in Coles Creek Chute—turn up past head of II—more to run chan perhaps—had only 2 casts of shoal water—bars in chute 4 ft out—big slough up middle, start fm mid of deepest Bd in II—bel. ft of main hd-of-II timber—& hd say 2 or 3 times open on r. h. pt (*n'importe,* run by judgment—better.

Despite the signs of impending conflict—troops gathering at strategic points along the shore, the bolstering of fortifications, mounting hostility in southern ports toward northern boats—Clemens' river notes remain professionally noncommittal. His last verifiable trips before steamboat traffic stopped were made from Saint Louis to New Orleans on 10 April, with a return to Saint Louis on 25 April. Although Clemens' notes do not reflect any awareness of the disastrous effect the war would have on river commerce, his growing professional ease did allow him to intersperse unrelated matters among his piloting annotations. These other entries are scattered throughout and resemble the memoranda in Clemens' first notebook—French grammar lessons, New Orleans addresses, a few lines of poetry, some bars of music, and a laundry list which documents the usual costume of a river pilot. Clemens returned to Voltaire, quoting the opening remarks in "*Dialogue Entre un Philosophe et un Contrôleur Général Des Finances*" (1751):

"Savez-vous qu'un ministre des fiances peut faire beaucoup plus de bien, et par conséquent être un plus grand homme que vingt maréchaux de France?" [#]

"*La vanitè n'est pas tant un vice que vous le pensez.* Si Louis XIV n'en avait pas eu un peu, son règne n'eût pas été si illustre. Le grand Colbert en avait; ayez celle de le surpasser. Vous êtes nè dans un temps plus favorable que le sien. Il faut s'èlever avec son siècle"

("Croyez qu'il n'y a rien d'utile que vous ne puissez faire aisèment.) Colbert trouva d'un côte l'administration des fiances dans tout le dèsordre où les guerres civiles et trente ans de rapine l'avaient plongèe. Il trouva de l'autre une nation lègére, (fickle,) ignorante, asservie<,> à des prèjugès dont la rouille (rudeness) avait trieze cents ans d'anciennetè. Il n'y avait pas un homme au conseil qui sût ce que c'est que le change: il n'y en avait pas un qui sût ce que c'est que la proportion des espèces, pas un qui eût l'idèe du commerce. A prèsent les lumières se sont communiquèes de proche en proche.

(*Copied.*)

Toll—toll—toll!
Way for a mighty soul
Unbar the gates of night
Woe—woe—woe!
It passeth—So!

shirts—1—1—1—1—1—1 6
Linen Pants—1—1 —2
White Cotton Socks—1—1—1—1—1—1 <4><5>6
Linen Coat—1 1
White hdkf—1—1<—1—1> <4> 2
[-----] Vest—1—1 2
Drawers—1—1 2
B[yron] Collars—1—1—1 3
Standing do—1 1
Blue Cot. Socks—1 1
26
Chambermaid —$2.00

pâté—pie
veloutè—velveting
Arretè—resolution
Cela me fait plaisir
De peur—de crainte que—lest
Encore que—even though—till—until (jusqu'à ce que)
Afin que—in order that
A moins que—unless
Avant que—before
En cas que—au cas que—in case [-]
Bien que—quoique—though

John Stevenson's house[8] is—

[8] Captain John A. Stevenson was a commission merchant and wholesale cotton dealer in New Orleans; he was a partner in Frellsen, Stevenson & Company. His residential address during the mid-fifties corresponded with the directions Clemens copied below the location of Magazine Market. Evidently he was familiar with Clemens' early journalistic ventures, for in 1882 Clemens would write to James R. Osgood about a recent discussion with Stevenson in New Orleans: "He has the article—my first—which made Capt. Sellers so angry. Said he would give it to me, but at the time I didn't think I needed it.—But I do. Won't you ask Bixby to get it for *you?*" (*MTLP*, p. 157).

Magazine Market[9] is between St. Mary and St. Andrew st.
On St. Mary st. between Nayades and Apollo sts. 2^{d} house on left—painted brown.

Margaret Leonard lives in Annunciation st bet. Phillipp and Sarreoperou.[10]

<Sitting under fig tree in Jackson st NO.>
<Pretty Cath Church [bel] Jackson st. N.O.>

"Dieu! qu'elle ètait jolie!"

Je suis allè chez vous hier, mais vous n'y êtiez pas—(but you were out)

On me l'a dit. Je suis bien fachè de ne pas <ne>n'y être trouvè

J'ai un projet dont je dèsire vous entretenir (speak about)

Je suis á votre disposition—service

Entr. IIIe—Si l'homme est ne mèchant et enfant du diable?—sub. 3^{d} [-----][11]
Allai au apotheke, et acheter trois sous de la longue epèce et le break en short pieces—et acheter trois sous de la short epice et le break en longue pieces et acheter trois sous de l'autre epèce et le break en square pieces—boil 'em down—donc allai à le barbière et causer le tête ètre razè—donce dormir sur la lit trois semaines —la première fait un plastre et le mit sur le tête—
Cela—veut-il une mal de dent?
Ah—Je pensait que vous eu mal de tête!

C'est bien facile—(easy) [#]

---

[9] This open-air New Orleans meat and vegetable market took its name from Magazine Street.

[10] Presumably Clemens meant Soraparu Street, but the New Orleans city directories contemporary with his piloting career do not list Margaret Leonard or her family.

[11] *Le troisième entretien* of Voltaire's *"L'A, B, C, ou Dialogues Entre A, B, C"* is entitled *"Si L'Homme Est Né Méchant et Enfant du Diable."* The nonsensical prescription which follows this title is apparently Clemens' own invention.

Pas si facile que vous le croyez—(think)

Comment donc cela (how so?)

Bien entendu—(of course)

Vous avez raison (are right)

Mais, alors, que comptez-vous, <a>faire? (intend to do?)

Vous feriez peut-etre bien
would do perhaps

J'en ai entendu parler
of it

Je le crois
it

Cela ne m'etonne pas que me conseillez-vous

Je vous conseille de ne pas trop vous <pes>presser[12]

Je ne dis pas cela

Vous <êtez>êtes[13] bien bon
kind

Où <([-]> vous retrouverai-je
meet

<[-]>Où vous voudrez. Donnez-moi un rendez-vous.
please appointment

Eh bien—chez moi—demain—à deux heures

<Je>J'y[14] serai.

Ailleurs—elsewhere

When Clemens temporarily (as he thought) gave up river piloting and departed for Carson City in July 1861 with Orion, he left his most recent

[12] Clemens wrote *re* over *es*.
[13] Clemens wrote *s* over *z*.
[14] Clemens wrote *y* over *e* and added the apostrophe.

piloting notebook in the custody of his mother. Jane Clemens used its blank pages to record household income and expenditures, and this document's survival may be due to her employment of it as an account ledger, from time to time, until 1870. Two of her memoranda are relevant to her son's notebooks since they concern loans Samuel Clemens made to fellow pilots while he was on the river. Horace Bixby was one of those who owed him money. On 14 October 1862 Jane Clemens wrote to her son about her anxiety that Bixby would renege on his $200 debt because of Samuel Clemens' supposed "secesh" sympathies (*MTBus*, p. 73). But her memoranda in this notebook indicate that her fears were not realized:

St. Louis August 12 1862
Rec'vd of Mrs Bixby on Sams note 10.00

Sept 16th 1864
rece'ed of Bixby <200.35> $235.00
paid Sam.
put in Will's hand $200—kept in my own hand $35.00

Another debt is documented on a slip of ruled blue paper which Jane Clemens tucked into the pocket in the leather notebook cover—a handwritten promissory note from Will Bowen to his fellow pilot:

$200.00
One day after date I promise to pay to Sam'l L. Clemens on order two hundred dollars without defalcation or discount
Wm Bowen
St Louis Mo
Feb 25th 1861

On the back of the neatly inscribed note Jane Clemens credited Bowen with payment of "one hundred dollars on within March 7th 1865" and computed the interest on $200 at 10 per cent until 4 January 1865—a total of $277.15. She also made a record of the transaction in the pages of the notebook: "March 7th 1865 Will Bowen paid me for Sam $100.00." Bowen eventually became irritated at Jane Clemens' persistent efforts to collect the remainder of the money, and on 25 August 1866 Clemens sent him a carefully worded letter of placation: "There has been a misunderstanding all around. You know I didn't want to take your note, but you insisted on it. And when I started across the plains to be gone 3 months & have the recreation we all needed (thinking the war would be closed & the river open again by that time,) I turned over a lot of notes for money I had loaned (for I did not know *what* might happen), to Ma, & among them yours—but I charged her earnestly never to call on you for a cent save in direst emergency, because, in all justice you could not be said to owe me a cent" (*MTLBowen*, pp. 12–13). The dispute was resolved, and the two men corresponded amicably thereafter.

Jane Clemens filled other pages of the notebook with itemized accounts of her personal expenditures and with the amounts of money which Orion and Sam sent to her from 1861 until 1870. She recorded a total of $2,242.55 contributed by her two sons during those nine years. The fluctuations in the family fortunes are reflected in these figures, for at first Orion's contributions were her main source of income, together with $297.75 which William Moffett provided in small payments before his death in 1865. By 1868, however, Samuel Clemens had virtually taken over her support, sending her steadily increasing amounts which were climaxed on 6 January 1870 when she received a check from him for $500, followed by another on 26 February for $300.

Notebook 3 now contains 144 pages, 54 of them blank. The pages measure 5⅝ by 2⅞ inches (14.3 by 7.3 centimeters) and are ruled with twenty-three pale gray horizontal lines and divided by pale brown vertical lines into four unequal columns in account book fashion. The page edges are marbled in red, black, and gold. The endpapers and flyleaves are white. The cover is of soft, stamped, black leather; the back cover extends beyond the width of the notebook to wrap around the fore-edge of the pages, meeting the front cover and terminating in a scalloped leather clasp that holds the notebook shut when slipped beneath a leather strap attached to the front cover; the extension of the back cover is lined with soft maroon leather. Between the back endpaper and the back cover is a pocket containing Will Bowen's promissory note and some newspaper clippings, probably placed there by Jane Clemens. Attached to this pocket is a green leather pencil holder. The cover has come loose from the pages and flyleaves. With the exception of some of Jane Clemens' entries in brown ink and the black ink bracket beside one of Clemens' river entries, all of the inscriptions in this notebook are in pencil.

IV

"By Way of Angel's... to Jackass Hill"

(January–February 1865)

THERE IS a gap of four years between Notebooks 3 and 4, a period for which no notebooks are known to exist. Following his experience as a Mississippi River pilot, Clemens helped form the Marion Rangers in the summer of 1861, after the outbreak of the Civil War. This informal connection with the Confederacy is described in "The Private History of a Campaign That Failed." Having had his "taste" of the war, Clemens "stepped out again permanently" and in late July 1861 took advantage of his brother Orion's recent appointment as Nevada territorial secretary to accompany him West. They arrived in Carson City in mid-August 1861. It was not long before Samuel Clemens caught the mining fever. His letters of the next months are replete with the details of his own mining endeavors in Humboldt and Esmeralda counties and with the statistics of his irrepressible stock speculations and transactions in "feet." It was from Aurora, Esmeralda County, that in the spring of 1862 he sent his first pieces to the Virginia City *Territorial Enterprise* over the pen name Josh. By the summer of that year he was beginning to doubt that he would strike it rich and, pressed for funds, in August he accepted a regular post as local reporter for the *Enterprise* at twenty-five dollars a week. He arrived in Virginia City near the end of that September and, except for assignments in Carson City in late 1862 to report the proceedings of the second Territorial Legislature of Nevada and again in late 1863 to cover the Nevada State Constitutional Convention and occasional trips to San Francisco, Lake Bigler [Tahoe], and Steamboat Springs, he remained there until 29 May 1864. On that date, after an exchange of abuse with James L. Laird, publisher of the Virginia City *Daily Union*, and the challenges to Laird which followed his accusation that the staff of the *Union* had reneged on its Sanitary Fund pledges, Mark Twain left for San Francisco with Steve Gillis, one of the *Enterprise* compositors and a close friend. The flight was probably to avoid ridicule and not, as he later claimed, to escape prosecution under a nonexistent "brand-new law" which made sending or carrying a challenge a penitentiary offense. (For an account of the entire Sanitary Fund controversy, see *Mark Twain of the "Enterprise,"* edited by Henry Nash Smith [Berkeley and Los Angeles: University of California Press, 1957].)

Clemens planned to stay in San Francisco for a month to dispose of some mining stock on Orion's behalf and then go East, but the market was not favorable. Two hundred dollars which he had asked Orion to forward to him in San Francisco was evidently not forthcoming, so in the first week of June he became a local reporter for the San Francisco *Morning Call*, probably at a salary of forty dollars a week; Gillis took a job as a compositor on the same paper. Mark Twain corresponded at least once with the *Enterprise* that month and also began weekly contributions to the San Francisco *Golden Era*. But it was the *Call* that demanded most of his time and energy in a fashion that he found oppressive since the paper's publishers allowed him little of the latitude he had enjoyed as "local" for the *Enterprise*. Working for the *Call* was tedious, he recalled in 1906, a "fearful drudgery, soulless drudgery, and almost destitute of interest" (*MTE*, p. 256) that began early in the police court and ended late in the theaters. By the autumn of 1864 he was reducing his commitment to the *Call*, for on 25 September he wrote his mother and sister:

> I am taking life easy, now, and I mean to keep it up for awhile. I don't work at night any more. I told the "Call" folks to pay me $25 a week and let me work only in daylight. So I get up at 10 in the morning, & quit work at 5 or 6 in the afternoon.

But his object was not entirely an increase in leisure, for he went on to inform them:

> I have engaged to write for the new literary paper—the "Californian"—same pay I used to receive on the "Golden Era"—one article a week, fifty dollars a month. I quit the "Era," long ago. It wasn't high-toned enough. I thought that whether I was a literary "jackleg" or not, I wouldn't class myself with that style of people, anyhow. The "Californian" circulates among the highest class of the community, and is the best weekly literary paper in the United States—and I suppose I ought to know. (TS in MTP; partially published in *MTL*, pp. 99–100)

Clemens had even more ambitious literary plans than this, however. On 28 September he informed Orion and Mollie Clemens that soon "I believe I will send to you for the files, & begin on my book," apparently to deal with material eventually to go into *Roughing It*, a project he was keeping secret for the moment. Preoccupation with such a book may have contributed to the growing neglect which precipitated his departure from the *Call*, although in *Roughing It* Mark Twain recalled that it was disappointment over a missed chance for a big mine sale (see note 17) that caused his indifference, and still later he attributed it to the suppression of a piece with "fire in it" condemning the persecution of an unoffending Chinese (*MTE*, pp. 256–257). At any rate, given the opportunity to resign around the middle of October 1864, Mark Twain promptly accepted. There followed the period in which, according to chapter 59 of *Roughing It*, he became "a very adept at 'slinking' ":

> I slunk from back street to back street, I slunk away from approaching faces that looked familiar, I slunk to my meals, ate them humbly and with a mute apology for every mouthful I robbed my generous landlady of, and at midnight, after wanderings that were but slinkings away from cheerfulness and light, I slunk to my bed. I felt meaner, and lowlier and more despicable than the worms. During all this time I had but one piece of money—a silver ten cent piece—and I held to it and would not spend it on any account, lest the consciousness coming strong upon me that I was *entirely* penniless, might suggest suicide. I had pawned every thing but the clothes I had on; so I clung to my dime desperately, till it was smooth with handling.

Actually, although he wasn't working regularly, Clemens was neither as miserably unoccupied nor as penniless as he insists. Between 1 October and 3 December 1864 he wrote ten weekly articles for the *Californian*, for which he received twelve dollars each. He was also contributing to the

Territorial Enterprise, for it was his criticism of police lassitude in the face of official corruption, published in Virginia City but also circulated in San Francisco, that helped hasten his departure for Jackass Hill. These now lost *Enterprise* dispatches had already made Clemens unpopular with San Francisco police chief Martin Burke when, late in 1864, Steve Gillis fled to Virginia City to avoid trial on charges resulting from a barroom brawl, and Clemens, Gillis' bondsman, found himself the object of Burke's displeasure. When Steve's older brother Jim offered Mark Twain the sanctuary of his cabin on Jackass Hill, a "serene and reposeful and dreamy and delicious sylvan paradise" (*MTE,* p. 360), he reportedly left San Francisco as he liked to think he had come, one step ahead of the police.

He arrived at Jackass Hill on 4 December 1864. He began Notebook 4 soon after New Year's Day 1865 with a highly elliptical recapitulation of his movements during the last half of the preceding year. The balance of the notebook reflects his activities until his return to San Francisco on 26 February 1865, for the most part consisting of a record of leisurely travels around Tuolumne and Calaveras counties. Chief among these was his four-week visit in January and February to Angel's Camp, where Jim Gillis had a pocket mining claim. Inclement weather limited Clemens' attempts to mine with Gillis, but even his brief experience of pocket mining had associative significance for him. While he and Gillis were stormbound during their first two weeks at Angel's Camp, Clemens jotted down reminiscences of his own mining days in Nevada, several of which he later expanded in *Roughing It.* On 8 February, probably to break the monotony of their days, Clemens, who in 1861 had joined Polar Star Masonic Lodge No. 79 in Saint Louis and in 1862 had attended meetings of the Carson City lodge, served as junior deacon at a meeting of Bear Mountain Masonic Lodge No. 76. The weather had cleared, but for the most part the fine days that came, like the rainy ones that had ended, were passed exchanging tales with Jim Gillis, with Dick Stoker, who came over from Tuttletown to visit, and with the regular patrons of the Angel's Hotel saloon. A number of these anecdotes and incidents, and others he heard at Jackass Hill and elsewhere, are recorded or alluded to in Notebook 4. Although the 1855 notebook gives clues about Clemens' biography which are relevant to the sources for his fiction and the two notebooks recording piloting information are clearly relevant to *Life on the Mississippi,* Notebook 4, with its combination of present and recollected experience, is the first that can accurately be considered a writer's notebook. Despite its brevity this notebook contains a considerable amount of literary material used in works that span Mark Twain's career. The note which proved to be most immediately useful to Clemens was the synopsis of what became "The Celebrated Jumping Frog of Calaveras County," but there are also a number of entries later developed in *Roughing It* and *Huckleberry Finn* and others that would not emerge again until his Autobiographical Dictations. Mark Twain's retentiveness of his source materials is demonstrated by the almost thirty-year interval between the 1893 writing and publication of "The Californian's Tale" and the original note for it in this notebook.

There is evidence of an awareness of his audience in the broad humor and scatological references of the long entry about the "Great Vide Poche Mine," perhaps intended for a reading before a male gathering. This frankness strongly contrasts with the mild language of the most daring sketches and "hoaxes" Mark Twain had written for publication, even in the permissive *Territorial Enterprise*. Mark Twain's ambivalent attitudes toward profanity and propriety are present in this notebook, particularly in the juxtaposition of his familiar modifications "d–d" and "G– d–dest" and the weak disguise *merde* with vulgarisms such as *piss-ants* and *ass*.

The conjunction in Notebook 4 of shorthand symbols, French words or phrases, and an unusual incidence of erratic abbreviations and simplified spellings forms a verbal texture uncharacteristic of any of Clemens' other notebooks.

Notebook 4 now contains 110 pages, 66 of them blank. At least one leaf has been torn out and is missing. Because it was designed to be used as an indexed memorandum or account book, right-hand pages at intervals are printed on their outside margin with an alphabet letter, and all but the last pages in the notebook are notched approximately 3⁄16 inch (0.5 centimeter), so that when the notebook is closed all of the letters are visible from the front. The unnotched pages measure 6⅝ by 4 1⁄16 inches (16.3 by 10.3 centimeters). The page edges are tinted blue. The pages are ruled with twenty-three blue horizontal lines and are divided by red vertical lines into four unequal columns in account book fashion. The endpapers and flyleaves are white. The notebook is bound in a stiff cover of tan calf. Clemens wrote "Use this on Mississippi trip." in ink on the front cover (see note 1), and someone, probably Paine, has written "1865" in ink on the front cover. The front cover, the front flyleaf, and the first 19 ruled leaves are loose; the rest of the notebook is only loosely attached to the spine, which is badly deteriorated. All entries are in pencil, except two later entries, which are in blue ink (see notes 34 and 37). Clemens used the same blue ink to inscribe use marks on several entries in this notebook. Most of the material so marked does not appear in his known writings. In four entries in Notebook 4 Clemens experimented with shorthand, mixing shorthand symbols and script letters. In the printed text of these four entries (identified in note 7) letters which appear in italics are transliterations of Clemens' shorthand.

Use this on Mississippi trip.[1]

(New Year 1865 (watch-<y>key to be returned to James N. Gillis, care Major A Gillis,[2] 12 m apres date.

(New

About 1st June left Va, N.T., 1864, & went to San F, Cal.
<Nov.>Dec. 4, went to Jackass <Gulch> Hill (Tuttletown,) Tuolumne Co—there until just after Christmas.
New Years 1865, at Vallecito, Calaveras Co

Tunnel under Vallecito Flat is 400 feet long—80 feet yet to run. [#]

---

[1] Mark Twain made this notation on the front cover of Notebook 4, apparently in 1882 just before his return to the Mississippi. This note, two later entries, and a number of use marks in the notebook were written in blue ink with the stylographic pen which Clemens used in the early 1880s.

[2] In a partially canceled passage in his Autobiographical Dictation of 19 January 1906 Mark Twain recalled that Angus Gillis, father of Jim, Steve, and Billy Gillis, had served under William Walker, who achieved fame with military expeditions into Mexico and Nicaragua in the mid-1850s: "The father received a bullet through the eye. The old man—for he was an old man at the time—wore spectacles, and the bullet and one of the glasses went into his skull, and the bullet remained there—but often, in after years, when I boarded in the old man's home in San Francisco, whenever he became emotional I used to see him shed tears and *glass,* in a way that was infinitely moving. . . . in the course of time he exuded enough to set up a spectacle shop with." In 1865 Mark Twain lived with the Gillis family at Angus Gillis' rooming house at 44 Minna Street in San Francisco.

New Years night 1865, at Vallecito, magnificent lunar rainbow, first appearing at 8 PM—moon at first quarter—very light drizzling rain.

New Years night—dream of Jim Townsend[3]—"I could take this x x x book & x x x every x x x in California, from San Francisco to the mountains."

(Daniel Lion's Den)[4]

Bly Gls was to take à Bal Quatre Juillet—failed à vient.—Elle dit "G D— B Gls!—G. D— B G!"[5]

Car'gton[6] met Madame D avec vieux chapeau sa mari's coat &c, boots, pick, shovel, & battaya, sur la bras—

"Ou est la vieu que vous avez taken up (Il était frightened.) [#]

---

[3] James W. E. Townsend, journalist on the Virginia City *Territorial Enterprise* and on the San Francisco *Golden Era* and other California newspapers, was known as "lying Jim" for his skill with the tall tale. In *Gold Rush Days with Mark Twain* (New York: Albert & Charles Boni, 1930, p. 182) William R. Gillis recalled that Townsend was the prototype for the Truthful James of Bret Harte's "The Heathen Chinee." He has also been credited with originating Mark Twain's "Jumping Frog" tale, a brief version of which appeared in the Sonora *Herald* in 1853, during the period Townsend was associated with that paper.

[4] On 5 November 1864 the *Californian* had published Mark Twain's "Daniel in the Lion's Den—and Out Again All Right," an account of a visit to the hall of the San Francisco Board of Brokers, in which he burlesqued stock-market jargon.

[5] This angry remark may be attributable to one of the "Chapparal Quails," Molly and Nelly Daniels, the "plump and trim and innocent" (*MTB*, p. 268) daughters of a family living in French Flat, not far from Jackass Hill. The Daniels sisters, "who boasted of having the slimmest waists, the largest bustles, and the stiffest starched petticoats in the entire locality" (Edna Bryan Buckbee, *The Saga of Old Tuolumne* [New York: Press of the Pioneers, 1935], p. 335), were much sought after by the young men of Tuolumne County, among them Billy Gillis and Mark Twain.

[6] Robert and Thomas Carrington had been among the first settlers of Jackass Hill. Thomas Carrington's wife Catherine had inadvertently made the first important quartz pocket discovery on Jackass Hill while looking for a turkey nest. "Mrs. Carrington . . . after a few days of searching found the nest. When she moved the eggs, she noticed, what was a matter of indifference to the bird, that the rocks on which the eggs were resting were seamed and in places crusted with gold. . . . The rest is mining history. Carrington made $100 to $300 a day for some years by grinding the rock in an old hand mortar" (Harriet Helman Gray, "A Story of Jackass Hill," unpublished, typed manuscript in The Bancroft Library, p. 12).

3^{d} Jan 1865 returned with Jim Gillis, by way of Angel's & Robinson's Ferry, to Jackass Hill.

<Miner's cabin, Jackass>
<*miner's*> *mi*ner's ca*b*in in Jac*kass:*[7]
<B> No *pl*a*n*king on the *fl*oor; <[-]> *old* <*punks*> bu*nks*, *p*a*ns* & <tra> *tr*aps o*f* *all* *k*inds—Byron Shakspeare, Bacon Dickens, & every kinds of only first class Literature[8]

The "Tragedian" & the *B*ur*n*ing Sha*m*e. No wo*men* ad*mi*t*t*ed[9] [#]

---

[7] In this entry, probably a description of Jim Gillis' cabin, and in the succeeding three entries Mark Twain experimented with shorthand, combining symbols with script letters when he did not know the appropriate notation. Letters that appear in italics in these entries are transliterations of the original shorthand.

[8] In "An Unbiased Criticism" (*Californian*, 18 March 1865, reprinted in *SSix*, pp. 158–165), Mark Twain would comment that "in most of those little camps they have no libraries, and no books to speak of, except now and then a patent-office report, or a prayer-book, or literature of that kind, in a general way, that will hang on and last a good while when people are careful with it, like miners; but as for novels, they pass them around and wear them out in a week or two." Some of the "first class Literature" noted here may have been borrowed at nearby Tuttletown, which Billy Gillis recalled had "a Literary Society, with a membership of three hundred, having a library of near a thousand volumes of standard prose and poetical works" (Gillis, *Gold Rush Days with Mark Twain*, p. 11).

[9] In his Autobiographical Dictation of 26 May 1907 (*MTE*, p. 361), Mark Twain recalled: "In one of my books–*Huckleberry Finn*, I think–I have used one of Jim's impromptu tales, which he called 'The Tragedy of the Burning Shame.' I had to modify it considerably to make it proper for print, and this was a great damage. As Jim told it, inventing it as he went along, I think it was one of the most outrageously funny things I have ever listened to. How mild it is in the book, and how pale; how extravagant and how gorgeous in its unprintable form!" The Tragedian may have been Jim Gillis, or possibly a character in a Shakespearean burlesque portrayed by Dick Stoker, who did appear in a private performance of the "Burning Shame" while Mark Twain was on Jackass Hill. On 26 January 1870, in a letter to Jim Gillis, Mark Twain remembered Stoker's part in that dramatization: "Wouldn't I love to take old Stoker by the hand, & wouldn't I love to see him in his great speciality, his wonderful rendition of 'Rinaldo' in the 'Burning Shame!' " (Edward L. Doheny Memorial Library, Saint John's Seminary, Camarillo, Calif.). All of the elements of this entry recur in *Huckleberry Finn* where the King and Duke perform "The King's Camelopard or The Royal Nonesuch," the expurgated version of the "Burning Shame," and also appear as "*World-Renowned Tragedians*" in renditions of ridiculously incongruous Shakespearean quotations.

The Trag & the broiled tur*n*ips
George & the stewed *plums*[10]

O*l*d To*m* watching by the ho*l*e whi*l*e *Dick* wor*ked* & running away with his *tail* enlarged when a *stranger* appeared.[11]

J imagine me married to N Dnls & on the hillside ground sluicing for bark

J's Plums & Garlic

Jan 22, 1865.

Angels', Ben Lewis', Altaville, Studhorse, Cherokee, Horsetown, <J>

Excelsior man bought privilege of "raising hell" in Stockton—party burlesqued him.

Meade throwing down & stamping cap when pokt found—only 700.

J's manner of encouraging himself when chasing an unpromising pkt all over hillside in Calaveras.

"White man heap savvy too much—Injun gone in—."

Squirrel hunt at Ben Lewis. [#]

---

[10] This allusion to another brother, George Gillis, and "J's Plums & Garlic," below, may refer to versions of an anecdote Mark Twain would record at length in his Autobiographical Dictation of 26 May 1907 (*MTE*, pp. 362–364). There he spoke of Jim Gillis' encounter with "some wild fruit that looked like large greengages" but were "all acid, vindictive acid, uncompromising acid." In order to justify the "fervent praises of that devilish fruit" produced by his "energetic imagination," Gillis stubbornly prepared the plums: "Oh, he was a loyal man to his statements! I think he would have eaten that fruit if he had known it would kill him. . . . that great-hearted Jim, that dauntless martyr, went on sipping and sipping, and sipping, and praising and praising, and praising, and praising, until his teeth and tongue were raw. . . . It was an astonishing exhibition of grit, but Jim was like all the other Gillises, he was made of grit."

[11] This incident wasn't used in chapter 61 of *Roughing It*, which Mark Twain devoted to Dick Baker and his cat Tom Quartz. He later admitted, "Baker was Dick Stoker, of course; Tom Quartz had never existed; there was no such cat, at least outside of Jim Gillis's imagination" (*MTE*, pp. 361–362).

Two sweethearts each with a glass eye.[12]

Morgan, Carson Hill Rock weighs 108—104 of it pur gld—<sold> vendue for 24,000[13]
Tk out 870,000 in 17 <d>jours.

Angels—best pros on Tuesday 24 Jan

Morgan Mine—2,908,000 in 7 mois. Taken up originally by New Yorkers who had lived a long while in The South.

Mine stopped for ten or 12 years on an injunction & Judgment for 80 agst one shareholder <—staid i>—constable put the creditor in possession of the whole claim instead of the single share, for $10—staid in law from 52 or '53 until Jan. '65—& was decided in favor of the Co.—lawsuit cost nearly 20,000.[14]

Beans & coffee *only* for breakfast & dinner every day at the French Restaurant at Angel's—bad, weak coffee—J told waiter must made mistake—he asked for café—this was day-before-yesterday's dishwater.

Loud femme—Did you see who came in the <stage> voiture? No. Why not? Didnt care a d—n. You're no ac/—take no interest in anything. [#]

---

[12] This note for a sketch reappears in expanded form in Notebook 5, p. 158, where it is associated with the uncouth Mr. Brown, Mark Twain's imaginary travel companion.

[13] The Morgan mine was a fabulously rich claim located on Carson Hill, "the classic mining ground of California" (Titus Fey Cronise, *The Natural Wealth of California* [San Francisco: H. H. Bancroft & Co., 1868], p. 264). A number of huge nuggets are reported to have been discovered there, one of which was claimed to be almost twice the size of the one Mark Twain notes.

[14] There are varying accounts of the legal entanglements over the Morgan mine, none of which exactly corresponds to Mark Twain's version. This mine had been discovered in 1850, either by Alfred Morgan or by John William Hance, who named it for Morgan, one of several associates. It reportedly yielded $2,800,000 between February 1850 and December 1851, but in 1852 the original owners were driven off by a band of ruffians and prospectors—perhaps recruited by a disfranchised partner named Finnegan—who contended that their holdings far exceeded the footage they could properly claim in proportion to that allowed individual miners. The claim-jumpers worked the mine until 1853, when the courts ordered them to yield it to Morgan. Upon their refusal to do so, Morgan armed a small band of followers

Old Mrs. Slasher—Englishwoman 45 yrs old—married merchant of 38—wears breeches—foulmouthed b—h. Tom found her blackguarding little Mrs. S last night, <w> had her cornered & holding her two small children behind her. Said <—>she— "An don't I know you—you're only a common strumpet & both them brats is bastards. And here is Mr Tom will say the same.<"> Tom said she was a distempered d—d old slut & recommended <sc>a dose of scalding water for her. The little woman's husband came in at this juncture, & <Mrs. Slash> mildly begged Mrs Slasher to go home until she was sober. She turned on him & said he was a rounder & had gotten a bastard by a Wallah. Tom suggested that the d—d old pelter be bundled neck & crop into the creek.

Hardy has sold his part of the Union copper mine at Copperopolis for 400,000. He was in the original location—cost him nothing—got about 40,000 out in dividends heretofore.[15]

Geo N. Marshall, Geo. Hurst & another have sold a new mine in Humboldt <in>for $3,000,000 in N. York.[16]

Jo— [*blank*] has sold a Humboldt mine in NY for $100,000. Herman Camp has sold some Washoe Stock in New York for $270,000.[17] [#]

---

and laid siege to the property, winning and then losing it without firing a shot. This did not conclude the dispute, however, for the mine remained under litigation for years, and it apparently wasn't until 1867 that mining was fully resumed.

[15] On 23 January 1865 the *Alta California* reported that Thomas Hardy, one of the founders of the "celebrated Union Copper Mine," had sold his quarter-interest for a price "we did not ascertain; but some idea can be formed of its value from the fact that the whole claim has, by shrewd calculations, been estimated at two millions of dollars." Later estimates of Hardy's price have been as low as $375,000 and as high as $650,000.

[16] In chapters 55 and 58 of *Roughing It*, Mark Twain would discuss the 1864 sale of the Pine Mountain Consolidated mine in Humboldt County, Nevada, by William M. (Sheba) Hurst, Amos H. Rose, and George M. Marshall, local reporter for the Virginia City *Daily Union*. Although he would claim to have been offered Marshall's place in the partnership, the disinterested tone of this entry, in which he miswrites the names of two of the partners and omits that of the other, suggests that his knowledge of the mine was in fact acquired at second hand.

[17] On 13 December 1865, in a letter to his brother Orion, Clemens described

Narrow Escape.—Jan 25—<18[0]5>1865—Dark rainy night—walked to extreme edge of a cut in solid rock 30 feet deep—& while standing upon the extreme verge for half a dozen seconds, meditating whether to proceed or not, heard a stream of water falling into the cut, & then, my eyes becoming more accustomed to the darkness, <I> saw that if the last step <I had> taken had been a hand breadth longer, <I> must have plunged in<to the abyss & lost my life. One of my feet projected over the edge as I stood.>

Tom Deer[18] (25th) is jubilant over having won the Morgan Mine lawsuit.

T.—Age 38—stature 6, weight 180. Parentage Va & N.Y. Light hair & blue eyes. Educated & well informed. Been on St Lawrence river. Been engineer & <clerk> 2d clerk on great rivers of the West. "Ranger" in early days of Texas; Indian fighter, soldier & clerk in office of one of Gen Taylor's staff—consequently was in principal battles. Fought Indians in <L>lower end of Cal. Came to upper Cal in '49 excitement from Mexico. Was in Washoe in '60—was Lieutenant in Pi Ute War in Capt Fleeson's Co under command of Jack Hays. Has worked silver mines there & gold mines in Cal for 12 or 15 yrs. Keeps Ky rifle has had 20 yrs. Milling & assaying—good cook. Reads writes & speaks Spanish & French.

Mountaineers in habit telling same old experiences over & over again in these little back settlements. Like Dan's old Ram,[19] whih

---

Herman Camp as "an old friend of mine—a 'rustler,' an energetic, untiring business man & a man of capital & large New York business associations & facilities" who "offered me half, 2 years ago, if I would go with him to New York & help him sell some mining claims, & I, like a fool, refused. He went, & made $270,000 in two months. . . . Men from New York tell me that Camp's mines have given better satisfaction than any that were sold in that market; he was shrewd enough to sell them well."

[18] No Tom Deer is mentioned in accounts of the struggle for the Morgan mine, nor was a settlement of the case reported at this time. In a notebook kept between 22 June 1897 and 24 March 1900, Mark Twain twice mentioned Tom Deer, first as "Tom Deer the Ranger (& liar?)" and then, in a list of lecture topics, as "Tom Deer & the explosion."

[19] This tale, attributed to Jim Blaine in chapter 53 of *Roughing It*, is again

he always drivels about when drunk. And like J's account of the finding of the Cardinel, Morgan (or Carson Hill), Excelsior, Isbell, (Vallecito,) Ish (Oregon,) Raspberry,[20] Saulsberry & other great pockets, & the sums they produced in a few days or weeks (50 to 100 lbs gold a day).

Met Ben Coon, Ill river pilot here.[21] Capt Whitney[22] is in San F. [#]

---

referred to as "Dan's old Ram" in Notebook 5, p. 172, but there is no evidence to indicate that Mark Twain's original source was Dan De Quille, his former associate on the Virginia City *Territorial Enterprise*.

[20] The accepted account of Bennager Raspberry's discovery of gold is probably typical of the legends in the mountaineer's repertoire. While hunting near Angel's Camp, Raspberry "shot a ramrod from his gun after it had become jammed. The ramrod landed at the roots of a manzanita bush. In pulling out the rod, Mr. Raspberry found a quartz vein and took out $700 that same afternoon, $2,000 the next, $7,000 the third day, and worked the vein at a huge profit for months" (*Ghost Towns and Relics of '49* [Stockton, California: Stockton Chamber of Commerce, 1948], p. 17).

[21] Ben Coon has generally been recognized as the originator of the "Jumping Frog" tale, but Mark Twain made no explicit connection between this entry and the later synopsis of the story of "Coleman with his jumping frog" (p. 80). In "An Unbiased Criticism," published in the *Californian* on 18 March 1865 (reprinted in *SSix*, pp. 158–165), he wrote of an ex-corporal Coon, "a nice bald-headed man at the hotel in Angels' Camp," whose deadpan, sleepy manner accords with the later, exaggerated, depiction of the "Jumping Frog's" narrator as "a dull person, and ignorant; he had no gift as a story-teller, and no invention; in his mouth this episode was merely history—history and statistics; and the gravest sort of history, too; he was entirely serious, for he was dealing with what to him were austere facts, and they interested him solely because they *were* facts; he was drawing on his memory, not his mind; he saw no humor in his tale, neither did his listeners; neither he nor they ever smiled or laughed" ("Private History of the 'Jumping Frog' Story," *North American Review* 158 [April 1894]: 447). Neither description, unless intended as a reversal of reality, fits Ross Coon, the "young, dandified" bartender with "yellowish-brown sideburns" in the Angel's Hotel, who allegedly "drew his chair close" to Mark Twain and "in his droll, inimitable way drifted slowly through the [Jumping Frog] yarn" (Edna Bryan Buckbee, *Pioneer Days of Angel's Camp* [Angel's Camp: Calaveras Californian, 1932], pp. 21, 22). Evidently on the basis of information supplied by Mark Twain, Albert Bigelow Paine dismissed both Ross Coon and one Coon Drayton as sources for the "Jumping Frog." He was unjustified, however, in implying that "Mark Twain's notes, made on the spot" (*MTB*, p. 271) definitively identify the teller of the tale as Ben Coon.

[22] Probably Captain James Whitney, president of the California Steam Navigation Company. The son of an Ohio steamboat builder, Whitney had first taken up his father's trade and then for sixteen years pursued his own "favorite vocation,

D—d girl always reading novels like The Convict, Or The Conspirator's Daughter,"[23] & going into ecstasies about them to <me> her friends.

Old woman who visits around & then comes home & tells all she finds out about her neighbors—gives them hell to each other, also—although she is sweet enough to a womans face.

Jan. 23, 1865—Angels—Rainy, stormy—Beans & dishwater for breakfast at the Frenchman's; dishwater & beans for dinner, & both articles warmed over for supper.

24th—Rained all day—meals as before

25—Same as above.

26th—Rain, beans & dishwater—tapidaro[24] beefsteak for a change—no use, could not bite it.

27th—Same old diet—same old weather—went out to the "pocket" claim—had to rush back.

28th—Rain & wind all day & all night. <Beans> Chili beans & dishwater three times to-day, as usual, & some kind of "slum" which the Frenchman called "hash." Hash be d—d.

29th—The old, old thing. <Jim says> We shall *have* to stand the weather, but as J says, we *won't* stand this dishwater & beans any longer, by G—.

30th Jan.—Moved to the new hotel, just opened—good fare, & coffee that a Christian may drink without jeopardizing his eternal soul.

W Bilgewater, says she, Good God what a name.[25] [#]

---

running steamboats on the waters of the Ohio and Mississippi." In 1849 he had come to California, where he "immediately engaged in steamboat building and in navigation on the San Joaquin and Sacramento rivers" (Sacramento *Daily Union,* 28 December 1865).

[23] Ned Buntline's *The Convict; Or, The Conspirator's Victim* (New York: W. F. Burgess) had been published in 1851.

[24] Properly *tapadera,* the leather cover on a Mexican stirrup.

[25] The people alluded to in this entry cannot be identified. Mark Twain's partiality to the name Bilgewater is evident from its recurrence in his works. He first used it in "Angel's Camp Constable" (DV 408), an unpublished early sketch about one of "the venerable Simon Wheeler's pet heroes," although neither of the Angel's

<"> Dick Stoker came over to-day, from Tuttletown, Tuolumne Co.

Boden crazy, asking after his wife, who had been dead 13 years—first knowledge of his being deranged.[26]

In Angels in '50, Americans shot down & killed 12 Mexicans in 5 days.[27]

In Tuolumne Co in '51, <2,000>4,000 Chinamen had a pitched battle—fought all day—only one killed.[28] [#]

Camp constables at this time bore the name. In a letter to the *Alta California* written on 20 December 1866 Mark Twain reported that just before his departure from San Francisco on the steamer *America* "Bilgewater arrived with a keg of quartz specimens, to be delivered to his aunt in New York" (*MTTB*, p. 12). In chapter 77 of *Roughing It* a Colonel Bilgewater is mentioned by Markiss, the Maui liar, and in chapter 19 of *Huckleberry Finn* Bilgewater becomes the Dauphin's corruption of Bridgewater, the Duke's alleged title.

[26] In 1893 Mark Twain expanded this note into "The Californian's Tale," published that year in *The First Book of the Authors Club; Liber Scriptorum.*

[27] In the early 1850s such attacks were frequently directed against the gold country's large foreign population, particularly the Mexican and Chinese elements, whose presence was bitterly resented by American miners. Antagonism toward the Mexicans, in many cases residents of California before the Americans, led the California legislature to establish in 1850 a monthly "foreign miners tax" of twenty dollars, which was often repeatedly levied without authorization by disreputable individuals seeking grubstakes. The tax was repealed the following year, when a mass exodus of Mexican miners depressed the profits of gold-country merchants. In 1852, however, a second tax was passed which was finally established at four dollars a month, this time directed against the Chinese, who were arriving in large numbers as low-paid contract laborers. This tax was still in effect while Mark Twain was in California, for he commented on its abusive application in chapter 54 of *Roughing It.* Nevertheless, by 1860 most of the foreign residents who hadn't been driven off had been assimilated, often as wage laborers for American miners, and the agitation against them had largely subsided.

[28] Probably the battle between the Sam-yap and Yang-wo tongs which took place near Table Mountain in Tuolumne County on 26 September 1855. While law officers stood by and watched, twenty-one hundred Chinese miners, reportedly wielding "tridents, skewers, pikes, daggers and bludgeon irons" as well as "a dozen or more muskets" engaged furiously for several hours. Nevertheless, when exhaustion put an end to the hostilities, it was discovered that "the total casualties to both tongs were four killed and seven wounded" (Buckbee, *Old Tuolumne*, pp. 79–80).

Feb 3—Dined at the Frenchman's, in order to let Dick see how he does things. Had Hellfire soup & the old regular beans & dishwater. The Frenchman has <3>4 kinds of soup which he furnishes to customers only on great occasions. They are popularly known among the Boarders as Hellfire, General Debility, Insanity & Sudden Death, but it is not possible to <the>describe them.

Little seventy-five-year-older.

<J[im]>J & me talking like people 80 years old & toothless.

Camp meeting exhorting, slapping on back till make saddle boils. "I've prospected all religions & I like the old Meth. best after all.
Bear Hunter next.
Indian fighter
Gambler.
Stage driver
Washoe Flat Copper gold silver

J etait appellé "Aristocrat" parce <queil>qu'il s'habiter dans un chemise blanc.

Feb. 6—Blazing hot days & cool nights. No more rain.

"Odd or Even"—cast away at Honey Lake Smith's.[29]

Billy Clagett moved fifteen steps from camp fire by the lice crawling on his body.[30]

Man in San F jumped lot & built house on it propped on low pins

---

[29] "A sort of isolated inn on the Carson river," where, as described in chapters 30 and 31 of *Roughing It,* Mark Twain had been stranded by flood for more than a week in January 1862. In a letter dated 12 February [1866] to the *Territorial Enterprise* (Yale Scrapbook), he recalled that "the whole place was crowded with teamsters, and we wore out every deck of cards on the place, and then had no amusement left but to scrape up a handful of vermin off the floor or the beds, and 'shuffle' them, and bet on odd or even."

[30] In the winter of 1861/1862 William H. Clagett, a lawyer and Keokuk, Iowa, friend, who in the early 1860s served in both houses of the Nevada legislature, had accompanied Mark Twain on the Humboldt silver hunt described in chapters 27 through 30 of *Roughing It*. Mark Twain did not include this incident in his account of their Humboldt experiences.

—hogs used to congregate under it & grunt all night—man bored holes in floor & his wife poured hot water through—hogs struggling to get out hauled the house down the hill on their backs & the <house> lot was re-jumped by its proper owners early in the morning.[31]

Bunker's <ge>great landslide case of Dick Sides vs. Rust—Rust's ranch slid down on Sides ranch & the suit was an ejectment suit tried before Gov Roop as Judge Referee, who gave a verdict in favor of defendant.[32]

Chinese Theatre[33]

<D[----] D[*three words*]> Pi Ute war dance on hills back of Angels'. [#]

---

31 A version of this story was also told by William R. Gillis in his *Gold Rush Days with Mark Twain* (pp. 242–245). Gillis' "A Sudden House Moving" concerns the pet pigs of "a little Holland Dutchman," who is neither provided with a wife nor involved in claim-jumping.

32 Mark Twain's account of this incident was first published as "A Rich Decision" in the San Francisco *Morning Call* of 30 August 1863. He subsequently reworked it twice, first for the Buffalo *Express,* where it appeared on 2 April 1870 as "The Facts in the Great Landslide Case," and then for chapter 34 of *Roughing It.* (For an extended account of the relationship between the three versions, see *The Great Landslide Case,* ed. Frederick Anderson and Edgar M. Branch [Berkeley: The Friends of The Bancroft Library, University of California, 1972].) Richard D. Sides, a Nevada landowner, cattle rancher, horse breeder, and silver miner, and Tom Rust, a Washoe Valley farmer, were the prototypes for the practical jokers who enlist the aid of Isaac Roop, former provisional governor of Nevada Territory, in confounding Attorney General Benjamin B. Bunker, in the later versions thinly disguised as General Buncombe. While in Nevada, Clemens had maintained an ambivalent relationship with Bunker. Although on friendly enough terms with the attorney general to accept him as a traveling companion on at least two occasions, Clemens' reports of him were consistently contemptuous. On 30 January 1862 he had written his mother of a horse named Bunker, a "poor, lean, infatuated cuss" whose forward progress was impeded by a penchant for deep reveries in which he would "go on thinking, and pondering, and getting himself more and more mixed up and tangled in his subject" until he would have to "stop to review the question" (*PRI,* p. 30). And on 8 March of the same year he informed Billy Clagett that Bunker was a "d—d old Puritan" who cheated at cards.

33 On 25 June 1865 the San Francisco *Call* noted:

> The almond-eyed manipulators of Celestial chop-sticks and terrestrial chickens have fitted up a theatre on the first floor of the Globe Hotel, corner of Dupont

Coleman with his jumping frog—bet stranger $50—stranger had no frog, & C got him one—in the meantime stranger filled C's frog full of shot & he couldn't jump—the stranger's frog won.

Wrote this story for Artemus—his idiot publisher, Carleton gave it to Clapp's Saturday Press.[34]

Time Bob Howland came into Mrs. Murphy's corral in Carson, <k>drunk, knocked down Wagners bottles of tarantulas & scorpions & spilled them on the floor.[35] [#]

---

and Jackson streets, which is to be opened during the present week. Any white man will be permitted to go in and enjoy the "divine racket," and inhale the heavenly odors of the entertainment, for four bits.

Mark Twain may have visited this theater, which is not listed by name in directories of the period, after his return to San Francisco. However, none of the surviving dramatic criticism he contributed to the *Territorial Enterprise*, the *Golden Era*, the *Californian*, and the San Francisco *Dramatic Chronicle* mentions it.

[34] This note was written in blue ink across the preceding entry, Mark Twain's original notation for the "Jumping Frog" story. On 26 February 1865, upon his return to San Francisco, he would find a letter from Artemus Ward requesting a contribution to the forthcoming *Artemus Ward, His Travels* (New York: Carleton, 1865). Mark Twain would note then (see p. 82) that delay in receipt of Ward's letter had already made it too late to comply. This assumption may in part explain why it wasn't until mid-October that he wrote his version of the "Jumping Frog," apparently after repeated invitations from Ward (see Edgar M. Branch, "'My Voice Is Still for Setchell': A Background Study of 'Jim Smiley and His Jumping Frog,'" *PMLA* 82 [1967]: 597, 599). By that time it was indeed too late, and George W. Carleton, Ward's publisher, passed the sketch on to Henry Clapp, who published it on 18 November 1865 in the New York *Saturday Press*, where it reached an enthusiastic audience and from which it was widely reprinted. On 20 January 1866, Clemens suggested in a letter to his mother and sister that Carleton had done him a service by omitting the "Jumping Frog" from Ward's book, "a wretchedly poor one, generally speaking, and it could be no credit to either of us to appear between its covers" (*MTL*, p. 101). Nevertheless, ten years later he recalled in a letter to William Dean Howells that "Carleton insulted me in Feb, 1867" (*MTHL*, p. 132), which indicates it was the publisher's rejection of *The Celebrated Jumping Frog of Calaveras County, and Other Sketches* (published in New York by C. H. Webb in 1867) that caused the antagonism registered here.

[35] In 1861 Robert M. Howland had been appointed town marshal of Aurora, Esmeralda County, Nevada, by his uncle, Governor James W. Nye, and in August and September of that year he had been a delegate to the Union party convention in Carson City. While in Carson City he boarded, along with Samuel and Orion Clemens and the rest of Governor Nye's entourage, at Mrs. Margret Murphy's

Louse betting by <sold> discharged soldiers coming through from Mexico to Cal in early days. The man whose louse got whipped had to get supper. Or place them on the bottom of a frying pan—draw chalk circle round them, heat the pan & the last louse over the line had to get supper.

Jim story of Kilien & his method of furnishing lodgings to strangers so they could carry off some of the lice.

Feb. 20th 1865.

Left Angels with Jim & Dick & walked over the mountains to Jackass in a snow storm—the first I ever saw in California. The view from the mountain tops was beautiful.

Feb. 21—On Jackass Hill again. The exciting topic of conversation in this sparse community just at present (& it always <in> *is* in dire commotion about something or other of small consequence,) is Mrs. Carrington's baby, which was born a week ago, on the 14th. There was nothing remarkable about the baby, but if Mrs C had given birth to an ornamental cast-iron dog big enough for an embellishment for the State-House steps I don't believe the event would have created more intense interest in the community.

Had to remain at Jackass all day 21st, on account of heavy snow storm—inch deep, but all gone, sun out & grass green again before night.

23d—Could have walked to Sonora over Table Mountain in an hour, & left immediately in the stage for Stockton, but was told it was quickest to take a horse & go by Copperopolis, 12 miles distant. Came down, accordingly—arrived here in Copper at dusk.

---

boarding house, the "ranch" operated by "a worthy French lady by the name of Bridget O'Flannigan" in chapter 21 of *Roughing It*. In *Roughing It*, Mark Twain wrote that one night, during a "Washoe Zephyr," "Bob H——— sprung up out of a sound sleep, and knocked down a shelf with his head," freeing a collection of tarantulas, which terrorized the occupants of the room. No mention is made of Wagner in *Roughing It*, and no one by that name has been identified as a boarder at Mrs. Murphy's. In the early months of 1862 Howland was one of Mark Twain's mining partners in Aurora.

24th—D—n Copperopolis—the big ball last night was postponed a week; instead of leaving this morning, the stage will not leave until to-morrow morning.

Have lost my pipe, & cant get another in this hellfired town. Left my knife, merschaum & toothbrush at Angels—made Dick give me his big navy knife.

Went down in the great "Union Copper mine" this morning 300 feet & throughout all the ramifications of its six galleries & numerous drifts. In some places vein 18 inches wide & in others as many feet—all very rich. <I>Mr. Hardy sold his half of it a week or so ago for $650,000 (greenbacks.)

This is a pretty town & has about 1000 inhabitants. D—d poor hotel, but if this bad luck will let up on me I will be in Stockton at noon to-morrow & in San Francisco before midnight.

25th—Arrived in Stockton at 5 P.M.

26th—Home again—home again at the Occidental Hotel,[36] San Francisco—find letters from "Artemus Ward" asking me to write a sketch for his new book of Nevada Territory travels which is soon to come out. Too late—ought to have got the letters 3 months ago. They are dated early in November.

Refer back.[37] [#]

---

[36] Mark Twain first took up residence at the Occidental Hotel on 8 June 1864 as he was beginning to report for the San Francisco *Call*. Soon after, in a piece called "In the Metropolis," he remarked:

> To a Christian who has toiled months and months in Washoe; whose hair bristles from a bed of sand, and whose soul is caked with a cement of alkali dust; whose nostrils know no perfume but the rank odor of sage-brush—and whose eyes know no landscape but barren mountains and desolate plains; where the winds blow, and the sun blisters, and the broken spirit of the contrite heart finds joy and peace only in Limberger cheese and lager beer—unto such a Christian, verily the Occidental Hotel is Heaven on the half shell. He may even secretly consider it to be Heaven on the entire shell, but his religion teaches a sound Washoe Christian that it would be sacrilege to say it. (*Golden Era*, 26 June 1864, reprinted in *WG*, pp. 74–76)

[37] This note was written in blue ink across the preceding entry at the same later time that Mark Twain similarly inscribed a comment on his 1865 "Jumping Frog" entry.

Scene—In a country cabin in Mo.—Traveler asks 3 boys what they do—last & smallest says "I <e>nusses Johnny, eats apples & totes out merde."

Scene—Woods in Cal in early times—one-armed man finds man tied up to tree—says "They tied you up, did they?"—yes. "Your'e tied tight, are you?—yes. Can't get loose?—No—"Then by — I go [*indecipherable shorthand word*] you myself."

Scene—Pacific street wharf—arrival of Sacto boat—Hackmen judging by <p> dress of passengers & not wasting breath on such as are not likely to want a carriage. One comes up to Mr. Derrick (who looks seedy), & says:

"Want a car.—O Jesus!" & turns away disgusted.

Another said to Jim Gillis—"No—don't want a carriage?—O I'll tell you what the feller wants—he wants a dose of salts."

Bald white head, like a billiard ball in a nail grab.

Mem—Must finish Mrs Fitch's tragedy, where the Injun chief siezes the halfbreed child by the ancles, suddenly substitutes a dummy & dashes its bloody brains out against a white dead-wall rather to the disgust of the audience than otherwise.[38]

Constitution U.S, Whole Duty of Man & other light reading.

Had a breath like a buzzard.

The d—d old sow!

Exercise—"Lesson VI" [#]

---

[38] Since it is unlikely that such a play had ever been conceived by Anna M. Fitch, "an able romancist of the ineffable school," Mark Twain may have contemplated a burlesque of the writer, whose work featured heroes who were "all dainty and all perfect" and heroines who "talked nothing but pearls and poetry." In chapter 51 of *Roughing It*, Mark Twain would describe his abortive involvement, along with Mrs. Fitch, her husband Thomas, and others, in a collaborative novel to be run serially in Thomas Fitch's short-lived literary weekly, the Virginia City *Occidental*. Among Mrs. Fitch's later works was a domestic novel, *Bound Down, or Life and Its Possibilities* (Philadelphia: J. B. Lippincott & Co., 1870).

Sallow faced <sore-faced> child, with sores on its face like a fruit-cake.

Couldn't been colder if I had swallowed an ice-berg.

The Tragedy of Othello—first part seen from dress circle—last part from private box.

Report[39]

Of Prof. G—to accompany Map & Views of the Great Vide Poche Mine, On Mount Olympus, Calaveras Co.

Prof. G—begs leave to report that he has thoroughly examined

[39] The following sketch constitutes one of the few examples of sustained composition in Mark Twain's notebooks. Its scatological quality makes clear it was con-

the grounds of the Great Vide Poche Company on Mount Olympus, & after the most careful deliberation & exhausting reflection, has arrived at the conclusion that if there is anything there, they haven't got it yet.

That there is a fine field for labor within the limits of their possessions is indisputable, for by an estimate based upon the amount of work already done & the results achieved by it, the Prof. is enabled to hazard the conviction that a similar ratio of labor, with similar & undiminished results, may be expended upon the mine for many centuries to come without exhausting the field of operations or sensibly <impairing> affecting the chances they now have. It is the unprejudiced opinion of the Prof that as long as there is anything left of Mount Olympus the Company will have as good a show as they have got now.

By reference to the Map it will be seen that the course of the principal lode or vein is apparently uncertain & irregular, & has the general direction of a streak of lightning. The map is not <ap>absolutely correct in this matter, the vein being really almost straight, but at the time the Prof was drawing it, seated upon a log, he was persistently besieged by piss-ants, & the acute angles in the course of the vein <will bear ample tes> demonstrate with singular fidelity the extraordinary suddenness & fury of their assauts.

This mark (o) in the map, signifies a shaft. The company have sunk some 250 of these, varying in depth from 6 inches to 2 feet, & in diameter from 10 inches to 3 feet. This mark (o═o) stands for a cut or drift connecting two <shafts> or more shafts. One of

---

ceived for an exclusively male audience, perhaps as an informal after-dinner speech. Although *vide poche*, or empty pocket, has obvious satirical effect in this piece, the phrase also had prior associations for Mark Twain. As late as 1841 Carondelet, a village just south of Saint Louis, was still being referred to as Vide Poche, an earlier name, which reportedly had derived from "the financial state of the domestic treasuries of its inhabitants" (*The Valley of the Mississippi*, ed. Lewis F. Thomas, [1841; reprint ed., Saint Louis: Joseph Garnier, 1948], 2:39). Mark Twain's familiarity with Carondelet is indicated by references to it in "Villagers of 1840–3" (*HH&T*, p. 32) and in his *Autobiography* (2:186).

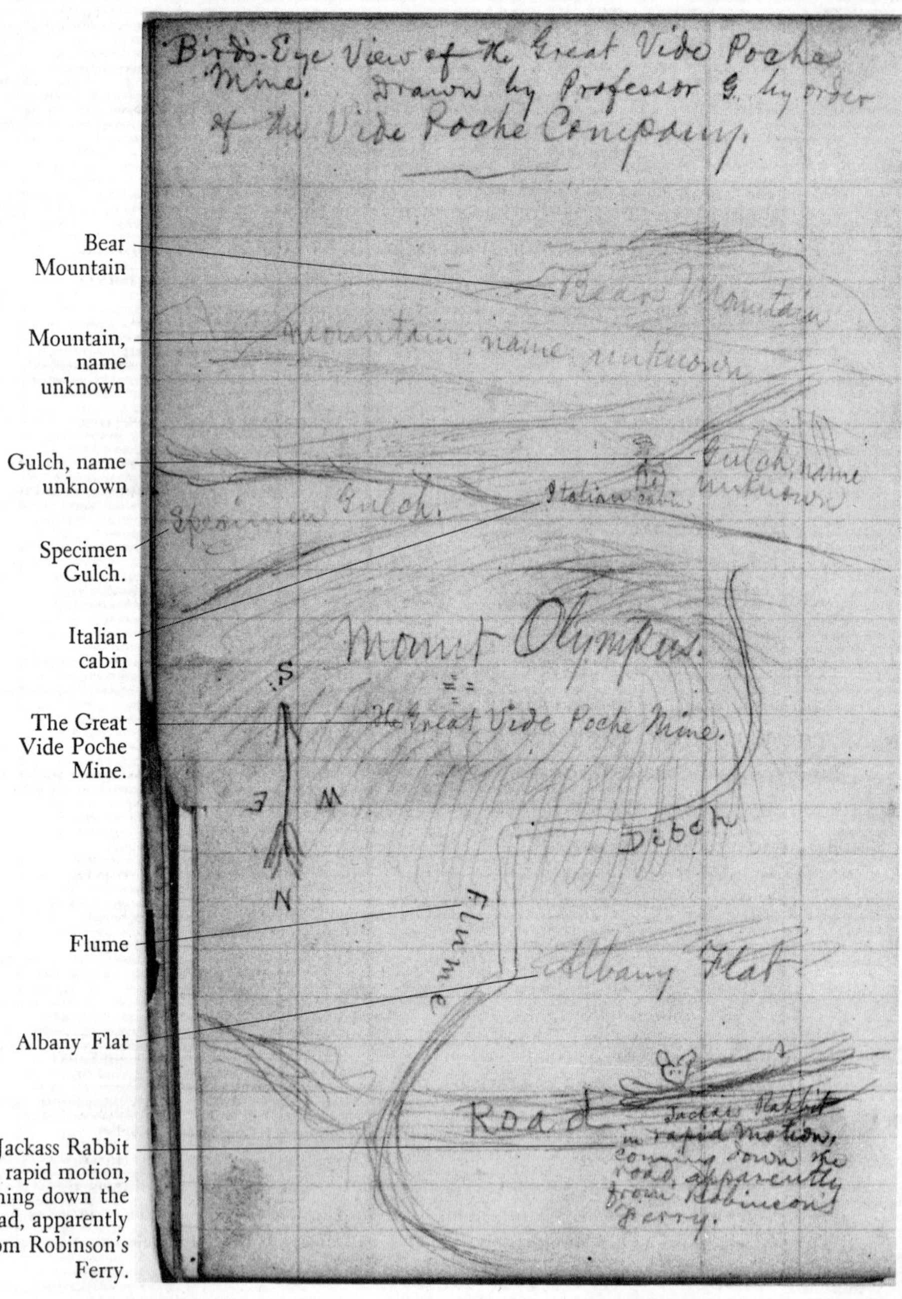
Birds-Eye View of the Great Vide Poche Mine. Drawn by Professor G. by order of the Vide Poche Company.
Bear Mountain
Mountain, name unknown
Gulch, name unknown
Specimen Gulch.
Italian cabin
The Great Vide Poche Mine.
Flume
Albany Flat
Jackass Rabbit in rapid motion, coming down the road, apparently from Robinson's Ferry.
S
N
Ditch
Road

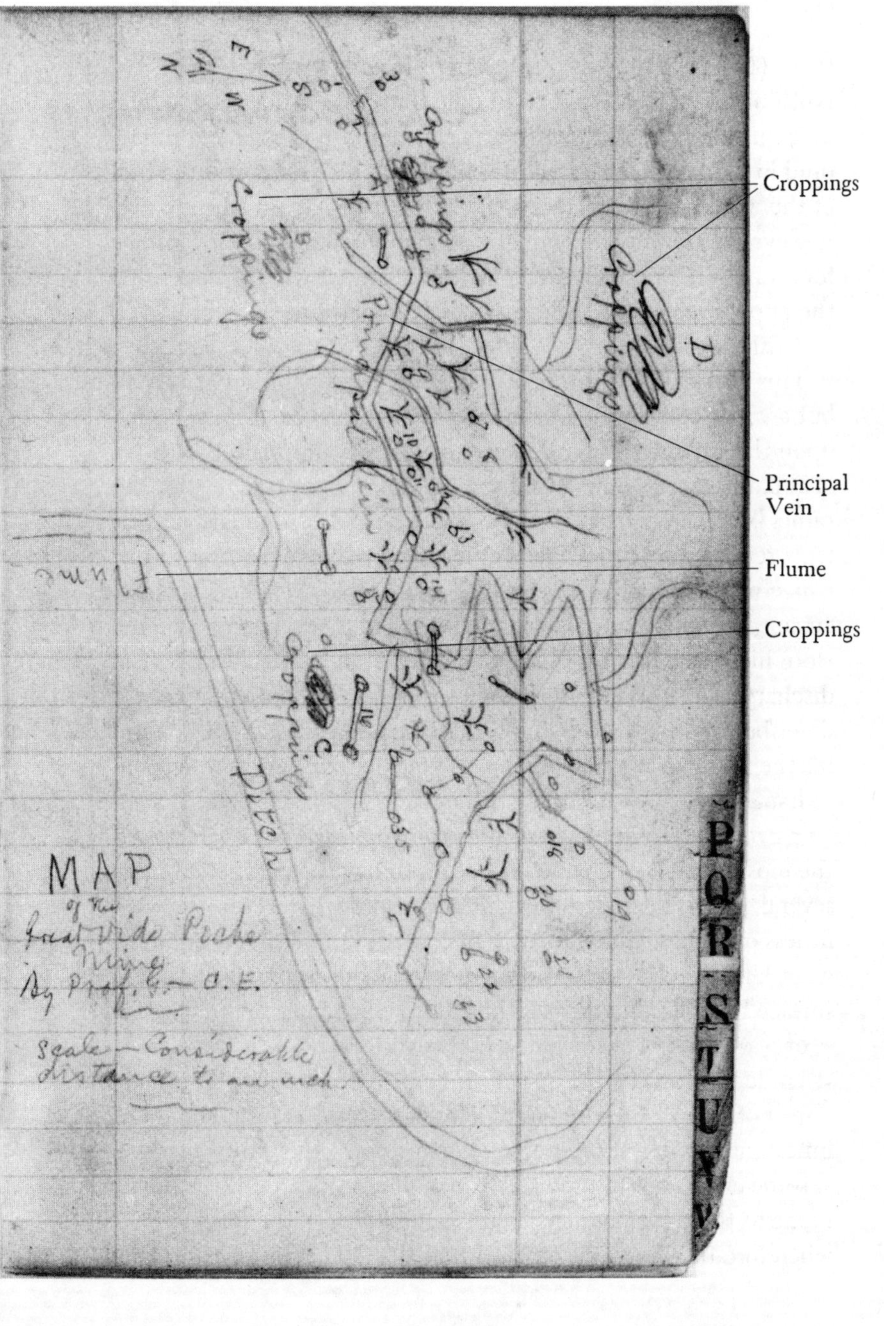
Croppings
Principal
Vein
Flume
Croppings
MAP
of the
Great Vide Poche
Mine
By Prof. G— O.E.
Scale—Considerable
distance to an inch.

these (No 72), is some 30 feet long, 2 ft wide & 1 foot deep. Nothing was found in it except mud, but it is encouraging to know that this mud was not in any respect inferior to the general run of mud in Calaveras Co. It has been judged best to suppress the results of the washings from the various shafts. It can do no harm to say, however, that if any individual who had purchased the V.P. mine for a vast sum of money were made acquainted with those results, the knowledge would be likely to fill him with the liveliest astonishment.

This mark (¥) is meant to signify chapparal, but it can afford but a vague conception of the excessive prevalence of that shrub upon the premises. Indeed, had the professor put in all the chapparal, there would have been no room left in the map for the mine. Not having had time to make a scientific examination of this truly remarkably shrub, the Prof is forced to make use of information concerning it which he derived from an employé of the Co who was engaged in chopping it down, & who <had> was resting a moment from his labors to wipe the perspiration from his forehead & discharge some blasphemy from his system. This person did not describe it minutely—he simply answered, in general terms, "Stranger, it's the G— d—dest truck that ever *I* tackled, & it's nearly lightnin' to hang on when you get ketched in it."

<Fro> The croppings upon the Great Vide Poche vein are of the most diversified character, & seem to have been assigned to their several <placed>places without any regard whatever to the eternal fitness of things. Consequently an expert can tell no more about what kind of rock <in>is underneath by the croppings on the surface here than he can tell the quality of a man's brain by the style <of> & material of the hat <that covers his head.> he wears. <Under unmistakeable quartz croppings the prof found nothing but slate.> Some of these croppings are slate, some granite, some limestone, some grindstone, some soapstone some brimstone, & <some even> even some jackstones, whetstones 'dobies & brickbats. None of these various articles are found beneath the surface, wherefore the Prof feels satisfied that the Company have got the

world by the ass, since it is manifest that no other <part>organ of the earth's frame could possibly have produced such a dysentery of disorganized & half-digested slumgullion as <this.> is here <present.>presented.

Upon one pile of these croppings the prof found a most interesting formation—one which, from its unusual conformation & composition at first excited in his breast <the> a frenzy of professional enthusiasm. The deposit was cylindrical in form, & 3 inches long by ¾ of an inch in diameter, tapering to a point like the end of a cigar at one end & broken off square at the <en>other, exposing several projecting fibres resembling hairs. The object was <gray in color> of a dull light gray color, dry & capable of disintegration by moderate pressure between the fingers. The professor at once applied the tests of handling, smelling & tasting, & was forced to the conclusion that there was nothing extraordinary about the seeming phenomenon, & that it had doubtless been deposited on the croppings by <a>some animal—a dog, in all probability.

In conclusion the Prof begs to assure the Company that splendid results must infallibly follow the thorough development of the Great Vide Poche Mine, & that if they continue to labor as they are doing at present, this development <u>will unquestionably be accomplished ultimately. It is only a matter of time,—or at any rate of eternity.

W Bilgewater

Jesus Maria (Suce Mariea)[40]

<Jan.> February 1st—Saw L. Mark <Wrigh>Write[41] in a

---

[40] A Jesus Maria Creek and settlement in Calaveras County "were named for a Mexican by that name who raised vegetables there in the mining days. . . . The local pronunciation is so͞os mȧ-rē′-ȧ" (Edwin G. Gudde, *California Place Names*, rev. and enl. ed. [Berkeley and Los Angeles: University of California Press, 1969], p. 157).

[41] Samuel Clemens met Laura M. Wright, "the only girl he had any trouble forgetting" (*MTBus*, p. 51) in New Orleans when he was twenty-two and she was in her early teens. Their three-day romantic interlude ended abruptly with the departure of the *Pennsylvania*, the boat on which Clemens was an apprentice pilot. The

dream ce matin-ce—in carriage—said good bye & shook hands.

[*three lines of undecipherable shorthand*]

---

two corresponded for a time, but Clemens was under the impression that his letters were being intercepted, and he didn't attempt to see her again. Nevertheless, he seems to have kept well informed about her, for on 25 September 1864 he asked his mother and sister: "What has become of that girl of mine that got married? I mean Laura Wright." And on several later occasions she again came to his mind. Between March 1880 and January 1882, by then Laura M. Dake, a Dallas schoolteacher, her presence pervaded Mark Twain's correspondence with twelve-year-old David Watt Bowser, one of her pupils (see Pascal Covici, Jr., ed., "Dear Master Wattie: The Mark Twain-David Watt Bowser Letters," *Southwest Review* 45 [1960]: 104–121). On 26 May 1885 she was the subject of a bittersweet notebook entry that marked the anniversary of their parting and recalled her prediction of a future meeting. In fact, the two did not meet, nor did they communicate until 1906, when, a "world-worn and trouble-worn widow of sixty-two," Laura Dake appealed to Mark Twain "for pecuniary help for herself and for her disabled son. . . . She is in need of a thousand dollars, and I sent it" (AD, 30 July 1906).

V

"Drifting About the Outskirts of the World"

(March, June–September 1866)

THERE IS an interval of slightly more than a year, from the end of February 1865 to the beginning of March 1866, between Notebooks 4 and 5. Mark Twain thought this period worthy of only a single paragraph in chapter 62 of *Roughing It*:

> After a three months' absence, I found myself in San Francisco again, without a cent. When my credit was about exhausted, (for I had become too mean and lazy, now, to work on a morning paper, and there were no vacancies on the evening journals,) I was created San Francisco correspondent of the *Enterprise*, and at the end of five months I was out of debt, but my interest in my work was gone; for my correspondence being a daily one, without rest or respite, I got unspeakably tired of it. I wanted another change. The vagabond instinct was strong upon me. Fortune favored and I got a new berth and a delightful one. It was to go down to the Sandwich Islands and write some letters for the Sacramento *Union*, an excellent journal and liberal with employés.

Although no notebook and little correspondence or other contemporary documentation has survived, a number of details can be provided to expand

and modify this abbreviated account. It is clear, for example, that Mark Twain did not depend entirely on credit in 1865. Contributions to the *Californian*, occasional pieces in the *Golden Era*, and correspondence for Joseph Goodman's Virginia City *Territorial Enterprise* helped support a bohemian existence during the spring, summer, and fall of that year. On 19 October Clemens informed Orion and Mollie that he intended "to work in dead earnest" to get out of debt by writing regularly for the *Territorial Enterprise* and the San Francisco *Dramatic Chronicle:*

> Joe Goodman pays me $100 a month for a daily letter, and the Dramatic Chronicle pays me or rather *will* begin to pay me, next week—$40 a month for dramatic criticisms. Same wages I got on the *Call*, & more agreeable & less laborious work.

In the same letter he belittled his emergent creative awareness in order to exhort Orion to become a "preacher of the gospel," a profession he himself had despaired of attaining:

> I have had a "call" to literature, of a low order—*i.e.* humorous. It is nothing to be proud of, but it is my strongest suit, & if I were to listen to that maxim of stern *duty* which says that to do right you *must* multiply the one or the two or the three talents which the Almighty entrusts to your keeping, I would long ago have ceased to meddle with things for which I was by nature unfitted & turned my attention to seriously scribbling to excite the *laughter* of God's creatures. Poor, pitiful business! . . . *You* see in me a talent for humorous writing, & urge me to cultivate it. But I always regarded it as brotherly partiality on your part, & attached no value to it. It is only now, when editors of standard literary papers in the distant east give me high praise, & who do not know me & cannot of course be blinded by the glamour of partiality, that I really begin to believe there must be something in it. (*My Dear Bro: A Letter from Samuel Clemens to His Brother Orion*, ed. Frederick Anderson [Berkeley, California: The Berkeley Albion, 1961], pp. 6–8)

Mark Twain's first great success with an eastern paper was imminent. On 26 February, upon his return from the Mother Lode country, he had written in Notebook 4, p. 82:

> home again at the Occidental Hotel, San Francisco—find letters from "Artemus Ward" asking me to write a sketch for his new book of Nevada Territory travels which is soon to come out. Too late—ought to have got the letters 3 months ago. They are dated early in November.

By the time his sketch, "Jim Smiley and His Jumping Frog," apparently written between 16 and 23 October, was ready, it was indeed too late for inclusion in *Artemus Ward, His Travels* (New York: Carleton, 1865) and was instead offered to the New York *Saturday Press*, where it appeared on 18 November 1865. Acclaim was instantaneous, and the sketch was widely reprinted. Fed by this unexpected success, Mark Twain's impatience with the routine of daily newspaper reporting, even of the "more agreeable & less laborious" kind, grew. Anxious perhaps for a reason to appear on the eastern scene of his "Jumping Frog" triumph, on 13 December 1865 he wrote Orion of a plan to dispose of the Clemens property in Tennessee. He would accomplish this with the assistance of Herman Camp, a mining acquaintance with New York business connections:

> He leaves for the east 5 days hence—on the 19th. I told him we had 30,000 acres land in Tennessee, & there was oil on it—& if he would send me $500 from New York to go east with, $500 more after I got there, & pay all my expenses while I assisted him in selling the land, I would give him one-half of the entire proceeds. . . .
>
> Now I don't want that Tenn land to go for taxes, & I don't want any "slouch" to take charge of the sale of it. I am tired being a beggar—tired being chained to this accursed homeless desert,—I want to go back to a Christian land once more —& so I want you to send me immediately all necessary memoranda to enable Camp to understand the condition, quantity & resources of the land, & how he must go about finding it. He will visit St Louis & talk with the folks, & then go at once & see the land, & telegraph me whether he closes with my proposition or not.

Clemens later recalled that Camp "agreed to buy our Tennessee land for two hundred thousand dollars. . . . His scheme was to import foreigners from grape-growing and wine-making districts in Europe, settle them on the land, and turn it into a wine-growing country." But Orion, then a temperance advocate, "said that he would not be a party to debauching the country with wine" (*MTA*, 2:320). His schemes for riches and release at an end, Mark Twain continued to write for the *Enterprise* during the tedious winter of 1865/1866. He exorcised some of his frustration in a journalistic feud with Albert S. Evans, a reporter and editorial writer on the *Alta California*, who used the pseudonym Fitz Smythe in San Francisco and signed himself Amigo in dispatches to the Gold Hill *Evening News*, a rival of the *Enterprise*. In the course of this sometimes bitter exchange, Mark Twain launched an attack on the San Francisco police, who were championed by Fitz Smythe. A similar attack had contributed to his hasty departure from San Francisco in December 1864, and in late 1865 and early 1866 this new one was signaling his readiness to leave again. In a letter of 20 January 1866 Clemens complained to his mother and sister: "I don't know what to write—my life is so uneventful. I wish I was back there piloting up & down the river again." He went on to express unhappiness at having foregone a recent opportunity to get away, at least temporarily:

> That Ajax is the finest Ocean Steamer in America, & one of the fastest. She will make this trip to the Sandwich Islands & back in a month, & it generally take a sailing vessel three months. She had 52 invited guests aboard—the cream of the town—gentlemen & ladies both, & a splendid brass band. I know lots of the guests. I got an invitation, but I could not accept it, because there would be no one to write my correspondence while I was gone. But I am so sorry now. If the Ajax were back I would go—quick!—and throw up the correspondence. Where could a man catch such another crowd together?

Clemens' desire for escape found expression in a sudden proliferation of literary projects, a reaction to stress or boredom that was to be characteristic throughout his life. According to the 20 January letter home, in the works were commissions to write for the New York *Weekly Review* and the New York *Saturday Press* and a collaboration with Bret Harte on a book of sketches and a book-length burlesque of "all the tribe of California poets" which would "just make them get up & howl." He also noted a rumor current in San Francisco that Mark Twain "has commenced the work of writing a book . . . on an entirely new subject, one that has not been written about heretofore," commenting:

> The book referred to . . . is a pet notion of mine—nobody knows what it is going to be about but just myself. Orion don't know. I am slow & lazy, you know, & the bulk of it will not be finished under a year. I expect it to make about three hundred pages, and the last hundred will have to be written in St Louis, because the materials for them can only be got there. If I do not write it to suit me at first I will write it all over again, & so, who knows?—I may be an old man before I finish it.

The need to return to Saint Louis suggests that this book was to deal with material later to appear in *Life on the Mississippi*, but there is no indication that it, or any of the other literary projects of the moment, were advanced from the planning stage. Still at loose ends in late February, after the return of the *Ajax* from Hawaii, Clemens made a brief trip to Sacramento whose purpose may be inferred from a letter of 5 March in which he jubilantly informed his mother and sister:

> I start to do Sandwich Islands day after tomorrow . . . in the steamer "Ajax." We shall arrive there in about twelve days. . . . I am to remain there a month and ransack the islands, the great cataracts and the volcanoes completely, and write twenty or thirty letters to the Sacramento *Union*—for which they pay me as much money as I would get if I staid at home. (*MTL*, p. 103)

The pleasure junket he had regretted declining some six weeks before had materialized again, this time as a roving commission. But if Mark Twain's assignment was in fact to write a letter a day for a month to report all that was important in Hawaii, its offer as well as its blithe acceptance suggest an innocence about these islands whose geography alone would have made compliance impossible. Still, boredom with the routine of his life in San Francisco precluded sober consideration of the conditions of escape. Two days after the exultant letter, Mark Twain went on board the *Ajax* and made his first entries in Notebook 5. Almost immediately he began gathering advance information about Hawaii from residents among the passengers. Although he diluted this seriousness of purpose with a readiness to yield to "the most magnificent, balmy atmosphere in the world" (Notebook 6, p. 192), the fact that he needed four months to "ransack" the Sandwich Islands was the result not of indolence, and not only of geography, but rather of the islands' variety and amplitude as subject matter.

The year 1866 was a watershed in Mark Twain's career, ending his period of apprentice journalism and introducing him to the expansive and independent labor that would culminate in the book-length travel narratives that established and propagated his fame. It marked a corresponding period of change for Hawaii. For by that year an era that had seen the Sandwich Islands become a sometimes volatile blend of mission and saloon had already begun to draw to a close, and the reign of the missionary and the whaler as dominant and conflicting forces in Hawaiian life was ending.

In the late eighteenth and early nineteenth centuries their location had made the Sandwich Islands a provisioning stop and trading center for merchant cargo ships. After 1820 Hawaii became an important whaling port, and it was the whaling industry, particularly in the years from 1843 to 1860, that was most important to its commercial development. The island complex was soon a service area for whalers, offering those commodities essential to the enterprise: provisions, shipyard facilities, seamen recruits, taverns, women. After 1850 Hawaii even sent out a few whaling ships of local registry. But by the early 1860s a decline had set in, the effect of a scarcity of whales, competition from the growing petroleum industry, and the Civil War, which brought the destruction of many United States whalers by Confederate privateers and the laying up of others. After the war there was some recovery and widespread hope for more, but the bright prospects Mark Twain envisioned in an early letter to the Sacramento *Daily Union* probably reflected the forced optimism of Honolulu businessmen too accustomed to the easy profits from whaling to readily face reality. In fact, although it was not to proceed without reverses, the transformation to an agricultural economy had already begun, boosted by a Civil War boom in Hawaiian sugar, a smaller boom in rice cultivation, and some success in the production of cotton. And there were clear indications of what was to be Hawaii's greatest twentieth-century industry, the tourist, for in 1865 there had already been talk of the need for a first-class hotel in Honolulu, and the volcano Kilauea on Hawaii was attracting enough visitors for a new hotel to open there shortly before Mark Twain's arrival. Mark Twain's reporting of this economic ferment was influenced by a sense of mission, and in some of his *Union* letters he seems almost an evangelist for American capitalism, fervidly urging the commercial exploitation of the Sandwich Islands.

The influence of the whaler in Hawaii's early commercial history was matched in social and political areas by that of the American Protestant missionary. Late in 1819, just after the arrival of the first whalers, and with the missionaries already en route, a fortuitous series of events prepared the Hawaiian soil for seeding with Christianity. Fortified by drink and impelled by a strong-willed female chief in rebellion against restrictions imposed upon women, Kamehameha II sanctioned the existing disaffection with the kapu, or tabu, system by dramatically violating the interdiction against the mixing of the sexes at meals. Encouraged by the failure of the gods to take immediate revenge, the king proceeded to order the destruction of their images and the desecration of the temples. Thus, the Sandwich Islands discarded the religion that was an integral part of its social and political system. Into the void sailed the New England missionaries, fearing the worst kind of resistance and finding instead that God had rewarded their faith and readiness for self-sacrifice by eliminating the competition. The missionaries' righteousness would probably have carried opposition before it in any case, but this turn of affairs fortified them for the initial encounter with the native condition and the subsequent difficulties of adjusting it to their own conception of morality and social order. Despite injunctions from the American Board of Commissioners for Foreign Missions, their controlling agency, the missionaries found it impossible to avoid assuming political as well as religious control of the Sandwich Islands, particularly when called upon by the king and chiefs to extricate them from difficulties with foreigners. Although theirs was a benign foreign intervention, at least in intent, the missionaries had no greater sense of the worth of the native way of life than the whalers, merchants, and grog-shop proprietors with whom they were frequently in conflict and from whom they were sometimes under physical attack. In the three decades after their arrival, particularly in the 1840s, the era of their greatest participation in government, the missionaries affected every aspect of Hawaiian life, supplying and enforcing an ideal of industry and self-denial and transforming the nation from a feudal autocracy to a monarchy with a constitution and an imposing bureaucracy that included a national assembly, cabinet, civil service, and independent judiciary. A good example of the profundity of missionary intercourse in Hawaii is the career of Gerrit Parmele Judd, whom Mark Twain met in Hawaii and mentions with approval and admiration in Notebook 5.

It would be difficult to overestimate the influence Judd had during the reign of Kamehameha III. He went to the Sandwich Islands in 1828 as a missionary doctor, but his activities as adviser to the king and chiefs soon took precedence over all other endeavors, leading him in 1842 to resign from the mission to devote himself entirely to government affairs. For more than ten years Judd literally "*was the government*" (Notebook 5, p. 115), holding successively the offices of minister of foreign affairs, minister of the interior, and minister of finance and enjoying almost dictatorial authority. His achievements were in accord with his power. Within a few years of his entry into the service of Kamehameha III, the government debt was liquidated. By the end of the reign of Kamehameha III in 1854, government income had been increased nearly eightfold and expenses were well in hand, a condition reversed during succeeding administrations, so that by the time of Mark Twain's visit the government was again in debt. Until he became convinced of the necessity of annexation to the United States, Judd was an indomitable proponent of Hawaiian independence who played a crucial role in maintaining Hawaiian sovereignty in the face of challenges by England and France. During his political career the man Herman Melville called "a sanctimonious apothecary-adventurer" in *Typee* managed to alienate almost every element in the Sandwich Islands' foreign population—Americans as well as nationals of other countries, missionaries as well as merchants—by his unyielding insistence that they emulate his loyalty and commitment to Hawaii and by an unfortunate though understandable habit of identifying the government with himself. Judd's strict temperance opinions upset not only the merchants and whalers, but also Prince Alexander Liholiho (Kamehameha IV), who found revenge for the moral rigidity of his upbringing in political opposition to Judd. Attempts to impeach Judd were made in 1845 and 1848, but it wasn't until 1853 that his opponents finally succeeded in forcing his retirement. When he left office, Judd, who in 1843 had rejected the chiefs' offer of the entire Manoa Valley, a fertile area on Oahu facing Waikiki Beach, had only a thousand-dollar annuity to support a wife and eight children and tried a variety of enterprises, agricultural and commercial, to meet his expenses. Despite indifferent success, he lived in Hawaii for the remainder of his life. When he died in 1873, his estate amounted to about $50,000, only a fraction of what it might have been had he been willing to take advantage of his political position.

By the 1840s and 1850s the Protestant monopoly was beginning to break down, even though Judd and the other missionaries were becoming an integral and permanent part of the Hawaiian community, assuming citizenship, acquiring title to lands, engaging in secular pursuits, all with the approval of the American Board of Commissioners for Foreign Missions, which desired to prevent their exodus by allowing them these means of providing for growing families. In 1839/1840 the Roman Catholics and in the 1850s the Mormons had established Sandwich Islands missions. In the early 1860s the Anglicans would also do so, and though this last addition to the ranks of their rivals was most bitterly resented by the original missionaries, it did not so much weaken their influence as indicate that it was already weak. For Kamehameha IV (1855–1863) and Kamehameha V (1863–1872) were the first rulers raised entirely under American missionary auspices. Both had become strong monarchists and adherents of the Anglican church in reaction against the rigid political and religious principles of their childhood teachers. Both seemed to present a political threat to the ambitions and security of Americans resident in Hawaii.

During the first half of the nineteenth century, through a succession of treaties and agreements, England, France, and the United States had, not always delicately, jockeyed for position in Hawaii. The two European empire-builders sometimes threatened to take influence away from the United States with intimidating displays of naval force. If the United States eschewed forceful tactics, it may have been partly because it had the wisdom to let biology accomplish what diplomacy of the gunboat variety could do only with more difficulty and less permanence. For the foreign community was disproportionately American, and the United States was inevitably on the way to assuming control by populating the islands with Americans and part-Americans, descendants of merchants and the prolific missionaries. Mark Twain recognized this means of achieving ascendancy and contended that "the main argument in favor of a line of fast steamers" between San Francisco and Honolulu was that "they would soon populate these islands with Americans, and loosen that French and English grip which is gradually closing around them" (Sacramento *Daily Union,* 17 April 1866, *MTH,* p. 266). Political possibilities were, of course, bound to economic realities, and the most significant of these was Hawaii's growing dependence upon the United States. There was a certain innocence about the attempts of the Hawaiian government to secure a reciprocity treaty to further and formalize its economic connection with the United States while at the same time trying to persuade the United States to enter into a tripartite treaty with England and France to guarantee Hawaiian independence. A sense of the relentlessness of the assimilation process was a cause of the definite unease that existed in Hawaii in 1866. Kamehameha V feared American political and economic domination, and his desire to keep Hawaii independent helped create an impression among Americans that official policy was anti-American. The resulting tension was exacerbated by the attitudes of the English and French officials in Hawaii who, although not actually plotting to annex the islands for their respective countries, were conspiring to preserve their independence from the United States.

What Mark Twain made of this is recorded in Notebooks 5 and 6 and in his twenty-five letters to the Sacramento *Daily Union.* The latter were a mélange of tourism, chauvinism, easy ridicule of the remnants of native culture, and exhortations to California capitalists, all set forth in a fashion which, for all its frequent insensibility, was making literature out of the materials of a travel guide. Clemens' travel itself was extraordinary. After he had been in Honolulu for about two weeks preparing his first letters for the *Union,* he wrote his mother and sister: "The steamer I came here in sails tomorrow, and as soon as she is gone I shall sail for the other islands of the group and visit the great volcano—the grand wonder of the world. Be gone two months" (SLC to Jane Clemens and Pamela Moffett, 3 April 1866, *MTL,* p. 104). At about the same time he composed an overambitious itinerary of the six major islands (see Notebook 6, p. 229), part of which, however, he wasn't able to carry out. Although many of the particulars of his peregrinations cannot now be recovered, the general sequence is clear. He remained on Oahu from his arrival on 18 March until about mid-April, when he went to Maui by small island schooner, returning to Honolulu on 22 May. On 26 May he departed again, this time for the island of Hawaii and the volcano Kilauea. After a hasty three-week survey of Hawaii, which "ought to have taken five or six weeks" (SLC to Jane Clemens and Pamela Moffett, 21 June 1866, *MTL,* p. 106) and which did produce an incapacitating case of saddle boils, Mark Twain returned to Honolulu on 16 June. He planned to spend three weeks on Kauai, but the arrival in Honolulu of the Anson Burlingame party on 18 June and the survivors of the *Hornet* shipwreck on 23 June, as well as the lingering effects of his Hawaii trip, kept him on Oahu until his departure for San Francisco on 19 July.

This almost constant movement helps account for irregularities in Mark Twain's Hawaiian notebooks. The sequence of his notes is sometimes confused, not merely because of his practice of inserting entries at random, but primarily because of his alternation between Notebooks 5 and 6 and the loss of an intervening notebook.

It was on 11 March, while still aboard the *Ajax,* that Mark Twain first shifted from Notebook 5 to Notebook 6. After misplacing the former, he began the latter by recapitulating briefly his observations of the first four days of the voyage. He continued to use Notebook 6 for the balance of the down trip and in Honolulu until early April. There is then a gap in the notebooks corresponding to his eight weeks of interisland travel. Sometime after his final return to Honolulu on 16 June, apparently in the last days of the month, Mark Twain recovered Notebook 5 and with one exception (see Notebook 6, note 142), used it exclusively during his remaining weeks in the Sandwich Islands, on the voyage to San Francisco, and for about a month after his return.

The period embraced by the unrecovered notebook is thus apparent. On 22 May, the day he returned from Maui, Mark Twain had informed Mollie Clemens that in five weeks there "I have not written a single line, and have not once thought of business, or care or human toil or trouble or sorrow or weariness" (*MTL*, p. 106), but this disclaimer must have referred only to sustained formal writing. It would have been so uncharacteristic of Mark Twain not to make notes, particularly when his Maui observations would be needed for letters to the *Union*, that it must be assumed that a notebook which succeeded Notebook 6 and preceded the return to Notebook 5 no longer exists. Indications of the contents of this unrecovered notebook can be found in the Sacramento *Daily Union*. In a letter published on 21 May (*MTH*, p. 301) Mark Twain asserted: "I seldom place implicit confidence in my memory in matters where figures and finance are concerned and have not been thought of for a fortnight." Nevertheless, his surviving Hawaiian notebooks contain only fragments of the statistical information about Hawaiian agriculture and commerce that appeared in the *Union*. Again, in a letter printed on 30 August (*MTH*, pp. 379–380), Mark Twain reproduced inscriptions from the monument to Captain Cook which, while on Hawaii in June, he "with patience and industry" had copied in his notebook but which appear neither in Notebook 5 nor in Notebook 6. In fact, there is little correspondence between the *Union* letters devoted to events of late April, May, and early June, which were not written until mid-August in San Francisco, and the extant notebooks. Some information Clemens must have gathered during that period occurs sporadically in Notebook 5, but, given the associative and recollective tendencies of his mind, such notes probably repeat material originally recorded in the unrecovered notebook. As late as 20 August, a week after his return to San Francisco, the missing notebook was still in his possession, for on that date he quoted the following entry from it to his mother and sister:

> On board ship Emmeline, off Hawaii, Sandwich Islands: Corn-bread brickbats for dinner today—I wonder what Margaret [probably Margaret Sexton, formerly a boarder in the Clemens home] would think of *such* corn-bread? (journal letter to Jane Clemens and Pamela Moffett, 30 July–20 August 1866, TS in MTP)

In addition to the missing notebook, there are other lacunae in the Sandwich Islands materials. As would be expected, no drafts of Mark Twain's Sacramento *Daily Union* letters have survived. Nor is there any significant documentation of his relationship with Anson Burlingame, United States minister resident to China, whom Mark Twain later lauded for having directed him to the paths of propriety and success (*MTA*, 2:123–126). Burlingame receives only passing mention—and that only once—in Notebook 6, although it was he who interviewed the survivors of the *Hornet* fire while Mark Twain, prostrate with saddle-boils, managed to take notes for what was to be his most celebrated piece of reporting. Mark Twain won the confidence of *Hornet* captain Josiah A. Mitchell and passengers Samuel and Henry Ferguson and was allowed to make longhand copies of their diaries during the return voyage to San Francisco, but these copies, the basis of his subsequent *Hornet* writings, have never been located. The few excerpts from the Ferguson and Mitchell journals which occur in Notebooks 5 and 6 are certainly too fragmentary to be a complete transcription. Although it is possible that some of these lost materials were included in the missing travel notebook, their length suggests that they were separate documents. At any rate, it is clear that the Hawaiian record is not complete with Notebooks 5 and 6.

Notebook 5 is largely a shipboard diary, devoted to Mark Twain's journeys to and from the Sandwich Islands. Unlike the quick eleven-day steamer trip down, the voyage to San Francisco, which occupies a major part of the notebook, extended monotonously over twenty-five days aboard the clipper *Smyrniote*. Mark Twain occupied himself with considerations, sometimes angry ones, of Hawaii's past and future, speculated about the missionary temperament, talked with the other passengers—particularly Captain Mitchell and the Ferguson brothers and the Reverend Franklin S. Rising, a Nevada acquaintance—made notes for a *Hornet* article he planned to write for *Harper's* and for other sketches, read, and was lulled into reveries of childhood. As the tedious voyage dragged on, his true creative inspiration began to emerge. Hackneyed ideas for a collection of eloquent public addresses and for cheap burlesques gave way to notes which anticipate passages in *Huckleberry Finn*, *Tom Sawyer*, and *Roughing It*.

Clemens also filled the time with a long journal letter to his mother and sister, sometimes copying passages from his notebook into the letter and other times transferring material from the letter to the notebook. He began this letter on 30 July with the explanation: "I write, now, because

I must go hard at work as soon as I get to San Francisco, and then I shall have no time for other things." After arrival on 13 August his first task was to finish his letters to the Sacramento *Union,* eight of which were yet to be published. On 20 August he was able to report: "I have been up to Sacramento and squared accounts with the *Union.* They paid me a great deal more than they promised me. I suppose that means that I gave satisfaction, but they did not say so" (journal letter to Jane Clemens and Pamela Moffett, 30 July–20 August 1866, TS in MTP). In the months after his return he found time to work on a book based on his Sandwich Islands letters, but in early 1867 he gave up trying to secure its publication. He completed an article for *Harper's* about the *Hornet* in time for it to appear in December as "Forty-Three Days in An Open Boat," unfortunately attributed to "Mark Swain." But perhaps the most significant use of his initial foreign experience came on 2 October 1866, when he gave his first Sandwich Islands lecture at Maguire's Academy of Music, a performance which, according to his own later reckoning, he repeated one hundred fifty times. After a brief visit to Sacramento in mid-September to report on the thirteenth annual fair of the California State Agricultural Society, again for the *Union,* Mark Twain spent most of the fall and early winter of 1866, a period for which no notebooks are known to exist, on an extended lecture tour of California and Nevada towns. Some of these towns are described in three "Interior Notes" to the San Francisco *Bulletin,* published in late November and early December. The lecture tour ended with a farewell discourse on the Sandwich Islands and a portentous tribute to San Francisco's coming brilliance at Congress Hall on 10 December 1866, just five days before his departure for New York. At one time Clemens had considered taking the new mail steamer to China at the invitation of Anson Burlingame, but although "everybody says I am throwing away a fortune in not going in her" (SLC to "My Dear Folks," 4 December 1866, *MTL,* p. 122) he was occupied with a new assignment as traveling correspondent for the *Alta California,* was enjoying the prospect of a world tour, and was content to be going home for the first time in more than five years.

More than once he would return to the Sandwich Islands in his writings, for despite the early failure he did not give up his plans for a Sandwich Islands book. On 20 December 1870 he informed Albert F. Judd, the son of Gerrit P. Judd and later chief justice of Hawaii: "I am under contract to write 2 more books the size of Innocents Abroad (600 pp 8vo.) & after that I am going to do up the Islands & Harris. They have 'kept' 4 years, & I guess they will keep 2 or 3 longer." Just two years later Mark Twain's Sandwich Islands letters and notes, perhaps still in the form of the manuscript of the 1866/1867 book, provided needed material for *Roughing It*. Even this did not satisfy his literary ambitions regarding Hawaii, however, and in 1884 he began a Sandwich Islands novel about Bill Ragsdale, a "half-white" interpreter in the Hawaiian legislature whom Mark Twain had known in Hawaii. Ragsdale had later given up a "prosperous career" and the "beautiful half-caste girl" he was about to marry when he discovered he had leprosy and committed himself to Hawaii's leper settlement and "the loathsome and lingering death that all lepers die" (*Following the Equator* [Hartford: American Publishing Company, 1897], p. 63). The Ragsdale novel, Mark Twain wrote to William Dean Howells on 7 January 1884:

> will illustrate a but-little considered fact in human nature: that the religious folly you are born in you will *die* in, no matter what apparently reasonabler religious folly may seem to have taken its place meanwhile & abolished & obliterated it. I start Bill Ragsdale at 12 years of age, & the heroine at 4, in the midst of the ancient idolatrous system, with its picturesque & amazing customs & superstitions, 3 months before the arrival of the missionaries & the erection of a shallow Christianity upon the ruins of the old paganism.
>
> Then these two will become educated Christians, & highly civilized. And then I will jump 15 years, & do Ragsdale's leper business. (*MTHL*, p. 461)

Despite the seriousness of this outline, Mark Twain had comic intentions as well, for on the flyleaf of his copy of James Jackson Jarves' *History of the Hawaiian or Sandwich Islands* (Boston: James Munroe and Company, 2d ed., 1844), he made these notes, evidently at the time he was planning the Ragsdale book:

> The Mish have given native boys a college education—put in my horse-boy, translating Greek, &c but wholly helpless to earn a living where the land was *importing* mechanics!
>
> Let old Commodore curse the Mish & always be laughing at them.

And on the back cover of the Jarves history Mark Twain listed four books that must have been among those he told Howells he had stacked up on his billiard table while saturating himself with Hawaiian information: William Root Bliss, *Paradise in the Pacific; A Book of Travel, Adventure, and Facts in the Sandwich Islands* (New York: Sheldon and Company, 1873); Charles Samuel Stewart, *Private Journal of a Voyage to the Pacific Ocean and a Residence at the Sandwich Islands in the Years 1822–25* (New York: John P. Haven, 1828); Rufus Anderson, *The Hawaiian Islands: Their Progress and Condition Under Missionary Labors* (Boston: Gould and Lincoln, 1865); George Leonard Chaney, *"Alo'ha": A Hawaiian Salutation* (Boston: Roberts Brothers, 1880 [© 1879]). But although Mark Twain's plans and preparations for the Ragsdale novel were considerable, the work seems to have been abortive, and only fragments of it survive.

Throughout his career references to Hawaii would persist in many of Mark Twain's writings, but it was as a lecturer that he presented his best-known comment about the islands, the evocative "prose poem" delivered on 8 April 1889 at a reception at Delmonico's in New York for two touring baseball teams that had stopped briefly in Honolulu:

> No alien land in all the world has any deep, strong charm for me but that one, no other land could so longingly and so beseechingly haunt me sleeping and waking, through half a lifetime, as that one has done. Other things leave me, but it abides; other things change, but it remains the same. For me its balmy airs are always blowing, its summer seas flashing in the sun, the pulsing of its surf-beat is in my ear; I can see its garlanded crags, its leaping cascades, its plumy palms drowsing by the shore, its remote summits floating like islands above the cloud rack; I can feel the spirit of its woodland solitudes, I can hear the plash of its brooks; in my nostrils still lives the breath of flowers that perished twenty years ago. (*MTH*, p. 217)

In 1881, in a wistful letter to Charles Warren Stoddard, Mark Twain spoke of abandoning care and distraction and fleeing to the solitudes of Hawaii, but in 1895, while on his debt-paying world lecture tour, a cholera outbreak in Honolulu frustrated his desire for a nostalgic return to "the loveliest fleet of islands that lies anchored in any ocean" (SLC to H. P. Wood, 30 November 1908, *MTH*, pp. 242–243). The 1866 trip to Hawaii, Clemens' first excursion outside the North American continent, initiated the familiar conjunction of travel and literature that would establish his fame with *Innocents Abroad* and *Roughing It,* would be revived for *A Tramp Abroad* and *Following the Equator*, and would influence the narrative form of such important works as *Huckleberry Finn, Life on the Mississippi,* and *A Connecticut Yankee*, all of which are narrated by travelers.

Apologize or Fight

—"If he means the editor of this paper when he speaks of his vision having been blessed once alone with the long green swell of the Pacific.+"

Eloquence—
Th. Parker's funeral sermon on Danl Webster—Picture of Webster standing amid the "fire & smoke & thunder of his own eloquence."

Brown's disease of the heart—Stomach—takes ~~sug~~ whisky 3 times a day in which sugar cane has been steeped—cant carry cane com

variety, 20 ~~[illegible]~~ kinds
plain sugar.

People bring all manner of diseases to the S.I. & keep the people always in danger.

Sarcasm
Henry Clay's "Gentlemen the monument still stands."

8

Old sailors dig nothing in the Hornet's boat but spin fo'castle yarns ~~Jack Hatter~~ about ships & former captains & how the grub was, & what for cook for cabin-house was, &c—& Jack & others like them who could barely read & couldn't sign their

Notebook 5 now contains 182 pages, 27 of them blank. They measure 6 13/16 by 4 inches (17.3 by 10.1 centimeters). Each page is ruled with twenty-four blue horizontal lines and divided by red vertical lines into four unequal columns in account book fashion. The page edges are marbled in red, black, and gold; the endpapers and flyleaves are white; and the cover is stiff tan calf. Notebook 5 is worn with use, and it is possible that leaves no longer traceable are missing; the binding has been repaired recently. There are single entries in ink on the front and back covers and numerous entries on the flyleaves and endpapers. Most entries are in pencil, with scattered notes in brown ink. The front cover was dated "*1866*" in ink, apparently by Paine.

Paine's penciled use marks appear throughout, in addition to Clemens' usual use marks. Clemens also imposed on many entries in this notebook a system of symbols and numbers in pencil that are now only partially understandable (see illustrations). The significant symbols, which are represented or described in the present text immediately following the entries across which they were written, are: a spiral on entries concerning the *Hornet* shipwreck, the number 8 written over examples of historical eloquence, and a 78 used to designate contemporary anecdote, quotation, and other potential literary material (although most of this material does not appear in Clemens' extant Sandwich Islands writings). The categories designated seem sufficiently clear, but it has not been determined why Clemens selected these particular symbols.

Bibliography of Related Materials

The following bibliography gathers the sources most consistently used to document Mark Twain's Sandwich Islands notebooks. A number of additional studies and articles of more circumscribed use are cited in notes, where appropriate. Contemporary files of the *Pacific Commercial Advertiser*, the *Hawaiian Gazette*, and the *Daily Hawaiian Herald* provided a variety of information, as did issues of *The Friend*, an important Honolulu temperance periodical. The *Hawaiian Almanac and Annual* series, published for many years by Thomas G. Thrum, was frequently consulted for its retrospective notes and articles about Hawaiian life at the time of Mark Twain's visit. All of these sources were supplemented by reference to works too numerous and sometimes too ephemeral to mention, more important in establishing a sense of period than for providing specific annotations. At several points in the preparation of the Sandwich Islands notebooks, information and counsel were most graciously supplied by Agnes C. Conrad, Hawaiian state archivist.

Alexander, William De Witt. *A Brief History of the Hawaiian People*. New York: American Book Co., [1891].

Anderson, Rufus. *The Hawaiian Islands: Their Progress and Condition Under Missionary Labors*. 3d ed. Boston: Gould and Lincoln, 1865.

———. *History of the Sandwich Islands Mission*. Boston: Congregational Publishing Society, 1870.

Andrews, Lorrin. *A Dictionary of the Hawaiian Language*. Honolulu, 1865.

Bradley, Harold Whitman. *The American Frontier in Hawaii: The Pioneers, 1789–1843*. Stanford, California: Stanford University Press, 1942.

Daws, Gavan. *Shoal of Time: A History of the Hawaiian Islands*. New York: Macmillan, [1968].

Frear, Walter F. *Mark Twain and Hawaii*. Chicago: Lakeside Press, 1947.

Judd, Laura Fish. *Honolulu: Sketches of Life in the Hawaiian Islands from 1828 to 1861*. Edited by Dale L. Morgan. Chicago: Lakeside Press, 1966.

Kuykendall, Ralph S. *The Hawaiian Kingdom*. 3 vols. Honolulu: University of Hawaii Press, 1938–1967.

Morgan, Theodore. *Hawaii: A Century of Economic Change, 1778–1876*. Cambridge: Harvard University Press, 1948.

Pukui, Mary Kawena, and Elbert, Samuel H. *Hawaiian Dictionary*. Honolulu: University of Hawaii Press, 1971.

Ch 19—440
20 479
21 505
22 533
23 555
24 (old page) 452[1] [#]

---

[1] This table of chapter and page calculations was inscribed on the front cover of the notebook. Mark Twain must have compiled it after his return to San Francisco while working on the Sandwich Islands book he completed by early 1867 (see headnote and note 166). Much of the matter of the manuscript probably found its way into chapters 62 through 77 of *Roughing It*.

"Wife perfect but blamed if she suits *me*"

Rev. Franklin S. Rising.

3 Bible House N.Y.[2]

Mark Twain.

Ferns, pendulous, creeping[3]

<March 7, 1866.>

<[*one or two words*]>

A. Gamble—Unk[4]

---

[2] On 19 December 1868, upon learning of Rising's death early that month in the disastrous Ohio River collision of the steamers *America* and *United States,* Samuel Clemens recalled his friend, the prototype for the fledgling minister in chapter 47 of *Roughing It,* in a letter to Olivia Langdon:

> He was rector of the Episcopal church in Virginia City, Nevada—a noble young fellow—& for 3 years, there, he & I were fast friends. I used to try to teach him how he ought to preach in order to get at the better natures of the rough population about him, & he used to try hard to learn—for I *knew* them & he did not, for he was refined & sensitive & not intended for such a people as that. . . . Afterward I stumbled on him in the Sandwich Islands, where he was traveling for his health, & we so arranged it as to return to San Francisco in the same ship. . . . We were together all the time—pacing the deck night & day—there was no other congenial company. He tried earnestly to bring me to a knowledge of the true God. In return, I read his manuscripts & made suggestions for their emendation. We got along well together.

Upon arrival in San Francisco, Rising would embark for New York to become secretary of the Church Missionary Society of the Episcopal Church of the United States, which had offices at this address in Bible House, headquarters of the American Bible Society, in Astor Place, New York City.

[3] An example of Mark Twain's increasing use of the notebooks as a repository for literary material. This combination of adjectives, noted upside down on the front endpaper, was borrowed from a passage in Manley Hopkins' *Hawaii: The Past, Present, and Future of Its Island-Kingdom* (London: Longman, Green, Longman, and Roberts, 1862):

> The sides of the hills are clothed with verdure; even the barren rocks that project from among the bushes are ornamented with pendulous or creeping plants of various kinds; and in several places beautiful cascades leap down the steep mountain's side into flowing rivulets beneath. (pp. 50–51)

Mark Twain commented on other passages from Hopkins' controversial book in Notebook 6.

[4] On 10 September 1866, the opening day of the thirteenth annual fair of the

A. F. Smith O B.
E. M. Skagg—Gough
Barney Rice—Y Amer
Geo Gilbert—Q Pac

From San Francisco to the Hawaiian Islands per steamer "Ajax," Mch. 7, 1866.[5]

Man drawn up in sp^{t} d l'eau[6]

Prov 17 & 18—M[--]
Isaiah 14 & 40

May Wentworth
—Mrs. Newman
621 Bush st.[7]

<Mrs>Messrs. J. & S. Ferguson
35 Pine st.
New York.[8] [#]

California State Agricultural Society, the following horses competed in the pacing race at Union Park in Sacramento: Unknown, entered by Peter Gamble; Mike O'Brien, entered by E. F. Smith; Dick Gough, entered by E. M. Skaggs; Young America, entered by Barney Rice; and Queen of the Pacific, entered by George Gilbert. Mark Twain was reporting the fair for the Sacramento *Daily Union,* and several pages of entries made at the stock grounds occur near the end of this notebook. This notation, written over the preceding two entries, is characteristic of Mark Twain's use of the flyleaf for observations made throughout the period of a notebook's use.

[5] The date of the second and last voyage to Honolulu made by the *Ajax,* operated by the California Steam Navigation Company. The *Ajax* proved unprofitable, and service was discontinued after its return to San Francisco on 15 April.

[6] This entry possibly derives from Henry Ferguson's observation of a waterspout which threatened the *Hornet* longboat (*The Journal of Henry Ferguson, January to August 1866* [Hartford: Case, Lockwood & Brainard Co., 1924], p. 98). Its occurrence here is a further example of Mark Twain's random use of the flyleaf, since he wouldn't read Ferguson's journal until late July.

[7] Mary Richardson Newman, whose pen name was May Wentworth, was a journalist for the *Golden Era,* editor of *Poetry of the Pacific: Selections and Original Poems from the Poets of the Pacific States* (San Francisco: Pacific Publishing Company, 1867), and author of several children's books. She lived at this address in San Francisco with her husband Charles, a miner.

[8] The firm of John and Samuel Ferguson, commission merchants, belonged to

7th—Got away about 4 P.M. Only about half dozen of us, out of 30 passengers, at dinner—balance all sea-sick.[9]

8th—Strong gale all night—shipp<ed> rolled heavily—heavy sea on this evening—& black sky overhead. Nearly everybody sick abed yet.

9—Woke up several times in the night—must have had pretty rough time of it from way the vessel was rolling.—Heard passengers heaving & vomiting occasionally.

Very rough, stormy night, I am told.

At Sea, March 9.

<I>Just read letters from home which should have been read before leaving San Francisco. Accounts of oil on the Tennessee land,[10] & that <worthless> <worthless> brother of mine, with his eternal cant about law & religion, getting ready in his slow, stupid way, to go to Excelsior, instead of the States. He sends me some prayers, as usual.

March 10—We are making about 200 miles a day. Got some sail

---

the family of Henry and Samuel Ferguson, survivors of the *Hornet* conflagration.

[9] This is the first entry in the body of Notebook 5. The previous entries were made on the front endpaper and flyleaf.

[10] Land in Fentress County, Tennessee, was purchased by John Marshall Clemens in the late 1820s and early 1830s in hopes of making the family fortune but was not finally disposed of—after much frustration and none of the anticipated profit—until many years later. The letters from home which so aggravated Clemens were probably related to the plans to sell the land he had been formulating in December 1865 (see headnote). On 22 May 1866 he wrote Mollie Clemens from Honolulu:

> It is Orion's duty to attend to that land, & after shutting me out of my attempt to sell it (for which I shall never entirely forgive him,) if he lets it be sold for taxes, all his religion will not wipe out the sin. It is no use to quote Scripture to me, Mollie,—I am in poverty & exile now because of Orion's religious scruples. . . . I always feel bitter & malignant when I think of Ma & Pamela grieving at our absence & the land going to the dogs when I could have sold it & been at home now, instead of drifting about the outskirts of the world, battling for bread. (*MTBus*, pp. 87–88)

And on 21 June he informed his mother and sister: "I expect I have made Orion mad, but I don't care a cent. He wrote me to go home & sell the Tenn. land & I wrote him to go to Thunder & take care of it himself. I *tried* to sell it once & he broke up the trade" (*MTBus*, p. 88).

on yesterday morning for first time, & in afternoon crowded *every*thing on. Sea-gulls chase but no catch.

10th—cont.

Three or four of the sea-sick passengers came to lunch at noon, & several of the ladies are able to dress & sit up.

Captain reports <over 335> 325 miles made in past 24 hours.

Found an old acquaintance to-day—never been anywhere yet that I didn't find an acquaintance.[11]

11th—<Ship> Magnificent day yesterday—sea as smooth as a river <w>ruffled by a land breeze. Occasionally ship rolled a good deal, nevertheless. Chief Engineer Sanford says reason is our head-winds (S. W.) smooth down the eternal swell that is always rolling down from N. W., but as soon as the contrary wind dies out, the old swell rolls the ship again, even in the calmest weather. N. W. is the prevailing wind far down through Pacific, but dies out toward equator—then round Horn comes up the S. E. wind, & its swell lasts up toward line—both swells die out & leave a space on each side of line smooth as glass & subject to calms.

11th Con—

Nearly everybody out to breakfast this morning—not more than ½ doz sick now.

<The old>

The old whalers aboard (Capt.s. Smith, Fish & Phillips[12]—two latter Shenandoah[13] victims—) say not more than 4 months smooth weather on this route a year. [#]

---

[11] Shorthand reporter Andrew J. Marsh, formerly Mark Twain's colleague in reporting Nevada legislative proceedings for the Virginia City *Territorial Enterprise,* was among the *Ajax* passengers.

[12] According to the *Ajax* passenger list, the ages of these "old" seamen were: Captain James Smith, 55; Captain A. W. Fish, 40; and Captain W. H. Phillips, 35. In Mark Twain's Sacramento *Daily Union* letters Fish became Fitch, Phillips became Phelps, and Smith became Cuttle (see Notebook 6, note 18).

[13] The *Shenandoah* was a Confederate privateer which destroyed a number of whaling ships in the Pacific, including some of Hawaiian registry. Its depredations contributed to the decline of the whaling industry in the Hawaiian Islands.

Butcher & Ayres visit the King.[14]

Wyhenas—<[W]>Hyenas.[15]

Leland arrested.[16]

Officers speak of the pleasant company on last voyage.[17]

11th Sunday—Old strd set <mn'> m'nif Sunday Ln^{c}h.[18]

S. Islanders never intended to work. Worse off now with all religion than ever before. Dying off fast. First white landed there was a curse to them.

Judd smart man—his own countrymen ruined him.[19]

---

[14] James J. Ayers, one of the founders of the San Francisco *Call* and a California acquaintance of Mark Twain, was in the Sandwich Islands at this time for health, recreation, and business, the latter culminating in his founding of the *Daily Hawaiian Herald*, which he published from 4 September to 21 December 1866. One of Ayers' Sandwich Islands acquaintances was James Price, whom he later described as "a leading butcher of Honolulu" (James J. Ayers, *Gold and Sunshine: Reminiscences of Early California* [Boston: Richard G. Badger, 1922], p. 219).

[15] In Mark Twain's letter in the Sacramento *Daily Union* of 19 April 1866 (*MTH*, p. 277) this phonetic resemblance appears as one of Mr. Brown's typical blunders in pronunciation.

[16] Mark Twain's "A Voyage of the Ajax" (*Territorial Enterprise*, 23 February 1866, reprinted in *The Californian*, 3 March 1866, as "Presence of Mind—Incidents of the Down Trip of the *Ajax*") included a comic account of the misadventures of Lewis Leland, manager of the Occidental Hotel in San Francisco, on the maiden voyage of the *Ajax* but made no mention of an arrest. As the next entry suggests, however, he may have been hearing further anecdotes about Leland from *Ajax* personnel.

[17] Although the number of celebrated passengers on the initial voyage of the *Ajax* did not fulfill the hopes of the publicity-conscious California Steam Navigation Company, several prominent people did make the trip. In addition to Leland and Ayers, the passenger list included the aging, but still well-known diva Madame Anna Bishop, said to be the prototype for Du Maurier's Trilby, and Kisaboro, a Japanese traveler who, it was remarked, wore two swords.

[18] Mark Twain's cancellation suggests an attempt to transcribe a slurred remark, perhaps by one of the three whalers who reportedly consumed nineteen gallons of whiskey in the first eight days of the trip (see Mark Twain's letter in the Sacramento *Daily Union* of 16 April 1866, *MTH*, p. 262). The speaker may have been instructing the steward to provide him "enough lunch" or commenting upon the magnificent or munificent lunch he had already provided.

[19] For a discussion of the career of Dr. Gerrit Parmele Judd, see the headnote to this notebook.

Each native must pay $8 annual tax, & worries himself to death as how going to do it. When come off whaling voyage may have $200—take & divide up as long as got a cent.

Judd always kept country out of debt & cleaned up his tracks—since been out country gone badly in debt. He went out poor as a rat. To prove his honesty, he *was the government* & might have cabbaged the whole country.

Allen, formerly Minister of Finance—now Chief Justice.[20]

Whalers like Kanakas better than any other sailors—temperate, strong, faithful, peaceable & orderly.

King always refused sign Constution—he altered one clause of it from universal suffrage to property qualification, & when they tried force him, & threatened streets run blood, he bade them good morning & said conference was ended.[21]

House of Nobles appointed by King, & Lower House elective.[22] Under Universal suffrage, Missionaries used vote their flocks for certain man, & then sit at home & control him. One member (missionary's son) said out loud in open <ne> house, he controlled eleven votes (a majority) in the House. [#]

---

[20] In return for nominating Zachary Taylor for the presidency at the Whig convention of 1848, Elisha Hunt Allen had been appointed United States consul in Honolulu. In 1853 he had become a member of the Hawaiian government, serving as minister of finance until 1857, when he was appointed chief justice of the Supreme Court of Hawaii.

[21] When Kamehameha V came to the throne in 1863, he refused to take an oath to support the constitution of 1852 because it did not conform to his view of the prerogatives of the crown. Opposed to universal suffrage, Kamehameha V advocated a property qualification for voting and for election to the Hawaiian House of Representatives, as well as other measures to increase the power of the monarch. When a constitutional convention called by the king failed to act to his satisfaction, he dissolved it and announced that he would provide the new constitution, which he did on 20 August 1864. Despite dissatisfaction with the constitution of 1864, it remained in force for twenty-three years, longer than any other Hawaiian constitution.

[22] By late May, when he was reporting on the Hawaiian legislature for the Sacramento *Daily Union*, Mark Twain had learned that it no longer was bicameral, having been reduced to a single chamber by the monarchist constitution of 1864.

King not married.[23] Well educated, & a <p>gentleman. Has a father[24] & sister living & will appoint successor.

Country will eventually pass into hands of foreigners—probably French.[25]

11th Cont.[26]

Fine day—good N. E. breeze. Fore spencer—fore-topsail—fore-to-gallantsail; <ji> lower stu'n sails—& fore-top-stu'nsl; jib &

---

[23] Kamehameha V, then thirty-six, never would marry. The facts of his bachelor life approach melodrama. Engaged as a young man to the High Chiefess Bernice Pauahi, Kamehameha V had relinquished his claims on her to permit her marriage in 1850 to Charles Reed Bishop of New York, later a prominent Honolulu merchant and public official. After the death of his sister Princess Victoria Kamamalu on 29 May 1866, the public demanded that the king marry in order to guarantee an undisturbed line of succession to the throne. Although in love with Dowager Queen Emma, the widow of his brother Kamehameha IV, the king did not propose marriage to her, feeling certain that reverence for her dead husband, as well as her own religious scruples and the disapproval of the Anglican church, to which the royal family belonged, would lead to his rejection. When he did authorize one of his ministers to approach Emma on his behalf, these intuitions proved correct. Even though Kamehameha V found himself unable to marry, he consistently resisted requests that he name a successor. At last, on 11 December 1872, just one hour before death, he informed Bernice Pauahi Bishop that he wished her to be his successor. Upon her refusal, the king, unwilling to offer the succession to Emma, died without naming a successor, thereby touching off a crisis of nearly a month's duration before a new king could be elected.

[24] Mataio Kekuanaoa, who for many years had been governor of Oahu, was now president of the Hawaiian legislative assembly.

[25] In 1865 Charles de Varigny, a former French consul and chancellor of the French consulate who had been minister of finance since 1863 and who was firmly opposed to United States influence in Hawaii, was named minister of foreign affairs. Varigny's elevation to the most crucial post in Kamehameha V's cabinet must have seemed ominous to Americans resident in Hawaii who remembered French involvement in local affairs between the 1830s and the 1850s. Although this entry indicates that some of the *Ajax* passengers were communicating their apprehensions to Mark Twain, his own later indifferent characterization of Varigny as a "merely sensible, unpretentious" man with "nothing particularly remarkable" about him (Sacramento *Daily Union*, 21 June 1866, *MTH*, p. 325) indicates he did not find him threatening or offensive.

[26] As explained in the headnote, it was on this date that Mark Twain misplaced Notebook 5 and shifted temporarily to Notebook 6.

flying jib—main spencer—gaff top-sail.—all canvass set. Made 230 miles past 24 hours—good run.

Missionary cousin got spittoon of old Gov. Young,[27] full teeth of enemies he'd killed—man to do nothing but take care of it, keep any one from getting hold some possession of his & pray him to death.[28]

Similar superstitions in south.

Only 65,000 natives in the whole groupe now—good many coolies & Malays brought there to work plantations & about 3,000 whites.[29]

English striving hard for supremacy—former King favored them—present favors Amer^ns^[30] [#]

---

[27] John Young, English boatswain of a United States vessel, was detained in Hawaii in 1790 after a massacre of natives by the captain of his ship. Young made one unsuccessful attempt to escape and then, persuaded by the good treatment he received from Kamehameha I, who was desirous of having foreigners in his service, he decided to remain in Hawaii. He became a trusted adviser to the king, aided him in his wars of conquest, and was given the status of a Hawaiian chief. Young was governor of Hawaii from 1802 to 1812.

[28] It is reported that when a native priest, jealous of John Young's influence with Kamehameha I, attempted in vain to pray him to death, Young responded in kind and was successful (Antoinette Withington, *The Golden Cloak* [Honolulu: Hawaiiana Press, 1953], pp. 66–67). This superstition figures in one of the surviving fragments of a Sandwich Islands novel Mark Twain attempted to write in 1884 (DV 111). There mass consternation results when the king's spittoon is stolen for use in praying him to death.

[29] According to the census of 1866, of a total population of 62,959, Hawaiians and part-Hawaiians accounted for 58,765, white immigrants for 2,200, with the balance made up of Chinese and other nationalities. In 1852 about 300 Chinese and in 1865 some 500 Chinese had been brought to Hawaii as contract laborers. Although Malaysia was discussed as a potential source, not for temporary labor but for permanent replenishment of the waning native population, apparently no large numbers of Malaysians were brought to Hawaii.

[30] It is difficult now to evaluate the comparative degrees of hostility felt toward the United States by Kamehameha IV and Kamehameha V. It is clear, however, that both kings were repelled by certain American political and social realities. Of royal birth, they naturally resisted attempts to turn their country into a republic on the American pattern or to simply make it an appendage of the United States. Racial prejudice, with which the royal brothers had several unpleasant encounters during a visit to the United States in 1850 (see note 120), was an important cause of

Mr. B. I quarrel with no man's proclivities—but mine must be respected—you can't make puns in my presence—I despise them, except they utterly bad. Such as the first animal created was chaos (a shay horse)—none other. It is so atrocious that it disarms—it stuns.[31] 78

Honolulu, June 29—visited the hideous *Mai Pake* Hospital & examined the disgusting victims of Chinese Leprosy.[32]

Rt. Rev. Bishop Maigret, Roman Cath.[33] In his huge church, congregation sit on the floor—has accommoda^{n} in the yard for native horses—shed for them to loaf in.

Honolulu, June 30 1866—attended funeral of Crown Princess Victoria Kamamalu Kaahumanu.[34] [#]

---

their displeasure with America. Resentful of the severe restraints placed upon him by his missionary tutors, Kamehameha IV may have been more antimissionary than anti-American. There is no doubt that his wife, Queen Emma, had strong British sympathies, particularly in religious matters, and it was during their reign that the Anglican church was established in Hawaii (see notes 78 and 80). Although Kamehameha V may have seemed less of an anglophile than his brother, there does not appear to be any support for the contention, contradicted at a later point in this notebook and also in Notebook 6, that he was more favorably disposed toward the United States.

[31] Although this remark has something of the tone of a remonstrance to the fictional Mr. Brown, it was probably meant for Anson Burlingame's nineteen-year-old son Edward, with whom Mark Twain was exchanging puns. The Burlingames had arrived in Honolulu en route to China on 18 June 1866; at about this time Mark Twain apparently recovered Notebook 5.

[32] Leprosy, known as *Mai Pake*, or "Chinese disease"—although there is no clear proof that it was imported from China—was present in the Sandwich Islands at least from the second quarter of the nineteenth century, but it wasn't until shortly before Mark Twain's visit that the government began to take measures for its control. Mark Twain must have seen the receiving station and hospital at Kalihi, about two miles west of Honolulu. Patients judged incurable at Kalihi were sent to an isolation settlement on a small peninsula on the north side of Molokai.

[33] Louis Desirée Maigret was the head of the French Roman Catholic mission to the Sandwich Islands. He presided over the Church of Our Lady of Peace in Honolulu.

[34] Victoria Kaahumanu Kamamalu, sister of Kamehameha IV and Kamehameha V and heir presumptive to the Hawaiian throne, was born on 1 November 1838 and died on 29 May 1866. Mark Twain devoted the major part of three Sacramento

July 3^{d} 1866—Saw star to-night on which counted 12 distinct & flaming points—very large star—shone with such a pure, rich, diamond lustre—lustrous—<nes> on a field on <deal>dead, solid black—no star very close—where I sat saw *no* other—

Moonlight here is fine, but nowhere so fine as Washoe.

All stars shine pure & bright here.

Brown called his horse Haleakala—extinct volcano—because if ever been any fire in him all gone out before *he* came across him. 78

Harris currency bill killed July 3—ayes 3, noes 31.[35]
Himself, Varigny & Dr. Smith[36] *aye*.

Say Honoluluans gossip—so do all villagers. [#]

Daily Union letters to a description of her funeral and the ceremonies of mourning held during the month her body lay in state in the royal palace (see note 64).

35 Charles Coffin Harris was an American lawyer. As attorney general and minister of finance Harris was a particularly influential adviser to Kamehameha V and an object of Mark Twain's critical attack. Ralph S. Kuykendall (*The Hawaiian Kingdom*, 3 vols. [Honolulu: University of Hawaii Press, 1953], 2:218) observed that Harris, who later served as minister of foreign affairs and as associate and chief justice of the Hawaiian Supreme Court, "deserved something better than the sneering obloquy heaped upon him by the American humorist [in the Sacramento *Daily Union*]. It is true that Harris had an unfortunate domineering manner, an air of superiority and condescension that infuriated some people and repelled many others; but he was a man of considerable natural ability, indefatigable industry, and unimpeachable personal integrity." Nevertheless, Harris' less than admirable performance during legislative proceedings on this currency bill, some of which Mark Twain probably observed, would have provided ample basis for an unfavorable impression of him. The bill was opposed by the consolidated force of the Honolulu business community, which saw no reason to issue unstable paper currency when sound specie was available. Harris, though apparently unmotivated by a desire for personal gain, repeatedly resorted to pompous indirection and innuendo in a misguided attempt to secure passage of his bill. On 3 July, after a foolish debate which was extended for nearly two months, the Hawaiian legislature denied Harris the face-saving device of withdrawing his bill and instead voted 31 to 3 to postpone it indefinitely.

36 Dr. John Mott Smith, Hawaii's pioneer dentist, had come to the Sandwich Islands from New York in 1851. In 1866 he was a Hawaiian legislator, chairman of the Legislative Committee on Finance, and editor of the *Hawaiian Gazette*, the government newspaper.

Young girls innocent & natural—*I* love 'em same as others love infants.

If a man ask thee to go with him a mile, go *with* him, Twain—Honolulu joke by Ed. Burlingame.[37] 78

Oudinot[38]

Wife perfect but d—d if she suits *me*. 78

Complete History of old K. I. by David Malo, containing appalling secrets, siezed & suppressed by K. IV., who was ashamed of his heathen ancestors & did not like hear them mentioned.[39]

Old Kanaka Gov. lost at sea, said innocently d—d fools, go back where started from & start fresh.[40] 78

Natives *will lie*. [#]

---

[37] In his Autobiographical Dictation of 20 February 1906, Mark Twain recalled the origin of this joke, which too frequent repetition had made "a seedy and repulsive tramp whose proper place is in the hospital for the decayed, the friendless, and the forlorn": "Mr. Burlingame's son—now editor of *Scribner's Magazine* these many years and soon to reach the foothills that lie near the frontiers of age—was with him there in Honolulu; a handsome boy of nineteen, and overflowing with animation, activity, energy, and the pure joy of being alive. He attended balls and fandangos and *hula hulas* every night—anybody's, brown, half white, white—and he could dance all night and be as fresh as ever the next afternoon. One day he delighted me with a joke which I afterward used in a lecture in San Francisco, and from there it traveled all around in the newspapers. He said, 'If a man compel thee to go with him a mile, go *with* him Twain' " (*MTA*, 2:125–126).

[38] F. A. Oudinot was a resident of Lahaina, Maui, who claimed descent from Charles Nicolas Oudinot, duc de Reggio, maréchal de France under Napoleon. Oudinot customarily celebrated French national holidays by dressing in a splendid French uniform and carrying a French flag. He was the prototype for Markiss, the teller of tall tales, in chapter 77 of *Roughing It*.

[39] David Malo (1793?–1853) was Hawaii's first superintendent of schools and the second native licensed to preach. His association with the Hawaiian chiefs provided him with the extensive knowledge of ancient Hawaiian history and customs he recorded in *Moolelo Hawaii*, written about 1840. Malo's history of Kamehameha I was apparently completed and suppressed around 1836, so that initial responsibility for its disappearance cannot accurately be assigned to Kamehameha IV, who was two years old at the time. In Notebook 6 (p. 228) Mark Twain recorded a more plausible version of these events.

[40] A popular story about Paul Kanoa, governor of Kauai from 1847 to 1877.

Italian Consul & wife rebels[41]—Capt. Davenport sent for Lt Cushing come & bring band—[42]

Got that sweet thing called Annie Laurie—no give 'em Hail Colum &c. 78

Removal of Eagle[43] by young midshipman Lord Beresford—Minister gave 'em till 10 AM next day restore it, or go on the reef

---

[41] Italian consul Dr. Charles F. Guillou and his wife, if they were Southern sympathizers during the Civil War, were definitely in the minority in pro-Union Hawaii.

[42] The incident alluded to here has not been identified precisely but must have occurred between 5 December 1865 and 3 February 1866 while the United States steam frigate *Lancaster*, commanded by H. K. Davenport, was on a diplomatic visit to the Sandwich Islands. Lieutenant Commander William B. Cushing had sufficient reason for celebration, for he was expecting a reward of $50,000 for "his services in blowing up the rebel ram *Albamarle*, during the rebellion" (*Pacific Commercial Advertiser*, 17 March 1866). Cushing's feat again became a topic of discussion in Honolulu just the day before Mark Twain's arrival, when the *Pacific Commercial Advertiser* reported that he had actually been awarded $16,100.

[43] The following events took place in the spring of 1865 and involved seamen of the British ship *Clio*, which was about to carry the Dowager Queen Emma on the first leg of a trip to England. Midshipman Charles De La Poer Beresford, the chief culprit, was a descendant of two ancient and martial families and had himself joined the navy in 1859, at the age of thirteen. Many years later, Admiral Lord Charles Beresford described this youthful escapade:

> A certain lady . . . bet me . . . that I would not pull down the American flag. That emblem was painted on wood upon an escutcheon fixed over the entrance to the garden of the Consulate. . . . Having induced two other midshipmen to come with me, we went under cover of night to the Consulate. I climbed upon the backs of my accomplices, leaped up, caught hold of the escutcheon, and brought the whole thing down upon us. Then we carried the trophy on board in a shore-boat. Unfortunately the boatman recognized what it was, and basely told the American consul, who was naturally indignant, and who insisted that the flag should be nailed up again in its place. I had no intention of inflicting annoyance, and had never considered how serious might be the consequences of a boyish impulse. My captain very justly said that as I had pulled down the flag I must put it up again, and sent me with a couple of carpenters on shore. We replaced the insulted emblem of national honour, to the deep delight of an admiring crowd. (*The Memoirs of Admiral Lord Charles Beresford*, 2 vols. [London: Methuen & Co., 1914], 1:58–59)

The other participants in the episode were American minister resident James McBride, British commissioner William W. F. Synge, and Captain Tourneur of the *Clio*.

at 25^c a day. On time—Lord was going to have carpenter do it—M^c said no Sir, with yr own hands—he complied.

Had it on board sewed up in gunny bag—

"No Sir, do it yourself, you took it down—the American eagle will not sully the hands of even a British Lord!" M^c not usually excited.

Brit. Commissioner Sing, very angry—said too bad to make a nobleman do such a thing.

Capt of ship a gentleman—said unfortunately had a man on board with too much money & family.—18 yrs old—bossed the ship—we hear great deal about nobles restrained on shipboard.

He turned water on at party at Sing's house—good joke—behaved like a puppy.

Took barber pole on board placed it as barricade across ward-room —30 ft long.

Took immens gilt boot & hung it aloft where flag of England flies—

Went round town drunk & shouting for Jeff Davis[44]

Young men cornered them in gin mill & were going to lam them—they sent for guard of marines.[45]

Not popular save with the Court.

When Harris went aboard flag-ship as she was about to sail Davenport insulted him—wanted know what he was indebted to for visit?—intimated broadly his room preferable to his company.

---

[44] "Feeling ran pretty high between the English and the Americans in the Sandwich Islands with regard to the American Civil War, which was then waging. It was none of our business, but we of the *Clio* chose to sympathise with the South" (Beresford, *Memoirs*, 1:58).

[45] On 13 May 1865, the *Pacific Commercial Advertiser* noted: "the night before the *Clio* left, a report was carried on board that some of the midshipmen were in danger of an assault from parties on shore. Upon learning it, the officer in charge called for volunteers to go on shore, and some forty men were landed with clubs. . . . The rumor arose from the fact that some four young Americans had made up their minds to try and stop the singing of the middies." According to the newspaper account, the Americans were objecting to the "mob of sailors and officers" who had gone through Honolulu singing "the 'John Brown' song with a chorus somewhat different from the original."

(Lancaster) = Ministers & all consuls & dignitaries staid away from Lancaster party—gave as excuse they had to attend Mrs Bishop's party following night & could not go to all.[46]

Navy boys well received—be good idea to have men-of-war there often—hear there is to be one stationed there.[47]

Population (native) still decreasing fast—3 deaths to one birth—12 per cent natives are over 60 yrs old—this from Amer. Minister

Congress ought see that steamer line runs to Hawaii.[48] [#]

---

[46] To counteract Great Britain's attentions to the Hawaiian royal family, the steam frigate *Lancaster* (see note 42) was under instructions "to cultivate the most friendly and cordial relations" with Hawaii's people and government (Kuykendall, *The Hawaiian Kingdom,* 2:206). Although the *Lancaster's* officers reportedly made a favorable impression, this entry suggests that its mission was not an unqualified success.

[47] The conclusion of the Civil War enabled the United States to comply with the wish of its citizens in Hawaii that there be frequent visits by United States warships to protect American interests there. In the summer of 1866, the U.S.S. *Lackawanna,* commanded by Captain William Reynolds, was assigned indefinitely to the Hawaiian Islands. It would arrive early in 1867, much to the annoyance of Kamehameha V, who feared for Hawaiian independence and felt a personal dislike for Reynolds, who, while stationed in the islands in the 1850s and early 1860s, had been a noisy advocate of annexation by the United States. Despite the king's resentment, the *Lackawanna* was not to be permanently withdrawn until May 1868.

[48] In 1865 the United States government had authorized the establishment of a federally subsidized ocean mail-steamship service between the United States and China, with Honolulu as one of the ports of call. The Pacific Mail Steamship Company, awarded the contract for the San Francisco–China line, objected to the Honolulu stop, maintaining that it lengthened the route and that Honolulu harbor facilities were inadequate for large ships. In January 1866, while controversy raged over the possible elimination of the Honolulu stop, the California Steam Navigation Company inaugurated its *Ajax* service between San Francisco and Honolulu. As a result of the Hawaiian government's refusal to subsidize any steamer service as long as Honolulu's inclusion in the San Francisco–China run remained possible, the local operation was abandoned in the spring of 1866. In his Sacramento *Daily Union* letters of 17 and 18 April, Mark Twain appealed for federal subsidy of direct service between San Francisco and Honolulu that would allow elimination of the Honolulu stop from the China run. California capitalists would have the means of carrying on rapid commerce with Hawaii, a necessity if they were to wrest economic control of the islands from the English and French. This was the compromise solution adopted by Congress early in 1867.

This is a *Republic* ruled by the shadow of a King & court—they dare not do any high-handed work.[49]

If Prince Bill is elected by Legislature he is a friend to Americans.[50]

Americans want annexation, of course, to get rid of duties.

It would be fair to have reciprocity anyway—then—no duties at either end, Cal would have entire S. I trade.

Southern Congressmen never would hear of reciprocity heretofore.[51] [#]

---

[49] The disposition of Kamehameha V to rule in fact as well as in name, which Mark Twain had already noted (p. 115), seems to invalidate this assessment of the Hawaiian political system. Nevertheless, an expanded version of this comment, published in the Sacramento *Daily Union* of 30 July 1866 (*MTH*, p. 354), indicates that he was concerned with the economic and social reality he thought he saw beneath the political facade: "The moneyed strength of these islands—their agriculture, their commerce, their mercantile affairs—is in the hands of Americans—republicans; the religious power of the country is wielded by Americans—republicans; the whole people are saturated with the spirit of democratic Puritanism, and they are—republicans. This is a *republic,* to the very marrow, and over it sit a King, a dozen Nobles and half a dozen Ministers."

[50] One of the most prominent potential successors to Kamehameha V was the High Chief William Charles Lunalilo, a cousin to the king and grandson of a half-brother of Kamehameha I, who enjoyed the unofficial title of *prince* and who was popularly recognized as having the best natural claim to the throne. Lunalilo's friendship for the United States would be evident during his brief reign (8 January 1873 to 3 February 1874) in his acceptance of American principles of government and by his appointment of a cabinet which, with one exception, was made up of Americans.

[51] A reciprocity treaty allowing free entry of Hawaiian sugar and a number of other products into the United States, desperately sought by Hawaiian planters and obstructed in the 1850s by Southern sugar and Northern wool interests, had most recently been denied consideration in 1864 because of President Lincoln's preoccupation with the Civil War. An 1866 campaign for reciprocity was doomed to failure by the usual antagonism of commercial interests represented in the United States Senate and by the opposition of some Americans in Hawaii, who believed reciprocity would prevent or postpone annexation. Mark Twain's comment here suggests the viewpoint of those who were willing to settle for reciprocity in the hope that the commercial ties fostered would lead inevitably to annexation, an argument of considerable weight in finally securing United States approval of a reciprocity treaty in 1876.

White men marry Kanakas—missionary girls marry German Jews.

In Kona, natives make living watching for adultery—fine $30 each.[52]

They *live* in the S. I—no rush—no worry—merchant gooes down to store like a gentleman at 9—goes home at 4, & *thinks no more* of business till next day— d—n San F style of wearing out life.

<D—m> D—n Kanakas ride along with you—walk whn you walk—gallop whn you gallop—trot when you trot—never say a word—perfect shadows—know all gospel but can't tell you the way to any place.

If cut a shark in two you die—a man who was to fish & divide up w^{h} Wilder[53] had to cut a shark in two—said 20 yrs ago would been afraid—w^{d} died—now believe in haole[54] doctrine—still <he did [---] on death> got a little sick & all natives came & said Because you cut shark—at last he said it *was*, & <did>died.

Kao-Kao,[55] Wilder's nurse, wanted native doctors—but superstition killed her—*she said the* natives say they going to die & they *do*.

Suppose been a native with Capt Mitchell[56]—he would have died sure. [*spiral*] [#]

---

[52] In 1866 a law against adultery became part of the Hawaiian penal code. The penalty it established for the male offender was "a fine not exceeding one hundred nor less than thirty dollars" and/or "imprisonment at hard labor not more than twelve nor less than three months" and for the female "a fine not exceeding thirty nor less then ten dollars" and/or "imprisonment at hard labor not more than four nor less than two months" (Robert G. Davis, *The Penal Code of The Hawaiian Kingdom* [Honolulu: Government Press, 1869], p. 21).

[53] Samuel Gardner Wilder, son-in-law of Dr. Gerrit P. Judd, was a planter and businessman who would later play an outstanding part in the development of Hawaii's interisland navigation system.

[54] According to Lorrin Andrews' *A Dictionary of the Hawaiian Language* (Honolulu, 1865), "A person with a white skin; hence, a foreigner."

[55] Kakau, the nurse of Gerrit P. Wilder, son of Samuel Gardner Wilder.

[56] After a journey of more than six weeks in a longboat, Captain Josiah A. Mitchell, master of the clipper ship *Hornet*, and fourteen other survivors of the ship's conflagration at sea arrived at Laupahoehoe, Hawaii, on 15 June 1866, just

All planters on the islands have begun too late—that <it>is reason why in debt—so slow about getting mill up that first cane has been matured 4 months when it is cut—then of course the first rattoons (*the* paying <g>crop & has the money in it,) gets no chance—first cane absorbed all vitality—& so the first rattoons yield nothing—Wyllie who ought to have taken off $100,000 (prices being high) took of 80 tons—debts are hanging there to-day in consequence—most of the plantations are in debt—to see their extravagance, it is a wonder they survive at all.[57]

Wailuku[58] begun right—consequence is, good paying property.

S. P. Kalama saved Dr Judd's life[59]—once when drunk he came

---

a day or two after Mark Twain's departure on the last stretch of his horseback tour of the island. Mark Twain made up for this near miss after the survivors' arrival in Honolulu on 23 June, when he wrote the story of the *Hornet* disaster for the Sacramento *Daily Union*, where it was given front-page publication on 19 July 1866. An excerpt from this letter was included under the title "Short and Singular Rations" in *The Celebrated Jumping Frog of Calaveras County and Other Sketches* (New York: C. H. Webb, 1867).

57 During the American Civil War sugar production replaced whaling as the staple industry of the Sandwich Islands. In 1860 Minister of Foreign Affairs Robert Crichton Wyllie had converted his Princeville plantation on Kauai from coffee to sugar in an attempt to profit from the boom in Hawaiian sugar. Although prices were high when Wyllie made the conversion, a decline set in after the war because of the renewed production of Southern sugar and a glut in the important San Francisco market caused by Hawaiian overproduction. Wyllie, who died nearly bankrupt, was only one of many who suffered. In the second half of 1866 and in 1867 there was widespread economic depression and considerable failure among plantation agents and planters who had gone heavily into debt during the boom period.

58 The Maui site of several large plantations Mark Twain had visited in April and May 1866.

59 On 16 January 1841 Simona P. Kalama, later a prominent government official, saved Dr. Gerrit P. Judd from death in the crater of the active volcano Kilauea. According to Dr. Judd, he was collecting specimens of gas and lava when:

> Suddenly I heard the report of an explosion; a fiery jet burst up from the center, and a river of fire rolled toward me. The heat was intense. I could not retrace my steps and face the fire, so I turned to the wall, but could not climb over the projecting ledge. I prayed God for deliverance, and shouted to the natives to come and take my hand, which I could extend over the ledge so as to be seen. Kalama heard me and came to the brink, but the intense heat drove him back. "Do not forsake me and let me perish," I said. He came again and threw himself

near riding into <Hen> Luther Severance & his young wife—scared the woman to death nearly—both wanted cowhide him—all arrived at Dr. Judd's—it was almost before the house—the lady to recover, the gent to cowhide & K to explain & apologize—gent. raised whip to strike—Miss Judd, taking a nearer look (near-sighted) exclaim "Oh, wait a moment—I believe it is K—" Well, who's K?—The story was told & the lady's wrath was dissolved in tears. Old K. gets drunk —is good & smart—leaves D^r^ to pay his debts.

"Mary, if you want no children, take glass water just as go to bed—*nothing else,* Mary, don't take anything else." 78

Horse begin to — like a thunder storm & in 15 minutes cinch would hang down 3 inches below horse's belly—"Another blast like that, & I'll have to get down & cinch him again 78

Rice fields look well.[60]

Saw Ukeke's 2-story house—relinquished Legislature on condition having it shingled.[61] [#]

---

on the ground, with face averted to avoid the heat, seized my hand with both his, and I threw myself out. The fire swept under as I went over the ledge, burning my shirt-sleeves and wrist, and blistering Kalama's face. (From a letter by Gerrit P. Judd, quoted in Laura Fish Judd, *Honolulu: Sketches of Life in the Hawaiian Islands from 1828 to 1861*, ed. Dale L. Morgan [Chicago: Lakeside Press, 1966], p. 150)

[60] Initiated originally for the market provided by the large Chinese population of the Sandwich Islands, rice cultivation had taken on the proportions of fanaticism in the early 1860s after experimental plantings of a new seed variety had yielded extraordinary returns. Even after the speculators dropped out, rice cultivation remained substantial, and by the mid-1860s rice was second in importance only to sugar among Hawaii's agricultural products.

[61] G. B. Ukeke, elected to the Hawaiian legislature in 1851 in the first election of popular representatives, was still an active legislator in 1866. A temporary resignation for the reason noted here would not, however, have been an unlikely action for the prankish Ukeke, who during the 1866 legislative proceedings on the controversial Harris currency bill (see note 35) suggested that dog's or pig's teeth be readopted as the medium of currency, since "paper money is not good for natives as their food is watery, and if they dropped any of the paper money into it, it would dissolve, and that would be the last of the poor natives' money" (*Pacific Commercial Advertiser*, 23 June 1866).

235 acres in cane at Wilders[62]—in fall will put in 90 more & take crop off the full amount—after a while the other two miles of the plantation will be planted & a portion of the present allowed to rest.

300 tons last year—consider it (2 ton per acre) a 300-ton plantation. Matures in 12 mos & always tassels in November.—rattoons the same of course—some of present crop is 3^d rattoons

Rice (Luther Severance) averages 1 ton an acre—has 100 acres in & buys 100 tons a year from natives & Chinamen—

Sometimes as high as 3 tons per acre.

Polished, it is worth 8, 9, & 10 cents in San F.

Unpolished, but merely hulled in the wheat thresher, it is worth 5 cts here to the Chinamen & they take a vast deal of it.

US duty on rice is 2½ cents a pound.

Make one crop a year <[-]>—COULD make 2, but the rat season intervenes—

The rice is not sown, but transplanted, 3 blades at a time—very slow & laborious.

Kao-Kao (or Kaukao) <d>Kaoka's nurse, (at Wilder's) died on Friday 13th July, 66, & was buried Sunday afternoon—pretty large crowd—coffin of Koa, with beautiful garland of gay flowers on it—it was wrapped in the blankets & tapa of deceased & mats—grave 3 ft deep—no dirt thrown on coffin—grave covered first with board.—natives have aversion to putting dirt on.

Her father died last week—nothing matter with the girl—just thought she was going to die.[63] [#]

---

62 In 1864 Samuel G. Wilder had become sole owner of the Kualoa plantation on Oahu in which he had previously been the partner of Gerrit P. Judd.

63 Elizabeth Kinau Wilder, wife of Samuel G. Wilder, later recalled:

> Mark Twain stayed with us for a week. While he was there, Kakau, Gerrit's nurse, died. The coffin was brought onto the veranda, and surrounded by wailing women. Kauka [rendered *Kaoka* by Mark Twain, this Hawaiian word for *doctor* was used by the natives in addressing Dr. Gerrit P. Judd, but it had also become a family nickname, applied to a dog, then to a horse, and here to the Wilders' son Gerrit] seized an umbrella, strode it like a horse, and galloped around the bier, while the natives groaned at the spectacle, and stretched out their arms to stop him. "Leave the child alone," said the humorist; "he will fight *his* way to

Old woman whose husband & daughter died same way is going to live in the tomb.

Pr. V. died in forcing abortion—kept half a dozen bucks to do her washing, & has suffered 7 abortions.[64]

Of the 17 children in Royal School in 47 only 2 have children living—one a ½ nigger & the other a ½ white—both illegitimate. The royal stock is dead out.

Wilder has lost 10 natives in a year—only 3 births.

Certainly were 400,000 here in Cook's time—& even in 1820—as far as you can climb the hills at Wilder's, there are stones piled up where they cleared for sweet potatoes.

Wilder has a school & church at his own expense—hires teacher & preacher & children of natives are free. Preacher $100 a year for 1 sermon a week—that is insures it to him—what natives don't pay he makes good. [#]

Heaven." Kakau's husband sat up all night, making a black alpaca coat to wear to the funeral, where Mark Twain followed him, in evident admiration. (*The Memoirs of Elizabeth Kinau Wilder*, ed. Elizabeth Leslie Wight [Honolulu: Paradise of the Pacific Press, 1909], p. 140)

[64] Accounts of the death at age twenty-seven of Princess Victoria Kaahumanu Kamamalu, whose sexual appetites were celebrated in native chants performed at her funeral, are suspiciously silent about the cause of death. Cognizant perhaps of the diplomatic wisdom of presenting the princess as the royal family wished her to appear—although she had suffered at least one widely known fall from virtue in the company of a Honolulu auctioneer—Mark Twain commented favorably on her character in his 16 July Sacramento *Daily Union* letter. In 1873, however, he would more candidly characterize her as "the christianized but morally unclean Princess" (letter in the New York *Daily Tribune*, 9 January 1873, *MTH*, p. 497), and still later he provided an account of her which expanded upon this early notebook entry:

> In the Sandwich Islands in 1866 a buxom royal princess died. Occupying a place of distinguished honor at her funeral were thirty-six splendidly built young native men. In a laudatory song which celebrated the various merits, achievements and accomplishments of the late princess those thirty-six stallions were called her *harem*, and the song said it had been her pride and boast that she kept the whole of them busy, and that several times it had happened that more than one of them had been able to charge overtime. (*LE*, p. 41)

Mapuaa Hog God—<Slid> had fight on hill with *Pele*—she drove him—he slid down Kaliuwa—escaped into sea—swam to Hawaii—took up & spit sea water into Kileaua, but couldnt put it out—made up w^{h} Pele—he <th> pulled land away (thus forming Kawaihae Bay,) & stuck it on North end of Isld.[65]

Have taken 40,000 watermelons from Wilder's this year—25 acres among cane.

Lincoln said, "You like McClellan— h—l on dress parade—no account in action." 78

Advertiser 12 or 1500 subscribers—Gazette 212½ by their own showing—Nupepa Kuakoa <28>25 to 2,800.
<Keaua>
Ke Au Okoa—2200 circ[66]

American unpopularity is easily explained—they are Americans, through & through—no cringing to royalty—free, outspoken <&> independent & fearless.

Horse with 11 styles of galloping—would be pleasing variety one at a time, but mixed, is bad. 78

25^{c} per doz—Why these eggs are spoiled—I know it—otherwise how could I sell them so cheap. 78

Princeville planta^{n} 3 tons—per acre.[67]

Kanaka fondness for big funerals—fellow died for one. 78

Policemen sing the half hours. [#]

---

[65] One of several versions of the legendary encounter between the hog-god Kamapuaa, local deity of the Kaliuwaa valley on Oahu, and Pele, goddess of volcanoes, who dwelt in the crater of Kilauea on Hawaii.

[66] The *Pacific Commercial Advertiser* and *Nupepa Kuakoa* were founded by Henry Whitney in 1856 and 1861, respectively. Whitney would later claim he had refused Mark Twain a job as reporter for the *Pacific Commercial Advertiser*, the spokesman for the American interests in Hawaii, reputedly on suspicion of laziness. The other two newspapers were established by the government in 1865.

[67] A further reference to Wyllie's unprofitable sugar plantation, discussed in note 57.

Brown's horse belch 2 or 3 times have to get down & cinch him. 78

I think if one of them were to slide into Paradise with *their* style of Christianity, St Peter would start him out again with a<n> <[e]> promptness that would be in the last degree surprising to him 78

"Good morning, Brown."[68]
"*Aloha!*"
"Have you been to breakfast?"
"*Aolé*"
<"Mr. Brown."
"Well! what's the *pilikia* now!">
When you going?
"Wiki-wiki."
Now see here Mr B. (impressively
Well, there *you* go again. That means pilikia, *I* know. <Out with it, then.> What's up now? I spose I've let go something that's aole-maitai."

"Give me your attention, Mr. B. ([------]) If you utter another of those cursed native words in my presence I'll brain you!

"Another of those cursed native words & I'll <comb your head with the bootjack!> brain you! It makes me mad. Every whiffet that comes here from Cal, picks up half a dozen of the commonest <native> Kanaka words the first week, & forever afterward he sandwiches them into his conversation. Now, you're at it, & you've got to stop it in <mighty> very short order. Here for the last two or 3 days you can't say "good morning" like a Christian, but with a wretched affectation of knowing the Hawaiian tongue, you must say "Aloha!" And you can't say "No," like a white man, but must either turn your right hand over quickly <[or s]> without speaking, or else say *aolé*-ah-owrie—if you are going toward the sea, you say you are

[68] The following draft of a conversation with Mr. Brown anticipates Mark Twain's scorn for affected use of foreign languages, as recorded in chapter 23 of *The Innocents Abroad*. It was not used by Mark Twain in his writings about the Sandwich Islands.

going "mar-*ki*" and if toward the mountains it is '<ma->mah-*ow*kah" — —if you would express such words as quickly & bad, you say "[kiki][69] & oni"[70] if you are in trouble of any kind, you are *pilikia*— I won't *have* it, Mr. Brown! It is a poor mean <presumption &>presumptuous affectation that has been indulged in by generation after generation of fools ever since Baalam's ass introduced <it th> it; & if I were you, Mr. Brown, I would be ashamed to subscribe to a custom that had such an origin.

"Mark, that's as much as to say that I'm *hoopilimeai*[71] to Ba—"

It is well that the <man> puppy escaped so expeditiously to the street, else I must have imbrued my hands in his gore. Nothing aggravates me like this contemptible fashion I have been abusing Brown about. <It> I am attacked with it every day by every silly stranger & tortured from the rising until the setting of the sun. But if Brown destroys my peace of mind again in this way, he shall die. The words are said.

Howries[72] talk so—

Honolulu, July 18/66

Have got my passport from the Royal d—d Hawaiian Collector of Customs & paid a dollar for it, & tomorrow we sail for America in the good ship *Smyrniote*, Lovett, master—& I have got a devilish saddle-boil to sit on for the first two weeks at sea.

"Why Ma, don't ask<e> the old thing to come in—he'll sit & sit & sit—& you'll never get rid of him!" 78

2—"Why Ma, it's one o'clock." 78 [#]

---

69 Mark Twain's inscription here is illegible, but its length and general configuration suggest that the word intended was either *kiki*, meaning *quickly*, or *wiki*, meaning *quick*.

70 Mark Twain mistakenly wrote *oni*, meaning *uneasy*, *restless*, for *ino*, which does mean *bad*.

71 *Hoopilimeaai* was pointedly defined by Mark Twain in the Sacramento *Daily Union* of 30 July 1866 (*MTH*, p. 349) as "Uriah Heep boiled down . . . the soul and spirit of obsequiousness" and offered as a description of Attorney General and Minister of Finance Charles Coffin Harris, who is discussed in note 35.

72 *Howries* is a phonetic spelling of *haoles* (foreigners). Mark Twain wrote this comment in the margin beside his purported conversation with Mr. Brown.

Put B's picture in Book.

All small villages are gossipy, but Honolulu heads them a *little*—they let me off comparatively easy, though, & I don't thank them for it because it argues that I wasn't worth the trouble of blackguarding. They only accused me of murder, arson, highway robbery & some other little eccentricities, but I knew nothing of it till the day I started. The missionary—I should say *preacher* <spirit> feature of insincerity & hypocrisy, marks the social atmosphere of the place.

A woman who keeps a dog won't do, as a gen^{l} thing.

Honolulu, July 19, 1866,

The Comet, with Howard[73] & Mrs. Spencer & Nellie & Katie[74] on board left at 2 P.M., with a great firing of cannon, & went to wind'ard (unusual)—we left peaceably in the *Smyrniote* at 4:30 P.M (Comet out of sight) & went in same direction. Now we shall see who beats to San Francisco.

Made 110 miles up to noon of Friday 20th, but were then only 10 miles from Oahu, having gone clear around the island.

On 21st made 179 miles

Sunday, 4th day out—lat. <28.21> 28.12. long. 157.42—distance 200 miles in the last 24 hours.

Monday July 23—5th day—lat. 31.34—longitude 157.30—distance 202 miles. [#]

---

73 Edward Howard was a foppish, proper Englishman who met Mark Twain at the Volcano House at Kilauea. Since he intended to journey across the United States, Howard became Mark Twain's touring companion so he could observe a "typical" American. A series of indelicacies and misadventures suffered in Mark Twain's company discouraged him about the prospective pleasure of his tour of the United States. During their joint excursion on the island of Hawaii Mark Twain persisted in introducing Howard as "Brown," claiming that he found the latter name "easier to remember" (*MTH*, p. 75).

74 The wife and daughters of Captain Thomas Spencer, master of a whaling ship who had become a prosperous merchant and ship chandler in Honolulu and Hilo after losing his ship in an assault by Gilbert Islands natives. In the second week of June, Mark Twain reportedly stayed at the Hilo home of the convivial Spencer, whose flamboyant and boisterous manner approached that of the nearly mythical Captain Ned Wakeman.

Literary Practice to form correct judgment—Teacher in S F school plans a novel—& makes pupils write it.

Show up Life at Sea & abuse "Life on the Ocean Wave."[75] 78

Petroleum for sore-backed horses.

Hospitality—Islanders been so often imposed on—J. Q. A Warren[76]

And the lion shall lie down with the lamb & the latter shall get up & dust. 78

Tuesday July 24—6th Day out—lat. <34.31> 34.31 N. long. 157.40 W. Distance 180 miles. Had calms several times. Are we never going to make any longitude? The trades are weakening—it is time we struck the China winds about midnight—say in lat. 36.

Wednesday 25th—lat. 37.18 long. 158.06—distance 170 miles. 3 P.M.—we are abreast of San Francisco, but seventeen hundred miles at sea!—*when* will the wind change?

Ship California loaded with grain at San F for China.—grain very scarce in Australia & China & very plenty in Cal.

Capt. Lovett's monkey story.[77] 78

Bp. Staley[78] & 5 ass'ts—

---

[75] Mark Twain's consistent desire to satirize popular romantic treatments of the sea, in this case Epes Sargent's buoyant escapist poem (set to music by Henry Russell), was here stirred by the becalmed monotony of the *Smyrniote* voyage to San Francisco as it had been stimulated on the down trip by the harsh reality of the *Ajax* fireman's lot (see the Sacramento *Daily Union*, 18 April 1866, *MTH*, p. 270).

[76] An aggressive agricultural journalist who was touring the Sandwich Islands. Mark Twain recorded some of his impositions in Notebook 6.

[77] Perhaps a version of an anecdote titled "A Monkey Trick" (in *Ocean Scenes, or the Perils and Beauties of the Deep* [New York: Leavitt, Trow, & Company, 1848], pp. 284–285), telling of a ship's monkey which abducts a passenger's baby and carries it aloft to dandle and comfort it in the rigging before returning it safely to the deck. Recurrent allusions in Notebook 5 to other pieces in *Ocean Scenes*—a collection of sketches dealing chiefly with mishaps at sea and intended to fill and instruct the leisure moments of "the intelligent mariner" (*Ocean Scenes*, p. vi)—suggest that Mark Twain found this book in the *Smyrniote* library.

[78] The Reverend Thomas Nettleship Staley, first Anglican bishop of Honolulu,

Nearly 50 Congregal (mostly native)[79]

Bp Maigret & 20 assts—

6 more Staleyites already appointed for isld Hawaii alone at $50 a month—

Thus in neighborhood of a hundred preachers to save 50,000 niggers, & they <dy> decreasing at rate 12 per cent. Double the preachers & you double this per cent. Now the idea of these d—d English coming in here & trying to gobble the work already done by Americans—it is just like them.[80]

There is more gospel here <tha> in proportion to population than any where else in the wide world!

25th July—lat. 29, N.—I was genuinely glad, this evening, to welcome the first *twilight* I have seen in 6 years,

No twilight in the S. Islands, California or Washoe. [#]

---

had arrived in late 1862 to be head of the Hawaiian Reformed Catholic church. Anglicanism was introduced at the request of Kamehamcha IV and Queen Emma, who considered English religious practices to be more consistent with monarchial government than New England Congregationalism.

[79] It wasn't until 1863 that the American missionaries in Hawaii undertook to train Hawaiian pastors and to assign them responsibility for small local parishes. In July 1866 *The Friend* reported a total of twenty ordained Hawaiian pastors. The number Mark Twain noted probably included natives in training for the ministry, since by 1870 there were forty-four native pastors in Hawaiian churches and another sixteen had gone as missionaries to Micronesia and the Marquesas.

[80] The sudden advent of the Anglican church caused much consternation and resentment among American missionaries and residents in Hawaii. Although they had been prepared to accept an Episcopalian clergyman, preferably an American, the establishment of an Anglican episcopate was regarded as a violation of the unstated agreement by which American Protestant missionaries confined themselves to islands north of the equator and left more southern islands to the English. Since affairs of the church were inevitably interpreted as machinations of the state, the English religious invasion seemed a prelude to a more general English intervention and raised the further possibility that France would feel obligated to exert herself more vigorously on behalf of her Roman Catholic mission in Hawaii. Despite some ambivalence toward American missionaries, Mark Twain shared their dislike of Bishop Staley and defended them against the encroachment of the English. "Our missionaries are our missionaries," he wrote at one point, "and even if they were our devils I would not want any English prelate to slander them" (Sacramento *Daily Union,* 16 July 1866, *MTH,* p. 331; see also his letter in the *Union* of 30 July, *MTH,* pp. 352–355).

Never mind—if you can find way in dark, guess I can follow that. 78

600
80
———
48000

Damon[81]—Oh—don't swear, friend, don't swear—that won't mend the matter.

Whaler—Brother Damon it's all very well for you to say don't swear, & it's all right too—I don't say nothing against it—but don't you know that if you was to ship a crew of sailors for Heaven & was to stop at Hell two hours & a half for provisions, some d—d son of a gun would run away." 78

Thursday 26—Got 50 miles above opposite San Francisco & at noon started back & are now running south-east—almost calm.—1700 miles at sea.

Jim Lampton & the dead man in Dr. McDowell's College.[82] 78

Where did you get that excellent venison at this time of the year? It isn't venison—it is a steak off that dead nigger.[83] 78

Friday 27—We are just barely moving to-day in a general direction southeast toward San F—though last night we stood stock still for hours, pieces of banana skins thrown to the great sea-birds swimming in our wake floating perfectly still in the sluggish water. In the last

---

[81] The Reverend Samuel Chenery Damon, pastor of the Oahu Bethel Church, is mentioned at greater length in Notebook 6.

[82] James Andrew H. Lampton was the half brother of Jane Lampton Clemens and a contemporary of her children, Pamela and Orion. Despite an aversion to the sight of blood, he attended the McDowell Medical College in Saint Louis, founded by Joseph Nash McDowell, a skillful though eccentric physician who encouraged his students to steal cadavers for dissection.

[83] "Forty-Five Days' Sufferings" (*Ocean Scenes*, pp. 180–184), an account of the tribulations of a crew stranded at sea in a ship that has lost shrouds and sails during a storm, includes a lurid description of the murder and consumption of a Negro who is part of the ship's cargo. Mark Twain's grotesque levity may be a reaction to the methodical butchery performed by the famished sailors, who took care to dress the meat before eating it and were even so provident as to pickle for later use what they couldn't devour immediately.

24 hours we have made but 38 miles—made most of that drifting sideways. Position at noon, 38.55 N. 157.37 W.

"Did Smutty tum down to see the baby?"

"Fly around gals—Monday morning—to-morrows Tuesday—next day Wednesday—middle of the week & no work done yet!"[84] 78

Tuesday & Friday bean day; Saturday fish day; Monday & Thursday duck <day> (or duff?) days. At 7 bells in the evening dog watch pump ship.

The sea is fully as level as the Mississippi—at least as smooth as the river is when ruffled by a very light breeze & swelling with a few dying steamboat waves.

We see *nothing* on this wide, wide, lonely ocean—nothing but some large sea-birds, sometimes a dolphin, & occasionally a Mother Cary's chicken—these latter persisting in flying *low*, indicating calm weather—the sailors say they only bring tidings of the coming storm when they fly *high*.

Poi not bad food—nor beans—time of flood[85] & famine 5 years ago in Esmeralda, none but the aristocracy had beans, for dessert. 78

The monotony of this calm! One can only tell the days of the week by the food—duff on Sunday, beans Tuesdays & Fridays, Salt Fish on Saturday &c.

Women kiss—& then, back turned, abuse each other like a couple wildcats.—female kissing is damnable custom. 78

Had an eye like an albatross.

"Yr mother had twins—<you> boy & a — the boy died—why how you have grown!" 78 [#]

---

[84] This quotation seems to be the product of the same impulse that produced Mark Twain's early Mississippi River sketch "Captain Montgomery," published in the *Golden Era* on 28 January 1866.

[85] The disastrous Walker River floods of late 1861 and early 1862, when Clemens was living in the Nevada county where he had one of his brief experiences as a silver miner.

A land bird came & hovered over the ship a while to-day—he is a long way from home—thought of the old song—"Bird at Sea."[86]

Ch. Eloquence—Prentiss' speech on Miss Murder Case[87]—Th. Parker's tirade against Webster.[88] 8

The stabbed dead man in my father's law office.[89] 78

Splendidly-colored lunar rainbow to-night.

Fishing for Goneys, but hooks too large—the birds bite freely, however.

Man tells Brown long thrilling adventure with no denouement to it—no point—& Brown abuses the same for working up his interest to no purpose. 78

Give sketch of 3^d^ Mate's belt—[90] [#]

---

[86] The song, with music by C. Meineke and words by Felicia Hemans, has been called "the most important maritime song of the 1830's" (Sigmund Spaeth, *A History of Popular Music in America* [New York: Random House, 1948], p. 78).

[87] Seargent Smith Prentiss, southern lawyer and politician, whose oratory reputedly struck awe in Daniel Webster, and whose prowess as a jurist was said to exceed even his skill as an orator, was prominent in two Mississippi murder trials in the 1830s. In 1831 it was Prentiss' speech for the prosecution that secured the death penalty for Alonzo Phelps, a scholarly highwayman-murderer. At one point during this speech Phelps was restrained from attacking Prentiss only by his own lawyer's confidence of acquittal. The second trial, perhaps more sensational, concerned the murder of Mississippi planter Joel Cameron by four of his slaves. In July 1835, having been engaged for a large fee by Cameron's partner, Alexander G. McNutt, who had vigorously spurred the prosecution and execution of the four slaves, Prentiss delivered an inflammatory speech that played upon white fears of Negro insurrection to wring from the jury the conviction of a fifth man, the free Negro Mercer Byrd, who had been discovered in possession of Cameron's watch. In a confession made just prior to his execution but suppressed by his lawyer, Byrd identified McNutt, a few years later elected governor of Mississippi, as the instigator of his partner's murder, apparently for financial profit.

[88] Here and below (see note 93) Mark Twain refers to Theodore Parker's controversial condemnation of Daniel Webster, delivered at the Boston Melodeon on 31 October 1852, one week after Webster's death, and disseminated widely through newspaper and pamphlet publication.

[89] Seen by the eight-year-old Sam Clemens and recalled in chapter 18 of *The Innocents Abroad*.

[90] John S. Thomas was third officer of the *Hornet*. In his letter in the Sacra-

Caught 2 goneys—they are all the same size—they measured 7 feet 1 inch from tip to tip of wings.

They made a wooden clog fast to him & let him go—a pitiful advantage for "godlike" man to take of a helpless bird.

Get photographs of the Hornets.[91]

The bird looked reproachfully upon them with his great human eyes while they did him this wrong.

Saturday 28 May[92]
—38.46—156.36—48 miles—*glassy* calm—had *sternway* awhile.

Actual distance—straight courses—ran by Hornet's long boat was 3,360 miles—devious make it 4,000 [*spiral*]

Apologize or Fight—"If he means the editor of this paper when he speaks of his vision having been blessed once more with the long green swell of the Pacific. &" 78

Eloquence—Th. Parker's funeral sermon on Danl Webster—Picture of Webster standing amid the "fire & smoke & thunder of his own eloquence."[93] 8

Brown's disease of the heart—stomach—takes <sug> whisky 3 times a day in which sugar cane has been steeped—can't carry cane conveniently, so <carrie> uses plain sugar. 78 [#]

---

mento *Daily Union* of 19 July 1866, Mark Twain cited Thomas as the primary source of his information about the *Hornet* wreck and the sufferings of its surviving crewmen.

91 Probably a reference to photographs of the Ferguson brothers and Captain Mitchell. On 13 July Mitchell had written in his diary: "Lunch^{d} at Am Hotel Fergusons about the same. Had pictures taken together for Hilo friends" (*The Diary of Captain Josiah A. Mitchell, 1866* [Hartford: Case, Lockwood & Brainard Co., 1924], p. 58).

92 Mark Twain intended to write "28 July." He was at this time reading the journals kept by the Ferguson brothers and Captain Mitchell during their ordeal in the *Hornet* longboat and inadvertently transferred the month from one of their notebooks to his own.

93 This particular phrase does not appear in published versions of Parker's speech, although elements of it pervade the frequently demonic word pictures he painted of Webster and his oratory.

People bring all manner of diseases to the S. I., & keep the people always in danger.[94]

Sarcasm

Henry Clay Dean's "Gentlemen, the monument still stands."[95] 8

Old sailors[96] did nothing in the Hornet's boat but spin fo'castle yarns <Jack & othe> about ships & former captains, & how the grub was, <l>& what for cook for lobscouse was, &c—& Jack & others like him who could barely read & couldn't sign their names to the ship's articles, blew all the time about rich parents, reared in lap luxury, &c & how high toned they were when at home & how magnif they lived! [*spiral*]

Packed like a midshipman's trunk—everything on top & nothing at hand. 78

A man can't know *any* thing about Dr. G. P. Judd from *talking* to him—but *read his writings*—he never *jumps* to a conclusion but when he arrives at one it is monstrous apt to be correct.—Writes *remarkably* clearly & concentratively—his state papers are models of clearness, perspicacity & sound judgment—statesmanship if you please. The whiffets who now hold office should not speak lightly of

---

94 Of the diseases brought to the Sandwich Islands, the most deadly was syphilis which dated from the arrival of Captain Cook in 1778. The *mai okuu*—cholera, or perhaps bubonic plague—reputedly destroyed over half the population around 1804. There were epidemics of influenza in 1826, mumps in 1839, and in the 1840s and 1850s outbreaks of measles, whooping cough, diarrhea, and smallpox, which took a combined total of many thousands of lives.

95 Prominent during the Civil War among Iowa Copperheads, the eccentric Dean was a Methodist circuit preacher, lawyer, and chaplain of the United States Senate, who was famous as a powerful and flamboyant public speaker. Mark Twain would recall Dean's oratory in chapter 57 of *Life on the Mississippi*.

96 In addition to Captain Josiah Mitchell, Third Mate John S. Thomas, and Henry and Samuel Ferguson, the following men—some of whom Mark Twain would mention in "Forty-Three Days in An Open Boat"—were refugees in the *Hornet's* longboat: Henry Morris, Joseph Williams, Peter Smith, C. H. Haartman, Antonio Cassero, John Ferris, Frederick Clough, Neil Turner, Thomas F. Tate, James Cox, John Campbell.

him—the equal to that shrewd, wise old head of his does not exist in the S. I. to-day.[97]

Rev. Lorrin Andrews[98] taught himself how to engrave & print on copper & he taught students (native) of Lahainaluna—they do it handsomely. He taught *himself* how to polish the copper.

Population 110,000—27 yrs ago—decreased 60,000 since.

Contrary to law native doctors & Kahunas have Kings written license ($10) to practice.

King is a heathen—an old sorceress has him under her thumb—picks out the fish he may eat—tells him <where> in what house he may sleep, &c. Accompanies him in all his excursions. He was educated in a Christian school but has never submitted himself to Christianity—discovered his predilections for heathenism in youth.

Great extinct crater of Mauna Loa is 24 miles circumference & <over 1200> 1,270 feet deep.

Great Crater on *Mauna Kea* is 27 miles circum & 1274 feet deep.

In a single voyage they grew old in the mariner's stormy experience. In this little voyage of 7 months of these 2 fresh young college students was crowded the sorrows, the privations, the bitter hardships & the thrilling adventures of a whole (long) lifetime before the mast! [*spiral*] [#]

---

[97] Complementing his ability as a writer of English, Judd had quickly become a master of the Hawaiian tongue. In 1834 he prepared a medical treatment book in Hawaiian for the use of both missionaries and natives. In 1835 he wrote *Anatomia*, a sixty-page textbook in which he established nearly all of the anatomical terms in the Hawaiian language. Judd also participated in the missionaries' translation of the Bible, completed in 1839.

[98] One of the pioneer missionaries, Lorrin Andrews became an adviser to the chiefs, then a judge and Supreme Court justice, but it was as educator and lexicographer that he became best known. Andrews helped establish and was the first principal of Hawaii's first high school, founded at Lahainaluna in 1831. He was the author of a large number of school texts in Hawaiian, including *Grammar of the Hawaiian Language* (Honolulu, 1854) and *A Dictionary of the Hawaiian Language* (Honolulu, 1865).

Sam[l] Ferguson is about 28—a graduate of Trinity College, Hartford—Henry is 18—a student of same college—Capt. says the boys were good grit—Henry's <showed> lip never quivered but once & that was when he was told that there was hardly the shadow of a chance for their rescue—and then the feeling he showed was chiefly at the thought that he was never to see his college mates any more. [*spiral*]

Chas Jackson, cook & Federal soldier at Jones'[99]—worked like a horse—was a genius & an intelligent one—a German—he saved the *lives* of 3 or 4 of the men, performing for them a service essential to them & one which no other man would have undertaken. He would swear like a trooper at his every day work, but on Sunday summoned the men by the Capt's permission & preached a feeling & sensible sermon from a well chosen Bible text. Suffers from a bad bayonet wound in the thigh—told me he served 3 yrs & was in many battles—shipped in a whaler for his health—got disabled—was put ashore at Jones who took care of him & pays him $6 a month—feels sincerely grateful to Jones & says will never leave him. Lost his papers, but the US ought to give the gallant Dutchman his pension anyhow—he treated me well & if this will serve him I shall be glad. Before I knew Jones well, I acted a little savagely—I apologize now that I know him better. [*spiral*]

D—d Englishman named Spencer[100] <co>came down first day —staid all day & bored the life out of the men—could not insult or drive him away. [*spiral*]

I have but one "specimen" saved from Hawaiian Kingdom—Hornet Third Mate's belt. [*spiral*] [#]

---

[99] John Jones was a storekeeper at Laupahoehoe on Hawaii, where the *Hornet* longboat was brought ashore. Although Mark Twain here identified Jones's steward as Charles Jackson, it is a Charles Bartlett whom Captain Mitchell's diary (p. 106) mentions gratefully in conjunction with Jones.

[100] On 17 June Henry Ferguson noted in his journal (p. 123): "Natives and some white men came in to see us, one big Englishman tormenting us exceedingly with well meant but ill timed attentions." This may have been the man Captain

Volcano Richardson[101] out of provisions 11 months on Guano island at Equator—sun red—days all same length—Capt who rescued him wrapped him in poi so he *absorbed* his food. [*spiral*] [102]

Capt Clark[103] went down to a guano Island to bring up a long boat & did so, with 3 or 4 natives—over a month making the trip up.

Simple <or> and Touching Eloquence—

<Effie> Jeanie Deans pleading for her sister before the Queen.[104] 8

Eloquence Simplicity—Lincoln's "With malice toward none, with charity for all, & doing the right as God gives us to see the right, all may yet be well.[105]—Very simple & beautiful 8

Boat[106] sailed 3,360 miles—it is 3,100 from N York to Liverpool.

"Don't fiddle—don't fiddle, my son—many a young man of noble promise has been stopped still & anchored at mediocrity just from learning to play on the fiddle. Avoid the awful seductions of the fiddle as you would avoid <the> a snare set for your undoing."

"But—"

"I tell you it draws your mind away from useful pursuits & [#]

Josiah Mitchell listed in his diary (p. 109) as "J. Spencer/Waimeu/Hawaii/Managing Waimeu Grazing Cop."

[101] Charles and Julius Richardson were cousins and partners in the Kapapala Ranch on Hawaii, where on 2 June Mark Twain stopped en route to the active volcano Kilauea. They were also proprietors of the recently opened Volcano House, Kilauea's first hotel. In a letter in the Sacramento *Daily Union* of 16 November 1866, Mark Twain would write of the comforts of the Richardsons' hotel.

[102] The only instance in which a spiral occurs on an entry not related to the *Hornet*, although the reference is to a similar disaster at sea.

[103] A Captain Clark was master of the interisland schooner *Alberni*, which belonged to the Hawaiian Steam and General Inter-Island Navigation Company.

[104] This incident occurs in chapter 37 of *The Heart of Midlothian*. Although Mark Twain read a good many of Sir Walter Scott's works, he may here be recalling Dion Boucicault's "Great Sensation Play, entitled Jeannie Deans," a popular adaptation of the novel presented in San Francisco shortly before he accepted his Sandwich Islands assignment.

[105] Paraphrase of a passage from Lincoln's second inaugural address, 4 March 1865.

[106] The *Hornet* longboat.

In 11 days these men were walking about the streets of Honolulu. [*spiral*]

Sunday <2>July 29. Overcast, breezy and *very* pleasant on deck. All hands on deck immediately after breakfast.

Rev. Franklin S. Rising preached, & the passengers formed choir.[107]

Very singular production—describe it. (They call it a cucumber. 78

No less gifted artist than Nature could have tied those knots in the excessively brief tails of Victor's cats.[108]

Dont forget the *Elephant* at the Pali.

"*Cannot* move back—*impossible?*—*Nothing* is impossible on Bunker Hill!" The vast multitude fell back with one impulse like a wave of the sea. —Webster.[109] 8 [#]

---

[107] Samuel Clemens' 19 December 1868 description of the Reverend Franklin S. Rising for Olivia Langdon (see note 2) included a romantic re-creation of the scene somewhat different from that present in this notebook:

> We were at sea five Sundays. He felt it his duty to preach, but of the 15 passengers, none even pretended to sing, & he was so diffident that he hardly knew how he was to get along without a choir. I said, "Go ahead—I'll stand by you—I'll be your choir."—And he *did* go ahead—& I was his choir. We could find only *one* hymn that I knew. It was "Oh, Refresh us." Only one—& so for five Sundays in succession he stood in the midst of the assembled people on the quarter-deck & gave out that same hymn twice a day, & I stood up solitary & alone & sang it! And then he went right along, happy & contented, & preached his sermon. . . . *Now* the glories of heaven are about him, & in his ears its mysterious music is sounding—but to me comes no vision but a lonely ship in a great solitude of sky & water; & unto *my* ears comes no sound but the complaining of the waves & the softened cadences of that simple old hymn—but Oh, Livy, it comes freighted with *infinite* pathos.

[108] "There is a breed of cats on Oahu, which have tails about two inches long, with a half-turn in them. They came here in this wise: Some sixteen years ago, a vessel arrived in this port, and the Captain applied to Monsieur Victor [Chancerel], then proprietor of the French Hotel, to furnish him with recruits (provender) for his vessel. This M. Victor promptly did, and the Captain pleased with his dispatch, invited him on board his vessels, and presented him with a male and female cat of the breed" (*Daily Hawaiian Herald*, 2 October 1866).

[109] On 17 June 1825 Daniel Webster delivered a stirring address to a vast audience assembled for the laying of the cornerstone of the Bunker Hill Monument.

> His voice was very clear and full, and his manner very commanding. Once, owing to the great press, some of the seats and barriers gave way, and there was a moment of considerable confusion, notwithstanding the efforts of those whose

Think of this prayer uttered in an open boat before uncovered famishing men in the midst of the Pacific Ocean & in the midst of a sea lashed to fury in the anger of a storm:

O most powerful & glorious Lord God at whose command the winds blow, & lift up the waves of the sea, & who stillest the rage thereof; we thy creatures, but miserable sinners, do in this our great distress cry unto thee for help. Save, Lord, or we perish! [110]—Prayers to be used in Storms at Sea. [*spiral*]

Think of the lonely ones drifting <about>abroad at large in that grand (tremendous) solitude & dreaming of home <und> & its idols under the (wonderful) <lustrous> torch-like stars of those far southern skies! It was a beautiful night—& those words in the tropics have a significance. [*spiral*]

5 o clock evening before made land, most magnificent rainbow ever saw & spanned the widest space—Capt sung out "Saved! Theres the bow of promise boys!" [111] When such a thing is seen at sea it is

---

duty it was to preserve order. One of these gentlemen said to Mr. Webster: "It is impossible, sir, to restore order." Mr. Webster replied with a good deal of severity: "Nothing is impossible, sir: let it be done." Another effort was made, and silence was obtained. (Account by George Ticknor, quoted in George Ticknor Curtis, *Life of Daniel Webster*, 4th ed., 2 vols. [New York: D. Appleton and Company, 1872], 1:249)

110 Condensed and paraphrased from a prayer written by Henry Ferguson in his journal of the *Hornet* voyage and wreck (pp. 139–140). During the voyage to San Francisco, Mark Twain was allowed access to the journals of both Fergusons and to the diary of Captain Josiah Mitchell, all of whom were *Smyrniote* passengers, but, except for the brief quotations and paraphrases that occur in this notebook, nothing survives of the longhand transcriptions he made. In "Forty-Three Days in An Open Boat" (*Harper's New Monthly Magazine* 34 [December 1866]: 104–113) Mark Twain would reproduce extensive excerpts from these personal records, and, despite his claim that "it did not appear to me that any emendations were necessary" (*Harper's*, p. 112), he in fact introduced a number of changes to heighten the dramatic effect of his material.

111 This incident may have been recounted to Mark Twain during the voyage to San Francisco. It is not mentioned in either of the Ferguson journals or in Captain Mitchell's diary. Henry Ferguson's journal entry for 14 June, the day before rescue, did begin with a simple observation and expression of hope: "Most lovely rainbow last evening, perfect bow with color most vivid and supplementary bow very distinct. Certainly it is a good sign" (*The Journal of Henry Ferguson*, p. 120). In "Forty-Three Days in An Open Boat," however, the entry attributed to him under

nearly always accompanied by the signs of coming squalls & tempests, but in this instance the sky was marvellously clear & entirely free from such signs. [*spiral*]

Sunday July 29—lat. 38.43 long. 154.55—Distance 80 miles

Eloquence

"You Zeke, you let that woodchuck go!" —Webster.[112] 8

They dreamed of all sweet music Imagine these poor fellows <awakened> creating in imagination at dead of night from their restless half-slumber by the softened distant music of Home Swt Home! [*spiral*]

Eloquence

"Forever float that standard sheet
Where breathes the foe but falls before us
With freedom's soil beneath our feet
And freedom's banner streaming o'er us!"[113] 8

There are factitious aids—surroundings & circumstances which often make a passage thrillingly eloquent which inherently possesses no such attribute—for instance, how Gen. Grant's simple response to Buckner who had <p> asked upon what terms he would stipulate or agree for the surrender of Fort Donaldson used to rouse the

---

this date incorporates language from Clemens' note: "Toward evening saw a magnificent double-rainbow—the first we had seen. Captain said, 'Cheer up, boys, it's a prophecy!—it's the bow of promise!' " (*Harper's*, p. 112).

[112] This entry and the later notation to "Write some more biographies of great men & women" (p. 153) suggest a plan for a piece about Daniel Webster similar to the "Biographical Sketch of George Washington" that Mark Twain had published in the *Golden Era* on 4 March 1866 (reprinted in *WG*, pp. 106–108, with the date misprinted as 1864). The apocryphal order from Daniel to his older brother Ezekiel must have been intended as a precocious manifestation of that eloquence of command which, as Mark Twain had already remembered, Webster displayed so impressively at Bunker Hill. These plans for burlesque biographies resulted in nothing more than the strained and undistinguished "Origin of Illustrious Men," which appeared in the *Californian* on 29 September 1866 (reprinted in *MTSF*, pp. 248–249).

[113] The last lines of "The American Flag" by Joseph Rodman Drake. This poem was included in *Ocean Scenes* (pp. 381–382).

multitude in the fierce days of the rebellion. "Unconditional surrender! I propose to move at once upon your works!"[114] 8

"I demand the surrender of this fortress in the name of the Great Jehovah & the Continental Congress!"[115] 8

Stately Eloquence

Washington Farewell Address.
Webster Reply to Hayne
Logan's Speech.[116]
Patrick Henry.

As solemn as the booming of a distant gun on a midnight sea.

<Why was it>
Conversation between the carpenters of Noah's Ark, laughing at him for an old visionary—his money as good as anybody's though going to bust himself on this crazy enterprise

Phenix—Why it ain't anything but a wheelbarrow your honor 78

Oudinot's bee & dog & lightning story—lightning came in at front door as he was just going out & drove him clear through & out at the back door.[117]

<Wthr Cck>
Bill of Fare—
Weather Cock

---

[114] A dramatized version of Grant's reply to Confederate General Simon Bolivar Buckner at Fort Donelson, Kentucky, on 16 February 1862.

[115] A paraphrase of Ethan Allen's demand for the surrender of Fort Ticonderoga on 10 May 1775.

[116] The speech delivered in 1774 to colonial officials of Virginia in which John Logan, or Tahgahjute, Mingo chief and warrior, reproached the white man for rewarding his friendship with the extermination of his entire family, which was wantonly killed during reprisals for an Indian robbery of some Ohio River land adventurers. Logan's speech received much contemporary publication both in America and England and became a declamation exercise in schools in the eighteenth and nineteenth centuries.

[117] Although a bee and a dog do figure in tales attributed to Markiss, the Maui liar, in chapter 77 of *Roughing It,* this lightning story does not appear there.

Pie—Sea-currents.
Gold fish $5 per 100.

Look at that Hornet boy, Brown—folks all wealthy, but he romantic, must go to sea & live this glorious Life on the Ocean Wave before the mast—cuffed around by mate & his fingers frozen—supposed to be a "Captain's pet" & derisively called "young gentleman sailor" by the men—always sad & sick at heart—always suffering—then 43 days in the boat—now sent home by the Consul, must work his way with a negro steward in menial offices, waiting on table & emptying the vomiting vessels of the passengers.

Romantic to see fine ship go to sea—sailor goes round the world but never into it, & is simple & ignorant as a child & knows nothing about it—is as green at 50 as a farmer's boy

Eyes stuck out like couple poached eggs— 87

If you want your soul gangrened with derision read a Utopian sea novel on board a ship.

While most men have a manner of speaking peculiar to themselves, no arbitrary system of punctuation can apply. Every man should know best how to punctuate his own MS.

Stick with only one end to it.

Mem—Head a letter with music.

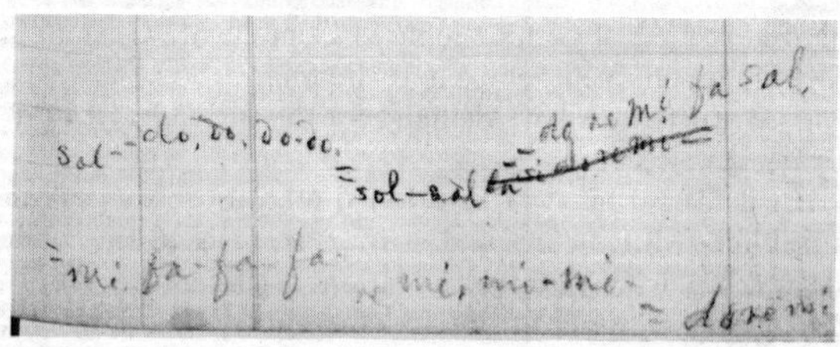

Monday July 30—
This is the fifth day of dead, almost motionless calm—a man can walk a crack in the deck, the ship lies so still. I enjoy it, and I believe

all hands do except the d—d baby. I write 2 hours a day & <s>loaf the balance. At this rate it will take me a good while to finish Ferguson's log.[118]

The yards are & *have* been braced up sharp & the ship close hauled on the wind—sailing within <6> six points of it they say, what <their>there is of it, <till> all through the calm, till last night they let up on her a point & put her on an easy bowline. Even going a point or two free is no gait for her, as it is for the Comet—<she> her best lick is dead before the wind—Heaven only knows when she ever find such a wind in this latitude & she heading straight east for San Francisco <&>on the 38th parallel & 1,400 miles at sea—

—Lat. 38.40; long 154.03—Distance 51.

The Larboard Ahoy![119]

THE KING—

<It riles me to hear an American (that [---]cking Harris) stand up & pay titular adulation to> this heathen blackamoor—to this

[118] On 30 July, Clemens wrote his mother and sister: "I have been copying the diary of one of the young Fergusons . . . to publish in Harper's magazine, if I have time to fix it up properly when I get to San Francisco" (journal letter of 30 July–20 August 1866 to Jane Clemens and Pamela Moffett, published with omissions in *MTL*, pp. 115–119). This was the journal of Samuel Ferguson, which makes up the bulk of "Forty-Three Days in An Open Boat." Mark Twain's use of the Ferguson journals in "My Début As A Literary Person" (*Century* 37 [November 1899]: 76–88), a revised version of the earlier *Harper's* article, would elicit a complaint from Henry Ferguson, then an Episcopal clergyman and professor of history at Trinity College in Hartford. Ferguson maintained that even in 1866 he had not anticipated verbatim quotation and had expected "that we should see what you had taken from the journals before the article was published" (Henry Ferguson to SLC, 8 December 1899). He was somewhat placated to learn that proceeds from the original article had been "sent to a church in Stamford," but he remained particularly offended by Mark Twain's failure to omit or alter the names of *Hornet* survivors mentioned in an uncomplimentary or equivocal fashion in the diaries. Although Ferguson declined Mark Twain's offer to suppress "My Début As A Literary Person," he made a number of suggestions for the alteration of offensive passages, all of which Mark Twain followed before including the article in *The Man That Corrupted Hadleyburg and Other Stories and Essays* (New York: Harper & Brothers, 1900).

[119] "Larboard Watch Ahoy!" is the last line of the chorus of "The Larboard Watch," a song by Thomas E. Williams.

man who remembers to this day, & grieves over a trifling unintentional offense offered in the US. years ago to his *private* individuality—*not* to his official <great> rank—& who hates America and Americans for it yet—but who is so guiltless of genuine, <true,> manly & kingly pride as to forget that his fathers, his whole people & his whole country have on the noted occasions <not far in the past,> to wh I have referred, been humiliated, insulted, wronged, abused—<yea, at least figuratively speaking,> spit upon & trampled under foot—by <the> two great *nations* (not insignificant, unofficial <& irresponsible> nobodies in a steamboat),—by two nations, England and France—<but,> <yet> and who to-day, purchased by the gimcrack & tinsel adulation those peoples have since conferred upon his house, <he> with a spirit proper to a soul that is capable of remembering a trivial <woul>wound inflicted upon its poor personal vanity & of forgetting a great national affront, licks the hands of the foreign princes who kicked & cuffed Hawaii-nei through her representatives his fathers.

The King gets his <cherished compliments> <cheap but> loved and cherished compliments from the English <Court> & his revenues from the Americans—his gew-gaws & cheap adulation from the one & whatever of real worth & greatness his country <is possessed of> possesses from the other—& with characteristic consistency he worships the men who have degraded his country & hates the strong & steadfast <American> hands that have lifted <it> her up.

Dam!

Royalty!—I don't think much of Hawaiian Royalty! Years ago, when the late King & the present King were only princes—youths—they traveled in the U.S. with the premier of the kingdom, Dr. Judd, an American. On one occasion, on board a Southern steamer, they did not go in to dinner as soon as the bell rang, & then there was no room for them.—They <f> were offended. The Capt however, as soon as he knew their national character, had a table set in a private room for himself & the 3, & entertained them in a manner befitting their high rank. That is Dr Js story & no doubt the true one.[120]

---

[120] Dr. Judd was witness to two racial incidents involving Princes Alexander

Other accounts say they went in to dinner, but observing their black faces, & uninformed of their rank, the steward enforced the rule of the boat excluding colored persons from the cabin table. They were naturally incensed, & all that could afterwards be done failed to wipe <fr> <out> from their minds the memory of the affront. Yet after all, it was one which was offered to them as unknown & merely *private* individuals, & being entirely unofficial, could not affect them as princes or their country through them, & should have been so received & so valued. The *men* only were insulted—not the princes[121] —& thus their *country* was no more insulted than if the affront had been offered to the commonest Kanaka in the realm. This King has never forgotten or forgiven that trifling stab at his little vanity.

But Great Britain, officially, through Sir Geo. Paulet, siezed the islands; in 43 abused, humiliated & insulted their King, K.3. in a bullying & overbearing manner threatened the destruction of the <helpless> little helpless capital town when it utterly at <his> the mercy of his heavy guns; and finally forced the acceptance of terms of so degrading a nature that in the hearts of a spirited people

---

Liholiho (Kamehameha IV) and Lot Kamehameha (Kamehameha V) while the three were in the United States in 1850 on a diplomatic mission:

> The princes' dark coloring led to a singularly ugly episode on the morning of June 4, as they boarded a train for Baltimore. While Dr. Judd was checking the baggage, a conductor "unceremoniously" ordered Alexander out of the railway car. . . . Alexander protested indignantly until Dr. Judd hurried in to the car and made the necessary explanations. Somewhat later, on a Hudson River boat, the princes were refused admittance to the dining salon. In later years, when he had come to favor Hawaii's annexation by the United States, Dr. Judd did his best to make light of both episodes. He insisted that the railway car was reserved for women and that the princes were excluded from the steamboat salon merely because they were too late for the first sitting. But Alexander, in particular, attributed the incidents to American color prejudice. . . . After having been cordially received in both England and France the princes developed a violent anti-American prejudice. (Gerrit Parmele Judd, IV, *Dr. Judd, Hawaii's Friend: A Biography of Gerrit Parmele Judd* [Honolulu: University of Hawaii Press, 1960], p. 186)

121 The journalist and diplomat Frederick Seward commented in his memoirs on reaction to the Hawaiian princes. Alexander and Lot, he wrote, "were educated, erect, graceful, and were royal princes. Washington society was disposed to adore their rank, but balked at their complexion. It was feared they might be 'black' " (Frederick W. Seward, *Reminiscences of a War-Time Statesman and Diplomat, 1830–1915* [New York: G. P. Putnam's Sons, 1916], p. 81).

the memory of them would rankle till the end of time.[122] K 5 has been carressed & flattered by British men-o-wars-men, & so he has forgiven that deadly insult & fawns upon the nation that gave it. So also with his dear friends the French, who treated his ancestor K 3 like dog—who, through Admiral —— marched gallantly upon this thoroughly harmless & entirely ornamental fort, &, unresisted, demolished it & spiked its guns—& then made the poor King sign an agreement the nature of which may be best be expressed by saying that through it, metaphorically, the French nation spit in the face of Hawaii-nei.[123] But dusky Queen Emma has been flattered and feted at the French Court,[124] & lo! K 5 is mollified & the atrocious acts of Admiral —— are forgotten!

This is Hawaiian Royalty!

First animal created Chaos (shay-horse)—for Burlingame.[125] 78

Missionary girl aged 17 on voyage to US: "Nov. 28, 1840—I am ashamed of myself many times a day for giving way to so much laughter, but there are so many witty remarks made that it is almost impossible for one *unaccustomed to hear them*, to refrain from it. I have heard more jokes, hyperbolical expressions & comical remarks *in one day*, since being on board, than I did *during the 17 years* of

---

[122] An emotion-charged account of events that occurred between February and August 1843, when, at the instigation of British officials, Lord George Paulet, in command of the frigate *Carysfort*, was in Honolulu to protect the interests of English subjects.

[123] Although in this case Kamehameha III was not forced to cede his kingdom and the actual French occupation of Honolulu under Admiral Legoarant de Tromelin lasted less than two weeks (from 25 August to 5 September 1849), it took almost three years of bitter litigation to produce even a temporary accord and ten years to achieve a final settlement, which was still not completely satisfactory to the Hawaiian throne.

[124] In 1865 and 1866 Dowager Queen Emma visited France and England, much to the dismay of the American residents of Hawaii. At the suggestion of Kamehameha V, she also visited the United States in order to help counter allegations of the royal family's dislike of America. On 17 October 1866 the *Daily Hawaiian Herald* would print a letter from Mark Twain describing Emma's arrival and reception in San Francisco on 24 September.

[125] Intended perhaps as a response to Edward Burlingame's pun on Mark Twain's name (see note 37).

my residence on the Sandwich Is. It is well for us to hear such things now, as we are going to a land where such expressions are used <d>more than at the S I"

(They made *me* feel like John Phenix in Boston when I perpetrated the diabolism of a joke in presence of mish families.) These mish come from Boston; quote J. P. <he>there.

Note the dire effect on a joke on a mish *child:*

"The children cannot bear <a> jokes, but take everything that is said to be truth, & often they are so <aff> distressed by <them> these things—not being able to understand them—<that> that they shed tears."

(The mish's are outraged by the levity of my letters, & have so expressed themselves—but in sorrow, not in anger.)

Aug. 1.—Lat. 38.50 N. Long 150.56 W.—Distance 100 miles.

Of Sounding in fair weather.[126]

Close-hauled—Brail up the mizzen & mizzen-staysail, let go the main-sheet, so as the sail will shiver, put the helm a-lee & brace the mizzen topsail square, so it'll back, you know. You keep the head-sails & the jib & staysails just as they were before, you understand, & haul taut & belay the <lay> lee-braces. When she's nearly lost her headway but is still coming to the wind, you heave the lead & you heave it quick, too—cussed quick, as you may say.

Would you mind saying that over again if it ain't too much trouble. (Repeat.)

Well, yes, I sh^d say so.

Going large—(Another method, w^h is preferable.)

Brace the headsails square, haul down the jib & staysails, without stirring the aftersails, & put the helm a-lee

Oh, yes, that is much preferable, I sh^d think.

Mem—Write some more biographies of great men & women. [#]

---

126 Mark Twain may have intended to use the following notes in a *Union* letter about the *Smyrniote* which would have paralleled his account of the *Ajax*. He did not, however, describe the return voyage in his Sandwich Islands writings.

Whitney about the cats.[127]

No—I'll tell you what's the matter with *you*—you have no conception of a joke—of anything but awful Puritan long-facedness & petrified facts. You have got *this* spirit on you.

(Here quote about jokes from Missionary's daughter.)

Missionaries have made honest men out of nation of thieves:
Instituted marriage;
Created homes;
Lifted woman to same rights & privileges enjoyed elsewhere.
Abolished infanticide.
″ intemperance
Diminished licentiousness (the hula, where copulation in public)
Given equal laws.
″ common Natives homesteads
″ whereby chief's power of life & death over his subject is taken away.

In a great measure abolished idolatry and (until this King & his Bishop Church) destroyed power of Kahunas (now however, King licenses them).

Have *well* educated the people.

Brown attempts to entertain company (in accordance with advice received from me,) <& is now> & accompanied by gaping & stretching of the company tells interminable story—something like Dan's old ram,)—& when abused <for> by me says it is *just* my style, & instances [illegible] gaping over my trip across plains in overland stage—says that when I got to <Jules> Julesburg Mrs. C. left, to Fort Laramie, Mrs. W. left; to Wind River Mountains & that remarkable circumstance of the Indians shooting Pony Express rider, Mr. G. left—Salt Lake City Mr. B left—Sacramento Mrs. L. left—

Changed subject then, didn't I?

---

[127] On 19 May 1866 editor Henry M. Whitney had reprinted in the *Pacific Commercial Advertiser* a passage about Hawaii's great variety of cats from Mark Twain's letter in the Sacramento *Daily Union* of 19 April.

Yes?

All gone but Miss M, warn't they?

Yes.—but *she* had stretched till her dress was too short for her & gaped till her mouth was enlarged—till you couldn't have gagged her with anything smaller than a keg of nails.

But She was *there* yet, <warn't>wasn't she?

Yes.

Very well, then—wasn't I smart?

Well, I' s'pose you think you was, anyway. It is curious, though, that generally there *anybody* body left when you get through.

And that time you was riding alone in Washoe—in the Humboldt Moun. & met the whole tribe of <Shon>Shoshone Indians & was just on the point of destroying them when something <told> whispered to you that they were not prepared to go to Paradise & you spared them. And I noticed that you didn't say anything about your being prepared to go to California, then, but you went—& you went mighty quick, too. 78

I see, now, stronger than ever before, the absurdity of our still retaining the crude, uncouth, inefficient, distressing orthography invented for us by our ancestors in a rude, ignorant, uncultivated age of the world. We have discarded their coarseness & obscenity of conversation; their groping & groveling superstitions; their slow methods of locomotion & transmission of intelligence—*why* should we retain their <vile> ugly & aggravating orthography?

I can't spell bow—some one will surely think I mean <bow> bo—can't spell bah—think I mean bah.[128]

Bad Jokes—Wonder there is any cylindrical shape left to the yards, they have been <">squared so often this voyage.

Mr Rising said this chicken <was prob> *might* have been with Cook 100 years ago—he didn't know, Henry Ferguson said "Been with him to-day, anyhow." [#]

[128] These opinions would find expression in 1876, when Clemens wrote *1601: Conversation As It Was by the Social Fireside in the Time of the Tudors* and in an Autobiographical Dictation of 7 November 1906 titled "Simplified Spelling" (*LE*, pp. 159–163).

Capt's dream 4th day of escaping alone to S F. & telling friend of disaster—teeth falling out meantime—said "Look there!"—most magnificent gold eagle against sky—presently it turned over & over & rolled into sky out of sight—Capt said "Must look out for the boat." The dream worried him for a week.[129] [*spiral*]

At Laupahoehoe could not sleep—surf on shore sounded as if he were covered wh canvas & still in boat. Every time Ferguson coughed[130] thought he said "Capt—Capt"—& got up & went to see.

Was always no more than dozing—always conscious in boat.

"This my son that was dead is alive again."[131] [*spiral*]

Be virtuous be happy don't apply to SI. 78

SI women much superior in manners—don't kiss & embrace women they hate. (Turn back.)

Speak of the other boats.[132]

Two women 5 babies—noisy—women silent—would enjoy funeral.

We have beautiful sunsets & splendid moonlight

Speak of the stone lions.

No sharks till in boat after ship burnt—then plenty. One grampus, bigger than boat. [*spiral*] [#]

---

129 Neither this entry nor the following one was based on incidents recorded in the journals of the Fergusons or in the diary of Captain Mitchell.

130 Samuel Ferguson had undertaken the *Hornet* voyage to recuperate after what his brother later termed "a severe attack of lung fever" (Henry Ferguson to SLC, 8 December 1899). This illness, aggravated by prolonged exposure, led to his death in the fall of 1866.

131 The Reverend Franklin Rising must also have observed the aptness of this phrase, for according to Captain Mitchell's diary (p. 64) he preached from the parable of the prodigal son on Sunday, 12 August.

132 After sixteen days at sea it was decided to separate the three *Hornet* lifeboats in order to increase the chances of there being some survivors. Food and water were divided, and the first mate's boat drifted away. Three days later, after a further division of stores, the second mate's boat separated from Captain Mitchell's longboat. Neither of the mates' boats was recovered.

Capt. says—

Sailor-like (great stupid children), hadn't been ashore till were growling about the grub, & not 3 till they were smuggling great slabs of pork through natives, to add to their rations of tea & ½ biscuit. One man nearly killed himself first day eating fruit—came near dying that night. Cox sat beside Capt on shore & was eating cocoanut—Capt. confiscated & threw it away—Cox thought hard treatment of a poor devil who been starving 43 days.

Sparkling & Bright.[133]

Floating away like a fountain's spray
Or the snowwhite plume of a maiden
The Smoke-wreaths rise to the starlit skies
With blissful fragrance laden.
Then smoke away till golden ray
Lights oe'r the dawn of the morrow
For a cheerful cigar like shield will bar
The heart from care & sorrow.

The darkeyed train of maids of Spain
Thro their orange groves trip lightly
And the bright cigar like gleaming star
And the <l>clasp of their lips burnt brightly.

It warms the soul like <a>the blushing bowl
With its spicy fragrance laden
And it lends a bliss like first warm kiss
On the glowing kiss of a maiden

White man he live berry long<er>
But the black man he <smell> live stronger
White man he smell berry stronger
But black man stronger 78 [#]

---

[133] Mark Twain has conflated the title of a song by Charles Fenno Hoffman with imperfectly remembered passages from Francis M. Finch's "Smoking Song." Although the fourth stanza borrows tone and language from Finch's work, it is apparently Mark Twain's invention.

Little more cider too

Man in Lynn can't get full wages unless he can work himself out of the shop every day by throwing shoes behind him.[134] 78

Aug. 3—The calm continues. Magnificent weather. Men all turned boys. Play boyish games on the poop & quarter-deck. Lay small object on fife-rail of mainmast—shut one eye, walk 3 steps & strike at it with fore-finger. Lay small object on deck, walk 7 steps blindfold & try to find it. Kneel—elbows against knees, hands extended in front along deck; place object against ends of fingers—then clasp hands behind back & try to pick it up with teeth & rise up from knees. Tie string around main-brace, turn back to it—blindfold—walk 3 steps—turn round 3 times—return & put finger on string. Tying all kinds sailor knots. Go aloft.[135]

This Brown told the girl her sweetheart had a glass eye & told the <sw>latter that the former had a glass eye. 78

Lie.

In gale, man sent up to saw off <In> topmast—blew all teeth out of saw. What y^{r} lat & longitude? I was in same storm, 3 degrees to eastward—teeth blew aboard of my ship. 78

Uncle Bicknell[136] came every day for 3 months (clouds always over head,) to old sea-dog Capt. Tolbert,[137] to ask if we are going to have any <more> rain—always same reply—"No rain to-day, Uncle Bicknell." At last, "yes, rain to-day, Uncle B." Fervently,

---

134 In 1866 this anecdote had little relation to the facts of shoe manufacture in Lynn, Massachusetts. The responsibility of individual workmen for the entire product had ended during the preceding ten years, with the replacement of small handwork shops by large steam factories using assembly-line techniques and machinery.

135 This passage, considerably revised, appeared dated 8 August in Mark Twain's journal letter to his mother and sister (*MTL*, p. 118).

136 Possibly James Bicknell, who had been part of the Hawaiian mission to the Marquesas Islands and who was on Oahu at the time of Mark Twain's visit.

137 Linton L. Torbert, a former sea captain, who had become a Sandwich Islands sugar planter and merchant.

"Well, I'm glad—I'm truly glad, *by God,* that we've got *your* consent!" 78

155 books on Hawaii—86 scientific papers—27 newspapers & periodicals, native & English—most of them dead. Few of these books readable.

There is this in favor of missionaries in all the South Sea Islands—they have saved many a white man's life, sometimes at risk of their own, & when *only* a mish could have had any influence with the abused & exasperated natives—(whites always the aggressors.)

"Can be better imagined than described"— d—n the man who invented it. Often, with 100 island books before me, I have thought, "now this piece of scenery is described in <one s>these, & I can steal & rehash—turn & find them shirking, with that hackneyed expression. or "What hath God wrought!"

Auwē! auwē, plaintive expression of distress.

Poor little lion back in the corner won't get any <Danl.>Daniel. 78

Sailors walk with hands somewhat spread & palms turned backward.

Horses & *Waimians* don't drink.[138]

Joe Goodman & the mouse in coffee. 78

Cat & painkiller. 78

Sunday, Aug 5, 1866.

Everybody cheerful—at daylight saw the Comet in the distance on our lee—it is pleasant in this tremendous solitude to have company.[139] [#]

---

[138] In chapter 76 of *Roughing It* Mark Twain would tell of mountain horses on Hawaii which, never having learned to drink running water, tried to chew it when it was offered to them. Waimea on Kauai, shut off by mountains from trade winds and clouds, was noted for its dryness.

[139] It was this persistent solitude, and the sense of indolence it brought, that touched off Mark Twain's surrounding recollections of the childhood incidents and superstitions that would figure so prominently in his later work.

Superstition.

Whence come the wise saws of the children?

Wash face in rain water standing on fresh cow dung to remove freckles.

Wash hands in rain water standing in old rotten hollow stump to remove <f> warts.

Stick pin in wart, get blood, then stick in another boy will transfer your warts to him.

Split a bean, bind it on wart <&> wait till midnight & bury at X roads in dark of the moon.

Niggers tie wool up with <threat>thread, to keep witches from riding them.

Onery orey ickery Ann—Phillisy &c

Eggs cheese, butter, bread, &c. These were regarded as infallibly impartial—as being regulated by destiny—fate if you please.

If those hymns were accepted at the Throne of Grace, (& we hope they were,) it was only because of the honest good intent with which they were sung, & not from any excellence there was in their execution. <It was>They were the worst singers that ever assembled on a ship's quarter deck.[140]

The End.[141]

But they were sustained <& p> & preserved through hunger & thirst & <storm> the dangers of the sea by that <Power> him <which>who miraculously fed the five thousand, & which said unto the winds & the waves "Be still!" & they obeyed him. [*spiral*]

To these poor forlorn & famished fellows, the green heights of Hawaii <was>were <like unto the> shadow of a great rock in a weary land." [*spiral*] [#]

---

140 On 6 August Clemens wrote his mother and sister: "I am leader of the choir on this ship, and a sorry lead it is. I hope they will have a better opinion of our music in Heaven than I have down here. If they don't a thunderbolt will come down and knock the vessel endways" (SLC to Jane Clemens and Pamela Moffett, journal letter of 30 July–20 August 1866, *MTL*, p. 117).

141 The following draft of a conclusion for Mark Twain's proposed *Harper's* article (see note 118) draws its piety from the journals of Henry and Samuel Ferguson. It was not used in "Forty-Three Days in An Open Boat."

Not even if it stung like a slight & was as bitter & lasted like the memory of a humiliation

After you have rudely (but heedlessly & unmaliciously) interrupted a narrative by breaking in with a remark (or handing a plate at dinner) addressed to the person to whom you are speaking, apologize, but don't insist on the story being finished—let the matter drop & the subject be changed—the head is gone from the story & it only insults & further aggravates the injured party to beg him to resume.

I reminded the Hornet sailor of the miraculous feeding of the 5,000, but with amazing gravity he crushed me with the argument that "there warn't none of them Portygheese there.[142]

I have no opinion of sailors as a class, but these were crazy. 78 [*spiral*]

Want to ship do you? Where have you sailed?

"Daown east. Went daown in a tar-sloop—went back in a kivered wagon." 78

Sailor ordered to steer on a star—got on another—said he had passed *that* star & got up to another. 78

<Monday, Aug 6.> Sunday Aug 5. Lat. 39.54—long. 142.13—Distance 80 miles.

I went with the parson (minister to see this poor miner die. <I bel> How do you feel—I believe I'm going to peg out. (Put in genuine pathos.[143] 78 [#]

---

[142] This argument is attributable to *Hornet* Third Mate John S. Thomas. Thomas had provided Mark Twain with information about a "Portyghee," probably Antonio Cassero (see note 96), who was "always of a hungry disposition" and at the onset of the disaster had plundered the ship's provisions of "bread enough, if economised in twenty-eighth-day rations, to have run the long-boat party three months" (Sacramento *Daily Union*, 19 July 1866, *MTH*, p. 342).

[143] This incident, which derives from Mark Twain's Nevada period, may have been recalled to him aboard the *Smyrniote* by the Reverend Franklin Rising. Although the entry evidences a pathetic intent, its language anticipates Scotty Briggs' vernacular assault upon the innocent young minister, Rising's fictional counterpart, in chapter 47 of *Roughing It*.

Harris coming in his old dug-out.—Br.

The Presentationer's Ready Speaker.[144]

Boy dipped the worm in the hot tea,—said "By G— you won't tickle *me* any more, I don't reckon." 78

Oudinot—Chimney got choked with smoke so thick had to *dig* it out.[145] 78

Wednesday, Aug. 8—800 miles <east> west of San Francisco—the calm is over & we have got a strong breeze. *This* sort of Life on the Ocean Wave will do—the ship is flying like a bird—she tears the sea into seething foam—& yet the ocean is quiet & sunny—so steady is the ship that I could walk a crack.

Only one dish meaner than stewed chicken, & that is grasshopper pie. 78

In my journal I find:[146]

"The calm is no more. There are 3 vessels in sight. It is so <cheering> sociable to have them hovering about us in this limitless world of waters. It is sunny and pleasant, but blowing hard. Every rag about the ship is spread to the breeze & she <sp> is speeding over the sea like a bird. There is a large brig right astern of us with all her canvas set & chasing us at her very best. She came up fast while the winds were light, but now it is hard to tell whether

---

144 Perhaps the title for a manual of impressive speeches, which the notations of eloquence in this notebook indicate that Mark Twain considered compiling.

145 One of the tall tales told by Markiss in chapter 77 of *Roughing It*.

146 The following two paragraphs correspond almost exactly to passages dated 8 and 10 August, respectively, in Clemens' 30 July–20 August journal letter to his mother and sister (*MTL*, pp. 118–119). It is likely that these paragraphs, more polished and less telegraphic in style than most notebook entries, were written in the letter first and later copied into the notebook. The second paragraph, describing the brig seen against the setting sun, was almost certainly added to the notebook later than the following paragraph beginning "Aug 13," which fills the bottom of the notebook page. Had that space been available, Clemens would have used it to continue the description of the brig instead of squeezing the addition into the margin as he did.

she gains or not. We can see the people on her forecastle with the glass. The race is very exciting.

Further along: She is to the setting sun—looks sharply cut & black as coal against a background of fire & floating on a sea of blood.

Aug 13—San Francisco—Home again. No—*not* home again—in prison again—and all the wild sense of freedom gone. The city seems so cramped, & so dreary with toil & care & business anxiety. God help me, I wish I were at sea again![147]

D—n it—when you go to sea, take some cans of condensed milk with you.

Latitude & Longitudes.

		Lat.	Long.	Distance
Monday, Aug	6	40.24	139.55	55
Tues	7	40.44	140.04	51
Wednes	8.	40.24	137.55	110
Thurs	9.	39.45	133.38	195
		(510 miles to San Francisco.)		
Friday	10th	39.23	130.58	122
Sat	11	39.00.	128.42	105
Sun	12	38.34.	126.33	98
Mon	13		123	Farralones at 11 AM

July 19 to Aug 13
25 days out.

O islands there are on the face deep
Where leaves never fade & skies weep.[148] [#]

---

147 In an unpublished passage in his 30 July–20 August journal letter Clemens informed his mother and sister that in his notebook under 13 August he found "the following terse & irreverent remark: 'Ashore again, & devilish sorry for it' " (TS in MTP).

148 An adaptation of lines from "The Pirate's Serenade," a popular song by the Scottish composer John Thomson with words by William Kennedy. Mark Twain's alteration of the last phrase, which originally read "skies never weep," is explained by his comment upon the same lines in a fragment of the Sandwich Islands novel he began in 1884: "The skies do weep, there, but the leaves never fade—*because* the skies weep" (DV 111). He would use these verses again in 1903 in *Christian Science*.

Man took plaster for wife's abdomen—druggist said formed of 2 Greek words, meaning stop both outlets to body—<m> must be cut in two—asked in morning for result—"Ab well enough, but domen blowed plaster all to hell 78

Girl used sausage & threw it out of window—beggar picked it up—said must be rich folks here, put butter on sausage. 78

Dogs so no account Nothing about them good but tails—Cut off dog's tail & throw the balance of the dog away.—Brown 78

Legend from Mailé Wreath.[149]

They need Bishop Staley's Missionary labors more in England than they do in H.I—<n>See London Labor & London Poor.[150] We <dont> can spare Mish's.

K III was uncle to IV & V—all papers were ready (in 1854) to cede the islands to a man fully empowered to represent the U.S. for $5,000,000—the King had signed & the chiefs were willing to sign, but the Prince Alex (K IV) was bitterly opposed—took the document & road away—persuaded the chiefs not to sign—& the King was poisoned—*didn't* die in a drunken fit—he was a genuine & a good old Kanaka.[151] [#]

---

149 A reference to a story Mark Twain had seen in a magazine sponsored by the Hawaiian Mission Children's Society (see Notebook 6, notes 59 and 60).

150 Henry Mayhew, *London Labour and the London Poor; A Cyclopaedia of the Condition and Earnings of Those That Will Work, Those That Cannot Work, and Those That Will Not Work* (London: G. Woodfall and Son, 1851).

151 This entry combines distorted versions of several episodes in Hawaiian history. The inclination of Kamehameha III to dispose of the burden of the kingdom can be dated at least as early as 1849, when, despondent over recent English and French incursions, he secretly instructed Gerrit P. Judd to negotiate sale of the Hawaiian Islands to "any King, President or Government or Agent thereof" (L. F. Judd, *Honolulu*, p. 317), should that seem necessary to insure protection against future depredations. Although Judd never had occasion to invoke this emergency authority, in the summer of 1852 he passed on to the Hawaiian government an offer of $5,000,000 from New York shipping magnate Alfred Grenville Benson for the purchase of the Hawaiian Islands, a proposal which does not seem to have received serious consideration. In December 1854, the death of Kamehameha III, as a result of illness precipitated by intemperance, ended a move toward annexation

Old Wyllie & the English triumphed.[152]

Like sweetheart of mine whose breath was so sweet it decayed her teeth. 78

The most tasteless chickens in the world are raised on the island of Hawaii—they stew them 78

A voyaging Kanaka woman's trunk is a thunder-mug.

I never was <cor> cheerfully & cordially received but at 3 or 4 places on the islands—I think they must have heard of me before—& yet in nearly every case I was treated <so> with such kind & considerate politeness that I seldom had cause to feel uncomfortable.

Most Americans who have lived any considerable time there all seem to have lost <their> whatever of impulsiveness, frank openness & warmth of feeling they may have possessed before, & become calculating, suspicious, reserved, <cold,> cold & distant. Don't believe w[d] welcome *any*body. They have cased themselves in a shell, & if by chance they are betrayed into coming out of it <f> <for> & displaying <some degree of> their old-time vivacity & naturalness, <they>for an hour, they withdraw into it again as soon as they cool down. There is <very little not> little sociability & genuine friendship existing among the families of foreigners living in the islands, though there is some show of it, by way of keeping up appearances. One wd expect the opposite from a class shut out as they are from the rest of the world. <Bu> They live within themselves—within their shells—and are not—if I may be allowed to suggest it—not happy.

I thought differently at first. I thought they were the happiest

---

then under way. Prince Alexander Liholiho (Kamehameha IV), who had been withholding his required consent by avoiding the negotiations, promptly terminated them upon assuming the throne.

152 After the death of Kamehameha III, Minister of Foreign Affairs Robert Crichton Wyllie had opposed further negotiations for annexation by the United States, not on behalf of England, but because of his commitment to the impractical idea of a tripartite treaty by which England, France, and the United States would guarantee Hawaiian independence.

people I had ever seen. They *do* look serene & contented, but they are not. Their hearts are not dead, but far away—at home.

women[153] They think often of home, & this absence of man's essence—his feelings, his affections, his interests—has much to do with their seeming <t[-]o>so indifferent & reserved no doubt.

Perls[154]

Had a hand like the hand of Providence & a foot that was more than a match for it.

Wyllie Private Secy to Recording Angel.[155] 78

Pearls at Ewa

K-I was promised man of war & parson by Vancouver—wrote & reminded British King about ship but not parson[156] 78

Said to preacher at Lahaina—"Faith preserve you?—Then jump from yon precipice (6,000 ft) & I'll believe[157] 78

Poem by K.IV

Like Honolulu town-clock 78

Brown call the Missionaries the Serious Family.[158] [#]

---

[153] Mark Twain interlined the word "*women*" with a caret, but the manuscript gives no further indication of its meaning in this passage.

[154] The significance of this marginal note and any relation it may have to the phrase "Pearls at Ewa" (p. 166.10), opposite it on the facing manuscript page, are unknown.

[155] Wyllie had died on 19 October 1865 after more than twenty years as minister of foreign affairs. Mark Twain is probably echoing speculation current at the time of his visit about the office Wyllie would inevitably assume in death, after his long attendance upon majesty in life.

[156] Captain George Vancouver visited the Sandwich Islands three times between 1792 and 1794 at the head of a British exploring expedition. It has been confirmed that in the course of extensive dealings with Kamehameha I, Vancouver promised the king a man-of-war armed with brass guns, but the promise of a clergyman remains an unsubstantiated Hawaiian tradition.

[157] This remark is quite consistent with Mark Twain's scorn for the Hawaiian Reformed Catholic church (see Notebook 6, pp. 197–198, and his letter in the Sacramento *Daily Union* of 30 July 1866, *MTH*, pp. 354–355) and, if actually made, was probably directed toward the Reverend George Mason, Anglican clergyman whom Mark Twain had planned to visit at Lahaina (see Notebook 6, p. 229).

[158] "The Serious Family" was the title of Morris Barnett's popular comedy

Scene 1 [159]

Trovatore—25 live shrouds, in feathered caps & with sheets around them. —Howl louder than ever when dinner bell<s> rings, & bust through green castle which waves & quake after them. Never saw hungry crowd in such hurry.

2—Shoved castlee aside & exposed a silvery blue moonligh landscape, with a railing in front & 2 steps—Woman came through gate when she could have jumped over the fence easier—

Another woman came from behind some trees that were so matted together that they looked solid.

Without any apparent reason for it, these 2 d—d fools fell to singing.

Principal one sang a long song then straddleed around while the applauded & then came back & sang it over again.

3—Fence alone for 3 minutes & impressive music—

Then a queer looking bilk with a gorgeous doublet, plumed smoking cap & white opera cloak hanging to heels come solemnly forward from somewhere till he got to the centre & then began to yell.

But a fellow in the kitchen with a piano crowded him down—

Then the chief woman came back & grabbed the fellow round the neck—Same moment knight in complet armor & with sheet round him rushes in & just saves self from going into orchestra—sensation—hell to pay, in fact.

Knight takes the woman & the other fellow comes forward & just wakes up everything.

<They>Then *they* take up his own tune & beat him at it.

---

about a fortune-hunting cleric's futile attempt to reform a pleasure-loving family. It had been most recently presented at Maguire's Opera House in San Francisco on 12 May 1865. The title was employed as an epithet for the missionaries by Mark Twain himself in a letter of 20 August 1866 (*SSix*, pp. 210–211) petitioning the publishers of the *Californian* for the paper's editorship. He claimed to be a "Moral Phenomenon" amply qualified by his own missionary experience in the Sandwich Islands to correct its deficient moral tone.

159 On the evening of 24 August 1866, Bianchi's Grand Italian Opera company presented *Il Trovatore* at the Metropolitan Theatre in San Francisco. Mark Twain's

This riles him & he draws his sword

Free fight—woman trying to stop it—false alarm—after singing & flourishing swords they rush off & the woman falls carefully down on the steps blowing the dust away from the spot where <his>her elbow is going to touch first.

2^{d} Act.

<Excellent>Exceedingly gay party of blacksmiths started in to improve a very good sort of a poker & didn't succeed—sung to much & didn't work.

That same knight came into the blacksmith shop with another woman—(you let him alone for always <find> being around when there is a woman to tag after

The women sang a good while, & then the d—d blacksmiths blasted away & tried to beat her. Then made a fizzle of it & knew enough to curl their tails & leave Thus the knight & the woman were left in sole possession of the blacksmith shop, but without anything to eat. <This> As usual, with the cheerful spirit this party have manifested from the first as soon as they found there was nothing to eat then fell to singing.

And as usual, they hadn't sung five minutes till there was a misunderstandg

The woman carries on dreadfully & the man stands & leans forward holding his blanket <out> out with outspread hands & looking as if he *would* help, if he could only think of something <that would> to do.

Finally she lets down on a bass viol box covered with bear skins, & he comes to his milk. They stand up & come to a musical explanation

This knight looks so stuffed & fat in his silver scale armor that he looked like some sort of a fish,

They have a long explana^{n} & rush off in high glee about something.

---

impulse to burlesque the production seems to indicate that he did not agree with the estimation of the *Alta California* of 25 August, which reported that the opera had been presented "in an unexceptionable manner." Mark Twain's dislike for opera persisted throughout his life.

2—The boss of the corpses & that plumed fellow came out in the dark before <that> a castle-gate to sing—<to serenade, likely. But they made so> <Then the> to practice, likely—the d—d fools—& the blacksmith shop <s>must be close by somewhere.

The Capt <of> soon froze out & left, but the other fellow blasted away by himself.

At 2 oclock by the bell the Capt came back—& of course those hungry ghosts piled in too, the moment they heard that dinner bell. But that plumed fellow fooled them for he kept singing there till they were about starved out—& then they left.

Serenading party heard in the woods—stage vacant—music beautiful—church music & a fine choir—it brought back the feathered chap & the ghosts & the Capt.—& d—n them they went to blatting & interrupted the choir—choked it off & then left.

Five minutes of solemn horn tooting in the orchestra—& then out comes a party of white dressed young women out of the wood (2½ AM)—one with a great black cross clasped to her breast—& she stood out & begun to sing.

In comes those fellows & the ghosts & & surprises & scares them—but the bold knight rushes in—of course—being so many women—from where the fence corner used to be, & grabbed the X woman & *she* was all right,

Then they stand off in two parties & sing. <[-]> I thought the knight was in for it once—he didn't know any more than to insult the whole crowd & he unarmed & 20 defenceless women to take care of—had him in the door. Drew sword but didn't kill him.

Arrval of 2 dozen ratty looking soldiers with brass helmets, coats with trunk tacks driven into them & broomstick lances—directly the knight grabbed the <wom> X, drew his sword & tried to shove—the corpses tried to prevent him, but the Soldiers took his part & so they struck a blow apiece & then <brought their> kept up a desultory sort of hacking here & there till the curtain fell—he holding his sword in a warding position & clasping fainting X.

Act. 3

Very handsome silk tent with splendid gold embroidered banner hanging at the door—row of other tents in distance—all those ghosts in a row armed with swords & singing—for hash, *of* course—I've got them spotted—they are expecting to hear that bell every moment.

They leave & the feathered chap comes out of the tent & goes to swelling around & singing—which disturbs the Capt of the Ghosts & *he* comes out of the tent to remonstrate

Then the ghosts fetch in the fat woman manacled.—& yowling as usual—the great overgrown scrubs, to impose on a woman. Sentinels—trunk-button fellows—pacing before the tents

Sing awhile & the woman tries to break away—d—d fool—they've got her in the door. Then *don't* she throw herself! They argue the <ch> case with her but no use—she'll be d—d if she *will* be satisfied, & keeps trying to get away—so they *took* her away—she's evidently breeding trouble for herself the way she is acting.

<T>Scene—2—That knight—with that X woman come into a mighty common looking country hotel & go to making love. She is dressed in white satin trimmed with silver lace & she has got his bulliest opera cloak on over his armor. He sends her off the stage.

He has lost his hat somewhere & he comes down to the footlight & sings about it in a way that shows he <considered> <put> set considerable store by it.

He went off finally to hunt for his hat, & in the meantime the curtain came down.

I went down to offer him mine, but they wouldn't let me behind.

Act 4—

That old original green castle—night.

Enter a conspirator with red rosettes on his slippers & a black table-cloth on—with a woman in black—(he leaves) she falls to serenading, all by herself—

Opposition serenade in the woods—all men's voices—very solemn stately & impressive—she had the good taste to dry up her screech while they sang, because it stood to reason that she couldn't <hold> keep up her end with them—

Then a fellow in the woods went alone on a <c>song about Leonore, & she started in to beat him, thinking she had caught him alone & had an easy thing, but the others broke in at once & helped him out. Grand—that chorus—inexprribly grand—she <woul>wound up the whole thing herself, tho' with a final screech—woman like, sh *would* have the last word. And then she took up her serenade & <b> blatted away till sh had had her sing out, & left.

Then the feathered chap came out of a neighboring house <&> with a soldier—sent him somewhere & went to sloshing around & singing till he came back.

His first blast fetched that same woman back—for she hadn't got far—& they two sang—she appeared to be wanting to make up with him—but he appeared to be telling her how circumstances over which he had no control rendered it entirely out of his power to accede. She even knelt to him.

Finally she happened to sing something he knew or it happened to strike his fancy, & he came right back & made up with her—it *was* a song he knew, for he sailed in & helped her sing it.

2—They shoved the castle aside—& showed the fat woman sitting on that viol box in a dungeon—chained, & only one poor oil lamp over her head while there were hundreds of gas burners all over the theatres—but *hell*—people never help an *unfortunate*—if she was in luck & wanted gas she could get it. The knight was with her<.>—always around where there is a woman—if that fat woman were in *hell* you could look for *him* there shortly.

Then they sang beautifully & feelingly to pathetic accompaniment.

Then she laid down on the viol case & he knelt—

Enter the X woman & a soldier with a torch & <th><slam> threw herself into the knights arms He argues with her—evidently don't like to have her there—thinks the fat woman won't like it no doubt—but it appears to be all right—she is asleep—but if they keep up that d—d yelling they are bound to wake her presently.

She sings in her sleep, poor devil—(the fat one,) & they help her out—*beautiful.*

Down comes the X woman to her knees—but it ain't any use—the knight turns his back on her—& so she sets down on the floor & spreads her hand across her breast—ostensibly to <c>feel her heart, but really to make up for the lowness of her low-neck dress—the knight (of course) comes & takes her round the waist & they sing.

Enter the feather chap & soldiers (in red striped breeches & high boots)

And *don't* he and she carry on, & she trying to faint & fall all the time & he holding her—but at last she *does* fall & <he &> he & all the soldiers leave—fat woman falls—flames show through cracks.

End.

(Letter Kanaka

A man *nevr* reaches that dizzy height of wisdom when he can no longer be led by the nose.

If <you>he had as many shirts as Ward they'd ruin him in the long run, anyhow.[160]

Fun to roll rocks—or rather, fun to see able-bodied Kanaka do it at 50^{c} a day.

Capt Barker's San Jose mule story—Ye come into the world wid disgraceful parentage & ye're goan out of it widout hope of lavin anny posterity behind ye—an ye ain't belonging in the works of God nyther—God made every baste & <bur>bird & crature that's in the world but <yersif>yersilf—& ye're the vile invintion of man!" 78

But of the horses in the world I prefer the gentle undulating motion of the Commodore's ass. 78

Passenger volunteers account of journey to Big Trees & Yo Semite—& then Dan's old Ram. 78 [#]

---

160 Mark Twain occasionally poked fun at S. W. H. Ward & Son, San Francisco manufacturers of men's shirts, whose aggressive, sometimes imaginative, advertising was well known to residents of the area. On 2 December 1866 the San Francisco *Morning Call* would notify its readers that "Prince Bill, the heir apparent of the Sandwich Islands, is a very nice, gentlemanly fellow, speaks two or three languages, plays a good game of billiards, dresses in good taste, and wears Ward's shirts, which he obtains from 323 Montgomery street."

<S>Tuesday 4th, 7 P.M.

Dennis, you didn't come to time—I was at the Hotel at the min[161]

These boys been mourned as dead for nearly 4—at least 3 months—think of the thrill of the first telegram to that home circle—"Crew & passengers of Hornet arrived safe!"[162]

Henry is more impressible & imaginative than Sam, or at least more demonstrative.

They covered from rain with old pieces of sail.

Capt. knew for days this murderous discontent was brewing by the distraught <&> air of some of the men & the guilty look of others—& he staid on guard—slept no more—kept his hatchet hid & close at hand—was not surprised at Henry's page.[163]

Frequently simple & touching language.
Offered watch for a ration.

Notes *on Henry Ferguson's* Log.—From day after the ship burnt till the 12th, he puts simply the (to him) eloquent word "Doldrums."

The storms during first fortnight he calls the awfulest rain squalls & the most terrific thunder & blinding lightning he ever saw, <closing> & black as ink in absence of lightning—caused to steer in all directions—rain 5 times as hard as in States

Saw waterspout on 17th—thinks might be pleasant sight from a *ship*.

---

161 This note, written on a page by itself, was intended for Denis E. McCarthy, Mark Twain's former associate on the Virginia City *Territorial Enterprise*. It was presumably interrupted by McCarthy's arrival for an appointment on 4 September 1866. The two men may have met to discuss plans for the lecture tour of California and Nevada towns that Mark Twain was to make under McCarthy's convivial management in October and November of that year.

162 Mark Twain inverted the notebook to isolate the following *Hornet* notes, evidently made in July or August while reading the Ferguson and Mitchell journals aboard the *Smyrniote*. The exact order of inscription remains somewhat unclear.

163 The final pages of Henry Ferguson's journal contain apprehensive notes exchanged by the two brothers concerning the ill-feeling shown toward Captain Mitchell and themselves by members of the crew in the longboat who had also expressed a disposition to eat human flesh.

Mentions the star mistaken for ship's light.

May 28—"Had out the photographs again to-day & I could not but feel that we should yet see them all again."

Distressed by another swordfish cavorting around the boat for some time—(immense one)—May 29.

June 5—The conspiracy.

" 6—Passed some sea-weed & something looked like trunk of old tree—but *no birds*—begining to be afraid islands not there. "Today it was said to the Capt & in the hearing of all that some of the men w^{d} not shrink, when a man was dead, from using the flesh, though they would not kill. Horrible! God give us all full use of our reason & spare us from such things!

At the stock grounds[164]—attendance—not under way yet.

List of Entries.

Thoroughbred Stallions }
Do "<">Do. Mares. } Pedigree
Mares & Colts other than Thor^{b}
Sucking Colts.
Graded Horses
Saddle " "
Roadsters.
Do "<">Do Mares
Draft Horses
Horses of all Work.
Jacks & Mules.
Jennets.
Durham Bulls.
Thor^{b} cows

---

164 Mark Twain collaborated in the Sacramento *Daily Union's* coverage of the thirteenth annual fair of the California State Agricultural Society, held in Sacramento from 10 through 15 September 1866 (see Edgar M. Branch, "Mark Twain Reports the Races in Sacramento," *The Huntington Library Quarterly* 32 [February 1969]: 179–186). The notes through "Both Races" were inscribed with the notebook still inverted, apparently because Mark Twain chanced to open it to the previous series of *Hornet* entries.

Graded Cattle.
Fine Wool Sheep—Spanish Meriño
Graded Sheep.
Goats
Swine

The Races

Time.
Remarks—trainers—track—Recapitulation

Both Races.

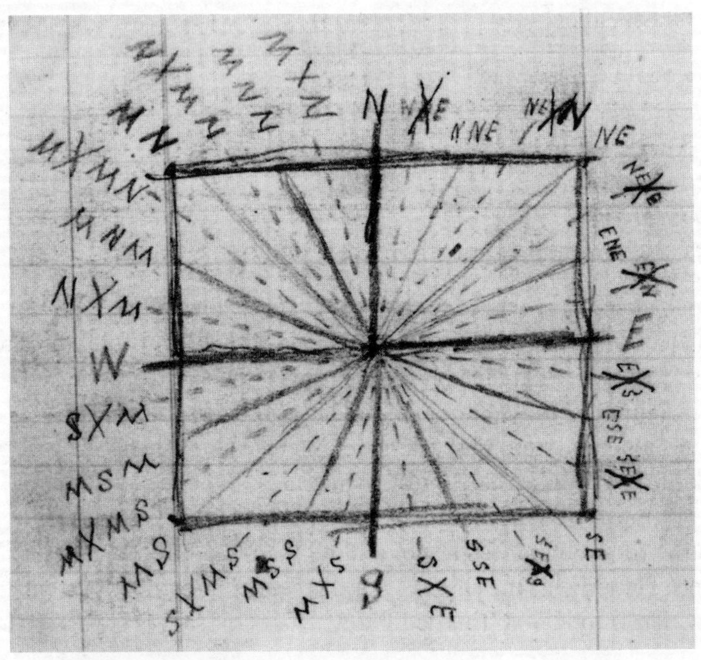

N., N×E, <NE×N>NNE, N.E.×N, NE

Lawrence Giles & Co
11 south W^{m} s^{t}
New York [#]

Mrs Osterhaus
540 Mission

Eugene Casserly[165] <out of> by Gen. Taylor out of Ellen Casserly Hanford sired Gen. Taylor out of Peggy Magee. Latham by Hambletonian out of a Morgan mare.

Union Hotel
Nevada
Ira Eaton & Williamson

Exchange Hotel
Grass Valley

2,000 . . . 1
4 2
8 4
20 10
100 50
15,000,000 <tons> pounds is 7,500 tons.

To <my mother whose gentle heart> hath always been gifted with an exquisite appreciation of the Good & the Beautiful, but unto whose (otherwise darkened understanding) grave and <solid> practical understanding even the mildest joke hath ever been a dark & bloody mystery, thse are affectionate[--] inscribed. She will mark the useful or contain a worthy moral, <but she> will march over the most <charmingly> elaborately humorous passages jokes with the tranquil indifference of a blind man treading among flowers. Happily for me she will not discover <no>the irreverent levity that is hidden in this ded.[166] [#]

---

165 The following names refer to horses Mark Twain observed competing in races or show events at the California State Agricultural Society Fair in Sacramento. All except Ellen Casserly are mentioned in the Sacramento *Daily Union's* reports of activities at the stock grounds.

166 A dedication drafted for a book made up from his Sacramento *Union* letters, which Clemens worked on late in 1866. By mid-January 1867 he could speak of

XYZS
XYS

Republic of Andorre,[167] on Southern slope of Pyrennees, 36 miles long & 30 wide—owe their independence to Charlemagne & have kept it ever since—are under protection of France & Spain—2,000 inhab—

"Give thy thoughts no tongue"—Polonius to his Son.

"Woe unto the faint-hearted."

600<[0]>
10 000
6000, 000

600
2000
[1]200000

<6 1[0]>
<12 2[0]>
<18 3[0]>
<[2-] [4-]>
<[30] 54>
<36 600 00 [pro--] ch[---] for U.S.> [#]

---

soon getting an "illustrated book on the Sandwich Islands in the hands of the printers" (SLC to E. P. Hingston, 15 January 1867, Lehigh University), but by May he admitted to his family that "I hardly think Dick & Fitzgerald [New York publishers whose literary list emphasized southwestern humorists] will accept the Sandwich Island book" (SLC to "Dear Folks," 20 May 1867); and the following month he informed them that "I have withdrawn the Sandwich Island book—it would be useless to publish it in these dull publishing times" (SLC to "Dear Folks," 7 June 1867, *MTL,* p. 127). A few years later *The Innocents Abroad* would carry a much more somber and conventional tribute to Jane Clemens, one which Mark Twain would afterwards too exclusively attribute to unconscious plagiarism of the dedication to Oliver Wendell Holmes' *Songs in Many Keys* (1862), which he had read while in the Sandwich Islands.

[167] The following entries, through the table of latitude and longitude, are written on the back flyleaf and endpaper of this notebook.

Smyrniote left 19th

—Noon 20th had made 110 miles
″ 21st ″ ″ 179 ″

Day	Date	Lat.	Long.	Miles
Sunday		lat. 28.12	long. 157.42	200 miles
Monday	23^{d}	31.34	″ 157.30	202 ″
Tuesday	24	34.31	157.40	180 ″
Wed	25	37.18	158.06	170^{m}
		DEAD CALM		
Thurs	26	38.53	158.24	100 miles
Friday	27	38.55	157.37	38 miles
Saturday	28	38.46	156.36	48—
Sunday	29	38.43	154.55	80
Monday	30	38.40	154.03	51
Tuesday	31	38.48	153.10	50
Wednes	Aug. 1	38.50	150.56	100
	2	38.54	147.59	138
	3	38.56	145.13	130.
	4	39.12	143.59.	63
Sunday	5	39.54	142.13	80
Monday	6	40.24	139.55	55
Tuesday	7	40.44	140.04	51
Wed	8	40 24	137.55	110
Thurs	9	39 45	133.38	195
Friday	10	39.23	130.58	122.
Sat.	11	39.00	128.42	105
Sun	12	38.34	126.33	98
Mon	13		123.	

S 10 to Farallones <[-]178>

1200 <38331>

530

1730

Sale of Is for 5 000 000

1854[168]

---

168 Written on the back cover (see note 151).

VI

"The Loveliest Fleet of Islands"

(March–April 1866)

NOTEBOOKS 5 and 6 were used in overlapping fashion, and the problems of their dating and their relation to each other are fully discussed in the headnote to Notebook 5.

Approximately one-quarter of Notebook 6 is devoted to the *Ajax* voyage to Hawaii and includes Mark Twain's notes about the ship and its officers, comments about his fellow passengers, and the Hawaiian information he solicited from them. The balance of the notebook is a record of his first weeks on Oahu, from arrival in Honolulu on 18 March 1866 until around mid-April, when he began his tour of the other islands. This section contains firsthand information about Hawaiian customs and the Hawaiian economy, accounts of some of the people he met, lists of places and things to investigate on Oahu and elsewhere, and a "Kanaka Lexicon" he compiled for his own use. At many points the notebook corresponds closely to his early letters to the Sacramento *Union*.

Notebook 6 now contains 160 pages, 18 of them blank. In design it is identical to Notebook 5, and its front cover, like that of Notebook 5, was dated "1866," probably by Paine. Its binding is broken, the back cover and portions of some gatherings are loose, and some leaves may have been lost. With the exception of two entries in brown ink, one in black ink (the final entry in the body of the notebook, inscribed more than two months later than the rest of the notebook), and an inscription on the back cover, also in black ink, all entries are in pencil.

In preliminary attempts to identify potential material for his Sacramento *Union* letters, Clemens employed two apparently independent systems of marks—asterisks and numbers—to distinguish individual entries. In connection with the same effort, he numbered the notebook's first 103 pages (through p. 220.7) and began to organize the marked entries in tabular form at the back of the notebook (p. 236). But the tentative and preliminary nature of both marking systems is evident in the very casual correspondence between marked entries and Mark Twain's published Sandwich Islands writings. Clemens' asterisks and numbers are discussed in notes 3 and 147. The asterisks and numbers appear in the present text at the beginning of the entries they designate, although Clemens' erratic habits of inscription sometimes led him to center them above or to place them at the ends of entries in the manuscript. Paine's use marks, of which there are many in this notebook, are not preserved here.

Steamer "Ajax"

Sailed from San Francisco for Sandwich Islands, Wednesday, March 7, 1866.

6 pounds ointment to salivate so they can't bite.

2 g [--] was a dwarf.

force habit—couldn't sleep without ch tobacco.

"Sleep! you might as well try to sleep with a coal of fire - - - - !"

"I feeds the hogs, tends Johnny & toats out"[1] [#]

---

[1] An expurgated version of the punchline of an anecdote Mark Twain recorded in full in Notebook 4 (p. 83).

March 7—Wednesday.—Left San Francisco 4 PM—rough night.[2]

8th—Thursday—Weather still rough—passengers nearly all sick.

9th—Better weather—several passengers came out.

10th—Saturday—Beautiful weather, & fine breeze—carrying all canvass.

11th—Sunday—Fine day, but rough night.

12th—Monday—Very rough & rainy all forenoon—foresail shredded last night.

Prevailing wind on this course is from N. W—so have heavy N. W. swell all time, even in finest weather. This dies out little above equator. S. E. breeze comes round Horn & dies out below Equator—so there is a space of glassy calm on both sides of line.

Rough weather on this route 7 to 8 months of year—spring, fall & winter—other 4 months beautiful weather.

* <1> 5[3] Grown white men & women, handsome & well educated, born in Hawaii.

1 <*> Lon[4] holding on by finger-nails & leaning to roll of ship like Capt. Cuttle. [#]

---

2 This is the first entry in the body of Notebook 6, the previous notes having been made on the front flyleaf and endpaper. The entries through that of 11 March were made after Notebook 5 was misplaced and constitute a brief recapitulation from memory of the first days of the *Ajax* voyage. Mark Twain left space after each of these entries for the addition of further recalled details.

3 Asterisks, sometimes circled and occurring as many as three times on a single entry, appear throughout the first 103 notebook pages (through p. 220.1). They represent a preliminary attempt to identify material for potential literary use, although not all of the entries marked were incorporated into Mark Twain's Sacramento *Union* letters. The numbers 1 through 5, which accompany many of the entries marked with asterisks—indifferently preceding or following the asterisks—belong to an apparently independent organizational system (see note 147 for a discussion of this code).

4 Probably the boy who, according to an *Ajax* passenger list published in *The Friend* on 2 April 1866, was traveling with Captain James Smith, called Captain Cuttle by Mark Twain.

<* 1> French Doctor—trav. gets $3,000 a year.[5]

<* 1> <3>2 whalers—Fish & Phillips—latter's vessel bonded—former's burned.

Brown[6]

Cowes, Steward—ancient in prof—fine catrer.

* 2 <6>Capacity 60 passengers in comfort—& 40 bunks between decks.

1000 to 1200 tons with coal for full trip on—capacity.

Pg—Dennis.[7]
Walking on the chickns.

<* 1> Restless—change pillow—turn over—roll out—tumbler fetch away—etc.

Island of Lanai has Mormon establishment—claim 5,000 converts —King won't let them practice polygamy though.[8] [#]

---

[5] Evidently a reference to Dr. Gambarelli Bechtinger, an eye specialist on his way from Venice to the Sandwich Islands, where he would open an office to offer consultation "in the English, French, German, Spanish, and Italian languages" (*Pacific Commercial Advertiser*, 21 April 1866).

[6] One of the *Ajax* passengers was W. H. Brown, an American merchant. It is impossible now to determine what traits this Brown may have contributed to Mark Twain's uninhibited literary figure, who had already appeared briefly in pieces written for the *Californian* and the *Territorial Enterprise* in 1865 and 1866 and would be more fully developed in the Sacramento *Daily Union* and *Alta California* travel letters.

[7] The ship's pig, which afforded the *Ajax* passengers much amusement until its demise. (See the Sacramento *Daily Union*, 17 April 1866, *MTH*, pp. 267–268.)

[8] As Mark Twain would later discover, the sanctioned Mormon colony was no longer on Lanai. A "City of Joseph" had been established there in 1854, but it nearly failed because of internal organizational difficulties. Walter Murray Gibson, an inspired—even visionary—adventurer, arrived in 1861 as a roving missionary of the Mormon church and stayed to become a newspaper editor, a controversial Hawaiian legislator, and by 1882, premier and minister of foreign affairs. Although Gibson temporarily revived the moribund mission, his irregular practices, including transfer of title to the Lanai property to himself, led to his excommunication from the Mormon church. The mission was forced to relocate, and in January 1865 land for a new settlement was purchased at Laie, Oahu. The new colony thrived, even though a number of City of Joseph saints chose to remain with Gibson on Lanai.

Missionary denominations are 4—American, Episcopalian, Catholic & Mormon.

Small island at extreme end of group [-] has been bought & is owned by a single individual, <& was for-> a<n> sheep ranch—Very rocky & barren—formerly place where sent convicts.

Another island owned by 2 men.

* 2 Shanghai Mail line[9]—5,000 ton ships—$500,000 subsidy—too big to go into Hon—can't carry *any* freight—always a sea on outside the reef, & can't always passengers come out in boats.

Going down *to* Hon, <wind pretty fair, but coming> would go down below 30th parallel to get trade winds—not so much out of way. But coming back will leave Shanghai & bend around north till above 40° to get benefit of the W winds—then come straight across, only drop down to strike S. F.—

So would have to make 1,000 to 1,200 extra on return trip, <& somewhere> though nothing much on down trip—lose a day at Hon going & another coming, & 4 to make extra 1,200 miles, is 6 or 7 days on trip—$1,500 a day ship expenses: $10,000 <out of> added to cost of trip.

50 tons coal a day $20

Louisiana plant cane every year—lasts 3 years. <Here can plant patch> Plant in Feb (1 crop year), commence roll in October. Here plant patch every week in year—roll every week in year—plant last 7 or 8 years. In Lou, precarious—always fear of frost—here *no* fear of it—no fear of anything. In Lou $300 an acre an extraordinarily large yield—as much as can be got out of it—here get $7 & $800.

One small refinery in Hon. [#]

---

[9] Mark Twain here recorded the essence of the Pacific Mail Steamship Company's case for excluding a Honolulu stop from its projected San Francisco–China line. He would expand upon this entry soon after arrival in Honolulu in a long letter published in the Sacramento *Daily Union* on 18 April (*MTH*, pp. 270–273), describing Hawaii's commercial significance for the United States and especially for California.

* Pine-apples begin come in next month.

* 5 Fancy milliners, & a newspaper H Gazettee in a place one is accustomed to think of as a land where <s>dark savages live & other dark savages come from some mysterious locality as they did with Crusoe, & have great battles & then eat up the prisoners. Then get in their canoes & disappear—where? Over the sea to dreamland, maybe.

* 5 "All the companies" (firemen) & "chf. Eng'r."

* <5> 5 Barbarism & high civilization so close together—religion refinement superstition bestiality.

<* 1> Weather side—good deal weather on all sides.

No reptiles or insects formerly save lice—mosquitoes produced by digging well.

No more water, s'il vous plait.

* Cool from 12 to sunrise—want bedclothes.

* Keep water in monkey[10]—get cool drink in window before sunrise—no ice or snow there—not enough foreigners.

Moa—(ghost) tuer any one qu'elle take pour Moa.[11]

Hawaians indolent & no tenacity of life—no vitality. For least possible excuse will lay down & die.

Never refuse to do a kindness <except> unless the act would work great injury to yourself, & never refuse to take a drink—under any circumstances.

Rise early—it is the early bird that catches the worm. Don't be fooled by this absurd saw. I once knew a man who tried it. He got up at sunrise & a horse bit him. Another [#]

---

[10] " 'Monkeys,' " Mark Twain wrote in the Sacramento *Daily Union* of 20 April 1866, "are slender-necked, large-bodied, gourd-shaped earthenware vessels, manufactured in Germany, and are popularly supposed to keep water very cool and fresh, but I cannot indorse that supposition" (*MTH*, p. 282).

[11] The moa was a Hawaiian wild chicken used in cockfighting.

Cant make stick with only one end.

* Tricks <[-]>upon Travelers.

Hotels <add>and stables add prices on steamer passengers.

American hotel.—hall with open windows at either end.

* Floriponda—long bell shaped white flower—on tree like fig—blooms once month—fragrant at night.

* Ginger flower—same the root comes from—<s>red striped white wax like flower when not in full bloom—very pleasant ginger fragrance.

* Cocoa—tamarind—oleander—

* 3 Tremendous solitudes of the Pacific—a lonely sea—no land in sight for ten days—& never a solitary ship in sight.

Consul at Honolulu—salary $4,000—no fees<.>, allowed—all go to Government.

Last quarter, entire Government fees, hospital revenues, &c., amounted to $21,000, as returned to American Commissioner.[12] All absorbed in Government expenses, & more called for.

Consul has *created* a system of private fees. For instance—clerical fees—such as powers of attorney & other notarial work—he gets it all to do, charges what he pleases, & keeps the money. For paying off a ship's crew he charges 2½ p.c. (Harbor Master has learned this dodge from him & charges same for native crews.)

Consul appoints Purveyor for Hospital.[13] Each sailor gets full

---

[12] This title was no longer in use, for in 1863, to compensate for its neglect of Hawaii during the Civil War, the United States had raised the rank of its diplomatic representative to minister resident. The minister resident at this time was James McBride, who had been appointed on 9 March 1863. McBride would be replaced just three days after Mark Twain's arrival in Honolulu, but he continued in office throughout the period of Mark Twain's visit, pending the arrival of his successor.

[13] The following bill of duplicities must have been based on information supplied by one of the Hawaiian residents aboard the *Ajax*. Honolulu consul Alfred Caldwell was abetted by his son-in-law and deputy Thomas Templeton Dougherty—particularly by Dougherty's manipulation of James M. Green, purveyor of the U.S.

suit clothing when he enters hospital, & another when he leaves. He & consul make about 100 per cent on these. Purveyor appointment should be taken from him & contracts let to lowest bidder.

Purveyor also gets about 85 cents a day for boarding each invalid, & out of this pays hospital rent—4 or $500 a year. Costs him 30 or 40 cents a day per man. Have had over 200 men in hospital at one time—400 suits clothing for season. No price set by Gov't on clothing. Present consul appointed his brother-in-law purveyor at first.

One consul took the $36 sailor fund home with him once (held sacred, now), <s>& had to disgorge—said he didn't know what to do with it. It must be kept here, because don't know what moment sailor may ship for home & call for his $24 out of it.

Dougherty venir w[h] $5000—has 125 to $150,000 in 4 yrs.

"Slops" are clothing, tobacco, &c, furnished sailors at sea & charged against them. Sailor's advance is $40—he may find $10 for boots which he got, $40 for boots which he didn't get, &c on return —be actually in debt—in which case the government fee of $1 for discharging him is remitted

"Long lay is the Captains & mates 10th 20th & 30th share of a whaling voyage.

"Short(?) lay is a common seaman's 120th of the same.

Captains swindle sailors out of every dollar they can by the slop system, & every cent so saved goes alone to owners. But the ungrateful owners, by false gauges of oil, quotations of markets, false sales, <&c> pretended non-sales & depreciation of price, &c, swindle the captains.

The consul, in buying the cargo from the sailors, reduce it some by putting it on gold basis, by leakage, shrinkage, margin for depreciation from ruling rates, &c, reduce the value of a cargo ⅔.

"Pulling" is the arrest of Capt by seamen for ill treatment. [#]

Marine Hospital in Honolulu. Official exposure of these fraudulent practices wouldn't come until the fall of 1866. It culminated in Caldwell's suspension early in January 1867.

Portuguese greenies often put on short lay of 300th—go to sea—learn how been swindled—desert first opportunity to ship offers more.

Governing classes & agriculturists first put $100 bonds on shipment of natives to break it up—then $300. As it hasn't succeeded, they will make effort coming session to prohibit their being carried away from islands altogether. Both papers support it.

Result will be to terribly inconvenience, cripple & possibly destroy commerce, whaling & guano trade.

<T>Planters like Kanaks best on the farm—industrious, tractable, can understand them, can get them in debt & keep them. Not so with coolies.

The *Tooker* matter is used as a great argument in favor of prohibiting shipment of Kanakas.[14]

Government Consular fees are:

Entry & deposit of ship papers—$5.

Shipping each man, 50 cents—$1 for discharging each.

Consul at Lahaina get $3000.

Consul at Hilo no <fees—ab> salary—fees about $600.

Physician here gets $4,500—no fees.

Young Thurston made 1st sermon in Fort street church Sunday eveing <before> 25th—his old father & mother (missionary 46 years) present—feeling remarks of minister in his prayer about the old people being spared to hear the son they had dedicated to the Lord—very affecting.[15] [#]

---

[14] On 27 November 1865 George S. Tooker, the notoriously tyrannical master of the American whaler *Mercury,* had been sentenced by a San Francisco judge to three months' imprisonment and fined one hundred dollars for beating, wounding, and starving a seaman, who apparently was a native of the Sandwich Islands. Indignation in Hawaii, already great over Tooker's cruelty, increased considerably early in 1866, when word arrived that President Andrew Johnson had pardoned him, thereby deflecting a punishment that had never seemed adequate.

[15] The Reverend Thomas Thurston, age thirty, son of the Reverend Asa Thurston and Lucy Goodale Thurston, members of the First Company of American Protestant Missionaries, returned to Honolulu aboard the *Ajax* after some eight years devoted to study at Yale University and at Union Seminary in New York City. On the evening of 25 March 1866, Thomas Thurston preached his first sermon on

Corwin salary $2,000—Damon $800 from American Seaman's friend society,[16] & $800 more. Old Thurston gets pension less than $700 from Amer. Mission <Socity.> Board.[17]

March 12, <Sunday.> Monday

<* 1> Roughest night of the voyage last night—ship rolled heavily.

<* 1> Still rougher this morning till 11 o'ck, when course was altered to W., which eased her up considerably.

Settee fetched away at breakfast, & precipitated 4 heavy men on their backs.

<* 1> Rev. Mr. Thurston, Capt Smith & family (Lon) Ye Ancient Mariner—Sea Monster—Capt Cuttle[18]—"Don't like gale

---

the text "And Jesus himself began to be about thirty years of age," at the Fort Street Congregational Church, then under the ministry of the Reverend Eli Corwin. This entry and the one following, both obviously out of sequence, were written apparently at random on the last of four pages which Mark Twain had originally left blank.

[16] Established in New York in May 1828, the American Seamen's Friend Society was a philanthropic organization zealously dedicated to the care of seamen. The society maintained sailors' homes, institutes, and bethels all over the world, and, in addition to caring for the shipwrecked and destitute, performed a repertoire of services for seamen, including letter-writing, provision of free meals and lodgings, and the maintenance of reading rooms ashore and loan libraries afloat. It also sponsored a variety of social, religious, and temperance activities intended to distract seamen from less savory amusements.

[17] On 29 June 1810, the General Association of Massachusetts Proper, "a recently organized body of conservative Congregational ministers, representing the more evangelical wing of the denomination" (William E. Strong, *The Story of the American Board, An Account of the First Hundred Years of the American Board of Commissioners for Foreign Missions* [Boston: The Pilgrim Press, 1910], p. 3) approved the desire of several Andover Theological Seminary students to undertake a mission to the heathen and created a nine-member American Board of Commissioners for Foreign Missions to regulate such activities. The American Board's first missionaries to the Sandwich Islands arrived in 1820.

[18] Mark Twain's sobriquets for Captain James Smith, the latter two suggested by John Brougham's popular dramatization of Dickens' *Dombey and Son*. In act 1, scene 1 of the play, although not in the novel, the rough-mannered, good-hearted Captain Ned Cuttle is referred to as "that old sea monster." In "A Voice for Setchell" (*Californian*, 27 May 1865) Mark Twain had expressed his partiality

holding on so close to change of moon—if holds 48 hours will hang on through the quarter."

"If wind don't haul around with sun won't have fair wind—no fair wind comes but comes with sun."

Yarns of force of sea—68 pounders on Helena, forty ft above water, in calm—Great Repub decks broke in—15,000 tons of <10> 30-ton rocks moved back 300 yards & left in winrow—decks stripped clean with gentle sea—27 stancions, &c.

Moral Phenomenon.

<* 1> Haven't reached the boasted d—d "trades" yet—may reach them to-morrow.

<1> Were ½ way (1,050 miles) at noon to-day.

Water taken in moderation cannot hurt anybody.

* 1 13th—Tuesday—Very rough again all night—had head winds & had to take in all sail—made poor run—weather fine this morning, but still head winds, & there being not a rag of canvass on to steady the ship, she rolls disagreeably, though the sea is not rough. <H>

* 1 14th—Wednesday—Good weather. I have suffered from something like mumps for past 2 days.

* 1 15th Thursday.

Dress by the latitude & longitude—Capt & Chf Eng came out in full summer rig to-day because by the sextant we are in lat. 26° though the weather don't justify it.

* 4 * 15th Thurday—Mumps—mumps—mumps—it was so decided to-day—a d—d disease that children have—I suppose I am to take a new disease to the Islands & depopulate them, as all white men have done heretofore. [#]

---

toward the production of Brougham's play which featured the well-known comedian Dan Setchell as Captain Cuttle.

* 2 Mr. Sanford Ch Eng been in US service 16 years—been in 7 battles in Mex & 6 in America.

2 * Mr Baxter, Mate, been on gunboat in the war, too. & Captain, Godfrey.

* 2 Heavily timbered, strong bolted ship.

* 2 3 watches, repeated of 8 bells each—each beginning at 12 o'clock & ending at 12. 1st watch <mo> evening—12 to 4—2^{d}, 4 to 8—3^{d}, 8 to 12. Morning watch midnight to 4, 4 to 8, 8 to noon.

In Honolulu, you can treat a <Kananka>Kanaka as much as you please, but he cannot treat you. No one is allowed to sell liquor to the natives, & an infraction of this law is visited with a heavy penalty. It is evaded by using back doors, as is the custom in civilized countries.

It is not lawful to hire out a horse or vehicle on Sunday—all such preparations must be made day before. This & the liquor law show where Hawaii's system of laws originated (with Missionaries,) & how firm a hold & how powerful a supremacy these people have gained by their 46 years of breeding & training voters & <law m> clannish law makers in their own ever-increasing descendants more than among the "fashionably" religious and decimating natives.

* 1 16th March—Friday—They say we shall be in sight of land to-morrow at noon. Good weather & a smooth sea for the past 2 days.

Dennis the hog was killed yesterday & served up for breakfast this morning.

* 1 The water begins to taste of the casks.

* 1 Brown's boots are all one-sided with bracing to the lurching of the ship—& his nose is skinned by a vomiting cup—thinks he will have cause of action against the company yet.

The usual chatter of the gens d'armes./servants.

4 * Passengers all <come> venir pour me voir.

* 1 Condensed steam water to cook with. [#]

8 demijohn<s> whisky.

* 3 Ye solemn glory of ye moon upon ye midnigt se.

* Old Gov. (native) on voyage between isles lost—turn around & go back where we came <[h - -]> from.

17th—St Patrick's Day—St Pat's Dinner & Dennis prematurely dead. Reported to be 160 miles from Honolulu at noon.

* 1 "Ship time"—(taken with the sextant reckoning every day at noon.)

Ye whalers at Euchre. "Who hove that ace on there?" <"You keep> "He kep' heavin' on 'em down so fast I couldn't tell noth'n 'tall <about> 'bout it." "Here goes for a euchre—by G— I'll make a point or break a rope-yarn<[-]>." Call small odd suit "blubber." "Now what'd you trump that for?<">—Your'e sailin' too close to the wind<.">—there, I know'd it—royals, stuns'ls—everything, gone to h—l. "That's my ace!—no t'aint—it's mine—you hove the King—

<No such> Not by a d—d sight!—rot my coppers if I <didn't> hove the King—leave it to Johnny here if I did."

* 1 Whaler drink—¾ of tumblerfull.)

Capt. Smith secesh.[19]

The Bullock named after Capt Dimond[20] because he <lay abe.> never got up for 5 days.

Brown & the Steward & waiters.

* 1 Stewardess.—Capts. always doctors. [#]

---

[19] In a letter to the *Alta California* from New York on 20 November 1867, Mark Twain would write of his dream of a passenger list for a world tour "made up of all sorts of people" who "could travel forever without a row." Among them he included "Admiral Jim Smith, late of Hawaiian Navy" (*TIA*, p. 312–313). That recollection of Smith and the present notebook entry indicate that he was the prototype for "the old Admiral" in chapter 62 of *Roughing It*.

[20] William H. Dimond, then a lieutenant in the Hawaiian Cavalry Company, had left the Sandwich Islands on 28 August 1864 to volunteer for service with the Union forces in the Civil War. He was returning as a captain of cavalry in the United States Army.

King strongly favors English, on account of attentions shown him when in England & the reverse shown him in the U.S. <(Va. planter said wouldn't sit at table w^{h} nigger)> & favors all foreigners much more than Americans—so, Americans are at discount in Honolulu, & possess small influence—on which account, & to curry favor, no foreigner will buy anything of an American which he can get of an Englishman. All money in hands of foreigners circulates among foreigners pretty exclusively, & on other hand, Americans who have any spirit retaliate by dealing with Americans pretty exclusively. The *American Hotel* is kept by a Dutchman.[21] Ten Americans there where one foreigner, but the "influence" plays the devil, nevertheless. <E[- - -]> All English men-of-war foster this partiality of the King by flattering him & showing him royal honors & attentions.

* 1 Night of 17th—Never could swear to being in the tropics by the weather till to-night—hot as hell in the state-rooms. Magnificent breezy starlight night & new moon on deck—everybody out.

* 1 Brown sleep in his shelf.

* 3 18th—8 A.M. Sunday—Land in sight on left—like a couple of vague whales lying in blue mist under the distant horizon.

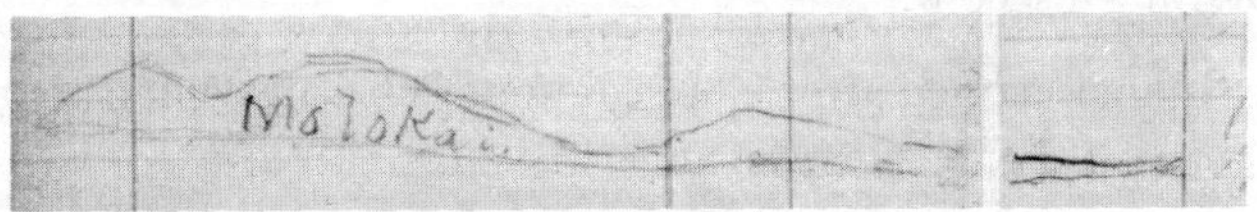

Oahu glinting in the sun through light mist—20 miles away.

* This is the most magnificent, balmy atmosphere in the world—ought to take dead man out of grave. [#]

21 The American Hotel in Honolulu, where Mark Twain was to stay and take meals, was operated by M. Kirchoff, a German.

"Dr. Gambarelli Bechtinger, $10 fee for medical attendance on Capt. Phillips"—& then ate $4 worth of Brown's lunch.

* Ch^n say—"Well, I don't care, my grandfather ate your grandfather."

American Ch^n say, "Well, I don't care, my <father> big brother can whip your <father> big brother if he wants to."

* 3 Flag of any kind at the fore calls a pilot.

* 3 We went in with stars & stripes at main-spencers gaff, & Hawaiian flag at the fore. The Union is the St George's Cross of England—balance is American flag except that there is a blue as well as a red & white stripe in it. The blue stripe makes it part of French flag. There is nothing national about it except the *number* of stripes—7—one for each inhabited island.[22]

* 2 Harp Engine laid horizontally—normal condition vertical—gives great compactness & leaves no portion of machinery above water line—Ajax was built for gun boat.

* 2 Temperature of fire-room (no ventilation,) 148°. Firemen only live about 5 years, & then probably don't mind hell much.

* 2 Screw 13 inches diameter, 70 feet long—flukes 13 feet diameter, 22½ feet p[--]

3 * Running past Diamond Head on about 100 foot water—beautiful light blue color—see shadow of bottom sometimes—water very transparent—water shames the pale heavens with the splendor of its brilliant blue.

* 3 Come to Waikiki 4½ miles before get to Honlulu—beautiful drive—fine road. [#]

[22] The genesis and evolution of the Hawaiian flag are still matters of some uncertainty. Except for the inclusion of a French influence, however, Mark Twain's description of the flag and its sources is generally consistent with the sometimes conflicting accounts by contemporary observers. Although earlier flags have been reported with seven stripes, the flag in use in 1866 was apparently one that had been introduced in 1845 which had eight stripes of white, red, and blue, symbolizing eight islands under one sovereign.

* 1 French D^{rs} odd positions & actions & dress—guitar—travels—head low & to leeward, heels on shelf—carried handsful grub away from table.

* 3 Arriv^{d} at noon Sunday—fired gun—10 days & 6 hours out—could have got in last night just after dark

3 * Channel very narrow but straight & well buoyed.—not wide enough for 2 ships at once hardly.

* 3 Custom House boat came off with flag.

<McMillan pilot>

* 3 McIntyre, pilot<.>—old burly gray bearded Scot.

* 3 King sat in two-horse buggy, alone, on wharf—big whiskers—old leather complexion—broad gold band on plug hat—band of gold around lappels of coat.

No—King's driver—speculation wrong.

* 3 Crowd 4 or 500

Females on horseback.

* 3 Sunday stillness—natives sitting in shade of houses on ground.

* 3 Absence of spring of ship to footstep.

* Walker, Allen & Co. have the major part of the sugar & molasses trade & give it to Brooks & Co's line

Brewer & Co will own & control major part of it in 2 months

* People here smoke manila cigars & drink everything.

* Aristocratic church—[23]

* * Long street darkest in the world, down to the Esplanade—width 3 buggies abreast.—couldn't get out of it & so found my way.[24] [#]

---

[23] The Hawaiian Reformed Catholic church, to which the royal family and several members of the government, including Attorney General Charles C. Harris, belonged.

[24] Probably Nuuanu Street, which ran from downtown Honolulu through the

* No native church to-night.

* Found Rev. Mr. Rising there.

* <American hotel>Hotels gouge<s> Californians—charges sailing passengers eight dollars a week for board, but steamer passengers ten.

* Charley Richards[25] keeps a tremendous spider & 2 lizards for pets. I would like to sleep with him if he would get a couple of snakes or so.

* Honolulu hospitality. Richards said: "Come in—sit down—take off your coat & boots—take a drink. Here is a pass-key to the <li> liquor & cigar cupboard—put it in your pocket—two doors to this house—stand wide open night & day from January till January—no locks on them—march in whenever you feel like it, take as many drinks & cigars as you want, & make yourself at home."

* Capt. Phillips said: "This is my end of the house & that is Asa's—the door's always open—the demijohns are behind the door —come in when you feel like it—take a drink, take a smoke—<pull> wash your feet <on>in the water pitcher if you want to—wipe 'em on the bedclothes—break the furniture—spit on the table-cloth—throw the things out doors—make yourself comfortable —make yrself at home.

* Capt. Drew—"Run agin me, will you, son of a b—— Dodge, will you, son of a b——? Run, will you, son of a b——

Challenged by imaginary English naval officer—<choos>chose harpoons—backed down—man of family—you touched my tender

---

Nuuanu Valley up to the Pali, the famous precipice over which Kamehameha I drove an opposing army to conclude his conquest of Oahu in 1795. In 1866 the street was inhabited by whalers and "gaudy women" awaiting trade in crowded coffee shops, and it resounded with the "fantastic babel" of dancing to violins, piano, and castanets (Gavan Daws, "The Decline of Puritanism at Honolulu in the Nineteenth Century," *Hawaiian Journal of History* 1 [1967]: 36).

[25] Charles L. Richards was a partner in C. L. Richards & Co., Honolulu ship chandlers and commission merchants.

point there, Charley. Was advised to leave—& did. Stopped at Robson's Said "If anybody asks for me, tell 'em I passed here at a ¼ past 9—P.—M." Had 2 miles of chapparal behind his house 1½ miles up valley. Said "If they kin find me there—*let* 'em!" Didn't show himself for 4 weeks.—Thought to cure him of drinking —he found 20 gallons Anderson's whisky on the place—drank it all up.

* 1 * * Our whalers drank 18 gallons whisky on way down—said they had to—if they couldn't show a good record, their owners would lose confidence in them.

T used by Catholics—L used by Protestants—natives use both —Towi & Lowi.[26]

13 letters in Hawaiian alphabet—each a distinct sound—3 vowels (o's) together sometimes, but each an independent sound—no trouble to learn to pronounce.[27] Have a large lexicon[28] & a small phrase-book.[29] [#]

---

[26] Mark Twain confused two pairs of interchangeable consonants, *t/k* and *l/r*. *Towi* and *kowi* (not *lowi*) were therefore the acceptable alternative forms of the word meaning "to press; to squeeze together." In devising an orthography for the Hawaiian language the American Protestant missionaries had preferred *k* to *t*. Mark Twain may have been led to believe that their Catholic rivals had opposed this choice by using *t* instead, but no evidence has been discovered to indicate that such was in fact the case.

[27] The Hawaiian language had seven consonants, *H*, *K*, *L*, *M*, *N*, *P*, and W, and the customary five vowels. A "guttural break," now known as a glottal stop, was represented by an apostrophe and may have been Mark Twain's thirteenth letter. Although contemporary experts did not seem to recognize this element as a separate consonant, considering it a variant of the sound represented by *K* in other Polynesian dialects, modern lexicographers have called it "the second most common consonant of the language" (Mary Kawena Pukui and Samuel H. Elbert, *Hawaiian Dictionary* [Honolulu: University of Hawaii Press, 1971], p. viii). Mark Twain's description of the pronunciation of vowels is substantially correct. Sequences of as many as six vowels may occur. Today, however, it is recognized that diphthongs do exist, although their elements are not as closely joined as in English.

[28] Lorrin Andrews, *A Dictionary of the Hawaiian Language* (Honolulu, 1865).

[29] Artemus Bishop, *Na Huaolelo a me na olelo kikeke ma ka Beritania a me ka olelo Hawaii, no na Haumana e ao ana i kela a me keia*. A *Manual of Conversations, Hawaiian and English. Hawaiian Phrase Book* (Honolulu, 1854).

* 3 King sitting on barrel on wharf fishing.

Gov. Domini's wife (native)—Gov. of Oahu—rides native fashion.[30]

* 3 King showed Asa Nudd greater attention than he ever showed foreign civilian before—in return for his hospitality in California.[31]

Water lemon.

Shittim wood

* <3> 1 Cigar man at San F. swindled me.

* 2 Whistler left day we arrived & Behring few days after—21 days out—both just in.—Onward is making long passage—not in yet.[32]

* Couldn't understand the bear-skin mats on floors—whalers bring them.

* Heavy dew.

<Ka-*meaa-meeah*><Ka-*meea-meeah*>

* 3 Ka-*meeah-mee*ah.

* Mr. Rising—first sprained & nervous prostration—worn out with study & labor—health not much improved

American Missionaries, who began the work on the islands & <have> really civilized & Christianized this people. And that church which claims to be the Hawaiian Established Church—King

---

30 John Owen Dominis, a native of New York State, was governor of Oahu. He was married to Lydia Kamakaeha Paki, who, as Liliuokalani, would reign as Hawaii's last queen.

31 Asa D. Nudd, a partner in Nudd, Lord & Co., San Francisco importers and wholesale dealers in wines and liquors, had spent two weeks in Hawaii in late January and early February 1866 as a passenger on the first round trip of the *Ajax*. His acquaintance with Kamehameha V must have dated from October 1849 or from August 1850, the two occasions on which the king, then Prince Lot Kamehameha, was in San Francisco as part of a diplomatic mission.

32 The barks *Whistler* and *Behring* had arrived from San Francisco on 15 and 16 March, respectively. The bark *Onward* had departed from Honolulu for San Francisco on 6 March 1866.

& royal family attend it. A<n> Bishop & several clergy of Church Eng sent out here, & then to give it an American cast,—brought over 2 or 3 American Episcopalians[33]

Question—whether this is not an indirect means of getting possession (by influence—treaty bet Fr & Eng is they shall never be disturbed in their independence)[34] French got possession of the Society & more recently the Marquesas by means of Romish Clergy.[35]

---

[33] Anglican Bishop Thomas Staley had come to Honolulu in 1862 accompanied by two English clergymen, George Mason and Edmund Ibbotson. At the beginning of 1865 the Reverend Peyton Gallagher came from the United States to assist Staley, and early the following year the Reverend G. B. Whipple, also an American, opened a station at Wailuku, Maui. The dispatch of American Episcopalian clergymen was not, however, the cynical maneuver Mark Twain indicates. Contemporary authorities, among them the Episcopal bishop of California, claimed that the English had initiated endeavors in Hawaii with the approval of the American Episcopal church, which, due to a lack of clergy and to the distractions of the Civil War, had been temporarily unable to collaborate. These explanations in no way alleviated the dismay of the pioneer American Protestant missionaries, who resented the Hawaiian royal family's undisguised preference for the Anglican establishment.

[34] On 28 November 1843, after protracted negotiations, complicated by Lord George Paulet's seizure of the Sandwich Islands in the name of the British crown (see Notebook 5, pp. 151–152), Great Britain and France had signed a joint declaration agreeing to consider the Sandwich Islands an independent state and promising never to take possession of any part of its territory. This declaration did not itself constitute a formal treaty, and the Hawaiian government was unable to secure the kind of treaty guarantees it wanted from Britain and France. The practical value of the joint declaration was perhaps best illustrated in 1849 by a brief but shocking invasion of Honolulu by French naval forces.

[35] Historians have pointed out that France did indeed use her missionaries, supported by timely displays of naval force, as a vanguard to gain prestige and influence in the Pacific. In 1838 and 1839 French ships had visited Tahiti [the Society Islands] to extort pledges of cooperation with French religious enterprises, in the latter year stopping at Hawaii as well and, under the threat of immediate hostilities, securing a site for a Catholic church in Honolulu, a promise of freedom of worship for Roman Catholics, and certain commercial and legal concessions. In 1842, shortly after taking possession of the Marquesas with the aid of missionaries there, the French returned to Tahiti and, finding compliance with an agreement of 1839 inadequate, coerced the government into yielding the islands as a French protectorate. Although France did not repeat these territorial appropriations in Hawaii, the French invasion of Honolulu in 1849, this time on a commercial and diplomatic, rather than a religious pretext, helped keep distrust of her intentions at a high level.

They sent priests here[36]—King said his people been rescued from idolatry—wouldn't have any more of it—sent them away. Man of war brought another priest disguised as merchant—found out—ordered away—ship threatened burn town—allowed remain under protest—ship brought back the banished priests from Mexico—one is now Bishop here & lives in palace.

We all know how France would regard treaty, if she could once get possession.

* Damon—"The Friend"—first issue 18th Jan 1843—never stopped but one <month—> year—Bethel preacher—asks no assistance in its issue from any religious society.

Began before there was a type set <w> anywhere from Cape Horn to Behring's Straits west of Andes & Rocky.

Beloved by all—he & wife always collecting & caring for the poor. Old whalers like him.[37] [#]

---

[36] What follows is a truncated and garbled account of events which occurred between 1827 and 1840 during establishment of France's Catholic mission in the Sandwich Islands. Bishop Louis Desirée Maigret, who had been in Honolulu since 1840 but who had not been a member of the first banished party of priests, did not live in a palace. The antagonism toward Maigret implied here seems as secondhand as the account of the coming of the French priests, since Mark Twain apparently would not himself meet or observe Maigret until late June (see Notebook 5, p. 118), when he would compose a tribute to him to appear in the Sacramento *Daily Union* on 30 July.

[37] Samuel Chenery Damon, Honolulu chaplain of the American Seamen's Friend Society and pastor of the Oahu Bethel Church, had come to Hawaii in 1842. On 1 January 1843 he began publication of *The Temperance Advocate & Seamen's Friend*, briefly called *The Friend of Temperance & Seamen* and then simply *The Friend*, a periodical concerned chiefly with the moral improvement of sailors. Damon, who by 1866 had completed slightly more than half his tenure as *The Friend's* editor and publisher, later liked to recall that he had initiated it at a time when "there was not a newspaper published in the English language at the Sandwich Islands, or any part of Polynesia, or even on the Western coast of North or South America, from Bherings Straights to Cape Horn . . . while in Oregon, California, Mexico, Panama, Peru and Chile not an English type had been set up" (Ethel Mosely Damon, *Samuel Chenery Damon* [Honolulu: Hawaiian Mission Children's Society, 1966], p. 12). Mark Twain's account of *The Friend's* publication history is slightly inaccurate, for according to Damon's statement in *The*

* Everybody use umbrellas—I don't have any use for them.

* Oh, islands there are
on the face of deep
Where the leaves never fade
& the skies never weep.[38]

* Went with Mr. Damon to his cool, vine shaded *home*[39]—you bet <your life>.

* No care-worn or eager, anxious faces in the land of happy contentment—God! what a contrast with California & Washoe.

Everybody walk at a moderate gait—though to speak strictly, they mostly ride.

* This house & chapel where he preaches were built by Seaman's Friend Society of NY—33—Rev. John <Dea> Diell[40]—here till '40—died of consumption on way home off Cape Horn '41—Damon arrived fall of '42, been here ever since—except visit home of a year, & one to Cal in '49—he & Gwynn made their debut in Cal at same time & both <sp> officiated at 4th July in Sac that year[41]—he made

---

Friend of 1 May 1862 it had been published semimonthly from 1845 to 1847, after which it had been published monthly with two intervals, May to September 1849 and February 1851 to May 1852.

38 Mark Twain's continuing attachment to these lines from "The Pirate's Serenade" by John Thomson and William Kennedy is discussed in Notebook 5, note 148.

39 An adobe house on the "narrow way called Pa'i'aina by Hawaiians, but soon known as Chaplain Lane" (Ethel Mosely Damon, *Samuel Chenery Damon*, p. 34). Mark Twain reportedly rented a room for some time at the corner of Fort Street and Chaplain Lane, next to the Damon home.

40 Damon's predecessor, who during his years in Honolulu so assiduously sought the patronage of sailors that some actually deserted the saloons for his church, much to the annoyance of the grog-shop proprietors, who on one occasion threatened to use violence to stop his proselytizing.

41 Damon delivered the opening prayer at the celebration held in Oak Grove, between Sutter's Fort and Sacramento City, on 4 July 1849. The holiday address was delivered by William McKendree Gwin, who had gone to California in 1849 to campaign for statehood and for his own election to the United States Senate. Elected one of California's first senators, Gwin held office from 1850 until 1861. In 1861 his attachment to John C. Calhoun and the Southern faction led to the first of two

prayer & G <was> <o[-]> spoke—while they were cutting down trees to build the town—only ½ dozen houses there.

He preached first sermon ever preached in Stockton—Whatsoever a man sowith, that shall he also reap. Man cleared out his bar for him.—only 2 houses there—one of them Weber's[42]—balance tents.[43]

* See Friend[44]

Sandwich Island Mirror—started here by R. J. Howard, Sept. 7, 1839.—lasted year or two. <First> Second, paper <in>ever printed in English.

First one was S. I. Gazette, by S. D. Mackintosh & Co, August 1836—lasted <a year or two,> to '39.

Hawaiian Spectator published quarterly Jan 38 to Oct 39—most excellent magazine—conducted by "an association of gentlemen."

Polynesian by J. J. Jarvis—June '40—died Dec 41

The Friend monthy, Jan 43 to present

Polynesian revived May 44—lasted 20 years—always paid its own way—others supportd by government.

Hawaiian Cascade Nov. 44 to Aug 45 by Hawaian Total Ab Union

Monitor, monthly, Jan to Dec 45. Rev. D. Dole.

<[-]>Friend May 65 Revenue derived by US Gov for [*one or*

---

imprisonments during the Civil War. Between prison terms Gwin attempted unsuccessfully to colonize Mexico with settlers from the South, and after this failure his public activities ceased.

[42] Charles Marie Weber, rancher, gold miner, and founder in 1847 of Stockton, California.

[43] Damon reported in *The Friend* of 1 December 1849 that he found Stockton "a city of tents, there being only two wooden buildings in the place" and that he "learned that a clergyman had never spent a Sabbath in the town." "On making known that I was a clergyman," he continued, "arrangements were made for holding services on board a vessel . . . used as a store-ship and moored alongside the bank." On Sunday 1 July 1849, Damon delivered his sermon on Galatians 6:7–8.

[44] The following information about early Sandwich Islands newspapers and periodicals was probably provided from memory by Samuel C. Damon with instructions to Mark Twain to examine the more inclusive list published in *The Friend* of 1 May 1862. Although not without uncertainties of dating, the list in *The Friend* would have prevented Mark Twain's confusion about the evolution of the *Polynesian,* which became the official journal of the government when it was revived.

two words] 400,000 Nat Ingols was the greatest accountant we ever had here—died lately in S. F.[45]

* American Com^r^ $7000 gold

May have a clerk—Gov^t^ pay $1,800.

* Landed Sunday—bells ringing for church—found 2 large native

---

[45] Facing this entry Mark Twain interleaved the following clipping from *The Friend* of 1 May 1865:

Rev. S. C. Damon, Editor of "The Friend," and my Reverend and Respected Friends, Singular and Dual:

The inherent modesty which is part and parcel of my nature received an abrupt shock the other day, when, by the *Whistler*, I received a copy of THE FRIEND, with the following item in its pages:

"It has been stated in print that the U. S. Government derives annually $400,000 from Custom House duties imposed upon Hawaiian products. Will Mr. Ingols, residing in San Francisco, please furnish some reliable statistics upon the subject? We know of no one who could do it better."

I tried at first to think it might be my brother James, who is computing clerk for Messrs. Kellogg, Hewston & Co., who was meant by the paragraph, "or any other man," save myself; but I afterwards came to the conclusion, on reading the letter of a common friend, in which he made allusion to "the call," that it was I, and I alone, who was the "Mr. Ingols." Such being the case, I will at once to the task, and point out how I think it can be made up with accuracy enough to form an approximate sufficiently correct for generalization. Let us first take the imports into San Francisco. The bulk of these are as follows:

Coffee, 14,854 lbs, duty 5¢ per lb.	$ 742.70
Molasses, 259,469 galls, duty 8¢ per gal.	23,757.52
Pulu, 664,600 lbs, (at 7¢ per lb, $46,522,) at 20 pr ct.	9,304.40
Salt, 308,000 lbs, at 18¢ per 100 lbs.	554.40
Sugar, 8,851,957 lbs, at 3¢. average duty	265,558.71
Rice, 377,978 lbs, at 2½¢ per lb.	9,449.45
Unenumerated, at least	2,000.00
Being for San Francisco alone fully	$311,367.18

Thus far I can go, but you will now have to call on Collector Allen for the details of the cargoes from the Islands to Oregon, Boston, and New Bedford. As the duty is mostly specific on Hawaiian produce, except Hides, Wool and Pulu, it will be very easy to calculate the duty on the amounts given by him. The bulk of the Portland cargoes were Sugar, say 1,000,000 lbs, which, with the molasses, would probably swell the duties collectable to $40,000. In round numbers, then, the duties collected on the Pacific coast of the United States would not be far from $350,000. The Eastern vessels' cargoes, as you well know, consist mostly of Oil transhipped from American whalers, and therefore duty free. The balance of their cargoes are Hides Wool and sundries. I think it would be safe to estimate that the whole of them did not pay over $50,000 to the Custom House. You will see, therefore, that the person who gave you the estimate of $400,000 as the amount of duties paid to the United States on Hawaiian productions, must have entered into a calculation of a somewhat similar nature to mine, and I venture to say that an elaborate research (outside of actual Custom House figures) will

Prot Cch—1 Cath do do—when landed all these in full blast.:[46]

* Rev. Eli Corwin Fort street Congregational—preached 8 years ago in San José for several years & was once Secretary of State Ag Soc Cal.[47]

* Bethel is oldest—30 yrs.

* We larm of man who preaches in what is called the King's Chapel (native cch)—Rev. H. H. Parker, son of one of the old Missionaries—a young man, born <e>& well educated here—never been away—*very* fine orator & thorough in native language.[48]

* College here 20 years old.[49] Rev. Mr. Alexander Prest, – – –

---

not vary the result for the year 1864, to the amount of $10,000 either way from $400,000.

All of which is respectfully submitted.

N. LOMBARD INGOLS,
Accountant and General Factor.

Ingols, at one time a resident of the Sandwich Islands, had died on 13 October 1865 at the age of forty-three. His calculations, taken from this clipping, appeared in Mark Twain's account of "The Importance of the Hawaiian Trade" in the Sacramento *Daily Union* on 18 April 1866 (*MTH*, p. 271).

46 Here Mark Twain pasted in an advertisement of Honolulu places of worship that ran in every issue of *The Friend* and listed the following six churches: the Seamen's Bethel, the Fort Street Church, the Stone Church, Smith's Church, the Catholic Church, and the Reformed Catholic Church, under the ministries of the Reverends Samuel C. Damon, Eli Corwin, Henry H. Parker, and Lowell Smith and Bishops Louis D. Maigret and Thomas N. Staley, respectively.

47 The Reverend Eli Corwin became pastor of the Fort Street Congregational Church in Honolulu in 1858 after serving as pastor of the Independent Presbyterian Church [First Presbyterian Church] of San Jose, California, from early 1852 until October 1858. He was recording secretary of the California State Agricultural Society during 1856.

48 The Reverend Henry Hodges Parker, whose father, Benjamin Wyman Parker, had come to the Sandwich Islands in 1833, was pastor of Kawaiahao Church in Honolulu, also known as King's Chapel and the Stone Church. Services there were regularly conducted in Hawaiian. Parker's knowledge of the Hawaiian language would later lead to his appointment to revise Lorrin Andrews' *A Dictionary of the Hawaiian Language*.

49 Oahu College was chartered in 1853 to train students in fields of Christian education, according to the principles of American Protestant Evangelical Christianity. It was an outgrowth of the school for missionary children opened in 1842 at Punahou, near Honolulu. Although intended to make it unnecessary to seek advanced education abroad, the school at Oahu never became a fully developed college.

Philologist—sent for that book poetry from Marquesas islands. born here—grad. Yale, 2d of class of 100—one of finest Greek scholars every produced[50]

Marquesas poorest group in Pacif—20 forigners—6000 natives.

* Sandwich most valuable in world.

* Week <be> ago this concert—*all* by natives—& managed <by> entirely by Hawians—& they raised $1175 <for>—proceeds—for an organ for King's chapel:[51]

* Papers.[52]

2 weekly native
{ N. "Kuakoa" }
Eng— { (Independent) }
and
"Okoa"
<(Light)>
2 weekly Eng.
"Advertizer"
and
"Gazette"
and
Monthly
"The Friend"

* Just issued the <l>Second volume law reports Supreme Court—elegantly printed & bound—800 pages—in a shape do honor to any printers.[53] [#]

---

[50] The Reverend William DeWitt Alexander was a member of a missionary family Mark Twain would visit at Wailuku, Maui, in April or May. Salutatorian of his class at Yale in 1855, Alexander had become professor of Greek at Oahu College in 1858 and in 1865 was named president of that institution. The book of poetry alluded to here has not been identified.

[51] Facing this entry Mark Twain attached a program for a "Grand Hawaiian Concert" held at Kawaiahao Church on 10 March 1866. He marked the program with a circled asterisk.

[52] Except for the braces, and the words "2 weekly native," "Eng—(Independent)," and "<(Light)>," the following list is in a hand other than Mark Twain's.

[53] Robert G. Davis, *Reports of a Portion of the Decisions Rendered by the*

* Could hardly find town in heart New England where Union sentiment was so strong as here during War.

Northern States Whalers.

* Hear a good deal of Opera singing around this town—& pianos.[54]

* Jim Ayres, McGeorge & Rising.

* Union Question.

N. Y. Eve Post Jan. 16, 1866:[55]

* Literature. 1 letter. [#]

Supreme Court of the Hawaiian Islands, in Law, Equity, Admiralty and Probate, 1857–1865 (Honolulu: Government Press, 1866).

54 An Amateur Musical Society had been organized in Honolulu in 1851. Its members seem to have been perpetually in rehearsal for the monthly concerts at which they sang "solos, duets, quartettes, and choruses from operas and oratorios, with piano, violin, and flute music" (L. F. Judd, *Honolulu*, p. 328).

55 The following newspaper clipping was attached here:

> This shows what is thought of the Bishop's American friend in the community in which he lives, and he will scarcely deny that the verdict of those American residents is entitled to consideration. They have shown themselves true patriots; long separation from the United States has not alienated their hearts from the land of their birth. Mark their course during the late rebellion; it is well worthy of notice and emulation. Their young men, scions of that Puritan stock the Bishop dislikes so much, enlisted in our Union army and navy; one, of whom we know, not able to go himself, kept a substitute in our army during the whole war. Very freely they gave personal service and money in defence of the land they had never seen, but which they had been taught by their parents to love. Our muster rolls show a brigadier-general, a colonel, a lieutenant-colonel, several lieutenants and numerous surgeons, natives or residents of the Sandwich Islands, and descendants of that despised missionary stock; while in money, they contributed to our Sanitary Commission the respectable sum of sixteen thousand one hundred and thirteen dollars and forty-three cents, being more than was given for the same object by either New Hampshire, Vermont, Rhode Island, Connecticut, Pennsylvania, Delaware, Maryland, the District of Columbia, Virginia, Ohio, Indiana, Illinois, Michigan, Wisconsin, Iowa, Minnesota, Kentucky, Louisiana, Idaho, Colorado or Nebraska; in fact, more in proportion to their numbers than was given by any state in the Union. Is not the judgment of such men entitled to as much weight as Bishop Staley's?

The influence of this clipping is evident in the martial depiction of the American missionaries Mark Twain included in his attack on Anglican Bishop Thomas N. Staley in the Sacramento *Daily Union* of 30 July 1866 (*MTH*, pp. 352–353).

<Anderson's> Andrews' Dictionary. 17,000 words[56]—printed here—same number as Richardsons first great dic^n 100 yrs ago.

* Sharks

Mrs McFarlane—volcano on Toahi[57]—30 miles from the house —eruption began slowly at <su>dusk—at 4 AM was shooting rocks & lava 400 feet high which w^d then descend in a grand shower of fire to the earth—<in w> crater overflowed & molten waves & billows went boiling & surging down mountain side just for the world like the sea—stream from ½ to mile & ½ wide & hundreds feed deep perhaps—over cattle, houses & across streams to the sea, 63 miles distant (7 years ago) ran into sea 3 miles & boiled the fish for 20 miles around—vessels found scores boiled fish 20 miles off—natives cooked their food there. Every evening for 7 weeks she sat on verandah half the night gazing upon the splendid spectacle—the wonderful pyrotechnic display—the house windows were always of a bloody hue—read newspapers every night by no other light than was afforded by this mighty torch 30 miles away. Crowds of visitors came from the other islands.

K IV & V were nephews of III, who adopted IV at his birth as his son & named him successor, though V was eldest.

IV was remarkable man—ambitious—proud, accomplished, profound in thought & wisdom—a deep thinker—ashamed of his family & did not like old K I & Cooks murder recalled—did not like to be reminded that he came of race of savages.—thought he was worthy of nobler origin—

Present King is penetrating—sound judgment—dignity—accomplished—has good sense & courage & decision—& became

---

[56] Lorrin Andrews himself estimated the number of words in his dictionary as "about 15,500" (*A Dictionary of the Hawaiian Language*, p. vi).

[57] This spectacular description of the January through August 1859 eruption of Mauna Loa, on Hawaii, provided by Mrs. Henry MacFarlane, wife of a Honolulu liquor merchant, is substantially confirmed by other contemporary accounts. *Toahi* is Mark Twain's phonetic approximation of *Kawaihae*, the name of a site on Hawaii about thirty-five miles north of Mauna Loa.

acquainted with business by long apprenticeship as Minister of Interior.

Prince Bill is very able man & accomplished gentleman—they have always been a wonderful family & the ablest in the land.

Missions.[58]

* The "Legend"[59]

* Children of missionaries all call each other cousins.[60]

Formed themselves into little Mis Soc—once month—have MSS paper—once ¼ select from it & print The Maile (Mily) (Vine) Quarterly.

* What'll you drink
Don't drink
But you *must*<?>
How much do you weigh
1 ton 2 ton—2200.[61] [#]

---

[58] Mark Twain would sometimes outline subjects for particular attention a few pages in advance, but as a notebook evolved he was not always able to restrict himself even to these loose boundaries. "Missions," which appears between "every" and "night" in the entry describing the eruption of Mauna Loa, was written and encircled at the top of a notebook page. It was probably intended to head a series of entries about missionary enterprises, but the pages allotted for this purpose were appropriated first to complete the rush of description of the volcano's eruption and then for the notes about Hawaiian succession.

[59] "The Legend of Ai Kanaka," an account of how a Molokai harbor came to be named Ai Kanaka (man-eater), appeared in the first number of the *Maile Quarterly* (see note 60).

[60] An outgrowth of the parent missionaries' custom of addressing each other as "brother" and "sister." In 1852 the Hawaiian Mission Children's Society, also known as the Cousins' Society, was organized for social and spiritual purposes in Hawaii and for the support of missionary children who themselves became missionaries to other parts of the world. The manuscript paper Mark Twain refers to was the *Maile Wreath*, a monthly magazine initiated in 1862, which was assembled from members' contributions, read at meetings of the society, and then circulated among those who had not been in attendance. From 1865 to 1868, in order to share parts of the *Maile Wreath* with "cousins," who lived at too great a distance to see the manuscript, a printed magazine, the *Maile Quarterly*, was mailed to subscribers.

[61] Part of the Hawaiian system of etiquette and insult which Mark Twain discussed in the Sacramento *Daily Union* of 22 May (*MTH*, p. 306).

* Capt Brown[62] Keeper City prison been tracing genealogical tree—found it takes root like a banyan every 6 months.

* Sea Island cotton—picked every day in the year—stalks cut off every January—no frost—sure crop—worth dollar a pound—in Liverpool or Havre worth *any* price—adulterate silk goods with it. 1,000 acres this land in bend of head of this Island worth $2 to $20 acre.

Raised <$> 30,000 lbs last year will raise 50,000 this. All that is needed is labor—industry—natives won't pick it every day—lazy & shiftless.

* Sailor's Home

* Best horses in the world—too d—d feeble to cut up any.

* Cows all <ded> dead this morning, I guess—no milk on ship or shore.

* Found the purser looking at naked women fishing, thro' spy-glass.

* By-word here—"Well, why didn't you say so?"

* Girls here have good, home faces.

* Climate here not as soft as at Santa Cruz, & the town not as beautiful as Havana, of course.

* Native printers at work in Gazette office.

* Royal Hawaiian (d—n those two i's) Agricultural Society)—MEM to visit it, & get its statistics.[63] [#]

---

[62] J. H. Brown, captain of the artillery in the Voluntary Military, was jailor of Oahu Prison.

[63] Organized on 13 August 1850, the Royal Hawaiian Agricultural Society was inactive after 1856 but continued to exist until September 1869, when it was formally dissolved. To the limited degree permitted by its scant finances, the organization sponsored scientific experimentation and the introduction of superior varieties of plants and animals. Its published reports, *The Transactions of the Royal Hawaiian Agricultural Society* (seven issued between 1850 and 1856), were undoubtedly the source for some of Mark Twain's information about Hawaiian agriculture.

* Also the American Legation.

* 9 large German firms here—some of them worth 3 or $4,000,000—trade largely DIRECT with Hamburg and Bremen.[64]

* Planters chained by merchants' advances & part ownership in their plantations—merchants also own in the sailing line—& so, the whole mercantile & planter interest is opposed to the steamship line.

* Jimpson weed.

* Native manner of tasting poi—blowing nose &c.

* More d—d bells ringing all the time day & night.

* Church built of lava blocks 5 by 1 foot—very full shells & pebbles—porous—dark cream color—laid in cement, stripes <20> 2 inches—looks checkered at little distance.[65] Big fine grounds.

* 1 Brown's boots all down at heel by Ajax.

* No tax on Real Estate?[66]

* Permission granted for three distilleries 18 months ago.

* Sandal wood.[67] [#]

---

64 During the 1850s, the formative years in Hawaii's commercial development, two dozen German business firms established themselves in Honolulu. Although the following decade saw the beginning of a decline in German influence, at the time of Mark Twain's visit the German firms still played a significant role in the commercial life of Honolulu.

65 Kawaiahao Church in Honolulu was built of blocks of coral, not lava. In his letter in the Sacramento *Daily Union* of 19 April (*MTH*, p. 275) Mark Twain correctly identified this characteristic Honolulu building material.

66 Although land taxes had been abolished in 1852, because of a pressing need to increase revenue the Civil Code of 1859 had imposed a tax of one quarter of one percent of assessed value, which was still in effect in 1866.

67 Sandalwood was Hawaii's first important export. During the first quarter of the nineteenth century it attracted large numbers of vessels, which transported it to China for use in the manufacture of incense. By the middle of the 1830s the once dense sandalwood groves had been almost totally destroyed. The abrupt contact with foreign values, the attendant corruption, and the severe hardships imposed on the people employed by the chiefs to gather the wood had pernicious effects that long outlasted this commodity.

See Mr. Rising about visit.

* Tabu.

* Get law books

* Color hair and build of peoples

* Smart—intelligent.

* Crowing chickens & bells, but few dogs

Thundering of the surf in the still night.

* Natives carrying bales of hay—B's joke.

* Whether hereditary chiefs still have sway

* No place where *public* education so widely diffused

* Children of ten—all read & write

* Boys sent here to school from Cal & Russian possessions.

* Custom of King & Nobles adopting children.

* Stranger's Friend Society—ladies.[68]

* Female riding apparel.

* Foreign Cemetery—2 miles up <isl> Nuuanu Vally

* American Seaman's Friend Society.

* Catholic Cemetery 1 mile out of town

* Native ditto

* Royal Tomb near palace grounds

* Koa tree[69] [#]

---

68 Mrs. Samuel C. Damon was the first president of this society, which was organized in 1852 as a counterpart to the Seamen's Friend Society to care for sick and destitute travelers.

69 The largest Hawaiian forest tree, whose splendid wood was used in the coffin of Princess Victoria Kaahumanu Kamamalu, which produced "a sort of ecstasy" in

* Grave of Kam the Great a secret to this day[70]

* What *Aloha* means.[71]

Visit City Prison

* The old, old fashion of gossiping & tale-bearing here. What they mostly talk about.

Aristocracy—exclusiveness marked.

Who are the exclusives, & what do they found it on?

Dress—fashion of foreigners

Ditto natives

Boys & girls in swimming [#]

Mark Twain (Sacramento *Daily Union*, 16 July 1866, *MTH*, p. 330). In 1908, in gratitude for his much-quoted testimonials to Hawaii, the Hawaii Promotion Committee would present Mark Twain with a mantel and accompanying breadfruit plaque of carved koa wood, "one of the handsomest pieces of furniture ever made in the Islands" (*MTH*, p. 242), for addition to Stormfield, his home in Redding, Connecticut. On 24 November of that year his secretary, Isabel V. Lyon, noted: "The Hawaiian mantel came today, but the beautiful Koa wood has been polished until it is terribly yellow, & it won't go anywhere." Mark Twain "declared it too offensive" and "suggested that all that wonderful shine be scraped off. So the men carried it to the garage to reduce its coloring" (Isabel V. Lyon Journal, 24 November 1908). The subdued mantel was installed at Stormfield on Mark Twain's seventy-third birthday, at which time he thanked the promotion committee, writing that "it is rich in color, rich in quality, & rich in decoration. Therefore it exactly harmonises with the taste for such things which was born in me & which I have seldom been able to indulge to my content" (SLC to H. P. Wood, secretary of the Hawaii Promotion Committee, 30 November 1908, *MTH*, facing p. 243).

[70] Near the end of this notebook Mark Twain recorded the traditional reason for the concealment of the bones of Kamehameha I, which were so well hidden that their location has not yet been determined. In "A Strange Dream" (New York *Saturday Press*, 2 June 1866), he would recount his imagined discovery of the remains of Kamehameha I in the crater of the active volcano Kilauea on the island of Hawaii.

[71] Mark Twain must have been impressed with the versatility of this common greeting, which was used to express love, affection, gratitude, kindness, pity, compassion, grief, and even "to salute contemptuously" (Andrews, *A Dictionary of the Hawaiian Language*).

Eating raw fish poi & lu-wow

Hoola-hoola

* <1> 3 Mosquito season—South (trade) wind does not blow yet.
Heated term

* Rain 4 months in year<.>—same months as ours

* Nearly all native women on it.

* $65 income entitles to vote.

Old Battle Ground.

Waikiki—Remains of Pagan Temple.

The Salt Lake

Site of an old Pagan Game

Fish Ponds.

Coral Reefs.

* Taro Plantations

Another Old Battle Ground at Wailueu

Feudal System—Reform of Landed System.[72]

* Correspondents publish from Sing Sing.

Feats of Horsemanship.

Remarkable Caves in Koloa

Femal Penitentiary on Koloa.

Indigo.

Silk

Valley of Cascades [#]

---

[72] A series of laws enacted between 1839 and 1850 supplanted the feudal system of landholding with individual ownership.

Lunar Rainbows

Objects of Superstition.

Legends.

Settlement of Californians

Modes of Travel

* Most here New Englanders.

* <S[-]>Look Contented but pine for Home

* Hear it in the Surf.

Coffee.

Evidences of Remote Antiquity on Hanalei.

Caves at Haena—Hanalei.

Subterranean Lakes

Native courage & size.

Significancy of native names.

Nomilu salt works.

Battle Ground of Wahi-awa.

Salt, Silk, Sugar, molasses, whisky Indigo, Cotton, coffee fruit, wood, tobacco.—11.

Traditions of Cook.

Russian fort at Waimea.[73] [#]

---

[73] The fort built at Waimea, Kauai, in 1817 under the direction of Georg Anton Scheffer, agent for the Russian American Company, which wished to establish regular commercial relations with the Sandwich Islands in order to secure a convenient source of supplies for its northern Pacific settlements and posts. The Russian presence at Waimea was brief. Soon after construction of the fort the king of Kauai, who had been supporting Scheffer's ambitious attempts to secure territorial as well as commercial concessions, drove the Russians off the island, apparently on orders from his overlord, Kamehameha I.

Wild cotton.

Birds, game, reptiles, insects, animals, beasts of prey.

Nohili, or Sounding Sands.[74]

* The island steamer[75]

* Island Postage Stamps.

* Photograph pictures

Fondness for tobacco<.>, but not whisky—laws against

Church law against smoking

Natives beautiful teeth—knocked out on death of relatives.

Haolē (man foreigner)

Make picture of men going to church in old native odds & ends.

* Cocanut groves.

* And Sharon waves
In silent praise
Her sacred groves of palm.[76]

Fondness for Horses

How tree [#]

---

[74] Nohili was an area on Kauai where the sand when walked upon sounded like the barking of a dog.

[75] The steamship *Kilauea*, built in East Boston for the Hawaiian Steam Navigation Company, had been brought to the Sandwich Islands in 1860 for interisland service. A combination of mechanical failures, accidents, and the financial difficulties of its various owners made for a record of intermittent performance. The *Kilauea* was incapacitated during a major portion of Mark Twain's visit, for on 13 January 1866 it had run aground on the reef at Kawaihae, Hawaii, and didn't go back into service until 4 June, after salvage, repair, and sale. It was the *Kilauea* which on 16 June would bring Mark Twain back to Honolulu after his extended tour of the island of Hawaii.

[76] From "Christmas Hymn" ("Calm on the listening ear of night . . .") by Edmund Hamilton Sears, also author of "The Angels' Song," the well-known Christmas carol beginning "It came upon the midnight clear."

Deserted Villages

More Cascades—in Palae.

Women more immoral there.

* Female mode of squatting.

Fleas.

Lice.

Big Cockroaches—came in ships

Wailing for the sick

Ceremonies for the dead.

* Houses have shutters to doors.

* Girl's head-wreath of flowers.

* Whirlwinds.

Disappointment in seeing no forests

* Hawaii a half-way house on the Pacif highway.

Salt by evaporation edge of town

* Damon's Library of Antiques.[77]

Shells.

Dog feast.

* 10,000 in '42.

* *Ohia* wreaths—crimson—& feathers.

* Mullet

* Kihei—wom riding dress.

* Odoriferous hala-nut—necklaces. [#]

---

[77] The Reverend Samuel C. Damon's large library supplied Mark Twain with historical information about the Sandwich Islands.

Awa—a drink[78]

Night-glasses used at Capt Finch's reception.[79]

Chnese musical kite

Site of tribe of Cannibals on Oahu.[80]

* Paper money here[81]

* Native wouldn't take dime for "rial"[82] 12½^{c}

Gain—purchase of slave—do of land—no frost—freedom from taxation

Expressive features grunts & gestures.

* Kona wind in winter

Falls of Wailua.

Lomi-lomi[83] [#]

---

[78] A native drink made from the root of the *kava* shrub, "so terrific that mere whisky is foolishness to it. It turns a man's skin to white fish-scales that are so tough a dog might bite him, and he would not know it till he read about it in the papers" (Mark Twain's letter in New York *Daily Tribune*, 9 January 1873, *MTH*, p. 496).

[79] The grand reception held at the royal palace on 15 October 1829 for Captain William Compton Bolton Finch and the other officers of the U.S.S. *Vincennes*, which was making a stop of almost two months' duration in the Hawaiian Islands. The splendid ostentation of this afternoon reception is indicated by the presence of night glasses—float-wick lamps or night lights in glass jars, normally used to light outdoor evening parties.

[80] In 1843, despite the missionaries' desire to believe that this practice did not exist in pre-Christian Hawaii, the missionary historian Sheldon Dibble had reluctantly confirmed the existence around 1700 of a tribe of about three thousand cannibals at Halemanu on Oahu (Sheldon Dibble, *A History of the Sandwich Islands* [Lahainaluna, Hawaiian Islands, 1843], pp. 133–135).

[81] Notes sometimes called silver certificates, backed by coin on special deposit in the Hawaiian treasury, had been authorized in 1859. Although historians are still uncertain whether they were issued in 1866 or 1867, this entry suggests that the notes were in fact in circulation in the former year.

[82] Laws passed in 1846 and 1859 had made United States coins the standard for Hawaii, but a large variety of foreign coins continued to fill the need for specie, among them the rial, or real, a Spanish and Mexican silver coin worth twelve and a half cents, the smallest coin the Hawaiians would willingly accept.

[83] "A kind of luxurious kneading or shampooing, and stretching and cracking

* Keep 2 pair in shoe shops—1 of 17^s & 1 of 5½

* In the single matter of importing ice, the steamer would make money. Worth $100 a ton Here worth $500 to $600 a ton here.[84]

Lignumvitae.

* Natives pay to get their poetry printed.

* Flying fish.

* Heated term, but there are but few flies in my room or hotel.

* Mosquitoes 2 kinds—day & night—1 black & white striped makes gray—night is little black fellow,—they leave befor daylight.

Liquor license $1000 a year—bonds to not keep open after 10 or before daylight—no recourse upon sailors—pay $3 duty on brandy & 10 per cent on wine. Rum business well cramped down—but few saloons notwithstanding great whaling depot.[85]

<M>Shanghier gets $3 for every man he recruits, & ten per cent

---

the joints, which served completely to renovate the system" (James Jackson Jarves, *History of the Hawaiian or Sandwich Islands* [London: Edward Moxon, 1843], p. 78) was originally of particular use in maintaining mobility in the gargantuan Hawaiian chiefs. Clemens attested to the efficacy of lomi-lomi on 4 May 1866, when he wrote his mother and sister that after a horse had kicked him across a ten-acre lot "a native rubbed and doctored me so well that I was able to stand on my feet in half an hour" (*MTL*, p. 105).

84 Ventures in importing ice—in 1852 from San Francisco, in 1853 from Sitka, Alaska, and in 1858 and 1859 from Boston—had not been successful, since too few Honolulu residents could afford the usual price of twenty-five cents a pound.

85 Acts passed in 1854 and 1862 had established an annual fee of $1,000, along with a bond of $1,000, for the licensing of retail liquor sales. Laws such as these were of little value in achieving the temperate community desired by the missionaries. Illegal production of liquor in the islands, as well as smuggling, would have defeated the temperance movement, even if there had not been a surfeit of dealers willing to operate in conformity with the licensing laws. In 1866 there were nine establishments licensed to retail liquor in Honolulu. Most of these called themselves hotels, but the designation was only technical, for "although a 'hotel' might offer lodging, more often it tendered nothing more than 'spirits'—then an overworked euphemism for hard liquor" (Richard A. Greer, *Downtown Profile: Honolulu A Century Ago* [Honolulu: Kamehameha Schools Press], 1966, p. 6).

of the sailor's advance ($40,) for Security. If the man isn't on board when the ship weighs anchor, Shanghier responsible <[-]> for the advanced money.

Sailor's Home—King gave the lot on condition Amer. <F>Sailor's Friend Soc w^{d} raise $5,000 within the year (55)—it was done—buildings & everything have cost $18,000—accommodates 40 men with bed & board all the time.[86]

Mrs Crabb foreman.

Bethel out back.[87]

Board for men, <is>& lodging, $5 week

For officers 6 "

Clerks & mech's of the town board at the officers' table.

* <M>Rode out this (22^{d}) morning, to <we> palace of late King Kam. IV, in Nuuana Valley—very fine grounds.

* Royal Tomb.

P.O. Regulations. Inter Island—2 cents ½ oz—5 when leaves <Is>Kingdom—3 cents U.S. & 2 for the ship. Thus single letter to US costs 10 cents.[88]

All postage must be pre-paid from *here* but not necessary to pay Hawaiian postage *from* U.S. here—no postal convention yet.[89]

P.O. Stamps very pretty. [#]

---

[86] Further conditions of the land grant by Kamehameha III for a Honolulu Sailor's Home were that no rum be sold on the premises, no "bad women" be kept there, and no gambling be allowed. The sailor's home officially opened on 1 September 1856 at an estimated total cost of $15,000.

[87] The Oahu Bethel Church, presided over by the Reverend Samuel C. Damon.

[88] The foreign postal rates had been established by Postmaster General David Kalakaua's Post Office Notice of 3 December 1864. Until 1 August 1859, when the domestic fee Mark Twain noted here was set, interisland mail had been transmitted without charge because of the missionaries' desire to encourage an educational exchange of letters between native correspondents.

[89] A mail contract signed on 30 July 1867 with the California, Oregon and Mexico Steamship Company, providing for twelve round trips per year for ten years between San Francisco and Honolulu, would be a prelude to the first formal postal treaty between the United States and the Hawaiian Kingdom, which was to go into effect on 1 July 1870.

* Gas Company died 10 yrs ago—stores don't keep open at night[90]

* No good livery horses—put em on ranch, Kanakas hire em out or ride em to death. Trick they played Wheelock by keeping their own blanket on sore-back horse. $7 a week. Brown bought one for $10. <[3]>50 cents for 2 bundles hay.

* Californians ought to come here twice a year to soothe down their harassing business cares.

* Board $8 & $10 a week—rooms $5 to $7, a week.—horses $1 to $2 a day.

* Not a toll-road in the Kingdom.

* Dr. Judd's, only house in the Hawaiian Kingdom that has got a chimney.

* Saw Kanaka woman catching fleas off a dog & eating them—she took a cat, but the cat was inclined to be quarrelsome—she suckled it at her own breast & then proceeded to prospect it for fleas.

* Saw dozen naked little girls bathing in brook in middle of town at noonday.

* But few Jews here & no Irish.

* French Padres.

Plenty water & bath-house to every dwelling—$25 a year. [#]

---

90 A Honolulu gas company had been chartered by a legislative act of 12 March 1859. According to a contemporary account, after a brief period when hotels and some other buildings were lighted with gas, "the resident manager of the Company, left for California, after mortgaging the works to parties here, for the purpose, as stated, of procuring necessary machinery and material. He never returned, and after a time, the enterprise was abandoned, entailing a considerable amount of loss on those who had gone to the expense of gas fittings for their houses" (Chauncey C. Bennett, *Honolulu Directory, and Historical Sketch of the Hawaiian or Sandwich Islands* [Honolulu: C. C. Bennett, 1869], p. 44). Despite the implication of chicanery, the account concluded curiously that the gas company's failure "was undoubtedly owing to the fact that the limited demand for gas was not commensurate with the outlay required to produce it."

* <Peo>Such a religious community where people go home from church 3 times a day to eat their meals.

2 Idols—(must visit them)

I've got a good horse, now—he ain't afraiid of a bale of hay.

Inquire about <Queen> La Reine. Ma, daugh^{r} of daughter of Gov. Young by D$^{r.}$ Rourke husband of her sister Fanny (in adultery)—adopted & educated.[91]

Capt. Tait[92]—60 Ch a day

Geo. Washington—aged <[-]>Va nego sailor Lord opens for him.

Hospital

4 Wards—capacity 132—32 in a ward—some <[-]> below
Portuguese idiot—victim of—
Shakes head time—hasn't spoken in 4 years.

Inverted bottles guard garden walks.

Prison & walls coral.

1000^{s} cats & nary snake.

Centipede.

Prostitutes (94) pay $5 a year license, & have to be examined every month & provided with certificate free from disease.[93] [#]

---

[91] Emma Naea Rooke, queen of Kamehameha IV, was the daughter of Fanny Kakelaokalani Young and granddaughter of John Young, who had achieved prominence as an aide to Kamehameha I. She was adopted in childhood by her maternal aunt, Grace Kamaikui Young, whose English husband, Dr. Thomas Charles Byde Rooke, had come to Hawaii in 1829, where he practiced medicine, held a number of government offices, and, according to an unsubstantiated rumor current at the time of Mark Twain's visit, fathered Emma Naea. Dr. Rooke's influence on Emma was great, and he has been held responsible for the English predilections which characterized her reign as queen.

[92] The following seven entries refer to a visit to the government prison in Honolulu.

[93] An "Act to Mitigate the Evils and Diseases Arising from Prostitution," passed

Have to take out a license ($10,) to have the Hulahula dance performed, & then if the girls dress for it in the usual manner, that is with no clothing worth mentioning, it must be conducted in strict privacy.[94]

Missionaries have busted out the national Saturday sports, pastimes & horse racing—also the 3 dance houses, within 2 years.[95]

If can see sky between the Pari or the adjacent mountain tops and the eternal masses of clouds that overhang that vicinity, it will be a pleasant, breezy day—the "trades" will blow.

A larkspur planted alongside any shrub here will protect the same from the prevailing blight.

This King ought to be grateful to the missionaries, because during all the years that the English & French were making trouble & creating complications & trying to get an excuse to sieze the islands, the wise counsels of these men saved Kamehamehas II, III & perhaps V from making any false step.[96] [#]

---

24 August 1860, required that prostitutes be registered, examined for disease at least every two weeks, and, if necessary, treated free of charge.

[94] The laws licensing the hula and restricting its performance to Honolulu, part of the Civil Code of 1859, were reportedly the product of Lot Kamehameha's (Kamehameha V) dismay at discovering that devotion to the dance had "demoralized the natives all through the country, and broke up all work" (R. A. Lyman, "Recollections of Kamehameha V," *Third Annual Report of the Hawaiian Historical Society* [1895]: 15–16).

[95] For the missionaries and some government officials dancing was as much of a menace as drinking. Throughout the 1850s unsuccessful attempts had been made to abolish the dance halls, which seemed responsible for the fornication and adultery which were perpetual embarrassments to Honolulu. Although a law restricting dance halls had been passed as recently as 1864, it was the decline of the whaling industry, and not this legislation, that was ending the dance hall era in Honolulu.

[96] Mark Twain does not overestimate the Hawaiian Kingdom's political indebtedness to American missionary advisers during most of the reign of Kamehameha II (20 May 1819 to 14 July 1824) and throughout the reign of Kamehameha III (6 June 1825 to 15 December 1854). Gerrit P. Judd was particularly useful in meeting challenges to Hawaiian sovereignty from England in 1843 and France in 1849. Missionary participation in government decreased considerably, however, during the reigns of Kamehameha IV and Kamehameha V, both of whom had been raised

Bishop received in '62 with great pomp.

Mrs. McFarlane's 2 boys riding on the hand-cart with the dead smallpox patients.[97]

Marshfield 2. P.M. March 25, 1866—Sunday—Mr. J. L. Lewis[98] —*Luau.*

Rev. Mr. Parker at great stone-church (native.) Native choirs—native girl played melodeon.

Reformed Catholic Church. Court religion.

Miss McF thought I was drunk because I talked so long.

Sunday, Mch 25 Luau at Marshfield—called at <Waikkiki> Waikiki, saw Mr. & Mrs Pratt Mrs <Do> Gov. Dominis & the Admiral of the Hawaiian Navy.[99]

Theory that a fresh water stream kills coral & <ma> keeps harbors clear.

Procession of 80 women, in white skirts, black bodies & tri-colored sashes, buried Thurston's child to-day.[100] [#]

---

under the repressive influence of the missionaries and felt a corresponding distaste for the principles of their teachers.

97 This incident, involving the children of Mrs. Henry MacFarlane, occurred during a major smallpox epidemic in the spring and summer of 1853. One of the boys, "young Henry MacFarlane," went along on the "notable equestrian excursion" to Diamond Head on Oahu, described in Sacramento *Daily Union* letters of 21 and 24 April 1866 (*MTH*, pp. 284–295). By December 1866 Henry MacFarlane had come to San Francisco, where Mark Twain found him working as "clerk at Wm. B. Cooke & Co's, Stationers, Montgomery Block, Montgomery street above Washington" (SLC to "Dear Miss Bella," 4 December 1866).

98 A Honolulu cooper, whose place of business was on King Street at the corner of Bethel Street. Marshfield was Lewis' residence at Waikiki.

99 There was no such official. Mark Twain may be referring to the person, probably Captain James Smith (see note 19), who in chapter 62 of *Roughing It* is portrayed as "the old Admiral" whose title "was the voluntary offering of a whole nation, and came direct from . . . the people of the Sandwich Islands."

100 Ed Hayden, five-year-old grandson of the Reverend and Mrs. Asa Thurston, who, along with his mother, Mary Hayden, and his uncle, the Reverend Thomas Thurston (see note 15), had come to Hawaii aboard the *Ajax*, died of croup on 24 March 1866 and was buried the following day.

Capt of one of M^c^Gee's[101] vessels dropped Warren[102] at certain point—M^c^Gee sent note by friend not to come—Warren sent immediately for explanation—which was returned instantly by letter, rather than let him *come* & get it.

M^c^Farlane told him Luther Severance wanted him postpone visit indef—would save him writing if he bring verbally. Place 26 miles fm here

Dr Wood[103] told him make himself at home—did—drank all brandy—ordered him get more—abused servants—found fault with horses—lost his purse & borrowed money—didn't want natives hunt for purse. [#]

---

101 Captain James Makee arrived in the Sandwich Islands in April 1843 to seek medical assistance after a murderous shipboard attack and remained to become one of Hawaii's leading merchants, shipowners, and planters. His Rose Ranch plantation at Ulupalakua on Maui, one of the showplaces of the Sandwich Islands and its most productive sugar plantation, was famed for its hospitality.

102 Before visiting the Sandwich Islands in the mid-1860s to gather seeds and farming information as the "accredited delegate" of the California State Agricultural Society, John Quincy Adams Warren had been connected with a number of agricultural publications as agent, editor, or publisher. His most significant labor had been as an agricultural correspondent, and his 1860 to 1862 letters to the *American Stock Journal* remain the best contemporary account of California farming. Although Warren succeeded in introducing a sheep-shearing machine to the Sandwich Islands, it was his boorish behavior rather than his agricultural competence which most impressed residents there. On 12 May 1866 the *Pacific Commercial Advertiser* would chide Warren about the startling Honolulu street scene in which he was brusquely dispossessed of his horse by the lady from whom he had purchased it with "an order for the value on the proprietors of the *American Flag*, in San Francisco, which they refused to pay." And on the same day the Honolulu paper carried a notice signed by the *American Flag's* publisher, which warned that Warren was "in no way connected as Agent or Correspondent, from and after this date." In September 1866, at the thirteenth annual fair of the California State Agricultural Society, which Mark Twain helped report for the Sacramento *Daily Union*, Warren would mount a gaudy display of his Hawaiian materials, including agricultural products, geological and aquatic curiosities, specimens of native insects, and life-size photographs of members of the Hawaiian court.

103 Dr. Robert W. Wood had come to the Sandwich Islands in 1839. For the next ten years he was physician at the United States Hospital for Seamen in Honolulu. In the late 1840s Wood became involved in sugar production which was to occupy him for more than twenty years. During this time he was instrumental in the introduction of improved methods of sugar cultivation and processing.

Staid 3 months at one house—owner left—he still staid a week—man sent him word to vacate premises.

Then he made a raid on the missionaries—remark made to missionary daughter 17 yrs old.

Agent for Cal State Ag Society—Cor. Am. Flag & various Ag papers.

Agent for various papers. Says he is going to write a book. Has got silk worm on the brain—got books full various kind leaves. Silk w on brain

Went & stole lot of seeds & a bamboo at <Inter> Ag. Bureau—made him bring latter back.

Laidies used to visit & welcome strange ladies—got fooled—have to have good recom. now.

Got *more* business on his hands—& don't keep any clerks & don't get any pay.

Aloha, Love, nui, great.

No word to express gratitude—can but lamely express virtue of any kind—prolific in epithets to express every degree & shade of vice & crime.

No word to express farewell—or good-bye.[104]

But give to me that good old word that comes from the heart Good-bye! you might translate that old song into Kanaka, to the last phrase, but there you would stick.

Is there any home?

All have a dozen mothers (friends)[105] and an expression signifying THE mother.[106] [#]

---

104 In this entry Mark Twain laments the lack of a distinct Hawaiian equivalent for each English expression, although these are all included among the many meanings of *aloha* (see note 71).

105 A reference to the Hawaiian foster relationship known as *hanai,* a sort of communal sharing of the responsibilities of parenthood.

106 Probably *luau'i makuahine,* meaning the "true mother."

Wail for joy & for sorrow with same noise.

Wash clothes well but beat them all to pieces.

The Bungalo Sam Brannan <won> won it from Shillaber—150 ft front—large colums[107]

Warren Sam Brannan's agent to repair Bungalo at cost $5,000.

None of the lineal <y>Young stock left but 2 daughters of a son of the old original Young.[108]

Capt. Adams—Scotsman—near 100—blind—been here 60 years[109] —with Sir Jno Moore at Corunna.[110]

If you don't know a man in Hon—call him Capt & ask him how many barrels he took last season—chances are he's a whaler.

Splendid Rainbow over the Pari

All classes splendid horsemen—raised in saddle. [#]

---

[107] On 15 November 1851, Sam Brannan, a prominent California pioneer and public figure, sometimes called "the first forty-niner," arrived in Hawaii aboard the clipper *Game-Cock* at the head of a filibustering expedition. It was Brannan's intention to convince Kamehameha III to place the kingdom in his hands and retire on an annuity. To house his followers Brannan purchased the Bungalow, a palatial coral-stone building on Richard Street built by Theodore Shillaber, a Honolulu merchant in the 1840s and later a merchant and landowner in San Francisco. After some ludicrous machinations, Brannan gave up his attempt to win control of the Sandwich Islands. He returned to San Francisco on 2 January 1852, to be greeted by the general scorn of that city.

[108] John Young, adviser to Kamehameha I, had six children by his two marriages to native women. Dowager Queen Emma, who was alive in 1866, was Young's grandchild by a daughter, not a son.

[109] Alexander Adams, born in Forfarshire, Scotland, in 1780, was a veteran of the Battle of Trafalgar and had also seen service with the British navy on the coasts of Spain and Portugal before coming to the Sandwich Islands in 1810. He became one of the most trusted members of the entourage of Kamehameha I, serving the king in civil as well as military capacities. Adams was captain of the royal ship *Kaahumanu* and in some sources is credited with creation of the Hawaiian flag during a voyage to Canton in 1817.

[110] In his letter in the Sacramento *Daily Union* on 25 October 1866, Mark Twain would parody "The Burial of Sir John Moore," Charles Wolfe's poetic tribute to the British lieutenant-general who died 16 January 1809 as a result of a wound in the famous battle at Corunna, Spain, during the Peninsular War with Napoleon's forces.

The female Pride of India tree bears a flower resembling the lilac, (sweet scented) about once a year, from which comes the seed by which the tree is propagated—the male blooms once in 7 years—tree is rapid growth

King out on his favorite white horse at night

No rowdies in Honolulu

King better executive officer that his late brother

Jennie McIntyre J S Walker[111] Eclipse[112]—30th.

Poi sure cure for whisky-bloats.

Combs on a stick & fish—squid mullet, &c in the market.

Raising the devil about the Ajax small pox patient—threatened to pull Sam Loller's house down.[113]

Sour Things—tamarinds (aggravated peanuts) & Chinese oranges.

Saturday as a gala day, no longer amounts to anything.

Balsam flowers

Takes one a good while to cramp & crowd & screw & diminish <his large notion> himself down to a conception of the smallness of this Island—this Kingdom—rides six or eight miles in any direction & here is the ocean bursting upon his view—seems as if he never will get the d—d island trimmed down as small as it really is.

Same way with planning a journey from Island to island on the map—sees the vast expanse of ocean between—thinks of talks about month-long drifting between 2 islands—& all at once notices

---

111 A partner in Walker, Allen & Co., "Importers and Commission Merchants—Dealers in General Merchandise, and Agents for the Sale of Island produce" (*Pacific Commercial Advertiser*, 21 April 1866).

112 A total eclipse of the moon occurred on 30 March 1866.

113 Sam Loller was proprietor of the Eureka Hotel & Restaurant on Hotel Street in Honolulu. No incidence of smallpox on either voyage of the *Ajax* has been discovered.

by latitude & longitude that the distance is insignificant—a mere degree—& then appreciates what had not struck him before—viz, that the long journeys speak of baffling winds & dreadful calms.

Low coral islands (Micronesia) little or no account for ag. purposes—but high volcanic first rate.

Shameful thrust at Rev. Wm Richards in Manly Hopkins (Consul General) book When he quit Missionary to help govern & get up the Domesday Book—says "Alas, ambition sometimes dwells beneath unstarched white cravats & suits of black alpaca."[114]

Also questions veracity of Americans in his preface.[115]

The American papers 600 each—the native papers 3,000 each—about 1,500 paid for—they don't make a cent—government helps foot bills. [#]

---

[114] William Richards, a member of the Second Company of American missionaries, arrived in Honolulu in 1823. He left the mission in 1838 at an urgent request that he become confidential adviser to Kamehameha III. Richards' immediate task was to educate the king and chiefs in the methods of government, with particular emphasis on the definition of their rights in dealing with foreigners. He later accepted diplomatic responsibilities and, for a short period that ended with his death in 1847, also held the office of minister of public instruction. The remark which Mark Twain quoted here came in the conclusion to a brief but biting portrayal of Richards in *Hawaii: The Past, Present, and Future of Its Island-Kingdom* (London: Longman, Green, Longman, and Roberts, 1862, p. 242) by Manley Hopkins, Hawaiian consul general in London, an exponent of Anglican church activities in Hawaii and an acerbic critic of the secular pursuits of the American missionaries. Hopkins' disparagement of Richards' abilities and motives had brought protest from Hawaii, particularly from the Reverend Samuel C. Damon in his review of the book in *The Friend* of 1 November 1862. Its second edition (London: Longmans, Green, and Co., 1866) may have been causing new concern at the time of Mark Twain's visit since, despite a "spirit of conciliation" promised in his preface, Hopkins had reproduced almost verbatim the text of his commentary upon Richards. Modern historical opinion has supported Richards' record of selfless devotion to the Hawaiian people, though acknowledging that his chief qualification for the post of king's adviser was his availability.

[115] In the preface to the first edition of his book Hopkins qualified a statement of indebtedness to James Jackson Jarves' *History of the Hawaiian Islands*, 3d. ed. (Honolulu: C. E. Hitchcock, 1847) with the comment that "a little circumspection is, of course, required in accepting the views of an American citizen on points wherein other nations are concerned" (Hopkins, *Hawaii*, 1862, p. xvi).

Soft voices of native girls.—liquid, free, joyous laughter.

Absence of news & carelessness regarding it—brig outside.—arrival from N. London.

Goin' to windward

Kanakas *will* have horses & saddles, & the women *will* fornicate—2 strong characteristics of this people.

Old style humming singing of Kanaka singing at Burgess'.[116]

W. C. Parke Marshal of Kingdom.[117] Jail.

Native lends his short, strong wooden pipe, fills it, & then with excess of hospitality lights it for you.

Natural Bob-tail cats.[118]

Bungalo

I wish Sherman had marched through Alabama

Darkest contry in world when moon don't shine.

<King> David Malo wrote Biography Kam. I, & legends—left it <with> at Lahaina for Prof Andrews—a princess stole it[119]—the King has got it won't give it up, because Royal family was down on Malo, & because Kam I did some hard things & they dont want them known.

Boo-hoo fever.[120] [#]

[116] Ed Burgess, "Honolulu's pioneer restaurateur" (Greer, *Downtown Profile*, p. 6), was proprietor of a saloon on Fort Street in 1866.

[117] William Cooper Parke, once a Honolulu cabinetmaker, had been commissioned marshal of the Hawaiian Islands in 1850, a position he held for thirty-four years. As marshal, Parke was responsible for the maintenance of public order, which duty he discharged by organizing and administering a Hawaiian police force.

[118] This variety of cat was brought to Oahu around 1850 by a visiting ship's captain. The occasion for his gift is described in Notebook 5, note 108.

[119] Harieta Nahienaena, daughter of Kamehameha I, was reportedly one of the last people to have seen Malo's book.

[120] Probably a corruption of *poo-hu-ai*, meaning "a pain; a disease; the headache" (Andrews, *Dictionary of the Hawaiian Language*).

Kanaka painted branch coral red & sold it.

Brown can't see those "trades"—they haven't

Boo-hoo—Feebleness, lassitude, indifference, no appetite, slight nausea, head & neck ache, achy all over.

It acclimates the patient—& don't hurt him—about home & sea-sickness—acclimates you—

<½ people>

All who have to buy wish Ajax would go—those who sell want her to stay.

Take <M>Spanish pistareens, worth 16 cts, for a quarter, & refuse a dime—

Go to Hilo, see Mr. Porter—use Dunn's[121] name as being in Tahiti in 54—go to Kileau (Vol) by advice of Porter)—Coming back get Capt let me ashore at Lahaina—there see Mr Mason[122]—use Dunn's name—go to Waialuka & surrounding plantations & thence to Makee's[123]—come back to Lahaina & go to Lainai & see Gibson's Mormons[124]—thence back to Lahaina & thence to Molokai by boat—thence back to Lahaina—then to Holulu—thence around Oahu—thence to Kauai—circuit & back to Honlula—(Hoffslacker on Kauia)—On Hawaii and Maui spend good deal time & make many inquiries.[125]

Sickness China

---

121 H. D. Dunn had come to Hawaii on the first trip of the *Ajax* and stayed from 27 January to 4 April 1866 to write a series of travel letters for the San Francisco *Bulletin*.

122 The Reverend George Mason, one of Bishop Thomas N. Staley's Anglican subordinates, resided at Lahaina, Maui.

123 James Makee's Rose Ranch at Ulupalakua, Maui. Mark Twain may have been directed there by Charles Warren Stoddard. Stoddard had stayed at Rose Ranch in 1864 while visiting with his sister, who was married to James Makee's son Parker.

124 The vestiges of the original Mormon settlement on Lanai (see note 8).

125 Mark Twain did not quite realize this ambitious itinerary. The actual sequence of his travels is discussed at length in the headnote to Notebook 5.

Mai pake—
China sickness[126]

O – K – <*L*>*M – H – L – M –*

April 3^{d}—[127]

Eliiboe[128]
Silver sheer leaf—

Prin Victoria
Mrs. Bishop
Prince William
David Kalu
Queen Emma's family.

Kammy's bones hidden <luc> at his own request, to keep them from making fish hooks of them—a superstition that hooks made of the bones of a great Chief would concentrate the fish.

War cloaks of the King K I's great grand father—of red black & yellow feathers.

Spear of giant 9 feet high.—700 years ago—know before 1500

Singing of natives very round & soft—has no sound of S in it.

Fetch the hearse we're going to take a drink. [#]

---

126 The incidence of leprosy in the Hawaiian Islands is discussed in Notebook 5, note 32.

127 On this date Clemens wrote his mother and sister:

> I went with the American Minister [James McBride] and took dinner this evening with the King's Grand Chamberlain [David Kalakaua, who would reign as King of the Hawaiian Islands from 12 February 1874 until 20 January 1891], who is related to the royal family, and although darker than a mulatto, he has an excellent English education and in manners is an accomplished gentleman. The dinner was as ceremonious as any I ever attended in California—five regular courses, and five kinds of wine and one of brandy. He is to call for me in the morning with his carriage, and we will visit the King at the palace. (*MTL*, p. 104)

Mark Twain in fact visited Iolani Palace on 4 April 1866, as evidenced by his signature in the guest register, along with that of *Ajax* purser Ormsby Hite.

128 This entry is so nearly illegible it may have been made on horseback. Mark Twain here refers to *ali'ipoe,* the Hawaiian name for canna.

Reciting of the native women in farewell to Mrs. Bishop, who is a chiefess, & only 3 removes from the throne.[129]

Islands $<100,000>150,000 in debt—holders wont give up the bonds, paying 9 p. ct.—treasury full money—have to devise ways to spend it could pay in 2 or 3 years

Perfect Gov't in miniature.

US. Won't recognize—Judge Allen remained Washington a year[130]

McBride Minister, ranks all other envoys here.[131]

H. I. have Chargé d'affairs in N. Y & London.

Have treaty of amity & commerce with U S.[132] but Mason Slidell & Benjamin killed a better one in 1856.—Seward & Fessenden favored Reciprocity.

King V parts hair in middle.

Turn thermometer upside down—make cool weather.

Deformed Catholic

Gallagher, Irish New Yorker, half-witted or crazy.[133]

American citizens gave carriage to Queen Emma, & she gave it to Bishop Staleys wife—Rough. She says her chiern never go into the street but the other chrn swear at them. [#]

---

129 High chiefess Bernice Pauahi and her husband, Charles R. Bishop, left Honolulu for San Francisco on board the *Ajax* on 4 April 1866.

130 Elisha Allen made two extended stays in Washington, in 1856/1857 in an attempt to influence passage of a reciprocity treaty, and in 1864/1865 again on behalf of reciprocity and to secure United States participation with Britain and France in a guarantee of Hawaiian independence. On neither occasion was Allen able to achieve the Hawaiian government's objectives.

131 Although the United States had raised the rank of its envoy to minister resident (see note 12), the French and English diplomatic representatives in Hawaii continued to hold the lesser title of commissioner.

132 The treaty signed on 20 December 1849, which established the general terms of United States–Hawaii relations until annexation. For a discussion of reciprocity, see Notebook 5, note 51.

133 The Reverend Peyton Gallagher, an American Episcopal assistant to the pastor of the Hawaiian Reformed Catholic Church in Honolulu.

The rose is red,
The violet is blue
The pink is pretty
And so—are *you.*[134]

Easily tell direction of trade wind here (toward sea) by bend of trees in Muana Valley[135]—wind or no wind they always seem in a storm

Judd's only house in Kingdom with a chimney—climate's indication.

Bake Houses

Harris Minister Finance & Acting Atty Gen.

Well enough for old folks to rise early, because done so many mean things all their lives cant sleep anyhow.

No native beggars.

King wouldn't receive Dr Anderson, Secy of Board of Missions.[136]

D^r. Judd, Prince Lott & late King traveling—went late to dinner—no places—Capt provided extra table.

Charybdis—officers said never saw anything like this service in Englnd.

Bishop received in carriage—old missionaries came on foot. [#]

---

134 Mark Twain squeezed in "are" after the dash and underlined "you." The rest of this rhyme is in another hand.

135 Mark Twain meant Nuuanu Valley on Oahu, site of Gerrit P. Judd's home.

136 The Reverend Rufus Anderson, foreign secretary of the American Board of Commissioners for Foreign Missions, had been in Hawaii in 1863 to assist in the development of a program to create an independent native church organization. Although not granted a private audience with Kamehameha IV, Anderson claimed that despite his prejudice against Americans the king was courteous to him personally and invited him to the public reception of the American minister resident, "where his attentions were all that could have been expected" (Rufus Anderson, *The Hawaiian Islands: Their Progress and Condition Under Missionary Labors,* 3d. ed. [Boston: Gould and Lincoln, 1865], p. 326).

Candles <t>done away with—also transparencies.

Repeated insults of English—*one* American—
Paulet
Capt. <Hammond> Hannam—King's carriage & house in palace yard—ran off with natives—2 ships chased—wouldn't receive Parke—shored natives on wnd side Island.[137]

More missionaries & more row made about saving these 60,000 people than would take to convert hell itself.

Americans have given religion, freedom, education, written language & Bible—

England & France have given insults.

Wouldn't pray for president before death—does now.

Russian vessel fired guns outside reef for Richmond taken—couldn't raise flags in harbor.

T. N. Hon—Call him Tom Honolulu.[138]

Minsters came armed aganst natives. canibals

Sold at auction

Yankee term of reproach—Yankee invention—rocky chairs.

Ride in Queen Emma's Carrige

Paid for washing in tobacco & brandy. [#]

---

[137] In November 1865, in violation of a law prohibiting the removal of natives, Thomas B. Hanham, captain and owner of the British yacht *Themis,* attempted to carry off a half-white woman, apparently on a dare from Minister of the Interior F. W. Hutchinson. A slapstick pursuit mounted by Marshal W. C. Parke, first aboard a Honolulu tug and then on board a makeshift gunboat, failed to apprehend Hanham, who nevertheless decided to relinquish the woman and landed her, as well as a half-caste man he also had with him, at Waialua, Oahu.

[138] Evidently this is Mark Twain's attempt at a fictional name for Bishop Thomas N. Staley. Letters by Staley were sometimes published in the Honolulu newspapers over the signature "T. N. Honolulu."

Severance[139] sold & Capt. Luce[140] took them to the auction—arms.

Bishop of Wialua—Mr. S. not at home—the Lord B in study

English Women wore mourning—deep—3 months—then white, trimmed with black ribands—men mourning also, for IV.[141]

Mattrass jackass feathers.

Fear reptiles in Bunk on Mary Ellen.

Rainbows every day at Honlulu.

Adultery—each $30 fine now.

July 4, 1866[142]—Honolulu—went to ball <—da> 8.30 PM—danced till 12.30—went home w^h^ MC[143]—stopped at Gen. Van Valkenburgh's room & talked with him & Mr. Burlingame, Col. Rumsey[144] & Ed. Burlingame until 3 AM 5th.—[145]

Kanaka Lexicon[146]

Walk in—Helemi moloko.

What's your name?

---

139 Henry Severance, a Honolulu auctioneer.

140 George H. Luce had been a Honolulu port pilot in the 1850s and in 1866 was road supervisor and tax collector for the District of Honolulu.

141 Kamehameha IV died 30 November 1863.

142 This entry, added in black ink on a blank page at the end of Notebook 6, which otherwise was used only in March and April, properly corresponds to the period covered by Notebook 5. Its placement here indicates Mark Twain's own confusion about the sequence of his Hawaiian notebooks.

143 James McBride, outgoing American minister resident.

144 Brevet Lieutenant Colonel William Rumsey, a Civil War veteran, was nephew and secretary to General Robert B. Van Valkenburgh, minister resident to Japan.

145 Mark Twain wrote to Will Bowen on 25 August 1866: "While I was there, the American Ministers to China & Japan——Mr. Burlingame & Gen. Van Valkenburg came along, & we just made Honolulu howl. I only got tight once, though. I know better than to get tight oftener than once in 3 months. It sets a man back in the esteem of people whose opinions are worth having" (TS in MTP).

146 The heading and first five phrases of this lexicon, apparently the beginning of

Wyko enoa.
Where do you live?
Mah-haerko hahlee.
How old are you?
Ah-heo-mah-ke-hekee.
How many brothers & sisters have you got?
Ah-heo-kaekoa-heaua-ah-kakunani.
Thy—kou
Who?—Owai—Who?—Owai
name inoa
Who art thou? Owai oe?
Who is that? Owai kela?
Who are they?—Owai lakou?
What is thy name? Owai kou inoa?
  " " his (or her) name) Owai kona inoa?
From whence came you? Maihea mai oe i hele mai nei?
Where are you going?—E hele ana oe mahea
What is this? Heaha keia mea?
What is that? Heaha kela mea?
This?—Keia—That, kela
What, heahu—thing, mea.
Kona, its.
Heaha kona inoa.
Is he gone?—Ua hala kela?
At what time did he go?—I ka wa hea kona hela ana?
<How>
Can you swim?—E hiki ia oe ka au?
How much do I owe you? Pehea ka nui o kuu aie ia oe?

---

a personal phonetic glossary Mark Twain intended to expand gradually while traveling in Hawaii, appear upside-down on the last page of this notebook. They were probably inscribed around the middle of March, when Mark Twain began using the notebook from the front for preliminary notes about Hawaii. The balance of the lexicon, copied or extrapolated from the small phrase book mentioned earlier (note 29), appears in normal position on the same page and on the recto of the back flyleaf and was added later.

What shall we 2 do? Heaha ka kaua e hana'i?
How old is your sister? Ehia na makahiki o kou kaikuwahine?
Aole—don't know

1 —page <4>, <5>, <10>, <25>, <26>, 27, 28, 32, 33, 34, 35, 37, 38, 42, 49, 51, 72,
2 — — 4, 6, 29, 30, 40, 51,
3 — — 13, 33, 38, 39, 41, 42, 44, 51, 52, 84,
4 — — 28, 33,
5 — — 9,[147]

Algeroba
fine foliage[148] [#]

---

[147] This system of numbers, 1 through 5, enclosed in symbols in the manuscript notebook (see the accompanying illustration), is keyed to entries on the first 103 pages, which Mark Twain numbered (through p. 220.7). The table is written across the top of the verso of the back flyleaf onto the top of the back endpaper. It constitutes Mark Twain's preliminary outline for his first five Sacramento *Daily Union* letters. It was made in late March or early April, when, shortly before setting out for Maui, he was almost certainly preparing an initial group of seven letters, all dated in March, for dispatch on the *Ajax*, which left Honolulu on 4 April and arrived in San Francisco on 15 April, one day prior to the appearance of his first letter in the Sacramento *Daily Union*. The correspondence between this schematic version and the finished letters is, however, a rough one. Some of the entries marked for inclusion in the first letter were not used at all, while others were incorporated into the second when Mark Twain decided to devote two letters to events of the *Ajax* voyage. Of the entries here indicated for inclusion in the second letter, those actually used were displaced to the third, and most of those intended for the third were reserved for the fourth, after which the outline was abandoned. (See note 3 for a discussion of the asterisks on most of the numbered entries.)

[148] In his fifth letter to the Sacramento *Daily Union*, published on 20 April, Mark Twain described the Honolulu algarroba, or carob tree, commenting that "my spelling is guesswork" (*MTH*, p. 279). The entry is written on the back of the flyleaf.

25
20
___
500

Boy dangled the worm in the tasse, & dit, G d yr ame, you not tkl mon <[-]> again[149]

J. Q. A. Warren is in here.[150]

---

[149] Written on the back endpaper with the notebook upside-down.
[150] Written on the back cover.

VII

"A Doomed Voyage"

(December 1866–January 1867)

ON 15 DECEMBER 1866, Mark Twain sailed from San Francisco on the North American Steamship Company's "opposition" steamer *America*, bound for New York via Nicaragua, "leaving more friends behind me than any newspaper man that ever sailed out of the Golden Gate" (SLC to "Dear Folks," *MTBus*, p. 89). Notebook 7 is his record of this journey. It is perhaps the most circumscribed of the early notebooks, covering less than a month in time and limited to the incidents of an itinerary that allowed little room for independent activity. Nevertheless, Notebook 7 has an obscure and difficult chronology which is complicated throughout by Clemens' habit of inserting retrospective notes. *Mark Twain's Travels with Mr. Brown* (New York: Alfred A. Knopf, 1940), edited by Franklin Walker and G. Ezra Dane, gathers Mark Twain's letters to the *Alta California* to provide an orderly chronological account of the journey, which helps illuminate Clemens' chaotic notebook.

To a great degree the difficulties presented by Notebook 7 reflect the complex voyage from San Francisco to New York. The Nicaragua passage, controlled by the North American Steamship Company, was accomplished by a combination of ocean, land, river, and lake conveyances. The *America*, under the command of Edgar Wakeman, completed only the first leg of the voyage, bringing Clemens to the port of San Juan del Sur on the Pacific coast of Nicaragua on 28 December 1866. Here there was a delay occasioned by a report of cholera on the Isthmus, an ominous forecast of the dangers that lay ahead. The disease had broken out among a party of six hundred passengers from New York, half of them soldiers, who had been stranded at San Juan del Sur for two weeks awaiting the *America.* They had arrived there too late to make their scheduled connection for California partly because their ship from New York, the North American Steamship Company's *San Francisco,* became disabled near Virginia and had to put into port to transfer them to another vessel. Clemens recorded their distress in his notebook (see pp. 258 and 296–297) and was no doubt apprehensive that the *San Francisco,* with so recent a record of poor performance was to convey the *America's* four hundred passengers to New York. In fact, the routine discomforts of travel in such numbers—registered in Notebook 7 in Mark Twain's many complaints of second-cabin passengers' impositions—were to be exacerbated aboard the *San Francisco* by three mechanical failures while cholera spread among the passengers.

On 29 December, leaving the stranded travelers to board the *America,* Clemens and the other disembarked passengers, distributed among carriages or mounted on horses and mules, began the "twelve-mile journey of three hours and a half, over a hard, level, beautiful road" (*MTTB,* p. 40) to Virgin Bay and the shores of Lake Nicaragua, where they boarded a steamer. After an afternoon and a night on the lake steamer they arrived at Fort San Carlos on the San Juan River. There at about 4 A.M. on 30 December they boarded "a long, double-decked shell of a stern-wheel boat, without a berth or a bulkhead in her—wide open, nothing to obstruct your view except the slender stanchions that supported the roof" and "started down the broad and beautiful river in the gray dawn of the balmy summer morning" (*MTTB,* p. 47). At Castillo, where they had to go ashore to bypass dangerous rapids on foot and change to another stern-wheel steamer, the *Cora,* Clemens and his companions stopped for a lunch of fruit, eggs, bread, and coffee. Here and throughout the river segment of the trip Mark Twain's notes reflect his attention to the topography of Nicaragua. Recalling perhaps the fine response to his romantic word-portraits of Hawaii on his recent California-Nevada lecture tour, he composed lengthy descriptions of the physical features of Nicaragua, which he later incorporated into his *Alta California* letters.

After a night "tied up at the bank within 30 miles of Greytown" (*MTTB*, p. 53), the *Cora* arrived at the coast on 31 December. Clemens spent the night ashore in Greytown and began the new year "in the midst of a heavy sea and a drenching rain," as the passengers bound for New York were shuttled by small boat to the *San Francisco*. The *San Francisco* had been at sea only about a day when, on 2 January 1867, Clemens noted, "Two cases of cholera reported in the steerage to-day." At this point Notebook 7 becomes the log of a desperate race against a spreading epidemic, first to Key West, where the *San Francisco* stopped for provisions and fuel on 6 January 1867, and then to New York, where it finally made port on 12 January after a harrowing ten days.

In addition to the complexities of the trip, it is because Notebook 7 is a record made by Clemens while afflicted by an undetermined illness and captive to fearful surroundings that this journal makes unusual demands on the patience of a reader. The effect of the developing epidemic on board the *San Francisco* is evident in the increasing morbidity of Clemens' notes after the departure from Greytown. "All levity has ceased," he wrote at one point, and indeed there was no renewal of the foolish deck games that had been popular aboard the *America*. By 5 January, when six people were ill and the ship seemed a "floating hospital," Clemens' preoccupation with his own chances of surviving and his pity and compassion for the dead and dying dominate the notebook. He sought distraction in Victor Hugo's *Toilers of the Sea* and in an attempted burlesque of that book, but he soon gave up both the reading and the satire. Other entries are less sustained than in the portion of the notebook used during the thirteen days aboard the *America*. There Clemens had transcribed entire anecdotes told by Ned Wakeman. He may originally have intended to write his *Alta* letters as he went, but during the whole trip he finished only one letter, which he sent back to San Francisco on the *America*. The six letters which complete his account of the journey did not begin to be published until more than a month after his arrival in New York, two appearing in late February, three in mid-March, and one at the end of that month. Upon arriving in New York on 12 January, Clemens telegraphed the bare details of the cholera-shadowed voyage to the *Alta*, but San Francisco readers had to wait until March for the full version. Clemens was determined to get full value from all of the events of the passage from San Francisco, the happy ones as well as the tragic. In few other instances is there so prolonged and direct a correspondence between the raw material of a notebook and its final literary expression.

Notebook 7 provides other evidence of Clemens' developing conception of himself as a professional writer. He was careful to preserve the moments of retrospection that were his characteristic response to the boredom inevitable on any voyage. Sometimes such notes are related to past incidents of the journey, but often they recall events from earlier periods, including a significant number that would be incorporated in *Roughing It*. Characters in Notebook 7 were to reappear regularly in Mark Twain's writings. He continued to employ Brown, the vernacular figure frequently present in Notebooks 5 and 6, and he introduced the Bore, a fellow passenger of persistent foolishness, who would figure in various guises in later travel accounts. More than anything else, however, it is Mark Twain's record of Captain Edgar Wakeman's manner and flamboyant anecdotal style that gives this notebook artistic substance.

Wakeman's place in Mark Twain's imagination is evident not only in the recurrent notes about him in this and succeeding notebooks, but also in his numerous appearances in Mark Twain's fiction. The first is the Captain Waxman of the *Alta California* letters, but Mark Twain also accurately portrayed Wakeman in 1872 as Captain Ned Blakely in chapter 50 of *Roughing It* and in 1877 as Captain Hurricane Jones in "Some Rambling Notes of an Idle Excursion." Other treatments of Wakeman were less successful. In 1868 Mark Twain began "Captain Stormfield's Visit to Heaven," based on a dream Wakeman recounted to him when the two met again during Mark Twain's return voyage to California that year. Mark Twain continued to work on this piece in the seventies, in 1881, and was still engaged by it in the early 1900s, finally publishing it as an "Extract from Captain Stormfield's Visit to Heaven" in *Harper's Magazine* in December 1907 and January 1908 and in book form in October 1909. In 1905 he worked on a manuscript he called "The Refuge of the Derelicts" about an aged Admiral Stormfield, who runs a haven for "Life's failures. Shipwrecks. Derelicts, old and battered and broken, that wander the ocean of life lonely and forlorn" (*FM*, p. 186). Mark Twain claimed that this manuscript concerned "an ancient admiral, who is Captain Ned Wakefield under a borrowed name" (AD, 30 August 1906). The composite name *Wakefield* was a significant slip, for although distance in time led Clemens to believe he was again portraying Wakeman, in none of the Stormfield pieces could he recapture Wakeman's idiom and idiosyncrasies. He revived Wakeman's character only in small measure, and even that by assertion rather than art.

Except for the brief meeting in 1868, Clemens never saw Wakeman again, although he heard about him on several occasions. In 1872 Mark Twain was solicited to write an appeal for assistance to relieve the Wakeman family, which was in financial trouble and in danger of losing its home. On 3 December of that year he responded with a letter calling upon Wakeman's "old friends on the Pacific Coast" to "take the old mariner's case in hand . . . and do by him as he would surely do by them were their cases reversed," which was published in the *Alta California* on 14 December 1872. Although Mark Twain was not listed among the contributors to the Wakeman fund, on 19 January 1873, Mrs. Wakeman wrote to thank him "for the kindness which prompted you in sending your timely letter to the *Alta.* Our home is once more our own, and we feel the kind and prompt assistance extended by the Capt's. California friends, is to be attributed to that letter." Clemens later recalled that the need for his aid had been occasioned by Wakeman's death and that the sum proposed for the relief of the family was raised "in an hour" (AD, 29 August 1906). In fact, this was not the case. The $4,750 necessary to pay the mortgage on the Wakeman home had been raised only after several weeks and a second appeal, this time not directly involving Mark Twain, although alluding to his *Alta* letter. Nor had Wakeman died. He had, however, suffered a paralyzing stroke that made it impossible for him to work. Mark Twain's mistaken recollection that Wakeman died in 1872 was coupled with a curious failure to recall a last pathetic appeal. On 12 February 1874 he received a request from the captain, then only a little more than a year from death, for "about ten days with you" to discuss collaboration on a biography "full of the most remarkable incidents thrilling adventures both on the Sea and Land" which "When Clothed by your able and incomparable Pen. in Such Brilliant Robes that the readers will be unable to Judge the difference between facts and fiction . . . will have a Big Sale." Don't "take Hold of any other Book unt[il] you have done With Mine . . . I want you and your [memor]y to write my Life so I Shall Die Contented," Wakeman entreated, but Clemens was already occupied with lecture commitments and a number of literary projects. Consequently, on 18 March 1874 he informed his brother Orion:

> I have written him that *you* will edit his book & help him share the profits, & I will write the introduction & find a publisher.

There is no indication that either Orion Clemens or Wakeman seriously considered this offer. Several months later, while traveling to Panama, the Reverend Joseph Twichell discovered Wakeman among his fellow passengers. On 22 August 1874 Twichell wrote Mark Twain that Wakeman "had a good deal to say about your books which he admires enthusiastically":

> By and by he told me of his having written to ask you to write up his career, and expressed himself as much disappointed that you declined the job. And, really, I was sorry myself that you had to refuse him. 'Twould have done him so much good to have you for his chronicler.

Twichell thought Wakeman "a titanic commentator on the old Testament" and Mark Twain later used his report of Wakeman's "adventure of Isaac with the prophets of Baal" in "Some Rambling Notes of an Idle Excursion." Wakeman's own adventures, finally edited by his daughter, appeared in 1878 as *The Log of an Ancient Mariner* (San Francisco: A. L. Bancroft & Co.). But Mark Twain's refusal to work with Wakeman cannot be attributed to a lack of belief in the literary value of Wakeman's character and anecdotes. For Notebook 7, a writer's notebook in the fullest, most immediate sense, provides primary evidence of Mark Twain's intention to use Wakeman and Wakeman's "most remarkable incidents thrilling adventures" as literary subjects long before he was invited to do so by the captain himself.

Notebook 7, used between 15 December 1866 and 12 January 1867, now contains 214 pages, 38 of them blank. The pages measure 6⁹⁄₁₆ by 4 inches (16.7 by 10.2 centimeters), and their edges are tinted blue; otherwise the book is identical in design and format to Notebook 5. All the gatherings have come loose from the binding, and many single leaves have come loose from the gatherings. Entries are in pencil with occasional revisions in various inks. Use marks in blue ink and in pencil, probably Paine's, appear throughout the notebook; Clemens drew wavy lines in brown ink through some entries toward the end of the notebook to indicate use. There are several pencil entries on the flyleaves and endpapers and a single entry in ink on the front cover. Paine, or possibly Clemens, wrote the date "1866" on the front cover in ink.

San Francisco, Cal, to
New York,
via
San Juan & Greytown—
Isthmus.[1]

* Chinese send dead home[2]

* Have no fear of death & suicide is common, because belive soul flies at once to China

Kin[d][3]

A little

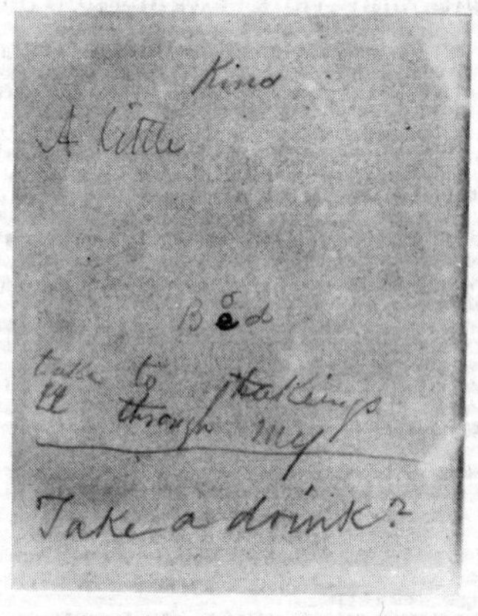

o
Bed

take to <[m]>takings
<u>U through my

Take a drink? [#]

---

[1] This entry was written lengthwise on the front cover of the notebook. The date "1866" was also added to the front cover, probably by Paine, but perhaps by Clemens.

[2] Mark Twain amplified this entry, written on the front endpaper, in an extended passage in chapter 54 of *Roughing It*.

[3] The words in the illustration are written on the front flyleaf, upside-down in relation to the entries that precede and follow them. The passage, here reduced to half size, includes three rebuses, which may be read "A little more than kin, and less than kind," "a little darkey in bed with nothing over it," and—despite false starts and one wrong word—"You undertake to overthrow my undertakings." The last line, which does not seem to be a rebus, may refer to Mark Twain's abstinence aboard the *America*, occasioned by the unidentified illness mentioned recurrently in this notebook.

Departure fm S.f.

Sailed from San Francisco in Opposition steamer America, Capt. Wakeman, at noon, 15th Dec. 1866.[4]

Pleasant, sunny day, hills brightly clad with green grass and shrubbery.

Runaway Match—boarded by irate father & bogus policeman—repulsed by passengers—love victorious.

First night great tempest—the greatest seen on this coast for many years—though, occupying an outside berth on upper deck it yet did not seem so rough to us as it did to those below, & we remain in bed all night, while the other passengers, realizing the great danger all got up & dressed.

The ship was down two much by the head & just dogged fought the seas, instead of climbing over them.

Nearly everybody seasick. Happily I escaped—had something worse. Lay in bed, 16th & rec'd passengers' reports.[5]

A sea that broke over the ship about midnight carried away twenty feet of the bulwarks forward, & the forward cabin was drenched with water & the steerage fairly flooded <&>

a case of <w> claret *floated*, in a state room in the forward cabin<. [¶]S>—then the water must have been 6 inches deep—if a box of claret would float or wash at all.

A man's boots were washed to far end of room.

Various things were afloat.

---

[4] This is the first entry in the body of the notebook. The *America* belonged to the North American Steamship Company and made connection for New York in Nicaragua. It ran in opposition to the steamers of the older Pacific Mail Steamship Company, which followed the Panama route.

[5] In the *Alta California* (*MTTB*, pp. 15–17) Mark Twain presented an account of this storm as if from personal observation. Although he avoided public mention of his lingering and mysterious illness, apparently contracted in late October 1866 while lecturing in Nevada, it was not so personal as to require concealment. On 4 December 1866, he had written "Dear Miss Bella," an acquaintance he had made the previous summer during his journey from Honolulu to San Francisco, that he had "been intending to call—but I am still unwell & take no pleasure in going out. I leave for New York in the Opposition steamer of the 15th inst., & I do hope I shall be well by that time."

Must have been *flooded* in steerage.

They *prepared the boats* for emergencies.

Old ship Capt of 28 yrs experience (is the old Capt *always* on hand?) said he had never seen the equal of this storm. He instructed a friend to stay by him till all but the ship's officers were adrift, & he & they would make a raft—"curse the boats" in such a sea." (& such bd lot passen)

Men were praying all about the cabin on their knees. <W>Brown[6] went to one & said—"What's matter?" & he said "O, don't *talk* to me—Oh my!"

Passenger said he had served 14 yrs at sea—but considered his time was come now <—still, went about> —still, said "if anybody can save her its old Wakeman."

I perceive by these things that we might have gone to the bottom unaware that we were in danger—why the Ajax[7] cut up worse in a dead calm.

Capt W. said last night's was heaviest storm he had ever experienced on this coast. in 3 years.

Man said every single soul—officers, servants & all—under the ship's pay, were on *active* duty most of the night & everywhere, on deck or below, regardless of station, in books.

Sunday 16—This is a long, long night. I occupy lower berth & read & smoke by a ship's lantern borrowed from <s>the steward (I won the middle berth, but gave it to Smith[8] because he is seasick, & we have piled our apples, limes, wines, books & small traps in the upper one.)

---

[6] There were two passengers aboard the *America* whose surnames were Brown and one named Brown Bryant. Although they could have furnished few general characteristics for Mark Twain's fictional companion, whose personality had been well established in the Sacramento *Union* letters from Hawaii, they may have provided some of the ludicrous behavior attributed to him on this trip. The cancellation here suggests that Mark Twain is crediting his Mr. Brown with a remark made by a passenger other than one of the real Browns aboard.

[7] The California Steam Navigation Company ship on which Mark Twain traveled to Hawaii in March 1866.

[8] In this case, not a fictional name. Mark Twain's cabin partner was P. P. Smith.

I don't know what time it is—my watch has run down,—I think it is 7 bells in the 3^{d} watch, but I am not certain, the wind may have blown <it> away one tap of the bell—we hear it very faintly away up here, anyway.

"People beginning to die off fresh in Islands with influenza—guess civilization & gospel taking new start—Brown.[9]

Capt W—Riding in a carrage! Belay! Don't talk to me about riding in a carrage—I got enough of that, with Hill—in Newburyport, twenty years <g>ago, now, I reckon.

We went to the livery concern—it was Sunday morning & I was stove in, wore out, crippled up, with all the different kinds of rheumatics you can find in the medicine books—& Hill chartered a horse for the voyage, & a <flim> clean clipper-built concern for to carry the passengers—but I <says,>said

'Look-a-here! are you the chief mate of this establishment?—because I want you to understand that I'm a cripple—I can't move hand nor foot, & I want a horse that *one* man can steer, <y>do you see?'

And he says '<he>Here, take out that horse & put in this one—black, the first one was, & wicked—stood up with his figure-head in the clouds—white the last one, but <not> wicked, too, I <thought> judged—anyway I didn't hardly like the cut of his jib—& I said as much to Hill—I said, "Here, now, take some of that rattlin' stuff & reeve it through his fair-leaders there forrard, & sieze it onto his fore-ancle, so as if we got in a tight place & he missed stays or run away we could fetch him up <on> with a round turn—couldn't do much on <[--]> 3 legs I don't suppose?"

But no,—*I* didn't know anything about it, Hill knowed it all. So we cast <loose> off & got under way,/stood out to wind'ard & it

[9] In the first half of December 1866 word had reached San Francisco of an influenza epidemic in Hawaii. On 15 December, the day of Mark Twain's departure for Nicaragua, the *Daily Evening Bulletin* published its Hawaiian correspondent's report that "The epidemic—influenza, accompanied with chills and fever—has been making sad havoc among the natives. . . . In Honolulu, they have been dying off at the rate of ten or twelve a day."

was all fair sailing till we sighted a fleet of sheep or something or other of that kind, & then bloody murder how he did shake out his reefs & howl before the wind! Go?—go ain't no name for it!—over gardens & orchards & dogs & cats, curb-stones & children—round this corner & then around that—everybody yelping, everybody skurrying out of the way, nobody trying to stop him—I says "Luff, in the name o' God! & let him go about!—because I see right ahead of us a little cove with a bulkhead across the other end of it—& Hill he put her down hard-a-port—but it was too late—it warn't no use—she missed stays & down she went like a rocket into that cove & fetched up like the staving of a ship-of-the line agin that d—d bulkhead!—& out we went & Hill & me—I was on the port side & the minute she struck she swung, broadside on, & I went over that bulkhead like a shot & Hill cleared the starboard bulwarks & struck on his shoulder & scoured the harness off of him & peeled the hide, too, & the<[re]> horse—hell! there warn't enough of him left to hold an inquest on!<"> shaking like a sick monkey on a lee back-stay. Eight bells, did you say?—very well, let her go just as she heads an hour & a half & then put her half a point more southerly. I've got to <[f]>go forrard a minute, boys, take it easy & amuse yourselves."

"Well?" said Brown.

"Well?" said I.

"Well, how was it?"

"Didn't you hear the story?"

"Yes,—but I don't understand them sailor terms. What was the trouble anyway?"

I disdained to answer, & left Brown to figure it out himself.

18th—The young runaway couple, after co-habiting a night or two, were married last night by the Capt's peremptory order, in presence of 5 witnesses.[10] [#]

---

[10] A statement by the Reverend St. M. Fackler (Edgar Wakeman Papers, San Francisco Public Library), who performed this ceremony, gives its date as 18 De-

20th—<Saturday—> Thursday—<Cap>At noon, 5 days out from Sanfrancisco, abreast high stretch of land at foot of Magdalena Bay, Capt came & said, "Come out here (we had just got into warm weather & covered the whole after part of the vessel with awnings, making it extremely cool & shady for December)—"I want to show you something"—took the marine glass.—

Scene—Two whale ships at anchor under the bluffs—one listed & hoisting vast mass of blubber aboard.

Said "Now to-night they'll try it out on deck & it'll <like>look like the whole ship's on fire. The first time I ever see it was in '50—I come along here just after dark, see a ship on fire apparently—*I* didn't know the country—didn't dare to go in there with the ship, so I sent a boat's crew & said "Pull for your lives d—n you—& tell the Capt I'll lay here if it's a week & render him all the assistance *I* can & then carry his people to Sanf."

Well, we laid to & waited & waited—all the passengers on deck & anxious for the boat to come back & report—but 10 ock, no boat —11 ock—no boat—passengers begin to get tired & sidle off to bed —12 oclk—no boat—every passenger give up & went below except one old woman & by G-d, she stuck it out & never took her eyes off the fire.

By & bye <&>at 12.30 back the boat come & me & the old woman crowded to the lee rail to see & hear it all,—couldn't see no extra men.

The officer of the boat stepped on deck & lifted his hat & says— "The capt of the ship sends great gratification—great obligations & thanks for your trouble & your good intentions but he ain't in trouble but quite the reverse—is full of oil & ready to up anchor to-morrow & is giving his crew a big blow out on deck & is illuminating—sends his good wishes & success & hopes you'll accept this boat-load of A 1 <sea-turtles>sea-turkles."

The old woman leaned over the rail & shaded her eyes from the

---

cember 1866. The couple whose arrival was heralded at the beginning of this notebook as "love victorious" were Lawrence Dunn and Emma Bayer. Mark Twain was not among the witnesses.

lanterns with her hand & she see them varmints flopping their flippers about in the boat & she says:

"For the land's sake—I've sot here & sot here & sot here all this blessed night cal'lating to see a hull boat-load of sorrowful roasted corpses, & now it ain't nothing after all but a lot of nasty turkles—it's too dern bad!"

Sent compliments with the Capt. to the whale ships.

8 AM Dec. 21—Crossed tropic of Capricorn—Cape St Lucas —now abreast Gulf of California.

Genius.

Genius is <a>exceedingly rare, <&, like gold & precious stones, is chiefly prized because of its rarity.>

<Genius is a> <Genius consists of a peculiar mental organization which enables a man to dash off wierd, wild, incomprehensible poems with astonishing facility, & then prompts him to go & get <howling> booming drunk & <lie> sleep in the gutter.> Geniuses are people who dash off wierd, wild, incomprehensible poems with astonishing facility, & then go & get booming drunk & sleep in the gutter.[11]

Genius elevates <its possessor> a man to ineffable speres far above the vulgar <earth> world, & fills his soul with a regal contempt for the gross & sordid things of earth

It is probably on account of this that people who have genius do not pay their board, as a general thing.

<Genius is>Geniuses are very <pe>singular.

If you see a young man who hath <a> frowsy hair & a distraught look, & affects excentricity in dress, you may set him down for a genius.

If he sighs about the degeneracy of a world which courts vulgar opulence & neglects *brains,* he is undoubtedly a genius.

---

[11] In order to preserve Mark Twain's revisions without sacrificing intelligibility, this paragraph has been rendered as though he recopied it entirely each time he shifted his intention, producing a form that varies considerably from the appearance of the original. For a description of the process of revision, see Details of Inscription.

If he is too proud to accept of assistance, & spurns it with <as lordly an>a lordly air at the <very> same time that he knows he can't make a living himself to save his life, he is most certainly a genius.

If he hangs on & sticks to poetry notwithstand^{g} sawing wood comes handier to him, he is a true genius.

If he throws away every opportunity in life & <crushes> wears out the affection & the patience of his friends & <then> then complains in sickly rhymes of his hard lot, & finally <persists,> in spite of the sound advice of persons who have got sense but not any genius, persists in going up some <infamous> back alley & dying in rags & dirt, he is beyond all question a genius.

<But above all things, as I said before, to deftly throw the incoherent ravings of insanity into verse & then rush off & get booming drunk, is the surest of all the different signs of genius.>

Brown's Ranch—11 men he killed buried together & self at head[12]

First 26 buried in Va killed.[13]
First 6 buried in Carson—

At sea Dec. 22, '66—About lat. 19 N.—Passengers have been singing several days—now the men have come down to leap-frog,

---

12 Sam Brown was a Nevada desperado notorious for preying upon defenseless men. On 6 July 1861, Brown's thirtieth birthday, Henry Vansickle, an unassuming innkeeper, unexpectedly responded to a death threat from Brown by dispatching him at close range with a shotgun after a prolonged horseback pursuit. Some accounts of Brown's career place the number of his victims at eleven, but others assert that he actually killed sixteen. A popular legend held that Brown maintained a private cemetery for his victims. In chapter 48 of *Roughing It* Mark Twain would recall that the deference "paid to a desperado of wide reputation, and who 'kept his private graveyard,' as the phrase went, was marked, and cheerfully accorded."

13 "The first twenty-six graves in the Virginia cemetery were occupied by *murdered* men. So everybody said, so everybody believed, and so they will always say and believe. The reason why there was so much slaughtering done, was, that in a new mining district the rough element predominates, and a person is not respected until he has 'killed his man'" (*Roughing It*, chapter 48).

boyish gymnastics & tricks of equilibrium—& sitting on a bottle with legs extended & X[d], & threading a good sized needle.

My man-of-war hammock on the promenade deck aft is a good institution & <is not> the swinging of it affords exercise.

Wakeman's Boat-Disengaging invention[14]

22[d] Dec—Midnight—smooth sea—or rather just rippled with a pleasant breeze—perfectly fair wind—yards squared—<glid> splendid *full* moon—ship gliding along placidly in full view of Mexican shore—all in bed but me—night too magnificent—temperature too soft, balmy, delicious.

23[d] Sunday—Brown—Goin to be in Gulf Tehuantepec 25th—instead going down shore as ordered, where easy sea, old man going to get up splendid Christmas Dinner & hold her out 4 points—all hell couldn't eat a bite in that sea & keep it on his stomach.

Capt W's Condors (full of epicures) that turn sheep inside out.

Rats that left the sinking ship.
Do do do —& hauled up a sick comrade.

Educated porpoises in Australia[15]—tattooing & driving feathers in head to grow.[16] [#]

---

[14] In *The Log of an Ancient Mariner* (p. 240) Wakeman claimed that on a voyage from San Francisco to New York he "invented the best detaching gear, to let go a boat from the davits, that has ever been invented." Just before this voyage Wakeman apparently tried to interest the *America's* proprietors in his device, for on 12 December 1866 William H. Webb, president of the North American Steamship Company wrote him:

> Should be pleased to see model (if already made) of your plan of sending down topmasts, disengaging boats etc, but do not wish you to incur the expense of models etc expressly to be sent here, for many such arrangements are now before us here. (Edgar Wakeman Papers, San Francisco Public Library)

[15] Apparently this is an allusion to a version of a tale which appears in *The Log of an Ancient Mariner* (pp. 194–195) concerning a friendly porpoise, which Wakeman was prevented from killing because it was believed to be the reincarnation of an Australian native.

[16] Wakeman recalled that among the natives of Australia tattooing was "performed by cutting the person all over with sharks' teeth and sharpened shells, and

Hanging the negro in the Chinchas.[17]

23[d] Dec. Sunday—Morning service on Prom deck by Fackler—organ & choir

I had rather travel with that old portly, hearty, jolly, boisterous, good-natured old sailor, Capt Ned Wakeman than with any other man I ever came across. He never drinks, & never plays cards; he never swears, except in the privacy of his own quarters, with a friend or so, & then his feats of fancy blasphemy are calculated to fill the hearer with awe & <the liveliest> admiration. His yarns—

Just as I got that far, Capt. W. came in, sweating & puffing—for we are off the far southern coast of Mexico, & the weather is a little sultry—& said he had "tore up the whole ship" (he scorns grammar when he is exercised about anything)—had "tore up the whole ship" to <rig> build a pulpit at the after compass & rig benches & chairs <athward>athwart the quarter deck & bring up the organ from the cabin & get everything ship-shape for the parson in the forward cabin who is going to preach us a sermon this beautiful December morning.

"And d—d the<m> passengers," said he, "as soon as they found they were going to be sermonized, they've up anchors & gone to sea!—clean gone & deserted!—there ain't a baker's dozen left on the after deck. They're worse than the rats in Hon—Hello! go forrard & tell the mate to let her go a couple of points free—in Honolulu. Me & old Josephus—he was a Jew, & got rich as Creesas in San f

---

then throwing hot ashes and embers into the wounds, thus burning the patient all up into the most horrible of sights." The natives, he continued, "were an awful looking set of savages. They stick the quills of some large bird through their scalps, and pitch them around with the gum of some tree until it grows fast between the quills; then they tie their woolly hair up into bundles, like fingers, by winding strings around, until their heads look like the devil" (*The Log of an Ancient Mariner*, p. 188).

[17] Mark Twain would use this anecdote in chapter 50 of *Roughing It*. There, however, it is a white man who is hanged in the Chincha Islands by Captain Ned Blakely, one of Mark Twain's fictional counterparts to Wakeman, for the murder of the Negro mate of Blakely's ship.

afterwards—we were going home passengers from the Sa I[18] in a bran new brig on her 3^{d} voyage—& our trunks were down below—he went with me—laid over one vessel to do it—because he warn't no sailor & he liked to be with a man that was—& the brig was sliding out between the boys & her headline was paying out ashore—there was a wood-pile right where it was made fast on the pier—when up come the d—dest biggest rat—as big as any ordinary cat, he was—& darted out on that line & cantered for the shore!—& up come another—& another—& another—& away they galloped over that hawser—<one with his nose right> each one treading on tother's tail—till they were so thick you couldn't see a thread of the cable—& there was a procession of 'em 300 yds long over the levee like a streak of pissants—& the Kanakas, some throwing sticks from that woodpile & chunks of lava & coral at 'em & knocking <th> 'em endways & every which way—but do you spose it made any difference to them rats?—not a particle—not a particle, bless your soul!—<&> they never let up till the last rat was ashore out of that bran new beautiful brig. I called a Kanaka with his boat, & he hove alongside & shinned up a rope & stood off & on for orders, & says I,

Do you see that trunk down there?

"Ai."

"Clatter it ashore as quick as God'll let you!"

Solomon the Jew—what did I say his d—d name was?—anyhow he says,

What are you doing Capt

And I say, DOING<?>!—why I'm a taking my trunk ashore—thats what *I'm* a doing?

Taking your <s[-]>trunk ashore?—why bless us, what is that for?

What is it *for?* says I?—do you see them rats? <T>Do you notice them rats a leaving this ship? She's doomed sir!—she's doomed! Burn't brandy wouldn't save her, Sir!—she'll never finish this voyage. She'll never be heard of again, Sir.

---

[18] In his haste to transcribe Wakeman's anecdote Mark Twain used this unusual abbreviation for the Sandwich Islands, similar in form to the abbreviation of San Francisco which immediately precedes it.

Solomon says, Boy, take that other trunk ashore, too.

And don't you know Sir that brig sailed out of Honolulu without a rat aboard & was never seen again by mortal man, Sir!

We went in an old tub so rotten that you had to walk easy on the main deck to keep from going through—so crazy, sir that in our berths when there was a sea on, the timbers over head worked backards & forrards 11 inches in their sockets—just like an old <wicker> basket, Sir!—& the rats were as big <&>as greyhounds & as lean sir! & they bit the buttons off our coats & chawed our toe-nails off while we <slee>slept & there was so many of them that in a gale once they all <run> scampered to the starboard side when we were going about & put her down <so>the wrong way so that she missed stays & come <precious> monstrous near foundering! But she went through safe, I tell you—becus she had rats aboard.

(Out at the door & back again in 2 minutes.)

"Everything's set—the passengers are back again & stowed—& the parson's all ready to cat his anchor & get under way. Everybody ready & waiting on that choir that was practising & <blatting>blattin' & blatt'n all night & now ain't come to time.

(Out again & back ½ a minute.)

D—n that choir!—they're like the fellow's <hog> sow—had to <pull> haul her ears off to git her up to the trough, & then had to pull her tail out to get her away again." But rats! Don't tell me nothing about the talent of rats! It's been noticed Sir!—notes has been taken of it, Sir!—& their judgment is better than a human's Sir! Didn't I hear old Ben Wilson, mate of the Empress of the Seas —as true a sailor & as gallant a ship as ever rode a gale—didn't I hear him tell how, seventeen years ago when he was <ly>laying at Liverpool Docks empty—empty as a jug—& a full Indiaman right alongside—full of provisions & corn & everything that a rat might prefer, & going to sail <to-morrow—> next day—how in the middle of the night the rats all left her & crossed his decks & went ashore—every <devilish> cussed one of 'em sir!—every *one* of 'em—& finally—it was moonlight—he saw a muss going on by the capstan of that other ship & he slipped around & there was a dozen old rats layin their heads together & chattering about something & looking down the forrard hatch every now & then—& finally they appeared to have got their minds made up, & one of 'em went aft & <brought> got a scrap of an old stun'sl, half a foot square, & they bored holes in the corners with their teeth & bent on some long pieces of rattlin-stuff <& then>—made a sort of a little hammock of it you understand—& then they lowered away gently for a while & stopped—& directly they begun heaving again & up out of that forrard hatch—in full view of the mate who was a watching, you see—up comes that little hammock with a poor old decrepit sick rat on it!—& they carried him ashore & they all went up town to the very last rat—& that ship sailed the next day for India or Cape o' Good Hope or Somewhers, & the mate of the Empress didn't sail for as much as 3 weeks—& up to *that* time that ship hadn't been heard from Sir!

D—n that choir, I must go & start 'em out—this sort of thing won't do.

Christmas Eve—9 P.M. Me & the Capt & Kingman out forward—

Capt. said—Don't like the looks of that point with the mist outside of it—hold her a point free.

Quartermaster (touching his hat)—The child is dead sir."
<Wh>(Been sick 2 days.—) What are yr orders.

Capt. Tell Ben to send the D$^{r.}$ for the parson to speak to the grandmother & the mate to speak to the young mother—bury at seat at daylight or preserve in spirits & bury at San Juan (Depart)

Capt.—Store-keeper don't you know you are out of your place here forward with the officers on watch—nobody ever tell you that?

S—No sir?

C—Well it ought to have been the first thing told & you wouldnt have made any mistake (Departure of S)

D—arrived & C told him to find out wishes of mother.

C—If it was mine I'd preserve it cost what it might—but poor thing—God's will be done.

Mate w^{h} Mother—Madam, you say the grandmother wants it

buried at sea at daylight—right—but you have yr say—whatever you wish *that* shall be done. (Exit) (11 AM. tomorrow—C—Enter in log—died at 9 PM.

Had sharks, whales, porpoises, dolphins—purser (Dodge's) phosphorescents)—70 miles.

Christmas Eve—Second time we have put $2 worth of Euchre on Kingman & Trueman—Roon 14 still ahead.[19]

Met old friend at San Juan.

First thing seen among tropical scenery was Try Ward's shirts! —Brown.[20]

On San Juan River.

The d—d fool[21] who asks you an infinity of questions, & persists in believing you know all about the country.

What kind of a bird is that?
Don't know.
Macaw, <perhaps>phaps?
Don't know.
Might be a parrot or a cockatoo, likely?
Don't know (& don't care a d—n) you would like to say.

---

[19] Although Mark Twain admitted in the *Alta California* that "we used to be very regular about getting the room crammed full of cigar-smoke and boys, and listening to the purser's infamous old stories, and playing pitch seven-up till midnight" (*MTTB*, p. 62), he described a more solemn Christmas Eve than this entry suggests:

> It has been an exceedingly quiet Christmas Eve, to-day. It is because a young child of one of the cabin passengers is lying very ill—suddenly taken last night—and so no one is willing to be noisy, or even passably cheerful, for that matter. All act as if they were related by blood to the child. And it is natural it should be so—a ship's passengers on a long voyage become as one family. (*MTTB*, p. 34)

[20] A reference to the ubiquitous advertisements of S. W. H. Ward & Son of 323 Montgomery Street in San Francisco, manufacturers and retailers of men's shirts (see Notebook 5, note 160).

[21] This figure, in several permutations, was to be a stock character in Mark Twain's travel writings. Perhaps his closest counterpart is the "grave, pale young man" with a proclivity for asking foolish questions in "Some Rambling Notes of an Idle Excursion" (*Atlantic*, October 1877–January 1878).

Oh, my, what kind of a tree is that standing in the water with the splendid blossoms on it?

Don't know.

Blossoms look like passion flower, tho' no passion blossom was ever so large, maybe—couldn't be a passion-*tree* could it?

Don't *know*.

Lord, see that alligator climbing out right close to where that monkey is swinging from a limb by his tail—can't be after the monkey, can he?

Don't know.

Reckon the alligator couldn't catch the monkey, could he?

<[I'm d]> I wish I may be eternally d—d if I know.

While gazing up a little narrow avenue, carpeted with greenest grass & walled with the thickest growth of bright ferns & quaint <&>, broad-leaved trees whose verdant sprays spring upward & outward like the curving sprays of a fountain—an avenue that is fit for the royal road to fairy land, & is closed with a gate of trellised vines stretching their charming maze of festoons, bright with beautiful blossoms athwart—some scoundrel interrupts with

You'd ought to gone ashore there where we wooded—bannaner trees till you couldn't rest!—leaves on 'em 7 foot long & a foot & a half wide—& natives doing something or other with the coffee trees —what is it?—& what do you spose they was doing it for?

I got up & left.

San Juan Bay—neat little semi-circle shut in by wooded hills. Fine breeze.

Must remain this afternoon & leave early in AM on <ac/>ac. of cholera—brought by Santiago—300 soldiers & several hundred passengers—26 deaths among former & 9 of latter & 40 natives—all in past 10 days—all subsided now.[22]

Left San Juan Dec. 28 in carriages & horses—hellfiredest sorebacks in world.—we in No 28—ahead of 16.—native drivers armed with long knives—native soldiers—barefooted w^h muskets. [#]

---

22 Mark Twain's later report on these events is on pages 296 and 297.

Threatened war between 2 candidates for Presidency of Repub of Nicaragua—case of contested election—present Pres. going to hold his posish & whip both parties.[23]

Numbered by varas—100 to Virgin Bay—12 miles—8 to a mile.

Long procession of horsemen & hacks—beautiful road & cool rainy atmosphere.

All on lookout for wild monkeys.

Orange, banana, aguardente, coffee, hot corn, carved cups—stands—pretty native women—ruffles around bottom of dress.

Snake cactus clasping trees.

Calabash trees.

Threatened bloodsheed bet. passengers & drivers.

One hack broke down.

Music & beautiful bouquets.

Comfortable boat—beautiful breezy lake—2 circus tent mountains—cloud-capped—wooded densely to summits save where lava passed—one 4,200 ft—other 5,400—look higher—very beautiful with their solid crown of clouds, & rising abruptly from water—coffee, cattle, tobacco, corn,—all sorts of ranches on them—raise everything w^h no trouble—splendid temperature.

Walker at Virgin.[24] [#]

---

[23] In December 1866, General Tomás Martínez was completing a second four-year term as president of Nicaragua. A belief that Martínez planned to retain his office for life had led to some attempts at revolution, but these were easily suppressed, and Martínez proclaimed himself innocent of dictatorial intentions. Although he was not a candidate for a third term, his support was instrumental in the election of Fernando Guzmán, a close personal friend, who would take office on 1 March 1867.

[24] The battle of Virgin Bay, fought on 3 September 1855, was William Walker's first victory in his Nicaragua filibuster campaign. Walker seized control of that country and in 1856 had himself inaugurated president, the initial step in his plan for Central American conquest and federation. He was overthrown the following year, and his attempts to return were abortive. In 1860 he was arrested after a landing in Honduras and was executed by a firing squad.

<St>Changed boats & started down lovely San Juan river at 4 AM, saluting old Fort San Carlos at head w^{h} 3 whistles—

<Alli> Bank full—spots of grass—trees like cypress—blossoming trees—trees so festooned w^{h} vines that look like vine-clad towers of ancient fortresses—great tree ferns & tall graceful clumps of bamboo—all manner of trees & bushes—& all thick enough anyway & then so woven together with a charming lace-work of vines that monkey can't climb through.

Walkers privateer near shore—a little green island—nothing visible but the great fore-&-aft braces, with bright green trees right between them springing up out of a thick carpet of green grass

On <San> first San Juan River steamer—man at <gang> companionway asked me—"None but 1st cabin allowed up here—*you* first cabin?" (with a most offensive emphasis on the italicised word)—& let a whole sluice of steerage pass unchallenged—quite a compliment to my personal appearance!

On 2^{d} river boat challenged me faithfully & passed the other 1st cabin unchal.

The jew. busted out & onto the other boat by sheer hard work—he kept back his 2^{d} cabin ticket & tried hard to play his 1st cabin *dinner* ticket on the sentinel.

Complained that the purser gave him no state room when a number of 1st C lay on floor.

Capt. W. crotoned him & yet he was back to the 7 PM lunch in his quarters.[25]

Town of <San Carlos> Castillo—where we walked 300 yds & changed boats below Rapids.—old romantic dobie castle of a fort

---

25 In the *Alta California* (*MTTB*, p. 36) Mark Twain preferred to obscure this cruel aspect of Wakeman's humor and attributed the administering of purgatives to "the jew" to unnamed passengers.

on top of steep grassy dome 200 ft high—14 houses under hill & dense vine-clad foliage appearing <on> beyond.

Old son of ——— bored me again with questions & information—had been there once before for 2 days.

Native thatched houses—coffee, eggs, bread, cigars & fruit for sale—delicious—10 cents buy pretty much anything & in great quantity.

Californians can't understanding how 10 or 25 cents can buy a sumptuous lunch of coffee, eggs & bread.

Vine festoons terrace & conceal hills like a web—couldn't believe they were hills at all except that upper trees tower too high to be on the bank level.

Dark grottos, fairy harbors—tunnels, temples, columns, pillars, towers, pilasters, terraces, pyramids, mounds, domes, walls, in endless confusion of vine-work—no shape known to architecture unimitated —& all so webbed together with vines that short distances within only gained by glimpses.—monkeys here & there—birds warbling—gorgeous plumaged birds on the wing—Paradise itself—the imperial realm of beauty—nothing to wish for to make it perfect.

The changing vistas of the river—corners & points folding backward—retreating & unveiling new wonders <of> beyond—of towering walls of verdure—gleaming cataracts of vines pouring sheer down from 150 feet & mingling with the grass—wonderfull waterfalls of glittering leaves as <smooth> deftly overlapping each other as the scales of a fish—a vast green wall—solid a moment, —then as we advance, changing & opening into gothic windows, collonades—all manner of quaint & charming shapes (D—n the blackguard with the <plug hat> damaged plug hat on who is looking over my shoulder as I make these notes on the boiler deck)

Cocoanuts for sale at San Carlos (shows we approach the sea—don't grow in the country.

Saw at San Carlos the first osage trees of the trip—my favorite tree above all others.

The <Nun> Hamlet's ghost. (with the flabby dead, expressionless, Hamlets ghost's countenance & dingy white veil).

The <u>Undertaker her husband—bony, sallow, heavy whiskered, cadaverous, unsociable.

The Nun—tall, hair plainly dressed, sweet, good, quiet countenance.

The Little Wdo—

K's mere—shriveled countenance, little villainous black bead eyes—no brains but a love of admiration that goeth even beyond her sex.

(Man overboard!—(rush!)

Alligators! (rush)—from side to side of boat.

Mrs. Grundy (all in brown) d—d old meddling, moralizing fool—said I was no better than I ought to be—told on the young couple—told on the gay party at the mock raffle in after cabin at San Juan—said they were 2[d] class.

Kingman, <S>Walker & Smith the good boys.

Capt Snow the accommodating gentleman

Brown, Col. Baker, Scipio, & several lad & gents unknown. The Choir—sung the d—dest, oldest, vilest songs—such as Marching thro' Geo, <J> When Jno comes Marching—Old Dog Tray—Just before the Battle, Mother—What is Home whout a mother—

When they sang hymns, they did well & made good music—but d—n their other efforts—<they never> & besides, they never invited me to sing, anyhow. "Homeward was pretty, & touched a chord in every breast—it was *appropriate*—but what the devil is there in common (& so was Larboard Watch ahoy!) between the boundless & shoreless sea, the gemmed & arching heavens—the <w> crested billows—the <noble ship—> stately ship plowing her gallant way & leaving a broad highway of dazzling fire behind her—the thousand thoughtful eyes gazing abroad over the heaving sea & dreaming of the homes <they>that shall soon bless their sight again, thank

God!—and Dog Tray? I say what is there in common between these things & Dog Tray? D—n Dog Tray.[26]

The Petit Mo<-an>—whom I like *because* is a Mo'an.[27]

Brown has been instructing the Bore, that an alligator can't climb a tree—(the fellow says he *knew* that before,) but Brown goes into full explanations *anyhow*, notwithstanding his protestations & interruptions, & finally wears him out & drives him off—vanquishes the Bore—does it as I shrewdly suspect to avenge the fellow's boring me so—& yet has the modesty & the good sense not to come bragging about the exploit.

The German girl.

Jew's wife's Jewelry—raffled it off—she'd been dead six weeks—d—d lie.[28]

Jew was stopped on the plank (after we had served notice) offered dinner ticket—was told it wouldn't do—said it was in his *trunk*—absurd—he is no fool, to carry such a thing in his trunk.

Walker's privateer No. 2—10 miles below San Carlos Rapids

Saw island 200 feet long grown over with thickest grass—locomotive boiler & steam drum sitting straight up,—the pyramidal walking beam timbers standing up behind them & completely swathed in green garlands & festoons of vines & shaded by low bright green trees.

Doking the Jew.

Take part of the Jew's familiarity on <myself> a white passenger

---

[26] A line is drawn from this sentence to "Homeward" (p. 262.25). Probably Clemens considered reordering the passage, which contains a line from Thomas E. Williams' song "The Larboard Watch," but when printed in the *Alta California* (*MTTB*, p. 59) it appeared as he originally inscribed it here.

[27] Possibly a reference to a native of Missouri who was among the *America* passengers.

[28] Mark Twain wrote to the *Alta California* (*MTTB*, p. 35) that the passengers became particularly incensed with "the jew" when "they reflected that he won all the jewelry himself that was worth having" and "what they got was pinchbeck."

—first few days was sick, & accepted Capt's invitation to lie on his sofa where it was cooler than in a state room—the Jew (in good health, though not to our thinking a white man,) presumed so far as to take the same liberty & curl up there every day to exhibit himself for the envy of passengers not captain's pets.

The country through w^h this San Juan River passes was made to look at & travel through—but not to live in

It is shrewdly believed that this is *not* an Opposition—that it is kept up to *keep off* real opposition & they keep the other for people who wish to travel select & are willing to pay big price for it.

They only show spasmodic Opposition prices occasionally to keep up appearances. They dont *want* this to be popular.[29]

Hills 6 or 800 feet high<t>, 40 or 50 miles below Castillo Rapids —steep & built of a dense architecture of delicate green domes of trees & each dome <so ench> splendid with sunshine on top & so enchantingly shaded off with indian summery films to absolute darkness & blackness—dome upon dome they rise from the level of the river timber high into the <crystal> sunny cloudless atmosphere—beautiful beyond all description—exstasy.

Tents & canopies of vines.

Tall straight clean white shaft of the Peruvian cedar all along (Cigar box wood.

Stately mahogany tree

Tall slender bastard or wild banana tree with neither limb nor leaf except at extreme top a graceful plume of long feathery leaves somewhat like cocoa-nut. [#]

---

[29] This claim of collusion between the Pacific Mail Steamship Company and the "opposition" North American Steamship Company was unfounded. In November 1867 the latter concern would initiate, in addition to its alternative route through Nicaragua, a "New Opposition Line Via Panama" with low rates for passengers and freight. The following spring the North American Steamship Company would transfer all of its ships to the Panama route, concentrating its resources for an intensified rivalry.

Many great lazy alligators lying on bank sleeping in the sun—bright plumaged parrots flying above the trees—birds with gay plumage & great hooked villainous bills—such as we see in the menagerie—long legged, long-necked birds that rise awkwardly from the edge of the jungle, crook their necks like an S, shove their long bills forward & thrust their long legs out behind like a steering oar when they flying—& monkeys capering among the trees—these are the signs of the tropics.

At first everybody apologised for coming this way—& said it must be done merely to see the country & get it off their minds—a sort of compulsory sense of duty—never should come this way again of course—but now, on the San Juan River with all this enchantment around us, & after going over what we have passed thro' & decided that it has been nothing but a comfortable, cheerful satisfactory pleasure trip, we all begin to confess that if we were already thro' our business in the States & ready to return, we should be uncommonly apt to come this way, after all.

Ben Holiday & Wells Fargo—the new Consolidated Co $10000000 capital—3 coaches a day after 1st April $100 apiece through to States—hurt steamers[30]

Mrs. Grundy—Cor. of <NO Delta—> Visalia Delta[31]—says

---

[30] On 1 December 1866 the *Alta California* had reported: "Negotiations which have been going on for several months for the reorganization and consolidation of the stage and express lines between the Missouri River and the Pacific Ocean have been completed within the last few days." Among the companies merging with Wells, Fargo and Company was Ben Holladay's Express and Stage Company. Following this entry Mark Twain pasted in a newspaper clipping stating that "BEN HOLLADAY made the trip from San Francisco to New York in sixteen days. He had his own relays of horses on the plains." In the margin of the clipping Mark Twain wrote "Sept 62." Ben Holladay's "prodigious energy" would become one of the subjects of an anecdote Mark Twain included in chapter 6 of *Roughing It*.

[31] The Visalia, California, *Delta* was a four-page weekly composed largely of advertisements. Its occasional correspondence was generally limited to agricultural and commercial affairs in neighboring communities. For the readers of the *Alta California* (*MTTB*, p. 27) Mark Twain made the point of this joke more readily available by having Brown refer to Miss Slimmens as a "sister correspondent" communicating with the *Hangtown Thunderclap of Freedom*.

everybody secesh—cornered said they *looked* so & she knowed they *was* so.

Said I was drunk all the time—<corner> said privately to K that I was on Christmas, anyhow, & thought it very cunning—was the only one dr. that day.

Said Truman & Brown collected a lot of money for the little widow & refused to give it up—(this said on the Steamer Sanfrancisco on Atlantic side first day out)—<K>T went after her howling & forced her to come on deck & state it publicly (silenced her husband) <—cornered>—said she'd *heard* it—repeated that she'd *heard* it—why, from *every*body—was offered $10 apiece for each she could find who had said so, & then said she was afraid they wouldn't like it—the d—d old lying hag!—haridan.

(Shape (from asylum at Stkton)—last button buttoned & invisible moustache.)[32]

Ace 1—Jack 11—Queen 12—King 13—91—so counted when 86 have been played, 5 will win—when 80 been played, Jack will win at faro.

The Stranger.[33]

O, give us a raffle
" " " " "
" " " " "
To help the poor stranger along.
" " " " " along, along,
" " " " " "

[32] "Shape" was the nickname given to Andrew Nolan, a young barber (see pp. 276 and 279). Mark Twain later dismissed the allegation of lunacy in a whimsical portrayal of Shape as the only passenger who remained aloof from the nonsensical deck games popular aboard the *America:* "With hat perched jauntily on one side of his head, and hands thrust into his coat pockets, he promenades the deck fore and aft, and admires his legs. They say he is a little 'cracked,' I don't know—the idea may have originated with Miss Slimmens of the *'Thunderclap'* " (*MTTB*, p. 29).

[33] The following verses, which catalog the offenses and sufferings of the passenger Mark Twain refers to as "the jew" in this notebook and as Isaac in his letters to the *Alta California,* were not used in his published accounts of this trip.

We'll chance his brass, his paste and
glass,
To help the sweet stranger along.

2d Chorus.

All that the stranger lacks in nose
(Repeat) 2 times
He neatly makes up in cheek.

What was that stuff he drank one day
(Repeat
In Capt Wakeman's room?

O but it was sinful,
(Repeat twice.)
To physic the stranger so.

Why didn't he travel with us?
(Repeat twice.)
'Cause his ticket for soup wouldn't go.

He comes from the second cabin
(Repeat twice.)
And gets the first choice of rooms.

This cheeky stranger's a nuisance
(Repeat twice)
In our o-pin-i-on.

New Year's Eve 1866.

Slept on the Cora on floor & hammocks at woodyard first night out from Castillo.

<Next> Started at 2 AM & got to Greytown at daylight Found Sanfrancisco there.—took them all day to transfer baggage & remove the 2 sets of steerage passengers.

K told 'em in joke up town our steerage & second cabin had smallpox & they <soo> anchored 'em out much crowded all night & wouldn't let any come ashore during the day.[34]

---

[34] In the *Alta California* (*MTTB*, pp. 54–55) Mark Twain would attribute this mischief to the fictional Mr. Brown, rather than to his friend Hector J. Kingman.

We stayed aboard most of day anchored out & slept up town—had to come to boat at 6 A.M. At 7, after keeping "*Active*" under steam good while & Capt Merry promising to send us aboard in her, changed his mind & sent us in surf-boats in rain-storm—our boat had to go to the "Managua" & finish her complement with 2^{d} cabin passengers—a dozen—& came near being swamped by them. Took <3> 3 hours to disembark the New York passengers & then we got under way.

Sandwiches.

Everlasting curses light on the man who invented the villainous little lamp they put in a man's state room on shipboard! That is as honest a prayer as ever I uttered.

The Jew all right—has purchased a first cabin ticket & sits at the right hand of the K who is his countryman.
"Shape" has the seat on his left.

The d—d second cabin passengers—(having nothing but standees hardly in their own den), are all buying into the first cabin—they have put Steuben into our upper berth (No. 1, starboard side, upper deck.)

I am in bed all day to-day (2^{d} Jan)—same old thing.

The Wandering Jew sat down by Miss Lander last night & began his grievances—the neglect of the passengers & so on, but something interrupted the recital.

Jan. 2—All right now, on this ship—got plenty of ice & ice water—no more melting here in the tropics.

That infernal monkey is having a perfect carnival all to himself. Smith & Kingman gave him a good square dose of straight brandy & now he feels his oats—one moment he is in the quarter boat abreast my room & the next he is at the top-gallant cross-trees & scampering wildly from rope to rope & capering out on the yards like a lunatic—the dizzy height, the blowing of the gale & the plunging of the ship have no terrors for *him*. [#]

A sailor scared the monkey a while ago & he jumped from the top-gallant yard-arm & caught a <st> backstay or something away down 20 or 30 feet below.

Mrs. Grundy & her husband (they are 2^d cabin) were permitted to occupy a room by some of the departing passengers before leaving Greytown, & he had his watch stolen.

Purser fine man.

I said monkey Brown's nephew—he said he was correspondent newspaper.

Jan 2. 1867.

Two cases of cholera reported in the steerage to-day.[35]

The <Labord> Larboard Watch ahoy.

We are running along in sight of the Mosquito Coast—saw a village a while ago.

Kingman's report of small-pox kept the steerage from getting ashore at Greytown, & now I don't more than half believe his report that there are 2 cases yellow fever below decks.

Got Capt's permission to have a safety lantern in my room.

<The> 4 PM Jan 2. The surgeon of the ship has just reported to the Captain in my hearing, that two of the cases are "mighty bad," & the 3^d "awful bad."

This is neither cholera nor yellow fever I suspect—these men have been eating green tropical fruit & washing it down with villainous aguardiente.

Mining Item.[36]

On Saturday Dec. 15, 1866, Washoe mines paid over $300,000 in dividends.

---

[35] This ominous note is the first of contradictory reports at the onset of a shipboard epidemic which resulted in seven deaths before the vessel arrived in New York on 12 January 1867.

[36] Although he misdated his note, Mark Twain evidently made it from the fol-

During the past 6 weeks dividends of 6 principal mines amounted to $519,000.

<Gross yield> <Dividends> Yield of ten <other> mines during October & November was over $2,000,000.

A ship is precisely a little village, where gossips abound, & where every man's business is his neighbor's.

The prospect of going into quarantine for 30 days is worrying the passengers like everything. Considering my present condition it would be the happiest thing that could happen to me.

7 PM—Neither of the sick men quite dead yet.

The ship has stopped her wheels.

Jew is transferred to a very narrow room far aft in the Saloon below where he has to go in edgeways & come out the same way

The Jew offered Capt Behm a pipe & some cards the first day—he respectfully declined—said he never received presents from passengers.[37]

Brown has found out why they call this North American S.S. Co. the Tri-Monthly Line—it is because it goes down one month & then tries next month to get back again.

---

lowing notice, which appeared in the New York *Tribune* on 17 December 1866 as part of a telegraphic dispatch from San Francisco:

> Over $300,000 was paid out in dividends to-day. The mines located on the Comstock lead and silver ores are yielding immense quantities of bullion. During the months of November and December, the dividends of six principal mines amounted to $519,000; and the yield of ten mines during October and November amounted to over $2,000,000.

The steamship *San Francisco*, which Mark Twain boarded in Greytown for the final leg of this trip, undoubtedly had copies of recent New York newspapers, including this issue of the *Tribune*.

[37] A similar episode had apparently taken place aboard the *America* at the outset of the voyage from San Francisco. Mark Twain reported to the *Alta California* (*MTTB*, p. 21) that "Broad-shouldered, kinky-haired Isaac"

> writes cards for a living, and came on board with a pack ready written and elaborately decorated with the familiar old tiresome flowers, cupids and birds of unknown species, for half the officers of the ship—and was surprised to learn that nautical etiquette forbade those gentlemen to accept of presents from passengers. He offered Captain Waxman . . . a meerschaum pipe (bogus) and was utterly confounded at its non-acceptance.

Brown came & woke me up at midnight to get this off, & it had peculiar pungency from the fact that the ship had been lying motionless on the dead calm water for <two hours> an hour fixing a bolt-head that broke this evening.

Passengers growl less this trip than I ever saw—but they *will* growl *some* on *all* trips, no matter how favorable every thing may be.

For Mayor & Custom House list—must be made up by purser, who makes it up according to his own notion thus:

Miss Smith 45—milliner—Ireland—California—(& she young & wealthy).

Mark Twain—Barkeeper—Terra del Fuego—Cal.

—Kingman—age 64—[--]

If his name is Molineux put him down a Frenchman—if O Flaherty, put him down Ireland—(these are Littlebridge's instructions to his boy clerk

Brown[38]

One of the sick men is dead. This calls for Rev. Fackler again. —9.10 P.M. poor *fellow*.

Nebraska, Dakotah, Nevada & Nicaragua—all splendid fast new ships building for the line—Nevada will be finished & ready to start around the Horn in 6 weeks—will make 15 knots all the time right along, with 20 pounds of steam.[39]

The man was buried overboard at a little past 10 PM.

Sent the America's surgeon along to take care of both sets of passengers over Isthmus

D—n these correspondents—I strike them everywhere. [#]

---

[38] Mark Twain revised this entry for inclusion in an *Alta California* letter (*MTTB*, pp. 79–80) as an excerpt from "Brown's Log-Book."

[39] In early 1867 the *Nicaragua* and the *Nevada* were put in service on the New York–Greytown circuit of the North American Steamship Company's Nicaragua route. In the fall of that year the *Dakota* was also put on the same run and the *Nebraska* began service between Aspinwall and New York on the company's "New Opposition Line Via Panama."

2d Jan. Midnight. Another patient at the point of death—they are filling him up with brandy.

2 Bells—The man is dead.

4 Bells—He is cast overboard. Expedition is the word in these crowded steerages.

Jan. 3.—Passed close to the Swan Islands at 9 AM—small, low, green-clad—they are guano islands—2 ships lying there taking guano.

Native women carry light, burdens on head—makes carriage erect & graceful.

Our Tropic Drink.

¾ pound of sugar, <&>
1½ " " ice
1 dozen limes,
1 lemon
1 Orange,
½ bottle of brandy.
Put in a ¾ gallon ice pitcher & fill up with water.

More baldheaded men in Cal than anywhere else.[40]

Mrs Grundy's name changed to Miss Slimmens

Second Cabin who have bought into the first are shoving themselves here there & everywhere so afraid everybody won't know it.

They have taken complete possession of the only upper Saloon on the ship—the Smoking Saloon aft—to the exclusion not only of the gentlemen but to all first cabin passengers. These things are not pleasant, but under the circumstances they cannot be helped. [#]

---

[40] In an *Alta* letter dated 2 February 1867 (*MTTB*, p. 88), Mark Twain noted that few of the elderly gentlemen he had observed on a visit to the Century Club, the New York association of "authors, artists and amateurs of letters and the fine arts," were bald: "It isn't that way in California. Most men are bald there, young and old. You know of a Sunday when it rains, and the women cannot go out, a church congregation looks like a skating pond. It is just on account of the shiny

Jan. 3—9.30 PM. Astonished to hear 3 bells strike—been sitting here reading so long I <thou> never thought of it's meaning anything else than half past 1 AM—took all my clothes off & *then* went to get ship time—find it is only 3 bells in the *first* watch. It is so stormy to-night that most of the passengers have gone to bed sea-sick long ago.

We are to be off the coast of Cuba to-morrow they say—I cannot believe it.

Folded his hands after his stormy life & slept in serenest repose under the peaceful sighing of the summer wind among the grasses over his grave.

Brown—yes, you're very sea-sick, ain't you?—you better take a little balsam co—

What!

He said "Oh, nothing,—don't mind me,"—but I <thought> half believed I heard him mutter something about Mrs Winslows Soothing Syrup for sick infants, as he went out.

Jan. 4.—Smith & Kingman sitting on the weather side of Lee deck this morning when a sea came aboard & completely drenched them—rough weather promised.

Capt.—who came aboard at Greytown where in 3 years he had worn out his constitution & destroyed his health lingered until 10 this morning & then died & was shoved overboard half an hour afterward sowed up in a blanket with 60 pounds of iron. He leaves a wife at Rochester N.Y. This makes the fourth death on shipboard since we left Sanfrancisco.[41]

Jan 4—3 PM—close in on N.W. corner of Cuba—long, flat, verdure-clad shore—Cape [*blank*] with a light house on it. [#]

---

bald heads—nothing else." And in another letter from New York on 16 April 1867 (*MTTB*, p. 142) he informed the *Alta* readers that in Saint Louis he had "noticed that few young men were bald-headed—which is not the case on the Pacific Coast."

[41] For more details about Captain Charles Mahoney, see page 279.

Miss Slimmens.

Air—Auld Lang Syne.

1

Miss Slimmens she's as <sweet> trim a lass
As any you can find—
  She always wears an old brown dress
All busted out behind

2

She talketh scandal all day long,
  With false malicious tongue—
She'd blast the brightest character
  That ever poet sung.

3

She said our ladies, one & all
  Were partisans of Jeff
And when they brought her to the scratch
  She proved it—oe'r the left.

4

On Truman she was monstrous hard,
  And hard she was on Brown
Said they'd a way of nipping cash
  Peculiarly their own.

5

She gave Mark Twain an awful shot,
  And Kingdom she did lift.
From White & Thayer the fur did fly
  Lord! how she snuffed out Smith!

6

She crowded Lewis till he swore
  If she would stop the war,
He'd take the cussèd newspaper
  She corresponded for.

7

She said 'twas funny Baker's charms
  No woman could withstand,
But if she saw where those charms lay

She wished she might be <cussed.> destroyed.

8.

Now dear Miss Slimmens take a hint,
From this rude song we've sung
And do belay your gossiping,
Trice/Dry up your blasted tongue![42]

Jan. 5.

We are to put in at Key West, Florida, to-day for coal for ballast —so they say—but rather for medicines, perhaps—the physic locker is about pumped dry.

Seven cases sickness yesterday—didn't amount to anything.

Col. Kinney pretty sick all night with Cholera or Cholera Morbus

Land ho! reported this morning—false news—no land in sight, of course.

Jan. 5—Continued.

"Shape" is said to be dying of cholera this morning.

Our servant boy, Jim, in this ship is first-rate—as good as Ben in the America.

Old Bum—comes around pretty regularly for his cock tail—broken down gambler of 15 years standing. Our room in this ship, as in the America is headquarters—& naturally all the more so here because there is no bar in this ship. I am sorry they stole that case of liquors or wine from us at Greytown,—not that I am drinking a drop, for I am not, for obvious reasons—but I am afraid the<y> boys will not have enough—we can replenish at Key West, but how about the quality?

There are half a dozen on the sick list to-day. The cursèd fools let the diarrhea run two or three days & then, <when> getting

---

42 Mark Twain composed this stanza before writing stanzas 6 and 7, which may have been added at a later time. He established their present order by interlining the numbers. Only stanzas 5 through 7 appeared in the *Alta California* (*MTTB*, pp. 63–64).

scared they run to the surgeon & <c>hope to be cured. And they lie like blazes—swear they have just been taken when the doctor of course knows better. He asked a patient the other day if he had any money to get some brandy with—said no—the ship had to furnish it—when the man died they found a $20 piece in his pocket.[43]

The d—d fools deserve to suffer some.

"Shape" has been walking the deck in stocking feet—getting wet —exposing himself—is going to die.

The disease has got into the second cabin at last—& one case in first cabin. The consternation is so great that several are going to get off at Key West (if quarantine regulations permit it) & go North overland.

The Captain visits every corner of the ship daily to see that it is kept in a state of perfect cleanliness.

Jan. 5—Continued—10 AM—The Episcopal clergyman, Rev. Mr. Fackler, is taken—bad diarrhea and griping.

All hands looking anxiously forward to the cool weather we shall strike 24 hours hence to drive away the sickness.

Like the bright light breadth of water around a ship—lightened by her paint.

12—"Shape" dead—5th death.—
"Shape" barber—only sick about 12 hours—usually eat rations for 4.

Rev. Fackler has made himself sick with sorrow for the poor fellows that died.

12.30 PM—The minister has got a fit—convulsion of some kind—so they are burying poor "Shape" without benefit of clergy. They don't wait many minutes after breath is out of the body.

There is no use in disguising it—I <b>really believe the ship is

---

43 Evidently Martin Sherlock (see p. 279).

out of medicines—we have a good surgeon but nothing to work with.

Just heard the Capt say "Purser put up an immense sign that all can read: '*No Charge for Medical Attendance Whatever!*'—put it so all can read it."

I told the Capt this morning that the fear of doctors' bills was one chief reason why the steerage passengers were concealing their illness till the last moment.

Jan 5.—2 PM—As the boys come to my room one after another (I am abed) I observe a marked change in their demeanor during the last ½ hour—they report that the Minister,<—>only sick an hour or <an> maybe two, is already very low—that a hospital has been fitted up in the steerage & he been removed thither.

Verily, the ship is fast becoming a floating hospital herself—not an hour passes but brings its fresh sensation, its new disaster—its melancholy tidings.

When I think of poor "Shape" & the preacher, both so well when I saw them yesterday evening, I <almost> realize that I myself may be dead to-morrow.

Since the last 2 hours all laughter, all levity has ceased in the ship—a settled gloom is upon the faces of the passengers.

Jan 5.—4 PM—The unfortunate minister is dying—he has bidden us all good-bye & now lies barely breathing. His name is Rev. J. G. Fackler, & he was on his way to the States to get his wife & family.[44]

The passengers are fearfully exercised, & well they may be, poor devils, for we are about to see our fifth death in five days, & the sixth of the voyage.—The Surgeon, a most excellent young man, a Mason, & a <p>first rate physician & one of considerable practice, has done all he could to allay their fears by telling them he has all the medicines he wants, that the disease is only a virulent sort of diarrhea, Cholera Morbus, &c.

---

[44] In fact, this was the Reverend St. M. Fackler, Episcopal clergyman from Boise City, Idaho. He had been seen off from San Francisco by a cousin, the Reverend J. G. Fackler, pastor of the Central Presbyterian Church. Mark Twain's confusion of the cousins, made public in his telegram in the *Alta* of 13 January 1867 (see pp. 296–297), would elicit an explanatory letter from the San Francisco clergyman which was published by the *Alta* three days later.

Discovering that he was a <Mason> XXX, I took him aside & asked him for a plain statement, for *myself alone*[45] & told him I thought I was man enough to stand the truth in its <most> worst form—

He then said the disease was *cholera* & of the most virulent type —that he had done all a man could do, but *he had no medicines* to work with—that he shipped the first time this trip & found the locker empty & no time to make a requisition for more medicines.

Jan. 5.—5 PM—That bolt-head broke day before yesterday & we lost two hours—

It broke again yesterday & we lost 3 or four hours.

It broke again this afternoon & again we lay like a log on the water (head wind) for 3 or 4 hours more.

These things distress the passengers beyond measure. They are scared about the epidemic & *so* impatient to get along—& now they have lost confidence in the ship & fear she may break again in the rough weather that is to come. I did not take any interest in the matter until just now I found the cursed little <boat>bolt was a sort of King-pin & that the <ship> engines must stop without it.

The passengers say we are out of luck & that it is a doomed voyage

It appears, though of course it is kept from the passengers, that there are 7 or 8 patients in the hospital down below.

Lightning.

Off the coast of <Mexico, under> Gautemala, above one of the 8 volcanoes (remember the beautiful Indian Summer there), we saw lightning flash out of a cloud for the first time I can remember in 5 or 6 years—we hoped it would thunder but it didn't.

MEM *Mem*—Get names of the dead from the First Officer to telegraph. [#]

---

45 Samuel Clemens had become a member of Polar Star Masonic Lodge No. 79 in Saint Louis on 10 July 1861, an affiliation he would maintain until 8 October 1869. His most recent known participation in Masonic activities had been in February 1865, when he had served as junior deacon at a meeting of the Angel's Camp lodge (see the headnote to Notebook 4).

Some misgivings, some distress as to whether the authorities of Key West will let our pestilence-stricken ship land there—but the Capt. says we are in sore distress, in desperate strait, & we *must* land, we *will* land, in spite of orders, cannon or anything else—we *can*not go on in this way.

If we do land, some of our people are going to leave—the doctor among them, who is afraid of the crazy machinery.

Sea in storm—caps crawling & squirming like white worms in the midst of ink.

The Dead. <—Je>

1 Harlan, Sacramento, baptized day <before> it died.—died 24 buried 25th

2 Jerome Shields, aged about 34—buried at sea<.> Jan. 2. His friend Patrick Burns, took charge of his effects, consisting of $55 in coin, a carpet bag containing clothing, letters a navy pistol <& a> & other small articles, <a> photographs &c. His friends reside in Waverly, Iowa. His brother-in-law, John Clark, lives at Pine Grove, Sierra County, Cal.

<J> 3 Martin Sherlock, of Irish descent, aged about 30, died & was buried at sea Jan. 3. He had no friends or acquaintances on board ship. His effects consisting of carpet sack, of clothing, <letters &> $20 piece, & <letters addressed to his Mother> letters from Mary Ann Sherlock, his mother, residing at Port Byron, Ill, are in possession on first officer.—

4 Capt Chas Mahoney, aged 40, late employe of Central American Transit Co, died of hemorrhage of the bowels Jan. 4. & was buried at sea. Has a family somewhere about Rochester, N.Y.

5 Andrew Nolan, about 20 or 21, barber by trade, died Jan. 5 & was buried at sea. Funds, $77. He belonged in Jersey City.

6 At 2.20 A.M. this Morning, Jan. 6, Rev. J. G. Fackler, Episcopal clergyman, of San Francisco.[46] At 2.30 we anchored at Key West (Florida,) & he will be buried on shore. Was bound for the States to get his family. [#]

[46] Actually the Reverend St. M. Fackler, from Boise City, Idaho (see note 44).

Only armed man going down on Sanf went around every Sunday distributing tracts among the passengers.

Sunday Jan. 6. 1867. We are out 22 days from San Francisco.

This Key West *looks* like a mere open roadstead, but they call it one of the best *harbors* in the world—they say the 100 little keys scattered all around keep of[47] sea & storm.

It seems to be a very pretty little tropical looking town, with plenty of handsome shade trees. It is very cool & pleasant.

The <fr>great frowning fortification is Fort Taylor & is very strong.

Brown says (on the Isthmus) now here's where the butter comes from.

We don't calculate to find any Key West folks in Heaven.[48]

7 Jan. 8. Chas Belmayne
8 Jan 11. P. Peterson[49]

A Novel
WHO WAS HE?

As I promised, I will now write you a novelette.
Gillifat was a man.
All men are men.
No man can be a man who is not a man.

---

[47] Mark Twain originally wrote *of*. A second *f* was added in what appears to be a darker pencil, probably the same used to inscribe the use marks which surround the entry. It is likely that the correction was made by Albert Bigelow Paine when he revised this entire passage, through the description of Fort Taylor, for inclusion in his edition of *Mark Twain's Notebook*.

[48] In describing the economy of Key West, Mark Twain claimed that it depended in part on overcharging passing ships for fuel and provisions and providing their passengers with "villainous" fare at first-rate prices and concluded that "if they keep on in that way, a Key Wester will be a curiosity in Heaven hereafter" (*MTTB*, pp. 70–71).

[49] The numbers preceding these names indicate they were inscribed here as belated additions to the list of dead passengers Mark Twain began to keep on 5 January. He left the back of the page with the list blank, probably for the inclusion of the names of more cholera victims.

Hence Gillifat was a man.

Such was Gillifat.

Too Many Cooks Spoil the Broth

At the corner of the beach furthest from the *Tremouille,* which is also between the great rock called Labadois & the Budes du Noir, two men stood talking.

One was a Dutchman

One wasn't.

Such is life.

Allons.

The Hair of the Dog will Cure the Bite.

The *Enfant* lay at anchor. The Enfant was of that style of vessel called by the Guernsey longshoremen a *croupier.*

They always call such vessels *croupiers.*

It is their name.

This is why they call them so.

A storm was rising.

Storms always rise <on>in certain conditions of the atmosphere.

They are caused by certain forces operating against certain other forces which are called by certain names & are well known by persons who are familiar with them. In 1492 Columbus sailed.

There was no storm but he discovered—

What?

A new world!

Oct. 23, 1835, a storm burst upon the coasts of England which drove ships high & dry <&>upon the land—a storm which carried sloops & schooners far inland & perched them upon the tops of hills.

Such is the nature of storms.

Let the Sinless Cast the first Stone.

The house was in flames. From the cellar gratings flames burst upward.

From the ground floor windows, from the doorways, from obscure crevices in the weather boarding flames burst forth.

And black volumes of smoke.

From the second story windows, flames & smoke burst forth—the flames licking the smoke hungrily—the smoke retreating,<—>from threatened devourment as it were.

The third story was a lashing and hissing world of gloomy smoke, stained with splashes of bloody flame.

At a window of the second story appeared a wild vision of beauty —appeared for a moment, with disheveled hair, with agonized face, with uplifted, imploring hands—appeared for a second, then vanished amid rolling clouds of smoke—appeared again, glorified with a rain of fiery <sp>cinders from above—& again was swallowed from sight by the remorseless smoke.

It was Demaschette

In another second Gillifat had siezed a ladder & placed it against the house.

In another moment he had ascended half way up.

A thousand anxious eyes were fixed upon him.

The<y> old mother & the distracted father fell upon their knees —looked up at him with streaming eyes—blessed him—prayed for him.

The roof was threatening to fall in.

Not a moment was to be lost.

Gillifat held his breath to keep from inhaling the smoke—then took one, two, six strides & laid his hand upon the window sill.

There are those who believe window sills are sentient beings.

There are those who believe that the moving springs of human action are the Principle of Good & the Principle of Evil—that window may, & they may not, have something to do with these.

It is wonderful.

If they have, where are the labors of our philosophers of a thousand years? If they have not, have we not God? Let us be content. Everything goes.

<Time is. The heavens are above us still. Everything goes.>

The fatal difference betwixt Tweedledum & Tweedledee.

The two men glared at each other eight minutes—time is terrible in circumstances of danger—men have grown old under the effects of fright while the fleetest horse could canter a mile—eight minutes

—eight terrible minutes they glared at each other & then—

Why does the human contract under the influence of <fear> joy & dilate under the influence of fear?

It is strange. It is one of the conditions of our being.

The human eye is round. It protrudes from the socket, but it does not fall out. Why? Because certain ligatures, invisible because hidden <by> from sight, chain it to the interior apparatus.

The pupil of the eye is also round. We do not pretend to account for this. We simply accept it as a truth. A man might see as well with a square pupil, perhaps, but what then? The absence of uniformity, of harmony in the species.

The human eye is a beautiful & an expressive feature. In November 1642, John Duke of Sebastiano insulted the Monseigneur de Torbay, Knight of the Cross, Keeper of the Seals, Grand Equerry to the King—insulted him grossly. What did Torbay do?

Split him in the eye.

In 1322 Durande Montesquieu broke a lance with Baron Lonsdale de Lonsdale—drove his weapon through the latters dexter eye. Hence the injunction, hoary with usage, Mind your eye.

Beautiful?

Without doubt.

<The>Nothing is Hidden, Nothing Lost.

The Tremouille lay at anchor. The two men had just finished glaring upon each other, Gillifat was upon the <last> uppermost round of the <latt>ladder, <when—> <[¶] You remember all these thi> the storm was about to burst forth in all its terrible grandeur when—

You remember all these people & things were <all> very close together—grouped in a mass as it were.

The dreadful climax was impending—fearful moment—when

Victor Hugo appeared on the scene & began to read a chapter from one of his books.

All these people & things got interested in his imminently impending climaxes & suspended their several <aims.> enterprises.

The flames & the smoke stood still.

The girl <stood> ceased to fluctuate<.> in the smoke.

<The> Gillifat halted.

The two men about to shed blood, paused.

The croupier slacked up on her cable.

But behold!

When after several chapters the climaxes never <came> arrived, but got swallowed up in interminable <phil> <metaphy> incomprehensible metaphysical disquisitions, columns of extraneous general information<s>, and chapters of wandering incoherencies, they became disgusted &—

Lo! a miracle!

The croupier up anchor & <left.> went to sea.

The two disputants <vamosed> left.

The (girl) disappeared for good.

Gillifat climbed down the ladder & departed.

The fire went out. Voila! They couldn't stand it.

V alone remained—

Victor was Victor still!

THE END.

(I pass. I withdraw from my contract. I cannot write the novelette I promised. In an insane moment I ventured to read the opening chapters of the Toilers of the Sea[50] & now I am tangled! My brain is in hopeless disorder. Take back your contract.

4 days without food.

Kingdom's father's discharge of the old gun.[51] [#]

---

[50] Mark Twain apparently undertook to read and then to burlesque Victor Hugo's *Toilers of the Sea* as distraction from the *San Francisco's* spreading epidemic. He did not include this burlesque in his *Alta California* writings, but in his letter dated 19 April 1867 (*MTTB*, pp. 152–153), and later in chapter 57 of *The Innocents Abroad,* he told of a hotel porter in Keokuk, Iowa, who presented him reading matter which included *The Toilers of the Sea* and thus precipitated his departure for a rival hotel.

[51] This entry and the one that follows refer to anecdotes told by Hector J. Kingman, for in the *Alta California* (*MTTB*, pp. 74–77) Mark Twain attributed two of these stories to Kingdom, Kingman's fictional counterpart. In the "Legend of the Musket" Kingdom related that his father's "shoulder was set back four inches,

<4 days without food.>—Kingdom's chicken-hawk with a crow's tail. Send it to Prof. Hagenbaum, Albany.

Trout with broken tail—Thought you might like to send it to Prof. H. Albany.

Sunday Jan. 6—*Cont.* Rev. J. G. Fackler was buried here at Key West at noon, by Episcopal Minister.

Our Doctor told me it was Asiatic Cholera, but they must have deceived the port surgeon else they wouldnt have let us land.[52]

I attended Episcopal service—heap of style—fashionably dressed women—350 of them & children & 25 men.

Don't see where so much dress comes from in a town made altogether of one & 2 story frames, some crazy, unpainted and with only thick board shutters for windows.—no carpets, no mats,—bare floors—cheap bloody prints on walls.

Only about 10 or 12 houses with any pretensions to style—& *one half* of these are military officer's quarters. As <most of> half the style went *up* the street, I think they must have been military.

The contribution box fooled me—I heard no money dropping in it, & the paper currency never occurred to me.

Men stylishly dressed, & with yellow ribbon cravats.

Town full of cocoa-nut trees of the many-leaved, low, branching pattern—very pretty.

Girls singing in most houses.

Haven't seen a really pretty woman in town.

Roads are in 3 paths, with grass between—very few prints of wheels, or horse shoes, or cows hoofs either, for that matter—saw

---

and his jaw turned black and blue, and he had to lay up for three days" after firing an old gun that a hired hand had induced Kingman to charge with "10 balls and 5 slugs" and "three or four handfuls" of powder. In "The Tale of the 'Bird of a New Specie' " Kingdom recalled how he and his brother had introduced a crow's tail into a "chicken-hawk's transom" and temporarily convinced their father and uncle it was a new species of bird worthy of being sent "to Professor Hagenbaum, at Albany."

[52] Within a day Mark Twain's disenchanting experiences in Key West would provide him a sardonic explanation for the *San Francisco's* routine reception there despite the epidemic on board (see pp. 287–288).

only one cow & two riding horses & one carriage—guess they go foot back mostly.

Duty on Havana cigars 300 per cent—on raw tobacco 35 only—so, import tobacco & then make cigars.

We bought 700 superb cigars at $4 a hundred—<bette> greenbacks—better cigars than could get in Cal for $25 a hundred in *gold*. Town is full of good cigars.

<T>Got up a dinner party in town—our own claret & champagne was good, & there was nothing else good about the dinner except the fried eggs—& *they* didn't hold out.

This is really a big town—big enough to hold over 2,000—though many houses seem deserted. Business mostly gin-mills—thats is for soldiers. It answers the question "What in the very devil is there here to support a population on this little barren rock in the sea with no market no commerce, no communication with the world—not even a visible garden on it?" The fortification & the military establishment support it. Remove them & the town would go to the devil.

<A>The people are very poor. A citizen said—"They'd sell the very shirts off their backs.

A steamer from N.O. to Havana touches here. Result, many Spanish here.

We passed through the nigger quarter—many black & jolly rascals here.

But those houses with no windows (only thick board shutters) beat my time.

They put me in the aftermost seat in cch with the niggers d—n them. They always gauge *me*, somehow or other.[53]

They take greenbacks here for everything.

I cannot yet realize that I am back in America again. [#]

---

[53] For publication in the *Alta* Mark Twain modified this entry to "I attended Episcopal service, and they gauged me at a glance and gave me a back seat, as usual" (*MTTB*, p. 72).

Some of the passengers who were scared by the Cholera wanted to go to NO, but the steamer was too uncertain—they will go on to N.Y.

The surface of the ground is a coarse white sandstone like fish-eggs stuck together.

The island is hardly raised above sea level.

The eternal cactus (large prickly pear) grows all over these chapparals—& a tree which looks like inferior orange—& in all the yards are cocoa-nuts & tamarinds—rose of <S>sharon, oleander & a thing which looks like century plant.

Stopped here at Key West at 3 oclock this morning—it is midnight now.

All over the ground everywhere at Greytown are the pretty blossoms of the sensitive plant, like pink bachelor's button—touch or even breathe upon it & it <dries> shrivels up.

Siempre vivre.

That lousy dinner for 11 adults & 2 children at Key West (we having but 2 dishes & 1 kind pie & 1 of cake & furnishing our own wine) cost $24. *This* is the way these thieves live.

The little doctor is all right now—got medicine enough to go around the world—he is a fine man—worked hard & was up all night, often.

Our <wines> brandy here (good article) cost $15 a gallon—$40.

Key West, <6>7th

21 passengers left the ship here, scared—among them the Jew, the Undertaker, <& [--]y> Goff, (<l>Let apples rot)

Some of them gave dinner & berth <to fr> tickets to remaining friends in the steerage! It would go down with the purser. I am glad they are gone, d—n them.

Jan. 7. Capt. Behm has <p>just poked his head in at the

window to say how lucky we were not to be quarantined at Key West (we are off—have just turned the pilot boat adrift)

Lucky! Damnation!—if I have got Key West put up right they would receive War, <P>Famine Pestilence & Death without a question—call them all by some fancy name & then rope in the survivors & sell them good cigars & good brandies at <r> easy prices & horrible dinners at <a> infamous rates. *They* wouldn't quarantine *any*body—they say Come! & say it gladly—if you brought destruction & hell in your wake. They rely upon the salubrity of their climate, & its famous healthfulness for immunity from disease.

1st Cal steamer in 2 yrs

Brown

Kingdom's fellow who went on stage & examined prof's head & said it was first time he ever saw such a peculiar head—ever saw ignorance & pusillanimousness so remarkably combined—prettiest fight there in about a minute you ever saw.

More cheerfulness at table this morning than ever before—even descended to trifling—the mustard pot & a large potato on a fork were kept traveling from hand to hand all round our (the purser's) table all breakfast time.

Key West prices: Putting coal aboard $2 a ton—in N.Y. 25 cents —Pilotage $108. Making a bolt, $50. They say it was first Cal steamer has touched there in two years—so they scorched us.

<Oliphant> Oliver tried to get the Capt. for $100 to contract not to bury him at sea in case he died—Capt refused, so Oliver went ashore at Key West at 9 P.M.—the last man.

Brown calls the Monkey Cor. of Nicaragua Transcript.
Sewing society for the monkey.

Ship—Key West $2,011.—100 tons coal. & provisions & medicines.

<B>Via Panama ship would direct N.E. just to E of Jamaica, <th>& thence through the Windward passage between Isles of

Cuba & St Domingo, thence up through midst of the Bahamas straight up the 74th meridian (the one N. York is on.

Via Nicaragua, ship passes same way—or up through W end of Carribbean Sea,—thence nearly N.W. through channel of Yucatan, between Yucatan & Cuba (almost touching the latter—thence sharp N.E (<m>or more Eastwardly than that) skirting Florida —thence cut across (N. by E.) the bend in Florida, Ga. N. & S. Carolina, to C. Hatteras, thence on 74° upward.

2850 from San Juan del Sur to S. F.
24,00 from San Juan to N. York.
2,850
2,400
———
5,250

The d—d 2^{d} cabin passengers lay & loll in our smoking saloon all the time. It

Jan 7. 18 invalids yesterday—only 13 to-day—only 2 really dangerous—one of them was getting along handsomely, but got drunk & took a relapse.

The noblest cigars in the world at Key West for $6 per 100.—smuggled from Havana.

Sewing Society

They have dressed the monkey up in black pants & vest & a <coat> roundabout & cuffs of a bright <curt> red & yellow curtain calico pattern, & paper collar—& he looks gay scampering among the rigging.

Oliver had 380 cholera articles cut out.

Capt Wakeman's advice to the new married couple.[54] [#]

---

[54] Wakeman's advice to the runaway couple he married by "peremptory order" appears at length in the *Alta California* (*MTTB*, pp. 24–25). Although the Captain's "homely eloquence" is structured by a sustained naval metaphor and sprinkled with seaman's language, this brief note was apparently sufficient to recall it to Mark Twain and to prompt his powers of imaginative re-creation.

Kingman found his long girl <in>he is in love with sitting by the taffrel picking her nose with a sliver. He's in love with her.[55]

Katy's mother swear—been vomiting on her in 2ᵈ cabin.

Wakeman cursing the man who <whine> came whining to him after gambling away his money.

Monkey man won $100 by the old string game from, steerage passenger—latter came whining & complaining monkey man was a gambler.

Monkey on the tarred ropes.

Dr. Grey.

<Belmay> Belmayne died Jan. 8, & was buried at sea. abreast of Florida.

The temperature of the Gulf Stream here (they try it every 2 hours for information Navy Dept.) is 76°—atmosphere 72. We are comfortable enough now while we are in this fluid stove, but when we leave it at Cape Hatteras Lord! it will be cold!

The speed of the stream varies from ⅓ m to 3½ <m>knots an hour. We have been making 200 & 210–20 m a day, but now in this current we can turn off 250–60–75.

The old man has wonderful charts compiled by Lt. Maury,[56] which are crammed with shoals, & currents, & lights & buoys & soundings, & winds & calms & storms—black figures for soundings, bright spots for beacons, an interminable tangle like a spider's web of red lines denoting the tracks of hundreds of ships whose logs have been sent to Maury.

---

55 Mark Twain later used this entry as the basis for Brown's journal comment: "Found my old girl setting in her old place by the taffrail, sighing and pensive, just as she always is, and also reading poetry and picking her nose with a fork. I cannot live without her" (*MTTB*, p. 79).

56 Matthew Fontaine Maury, oceanographer and naval officer. Maury's charts, the product of his own research, supplemented by information provided by seamen grateful for his work, established shorter ocean passages, allowing for vast savings of time and money. In 1855 he had published *The Physical Geography of the Sea*, the first textbook of modern oceanography.

"They that go down to the sea in ships see the wonders of the great deep.

Man on a midnight sea where all looks alike, measuring from star to star & knowing precisely where the ship is.

We stop at Greytown 2 weeks out & get papers from N.Y. which tell all about us. Stop at Key West & get more N.Y. papers which contain news *we* only ought to know.

8m 8 Usual run 210–20 per 24^{h}

In the strongest current of the Gulf Stream at 4 this morning, off Jupiter Inlet—say 3½ m. Numerous bets we wouldn't make 250 miles.—we made 271 in the 24<^{h}> hours ending at noon.

The next 24, current not so strong, but wind coming around promising to <let us go f> be free at any rate & maybe fair—so we may do it again.

350 m from Key West.

Jan. 8.

Growl in steerage—why did they *go* in the steerage? Growl in the 2^{d} cabin—why did they *go* in 2^{d} cabin?

They have more privileges than 1st cabin.

That dirty Dutchwoman & her 2 children—none of them washed or taken off clothes since left Sanf—belong in 2^{d} cabin—ought to be in <hell>—<husb> purser started them out of the smoking room to make room for card party—Dutchman brought them back soon & said she was sick & *should* stay there.

Well, the woman *is* sick, & if they don't take sanitary measures, she'll stay so—she needs scraping & washing.[57] [#]

---

[57] In the *Alta California* (*MTTB*, p. 26), Mr. Brown makes similar remarks about one of the *America's* passengers, attributing them to "old Slimmens":

> She says she knew that innocent old fat girl that's always asleep and has to be shovelled out of her room at four-bells for the inspection, and always eats till her eyes bug out like the bolt-heads on a jail door . . . and knows the clothes she's got on now she's travelled in eleven weeks without changing—says her stockings are awful—they're eleven weeks gone, too—and when she complained of the weather being so hot, old Slimmens said "Why don't she go and scrape herself and then wash—it would be equal to taking off two suits of flannel!"

Tradition of a snow storm in Sanf—<3> 13 yr ago.

Table talk.

Dinner table talk at Sea—what became of the boy that stood on the burning deck?[58]

No inquest.

Extracts from Brown's Journal.[59]

Condensed Milk.

Key West.

$1250

Coal 100 tons	$1,206.00
Labor on it $2	205[.]00
Burying Minister	30.00
Port Doctor Quar Off	10.00
Provisions	124.45
2 bolts ($1.50)	50.00
300 lbs Beef	56.00
Drugs & Meds	221.75
	< >
	<1903.20>
Pilot	$108.00
(13. ft. 6 in.—$4 per foot)	
Total	$2,011.20.

Soaked banana & plantain in brandy & got the monkey tight—sport. Jan 9.

Brown in love w[h] long woman—in heaven holding her head to vomit when she is sea-sick [#]

---

[58] This is an allusion to Felicia Dorothea Hemans' poem "Casabianca."

[59] "I captured Brown's journal," Mark Twain informed readers of the *Alta California* (*MTTB*, pp. 79–80), "and I mean to make an extract from it, whether it be fair or not." He then attributed to Brown revised versions of two entries from this notebook (see notes 38 and 55).

Bridget going out to borrow a washtub from the Mormons.[60]

Jan. 10, 1867.—26 days out from Sanfrancisco to-day—at <7 AM> noon we shall be off Cape Hatteras & less than 400 miles south of New York—(day & a half's run.)

We shall leave this warming pan of a Gulf Stream to-day & then it will cease to be genial summer weather & become wintry cold. We already see the signs—they have put feather mattresses & blankets on our berths this morning.

It is raining—warm.

Geo. Wilson & party in Death Valley, dogged by Indians, poisoned a mule & left it—went there next day & found mule devoured & 42 armed warriors laid out around him.

Man in Humboldt declined to go out & hunt Indians—said he hadn't lost any.[61]

Curry[62] sold 600 feet of Gould & Curry for $2,600. Gould sold 600 feet for $250, an old plug horse, a jug of whisky & a pair of blankets.

A man sold 26 feet of Ophir or Yellow Jacket for an old plug horse—called him the $26,000 horse.

---

60 In chapter 25 of *Roughing It* Mark Twain would write of the Irish Catholic "hired girl" of some "orthodox Americans" whose ability to "get favors from the Mormons" was a mystery until "one day as she was passing out at the door, a large bowie knife dropped from under her apron, and when her mistress asked for an explanation she observed that she was going out to 'borry a wash-tub from the Mormons!' " The recollected Western incidents which occur in the following pages alongside recalled events of this trip to New York suggest Mark Twain's increasing boredom with the journey.

61 This entry and the preceding one, although not in the published version of *Roughing It*, were lined through in ink in the same fashion and apparently at the same time that Mark Twain lined out six adjacent anecdotes (see notes 60, 62, 63, and 68) and "Tradition of a snow storm in Sanf–<3> 13 yr ago" (p. 292), all used in that book. All nine stories may have been incorporated in a now unknown early sketch or an early manuscript of *Roughing It*.

62 The following three anecdotes all appear in chapter 46 of *Roughing It* with their statistics somewhat revised.

100 feet <(>of Ophir (the present Mexican) was segregated for a stream of water as large as your wrist to some Spaniards. Afterwards worth $18,000 a foot.

Jan. 10—Rainy. At 11 AM 18 miles from Cape Hatteras—thence to N.Y. 320 miles.

8 sick—5 diarrhea—3 convalescent—2 better.

Plug hat & white shirt in the mines.[63]

Jan 10.—Passing out of the Gulf Stream rapidly—at 2 PM the temperature of the water had fallen 7 degrees in half an hour—from <6>72 down to 65—we are about out of the warming pan & already the day is turning cold & overcoats coming into vogue.

At 2.30 P.M. Temperature of water 2 degrees low—[only] 63.

A 3 PM. Temperature Water 61.

<Jno Henning—wheeling dirt—crazed by money—Softening brain—gibbering idiot.[64]

Henderson—car conductor.>

Jan. 10, 11.30 PM—Dark & stormy & the ship plunging considerably. <Have> It is villainously cold. Have just come forward from the purser's room & felt something blow in my face like snow—think it was—but too dark to tell. [#]

---

[63] According to chapter 57 of *Roughing It,* such attire was sure to provoke a violent reaction from the California gold miners, who "hated aristocrats" and "had a particular and malignant animosity toward what they called a 'biled shirt.' "

[64] John S. Henning was an early settler of Nevada Territory, where he became acquainted with Mark Twain. In the mid-1860s he was a partner in the Adelphi Hotel Company, proprietors of the Cosmopolitan Hotel on the corner of Bush and Sansome streets in San Francisco. Mark Twain had covered the riotous opening of the Cosmopolitan for the *Call* of 1 September 1864 (see "The Cosmopolitan Hotel Beseiged," *Clemens of the "Call": Mark Twain in San Francisco,* ed. Edgar M. Branch [Berkeley and Los Angeles: University of California Press, 1969], pp. 58–59). This entry may explain why around 1867 Henning ceased to be associated with the Cosmopolitan Hotel and seems to have disappeared from San Francisco.

Mean W.

That whining puppy—scared at the storm first night out from Sanfrancisco—his little wife out observing the signs of the weather.

He whined all the way down & was nursed by her.

He lay & whined on the lake boat & she sat up all night & fanned him. The sofa in the social hall was coolest place & she wanted it—he wouldn't give it up—she tried the stateroom—too hot—came back & fanned him all night.

<She sat up in> On the last boat on the San Juan, she slept in a grass hammock without blankets & he lay on the deck on the blankets & whined as usual.

At Greytown he went ashore & wouldn't let her go.

In the Atlantic he was scared to death about the cholera—she sat by his bedside & fanned him two whole days & he whining with a pitiful headache which he feared was cholera—yet he went to his meals regularly.

At Key West scared out of his wits, he wanted to desert the ship & sail for Havana or New Orleans—& said it was his *wife* who proposed it & *he* was not in favor of it—the liar—I had just heard her regretting his determination

At Key West he got into that dinner arrangement—wanted to pay his share, as Capt Snow & I were the only invited guests but took good care not to recollect it afterward.

<Went into the ⅛> Took ⅛ share in the $40 worth of brandy at Key West & has not paid his $5.

Gives his waiter old clothes instead of money.

Jan. 11, 7 PM—Been in bed all day to keep warm—fearfully cold. We are off Barnegat—passed a pilot boat a while ago.

We shall get to New York before morning.

The d—d crowd in the smoking room are as wildly singing now as they were capering childishly about deck day before yesterday when we first struck the cold weather [#]

Out four weeks—28 days—at noon, Saturday Jan. 12, 1867 from Sanfrancisco.

Friday night 11.

2 Bells—P. Peterson <, the paralytic,> has just died dropsy—the Highland Light, the light ship, & several other light at entrance to New York harbor in full view—<they are burying him at sea.> This is the <7th or 8th> 8 death this voyage. Bury him ashore as we are now on soundings.

(Chas.)

Kingdom's <candi> opposition candidates one of whom got the other to write him a little speech—his sole canvass capital—Opp always led off & always rung in the little speech & took all the winds out of his sails

N.Y. Jan. 12.[65]

Arrived to-day, 27½ days out.

<Infant child of Mrs. Harlan of Sacramento died buried at sea Christmas day.>

At San Juan found 700 passengers from Santiago de Cuba (300 of them soldiers been left by Moses Taylor[66] & placards were posted

---

[65] The following long entry, through "Names of dead," is the draft of a telegram Mark Twain sent to the *Alta California* to provide immediate details of the cholera outbreak aboard the *San Francisco*, since he had not yet decided how he wished to present his account of the journey. The telegram was given front-page publication on 13 January 1867. On 17 January, the day of the *America's* return to San Francisco, the *Alta* would note: "We are in receipt of a letter from our correspondent, 'Mark Twain,' but it was sent from this side of the Isthmus and does not mention the cholera." With the exception of this letter, sent to San Francisco aboard the *America* and published in the *Alta* on 18 January 1867 (*MTTB*, pp. 11–19), Mark Twain's narrative of the journey from San Francisco, although substantially drafted in this notebook, was not put into letter form until after his arrival in New York. A second letter did not appear in the *Alta* until 22 February, and it was not until 17 March that Mark Twain's account of the cholera epidemic began to be published.

[66] This group, actually of 600 passengers, had left New York on 20 November 1866 aboard the North American Steamship Company's *San Francisco*. When the

on the America saying cholera very bad among soldiers & requiring passengers remain on board till next day

Found steamer San Francisco at Greytown with 600 more passengers for America's return trip 1,3,00 in all. Wild reports of cholera deaths reaching <200>250 on Isthmus. After some trouble got prefect & other officer's reports found only <27> 9 passengers & 27 soldiers died of Cholera.

If any those passengers remain on Isthmus, <they run some risk of cholera th> cholera may attack them again,—they are so imprudent in eating & drinking,—tho disease had stopped when we passed through, it was said. If America carries them all, cholera will be nearly sure to break out among them. Do not telegraph this to scare, but to warn & enable you to take proper precautions.[67]

Left Greytown in Steamer Sanf Jan. 1.

San Francisco became disabled near Fort Monroe, Virginia, it put into port there, and the passengers were transferred to the company's *Santiago de Cuba*. This ship reached Greytown on 6 December but because of strong winds could not land its passengers for another nine days. Upon crossing the isthmus they discovered that the steamer *Moses Taylor* had departed from San Juan del Sur without them, compelling them to await the arrival of the *America* for transport to San Francisco. Mark Twain later notified the *Alta California* (*MTTB*, p. 39) that this "vast shipload of passengers had been kept in exile for fifteen days through the wretched incompetency of one man–the Company's agent on the Isthmus."

[67] Mark Twain's telegram undoubtedly aggravated fear of a cholera epidemic in San Francisco. On 16 January 1867, the *Alta California* found it necessary to refute "Exaggerated Rumors" that the *America* had arrived the previous day carrying cholera which had "killed two hundred and fifty of her passengers." The *America* did not actually arrive until about 12:30 A.M. on 17 January. That day the San Francisco quarantine officer reported:

> Of the thousand passengers on board, five soldiers and four civilians died of cholera on the passage . . . the condition of the vessel is very favorable, but as a matter of precaution it is deemed necessary to put her in quarantine. The passengers will be landed at Saucelito, and sheltered by tents. . . . The number of days for the quarantine is not yet determined. (*Alta*, 17 January 1867)

Despite this uncertain conclusion, on 18 January the *Alta* could report that "no real Asiatic cholera exists at this time among the passengers, civilians, or soldiers." Plans for a prolonged quarantine were abandoned, and by unanimous vote of the San Francisco Board of Health steam tugs were allowed to disembark cabin passengers in San Francisco on 18 January and steerage passengers the following day.

Infant child Mrs. Harlan of Sac, died, spasms, Dec. 25, before reaching San Juan. <[¶] Lef>—Buried at Sea

Left Greytown Jan. 1. Next day <2>3 cases in steerage believed to be cholera. One died that night—one on 3^{d}, one on 5th one on 6th, one on 8th—all <currently reported> believed by passengers to be cholera. Two other deaths, other diseases.

Put in at Key West 6th, for some few supplies, but chiefly to allay fright & distress of the passengers.—Many steerage prostrated with diarrhea. Twenty-one worst scared passengers deserted the ship there when was no longer occasion for fear.

Names of dead—

<Water's joke—spring of '49.>

Man in Washoe moved ranch above high water mark.[68]

Carson—Give us this day our daily stranger.[69]

Pet phrases—in S I "indigenous."

<N.>Cal & <N.Y> Atlantic states "peek" instead of "peep."

Reckon—cal'late—guess

Pronunciation—N. England, glahs for glass.[70] [#]

---

68 Apparently an allusion to the "great landslide case" incident that Mark Twain used as a literary subject on three occasions, the last time in chapter 34 of *Roughing It* (see Notebook 4, note 32).

69 In chapter 51 of *Roughing It*, Mark Twain would claim that Thomas Fitch, editor of the short-lived Virginia City literary paper, the *Weekly Occidental*, "once said of a little, half-starved, wayside community that had no subsistence except what they could get by preying upon chance passengers who stopped over with them a day when traveling by the overland stage, that in their Church service they had altered the Lord's Prayer to read: 'Give us this day our daily stranger!'" Mark Twain's own recent experiences in Key West (see pp. 287–288) probably recalled Fitch's remark to him at this time.

70 In his *Alta California* letter dated 16 April 1867 (*MTTB*, pp. 141–142) Mark Twain would enlarge upon the observations of regional pronunciation noted in these three entries.

Notice.[71]

The usual Entertaining Spectacle of Dutch Babies and Sea-Sick Steerage Passengers, (in their customary engaging and truly extraordinary attitudes,) will be exhibited

THIS EVENING,
Jan. 8, 1867.

In that portion of the Ship distinctly set apart *"For the Gentlemen of the First Cabin Only,"* (but more familiarly known as the "Teutonic Nursery.")

Admission—Steerage, Second Cabin & Babies *free.* as usual. First Cabin passengers may look in at the windows—One Dollar, coin.

Regulations.

Song "Pass Under the Rod,"

Larboard Watch.[72]

2 cases 2^{d}—

---

[71] Twenty-four blank pages intervene between the previous note and this entry, written on the back flyleaf with the notebook inverted. In conjunction with "Regulations," inscribed after it on the last ruled page with the notebook still inverted, this notice may have been the beginning of an extended parody of ship's rules, much like one Mark Twain would compose aboard the *Quaker City* in a notebook used on that voyage (see p. 329).

[72] "The Larboard Watch" by Thomas E. Williams was one of the songs presented by the choir of passengers aboard the *America.* They may also have sung Mary S. B. Dana's "Passing Under the Rod," although Mark Twain does not mention that song in his *Alta California* letters. The last three entries were inscribed at random on the back flyleaf of the notebook.

VIII

"The Great Pleasure Excursion to Europe and the Holy Land"

(May–July 1867)

NOTEBOOK 8 was evidently begun in mid-May 1867, less than three weeks before Clemens sailed in the *Quaker City* for Europe and the Holy Land. It is the first of three surviving *Quaker City* notebooks and contains notes that Clemens made primarily for his letters to the San Francisco *Alta California*, and so by extension for his first major book, *The Innocents Abroad*. He did make some early notes in New York for letters he sent to the *Alta* before the trip began, but by far the largest portion of the notebook was filled with his initially enthusiastic record of the excursion, as the travelers made their way across the Atlantic to the Azores, then to Gibraltar and Tangier. He discontinued Notebook 8 shortly after 2 July as the ship sailed for Marseilles, although he added several brief entries at a later time. Clemens used most of his notes in sequence, elaborating on them in four letters to the *Alta* and one to the New York *Herald*. Since his newspaper letters often provide the best possible annotation for the notebook, the reader should consult them, along with *The Innocents Abroad*, which Clemens composed from the letters, incorporating revisions, and making additions occasionally supplied by these *Quaker City* notebooks. The letters from New York sent before departure have been collected in *Mark Twain's Travels with Mr. Brown,* edited by Franklin Walker and G. Ezra Dane (New York: Alfred A. Knopf, 1940). The letters from the excursion itself appear in *Traveling with the Innocents Abroad,* edited by D. M. McKeithan (Norman: University of Oklahoma Press, 1958).

The interval from January 1867 (when Notebook 7 breaks off) to mid-May 1867 (when Notebook 8 begins) was a period of considerable stress and activity for Clemens. He may simply have been too preoccupied with work to keep a notebook, or it may have been lost. Except for a six-week excursion to Saint Louis in March and April, most of the undocumented period was spent in New York. It was very much changed from the city he had first visited in 1853: "I have at last, after several months' experience," he wrote the *Alta* on June 5, "made up my mind that it is a splendid desert—a domed and steepled solitude, where the stranger is lonely in the midst of a million of his race" (*MTTB,* p. 259). In three long letters to the *Alta,* all written in February, he inspected varied aspects of city life, ranging from a performance of Broadway's notorious burlesque, *The Black Crook* ("It is the wonders of the Arabian Nights realized"), to an afternoon church service known as "Bishop Southgate's matinee"—each, as he said of the bishop, "in pursuance of my desire to test all the amusements of the metropolis" (*MTTB,* pp. 86, 95). The cure for his restless loneliness, however, was not to be found in New York's amusements, but in the chance to go to sea again.

The strain of urban life seems to have overtaken him as early as February 23, when he wrote to the *Alta* that he was suffering from "the blues" and that his "thoughts persistently ran on funerals and suicide" (*MTTB,* p. 101). The immediate cure was "the monster they call the Russian Bath," but soon afterward—seven weeks after landing in New York—he hit upon a more congenial way to fulfill his obligations as correspondent. "A great European pleasure excursion for the coming summer," he wrote the *Alta* on March 2, "promises a vast amount of enjoyment for a very reasonable outlay." He went on to describe the extensive itinerary and to specify what kind of a trip these "prominent Brooklynites" had envisioned for themselves. "Isn't it a most attractive scheme?" he asked. "Five months of utter freedom from care and anxiety of every kind, and in company with a set of people who will go only to enjoy themselves, and will never mention a word about business during the whole voyage. It is very pleasant to contemplate" (*MTTB*, pp. 111, 113). The prospect of life aboard ship was so pleasant, in fact, that he resolved to go if the *Alta* would extend his roving commission and pay the $1,250 fare. Even before the paper's response was known, Clemens made a down payment, and then happily left the city for Saint Louis, where he lectured, wrote newspaper articles, and after six weeks said farewell to his family.

When Clemens returned to New York in mid-April, he still had much to do before the ship would sail, and April and May found him increasingly busy. His literary ambition seems clear: to make "Mark Twain" as familiar and acceptable to sophisticated eastern readers as he was already on the Pacific Coast. "Make your mark in New York, and you are a made man," he wrote the *Alta* on May 17. "With a New York endorsement you may travel the country over . . . without fear—but without it you are speculating upon a dangerous issue" (*MTTB*, p. 176). He had five of his Sandwich Islands letters reprinted in the New York *Weekly Review*, and by the time of departure he would place seven fresh articles with the New York *Sunday Mercury*. In late April Charles Henry Webb published Clemens' first book, *The Celebrated Jumping Frog of Calaveras County, and Other Sketches*, which, as the sympathetic reviewer in the *Times* suggested, was calculated to introduce Mark Twain "to the lovers of humor in the Atlantic States" (1 May 1867). Finally, he asked Frank Fuller to assist him in arranging his first lectures before a New York audience—on May 6, 10, and 16.

On his return from Saint Louis he moved to more sophisticated lodgings from his usual quarters at the Metropolitan Hotel—which was known as "the resort of Californians and people from the new States and Territories" (Junius Henri Browne in *The Great Metropolis* [Hartford: American Publishing Company, 1869], p. 394). On April 19 he wrote his family from the Westminster: "Direct my letters to this hotel in future. I am just fixed, now. It is the gem of all hotels. I have never come across one so perfectly elegant in all its appointments & so sumptuously & tastefully furnished. Full of 'bloated aristocrats' too, & I'm just one of *them* kind myself."

Like the Westminster, the *Quaker City* excursion seemed to offer physical luxury and social prestige. He wrote the *Alta* on April 30:

> Our ship in which we are to sail for the Holy Land, is to be furnished with a battery of guns for firing salutes, by order of the Secretary of the Navy, and Mr.

> Seward has addressed a letter to all foreign powers, requesting that every attention be shown General Sherman and his party. . . . I have got a handsome state room on the upper deck and a regular brick for a roommate. We have got the pleasantest and jolliest party of passengers that ever sailed out of New York, and among them a good many young ladies and a couple of preachers, but we don't mind them. Young ladies are well enough anywhere, and preachers are always pleasant company when they are off duty. (*MTTB*, pp. 165–166)

As Stephen M. Griswold recalled, years later: "Mr. Beecher contemplated writing a Life of Christ. He expressed a desire to visit the sacred places of Palestine . . . and wanted several members of Plymouth Church to go with him" (*Sixty Years with Plymouth Church* [New York: Fleming H. Revell Co., 1907], p. 153). Captain Charles Duncan's prospectus for the voyage assured Clemens, moreover, that the "select company" could be "easily made up in this immediate vicinity, of mutual friends and acquaintances" (*The Innocents Abroad*, chapter 1). The presence of Beecher and his congregation, accompanied by General Sherman, was designed to assure the congeniality as well as the proper social standing of the passengers, who were to be approved by the "merciless" Committee on Applications. After paying his passage on 15 April, Clemens wrote to his family:

> A newspaper man came in & asked how many names were booked & what notabilities were going, & a fellow (I don't know who he was, but he seemed to be connected with the concern,) said, "Lt. Gen. Sherman, Henry Ward Beecher & Mark Twain are going, & probably Gen. Banks!" I thought that was very good—an exceedingly good joke for a poor ignorant clerk. (The Clifton Waller Barrett Library, University of Virginia)

Clemens may have begun to feel that the joke was really on him when, early in May, Beecher withdrew from the excursion. The immediate consequence was that forty members of Plymouth Church who had planned to accompany their pastor also declined to go. Three weeks later, General Sherman publicly announced that he would be detained by the Indian wars and could not travel with the excursion.

The withdrawal of both men had financial consequences as well as diminishing the prestige of the excursion. Captain Duncan, who had been planning the trip as early as November 1866 and who had a personal interest in the financial success of the venture, found his passenger list well short of the one hundred ten travelers he had expected. With only weeks left before departure, it was clearly no longer possible to assemble a select company from mutual friends and acquaintances. As the passenger list shows, a large proportion of the passengers came from Ohio and other western states, and relatively few from Brooklyn, or even the East Coast. The religious influence of Plymouth Church would not now be exerted through the worldly and genial Henry Ward Beecher, but rather through that "psalm singing hypocrite"—as the ship's co owner Daniel Leary called him—Captain Charles Duncan. Moreover, the pleasant and sophisticated companions that Clemens anticipated became instead a solemn and provincial, although prosperous, group of elderly tourists. When the trip was over, Clemens would write Mrs. Fairbanks, one of the few friends he made on the voyage, that there were only eight of the sixty-five passengers that he cared to remember:

> My opinion of the rest of the gang is so mean, & so vicious, & so outrageous in every way, that I could not collect the terms to express it with out of any less than sixteen or seventeen different languages. Such another drove of cattle *never* went to sea before. Select party! Well, *I* pass. (*MTMF*, p. 5)

Clemens had felt some anxiety about his fellow passengers even before sailing. To the *Alta* he reported encountering one passenger who seriously asked the captain whether "the excursion would come to a halt on Sundays" and when told that it would not, betrayed his shallow piety. "I thought I perceived that he was not good and holy, but only sagacious, and so I turned the key on my valise and moved it out of his reach. I shall have to keep an eye on that fellow" (*MTTB*, pp. 276–277). But, as the notebook shows, the dichotomy between pilgrim and sinner that he was to exploit in *The Innocents Abroad* was actually preceded by a more general dissatisfaction with the passengers. The three travelers that he sketches in the notebook as the voyage begins are all ridiculed for their lack of sophistication, coarseness, and naiveté. As he wrote John Russell Young of the New York *Tribune* after the voyage, what he really yearned to ridicule was "the Quaker City's strange menagerie of ignorance, imbecility, bigotry & dotage" (Library of Congress).

Clemens' most immediate concern before departure was the preparation of letters to the *Alta*. Those he sent show him methodically generating copy—by visiting the Society for the Prevention of Cruelty to Animals, the Midnight Mission for prostitutes, the New York Travellers' Club, the Blind Asylum. He reported on the exhibition at the Academy of Design, on Albert Bierstadt's latest painting, the most recent New York crimes, and a variety of touring San Francisco performers who were appearing in New York. Despite his restless enterprise, by mid-May he found himself seriously behind on his *Alta* correspondence. On May 20 he wrote his family: "Don't—*don't* ask me to write, for a week or two. I am 18 *Alta* letters behindhand, & I *must* catch up or bust. I have refused all invitations to lecture in the interior towns of this & neighboring States, & have settled down to work." But his own lack of inspiration and the oppressiveness of New York combined to prevent him from completing more than six letters. "I have just written myself clear out in letters to the *Alta*," he wrote his family on June 7, "and I think they are the stupidest letters that were ever written from New York. Corresponding has been a perfect drag ever since I got to the states. If it continues abroad, I don't know what the Tribune and Alta folks will think" (*MTL*, p. 127).

Clemens' mood gradually darkened as he waited impatiently for the ship to sail, trying at the same time to generate copy for the *Alta* in New York. Both his public and his private letters reveal a harried, restless state of mind that would not be dispelled for several weeks. On June 1, probably aware of Captain Duncan's deteriorating passenger list, Clemens wrote his family:

> I know I ought to write oftener . . . but I cannot overcome my repugnance to telling what I am doing or what I expect to do or propose to do. . . . It isn't any use for me to talk about the voyage, because I can have no faith in that voyage till the ship is under way. How do I know she will ever sail? . . . All I do know or feel, is, that I am wild with impatience to move—move—*move!* (*MTL*, p. 125)

On June 7, just before departure, he seemed filled with vague feelings of guilt—for not helping his brother more, for not writing oftener, perhaps for going away at all.

> My mind is stored full of unworthy conduct toward Orion and towards you all, and an accusing conscience gives me peace only in excitement and restless moving from place to place. If I could say I had done one thing for any of you . . . I believe I could go home and stay there and I *know* I would care little for the world's praise or blame. . . . You observe that under a cheerful exterior I have got a spirit that is angry with me and gives me freely its contempt. I can get away from that at sea. (*MTL*, p. 128)

The attraction of "restless moving from place to place" and of the sea voyage seemed to enlarge even though the prospect of genteel association faded. On the same day Clemens wrote Will Bowen that although he anticipated five or six months of a "jolly, sociable, homelike trip," when it was over "if we all go to the bottom, I think we shall be fortunate. There is no unhappiness like the misery of sighting land (and work) again after a cheerful, careless voyage. They were lucky boys that went down in sight of home the other day when the Santiago de Cuba stranded on the New Jersey shore" (*MTLBowen*, p. 15). And perhaps even more explicitly, he confided similar feelings of depression (blaming them on New York) to his *Alta* readers:

> There is something about this ceaseless buzz, and hurry, and bustle, that keeps a stranger in a state of unwholesome excitement all the time, and makes him restless and uneasy, and saps from him all capacity to enjoy anything or take a strong interest in any matter whatever—a something which impels him to try to do everything, and yet permits him to do nothing. . . . This fidgetty, feverish restlessness will drive a man crazy, after a while, or kill him. It kills a good many dozens now—by suicide. I have got to get out of it. (*MTTB*, pp. 260–261)

Finally, on June 8, he did leave. Even though rough weather confined the ship to New York harbor for two days, he was glad simply to be aboard. In chapter 2 of *The Innocents Abroad* he would recall that despite the inauspicious weather he had felt the "cheering influence" of the sea and when he retired that night was "rocked by the measured swell of the waves, and lulled by the murmur of the distant surf" until he passed "tranquilly out of all consciousness of the dreary experiences of the day and damaging premonitions of the future." The notebook reflects his change of mood with a drastic shift away from the elliptical, desultory New York notes to a series of extended sketches of fellow passengers and a burlesque of the ship's regulations. His depression found relief in private vituperation and ridicule that had obvious literary potential. The spark of the future book is even recorded in somewhat cryptic fashion: "Stupid remarks & ? from ? every now & then—make him a character" (p. 340).

Despite his initial testiness, Clemens seems to have joined, and even to have helped initiate, various shipboard activities: a birthday party for the captain's wife, a social club to discuss routes of travel and points of interest, a mock trial, a debating club. The captain's log records some of the other amusements provided during the sometimes stormy passage to the Azores: Bloodgood Cutter read repeatedly from his verse; stereopticon slides were shown; and the *Quaker City* trio provided several evening concerts and music for religious services and for the first of the shipboard dances. Clemens attended these functions, but seems to have found as much contentment in playing cards or dominoes, smoking, and drinking late into the night. "Horse-billiards" on the foredeck also attracted him: "[It] is a fine game. It affords good, active exercise, hilarity, and consuming excitement. It is a mixture of 'hop-scotch' and shuffle-board played with a crutch" (*The Innocents Abroad*, chapter 4).

The ship arrived in the port of Fayal on June 21, and Clemens began taking notes in earnest. The ship's company was entertained by the United States consul, Charles Dabney, whose sister Clara wrote her family on the occasion that "one young man had his note book out all the time and remarked as I gave him some verbena, 'I am taking notes as I am a correspondent of a paper' " (Roxana Lewis Dabney, *Annals of the Dabney Family in Fayal*, 3 vols. [Boston, n.d.], 3:1292). Clemens was not the only one with a notebook, of course, and certainly not the only newspaper correspondent. "Everybody taking notes," he recorded in his notebook, "cabin looks like a reporters congress" (p. 344). He was, however, the most professional and the most thorough of the various correspondents. Before leaving New York he had heard from John J. Murphy of the *Alta*, "Your only instructions are that you will continue to write at such times and from such places as you deem proper, and in the same style that heretofore secured you the favor of the readers of the *Alta California*" (*MTB*, p. 310). In his Autobiographical Dictations Clemens would recall that he contracted to write fifty letters at twenty dollars per letter, an extension of his original agreement made before leaving California (*MTA*, 1:243).

Clemens also arranged to correspond with two eastern newspapers. He agreed to write for the New York *Tribune*, which, as he told John McComb, had a circulation of 200,000. He wrote Will Bowen on June 7 that he planned to write "two letters a month" for that paper "till we reach Egypt, and then I have to write oftener" (*MTLBowen*, p. 16). He eventually completed only seven letters to the *Tribune* and, as he told his family on November 20, felt "ashamed to go to the Tribune office almost—they have treated me so well & I have not written them a third of the letters I promised" (*MTBus*, p. 95). Clemens also agreed to write several letters (to appear unsigned) for the rival New York *Herald*, and three brief letters were actually published. Significantly, however, he declined to continue his contributions to the New York *Weekly Review*. "Like all other papers that pay one splendidly," he told his family on June 1, "it circulates among stupid people and the *canaille*" (*MTL*, p. 126). He was striking out for the larger audiences of New York, and he was willing to make sacrifices for more sophisticated ones.

Novelty was the attraction of Fayal. Clemens took notes on local customs and sights, later marshaling "a paragraph of dry facts" for the *Tribune* because "the Azores must be very little known in America" (*TIA*, p. 16). And he wrote the *Alta* enthusiastically about an excursion into the hills and valleys of the island: "There was that rare thing, novelty, about it; it was a fresh, new, exhilarating sensation, this donkey riding, and worth a hundred worn and threadbare home pleasures" (*TIA*, p. 8). When the *Quaker City* left the Azores on June 23 bound for Gibraltar, the ship encountered six days of stormy passage. Evidently not yet completely at odds with the religious faction, Clemens led the day's devotions on June 24. But for the remainder of the time he smoked and played dominoes, unable to play "horse-billiards" on the stormy deck. Captain Duncan found little to enter in the log: "Nothing of special interest" happened on June 26, and "Nothing of interest" marked the next day.

On June 29 they arrived at Gibraltar, but their first European port seems to have held only mild interest for Clemens. After touring the town, he told his *Alta* readers that one might "easily understand that a crowd like ours, made up from fifteen or sixteen States of the Union, found enough to stare at in this shifting panorama of fashion," but the implication remains that he himself was not impressed (*TIA*, pp. 22–23). They toured the military installations and some archaeological sites, and Clemens wrote to his family on June 30 that he was "clear worn out with riding and climbing in and over and around this monstrous rock and its fortifications" (*MTL*, p. 129). He pondered traveling through Spain to Paris with Moses S. Beach and others, but through indecision was excluded from that party when it sailed for Cadiz.

If he was disappointed in missing that adventure, his reaction seems to have been merely a stronger resolve to do something even more exciting. "Now as to Tangiers there shall be no pulling & hauling—we will *go*. I shall answer no questions, & *not listen* to any d—d fears, surmises, or anything else," he wrote in the notebook (p. 351). It was, in fact, a daring and somewhat dangerous trip, but with the *Quaker City* delayed at Gibraltar for coaling and boiler work, there was just enough time to sail across the strait to Morocco and visit the second oldest city on the itinerary. On Sunday morning, June 30, Clemens set out with six fellow passengers—Major

James Barry, Dr. Jackson, Dan Slote, Frederick Greer, Colonel Foster, and Colonel Denny—guided by an English merchant named Redman. The rest of the passengers went to church.

As the notebook and his newspaper letters testify, Clemens found the city entirely and excitingly strange. "This is jolly!" he exploded in his *Alta* letter.

> This is altogether the infernalest place I have ever come across yet. Let those who went up through Spain make much of it—these dominions of the Emperor of Morocco suit me well enough. We have had enough of Spain at Gibraltar for the present. Tangier is the spot we have been longing for all the time. Everywhere else one finds foreign-looking things and foreign-looking people, but always with things and people intermixed that we were familiar with before, and so the novelty of the situation lost a deal of its force. We wanted something thoroughly and uncompromisingly foreign . . . nothing to remind us of any other people or any other land under the sun. And lo! in Tangier we have found it. (*TIA*, pp. 25–26)

They visited the American consul resident in the city, Jesse H. McMath, who was apparently glad to entertain these Americans with gossip about consular history and information on local customs and practices. Engaging a guide, Sadi Mohammed Lamarty, the party toured the city on their first day, and spent part of the second on a brief, uneasy ride outside its walls. They narrowly escaped Moorish wrath when Clemens prevented Major Barry from heedlessly entering a mosque, forbidden by custom to "Christian dogs." Clemens took voluminous notes on local history and legend, filling nearly one-third of the notebook. These notes furnished him more than enough material for two letters to the *Alta*, which overflowed with chaotic details of their new experiences. In fact, concluding the second of these letters, Clemens threw up his hands: "I find I cannot write up my notes, and so I will stop" (*TIA*, p. 35).

Returning to the ship late on July 1, he wrote his family in the same vein of enthusiasm: "I would not give this experience for all the balance of the trip combined. This is the infernalest hive of infernally costumed barbarians I have ever come across yet" (*MTL*, p. 130), a comment that records the height of his excitement rather than any contempt for Tangier. "It seems like profanation to laugh, and jest, and bandy the frivolous chat of our day amid its hoary relics" (*TIA*, p. 27). Unlike the disappointment that he would feel in Turkey and Palestine, his excitement here exceeded even his expectations:

> Here is not the slightest thing that ever we have seen save in pictures—and we always mistrusted the pictures before. We cannot any more. The pictures used to seem lies—they seemed too wierd and fanciful for reality. But behold, they were not wild enough—they were not fanciful enough—they have not told half the story. Tangier is a foreign land if ever there was one. And the true spirit of it can never be found in any book save the Arabian Nights. (*TIA*, p. 26)

Nevertheless, his earlier restlessness persisted, and the brevity of the visit to Africa undoubtedly contributed to its success. Clemens himself concluded that "Tangier is full of interest for one day, but after that it is a weary prison" (*TIA*, p. 35). The returning adventurers brought Moorish tobacco pipes, Moroccan dates, and "full, flowing, picturesque Moorish costumes . . . purchased in the bazaars of Tangier" (*MTL*, p. 131). And during the last shipboard dance the "Tangier 3" (Clemens, Slote, and Dr. Jackson or Frederick Greer) cavorted in their oriental finery. That midnight Clemens remarked on the end of the adventure. "After all this racing, & bustling & rollicking excitement in Africa" he wrote in the notebook, "it seems good to get back to the old ship once more. It is so like *home*. After all our weary time, we shall sleep peacefully to-night" (pp. 367–368). The quest for novelty would resume the next day, however, as the ship steamed toward Marseilles, where Clemens planned to disembark and take the train to Paris.

The passenger list derives ultimately from that given by Paine in *Mark Twain: A Biography*, pp. 1609–1610, but uses and sometimes corrects the fuller list given by Dewey Ganzel in *Mark Twain Abroad: The Cruise of the "Quaker City"* (Chicago: University of Chicago Press, 1968), pp. 319–322. Passengers who figure prominently in *The Innocents Abroad* have been marked with asterisks. When Mark Twain referred to a passenger by a nickname, it follows the formal name in quotation marks.

Passengers

Allen, Anthony Bezenet. New York, N.Y.
*Andrews, Dr. Edward ("The Oracle"). Albany, N.Y.
Barry, Major James G. Saint Louis, Mo.
*Beach, Moses Sperry. Brooklyn, N.Y.
Beach, Miss Emeline. Brooklyn, N.Y.
Beckwith, Thomas S. Cleveland, Ohio
Bell, Mr. and Mrs. R. A. H. Portsmouth, Ohio
*Birch, Dr. George Bright. Hannibal, Mo.

Bond, Mr. and Mrs. John W. Saint Paul, Minn.
Bond, Miss Ada. Saint Paul, Minn.
Bond, Miss Mary E. Plaquemine, La.
Brown, Dr. M. Circleville, Ohio
Brown, Miss Kate L. Circleville, Ohio
Brynam, John. Philadelphia, Pa.
*Bullard, Rev. Henry. Wayland, Mass.
Chadeyne, Miss Carrie D. Jersey City, N.J.
*Church, William F. Cincinnati, Ohio
*Clemens, Samuel Langhorne ("Mark Twain"). San Francisco, Calif.
Crane, Dr. Albert. New Orleans, La.
Crane, Albert Jr. New Orleans, La.
Crocker, Mr. and Mrs. Timothy D. Cleveland, Ohio
*Cutter, Bloodgood Haviland ("Poet Lariat"). Little Neck, Long Island, N.Y.
Davis, Joshua William. New York, N.Y.
Decan, Nathan. Long Island, N.Y.
*Denny, Col. William R. ("The Colonel"). Winchester, Va.
Dimon, Mr. and Mrs. Fred. Norwalk, Conn.
Duncan, Mrs. Charles C. Brooklyn, N.Y.
Duncan, George. Brooklyn, N.Y.
Duncan, Henry E. Brooklyn, N.Y.
Elliott, P. A. Columbus, Ohio
Fairbanks, Mary Mason (Mrs. Abel W.). Cleveland, Ohio
Foster, Col. J. Heron. Pittsburgh, Pa.
*Gibson, Dr. and Mrs. William. Jamestown, Pa.
Green, Mrs. J. O. Washington, D.C.
Greenwood, John Jr. New York, N.Y.
*Greer, Frederick H. ("Blucher"). Boston, Mass.
Griswold, Mr. and Mrs. Stephen M. Brooklyn, N.Y.
Grubb, Gen. B. B. Burlington, N.J.
Haldeman, Hon. Jacob Samils. Harrisburg, Pa.
Heiss, Goddard. Philadelphia, Pa.
Hoel, Capt. W. R. Cincinnati, Ohio
Hutchinson, Rev. E. Carter. Saint Louis, Mo.
Hyde, Hon. James K. Hydeville, Vt.
Isham, John G. Cincinnati, Ohio
*Jackson, Dr. Abraham Reeves ("The Doctor"). Stroudsburg, Pa.
James, William E. Brooklyn, N.Y.
Jenkins, Frederick P. Boston, Mass.
Kinney, Col. Peter. Portsmouth, Ohio
Krauss, George W. Harrisburg, Pa.

*Langdon, Charles Jervis (possibly the "Interrogation Point"). Elmira, N.Y.
Larrowe, Miss Nina. San Francisco, Calif.
*Leary, Daniel D. New York, N.Y.
Lee, Mrs. S. G. Brooklyn, N.Y.
Lockwood, Mr. and Mrs. E. K. Norwalk, Conn.
May, J. M. Janesville, Wis.
McDonald, Louis. Bristol, England
Moody, Capt. Lucius. Canton, N.Y.
*Moulton, Julius ("Moult"). Saint Louis, Mo.
Nelson, Arba. Alton, Ill.
Nesbit, Dr. Benjamin B. Louisville, Ky.
Nesbit, Thomas B. Fulton, Mo.
Newell, Miss Julia. Janesville, Wis.
Otis, William Augustus. Cleveland, Ohio
Paine, C. C. Pa.
Park, Rev. A. L. Boston, Mass.
Park, Miss. Boston, Mass.
Parsons, Samuel B. New York, N.Y.
Payne, Dr. and Mrs. James H. Boston, Mass.
Quereau, Rev. George W. Aurora, Ill.
Sanford, S. N. Cleveland, Ohio
Serfaty, M. A. Gibraltar
Severance, Solon Long. Cleveland, Ohio
Severance, Emily C. (Mrs. Solon L.). Cleveland, Ohio
Sexton, Nicholas. New York, N.Y.
*Slote, Daniel ("Dan"). New York, N.Y.
*Van Nostrand, John A. ("Jack"). Greenville, N.J.
Willets, Samuel. Islip, Long Island, N.Y.

SHIP'S OFFICERS

Duncan, Charles C. Captain
Bursley, Ira. Sailing Master and Executive Officer
Jones, William. Second Officer
Burdick, Benjamin. Steward
Harris, John. Chief Engineer
Vail, Robert. Purser
Pratt, William A. Quartermaster

Notebook 8 now contains 198 pages, 71 of them blank. At least two leaves have been cut out and are missing, and it is possible that other leaves no longer traceable are also missing. The notebook is identical in design and format to Notebook 7, but its binding has been repaired recently. Most entries are in pencil; occasional entries and several use marks are in brown ink. Clemens probably used brown ink when he returned to his notes while writing the *Alta* letters. All occurrences of brown ink, including use marks, which Clemens made by striking through an entry, are reported in Details of Inscription. Paine made use marks in black pencil throughout.

Clemens did not fill the notebook consecutively from first page to last, so the left-to-right sequence of pages does not necessarily correspond to the chronological sequence of entries. Two main sequences can nevertheless be distinguished. Beginning on the ninth page, Clemens filled most of twenty-one consecutive pages with his notes on New York City (from mid-May through the first week of June 1867). He then turned the notebook end-for-end and wrote his notes on the *Quaker City* voyage in a second sequence covering most of 114 pages (from June 8 through early July 1867). From time to time during the trip he turned to blank pages selected at random to enter lists that he wished to keep distinct from his day-to-day entries.

The chronological sequence of entries, when it can be determined, has been preferred to the physical sequence. Although entries on flyleaves and endpapers (and two entries on the back cover) are printed in the order in which they appear in the notebook, the two main sequences and the various lists are printed in chronological order. All deviations from physical sequence are reported in Details of Inscription and described in the notes.

Bibliography of Related Materials

The following books are those most immediately relevant to a study of Clemens' *Quaker City* notebooks (8–10) and *The Innocents Abroad.* They provide the letters he constructed from the notebooks, an independent history of the voyage, and a distinguished analysis of the evolution of the book. A number of more obscure texts (cited in the notes) have, however, been used to annotate these notebooks: Captain Duncan's log in the Patten Free Library of Bath, Maine, quoted with the permission of John E. Duncan; travel letters written by two of Clemens' friends, Mrs. Fairbanks and Mrs. Severance; and a variety of travel letters by several other passengers, graciously made available by Leon T. Dickinson.

Ganzel, Dewey. *Mark Twain Abroad: The Cruise of the "Quaker City."* Chicago: University of Chicago Press, 1968.

McKeithan, D. M. *Traveling with the Innocents Abroad.* Norman: University of Oklahoma Press, 1958.

Smith, Henry Nash. "Pilgrims and Sinners." In *Mark Twain: The Development of a Writer.* Cambridge: Harvard University Press, Belknap Press, 1962.

Walker, Franklin, and Dane, G. Ezra, eds. *Mark Twain's Travels with Mr. Brown.* New York: Alfred A. Knopf, 1940.

LK[1]

<Qel> Quel est votre nom & how the h—l do you spell it.

Brown letter to French girl (or landlord)[2]
Il ne se corrigera jamais.

Tangier 3[3]

Mark Twain—
Correspondent San F. "Alta"
Westminster Hotel, N.Y.[4] [#]

---

[1] The first four entries were made on the front endpaper at different but undetermined times; the third and fourth are in the brown ink which Clemens probably used to write his *Alta* letters and which he used intermittently in this notebook.

[2] Clemens referred twice more to Mr. Brown's "French" letters later in this notebook (see pp. 320 and 336), but he did not use the anecdote until he wrote to the *Alta* from Lake Como in July. In that letter Brown is reported to have written a complaint to his landlord in a barbarous mixture of broken French and American slang: "Brown said he guessed the old man could read the French of it and average the rest" (*TIA*, p. 56).

[3] Clemens wrote to his family on 2 July: "We had a ball last night under the awnings of the quarter deck, and the share of it of three of us was masquerade. We had full, flowing, picturesque Moorish costumes which we purchased in the bazaars of Tangier" (*MTL*, p. 131). The "Tangier 3" were probably Clemens, Dan Slote, and either Dr. Jackson or Frederick Greer.

[4] On returning to New York from Saint Louis in mid-April 1867 Clemens, who

Edwin Lee Brown
Lecture Man,
Chicago.[5]

Upton—Place de la Bourse No. 12.[6]

Billy Fall—[7] [#]

---

had corresponded for the San Francisco *Alta California* since December 1866, moved from the Metropolitan Hotel to the more elegant Westminster Hotel, where he lived until the *Quaker City* departed on 8 June. He scrawled these lines in bold letters diagonally across the front flyleaf.

[5] Brown was former corresponding secretary of the Associated Western Literary Societies and in 1866–1867 was president of the Young Men's Association (also known as the Chicago Library Association). From Naples on 7 August Clemens would write his business agent, Frank Fuller: "Don't make any arrangements about lecturing for me, I have got a better thing in Washington . . . better than lecturing at $50.00 a night for a Literary Society in Chicago and paying my own expenses" (TS in MTP). The job he anticipated as private secretary to Nevada's Senator William M. Stewart soon gave way to the task of writing *The Innocents Abroad*, and Clemens did eventually lecture to the association on 7 January 1869, six months before the book was published. Clemens wrote this entry lengthwise on the front flyleaf for easy reference.

[6] Mark Twain wrote to the *Alta* on 19 April that "Mr. M. G. Upton, the ALTA Washington correspondent during the last session, sailed for his new post, at Paris, on Tuesday [16 April]. You are fortunate in having such an able correspondent at the Exposition" (*Alta California*, 2 June 1867; omitted from *MTTB*). Clemens recorded Upton's Paris address at the bottom of the front flyleaf, possibly intending to make use of it when the *Quaker City* excursion arrived in Europe.

[7] Although Mark Twain identifies Billy Fall as "Wm. C. Fall" in his *Alta* letter dated 17 May 1867, Franklin Walker has suggested that he actually meant William H. H. Fall, "who had operated pack-trains over the Sierra to the Washoe silver mines" and who was well known in San Francisco and Nevada (*MTTB*, pp. 168, 290). One month earlier, in his 19 April *Alta* letter, Mark Twain said that Fall planned to leave New York no later than 21 April "to take a position under Surveyor General Safford, of Nevada" (*Alta California*, 2 June 1867; omitted from *MTTB*). Evidently Fall did not leave as planned, for in his 17 May *Alta* letter Clemens reported that two days earlier Fall "got into a quarrel with Harry Newton, an old citizen of Esmeralda . . . and they fired several pistol shots at each other" and wounded a bystander. Fall was arrested but soon released when no one appeared to press charges (*MTTB*, pp. 168–169, 290). This entry appears following three blank leaves and one leaf containing Clemens' charges against Captain Duncan,

Johnny Skae[8] & Santiago[9]

Show you my sore finger

Hudson street—in 8th ave car, see shab old fash—scoop bonnets & long gored dresses—University Place, see new fash & all manner elegance

Blind Asylum <3d.><34> 33 & 34th & 9th Ave.[10]

X <Gathers>Gathering punkins[11] [#]

---

which are printed in their appropriate chronological position at the end of the notebook.

[8] John William Skae, superintendent of the Hale & Norcross mine in 1863 and part-owner of the Virginia City and Gold Hill Water Works, made and then lost two fortunes by speculating on Nevada silver mine stocks. As Edgar Branch has pointed out, Skae "constantly pops up in Mark Twain's imaginary adventures" and "foreshadows later traveling companions" in Clemens' *Californian* sketches (*LAMT*, p. 116). In this instance, however, Clemens merely reminds himself to tell his *Alta* readers that Skae had arrived in New York, a fact that he mentioned in the 26 May *Alta* letter where he also discussed the wreck of the *Santiago* (*MTTB*, pp. 229–231, 236). Since Skae arrived in the steamship *Ocean Queen* on 25 May, the entry can be clearly dated.

[9] According to the New York *Times* for 23 and 24 May 1867, the steamer *Santiago de Cuba* ran aground at Absecom Beach, New Jersey, on May 22. Five passengers and two crew members drowned while trying to reach shore. Captain Charles F. W. Behm, who had commanded the steamship *San Francisco* which brought Clemens from San Juan del Norte, Nicaragua, to New York, was later accused by the *Santiago's* passengers of gross negligence, intoxication at the time of the accident, and apathy during the landing. Mark Twain's account to the *Alta* was written on 26 May and was defensive of the captain: "I hope Captain Behm will come out of this difficulty with a clear record, and somehow I cannot help but think he will. All who have sailed with him would be glad to see him found blameless in this matter" (*MTTB*, p. 231).

[10] Clemens visited the New York Institute for the Blind on 22 or 23 May. (See notes 22–24.)

[11] This and the following eighteen entries (through that beginning "Sunset on the sea") were made when Clemens viewed the National Academy of Design's forty-second annual exhibition, which (as he told his *Alta* readers on May 28) "the art critics have been so diligently abusing . . . for weeks past" (*MTTB*, p. 238). Although Mark Twain maintained that he was "not cultivated enough to see the dreadful faults that were so glaring to others' eyes," he marked this and seven subsequent entries with a marginal *X*, presumably in order to remember to mention each in a paragraph criticizing their hackneyed subjects. "I suppose," he concluded,

X <192> Pile of Cats[12]

Libertines in German hostel & Bro & Sister[13]

Squirrels on a spree

X Dogs looking out window
X Cows wading a branch sunset

X Bunches grapes, apples, strawberries, glass wine, &c on table—women take most kindly to these.

X Naked libels marked Eve.

X Other naked women—marked Spring Summer &c—all family likeness & <all short> out of shirts

Some botches & some that are not

<T>D—n the water-color pictures—they never look like perfect imitations of nature & the finest of them are coarse

No historical pictures whatever save Lincolns Entry into Richmond[14] & a poor warrior portrait or so

Sea-views & woodland & mountain-views & storms all beautiful. [#]

---

that "I have gone and done the very same thing the art critics do—left unmentioned the works I liked, and mentioned only those I did not like" (*MTTB*, pp. 239, 241).

[12] The Academy's *Catalogue of the Forty-second Annual Exhibition* (New York, 1867) identifies item 192 as "Cat and Kittens" by George B. Butler, Jr.

[13] Clemens singled out "two pictures that suited me" in his *Alta* letter of May 28: "One of these pictures represented two libertines of quality teasing and jesting with a distressed young peasant girl, while her homely brother, (or sweetheart, may be,) sat by with the signs of a coming row overshadowing his face. The other was racy. In a little nook in a forest, a splendid gray squirrel, brimful of frisky action, had found a basket-covered brandy flask upset, and was sipping the spilled liquor from the ground" (*MTTB*, pp. 239, 240). The two paintings were probably "Unpleasant Vicinity" by H. Hiddeman and "The Hunter's Flask" by William Holbrook Beard.

[14] Dennis Malone Carter's "Lincoln's Drive Through Richmond" was dismissed as "execrable" in Mark Twain's *Alta* letter. He was both surprised and puzzled by the absence of historical paintings "after four or five years of terrible warfare. . . . What do you suppose is the reason?" (*MTTB*, p. 241).

X <G>Fille swg[g] on gate.[15]

That island in tropical lake surrounded by <trees> <j>impenetrable jungle of trees & all woven together in an impenetrable web of vines & flowers—water still & glassy & glowing with pictures of the shores—two lonely birds winging their way across the lake—the <woods> forest on the further side dim <with> <&>with a gossamer mist—dead solitude & loveliness[16]

Architecture of Academy[17]

Sculpture—fine Eve with 3 apples[18]

Pillar of fire—good[19]

Sunset on the sea[20]—streak of gold across misty Indian summery blue waves

Greely & Jeff.[21] [#]

---

[15] Mark Twain mentioned "Girl Swinging on a Gate" in the *Alta* paragraph criticizing hackneyed subjects. The actual title and artist have not been identified from the *Catalogue*.

[16] Probably this is "Lagoon, in Nicaragua" by Martin Johnson Heade. Mark Twain used this description in his *Alta* letter of May 28.

[17] The building which housed the National Academy of Design had been completed in 1865. In his *Alta* letter Mark Twain ridiculed its "infamous flummery and filagreed gingerbread. . . . The Academy people call their costly stack of architectural deviltry 'the Moorish style'—as if the atmosphere of antiquity and poetry and romance, that cast a charm around that style in its ancient home beyond the seas, could be reproduced here in the midst of railroads and steamboats, and business rush and clamor" (*MTTB*, pp. 241–242).

[18] Mark Twain commented on the number of apples Hiram Powers had given to Eve in this famous marble statue: "I thought our common mother only plucked one apple. When this sculptor makes another Eve he had better get her a basket" (*MTTB*, p. 241)

[19] By Lemuel Maynard Wiles. It was not "good" enough to be mentioned in the *Alta* letter.

[20] Most likely this was "Sunrise on the Seashore" by Sanford Robinson Gifford.

[21] On 13 May 1867 Horace Greeley signed a $100,000 bail bond to end the two-year pretrial imprisonment of Jefferson Davis. Mark Twain's account to the *Alta* (dated 28 May 1867) acknowledged Greeley's "courage and independence" but criticized his action "because the millions he represented would not have done it" (*MTTB*, pp. 242, 243). The following entry suggests ironically that Greeley might

Greeley Bail for Max.

Wednesday—[22]

60 boys & 60 girls—3 tables each.
2 tables for tchs
124 pupills
Brooms
Mattrass
Bead
Knitting
Need No 6—could thread No 10—with 3^{d} finger & with mouth.[23]

Talk & knit & gossip & get very noisy at times—especialy at dinner—
27 knitters
Naturally enough, most of them stoop painfully—many have drawn features—& <are al>all are rather homely, several desperately so.

Young lady read 9th Ch II Corinthinans

though—whereof
lo.—
behold[24] [#]

---

be expected to react in the same way to the plight of Emperor Ferdinand Maximilian Joseph of Mexico, who had been deposed on 15 May and who would be executed on 19 June.

[22] This and all subsequent entries through "Maps" (p. 320.1) are the notes Clemens made on his visit to the New York Institute for the Blind. These entries appear after four blank pages and were probably written before Clemens' notes on the exhibition at the National Academy of Design. Mark Twain expanded upon almost all of these rather cryptic notes in the 23 May *Alta* letter (see *MTTB*, pp. 214–220).

[23] Clemens reported in his 23 May *Alta* letter that a "matron gave a girl a needle, in order to show how deftly she could thread it–a girl who was as blind as a brick bat. The needle was a No. 6, the matron said, and I judged that the thread was about No. 14. . . . The girl did it, and quickly. Then the same service was required at the hands of another girl, and she performed it, too, but in an unusual way–she put the end of the needle in her mouth and worked the thread through the eye with her tongue. The matron said either of them could thread a No. 10 needle with great facility" (*MTTB*, pp. 217–218).

[24] Clemens described the use of Braille by blind readers: "One of the girls read

Maps

Billy Fall[25]

Billy Fall

Santiago.

French letter from Brown to the landlord.[26]

Instruc^{ns} to Passngrs[27]

Passport.[28]

No. Passengers. 81[29] [#]

---

the ninth chapter of Second Corinthians for me. She spelled the words rapidly with her fingers, and when she came to familiar biblical words like wherefore, therefore, lo, behold, etc., she recognized them with a single nervous touch and went on. She made no mistakes" (*MTTB*, p. 219).

25 After reporting in his 17 May *Alta* letter that Fall had been put in jail for taking part in a gunfight (see note 7), Clemens observed in his 18 May letter that "Billy Fall is released, a friend of his tells me. Nobody appeared against him" (*MTTB*, p. 290). It is not clear why Clemens mentioned Fall again here nor why he wrote the name twice (at the bottom of one manuscript page and at the top of the following page).

26 This entry is in brown ink. It may have been at this time that Clemens entered the idea for the anecdote on the front endpaper.

27 Mark Twain indicated in *The Innocents Abroad* that subsequent to the official "programme" of the excursion "a supplementary programme was issued which set forth that the Plymouth Collection of Hymns would be used on board ship. . . . This supplementary programme also instructed the excursionists to provide themselves with light musical instruments for amusement in the ship; with saddles for Syrian travel; green spectacles and umbrellas; veils for Egypt; and substantial clothing to use in rough pilgrimizing in the Holy Land. Furthermore, it was suggested that although the ship's library would afford a fair amount of reading matter, it would still be well if each passenger would provide himself with a few guide-books, a Bible and some standard works of travel" (chapter 1).

28 Clemens applied for a passport on 20 May 1867 with Captain Duncan as a witness.

29 Expectations about the number of passengers that planned to sail with the *Quaker City* varied from day to day. Duncan originally planned for 110; on 28 May Clemens wrote the *Alta* that 85 had been booked "and more are to join at Marseilles" (*MTTB*, p. 247). The precise number has not been established, but Clemens later gave the number as 65 (*TIA*, p. 310).

Bret Harte.[30]

Racing—[31]

Webb's quarrel with Perkins

Beirstadts Domes of the Yo Semite.[32]

Butman's Log & red[33]

Apochraphal Bible.[34]

<R>K P [S][35]—a man who says his hoary smart things & tells his keen anecdotes & enjoys your applause—but forgets & does the same old things on you some other time. A man made up of *old* things, always repeating them & not often originating anything new.

Johnston—My God have I been ——— my grandmother! [#]

---

[30] The last known letter to Harte from Clemens before the excursion departed was written on 1 May 1867, several weeks before the probable date of this entry. Clemens wrote: "The book is out, and is handsome. It is full of damnable errors of grammar and deadly inconsistencies of spelling in the Frog sketch because I was away and did not read the proofs; but be a friend and say nothing about these things. When my hurry is over, I will send you an autograph copy to pisen the children with" (*MTL*, p. 124).

[31] In his last *Alta* letter (6 June) before sailing, Clemens mentioned having seen "the horse 'Dexter' trot a race—but then I know but little about horses, and I did not appreciate the exhibition" (*MTTB*, p. 277).

[32] Albert Bierstadt had been exhibiting his "Domes of the Great Yo Semite" at 51 West 10th Street for the benefit of the Ladies' Southern Relief Association since 26 April. On the day after the exhibition closed, Clemens wrote his 2 June *Alta* letter which discussed the painting (*MTTB*, pp. 249–251).

[33] Possibly a reference to F. A. Butman, a Californian since 1857, who had recently shown his "Mount Hood, Oregon, View above the Lower Cascades of the Columbia River" at the National Academy of Design's annual exhibit.

[34] On 2 June Mark Twain wrote to the *Alta* that he had found "an edition of 1621 of the Apochryphal New Testament" in a local New York library. He called it "rather a curious book" and quoted several extracts dealing with the infancy of Christ (*MTTB*, pp. 251–254). The passage, condensed and revised from the *Alta* letter, became part of chapter 51 of *The Innocents Abroad.*

[35] The identity of the man whose scrawled initials Clemens noted here has not been discovered. The final very irregular S may well be the stenographic symbols for the letters *trk,* reflecting Clemens' attempt to further obscure the identity of his subject.

Jack Simmons[36]
Captured [by]
Indians

Corresp[e] for several papers.
Abuse each.

Must learn swear in 17 languages.[37]

Looks like he is waiting for a vacancy in the Trinity.[38]

Aprés vous, M[r.]

Return-ball
—assassinated
—made fortune
—rage year ago,
—puzzles 2 month
—toys on string now[39] [#]

---

[36] A. J. ("Jack") Simmons was the Speaker of the House in the second Territorial Legislature of Nevada. No evidence has been found linking Simmons and Indians. The obscurity of the entry is compounded by Clemens' careless scrawl. The word *by* may in fact be a brace connecting "Captured" and "Indians." Thus it is not clear whether Clemens meant to say that Jack Simmons captured Indians or was captured by them.

[37] In his 5 June *Alta* letter Clemens described his frustration with New York's eccentric street addresses and resolved that he would leave the city and not return until he had "learned to swear with the utmost fluency in seventeen different languages" (*MTTB*, p. 262).

[38] Clemens applied this simile to an unidentified *Quaker City* passenger. He acknowledged in his 6 June *Alta* letter that Henry Clapp had previously characterized the pompous Park Avenue minister "Rev. Dr. [Samuel] Osgood" in this language (*MTTB*, p. 276).

[39] Mark Twain worked these notes into an *Alta* passage on "Street Livelihoods," which described, among others, the peddling of puzzles made from iron rings and a current "popular rage" for "little painted horses, clowns, chickens, etc., suspended from India-rubber strings. . . . No invention, since the game of croquet, has reached such miraculous triviality" (*MTTB*, pp. 254–255). He concluded by moralizing on the fate of the inventor of these toys. The New York *Times* for 22 May 1867 reported that William T. Skidmore, a former police sergeant, had shot and killed William Bishop Carr with an air gun resembling a cane. "Mr. Carr was the inventor of what is known by boys as the 'Return Ball,' which is attached to an India rubber cord, and thrown a considerable distance when it returns to the hand. He made a

Hates her because she owned a lap-dog.[40]

Artemus Ward's body—[41]

Bridget Durgan[42]

Even the Young Men's Christian &c wouldnt do more than pray *politely* for a stranger.[43]

French virtue in woman: Only one lover & don't steal.

N.Y. <Dirt> Sweeping cart.

Music of nightly (midnight fire-alarm bells)—nobody cares

Bayard's motto—Sans peur et sans—culottes.[44] [#]

---

large amount of money out of the invention, and accumulated considerable property." Clemens moralized: "Riches will still take wings and fly away, and so also will life–and nothing can assist them in their flight better than an ex-policeman" (*MTTB*, p. 256). The entry has been struck through in brown ink, probably after Clemens completed the *Alta* letter dated 2 June 1867.

40 Although this note was apparently written before the *Quaker City* departed, it anticipates Clemens' reflections on the lap dog of Mrs. J. O. Green. See pages 329 and 330 of this notebook.

41 Although Artemus Ward had died on 6 March 1867 and been buried in England, his body was exhumed and shipped to the United States for burial in his native Maine. In the last paragraph of his 2 June (Sunday) *Alta* letter Clemens reported that the "body of poor Artemus Ward arrived here per steamer to-day, from England, . . . and will be forwarded to the old homestead in Maine on Monday, for final interment" (*MTTB*, p. 258). Artemus Ward was buried on 6 June 1867 at Waterford, Maine. The entry has been canceled in brown ink, probably after Mark Twain wrote his *Alta* letter.

42 Bridget Durgan was tried for the murder of Mrs. Mary Ellen Coriell and was found guilty on 31 May. She was hanged on 30 August in New Jersey in the presence of several hundred spectators, admitting her guilt only the day before. Clemens first discussed her case in his *Alta* letter of 26 May (where he spelled the name *Dergan*), but the present entry was probably used for his 5 June *Alta* letter, where her name appears with this (*Durgan*) spelling.

43 In his 5 June *Alta* letter Clemens expressed his impatience with the bustle and impersonality of New York, describing the alleged complaint of a fellow visitor to New York that the Young Men's Christian Association prayed for a stranger only because it was " 'customary, but didn't wish to be misunderstood as taking any personal interest in the matter' " (*MTTB*, p. 260).

44 A corruption of the phrase, *sans peur et sans reproche*, which traditionally characterized the legendary French hero Pierre Terrail, seigneur de Bayard (1476–1524).

union down

They have interrupted/interfered our sacerdotal perform^{s}/exercises

I thought they'd stopped your grog.[45]

The Cooper Indians[46]

Man wanted seat by Gen. Sherman[47]

Bring everything but gin—on ship.

The man that didn't want to travel on Sunday.[48]

Library will be furnished by Young Men's Chr. Ass^{n}[49] [#]

---

45 Clemens claimed, in his June 2 *Alta* letter, to have heard the anecdote which concludes with this phrase from "Capt. Summers." "Summers anchored his sloop-of-war off one of the Marquesas. . . . The next morning he saw an American flag floating from the beach, union down." When he inquired the reason from a "grave-looking missionary" he was told that " 'the natives have been interrupting our sacerdotal exercises.' " Summers was preparing to open fire on the troublemakers until the missionary explained that the natives "had only been breaking up a prayer-meeting," to which Summers responded: " 'Oh, devil take it, man, is that all? I thought you meant that they'd stopped your grog!' " (*MTTB*, p. 257).

46 In his 5 June letter to the *Alta* Mark Twain said that he was hoping to hear that "they have ordered General Connor out to polish off those Indians, but the news never comes. He has shown that he knows how to fight the kind of Indians that God made, but I suppose the humanitarians want somebody to fight the Indians that J. Fenimore Cooper made. There is just where the mistake is. The Cooper Indians are dead—died with their creator. The kind that are left are of altogether a different breed, and cannot be successfully fought with poetry, and sentiment, and soft soap, and magnanimity" (*MTTB*, p. 266).

47 "This fellow had tried to stipulate that his wife should be introduced" to the general's daughter and "that he should be permitted to sit next the General himself! And next, I suppose this flunkey would have waited to hold the General's hat while he washed his teeth" (*MTTB*, p. 276).

48 One of the *Quaker City* passengers inquired at Captain Duncan's office whether "the excursion would come to a halt on Sundays" (*MTTB*, p. 276). The issue of Sabbath-breaking recurred, at least in the fiction of *The Innocents Abroad*, when certain "pilgrims" insisted on riding rapidly to Damascus in order to avoid traveling on Sunday.

49 Dr. Abraham R. Jackson's New York *Herald* account of the Holy Land excursion mentions that the *Quaker City's* library, "with the exception of the books furnished by the passengers themselves, consisted of a score and a half of the 'Plymouth Collection' [of hymns] and two volumes of *Harper's Weekly*" (21 November 1867). Mark Twain would write to the *Alta* that "all our library, almost, was made up of Holy Land, Plymouth Collection and Salvation by Grace!" (*TIA*, p. 304).

Capt Behm—or Wakeman—Stop the boat you old pot-b—sonofab—

W— Stop her John,—stop her—some old friend of mine wants come aboard[50]

Dr. J. H. Pottinger
7th & Olive[51]

Fine Strawberris.

Tragedy Albany
Bro of Senator Cole.[52]

Quick & comple report.

Her^{ld} house telegraph.

Cor. fr Tribune·

Would not SAY served right, but think it, <nevertheless> anyway.[53]

Webb & his books & mag. articles.[54]

The China.[55] [#]

---

[50] Clemens' respect and affection for Captain Charles F. W. Behm (see note 9) prompted him to imagine Behm in the role usually assigned to his earlier friend, Captain Ned Wakeman.

[51] The Saint Louis city directory for 1870 lists Dr. John H. Pottenger at 1017 Olive Street. Probably shortly after returning from Saint Louis in mid-April Clemens entered the name in the top margin for future reference.

[52] On 4 June 1867 General George W. Cole shot and killed L. Harris Hiscock, a delegate to the New York Constitutional Convention, in Albany. General Cole alleged (and it was widely believed) that Hiscock had attempted to seduce the general's wife, according to the New York *Times* for 5 June 1867.

[53] This entry has been added lengthwise in the left margin and probably refers to the general agreement of the newspapers on Hiscock's guilt.

[54] Charles Henry Webb published *The Celebrated Jumping Frog of Calaveras County, and Other Sketches* in April 1867. In this same period Webb reissued his own popular burlesque, *Liffith Lank; or, Lunacy,* and published his *St. Twel'mo; or, the Cuneiform Cyclopedist of Chattanooga,* a travesty of Augusta J. Evans' *St. Elmo* (1867).

[55] The Pacific Mail Line's new steamship *China* made a trial run on 4 June 1867 to a point thirty miles out from the New York harbor.

Racing.

708.

August Brentano,[56] a pop-eyed, squat, thick-set Jew with a deformed right hand & the general expression of a successful convict. Got—shelves on both of a 24 × 7 foot room & a counter down middle

Nef look at 'a Her[ld] got sum else to do but [work] at Herald.

Son of a b— has made money & it has made him

Summer is here[57]

Mint Juleps.

Get Telemaque[58]
Dumas
Balzac.

Orpheus
Divorced[59] } [#]

---

[56] Although August Brentano did not open his Literary Emporium until 1870, in 1867 he was operating a "news emporium" at 708 Broadway. It had been described as early as 1865 as a "fashionable literary rendezvous" (New York *Saturday Press*, 5 August 1865, pp. 8, 15). And in 1866 Henry Clapp had written that "in addition to having the most extensive newspaper and periodical depot in the city, he is taking rank among the leading booksellers on Broadway" (New York *Saturday Press*, 26 May 1866, p. 4). Clemens originally wrote "Brentano . . . down middle"—then added Brentano's first name and the number of his Broadway address above the original entry.

[57] In his 19 May *Alta* letter Clemens had complained that New York had been "wretchedly cold every night, and a good many of the days, too—most of them, I think. And, as for rain—well, it is California in winter all over again, and all the time" (*MTTB*, p. 195). This entry can be clearly dated, however, because on 30 May the New York *Herald* reported that the "temperature yesterday was somewhat of a surprise after the curious weather which has been a sojourner with us since the advent of what ought to have been spring. The season seems to be making up for the deficiency in caloric which characterized its earlier stages, and yesterday bestowed upon us a genuine summer day."

[58] François de Salignac de La Mothe-Fénelon's *Les aventures de Télémaque, fils d'Ulysse.*

[59] Robert Henry Newell, who wrote humorous sketches for the New York Sunday *Mercury* under the pseudonym of Orpheus C. Kerr, had actually been divorced from Adah Isaacs Menken in October 1865, although the *Alta* of 24 April 1867

Paris Exposition.[60]

Kohler & Frohling—Wines—at Paris Exposition—Californian—Perkins' Stern & Co request.

3800 miles by longitude from N.Y. to Gibraltar.

2,726 miles by longitude from N.Y. to the Azores.

1,160 miles by longitude from the Azores to Gibraltar.[61]

---

insisted that the New York court had only recently granted the divorce. Clemens commented on Miss Menken's various husbands and lovers in his *Alta* letter of May 17: "She has a passion for connecting herself with distinguished people, and then discarding them as soon as the world has grown reconciled to the novelty of it and stopped talking about it" (*MTTB*, p. 170).

[60] In his letter to the *Alta* dated 19 May Clemens reported that he had visited the establishment of "Messrs. Perkins, Stern & Co., which is the New York department of the Kohler & Frohling house in San Francisco. . . . [California wine] is destined to become a very important article of trade, and the firm I speak of hope to get it all into their own hands eventually" (*MTTB*, pp. 192–193). The firm was exhibiting California wines at the Paris Exposition, and their "request" may have been for some publicity through his letters to the *Alta California*. The heading "*Paris Exposition.*" was added later than the original entry.

Beginning here, Clemens wrote the entries through "Tangier . . . o" (p. 328.27) at different times on the back endpaper and facing side of the flyleaf.

[61] These are the distances in statute miles between New York, the island of San Miguel in the Azores, and Gibraltar. (Because of bad weather, the *Quaker City* visited Fayal, one day closer to New York than San Miguel, the originally scheduled stop.) Although their meaning is not certain, the rough diagrams below this list may have been sketched to show the difference between a compass course and the great circle course between the same two points. On many maps and navigational charts, compass courses appear as straight lines, while great circle courses, which are actually shorter on the earth's surface, appear as arcs.

I spoke or was spking.[62]

Je parlais
Tu
Il parlait
Nous parlions
Vous parliez
Il parlaient

I shall or will speak.

Je parlerai
Tu parleras,
Il parlera,
Nous parlerons,
Vous parlerez,
Ils parleront

I should or would speak.

Je parlerais,
Tu parlerais,
Il parlerait,
Nous parlerions,
Vous parleriez
Ils parleraient.

Irving's Spain
Moors.[63]

	Alta	Tribune
Fayal	1	1
Gibral	1	0
Tangier	2	0[64] [#]

[62] On 26 May Clemens remarked in a letter to the *Alta* about the American exodus for Europe: "I am afraid the French language will not be spoken in France much this year. I shall feel mighty sick if, after rubbing up my rusty French so diligently, I have to run the legs off myself skirmishing around Paris, hunting for such a sign as '*Ici on parle Français*'" (*MTTB*, p. 236).

[63] Clemens may have read Irving's *The Alhambra: A Series of Tales and Sketches of the Moors and Spaniards* in anticipation of a visit to Spain (see note 119).

[64] Clemens records the letters he has sent from the Azores, Gibraltar, and Tangier. The second letter from Tangier is dated July 1.

Regulations[65]

Steamship Quaker City.

A strict observance of the following Regulations is requested:

Passengers are requested to divest themselves of their boots or shoes before occupying their berths, & to <remove the> wash before going to breakfast.

Passengers may eat at every meal specified in the rules, & may take all reasonable advantages, & eat all they fairly can, but [*blank*] & extraordinary stratagems are barred. No swapping false teeth allowed.

Holy Land Pleasure Excursion[66]

Steamer Quaker City

Capt C C Duncan

Left New York at 2 PM, June 8, /67

Rough weather—anchored within the harbor to lay all night.[67]

Br. said now this is River Jordan—where is that old Original faro bank.[68]

The Frenchy-looking woman with a dog[69]—small mongrel black & tan brute with long sharp ears that stick up like a donkey's & give

---

65 This burlesque was inspired by the official *Quaker City* ship regulations, which, according to Captain Duncan, were struck off on the ship's printing press on 24 June. The passage is separated by one blank leaf from the back flyleaf and by one blank page from the next entry.

66 Clemens inverted the notebook and began a fresh page as he set out on the great "Excursion."

67 Although the *Quaker City* left her berth at 2:00 P.M. on 8 June as planned, gale winds forced the ship to anchor in the protection of Gravesend Bay at 4:30 that afternoon.

68 The subject of "Mr. Brown's" pun may have been brought to mind by periodic raids New York police were making on faro banks, arresting owners and patrons and confiscating the gambling equipment.

69 Mrs. Severance wrote of Mrs. J. O. Green that she "seems not to be exactly sane, and has constantly with her a little black and tan terrier dog" (*JLS*, p. 7).

him an exceedingly wild & excited expression, even in his mildest moods. He has unbounded influence over his mistress (a married woman of 30, with dark skin, inclined to hairiness, & a general suggestion all about her of <ignorance> coarseness & vulgarity,); he jumps into her lap, & repeats it over & over again<;> & his damned spirit will not down till she takes him to her bosom, wraps her shawl about him & talks affectionate baby talk to him. When he is skirmishing about the cabin, she follows him anxiously about & interrupts his enterprises, because they are always of an improper & mischivous tendency,) & meanwhile she keeps up an interminable biography of him to the passengers, embellished with anecdotes illustrative of his general disposition <& general style.> & with stories of some of his most remarkable performances. The dog is noisy, & in the way, & his relations with his mistress are <too> so intimate as to be disgusting to the passengers. He may ———

The long-legged, simple, green, wide-mouthed, horse-laughing young fellow,[70] who once made a sea-voyage to fortress Monroe in the Oceanica, & now knows it all. He quotes eternally from his experiences upon that voyage, <"calls"> goes every anecdote one better, by a reminiscence from that voyage, & I am satisfied that we shall never hear the last of that very voyage. He will harp on it from here to Palestine & back again. He wears a monstrous compass slung to his watch guard, & consults it from time to time, keeps a wary eye on the binnacle compass to see that it does not vary from his & so endanger the ship <—&> he is loud, & affects <the> an extravagant devil-may-care boisterousness & freedom which he imagines to be characteristic of the man of the world. He says the most witless things & then laughs uproariously at them—& he has a vile notion that everything everybody else says is meant for a witticism, & so laughs loudly out when very often the speaker had spoken seriously, or even had meant to say something full of pathos. But this fellow

[70] Some aspects of this description forecast Clemens' portraits of Blucher and the Interrogation Point in *The Innocents Abroad*. It seems more likely, however, that the boisterous passenger was Clemens' friend Jack Van Nostrand of Greenville, New Jersey. Clemens' first impresssion of Van Nostrand may have been more

don't know. He laughs dreadfuly at *every*thing & swears its good, d—d good, by George. I wish he would f———

The innocent young man—who is good, accommodating,—pleasant, & well meaning, but fearfull green & as fearfully slow.[71] Began conversation in the smoking room with the remark that well, he believed the papers stated that Max had been captured at last—[72]

And got promptly snubbed by somebody who said the news was a week old. Then he exposed the fact that he had gone to sea without a passport.—

Then he wished to know how long sea-sickness lasted. He is on the other extreme from Legs—don't know anything at all. [<le>]

Came confidentially to me in a private place & seemed almost bursting with an idea—a new & dangerous guest to have about his premises. He said Said:

If you had got a panorama—any kind of a panorama—one of them old ones would do—why by gracious you could pay your way in the ship—any old panorama, you know—but I don't think likely you could with only just a lecture,—because them Italians & Arabs &—wouldn't go much maybe, except for the novelty, because they wouldn't understand a d—d you know. But if you had an old panorama, I should think likly you'd fetch them.

Sunday Morning—June 9—Still lying at anchor in N.Y. harbor—rained all night & all morning like the devil—some sea on—lady had to leave church in the cabin—sea-sick. [#]

---

negative than his later view, expressed in *The Innocents Abroad:* "One of our favorite youths . . . [is] a splendid young fellow with a head full of good sense, and a pair of legs that were a wonder to look upon in the way of length, and straightness, and slimness" (chapter 4).

[71] Almost certainly Charles Jervis Langdon, then not quite eighteen years old. Clemens remarked to Langdon, after the latter had interrupted a card game in the smoking room of the *Quaker City,* " 'Young man, there's a prayer-meeting forward in the dining saloon and they need you there' " (Jervis Langdon, *Samuel Langhorne Clemens: Some Reminiscences and Some Excerpts from Letters and Unpublished Manuscripts* [n.p., 1910?], p. 4). The illustration of Interrogation Point in chapter 7 of *The Innocents Abroad* bears a striking resemblance to contemporary photographs of Charlie Langdon.

[72] The report of Maximilian's capture had been published in the New York *Times* on 28 May 1867.

Rev. Mr. Bullard preached from II Cor. 7 & 8th verses about something.[73]

Everybody ranged up & down sides of <main> upper after cabin—Capt Duncan's little son played the organ—[74]

Tableau—in midst of sermon Capt Duncan rushed madly out with one of those d—d dogs but didn't throw him overboard.[75]

Several days at sea—four, I think—the beautiful weather we started with still continues—sunny days, sea just rippled by the summer breeze, & magnificent moonlight nights that <seduce every one out of the cabins, & make the promenade deck> bring everybody on deck, even the sea-sick ones.

<I am> <But—there>

But speaking of <sea in> sea-sickness, there certainly are more sea-sick people in the ship than there ought to be. I am more than ever satisfied, now, that we ought to have put to sea in the storm of Saturday. The ship is strong, & could have weathered it easily, <but> & everybody would have had a fearful four-hours' siege of sea-sickness & then been over it & done with it.

But alas! we sailed with a bright sky & an untroubled ocean, & so most of the passengers remain half-sick & half miserable, day after day, & they will never be otherwise until we touch land again.

I have got the bly-ak—& there's 8 doctors on board—spring chicken

Diaries.

Most of the passengers being unaccustomed to voyaging, are diligently keeping diaries [#]

---

[73] Mrs. Severance reported that the text read: " 'If there be first a willing mind, it is accepted first, according to what a man hath, and not according to what he hath not' " (*JLS*, p. 8), slightly modified from 2 Corinthians 8:12.

[74] Harry E. Duncan, "a nice boy of eleven years of age, plays church music very well indeed," according to Mrs. Severance (*JLS*, p. 7).

[75] The previous day Daniel D. Leary, one of the owners of the *Quaker City*, had been moved by the same impulse. He wrote his brother Arthur: "Duncan's sons have three or four dogs on board, and [an] accident will happen to them sure when nobody is looking (I mean the dogs)" (Lewis Leary, "More Letters from the *Quaker City*," *American Literature* 42 [May 1970]: 198).

Of a lady.

First Day—The ship rolls & pitches, & Oh, I am *so* sick!

Second Day—We met an emigrant ship to-day, full of Irish people.—From Ireland, doubtless.[76] Our captain got on the paddle-box & shouted Ship Wo-haw! or something like that, & the other captain shouted back through a horn & said he <wa> had been out thirty days. Then we started away, & gave the emigrants 3 cheers & waved our handkfs, & they gave us three cheers also, but did not wave their handkfs, but we thought nothing of it, because, as they had been out 30 days their handkfs were all dirty, likely. Still, I am *so* seasick.

Third Day—Mrs. S., who has got her face so sunburned since we left N.Y, made a conundrum on the promenade deck last night. She said, "Why is my face like a bird that is just about to fly?" Ans—"Because both are to soar." Ah, me, I am so sick!

Fourth Day—I am tired being at sea, & tired keeping journal, & very tired of being sea-sick. I do wonder where those Azores Islands <h>are hidden away in this boundless expanse of heaving water? I do so want to see the land & the green trees again.

Fifth Day—Chicken soup for dinner, but my heart is not in chicken soup. I care not for poetry, or for things to eat, or for dress. I have taken off my hoops & put away my waterfall, & all I take an interest in is being squalmish & getting to shore again. It *is* funny, but somehow I don't seem to care how I look.

Sixth Day—At last I am over it! I am not a bit sick any more. And how different everything looks to-day. Why the sea is beautiful —actually beautiful! & the soft south wind is balmy & gentle, & I almost imagine it has lost its <drea> nauseous odor of salt. I am like a new person. I take an interest in everything, now. Ah, yonder is that scrimp-nosed little doll trying to make herself so agreeable to Mr ——. I will just happen along there as if I were not noticing, & see if I don't spoil your schemes, Miss? [#]

---

[76] Captain Duncan recorded that at noon on 11 June the *Quaker City* hailed the *Emerald Isle*, which, according to the New York *Times*, had left Liverpool on 12 May.

Bloodgood H. Cutter.[77]

He is fifty years old, & small of his age. He dresses in homespun, & is a simple-minded, honest, old-fashioned farmer, with a strange proclivity for writing rhymes. He writes them on all possible subjects, & gets them printed on slips of paper, with his portrait at the head. These he will give to any man that comes along, whether he has anything against him or not. He has already written interminable poems on "The Good Ship Quaker City;" & an "Ode to the Ocean;" & "Recollections of the Pleasant Time on Deck Last night"—which Pleasant Time consisted in his reciting some 75 stanzas of his poetry to a large party of the passengers convened on the upper deck.

Here is a specimen of his work.[78]

Dan said to him, in a private conversation:

"It must be a great happiness to you to be able to sit down at the close of the day & put its events all down in rhymes & poetry like Byron & Shakspeare & those fellows."

"Oh, yes, it is—it is. There is no pleasure like it in the world."

"Yes—& I should think that when a man was gifted in that way, more would be expected of him than from common people—from people who ain't poets. You'd be expected, you know, to keep that talent going at all reasonable times, & never lose an opportunity. It's a duty you owe to your countrymen & your race, you know."

"I know. I appreciate it. I *do* keep it agoing. Why bless your soul, many & many a time when everybody else is asleep, you'll find me

---

[77] Clemens often seemed more embarrassed than amused by Cutter, and he mentions him only twice in the *Alta* letters, first in the 30 June letter from Gibraltar. When Mark Twain wrote *The Innocents Abroad*, he dubbed Cutter "Poet Lariat" because Dr. Edward Andrews ("The Oracle") "always distorted the phrase 'Poet Laureate' into Poet Lariat" (*MTMF*, pp. 89–90). Cutter eventually published *The Long Island Farmer's Poems, Lines Written on the "Quaker City" Excursion to Palestine, and Other Poems* (New York, 1886). Clemens separated this sketch from earlier entries by two blank leaves and from subsequent ones by a single blank page.

[78] Clemens left space for the "specimen" but did not supply one here, possibly because he included a couplet by Cutter at the end of the dialogue between Cutter and Dan Slote that follows.

writing poetry.—And when I feel it coming on, there's no let up to me."

"That's it! that's it! Often, no doubt, when you're talking to people, or looking at anything, or eating dinner, it comes on you, & every thought that clatters through your head fetches up <a>with a rhyme at the end of it—pure, honest, natural born poetry—ain't it so?"

"Bless your soul, yes. Many's the time I've had to leave my dinner & many's the time I've had to get up in the night when it came on me. At such times as that, I can't any more talk without rhyming than you could put fire to powder & it not go off. Why, bless me, this ship may go to the bottom any moment & drown us all—but what of that?—

Whether we're on the sea or the land,
We've all got to go at the word of command—

"Hey?—how's that?"

Thursday, June 13, 1867—On board Steamer Quaker City at sea, 12 M—lat. 40, long 62—560 miles from New York, ¼ of the way to the Azores—<in last> just 3 days out—in last 24 hours made 205 miles. Will make more in next 24, because the wind is fair & we are under sail & steam both, & are burning 30 tons of coal a day & fast lightening up the ship.

Friday—Shipped a sea through the open dead-light that damaged cigars, books, &c—comes of being careless when room is on weather side of the ship.

Friday, June 14—Mrs. C. C. Duncan's 46th birth-day festival in the after-cabin.[79] [#]

[79] As Duncan recorded in his log, Clemens, Moses S. Beach, and Dan Slote were appointed to escort Captain and Mrs. Duncan into the main saloon for the festivities. Dr. Albert Crane spoke briefly, followed by the main speaker, the Reverend E. Carter Hutchinson, then Dr. Edward Andrews, and finally Clemens himself. Mrs. Severance recorded most of what he said: " 'This is Mrs. Duncan's birthday. I make this statement to gain time. You have spoken of her youthful appearance, but I think she is old. Our life is not counted by years, but by what has been seen and accomplished. Methuselah was but a child when he died, though nine hun-

Saturday, 15—Trial in the Circuit Court of the Commonwealth of Quaker City, of Robert Vail, Purser, charged with stealing an overcoat belonging to Sam Clemens. Judge Crane presiding. Rev. Henry Bullard Clerk, Dan Slote Sheriff, Moses S. Beach, Crier of the Court, Dr. Jackson, Surgeon of the Ship, Counsel for the State, Sam Clemens & Capt Duncan Counsel for the defendant.—Six Jurymen. Eight witnesses examined. Speeches made. <Verdict> <Ali> Alibi proven—also insanity of def't. Verdict guilty, with recommendation to mercy. Sentence inflicted on junior counsel in absence of <c>the criminal—solitary confinement on straight whisky in room 10 for one hour & may God have mercy on your soul.[80]

Curiosity—Genuine Nubian chancre.

Brown's letter to French girl.[81]

Capt Wakeman & the nigger hung.[82]

Evasive answer

Physician sands nearly run out.

Thought they shut off your forncation[83]

The surest sign of quack is picture of some ignorant stupid ass in

---

dred and sixty-nine years old. The world did not improve any while he lived,—he tended his flocks just as his fathers did, and they none of them knew enough to make an iron fence. Mrs. Duncan has lived to see great improvements. . . .' The whole of his remarks were humorous" (*JLS*, pp. 12–13). Daniel D. Leary, writing to his brother Arthur on 1 July, gave a more cynical view of the proceedings: "a meeting was called, bunkum speeches made and the old woman crowned with myrtle. It was too ridiculous" (Lewis Leary, "More Letters from the *Quaker City*," p. 199). For a fuller account of Clemens' remarks, see Dewey Ganzel's *Mark Twain Abroad*, pp. 44–45.

80 Mrs. Severance wrote that the "Court was very well conducted, and proved a laughable affair. Mr. Clemens is the ruling spirit and a capital person for ocean life" (*JLS*, p. 14). Room 10 was, of course, Clemens' stateroom.

81 See note 2.

82 This anecdote was first mentioned in Notebook 7, p. 253. Its fullest version appears in chapter 50 of *Roughing It*.

83 This is a variation on the punch line to the anecdote Mark Twain told in his 2 June *Alta* letter. See note 45.

horrible woodcut on a coarse lying, bragging handbill to be treasured by clowns & used in water closets by the rest of the world.[84]

Monday 17 June—Blackfish, whales <&> an occasional shark & lots of Portuguese men-of-war in sight

Brown distressed for fear the latter would attack the ship,.—jelly.—long tails & sting—burn,—reef in a storm—turn over in sun, wet sail & come up again—long tails hanging down—saw fleet of them.

These stay only between 35 & 45°—story of chartless ship telling where she was by seeing nautilli.

Caught a flying fish—it flew 50 yards & came aboard—can't fly after wind & sun dry their wings.

June 17—Lat. 40, long. 43 W—½ way between America & Portugal & away south of Cape Farewell, Greenland. Large school of spouting blackfish<.>—make the water white with their spouting spray.

June 19—Within 136 miles of the Azores at noon.

D^r & S get sea-sick at table—go out & throw up & return for more.

Singular—Find the full moon exactly in same spot every night at 8 oclock—for past 9 or 10 nights—because we move as fast as she does, & approach 15 to 20 minutes closer to sunrise every 24 hours, sailing directly east as we have been.

Started <the> a Social Club last night to discuss routes of travel, & chose Judge Haldeman[85] for President,—Rev Mr Carew[86]

---

[84] Probably a reference to Bloodgood Cutter, who, as Clemens wrote earlier in this notebook (p. 334), was composing doggerel verses "on all possible subjects, & gets them printed on slips of paper, with his portrait at the head."

[85] Jacob Samils Haldeman served in the Pennsylvania legislature from 1850 to 1855, and from 1861 to 1864 was United States minister resident to Sweden and Norway. Mrs. Severance wrote on 18 June: "He is a very peculiar man, I could imagine him to be a gambler. He wears a red flannel shirt on which are printed hunting figures. Every day he brings out a new necktie, and on his small feet he wears the tightest of patent leather boots. I am told he has been strongly addicted to drinking, and came abroad at this time to try to break up the habit. In endeavoring to do this, he is much of the time under the influence of morphine, and always appears exceedingly peculiar" (*JLS*, pp. 16–17).

[86] The Reverend George W. Quereau.

for Secretary, & <Mr>Moses S. Beach, Dr Jackson & myself as Executive Committee.

Dr Andrew & Capt Duncan enlightened the Club concerning the Azores & Gibraltar.[87]

After which Mr James gave Stereopticon views—promised us pictures of places we are going to visit, & his first was a view of Greenwood Cemetery![88]

Prayer Meetings every night.[89]

Sea so rough to-day we cant play horse-billiards for'ard.

Gr-r-(????)

The Quaker City Mirror is not issued very regularly.[90] [#]

---

87 Clemens neglected to mention that he was also one of the speakers who "enlightened the Club" with "remarks touching the ports to be visited," as Captain Duncan recorded (CCD, 19 June). His notebook entries on the Azores were influenced by the fact that, as he told the *Tribune* readers in his 23 June letter: "Out of our whole ship's company there was not a solitary individual who knew anything whatever about them" except that "they were a group of nine or ten small islands far out in the Atlantic, something more than half-way between New-York and Gibraltar. That was all." As he wrote in one of his final *Alta* letters, the ship's library had been of little help; nearing Gibraltar they "could hardly find out from any book on board whether Gibraltar was a rock, or an island, or a statue, or a piece of poetry." For these reasons he added "a paragraph of dry facts" to his 23 June *Tribune* letter (*TIA*, pp. 16, 304).

88 Mrs. Severance recorded that William E. James, the official photographer for the excursion, had introduced his magic lantern show with a picture of the well-known Brooklyn cemetery by saying, " 'They are mostly of places where we expect to go' " (*JLS*, p. 17). Clemens decided to include the grotesque joke in chapter 4 of *The Innocents Abroad*: James "advertised that he would 'open his performance in the after cabin . . . and show the passengers where they shall eventually arrive' . . . [and] the first picture that flamed out upon the canvas was a view of Greenwood Cemetery!"

89 Daniel Leary wrote his brother on 1 July: "As you are probably aware the captain is a psalm singer and quite a number of others on board and they managed to get up quite a 'revival' among themselves. They commenced with services once on Sunday, and finally we had it every evening and twice on Sunday, which did not suit myself or about a dozen other of the best people on board" (Lewis Leary, "More Letters from the *Quaker City*," p. 199).

90 According to Dr. Jackson in the New York *Herald* for 21 November 1867: "In a few hours the printing press was put in operation, and the first number of the

"Would be pity if we came in sight of the islands in the night when so dark we can't see them"—

Dan Slote said—

"See 'em in the morning"—

June 19—Up at 4 AM[91] to see Island of Corvo (small)—passed half way around its large neighbor Flores—very cold & windy—spray continually coming aboard in broad sheets & drenching the passengers.—Vineyards, gorges, ridges (sharp, velvety.) topped with seeming castles & ramparts—all green in bright spots & handsome.

(Constantinople)

Got so far east now that when it is next week here it is day before yesterday in San F.[92]

Brown wondered that his watch was so out of order that it lost 20 minutes every day—kept slowing her down till she hardly moved at all, but all to no purpose.[93] [#]

Quaker Mirror, a paper six by eight inches in size, appeared, and was supplied to subscribers at the modest price of ten cents per copy, the reputed editor and proprietor being a son of the manager [that is, Duncan]. As it only contained an editorial which had been published before in a New York daily, and which everybody on board had read, together with some advertisements from the same paper which nobody wished to read, it created but little enthusiasm, and the subscribers even cruelly withdrew their names, so that the first number of the *Mirror* was also the last."

[91] That is, early in the morning of June 20.

[92] On 20 June, when Clemens came in sight of the Azores, he was only about three hours ahead of New York time and seven ahead of San Francisco time. He inserted "(Constantinople)" above the original sentence to remind himself to use the joke in a letter from a more distant time zone, and on 22 August he wrote from Odessa: "The difference in time between Sebastopol and Sacramento is enormous. When it is six o'clock in the morning here, it is week before last in California" (*TIA*, p. 137).

[93] Brown would certainly have been confused if he had slowed his watch down to compensate for its losing twenty minutes each day. In his first letter to the New York *Tribune* Clemens corrected the error: William Blucher "from the far West" reports that he has " 'set that old regulator up faster and faster, till I've shoved it clear around, but it don't do any good; she just cleans out every watch in the ship, and clatters along in a way that's astonishing till it is noon, but then them eight bells always gets in about ten minutes ahead of her anyway' " (*TIA*, p. 11).

Stupid remarks & ? from ? every now & then—make him a character.

Also occasional rhymes from the poet.

June 19—Heavy gale down among Azores—threw Capt D. across cabin from dinner table, swept dishes away [p] dozen, & fetched away iron water cooler which smashed seat just vacated by Mr. Church.

Most folks in bed sick—tremendous sea running all afternoon—fierce gale—shall I NEVER see lightning & thunder any more?

Fellow in France 3 weeks—came back & couldn't understand his mother—So used to French money—how much *is* 50^c

75 cts!

Blodgett—Been so used to being called *Blojay* in Paris[94]

Brown

Like to see a man eat enough but I *do* hate to see a man sit down & eat a dinner & go out & heave it overboard & come back & eat & another like a dog

Questions for Debate.[95]

Which is the most powerful motive—Duty or Ambition?

<Who is> Is or is not Capt. Duncan responsible for the head winds? [#]

---

[94] Clemens frequently ridiculed this kind of affectation, and this entry probably prompted the passage in chapter 23 of *The Innocents Abroad* which described some "Americans abroad in Italy who have actually forgotten their mother tongue in three months—forgot it in France." Clemens also reported that a "lady passenger of ours tells of a fellow-citizen of hers who spent eight weeks in Paris and then returned home and addressed his dearest old bosom friend Herbert as Mr. 'Er-bare!' " The affectation was particularly annoying because of Clemens' prejudice against the French: "Oh, it is pitiable to see [the American tourist] making of himself a thing that is neither male nor female, neither fish, flesh, nor fowl—a poor, miserable, hermaphrodite Frenchman!"

[95] Although a precise date for this list of questions has not been established, the list has been moved to this position on the testimony of Captain Duncan's log that the ship's debating club first met on the evening of 20 June, the day before arriving at Horta. The list appears sandwiched between the entries at p. 365.9 and p. 366.4, where Clemens arbitrarily entered the questions on two separate, unfilled leaves toward the back of the book, writing with the notebook upside-down. Later in June, as he made notes on Tangier, he found the list in his way and wrote around it.

How can the passengers best see Spain consistently with the ship's route as laid down in the original programme?

Is a tail absolutely necessary to the comfort & convenience of a dog?—& if so would not a multiplicity of tails augment the dog's comfort & convenience by a constantly increasing ratio until his ability to carry them was exhausted?

Which is most desirable—the single or the married state?

<F>Azores.

June 21, Daylight—Arrived at the port of Horta, island of Fayal—island of Pico, where the fruits are, is opposite, & looks beautiful with its green slopes & snow-white houses.

Azores under Portuguese sway—old fort with six-pounders over 250 yrs old.

Mr. Dabney, <Jr.,> is American Consul. <He & his br> His father was here.[96] The family been here 60 yrs.

His 2 sons[97] married daughters of Webster of Parkman murder notoriety. One of these ladies said to Haldeman, "Well, I suppose you know who *we* are!"[98]

Consul's & Silver's[99] are superb grounds, with all tropical & other plants in them—15 acres in former—more in latter.

---

96 Charles W. Dabney was the current United States consul to the Azores. "His father" was the former consul, John B. Dabney.

97 Probably Samuel W. Dabney, who would succeed his father Charles as United States consul in 1872, and John P. Dabney, who would be appointed deputy consul in 1873.

98 Clemens told his *Alta* readers in his letter from the Azores that "Two of the junior Dabney's married daughters of Professor Webster, who was executed in Boston twelve or fifteen years ago, for the murder of Dr. Parkman. The girls were very young then, but highly educated and accomplished. The Webster family removed to Fayal immediately after their great misfortune came upon them, to hide their sorrows from a curious world, and have remained here in exile ever since. . . . I did not recognize them in the fine, matronly, dignified ladies we saw to-day" (*TIA*, pp. 4–5). Professor John W. Webster was hanged on 30 August 1850 for the murder of Dr. George Parkman.

99 Moses S. Beach wrote to the New York *Sun* that "the great attraction of the neighborhood seemed to be the gardens of Mr. Silviera, the only competitor in that line, of the Dabneys" ("Editorial Correspondence," 31 July 1867).

Full chaffinch & canaries.

Most superb russ pavements[100] & whitewashed lava walls & stone bridges I ever saw & *so* clean & neat.—Will last forever. So will the houses, which are of lava plastered with mud & painted white.

These snowy houses thickly clustered at the base & scattered upon the sides of the checker-boarded hills & <hav>half buried in luxuriant shrubbery, make of this one of the loveliest towns I ever saw.

Population of Horta, 10,000—nearly all <Portugu>Portugese. Pop. of Fayal 25 to 30,000.

Rode jackass on mattrass with sawbuck for a saddle, 10 miles among the hills ravines & beautiful scenery of the suburbs, with a troupe of barefooted noisy young patched & ragged devils following with gads. Paid 30 cents an hour for the jacks.

sekki-yo![101]

Everything calculated by reis (rays)—takes about a million of them to make six bits.

<Two hundred> A thousand reis make one dollar.

Brown having heard that prices were very moderate here, opened his heart & ordered dinner <on> for 8 of us. Here is the bill. It knocked him senseless:

Dinner for 8 <at>@ <$>3,000, r, ...	24 000
<C>Wine, <a>10 bot at 1,200	12,000
Cigars	2,000
	38,000 [#]

---

[100] Russ pavements were "composed of blocks of granite, set on a bed of crushed stone and cement" (John A. Kouwenhoven, *The Columbia Historical Portrait of New York* [New York: Doubleday & Co., 1953], p. 247). Clemens wrote to the *Alta:* "They talk much of the Russ pavement in New York, and call it a new invention—yet here they have been using it in this remote little isle of the sea for two hundred years! Every street in Horta is handsomely paved with the heavy Russ blocks, and the surface is neat and true as a floor—not marred by holes like broadway" (*TIA*, p. 9).

[101] A phonetic approximation of a form of the Portuguese verb *chegar*, sometimes used idiomatically to mean "get up!" In chapter 6 of *The Innocents Abroad*

All the hills are cultivated to their very summits <&> (4 to 600 feet) & look like checker-boards—

Export oranges to England from San Miguel, but that is about all. Used to export wine, but haven't been able to make any for 15 years.[102]

They raise corn here, mostly.

Cathedral Church (Jesuit) <Colle> nearly 200 yrs. old—the great altar a mass of gaudy gilt work[103]

Ball supporting ivory cross is bound with wood which they claim is from the true cross.

Walls of the chancel are faced with superb porcelain—figures life-size—pictures are varied, animated & exceedingly well executed. Blue.

My ears roar yet with the infernal din<ni> of those chattering, jabbering portugese vagrants.

2 papers published in the islands.[104]

Ladies gathered plenty of flowers, feather wreaths, ornaments in pith of fig tree, &c &c.

Wages for laborers 24 to 26 cents a day—mechanics twice as much.

Couple Custom House officers remained on ship all day to

Mark Twain wrote that the muleteers "banged the donkeys with their goad-sticks, and pricked them with their spikes, and shouted something that sounded like '*Sekki-yah!*'" He added the word in the left margin lengthwise, beside the previous paragraph.

[102] The vineyards of the Azores had been destroyed about 1854 by a parasitic fungus.

[103] Matriz Cathedral had been built in 1670 in the center of the old Jesuit college. Clemens told his *Alta* readers that its altar was "a perfect mass of gilt jim-cracks and gingerbread, and reminded me of the tawdry trumpery of the Chinese Temple in San Francisco" (*TIA*, p. 7).

[104] Two weekly newspapers, *O Fayalense* and *O Atlantico*, were being published in Horta at the time of Clemens' visit, but at least ten other papers were being published among the other islands, primarily San Miguel and Terceira.

examine all bundles carried ashore by <g>passengers—but both stayed on one side, while most of the people went off on the other.

Sentinels <& s>carry Sharpe's rifles & soldiers wear blue roundabout & white linen pants & have their boots blacked—<considering that> common soldiers best dressed people in Fayal (Port^{e})—& considering that most of the low class have no boots to black & no clothes to speak of, imagine that to be a common soldier must be a position of high dignity.

Place is full of shoe shops yet everybody go barefoot.

Women wear a blue cloak with a hood like a covered wagon & are the infernalest homeliest tribe on earth, perhaps. They say they are not virtuous—but I cannot see how the devil they can possibly be otherwise—for fornication with such cattle would come under the head of the crime without a name.

Have to lay to in a head wind.[105]

Woman waiting at corner for the wind to change   Rain flats the hood right out—is heavy but coarse texture.

Everybody taking notes—cabin looks like a reporters congress.[106] [#]

---

[105] Clemens wrote this sentence diagonally across the previous paragraph, and he wrote the next two sentences lengthwise in the margin and extending over the previous two paragraphs. The additions were probably made in connection with his 23 June letter to the *Tribune*, where he used these details to introduce an anecdote which is described in note 111. The *Tribune* letter discussed the cumbersome regional costume and read in part: "She was becalmed. Or rather, she was laying-to, around a corner, waiting for the wind to change" (*TIA*, p. 14).

[106] On 27 June Mrs. Severance remarked that there were

> at least a dozen correspondents for different papers: Mrs. Fairbanks, "Cleveland Herald"; Mr. Crocker, "[Cleveland] Leader"; Mr. Foster, "The Pittsburgh Dispatch"; Mr. Clemens, "The California Alta" and "The New York Tribune"; Mr. Beach, "The New York Sun"; Mr. Sanford (I think) for a Granville [Ohio] paper; Dr. Jackson for one in Philadelphia [the Monroe County (Pa.) *Democrat*]; Mr. Bullard for one in Boston; Dr. Hutchinson for one in St. Louis. Captain Duncan urged me very strongly to write for him a letter which he had promised to send to the "Independent," and I have done so, but I confess to feeling poorly satisfied with my effort." (*JLS*, p. 33)

In addition, Stephen M. Griswold and William E. James both wrote occasional letters for the Brooklyn *Daily Eagle*; John G. Isham for the Cincinnati *Commer-*

Commandant at fort was astonished to see Lisbon dates 2 weeks earlier—thought telegraph failed 10 yrs ago.

Donkey & family—donkey with pallet of thistles—folks with bedstead—no bedstead for the poor donkey.

Man asked if the States were joined together again.

Fayal, June 22.

Mules & family live all together in one small room—fire in centre—no escape for smoke save thro' small passages built in walls. Hardly a chimney in the city.

Saw no graveyards. They say they do not reverence their dead very highly, & only a few graves are well cared for.

Wheat is threshed by oxen in a hard room in the old scriptural way—"Ye shall not muzzle the ox that treadeth out the grain." Wheat is worth 70 cents a bushel, but flour $12 a barrel because of <this> their slow methods of threshing & grinding.

Corn is ground in private houses with a stone mortar & [*blank*]

In a windmill—10 bushels corn a day—man scrapes it thro' trough from hopper—Yankee would make a shaking table.[107]—The base of mill is stone up 10 ft—then wooden house so arranged as to turn around & shift sail when wind shifts. Near by have a mule mill to go when the wind don't blow.—

Their plow is a wooden board shod with iron.

Their harrow is drawn by hand & has teeth as small as a finger.

---

cial; Julius Moulton for the Saint Louis *Missouri Republican*, and Julia Newell for the Janesville (Wis.) *Gazette*. Only Mrs. Fairbanks, Moses Beach, and Julia Newell were as regular as Mark Twain in their correspondence, and no one wrote as much as he did. But the initial excitement of the Azores must have fired the ambitions of less experienced journalists, whose interest waned as the journey progressed.

[107] In his letter to the *Alta* Clemens commented on the contrast: "they scorn threshing-machines and all other unholy inventions with the true Jesuit wisdom, which says that ignorance is bliss and progress is sedition. . . . Now, how long do you suppose a Yankee would stand there before he would invent some way of making that trough shake, and feed the mill intelligently itself?" (*TIA*, p. 5).

Their <wagon> cart is a basket hauled by a cow & the axle & the wooden slab of a wheel *both* turn.

Civil Governor & a military governor both—latter takes precedence.

Country Volcanic.

Baalam's ass.

The party started at 10 A.M. Dan was on his ass the last time I saw him. At this time Mr. Foster was following, & Mr. Haldeman came next after Foster—Mr. Foster being close to Dan's ass, & his own ass being very near to Mr. Haldeman's ass. After this Capt. Bursley joined the party with *his* ass, & all went well till on turning a corner of the road <Capt. Bursley's> a most frightful & unexpected noise issued from Capt Bursley's ass, which for a moment threw the party into confusion, & at the same time <the> a portughee boy stuck a nail into Mr. Foster's ass & he <f>ran—ran against <Mr> Dan, who fell—fell on his ass, & then, like so many bricks they all came down—each & every one of them—& each & every one of them fell on his ass.[108]

Muleteers sang

We hang Jaf Deevez on sowly abbla tree
Glory halleluiah—and his soul go[109]

Left the Azores Sunday noon, June 22.[110] [#]

---

[108] The high spirits evident in this account were predictably excluded from Clemens' *Alta* letter from Horta. Their "ten-mile excursion" around the "breezy hills and through the beautiful cañons" of Fayal was momentarily interrupted when Brown's donkey "turned a corner suddenly, and Brown went over his head. And, to speak truly, every mule stumbled over the two, and the whole cavalcade was piled up in a heap" (*TIA*, pp. 9, 8).

[109] Julia Newell and Moses Beach also reported that the muleteers sang a corrupted version of "John Brown's Body." Beach wrote that the last line of the song was distorted to " 'Lowry-allelu-a-go marchy on-no' " ("Editorial Correspondence," New York *Sun*, 31 July 1867). Clemens wrote to the *Alta* that the last two lines were "*We 'ang Jeffah Davis on sowlah applah tree, / So we go molloching on!*" (*TIA*, p. 10).

[110] The sketch of Pico's silhouette and the view of its mountain (p. 347) were presumably drawn as the ship departed "Sunday noon" June 23.

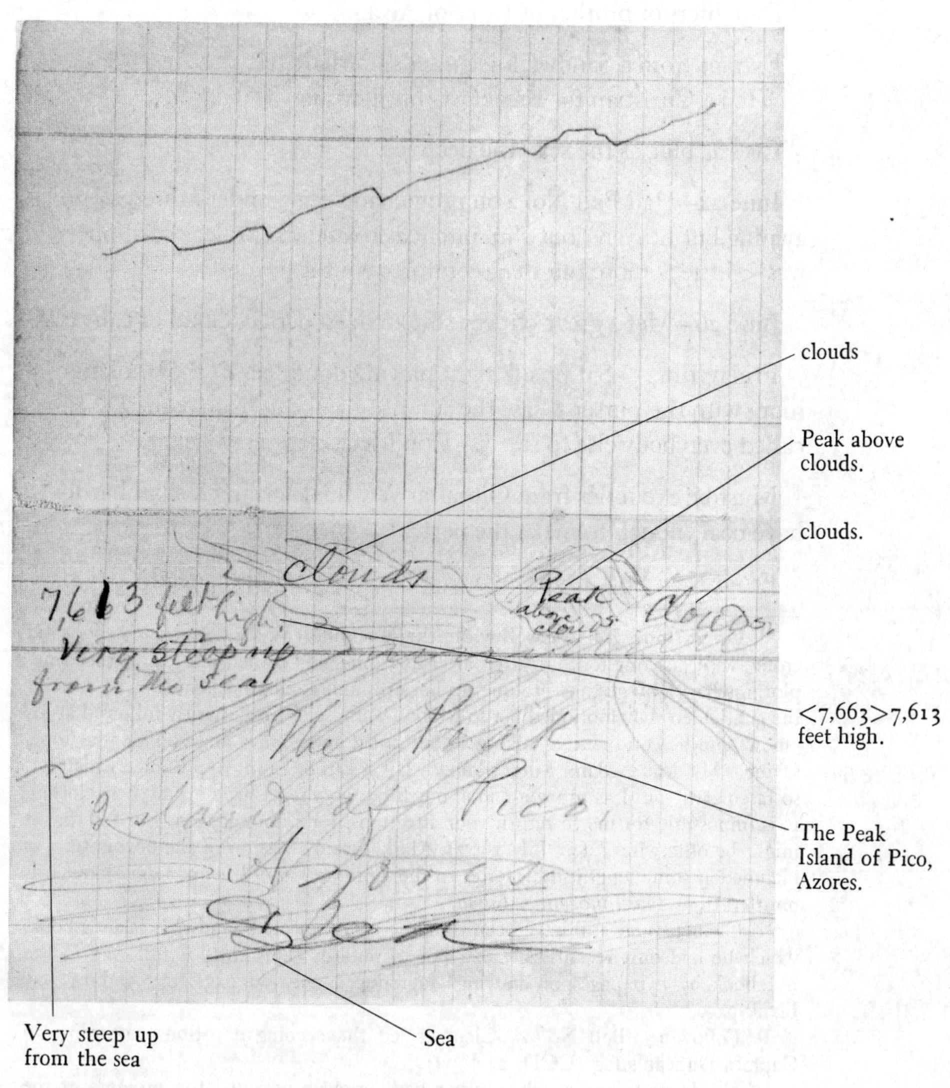
7,6[?]3 feet high.
Very steep up
from the sea
clouds
Peak
above
clouds
Clouds,
The Peak
Island of Pico,
Azores
Sea
clouds
Peak above
clouds.
clouds.
<7,663>7,613
feet high.
The Peak
Island of Pico,
Azores.
Very steep up
from the sea
Sea

Madame, these attentions are very flattering to me, but—[111]

Daughters of brother of Duke of Alva.

Extract from a Sandwich Islander's Journal:
"Had a Christian for Breakfast this morning."[112]

Eyes as blue as the sea (the deep sea.)

June 24—Had Ball No. 2 on promenade deck, under lanterns (no awning but heaven) but ship pitched so & dew kept deck so slippery, was <little> more fun than comfort about it.[113]

June 26—Met a great clipper ship under a perfect cloud of canvas.

Friday June — Sat up all night playing dominoes in the smoking room with the purser & saw the sun rise—woke up Dan & the Dr. & called everybody else to see it.—Don't feel <f> very bright.

Must be 150 miles from Gibraltar yet, this morning & shall hardly have coal enough to make the port.[114]

From New York to the Azores the sea was of a dull, dead,

---

[111] On 22 June, Julia Newell wrote the Janesville (Wis.) *Gazette:* "A poor old crone, with just one tooth, started after us from some corner, and commenced imploring charity by gestures, rolling up her eyes and kissing her hands to us. One of the gentlemen slyly motioned her to Mark Twain, so she persistently followed at his elbow, and he commenced talking to her in the most grave and confidential tone, saying—'My dear madam, I don't know what it can be in my appearance which has so fascinated you. I assure you I look much better when I have on my best clothes. It is impossible for me to return your affections, for I am engaged—but for that it might be otherwise' " (23 July 1867). Mark Twain's version of the encounter was included at some length in his letter to the *Tribune* (see *TIA*, pp. 14–15) but was omitted from *The Innocents Abroad*.

[112] Clemens may still have been thinking of a projected Sandwich Islands book, which he had only recently decided not to publish. This entry is followed in the notebook by two pages of drawings reproduced here on page 347 and by one blank page.

[113] Following "Ball No. 2" Clemens led the evening devotions, according to Captain Duncan's log (CCD, 24 June).

[114] Head winds and rough weather had seriously impeded the progress of the *Quaker City*, but there may have been another difficulty. Daniel Leary wrote to his brother on 1 July from Gibraltar that "the coal given us at New York was most miserable, 25% of it composed of slate. We never had more than eighteen lbs. steam when we should have had 25 lbs. average consumption 29 tons daily. Tell

mouse-colored blue—but from thence till now (within 150 miles of Gibraltar—we are just south of Cape St Vincent, Portugal, & Cape Blanco, Morocco,) it has been of a deep, splendid, lustrous purple-blue.)

Saturday, June 28.[115] Sailing along through the Straits, with Africa (bold, sand-spotted hills,) & Spain (a good deal like it) on either hand, 13 miles apart. Water green, not blue—splendid morning spring-like—

Saw the Moorish town of <Tarifa> Tangier in Morocco, sitting on a hill—<it>

Further along a tall bold hill in <Spain> Africa which must be one of the Pillars of Hercules.

Passed close to the little heavily-walled town of Tarifa, Spain, houses with pink-tiled roof—

The great Spanish hills beyond have rather barren looking sides & grey granite tops.

Old round stone towers here & there on the sea-walls—<lighthouses or> watch towers

Little <tower> town in lap of a valley nestling in shrubbery.

Splendid breeze & the white-winged ships speeding down the strait in the morning look beautiful.

Dr Andrews at breakfast said

"<Did th> Which side was the Pillars of Hercules on?

Both.

Some thinks different—Gibbon—(the old fool had been smelling in a guide book & was trying to play it for old information been festering in his brain.[116]

D'Oyly about this coal business, it was outrageous to pack off such stuff on us" (Lewis Leary, "More Letters from the *Quaker City*," p. 200).

[115] Saturday would have been June 29. Captain Duncan's log confirms that they entered the strait on that day.

[116] The foibles of Dr. Edward Andrews ("The Oracle") were roundly lampooned in Mark Twain's *Alta* letter of 30 June: " 'Some authors states it that way, and some states it different. Old Gibbons don't say nothing about it—just shirks it complete—Gibbons always done that when he got stuck—but there is Rolampton, what does *he* say? Why he says that they was both on the same side, and Trinculian, and Sobaster, and Syracus, and Langomarganbl—' " (*TIA*, pp. 23–24).

He said "I suppose them old ancients really believed the *goddess* Hercules lived there some time or other."

But while we stood admiring the cloud-capped peaks of Africa & its lowlands robed in misty gloom, "clouds & darkness are over it"—Scripture, & spoken of this particular locality.[117] a more magnificent sight burst upon us—a lordly ship with every rag of canvas set & sweeping down upon us like a bird.

All at once a thrill went through the whole ship & <every hat> with one impulse every hat & every hankerchief <wa>were swung aloft—she had flung the stars & stripes to the breeze! She dipped her colors gracefully by way of salute, & we answered—& so long as the gallant ship was in sight every eye followed her & every <sen> wafted a God speed after her.[118]

In a few moments <an> a lonely & enormous mass of rock, standing seemingly in the centre of the <s>wide strait & washed on sides by the <o>sea apparently, swung grandly into view, & it required no guide book to tell us it was famous <g>Gibraltar, that type of stability. It stood a 4 years siege.

Gibraltar—

Going through Spain or *not* going through Spain? What is the

---

[117] Clemens interlined the fragment " 'clouds & darkness . . . locality." below "robed in misty gloom," and above "a more magnifi-|" continuing into the right margin. When he came to write his 30 June *Alta* letter from Gibraltar, he described the African hills in his first paragraph: "their bases vailed in a blue haze and their summits swathed in clouds—the same being according to Scripture, which says that 'clouds and darkness are over the land.' The words were spoken of this particular portion of Africa, I believe" (*TIA*, p. 18). Clemens may have had Exodus 14:20 in mind, but the "cloud and darkness" mentioned there of course refer to a different part of Africa: Moses stretched forth his hand "that there may be darkness over the land of Egypt" (Exodus 10:21).

[118] Mark Twain's revisions of this passage in the 30 June *Alta* letter further point up his prevailing mood. After heightening the effect of the "Stars and Stripes" on his readers, he added: "Many a one on our decks knew then for the first time how tame a sight his country's flag is at home compared to what it is in a foreign land. To see it is to see a vision of home itself and all its idols, and feel a thrill that would stir a river of sluggish blood" (*TIA*, p. 19).

time to Paris?—60 hours<?>. Can we visit the Alhambra—Seville, Valladolid, the <Encin> [*blank*] and 50 other places? D—d glad when I *knew* it was too late & we couldn't go.

Now as to Tangiers there shall be no pulling & hauling—we will *go*. I shall answer no questions, & *not listen* to any d—d fears, surmises, or anything else.[119]

Blucher in Gibraltar blowing about being American to British officers—to hotel keepers—to commandants—to band-masters, whores, chambermaids, bootblacks—making an ass of himself generally.

Buying gloves of the seductive Spanish wench in the main street who said *I* knew how to put a glove on, & few did—(when I was tearing the worthless thing to pieces with my awkwardness) & taking this fearful sarcasm for a compliment I paid the price (50 cents) for a torn pair of Spanish kid gloves.[120] [#]

---

119 Evidently general indecision and the prospect of a sixty-hour train ride prevented Clemens from accompanying Moses Beach and several other passengers on a side trip through Spain (see note 123). The glowing report he sent the *Alta* on 1 July explains Clemens' determination to "go" to Tangier.

120 Dr. Jackson wrote to the Monroe County (Pa.) *Democrat* on 30 June that this incident "afforded some amusement, and at the same time exemplified considerable tact on the part of at least one of the persons concerned," and that it prompted Clemens to say that "he could not remember having ever injured that lady and consequently could not account for the amount of sarcasm she had bestowed upon him."

Blucher in the ———

King's Arms & Club House Hotels[121]—keep no register & never know who is in the house—send *me* to find my friends instead of a servant. Landlord lied about the Tangier boat.[122]

<Brown> Dan told to gather all manner of statistics, reports that brandy is 8 cents a drink, & cigars 3-pence.

More barber-shops here than shoe-shops in Fayal.

Many beautiful English & Spanish girls.

Beach & ½ doz. others went through Spain.[123]

Cave of Gen—something/Genesta in Europa Point (Rock of Gibraltar) find Roman implements showing Rome once held the rock—also, bones of mastodons & fossils of many animals that have always existed in Africa but never in Spain—there are apes on Gibraltar now (saw one) & Ape Hill on the African Coast facing Gibraltar <is now f> (One of the Pillars of Hercules) is now full of them—yet there are none in Spain. These lead to the belief that the narrow channel (13 miles) between the pillars was once dry land & the <300> low place where the neutral ground is was open sea.[124] [#]

---

[121] These were the two principal hotels in Gibraltar at this time and, according to *A Handbook for Travellers in Spain*, 4th ed. (London: John Murray, 1869), "old established and comfortable" (p. 328).

[122] What the landlord lied about has not been discovered, but Murray's *Handbook* for 1869 explained that "steamers leave Gibraltar several times a week for Tangiers, making the passage in about 4½ hours. The passage across the straits is agreeable, although the strong currents in the centre often occasion a heavy sea. . . . There is no mole nor landing-place, so passengers must first enter boats to approach the strand, and then make use of the backs of the Tangerine porters, who will wade with them ashore" (p. 338).

[123] According to Captain Duncan's log (30 June), Moses S. Beach, his daughter Emeline, Thomas S. Beckwith, the Reverend Henry Bullard, Charles J. Langdon, and S. N. Sanford had set out for Spain the previous day. They planned to sail for Cadiz, then overland to Madrid and across Spain to Paris, rejoining the *Quaker City* in Italy.

[124] Clemens' visit to the Genista caves sparked strong interest in the implications of geological and biological discoveries which had only recently been made. As he wrote to the *Alta* on 30 June: "In this cave, likewise, are found skeletons and fossils

The low place is very low & flat & is only ¼ mile wide between the Atlantic & Mediterranean & the "neutral ground" between the blue & white posts[125] is about 300 <miles> yards wide.

Tangier, Morocco.

Oran

Riffians from the Riff coast up by <Algiers>Algria—very barbarous tribe—driven down from the mountains by starvation—wheat crop failed—using chicken feed to make bread—small feed.

Emperor don't allow anything to be exported & so they don't raise any more wheat than necessary to live. Only 3,000 head cattle allowed

Only consuls &c can get horses out by paying £20 duty.

Cape Spartel light
Tarifa "
same[126]

Charts all say current always sets eastward—& so vessels from Mediteranean lay at Gibraltar weeks & make no attempt to beat down through Straits with adverse winds & get into Atlantic—whereas the current sets at stated seasons west & east both—get to Tarifa & take first of tide & follow Spanish coast apiece, & current will carry them through in spite of the wind.

flood tide goes to westward & ebb-t to eastward flood tide is from ape's hill to Trafalgar Bay & takes vessels out.[127] [#]

---

of animals that exist in every part of Africa, yet within memory and tradition have never existed in any portion of Spain save this lone peak of Gibraltar! So the theory is that the channel between Gibraltar and Africa was once dry land" (*TIA*, p. 22).

[125] Respectively, the British and Spanish sentry boxes.

[126] The lighthouse at Cape Spartel, Morocco, and the one at Tarifa, Spain, marked the southern and northern sides of the mouth of the Strait of Gibraltar.

[127] Clemens' perennial interest in nautical matters was probably stimulated by the boat trip to Tangier, which could only be reached from Gibraltar by going westward through the strait. The captain of the local steamer which made the trip several times a week doubtless knew what the "charts" and the foreign "vessels" did not. Clemens added these last two sentences across and in the left margin of the preceding paragraph at a later time, probably in an attempt to clarify how the flood tide could be used to counteract adverse winds.

Moroccans don't dare to get rich—Emperor get up some charge against him & confiscate.[128]

Nigger Consul from <Morr>Morocco to Gibraltar[129]—was a slave to former consul—bought his freedom—was left all his property —had become so smart & well posted in Gib affairs the Emperor gave him his master's place & he has held it for years. Kissed one old Moorish dignitary (who is very rich.

The shore towers are Spanish—Moroccans used to slip in with boats & carry off all the pretty women. England stopped it.

In Morocco, for theft, of cattle take off right hand & left foot. <Two> 2—one died (cut round the joint & break it off—hang up facing the market) the other got well by re-amputation by English surgeon.

Two little steamers in Gib & Tangier trade—will be another soon.

Murder in Morroco—behead.

Jew executed for helping to poison a (Sp.) consul—shot—3 of them. Put him at a distance like a target & bad marksmen practised on him a good while.[130]

Note the magnificently rich & soft bluish misty tint that veils Gib. [#]

---

[128] Mark Twain explained, in his first *Alta* letter from Tangier, that, since "there is no regular system of taxation," the "soulless despot" would "levy on some rich man and he has to furnish the cash or go to prison. So, few men in Morocco dare to be rich. . . . Every now and then the Emperor imprisons a man who is suspected of the crime of being rich, and makes things so uncomfortable for him that he is forced to discover where he has hidden his money" (*TIA*, p. 30).

[129] Hadji Said Quesus was Morocco's consular representative at this time.

[130] Between 1863 and 1867 there had been at least four cases of atrocities committed against Moroccan Jews. The incident referred to by Clemens is most similar to one that took place in the coastal town of Saffi. Clemens' account to his *Alta* readers does not mention that the victims were Jewish and wavers between sympathy for them (and antipathy for the Moors) and a kind of grisly humor: "Moorish guns are not good and neither are Moorish marksmen. In this instance they set up the poor criminals at long range, like so many targets, and practiced on them—kept them hopping about and dodging bullets for half an hour before they managed to drive the centre" (*TIA*, pp. 31–32).

Officers of garrison go to Tangier to shoot—wild boar, partrige, rabbits, hares, ducks.

Splendid dates exported from Morocco[131] (Barbary Coast)—that place in San F is well named Barbary Coast.

Fez.—Capital.[132]

Lady Hill visited Fez 6 w. ago—only European lady ever been there—no protection outside Tangier walls—must take escort.

Brass decimal coinage—silver real—copper coin 31 oz to dollar.[133]

When a poor Moor sees one of those scarce silvers dollars, asks permission to kiss it—been rich.

Money changers in the streets.

Gov. of Tangier (used to) have salary £5 or £6 a month but keeps 25 or 30 wives—snaked the cash that passed through his hands. —American political sagacity.

Emperor has no system of taxation but levies on individuals—made the old Moor by imprisonment confess where his money was hidden

Plow with crooked piece timber & oxen. Sp^s same. [#]

---

131 Mrs. Fairbanks reported to the Cleveland *Herald* that they "were rejoined by others of our passengers, who had made an excursion into Morocco and had returned in safety from the Emperor's dominions, bearing with them some forty pounds of the '*latest dates*' " (25 July 1867).

132 Since Fez was 130 miles southeast of Tangier, it is unlikely that Clemens traveled to the holy city. It was almost certainly Lady Hay (not Hill), wife of Sir John Hay Drummond-Hay, British minister resident to Morocco, who had made the unprecedented visit.

133 Currencies used in Tangier included Spanish, Moroccan, French, and even British coins. In his first letter from Tangier Clemens reported that "Brown went out to get a Napoleon changed, . . . and came back and said he had 'cleaned out the bank; had bought eleven gallons of coin, and the head of the firm had gone on the street to negotiate for the balance of the change.' I bought nearly half a pint of their money for a shilling myself" (*TIA*, p. 29). Clemens sent two "Moorish coins of Tangier" home to his family (SLC to "Dr. Folks," 2 July 1867, transcribed from the manuscript by Dixon Wecter in his corrected copy of *MTL*, p. 131; volume in MTP).

Tread out grain in Spain with oxen—probably same in <Africa> Barbary.

Moorish farmers live in thatched hovels—burn off brush & scatter a little grain.

Apparently no large timber in Barbary.

6 yrs ago Spaniards had long occupied Souta abreast Gib, above Ape Hill—Spaniard built house outside lines—Moor's destroyed it <<3>2 tim> twice Spaniard rebuilt & flagged—down again—war —only few miles to Tetuan, yet took Sp. many months to get there—didn't take the place, but extended their Souta possessions a little (low neck of land connects Souta with Ape Hill,) & got ($10,000,000?) indemnity—Spanish, Moorish & English customs officers of customs were placed at every Moor port down coast to take strict account of duties, & Emperor takes ½ & Spain ½—first Morrocco ever <had a> knew what her income was—Governors used to collect what they pleased & account to Emperor what they pleased.

Indemnity is about paid off now, & Morocco only country on earth without national debt.[134]

Small out of the way places the only ones you can learn anything about.

Immense No of Moors leave Tangier every year on pilgrimage to Mecca.

Can't go unless worth $100—Jew dodge—lend $100 & get it back before ship sails—charge for loan. [#]

---

[134] Spain, which had occupied Ceuta since 1580, declared war on Morocco in October 1859 and entered Tetuan (only twenty miles from Ceuta) in February 1860. After defeating the Moors, Spain signed a peace treaty in August 1860 which allowed for the payment of an indemnity of approximately $20,000,000. Britain, however, objected to Spain's holding Tetuan as a pledge until the indemnity was paid and so raised a loan in January 1862 to pay Spain £500,000 ($2,500,000). The entire indemnity was guaranteed by a lien on Moroccan customs receipts, which were shared equally by England and Spain until 1883 and then went to Spain alone until 1887. This last condition perhaps explains why, in Clemens' words, the "Emperor don't allow anything to be exported" (p. 353.9).

Man is entitled Hadji after made Pilgrimage—not so entitled before.

Never wash on entire pilgrimage—<w>go through motions with stones.[135]

Moorish wedding

Jewish wedding—woman sits with eyes closed for many hours.

Koran allows 4 wives & many concubines—
In *interior* Jews marry several wives.[136]

Cords of Jews in Tangier & Morocco.[137]

Stately splendid old dignified Moorish dignitary with moustache & beard & beads—tall—yellowish but nearly white—great peaked long sweeping blue hood & robe—& white turban of many folds.

They wear crimson sash—voluminous—around waist—robe—& bare legs—some other Arab robes are white & some blue striped.—some red skull caps. [#]

---

[135] In his second letter from Tangier Clemens reported that "from the time they leave till they get home again they never wash, either on land or sea. They are usually gone from five to seven months, and as they do not change their clothes during all that time, they are totally unfit for the drawing-room when they get back" (*TIA*, p. 33). This and the previous entry have been struck through in brown ink, probably after Clemens included them in his *Alta* letter.

[136] "Bigamy is also legal, though uncommon, especially among the Castilian section of the coast Jews, whose marriage contracts provide that a second wife may be taken only at the request of the first wife" (Budgett Meakin, *The Moors* [London: Swan Sonnenschein & Co., 1902], p. 443).

[137] This entry and the one above beginning "Koran" have been struck through in brown ink. Clemens used the entry about the Koran, but not this entry, in his Tangier letters. His fascination with the Jewish population in Morocco was, however, fully expressed: "Here are five thousand Jews in blue gaberdines, sashes about their waists, slippers upon their feet, . . . the selfsame fashion their Tangier ancestors have worn for a thousand years" (*TIA*, p. 27). And later: "Now these fellows worship just as Moses did; their habits and customs are just as they were in Biblical times; . . . all of which is to say that they are an inconceivably rusty-looking set now and consequently must have been in the days of the Old Testament—and how they ever came to be the chosen people of the Lord is a mystery which will stagger me from this day forth till I perish" (*TIA*, p. 33).

Trafalgar—we saw where Nelson fought—see it from Tangier on fair day—sailed by it in Quaker City.

Tangier snow-white town—scattered yellow houses—in little valley & on low hill-sides.

Took no baggage to Tangier but 5 bottles & 75 cigars.

Everything in these countries stone—durable—substantial—to last forever—strikes you evrywhere.[138]

Moorish little pipes & tobacco.[139]

A narrow court leading to the American Consulate General in Tangiers called Washington Street.

Snatched Maj. Barry out of the Moorish Mosque—would have been sacrilege—couldn't pray in there for a long time till it was purified—would have got a shoe over his head—years ago would have got a knife—they are very fanatical.[140]

English officer stepped in & the Moors chased him out & up street with shoes.

Frenchman went through—

Portuguese clock-mender—Moors couldn't mend it—<concluded>

---

[138] Clemens was right about the stone, but not about the durability of construction. "The material used in construction, rough stone and mortar work in which there is far too much of the latter, and that of an inferior quality, renders all the local buildings short-lived" (Budgett Meakin, *The Land of the Moors* [London: Swan Sonnenschein & Co., 1901], p. 95).

[139] Dr. Jackson wrote the Monroe County (Pa.) *Democrat*, somewhat naively, that "the Moors, like all orientals, are inveterate smokers. They do not generally use the tobacco plant, but a preparation made from the dried leaves of the hemlock, and which, in Arabic, is called *keef*. It is smoked in very small pipes and produces quickly a peculiarly soothing effect" (letter dated 2 July 1867). A typescript in the Mark Twain Papers indicates that Clemens brought home a "small moorish pipe & tobacco."

[140] This episode was reported in the second *Alta* letter from Tangier and in chapter 9 of *The Innocents Abroad*. In the first case the adventurer was Mr. Brown and in the second Mr. Blucher, indicating once again that the Brown/Blucher pseudonym was readily transferable.

"You know we permit donkeys when building—we'll let the Portuguese <c> take off shoes & go in & come out as a donkey."

Brown wanted to go in as a donkey.

Consul General McMeth at Tangier has nothing to do.[141]—But keeps his residence here because it is the most civilized port in Barbary—God help the other ports.

Tangier only remarkable for its fashions—not its civilization.

Tangier is an old Roman town—old Roman ruin.

Can't get into inside of Moorish house unless women are withdrawn—then see little.

The ancient Moorish Castle is a little town within a wall—& is the residence of the Bashaw—the office is pretty much hereditary—he is both military & civil. Has every power but life & death. He is absolute.

<Tabebe> El Tabeeb—Arabic for "The Doctor." Inflicted them on <the> Dr Jackson.

The well-dressed Moors—the learned & doctors in the law—go on mules but seldom show themselves. More well-dressed Moors in Gib than here.

Go to Mosque about 1 oclock on Friday (Sunday) & say their prayers an hour or two—bathe, & then go to work again—that is all of their Sabbath.

People in remote places ring in terribly old jokes, as original, imaging that the hearer has never heard them before, & are surprised at the faint laugh the ancient jest creates. [#]

---

[141] Jesse H. McMath had assumed the duties of United States consul at Tangier in 1862. Clemens described his visit with McMath in the second *Alta* letter from Tangier: "I noticed that all possible games for parlor amusement seemed to be represented on his centre-tables. I thought that hinted at lonesomeness. The notion was correct. . . . Tangier is full of interest for one day, but after that it is a weary prison. Mr. McMath has been here five years, and has got enough, and is going home shortly" (*TIA*, p. 35).

Naval squadron in Mediterranean go to Marseilles, to Gib. &c, but seldom or never touch at an African port,<—>the very places where they ought to appear *often* to awe the Moors & give them respect for America—can't overawe France at Marseilles.

Goldsborough gone with whole squadron to Cadiz to deliver up to Farragut.[142]

Moors went to Gib & came back *full* of wonder at the smoothing-iron Miantonomoh—staid 10 days—didn't come to Tangier where all the Moorish officers wanted to see her.

They have *heard* of the great American navy, but when the little Frolic & Swatara come, they say why are *these* they great ships?[143]

Consul says for God's sake, they judge by what they *see*—no newspapers—& *don't* send any small vessels.

Ticonderoga came & *astonished* the Moors talked about it a month[144] with great guns & great ship—<sen>stayed 2 days—sent by request of McMeth.

When big iron ship came to Gib, tried to get her here—Goldsborough wouldn't permit it.

Mr. Redman says Spanish are gaining great influence here by showing big ships & burning powder. Spain <consi> hated but considered greatest & most powerful nation on earth—just by SHOW.

Consul ratifies engineer's statements. If Spanish vice-consul gets into trouble with McMeth's vice-consul—Spaniard appeals to his Minister & up goes the case against America.

Spanish Minister makes a demand on Emperor of Morocco,

---

142 Admiral David Glasgow Farragut would relieve Rear-Admiral Louis Malesherbes Goldsborough as commander of the European squadron of the U.S. Navy on 14 July 1867 at Cherbourg, France. In addition to the flagship *Colorado*, the fleet included the *Ticonderoga, Augusta, Swatara, Shamrock, Canandaigua, Frolic, Miantonomoh, Guard,* and *Ino*.

143 The *Miantonomoh* was a very large ironclad, heavily armed, of 3,400 tons. The *Frolic* was only a small side-wheel steamer of 880 tons and the *Swatara* a slightly larger gunboat of 1,120 tons.

144 The *Ticonderoga* was a large, heavily armed, second-class screw sloop of more than 2,520 tons. Clemens interlined the fragment "talked about it a month" without a caret, above "Moors," breaking his original sentence.

instantly complied with—other nations worry through months of red tape but accomplish nothing.

<Six mi>

Before the war Spain was despised—feared now.

Indemnity $20,000,000.

Spain took Tetuan but gave it up.

Semmes was at Gibraltar, but on McMeth's demand, Emperor of Morocco ordered Moors to fire on Rebels if they came here.[145]

All American consuls have absolute control over all Americans here, & Moors have none over either consul or citizen.

Tunstall & Lt. Meyers of Alabama captured by American consul at Tangier. Tunstall *expatriated* & Meyers imprisoned—done in America.—sent home by Commodore.[146] [#]

---

[145] On 18 January 1862, early in the American Civil War, Captain Raphael Semmes had anchored his coal-less, disabled Confederate cruiser, *Sumter*, at Gibraltar. While at least five federal warships were occupied with guarding his sanctuary, Semmes went in search of coal, which he eventually procured, and patched the boilers, only to discover that they would not withstand operating pressure. After arranging to dispose of the ship and discharge the crew, Semmes left Gibraltar to return to the Confederate states on 14 April 1862. On 23 April 1863, according to contemporary State Department records, Consul McMath formally demanded that the Moroccan government deny port permission to Confederate ships, upon threat of seizure. The Moroccan government, probably reluctant to take sides in the conflict, did not comply until 23 September 1863, when the appropriate orders were issued to all the bashaws in the ports of Morocco.

[146] Clemens had obviously been gossiping with Consul McMath about Civil War days. On 19 February 1862, McMath's zealous predecessor as consul at Tangier, James De Long, had employed Moroccan soldiers to arrest two Confederate citizens: Tom Tate Tunstall, an Alabamian whom Lincoln had fired from his post as United States consul at Cadiz, and another Southerner, Lieutenant Henry F. Myers, paymaster of the Confederate privateer *Sumter*. Both men had come to Tangier in search of coal for the disabled *Sumter*, and their arrest by a foreign government at the behest of the American consul was certainly illegal. The two captives were placed aboard the U.S.S. *Ino* despite vigorous protest from other members of the foreign colony at Tangier. "When Lieutenant Commanding Josiah P. Creesy of *Ino* threatened the mob with his sword, they started throwing stones at the Union forces." The men were returned to Boston, imprisoned at Fort Warren, and eventually paroled. (See Charles G. Summersell, *The Cruise of C.S.S. Sumter* [Tuscaloosa, Alabama: Confederate Publishing Co., 1965], pp. 165–166.)

Any crime so heinous law provides no adequate punishment make him Consul to Tangiers

Roman fountain 2200 yrs old.

Outside of wall, remains of old Roman buildings—

Town <been> one of the oldest towns in world except Damascus—ancient history dates it<s> about time Hercules founded Cadiz—say 4,000 years ago.

Been in possession of Phenicians, Carthagenians, English, Moors, &c.

5 or 6 miles out, 600 ft high, complete bed of oysters.

Animals remain from sea up to 5 or 600 ft every inch.

Romans had this 2,600 years ago, [*blank*]

& when they invaded Gaul & Britain at [*blank*] AD, drew their grain from here.

The great battle which determined the religious status of this country was fought not many leagues from here <in> 1160 yrs ago, between Mahommedans & Christians & latter lost.

Moorish women cover their faces with their coarse white robes—to cover their inhuman d—d ugliness, no doubt.

Small donkeys

Bazaar—niggers—Arabs, &c.

Emperor don't know how many wives he has got—thinks it is 500.—take turns—Arabic

Walls of Bashaw—all damaged.[147]

The original nigger[148]

Many of the blacks are slaves <o>to the Moors—when can read

---

[147] On 6 August 1844 the French fleet had bombarded Tangier's walls and fortifications for three hours.

[148] In his first *Alta* letter from Tangier Clemens exuberantly catalogued the variety of "people that are foreign and curious to look upon" in that city, including "original, genuine negroes, as black as Moses" (*TIA*, p. 26).

first chapter of Koran (contains creed) can no longer be slaves—would have been well to adopt educational test for nigger vote in America.

Connection of Master with female slave frees her.

Population of Tangier is about 5,000 Jews, 14,000 Moors, Arabs & Bedouins, & 1,000 Christians.

Mt. Washington, named so by owner of country house there in 1793—back of town.

Saw remains of old Roman bridge at mouth of Fishing river (single arch) where Roman dock-yard was—built their ships & took grain in them to Britain 50 yrs before Christ.

Hercules is the representative of a character—that man landed at Cadiz w^h his lion skin on his shoulders & his club in his hand & founded it—came here <on> also (called Tingis, then) & conquered Anitus,[149] King of this Country, who lived also at the garden of Hesperides 70 miles down coast from here—savages here, then—Hercules met & killed him in these streets. These were savages, who lived in little huts, & ate only the natural fruits of the land. Canaanites came here when driven out by Joshua, & set up a pillar on w^h they inscribed:

We are the Canaanites, driven out of the Holy Land by the Jewish robber Joshua"[150]—been seen by Roman historians within 2,000 yrs. in these streets.

Cape Spartel, near here—Cave of Hercules—full of inscriptions—Herc took refuge <her> in that cave.[151] [#]

---

149 Antaeus.

150 Clemens probably read the passage, which derives from Procopius' *History of the Wars,* in one of the *Quaker City's* guidebooks or histories. Gibbon, in commenting on the Moors, says of this passage: "I believe in the columns–I doubt the inscription–and I reject the pedigree" (*The History of the Decline and Fall of the Roman Empire,* ed. Henry H. Milman, 6 vols. [Boston: Phillips Sampson, & Co., 1856], 4:142).

151 "An hour and a half's ride beyond the Cape [Spartel], at Mediána, are extensive caves opening on to the shore, which have been quarried immemorially for

Garden of Hesperides (golden fruit—oranges) was on an island in Elyxis—neither island nor garden remain.

Five days from here ancient city of which nothing is now known—statues. there yet.[152]

Gun-carriage remains of our contact with the Moors—Emperor declared war.

Streets 6 to 12 feet wide—no vehicles

When meet 5 Moors, 2 are Haemed—2 Mohaemmed & 1 Selim.

Game of checkers in ancient Treasury of Moorish Emperor's Palace—turbans & hoods & a negro with shaven head & a top-knot—lost their temper.

Leper boy—with great white splotches on his black body & covered with sores.[153]

Tell Moor Jews by noses.

Fellow with shoes off salaaming & praying in chapel near Treasury.

Moors hospitable—run out & offer hunters milk & kooskysoo—can't go in house.

Moorish woman who knows she is handsome will glance around, & no Moor in sight will unconsciously uncover the face.).
Moor won't look woman in face, nor she him.[154]

---

querns or mill-stones, and which are popularly held to be those of Hercules, described by Pomponius Mela" (Meakin, *Land of the Moors*, p. 111).

[152] Probably the Roman city of Volubilis, near Meknes, 125 miles south of Tangier. At the time of the *Quaker City* excursion these ruins were called Kasar Faráôn (Citadel of the Pharaoh) (Meakin, *Land of the Moors*, p. 280).

[153] "There are many cases of white spots, but leprosy is not very common. [Dr. Gerhard] Rohlfs considered the disease . . . usually described as leprosy, to be rather constitutional syphilis arrived at a stage unknown in Europe" (Meakin, *The Moors*, p. 211).

[154] Clemens used this and the previous paragraph in his second *Alta* letter from Tangier, distorting the truth of his note for humorous effect in a way which he

Marriage is contracted by parents—man never sees her before he is married—next morning, if she is sick or unchaste he can send her home—after reasonable time if she don't breed, discharge her—don't take her for better for worse.

Saw an animal whose father was a horse & his mother a jennet.

Moors reverence cats & will not kill them—during the war, & during the Spanish occupancy of Tetuan they ate up all the cats & the Moors will never forgive them.

Bell[155] & nigger water carriers.

Prompter in Gibraltar theatre—talked louder than actors—much hissing.

Consul M^c^Math—no society—keep plenty games—first week his wife & her sister cried all time.

Brown—Hadji—went to Mecca—busted himself—$10 on deck to Alexandria—been a busted community ever since.

Mrs. M^c^Math's little 4-yr old Katie, born in Tangier,—fluently speaks Spanish & Arabic, but knows no English—when very earnest, talks broken English & uses figurative language of the Arabs, & says by the beard of my father—by the good health of my mama, &c.

Rode through country—

Moors unsociable devils—never smile or bow—look "Christian dog." [#]

---

usually shunned: "I have caught a glimpse of the faces of several Moorish women (for they are only human, and will expose their faces for the admiration of a Christian dog when no he-Moor is by,) and I am full of veneration for the wisdom that leads them to cover up such atrocious ugliness. If I had a wife as ugly as some of those I have seen, I would go over her face with a nail-grab and see if I couldn't improve it" (*TIA*, p. 32). These two paragraphs have been struck through in brown ink; the last sentence of the *Alta* passage was deleted from *The Innocents Abroad*, chapter 9.

155 The *Quaker City* passenger, R. A. H. Bell of Portsmouth, Ohio. None of the other travelers to Tangier gives the incident in any detail.

J. C. L. Wadsworth, San Francisco—at Tangier, Morocco, April 27/67.[156]

Our <Arab> splendid looking Arab friend who has so faithfully served us ever since we got to Tangier is "Mohammed Lamarty."

Yours Truly

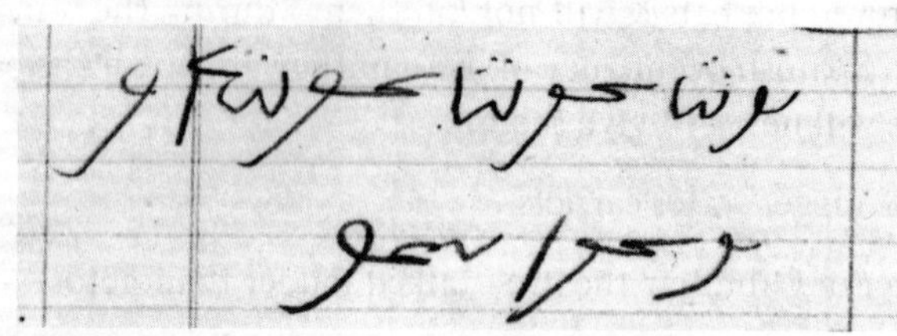

The Signature of <Sahib> Sadi Mohammed Lamarty.

During revolutions, Moorish or Spanish couriers, collecting on letters, swallow the gold, but marauders physic them & collect.

Rode outside the Tangier walls, but <&>did not enjoy it much on account of a notice in hotel warning travelers that it is very dangerous to get out of sight of town without guard of soldiers on account of the Riffians.[157] [#]

---

[156] James C. L. Wadsworth had been part-owner of the Gould & Curry silver mine in Virginia City from 1860 to 1864. After his resignation from the mining firm, his fortune declined until in 1870 he was almost penniless. San Francisco readers were familiar with him, for in his 2 February 1867 *Alta* letter Clemens had mentioned that "Jemmy" Wadsworth was staying at New York's Metropolitan Hotel. And M. G. Upton, the *Alta's* Paris correspondent, reported that Wadsworth had been in Paris in June (31 July 1867). Finally, Clemens noted in his second letter from Tangier: "Looking over the register of the Royal Victoria Hotel a while ago, I came across the name of J. C. L. Wadsworth, of San Francisco, under date of April 27th. How came he to wander to this out-of-the-way place?" (*TIA*, p. 35).

[157] The Riffians were the Berber tribes inhabiting the Rif Mountains of Morocco. Among the Berbers "highwaymen are in great repute, and plunder of passers-by is looked upon as a respectable means of subsistence" (Meakin, *The Moors*, p. 401). Murray's *Handbook for Travellers in Spain* (1869) instructed tourists traveling outside the city of Tangier "to apply to the English or U.S.A. consul for an escort," explaining that the escort, "usually selected from the sultan's body-guard," would be "responsible with his life for the safe return of his charge" (p. 339).

Basket of copper, & bronze coin at money-changers—½ peck—worth seven dollars.

Found a nation who refused to take a drink—wonderful—wonderful—*will* wonders never cease!

Got back to Quaker City at Gibraltar, Monday evening, <June>July 1, 1867.

The Queen's Chair—occupied during the long siege under Elliott—repeat—repeat—repeat—Brown. "Oh, d—n it,—I've got enough of that tiresome old yarn"[158]

Renew provisions every year—

Big reservoir: 210,000 bbls—can make from steam from sea water.

Left Gibraltar just as the sun was setting, July 1, 1867. The sunset was soft & rich & beautiful beyond description. I shall never forget what a dreamy haze hung about the silver-striped dome of the African Pillar—the <peak> city & headland of Soudah & the hills beyond the neutral ground, & how the noble precipice of Gibraltar stood out with every point & edge cut sharply against the mellow sky. Nor how like a child's toy the full canvassed ship looked that sailed in under the tremendous wall & was lost to sight in its shadows.

Beautiful star-lit night on the Mediterranean.

All we left behind are in snowy Gibraltar shoes, & our African party are gorgeous with yellow Moorish slippers.

Midnight, July 1.—After all this racing, & bustling & rollicking excitement in Africa, it seems good to get back to the old ship once

---

[158] It was commonly believed, but without any basis in fact, that the queen of Spain sat in the tower on the summit of the Sierra Carbonera during the Great Siege of Gibraltar (1779–1783), refusing to leave until the British flag had been lowered. Out of compassion for the queen, General George Augustus Eliott, governor of Gibraltar and commander of the British troops there, was said to have lowered the flag so that she might depart with honor. Clemens made the yarn, if possible, even more tiresome in chapter 7 of *The Innocents Abroad.*

more. It is so like *home*. After all our weary time, we shall sleep peacefully to-night.

Sleep makes us all Bashas.—(Moorish Proverb.

"Sleep joins the parted lovers' hands."

Hotel Bill at the Royal Victoria Hotel, Tangier, Morocco.

Breakfast for 8 ....$2.00
Ale . . . . . ″ 8 .... 8.00
Whisky . . ″ 8 .... 8.00
Brandy . . . ″ 8 . . . . <8>10.50
Dinner . . . . . .8 .... 2.50
Jackasses . . . .8 .... 3.25
Guides 2.00
Specimens for 3 ....32.75

July 2, <[1877]>1867.

The Mediterranean this morning is a paler blue than any other sea, perhaps, but the richest & most lustrous & beautiful color imaginable. 20 ships in sight all the time.

Tangier Jew wont touch fire on Saturday—steal though.

Curious the lord made *these* his chosen people.

What a good thing Adam had—when he said a good thing he knew nobody had said it before.

Oh for the ignorance & the confidingness of ignorance that could enable a man to kneel at the Sepulchre & look at the rift in the rock, & the socket of the cross & the <g>tomb of Adam & feel & know & never question that they were genuine.[159]

Gave away Mrs. Larrowe's room.—*favor*. *Promised* her a single room[160] [#]

---

159 This entry and the preceding one may have been written in late September, when Clemens visited the Holy Sepulchre in Jerusalem, or perhaps as late as the end of the excursion. They are on an otherwise blank page, apparently chosen at random, near the beginning of the notebook.

160 This and seven subsequent entries, a list of grievances which Clemens formu-

Gave her a seat *not* at his table.

Hypoc[r] about James at his table.

Promised take her under especial charge, yet tacitly refused to take her ashore in his boat.

Changed Andrews & Crane's rooms.

Took *especial* charge of Miss Chardeyne—yet is permitting her to make a questionable ———

Took Miss Newell under charge, & yet has never <made> paid her *any* attention.

Promised her a single room.

679 Broad st[161]
Room 66

New York to Azores Islands—Gibraltar—Tangier, Africa.

---

lated against Captain Charles C. Duncan, were possibly written after the excursionists reached Paris on 7 July. They appear on the first leaf of the notebook. Stephen M. Griswold wrote the Brooklyn *Eagle* that the "Quaker City party arrived at Paris without Captain Duncan, who prefers to stick to the steamer. We found several young ladies, who had been put under the Captain's charge, wandering about Paris on their own hook" ("Notes of European Travel," 6 August 1867).

161 This and the following entry are in ink on the outside back cover of the notebook.

IX

"A Funeral Excursion Without a Corpse"

(11 August–11 October 1867)

THE LAST dated entry in Notebook 8 (2 July 1867) left Clemens at sea, bound for Marseilles, while the entry bearing the earliest date in Notebook 9 (11 August 1867) marks his departure from the harbor of Naples. A notebook was certainly kept for the intervening period, but no evidence refutes Paine's surmise that the "notes of this period are lost. We shall never know just what memoranda he made on the spot of the doings" of his companions as they traveled to Paris, Genoa, "then by rail through Italy to Milan, Venice, Florence and the rest, joining the ship again at Naples" (*MTN*, p. 69). However, Mark Twain did include two references to this missing notebook in *The Innocents Abroad*. An engraving in chapter 19 ostensibly reproduces two pages from the notebook, even though the reproduction is obviously not a facsimile. On the right-hand page of an open notebook appears:

Picture by Titian in the Cathedral—
subject forgotten

size of a slate—
Priest said History of it was very curious
It was painted in the dark—
Train leaves at 10 AM—
October [*one unrecoverable word*]

On the left-hand page are the pencil dots recording the "astonishing clatter of reverberations" of "the most remarkable echo in the world" that Mark Twain witnessed just outside Milan. When Clemens saw specimen illustrations for *Innocents* in April 1869, he wrote Elisha Bliss: "Your idea about the 'Echo' diagram is correct—glad it is to be engraved" (*MTLP*, p. 19). It is conceivable that Clemens sent his original notebook to the engraver, who failed to return it. A passage in chapter 24 of *Innocents* indicates that the notebook was lost subsequent to the writing of the book: the travelers "were a little fatigued with sight seeing, and so we rattled through a good deal of country by rail without caring to stop. I took few notes. I find no mention of Bologna in my memorandum book, except that we arrived there in good season, but saw none of the sausages for which the place is so justly celebrated."

Notebook 9 takes Clemens through the remainder of the itinerary for the excursion, concluding with his departure from Alexandria and the voyage back through the Mediterranean, but omits all details of his brief trip through Spain, the Atlantic crossing, the stopover in Bermuda, and the arrival in New York on 19 November 1867. "We were all lazy and satisfied, now," Clemens wrote in chapter 59 of *Innocents*, "as the meager entries in my note-book (that sure index, to me, of my condition,) prove. What a stupid thing a note-book gets to be at sea, any way." Then, to make up for the absence of notebook entries or *Alta* letters covering the final stages of the journey, Mark Twain created a passage that he represented as a transcription from his notebook:

Sunday—Services, as usual, at four bells. Services at night, also. No cards.

Monday—Beautiful day, but rained hard. The cattle purchased at Alexandria for beef ought to be shingled. Or else fattened. The water stands in deep puddles in the depressions forward of their after shoulders. Also here and there all over their backs. It is well they are not cows—it would soak in and ruin the milk. The poor devil eagle from Syria looks miserable and droopy in the rain, perched on the forward capstan. He appears to have his own opinion of a sea voyage, and if it were put into language and the language solidified, it would probably essentially dam the widest river in the world.

Tuesday—Somewhere in the neighborhood of the island of Malta. Can not stop there. Cholera. Weather very stormy. Many passengers seasick and invisible.

Wednesday—Weather still very savage. Storm blew two land birds to sea, and they came on board. A hawk was blown off, also. He circled round and round the ship, wanting to light, but afraid of the people. He was so tired, though, that he had to light, at last, or perish. He stopped in the foretop, repeatedly, and was as often blown away by the wind. At last Harry caught him. Sea full of flying-fish. They rise in flocks of three hundred and flash along above the tops of the waves a distance of two or three hundred feet, then fall and disappear.

Thursday—Anchored off Algiers, Africa. Beautiful city, beautiful green hilly landscape behind it. Staid half a day and left. Not permitted to land, though we showed a clean bill of health. They were afraid of Egyptian plague and cholera.

Friday—Morning, dominoes. Afternoon, dominoes. Evening, promenading the deck. Afterwards, charades.

Saturday—Morning, dominoes. Afternoon, dominoes. Evening, promenading the decks. Afterwards, dominoes.

Sunday—Morning service, four bells. Evening service, eight bells. Monotony till midnight.—Whereupon, dominoes.

Monday—Morning, dominoes. Afternoon, dominoes. Evening, promenading the decks. Afterward, charades and a lecture from Dr. C. Dominoes.

No date—Anchored off the picturesque city of Cagliari, Sardinia. Staid till midnight, but not permitted to land by these infamous foreigners. They smell inodorously—they do not wash—they dare not risk cholera.

Thursday—Anchored off the beautiful cathedral city of Malaga, Spain.—Went ashore in the captain's boat—not ashore, either, for they would not let us land. Quarantine. Shipped my newspaper correspondence, which they took with tongs, dipped it in sea water, clipped it full of holes, and then fumigated it with villainous vapors till it smelt like a Spaniard. Inquired about chances to run the blockade and visit the Alhambra at Granada. Too risky—they might hang a body. Set sail—middle of afternoon.

And so on, and so on, and so forth, for several days. Finally, anchored off Gibraltar, which looks familiar and home-like.

Although the passage is arbitrarily dated, and although Clemens inadvertently placed Algiers ahead of Cagliari on the itinerary, the facts are essentially as he presents them. Mark Twain borrowed several details—the storm, the land birds blown to sea, and the flying fish—from Notebook 9. Although not a genuine notebook entry, the passage approximates what Clemens would have written if he had kept a record of the trip through the Mediterranean.

It had been an exhausting two months since the group had left Italy in early August, proceeding south past Sicily through the western isles of Greece to arrive finally at Athens. Encountering a strict quarantine for cholera, the party sailed almost immediately for Constantinople, although not before Clemens and three comrades made a surreptitious midnight excursion to the Acropolis. After three days in Constantinople most of the passengers sailed through the Bosporus to the Black Sea, and then visited Sebastopol, Odessa, and finally Yalta, where they were received by Czar Alexander II. Returning to Constantinople, they encountered a five-day delay for coaling and so saw more of the city than they had planned. But by early September they were bound for Smyrna, took a side trip to the ruins of Ephesus in their first encounter with ancient, biblical ground. By September 10 they had arrived in Beirut and the Holy Land, the climax of their voyage to the East. Despite unforeseen complications about transportation and routes, they soon divided into several small parties with itineraries to suit their members' varying tastes for roughing it. Clemens joined with Dr. Birch and William Denny (who had both gone along on the moonlight hike to the Acropolis), Dan Slote, Jack Van Nostrand, Julius Moulton, Joshua William Davis, and William F. Church in a three-week overland trip to Baalbek and Damascus, then down through the length of Palestine to Jerusalem, over to the Dead Sea, the Jordan, and Bethlehem, and then finally to Jaffa (Joppa), where they rejoined the ship. Leaving Palestine (which all the travelers found "lovely only in books") early in October, they spent several days in Alexandria, which seemed pleasantly European and modern. They traveled by train to Cairo and the pyramids, finally turning homeward on October 7. The last dated entry in Notebook 9 is for October 11 and appears slightly rephrased in the bogus notebook passage of chapter 59 of *The Innocents Abroad*: "At sea, somewhere in the neighborhood of Malta. Very stormy."

The notebook maintains the highly professional, detailed, and detached style that prevailed in the latter part of Notebook 8. Most entries were designed as brief memoranda of sights and incidents from which Clemens could construct his letters to the *Alta*. Since he tended to write those letters soon after the experience, it is only occasionally that we find extended, circumstantial accounts in the notebook. Leisure on shipboard encouraged greater expansion—both the trip to the Acropolis and the visit with the czar are given in some detail—but Notebook 9 was less a journal than a memorandum book, from which Clemens wrote his *Alta* letters and eventually *The Innocents Abroad*.

The factual, mnemonic form of the notebook demonstrates how Clemens' "reportorial instinct" worked. In a letter of 1875 he would counsel Dan De Quille, who was planning to write *The Big Bonanza,* to "bring along *lots of dry statistics*—it's the very best sauce a humorous book can have. Ingeniously used, they just make a reader smack his chops in gratitude" (William Wright Papers, The Bancroft Library). Clemens' use of this method is documented by the kind of detail he preserved. There is a sense of almost indiscriminate note-taking. Clemens' frequent, often phonetic, misspellings show that he recorded what he heard from guides and fellow travelers, as well as what he read in guidebooks. He traveled, as he would write in the preface to *The Innocents Abroad,* with the intention of eventually showing his reader "how *he* would be likely to see Europe and the East if he looked at them with his own eyes instead of the eyes of those who travelled in those countries before him." Penciled sketches, especially rough maps or panoramas, to jog his memory and keep the physical reality clearly before him, appear frequently and are sometimes labeled "(Not copied)" or "(This drawing is not copied)." He kept a scrupulous chronology of arrivals, departures, and delays—often to the hour—not because these details would be used directly for letters, but in anticipation of the need to reconstruct actual events. Julia Newell wrote scornfully to the Janesville (Wis.) *Gazette* of 30 November 1867 that in Jerusalem she had witnessed guides leading "travelers with the inevitable note book, swallowing and recording it all, with the greatest apparent credulity." Clemens' note-taking, however, was that of an ambitious, professional reporter at work.

Despite Clemens' remarkable stamina in traveling, sight-seeing, and not least of all in writing, the next two months were marked by fatigue and waning interest, especially in Turkey and Palestine. Only two events seemed to break the gathering pattern: Clemens' hike to the Acropolis and the audience with Czar Alexander Nicholas. The first probably endorsed his image of himself as the wild westerner, willing to defy law and physical danger for the sake of adventure, while the second flattered the emerging image of the polite and articulate writer, the man who would naturally be called upon to write the group's formal address to the czar.

The visit with Russian royalty was certainly one of the high points of the trip, both for Clemens and for his fellow travelers, but the origin of the visit is not entirely clear. Clemens says in his notebook that the original suggestion came from the friendly Russians at Sebastopol, and there seems no reason to doubt this private record. He also says there that for "certain reasons" they at first declined to seek an audience, "& everybody was sorry enough, very naturally." In his *Alta* letter he explained that "our time is so short . . . and more especially our coal is so nearly out, that we judged it best to forego the rare pleasure of holding social intercourse with an Emperor" (*TIA*, p. 134). But on 25 August in a letter home he indicated the fear of a rebuff: "we knew that a great English Excursion party, and also the Viceroy of Egypt, in his splendid yacht, had been refused an audience within the last fortnight, so we thought it not safe to try it" (*MTL*, p. 132).

Although the passengers were initially unaware of it, one of the motives that had led the owners of the vessel to charter the *Quaker City* for this excursion was their hope of finding a purchaser for the ship. This somewhat cynical exploitation of the high-minded plans initiated by members of the congregation of the Plymouth Church is documented by Daniel D. Leary's letter commenting on the decision to incorporate Yalta in the itinerary. Leary, who was a passenger, wrote to his brother on August 29 that he "was induced to go there in the hope that the steamer might tempt the Emperor to purchase. . . . I had telegraphed from Odessa at the suggestion of the Governor there to the Governor at Yalta, announcing my intention to visit the Emperor, so when we arrived an aide of the Governor came out to receive us, and invited me ashore to call on the Governor General, who said the Emperor would receive us the next day at the palace, which he did in a most cordial manner." Although commerce brought him to Yalta, it was not his only satisfaction: "Of course I was king pin, and walked about on the most familiar footing with the Emperor and Empress." And, he assured his brother, "they are splendid people and no mistake in going through the conservatories I had the Grand duchess Marie on my arm, what do you think of that?" (Lewis Leary, "More Letters from the *Quaker City*," *American Literature* 42 [May 1970]:201).

William E. James, for one, took a more sardonic view of Leary's inept commercial efforts in a letter published by the Brooklyn *Eagle* on 20 September 1867. James wrote that after the consul had read the address the czar was

> surrounded and buttonholed by [Leary] . . . urging him to come on board of the Quaker City; he stood there awhile, looking ill at ease and nervous, and finally

turned to get to the rest of the party to speak to them, but was headed off by Leary, who would post himself directly in front of him, with his mouth wide open, showing his teeth, and putting his hand on his shoulder, urging him to come on board; three times was this repeated.

Even though Leary's unsuccessful commercial ambition was known, his primary role in arranging for the reception itself was gratefully acknowledged by twenty-seven members of the *Quaker City* party. A petition addressed to him, thanking him for his "kindness in affording us an opportunity to visit the Emperor of Russia at Yalta" survives, and Clemens' name is among those on the list.

Clemens' enthusiasm in Notebook 8 for the foreignness of Tangier and his excitement about the illicit excursion to the Acropolis and the unexpected reception by the czar contrast with his relatively jaded reactions to Constantinople and Palestine. As Clemens traveled through Italy, the eagerness of the relatively green westerner gave way to the ennui of a homesick and occasionally chauvinistic traveler. "What," he wrote the New York *Tribune* on August 31, "is a Turkish bath in Constantinople to a Russian one in New-York? What are the dancing dervishes to the negro minstrels?—and Heaven help us, what is Oriental splendor to the Black Crook? New-York has fifty wonders where Constantinople has one!" (*TIA*, p. 132).

This disillusionment is consistently reflected in the reactions of Clemens, and of the other passengers, to the cities of the Near East, with their "picturesque" associations and reputations. Constantinople, seen "from a mile or so up the Bosphorus," Clemens wrote the *Alta*, "is by far the handsomest city we have seen." But "its attractiveness begins and ends with its picturesqueness. From the time you start ashore till you get back again, you damn it." Likewise, "Damascus *is* beautiful from the mountain. . . . If I were to go to Damascus again, I would camp on Mahomet's hill about a week, and then go away. There is no need to go inside the walls. . . . It is so crooked and cramped and dirty that one cannot realize that he is in the splendid city he saw from the hill top" (*TIA*, pp. 112–113, 194–195). The notebook entry is laconic, but firm: "got enough of Damascus. Don't want to see any more of it."

Julia Newell wrote to the Janesville (Wis.) *Gazette* on 3 September 1867 (published 31 October 1867):

> Out in the bay before the city which disputes with Naples the claim to the loveliest situation in the world, with the rays of the declining sun lighting up its innumerable gilded mosques and minarets, it seems in truth as fair a city as the sun ever shone upon—yes, as magnificent as the most vivid imagination could paint. But when we come to toil up the steep, rough, wretchedly-paved, filthy streets, picking our way through the miserable mangy curs asleep in the sun, and so thickly laid out as to hardly leave a path, we began to think that if *distance* ever did lend enchantment to the view, that statement is peculiarly true of Constantinople.

She found Jerusalem, "even without the aids of imagination and association, . . . imposing and beautiful, as from the distant hill tops it rises, gleaming against the sky. But when you are fairly within her walls, the spell is broken, and you find modern Jerusalem only another dirty Turkish town. . . . However prepared, I think that every one must feel a certain disappointment at the almost total obliteration of every trace of the Jerusalem of Holy Writ." And Moses S. Beach in his eighteenth letter to the New York *Sun*, spoke for the entire company:

> As a child, I supposed [Constantinople] to be a paradise on earth, and one of my greatest ambitions was to look upon its glistening domes and its forest of minarets while I listened to the oft-repeated calls of the faithful to prayer. That I have unravelled the enchantment and found in it but the effect of distance is not surprising; yet must I confess myself wholly unprepared for the utter disappointment experienced in common with nearly every one of my fellow passengers. . . . Except in size and in an unequalled beauty of position, Constantinople ranks among the least and last of the European cities.

Clemens found the East discomforting, even threatening, for other reasons. Remarking on the Moslem disdain for Christians he fumed: "I never hated a Chinaman as I hate these degraded Turks and Arabs" (*TIA*, p. 203). His irascibility extended to the people who surrounded and watched the sleeping travelers in Cesarea Phillippi:

> They sat in silence, and with tireless patience watched over our every motion with that vile, uncomplaining impoliteness which is so truly Indian, and which makes a white man so nervous, and uncomfortable and savage that he wants to exterminate the whole tribe. (*TIA*, p. 211)

The role of the western maverick, slyly puncturing the grandeur of European culture, as well as the smug pretentiousness of the eastern pilgrims, had been one of the chief pleasures of the early part of the voyage. But, confronted with cultures that had no pretense and that uncomfortably reminded him of his own western background, Clemens expressed a hostility that was often masked by genteel humor. Watching the women of Palestine gather camel dung for fuel, he remarked:

> I am susceptible, but even up to this very moment I have never taken what you might seriously regard as a shine to one of these young women. They are not fastidious enough for me. I may be too particular, but such is my bias, anyway. (*TIA*, p. 246)

The poverty of the landscape had become as offensive as the residents. At Capernaum he was reminded of the desolate parts of Nevada:

> This country reminds me of Washoe all the time. Take Washoe Valley, and you have this Valley of the Sources of the Jordan; take Washoe Lake and you have the Waters of Merom exactly; take the swamps that border it and you have the dwelling-place of the Bedouin goat herdsmen; take the forbidding mountains that surround the picture, and strip them of every tree, every shrub, and batter from their outlines every semblance of grace and beauty, and you have the mountains that border Merom. . . . They say it is a most favorable specimen of Palestine. If it is a favorable specimen of Palestine, surely Palestine is Washoe's born mate. (*TIA*, p. 227)

Yet, despite this dissatisfaction, Clemens continued to approach every jaunt and journey with energy and enthusiasm. Four days before beginning this notebook he wrote to Frank Fuller that he had "had a good deal of fun on this trip, but it is costing like Sin. I will be a busted community some time before I see America again. The worst of it is, that a ship is a bad writing desk and I can't write on shore because I have too much to see there. So I neglect my correspondence half the time and botch it the balance" (TS in MTP). Although he actually maintained a very regular correspondence, it seems clear that he was rarely tempted to stay on board to write or rest. While the ship was delayed at Constantinople, he walked throughout the town before leaving for nearby Scutari. Although disillusioned by Jerusalem, he set off on a three-day trip to the Dead Sea and Bethlehem. After three weeks of riding through Palestine, he sailed with relief for Egypt, where he and Jack Van Nostrand, unlike the rest of the travelers, immediately disembarked at Alexandria instead of waiting until morning. Toward the end of the voyage, when others hesitated and delayed, Clemens impetuously set out with three others for a grueling overland trip through Spain.

Clemens' disillusionment with Palestine did not diminish. When he reported the dream of a revised excursion in his *Alta* letter of November 20, he indicated his opinion of this portion of the trip. While a projected, idealized voyage with Ned Wakeman allowed forty days in London, forty in Vienna, forty in Rome, and so on, it allotted only a total of six days for Egypt, two days for Constantinople, and "two hours and a half in the Holy Land."

Notebook 9 now contains 184 pages, 21 of them blank. The pages measure 6½ by 3¹⁵⁄₁₆ inches (16.4 by 10 centimeters), and their edges are marbled in red, black, and gold. They are ruled with twenty-four blue horizontal lines. The endpapers and remaining flyleaf are white; the front flyleaf and at least the first ruled leaf have been torn out and are missing. The notebook is bound in a stiff cover of tan calf. The front cover and the first gathering are only loosely attached to the binding; portions of some gatherings have come loose altogether. Someone, probably Paine, has written "1867" in ink on the front cover. All entries are in pencil, with occasional blue or black pencil use marks made by Paine.

The great bulk of the notebook comprises a continuous journal, beginning in Naples and ending near Malta. But Clemens inverted the notebook to isolate at the back such entries as the petition to Captain Duncan, a sketch of Athens, a list of passengers, cryptic notes on Egypt, and the nubs of several jokes used in *The Innocents Abroad*.

On many notebook pages Clemens entered headings, some apparently written at the time of the initial inscription, some added later. These are usually simply such things as "Constantinople" or "Syria," but they occasionally include dates mentioned elsewhere on the page or on a preceding page. Since these headings, which serve to index the contents of the manuscript page, would interrupt the continuity of the printed page, they have been omitted here except at their first occurrence. Omitted headings are recorded as emendations. On the back cover Clemens wrote, in ink, a brief summary of his itinerary; this appears in the present text where the notebook is inverted (p. 447.4–6). A small piece of paper, with three entries on it, is pasted on the back cover, and these appear at page 447.7–9.

Sam L. Clemens—1867—Sept.[1]

Burial of Moses[2]

By Nebo's lonely mountain,
    On this side Jordan's wave,
In a vale in the land of Moab,
    There lies a lonely grave;
And no man dug that sepulchre,
    And no man saw it e'er,
For the "Sons of God" upturned the sod,
    And laid the dead man there.

That was the grandest funeral,
    That ever passed on earth;
But no man heard the trampling,
    Or saw the train go forth.
Noiselessly as the daylight
    Comes when the night is done,
And the crimson streak on ocean's cheek
    Grows into the great sun—

Noiselessly as the spring-time
    Her crown of verdure weaves,
And all the trees on all the hills
    Open their thousand leaves;
So without sound of music,
    Or voice of them that wept,
Silently down, from the mountan's crown
    The great/vast/grand procession swept.

---

[1] The entry appears lengthwise on the front endpaper; it was apparently written when Clemens was visiting Palestine in September.

[2] By Mrs. Cecil Frances Alexander. The poem has been neatly transcribed on the first four notebook pages and may have been set down from memory. Paine testified that Clemens "often repeated" his favorite stanzas in the Nevada days, and that the poem became "to him a sort of literary touchstone" (*MTB*, p. 217). Clemens entered the title in this notebook at p. 438.2, and he quoted part of the first stanza in his September 12 *Alta* letter.

Perchance the bald old eagle,
    On gray Beth-peor's hight,
Out of his rocky eyry
    Looked on the wondrous sight;
Perchance the lion, stalking,
    Still shuns that hallowed spot:
For beast & bird have seen & heard
    That which man knoweth not.

But when the warrior dieth,
    His comrades in the war,
With arms reversed, & muffled drum
    Follow the funeral car;
They show the banners taken,
    They tell his battles won,
And after him lead his masterless steed
    While peals the minute-gun.

Amid the noblest of the land
    Men lay the sage to rest,
And give the bard an honored place
    With costly marble drest—
In the great minster transept,
    Where lights like glories fall,
And the sweet choir sings & the organ rings
    Along the emblazoned wall.

This was the bravest warrior
    That ever buckled sword;
This the most gifted poet
    That ever breathed a word;
And never earth's philosopher
    Traced with his golden pen,
On the deathless page truths half so sage
    <S>As he wrote down for men.

And had he not high honor?
    The hill-side for his pall,

To lie in state while angels wait
With stars for tapers tall,
And the dark rock-pines, like tossing plumes,
Over his bier to wave,
And God's own hand in that lonely land,
To lay him in the grave!

In that deep grave without a name,
Whence his uncoffined clay
Shall break again—most wondrous thought!—
Before the judgment day,!
And stand, with glory wrapped around,
On the hills he never trod,
And speak of the strife that won our life
With the Incarnate Son of God.

O lonely tomb in Moab's land!
O dark Beth-peor's hill!
Speak to these curious hearts of ours,
And teach them to be still.
God hath His mysteries of grace,
Ways that we cannot tell;
And hides them deep like the secret sleep
Of him he loved so well.

Italy.

From Naples.

Sailed from Naples Aug 11 at 6 AM.[3] [#]

---

[3] The *Quaker City* arrived in Naples August 1. On August 7 a correspondent to the London *Times* reported that most of the passengers had "landed at Civita Vecchia, and many of them have come on by land. . . . In all there are 65 passengers, 80 having been expected, who will remain not more than 12 days, of which seven have been spent either in quarantine or in escaping from it *viâ* Civita Vecchia and Rome" (15 August 1867). Mrs. Severance noted that their departure was actually delayed until eight o'clock in the morning because Jacob S. Haldeman ("unfortunately a victim of intemperance") was late returning from shore. "After a man had been dispatched for him, he came rowing out rapidly in a boat with four oars, as he had seen the steamer moving round and had feared they had left him" (*JLS*, p. 106).

7 PM, with the western horizon all golden from the sunken sun, & specked with distant ships, the bright full moon shining like a silver shield high over head, <th>& the deep dark blue of the Mediterranean under foot & a strange stort of twilight affected by all these different lights & colors, all around us & about us, we sighted old Stromboli.[4]

How grand it looms up out of the lonely sea & how symmetrical. It is beautiful, now, with its dark blue just veiled under a pearly mist that half conceals & half discloses

8—The 2 jets of smoke have turned into one, a hundred feet broad—can't see how high—can't see it after it gets above the black background of the further rim of the crater.

(In Rome.[5]

Peter's footprints.

Peter's prison (Mamertine)—print of face—miraculous spring he made to baptise the soldiers—hole where he broke through.[6] [#]

---

[4] Apparently because his *Alta* letter for this period was lost in the mails, Clemens returned to his notebook when writing about Stromboli for *The Innocents Abroad.* This passage was inserted, with minor changes, in the second paragraph of chapter 32.

[5] The entries from here through "Chris Colombo" (p. 384.7) are evidently Clemens' recollections of his visit to Rome, which preceded the departure from Naples.

[6] Clemens' letter to the *Alta* from Rome was lost. In writing about "Old Monkish Frauds" for *The Innocents Abroad* he may have referred to these notes on Saint Peter: "we also [stood] in the Mamertine Prison, where he was confined, where he converted the soldiers, and where tradition says he caused a spring of water to flow in

Chateau Margaux Bath.[7]

New <St>Bronze Statue of Jupiter—<$30,000>$50,000—gave $36,000 for the land.[8]

Fellow in outskirts who sells urns of dead ashes 2,000 fr.

St Peter's chains—wipe, kis touch to forehead & necklace

<—>Napoleon & the Sultan[9]

In bronze! Appian Way!—Chris Colombo.

Sicily—Straits Messina.

Hard a case as Paul—got to knock him endways with a streak of lightning before <he woul> he could get religion through him.

Aug. 12.

Passed through Straits of Messina, between <I>Southern Italy & Sicily—2 miles wide in narrowest place.

Sylla on the one hand & Charybdis on the other.

<One of> Ulysses' companion died at Baia.

Passed close to city of Messina—mass of gas lights—

Greece.

Mount Etna not visible. [#]

---

order that he might baptize them. But when they showed us the print of Peter's face in the hard stone of the prison wall and said he made that by falling up against it, we doubted. And when, also, the monk at the church of San Sebastian showed us a paving-stone with two great footprints in it and said that Peter's feet made those, we lacked confidence again" (chapter 26).

[7] Margaux, in southern France, the source of Château Margaux wine, is also in the vicinity of several sea-bathing resorts. Clemens did not stay in or pass through this area, and it is not known what sort of bath he meant.

[8] Clemens probably refers to a fifteen-foot bronze statue of Hercules that had been excavated at the site of the theater of Pompey in 1864. According to *A Handbook of Rome and Its Environs*, 10th ed. (London: John Murray, 1871), Pope Pius IX purchased the statue for the equivalent of $50,000. Clemens explained in chapter 28 of *The Innocents Abroad* that its seller had just bought his farm "for thirty-six thousand dollars, so the first crop was a good one for the new farmer."

[9] Clemens fully expressed his opinion of the two monarchs, whom he had seen together in Paris, in chapter 13 of *The Innocents Abroad*.

Aug 13.

Been skirting along the Isles of Greece all day—western side—very mountainous—prevailing tints gray & brown approaching to red. Pretty little white villages surrounded by trees <nessel> nestle in little depressions & roost upon gentle elevations on the lofty table-lands with high perpendicular sea-walls. We see them all as if laid down on a map.

Splendid, rich carmine sunset.—fine sunsets are rare in Italy, or at least striking ones. They are lovely, often, but their loveliness is soft & rich—elegant, refined—never grand, splendid, gorgeous, like those in our cold Northern States.

The damnable public burial ground at Naple.[10]

The Piraeus.— Greece.

Aug. 14.

Entered the little narrow canal (500 yds wide & 2 miles long) & in between two light on reefs hardly wide enough for the ship—came in gallantly without chart or pilot.

The town extends most of the way around a deep circular  basin & is the cleanest, neatest 2 & 3-story of square cream-colored buildings we have seen. [#]

---

[10] Clemens apparently witnessed the grisly daily burial procedure at Campo Santo Vecchio. An American reporter, Frank Hall, had viewed the scene earlier that year and reported: "The dead for the day were brought to the pit's side, the priest who attends daily was there, the coffins were opened, that the priest and the custodian of the ground might see their contents. There was no need to be told that they were children of the poor—for among all there was not an adult corpse—their pinched, grinning faces and their dirty, tattered garments told all that and more. The priest murmured a short prayer, sprinkled each coffin with holy water, and then the sextons did their duty by taking their little bodies one by one and dropping them into the vault, where they fell with a crunching sound on the dead bones beneath. The last box was opened—can I ever forget the sight?—twelve infants packed in one box, and the sexton took them out one by one by the heel dropping them into the yawning pit as if they had been so many dead kittens" (letter written on 2 May 1867, Elmira [N.Y.] *Advertiser*, n.d.; clipping in MTP).

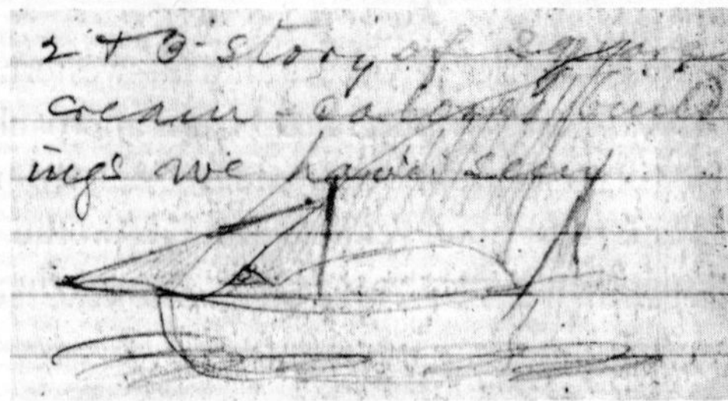

Boats are not pretty, but how they fly! & how exquisitely skillful these Greeks are in handling them. I would like to stay with them a while.

The sun is *very* bright & the atmosphere infinitely clearer & purer than that of Naples.

On Board Steamer[11]
Quaker City, Aug 14.

Capt C C Duncan

Sir—Whereas—

First—There is nothing to see at Sebastopol but a bare &

[11] Despite the objections enumerated below, Clemens did visit the battlefields of the Crimean War at Sebastopol when the *Quaker City* touched there. The petition was written with the notebook inverted, on two pages chosen at random near the back of the notebook, but has been moved to this position on the evidence of a clear date.

uninteresting battle-field where military fortifications *have been* but no longer exist—and

Secondly—Several among us <have>having stood <am> in the midst of <such> scenes of this character of infinitely greater importance in our own Country in the smoke & carnage of battle —and—

Thirdly—The remainder of our company having seen a sufficiency of such things after the battles were over—and

Fourthly—Since by leaving Sebastopol out of the excursion we can gain a precious addition of time for travel in Palestine,—

Therefore, Satisfied that <the minority> if a short trip be taken through the Bosphorus & into the Black Sea, all parties will be willing to forego the extension of it to desolate Sebastopol with its notable <pyr> pile of porter bottles, we respectfully request that you will alter your programme in accordance with the suggestion contained in this last paragraph.

Respectfully

Athens.[12]

Thursday, Aug. 15,/57.

<At>We were put into quarantine at once, yesterday, & rather than be cooped up at anchor remote from shore for 11 days, the Captain decided to <sail> lie still 24 hours & then sail direct for Constantinople.

It was <a>remarked by the commandant of the port (the Piraeus,) that guards would be set & a watch kept upon us, & that any one found breaking the quarantine by stealing ashore would be severely dealt with—& quarantine laws in these countries are usually harsh & even <cruel> unnecessarily cruel sometimes.[13]

---

[12] The second drawing of Athens on page 388 was made by Clemens on a page apparently chosen at random near the back of the notebook. It has been moved here in accord with its probable date.

[13] A *Handbook for Travellers in Greece*, new ed. (London: John Murray, 1854) remarked that "detention in a Lazzaretto has been defined [as] 'imprisonment, with the chance of catching the plague;' and its length and frequency formed, until within the last few years, a serious drawback to the pleasures of an Eastern tour. . . . The duration of quarantine sometimes amounted of old to the full probation of 40

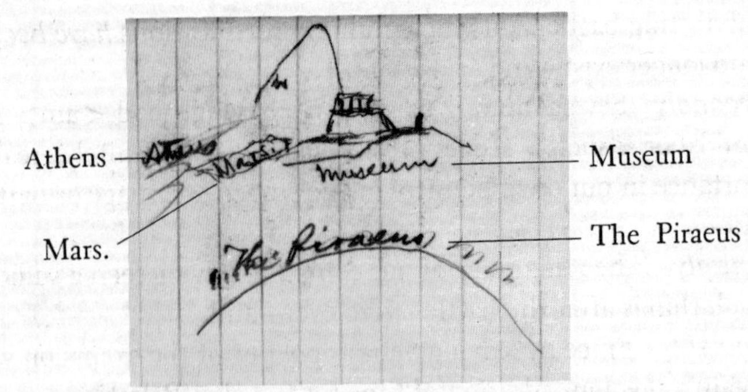

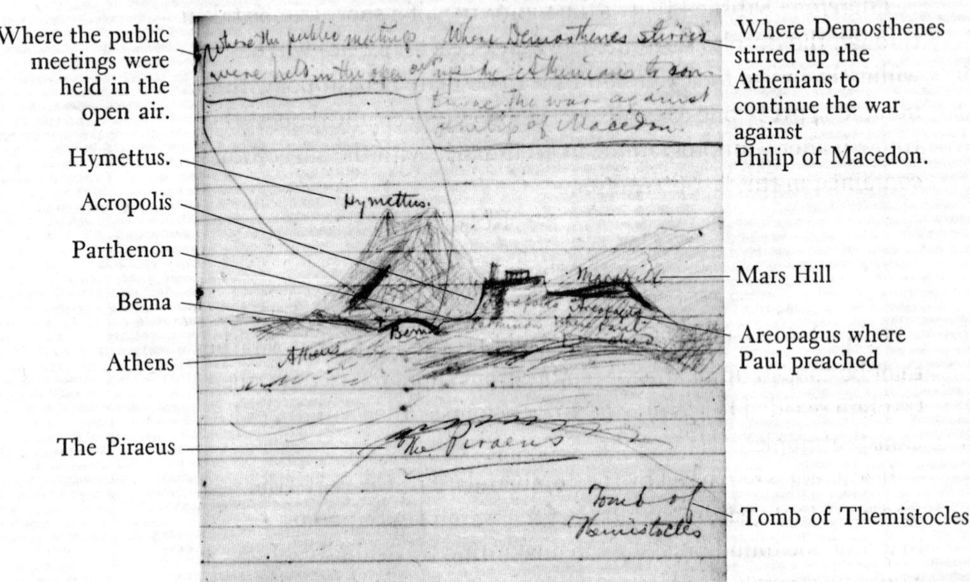

It was a bitter disappointment to the whole ship's company, to be so near to famous Athens & not be permitted to visit it. We could see the city vaguely defined in the distant valley with the glass, & <with the> with the naked eye we could see the grand ruins upon

days, from which the term is derived; and it rarely was less than 10 days, even when the vessel arrived with a *clean bill of health*" (p. 13). Recalling an incident of 1854 in which British seamen broke quarantine and, as a result, ten thousand people died, Mrs. Severance remarked that "one is not surprised to see the stringency maintained" (*JLS*, p. 113).

the Acropolis, & with the telescope could count the columns of the Parthenon.

Themistocles' Tomb.[14]

We imagined we could trace out Mars Hill (the Areopagus,) where Paul preached, the highest court was held 3 days in the year, & where Demosthenes thundered his Phillippics into the ears of the disheartened Athenians; we believed we could see the Museum Hill & the Pnyx. We cared little for Hymettus & Pentelicon.

At 11 o'clock at night Dr Jackson, Col. Denny, Dr. Birch & I, left the ship <&>in a boat & got set on shore outside the quarantine lines[15]—then <stran>straggled over the hills, serenaded by a hundred dogs, skirted the town under a <d>clouded moon, & in half an hour were safe beyond any chance of capture & fairly away for Athens. We could not find a road that seemed to lead in the right direction, & so, taking the tall steep mountain to the left of the Acropolis for a mark, we steered at it <for two hours> industriously over hills, throgh valleys, stony desert places, plowed fields & vineyards, & walked fast, too, for there was little time to spare if we would get back to the ship before the treacherous day should dawn.

We made the trip! (stopped occasionally by savages armed with guns, who rose mysteriously up out of shadows & darkness & said

---

[14] "As we enter the harbour, a sarcophagus, hollowed out of the rock at the water's edge, is seen, near which lie the fragments of a large column. This is called the monument of Themistocles,—most appropriately situated in sight of the scene of his great victory on the one hand, and the city he saved on the other" (Thomas Chase, *Hellas: Her Monuments and Scenery* [Cambridge, Mass.: Sever and Francis, 1863], p. 13). Clemens interlined this entry above "these countries" (p. 387.27) some time after completing the general description of Athens. He mentions the tomb again on p. 394.

[15] Years later William A. Pratt, quartermaster of the *Quaker City*, recalled that he "was told by the ship's captain, that aft some gentlemen wanted to go ashore after dark, but he said, 'Remember I don't give you any liberty to take that small boat.' Mr. Pratt understood what that meant. . . . These four men said they would take the chances if he would land them on a rocky point of land away from the Old Port and keep a lookout for their return. . . . Mr. Pratt says he did not sleep much that night, as he kept a constant watch for a peculiar whistle which he heard when the first call was made, but it was a close shave to avoid the quarantine boat, which was on the lookout for anyone who would dare to violate their law" (undated, unidentified newspaper clipping in MTP).

"*Ho!*" when we happened casually to be stealing grapes,) and stood under the towering massive walls of the ancient citadel of Athens—walls that had loomed above the heads of better men than we, a thousand years before the Son of God was born in <b>Bethlehem!

<At>It was between 1 & 2 oclock—the place was silent—the gates were shut—the devil to pay. Denny tried to climb over a ruined wall—knocked down a stone—somebody shouted from within, & Denny dropped!

We soon roused that fellow out—(the guard)—& entered the majestic ruin.

The *Propileia,* <—>the gateway to the temples of the Acropolis, is of lovely <[well r]>fluted columns, of white marble

Parthenon—8 × 17 columns—inner row same size columns but smaller Number—250 ft long, 100 wide.

Marble arm-chairs, bas-reliefs, entablatures, <sul> statues &c

Grim marble faces <looking> glancing up suddenly at you out of the grass at your feet,[16]

Temple of Minerva—small.

Temple of Hercules (with the six noble caryatides supporting the portico.

Huge reddish marble tower of rough, massive masonry, like a <cha>chimney—don't know what it was for.

Old ruined arches in the valley below our right.

The narrow rocky ridge & flight of steps & square rostrum on the Aeropagus or Mars Hill—sacred to memories of St. Paul & Demosthenes, Aristides, Themistocles &c.

But Athens by moonlight, from the bastions! The King's white palace & shrubbery garden flecked with mellow gas-lights! The

---

16 Clemens took one of these relics as a souvenir of his hike to the Acropolis. The small marble head is now in the Mark Twain Papers.

sharply defined windows, chimneys, *shingles*, almost, of every single house in Athens, in the <lus> splendid lustre that was pouring out of the Heavens, & even paling the scattering gas-lights! Athens spread out right underneath our feet, 200 feet below us, & the grand <old> white ruin of the Parthenon towering over our heads! <—such> <the>Athens by moonlight! When I forget it I shall be dead—not before.

We made the trip undisturbed save by the armed grape-guards & the seventeen million dogs that followed us thro' the Piraeus, & reached the ship at 4.30 <A.M.> this morning, just as the day was dawning. I sat up an hour <& saw> or two & saw a very beautiful sunrise—a rich <s>carmine flush that suffused all the Heavens behind the Acropolis like a blush!

At 6.30 after I had gone to bed, Mr. Griswold came & got my Moorish fez, & he & James & Crocker went ashore intending to steal away to Athens, but the guards discovered them before they went a thousand yards, & chased them—they say it was a close race, but they won the boat & escaped to the ship.

We sailed at noon. Of course the passengers are very sorry they could not go to Athens & the Acropolis, but it could not be helped—if many had made our trip <w>some of us would surely have got into trouble. It would not have been possible to avoid arrest if enough had left the ship to attract the attention of the people.

Through a friend, Bullard & Beach fared uncommonly well.[17]

Aug. 15.

Booming through the Grecian Archipelago with a splendid breeze. Many passengers sea-sick.

---

[17] Moses S. Beach and the Reverend Henry Bullard also managed to run the blockade successfully. As Mark Twain reported in chapter 32 of *The Innocents Abroad*, "They slipped away so quietly that they were not missed from the ship for several hours. They had the hardihood to march into the Piræus in the early dusk and hire a carriage. They ran some danger of adding two or three months' imprisonment to the other novelties of their Holy Land Pleasure Excursion. . . . But they went and came safely, and never walked a step."

Bloody sunset.

Splendid full moon—sea white with foamy waves & a hundred white-winged ships.

Passed a ruined temple—graceful, beautiful fluted white columns, standing lonely on a tall barren promontory overlooking the sea, —Curious place for it—the country utterly barren & uninhabited for miles in every direction.

Aug 16. *TROY*.

We are now, (11 AM., right abreast <of ancient> the Plains of Troy <&> a little rock 200 yds long with a light on it <& between it & the shore> (Asia Minor) <was the anchorage of the Greek vessels.>

The Plain of Troy is wide, & long & low—8 or ten miles back is a range of undulating hills. Half the Plain is covered with what seems to be green underbrush & the other half is sand.

We are making a straight break for the Dardanells & shall enter in an hour or two.

Mount Ida in the distance.

Plato & Diogenes were captured by pirates & publicly sold as slaves in the market place of Athens—Plato brought $500. by way of ransom.

Throughout Greece there were more slaves than freemen. If a man could publicly convict his freedman of ingratitude he could enslave him again.

Noon—passed abreast of Ancient *Troy*, & not long afterward <passed the> entered the Dardanelles (or Hellespont)—& after this passed the harbor whence Agamemnon's fleet sailed to the siege of Troy.

Further along, the tomb of Hecuba on one side & Ajax on the other.

Pericles was buried in the Ceramicus, the place set apart for such as fell in battle—a great honor, as he did not die <on>in battle. [#]

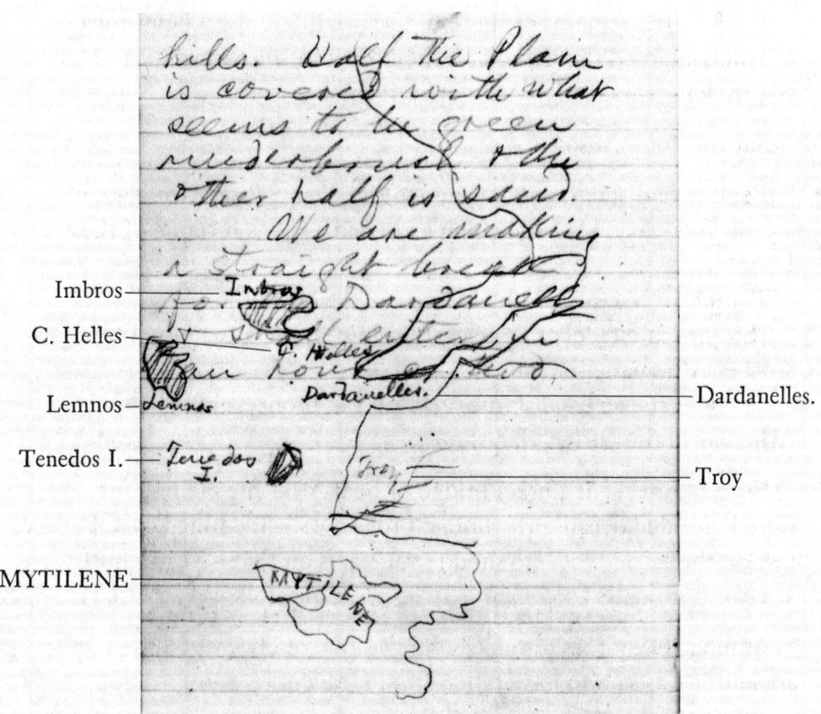

Plato—Aristotle,—Solon—Themistocles—Demosthenes—Diogenes—Socrates—Isocrates—Phocion—Pythagoras—Euripides. Praxiteles. Zeuxis painter—Pindar—Phidias—Euclid.[18]

Diogenes going about with his lantern in the moonlight, did not tackle our party.

At Athens we laid in a stock of honey from Hymettus.

The Athenians chose ten Generals to command their armies every year.—Philip of Macedon said they were fortunate—they could find ten every year, but he had never been able to find but one [#]

---

18 Clemens gave a similar list in his *Alta* letter for 15 August and said that he "wished that the illustrious men who had sat in [the Parthenon] in the remote ages could visit it again and reveal themselves to our curious eyes" (*TIA*, p. 106).

We saw the remains of the <w>sea-wall built by Themistocles & which inclosed the harbors of the Piraeus & the Munychiae—was 6½ m. long & 60 ft high.—about 10 ft thick

Saw his tomb, also.

Pericles had them built.[19] The <Propylieia>Propylaea is Doric —cost $2,000,000. (a sum which exceeded a year's revenue of the Republic.

Temple of Victory on the left.

(Statues in citadel of Pericles, Phormio, Iphicrates, Timotheus, & other Athenian Generals.)

(Yonder the colossal statue of Minerva (bronze,) which Athenians raised after Marathon.)

First architects of Xerxes bridge of boats over the Hellespont were beheaded because the bridge broke away—the hint was not lost on the second lot—no shoddy contracts on that—Xerxes host <2,500,000> 2,600,000 men & 2,500,000 camp followers crossed it.

Among the statues in the citadel was one of olive-wood so ancient it was said to have fallen from Heaven.[20]

(Just entering the Hellespont[21]—3 or 4 m. wide—guarded on either side by Turkish castles flying the crescent flag.—We are gaining faster on the French steamer since we have hoisted main & main topsails & jib—will catch him in an hour.

See a camel train on shore with the glass.)

Parthenon (<an>which is another Temple of Minerva)—It is Doric

Parthenon 226 ft long, 100 wide.—<69>70 high. <—all of gold & ivory,—$1,100,000 worth of gold.> [#]

---

[19] Clemens added this sentence, referring (in the plural) to the Doric columns of the Propylaea, at a later time.

[20] This was the statue of Athena Polias which stood in one of the shrines of the Erechtheum.

[21] The *Quaker City* entered the Hellespont at noon on August 16, according to Captain Duncan's log.

Statue of Minerva by Phidias, in complete armor & lance—36 ft high—all of gold & ivory—$1,100,000 worth of gold.

Square, deep tombs cut in the solid rock all about before you get to the Museum & also *in* the Museum hill (which is a high long rock only separated from the Acropolis & the Areopagus by a little narrow ravine.

Dardana.[22]

2 bells—afternoon—

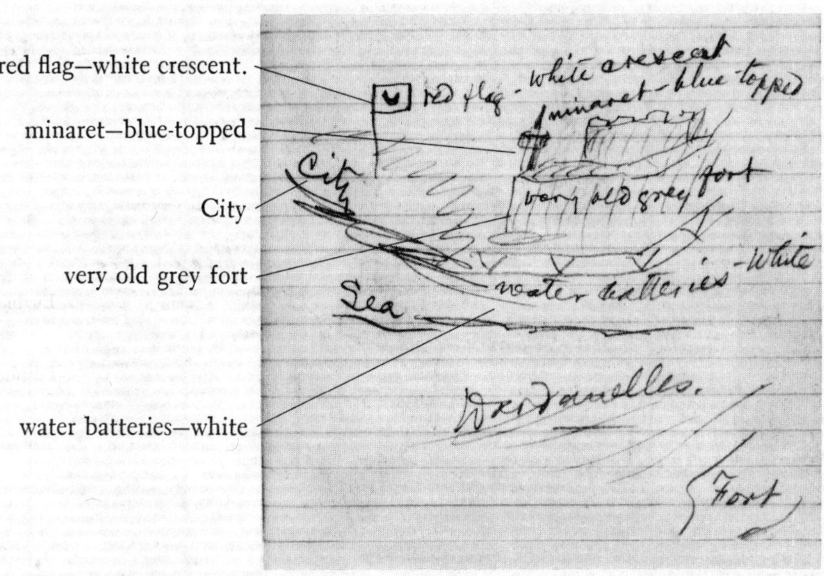

Stopped here for the health officer to come aboard.

Aug. 16.

Entered the Sea of Marmora at <6>5 in the afternoon, if I remember rightly. [#]

---

[22] Short for *Dardanelles.* Ships were required to stop here and present their papers before proceeding to Constantinople.

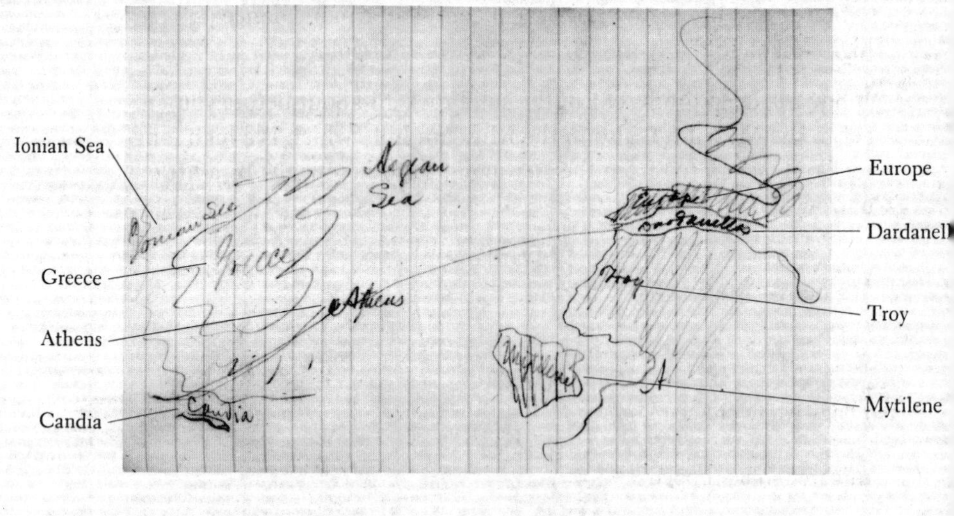

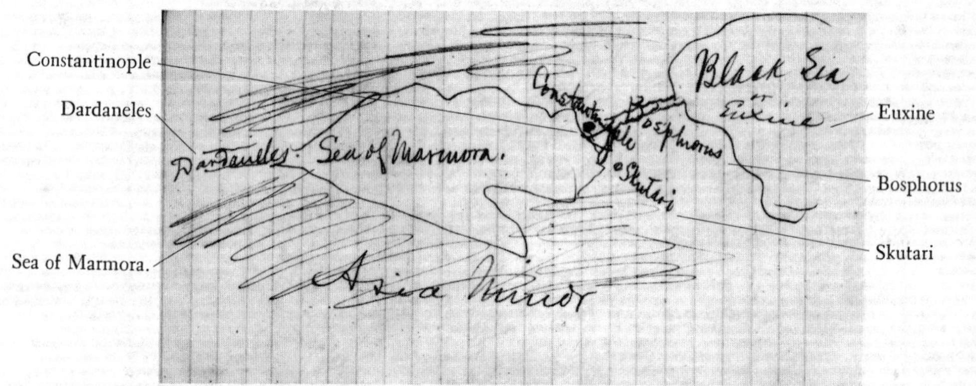

The Viceroy of Egypt passed us in his lightning yacht, like we were standing still—waved his hand to us.[23] He looks a good deal like his uncle (or his brother—which?) the Sultan of Turkey. [#]

[23] "At 4^{30} Vice Roy of Egypt passed in his Yacht Steamer beating us at least 2 Miles an hour" (CCD, 16 August 1867). "This yacht is of a splendid model, is the fastest vessel afloat, and was built at a cost which would shake the very bones of the chief of the Rothschilds" (James Eglinton Montgomery, *Our Admiral's Flag Abroad* [New York: G. P. Putnam & Son, 1869], p. 384).

Night—Rev. Mr. Bullard lectured on Athens, & I said a few words—same subject.

Turkey

Constantinople.

Aug. 17—Reached Consta[e] at daylight, & anchored in the mouth of the Golden Horn.

Standing on the Military Tower in the Plaza—[24]

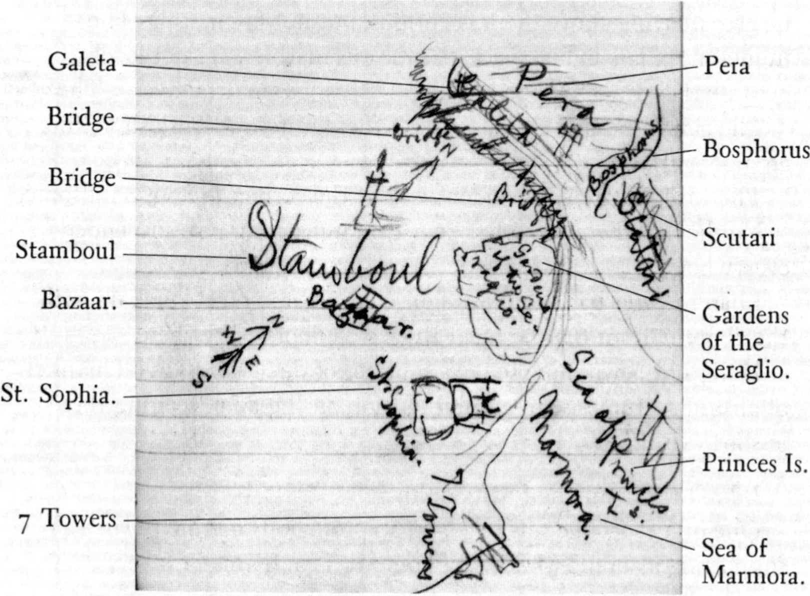

[24] The Serasker Tower stands in the plaza of the Seraskerat, or War Office. "From this point all parts of Constantinople, Pera, Galata, Scutari, the Golden Horn and its extension to the Sweet Waters, the Bosphorus, with its harbor and shipping, and all the natural and artificial beauty of its incomparable shores, the sea of Marmora with its islands, and the vast chain of mountains bounding the view in the distance, are all spread out before us as upon a map. Looking down upon the city itself, one can trace amid the vast sea of red tile-roofs the form and position of the bazars, the palaces, the colleges and public buildings" (Dr. Abraham R. Jackson, 19 August 1867 letter to the Monroe County [Pa.] *Democrat*). Clemens' drawing is of this view.

Visited the celebrated Mosque of San Sophia, near the Grand Seraglio Gardens, but found nothing there to go into ecstasies over. It is an immense structure, & its dome is very peculiar, being as great in diameter as St Peter's, perhaps, but enough flatter to be remarkable.

<The> It seems curious to see these eastern devotees going through with their extravagant ceremonies in a church that was built for Christian worship, & this strikes one more than anything else.

The painted bronze open-work capitals of the columns & the filagree inlaying above them is curious, but not fascinating. The numerous pillars in one piece, of precious marbles, are not lovely, because they are so chipped & dinted & rusty & unattractive. <The g>

The gaudy mosaics in the dome & their grotesque Turkish writing are not pretty.

The vast gilt circular wooden signs at the corners are not handsome.

Neither are the numberless coarse oil mugs for tapers suspended everywhere.

I had to enter barefoot, & caught cold & got my feet stuck up with the abominations that besmear the paved floors everywhere.

It was not bewitching to see a number of dirty varlets in all manner of absurd costumes sitting tailor-fashion on the floor, reciting their lessons.

I don't think much of San Sophia.

One other mosque was large, & had prodigious marble pillars (4) supporting its dome which were some 30 ft in diameter & very massive & imposing.

In another they had nothing more remarkable to show than several thousand unclean tame pigeons & some frowsy great trees in the open court of the mosque.

Obelisk—

Egyptian, was perfect—4,000 yrs old, 70 ft high, 12 or 15 at the base—20, maybe—one solid piece of granite & all its figures & hyeroglyphs unmarred by time. [#]

Grecian Obelisk—

Old, ratty, coarse stones, ragged, shaky—will tumble some day.[25]

Column of Serpents—

Bronze & broken—not astonishing.[26]

Fire tower—high—nothing more—noble view of the city from it.[27]

A better from the Sea or the Bosphorus.

New Moorish gateway—handsome.

1,000 columns under ground—curious—nothing more.[28]

Janizaries—

Grotesque wax-work museum—could have survived without seeing it.[29]

Turkish Singer—funny.

Sultanic Tombs—fine. [#]

---

[25] Dr. Abraham R. Jackson described this monument for his readers in the Monroe County (Pa.) *Democrat* as "the lofty square pillar of Constantine, built of blocks of marble and formerly covered by plates of brass. Many of the stones are displaced, and the upper portion of the structure threatens to fall" (letter dated 19 August 1867).

[26] This monument was "formed of three bronze serpents, the tails downwards, and the bodies twisted spirally as far as the necks; their heads spreading outward formerly supported the golden tripod of the priestess of Apollo at Delphi, whence this singular monument is generally supposed to have been brought" (*Handbook for Travellers in Constantinople, Brûsa, and the Troad* [London: John Murray, 1893], p. 41).

[27] Probably the "*Galata Tower* . . . which is one of the most striking features in Galata, [and] is now used as a *fire-station*. . . . From the Galata Tower travellers obtain the best *general view* of the city, and it should be one of the first places visited" (Murray's *Constantinople*, p. 16).

[28] The Cistern of Philoxenus in Constantinople was known for the striking effect made by its 1,001 supporting columns.

[29] The "*Museum of Ancient Costumes*, or *of the Janissaries* . . . contains a collection of old Turkish costumes on lay figures, which was formed by Sultan Abdul Mejid, and at one time kept in the Seraglio. . . . In no other place can the visitor obtain such a vivid impression of that strange old Turkish life which passed away for ever when Mahmûd II. introduced his reforms" (Murray's *Constantinople*, p. 70).

Women rather pretty with their veiled faces & flowing Oriental robes—but, flitting about in the magnificent distances of the dim arches of the great bazaars, look horribly like the shrouded dead abroad in the earth.

The Bazaars of Stamboul—wonderful.

The Dogs of Constantinople more so.[30]

Embroidered Jackets of gold & purple, blue & crimson—splendid—Persian shawls & fabrics—& Turkish—gorgeous.

Some people wear a fez, here.

"Can recommend my son as a smart boy & terrific liar—can cheat deftly" —Turkish.[31]

Haldeman's dauby pictures & his walking arsenal.[32]

Porters.
Grape-sellers
Seed-merchants.
Water-sellers.[33]
Turkish dinner.[34] [#]

---

30 "I never saw such utterly wretched, starving, sad-visaged, broken-hearted looking curs in all my life. . . . They are the sorriest beasts that breathe—the most abject—the most pitiful. In their faces is a settled expression of melancholy, an air of hopeless despondency" (*TIA*, pp. 123–124).

31 " 'This boy is worth his weight in broad pieces of a hundred—for behold, he will cheat whomsoever hath dealings with him, and from the waters of Marmora to the Euxine there abideth not so gifted a liar!' How is that, for a recommendation? The Missionaries tell me that you hear encomiums like that passed upon people every day" (*TIA*, pp. 121–122).

32 Probably this is a reference to Jacob S. Haldeman's acquisitions from the Bazaar: hastily painted pictures, and old, jewel-handled guns or swords—both commonly sold in Constantinople.

33 Dr. Jackson reported seeing "a train of men bearing water enclosed in pig-skins upon their backs. Pig-skins, used in this way are not ornamental. They always present the appearance of very bloated pigs with their heads and legs cut off; and no pig can appear gracefully when seen dangling upside down hanging by his own tail" (19 August 1867 letter to the Monroe County [Pa.] *Democrat*).

34 As Clemens wrote to the *Alta* from Constantinople late in August, "I never

Cripples.[35]

Terrific Costumes.

The Bosphorus

New Palaces—gems of <noble arc> elegant architecture—beat all in France & Italy.

The lovely Bosphorus, with its exquisite white marble palaces—they ARE palaces.[36]

Bohemian singing girls & beer.

Spinning & howling Dervishes.

75 Mahometans converted—used to be (suspected) imprisonment & death—is imprisonment yet.[37]

They say it has cost $2 000 000 for each Chinese convert—no better here.

40,000 suspected converts here in Con. [#]

---

want another one. The cooking apparatus was in the little lunch room, near the bazaar, and it was all open to the street. The cook was dirty, and so was the table. . . . That is all I learned about Turkish lunches. A Turkish lunch is good, no doubt, but it has its weak points" (*TIA*, pp. 127–128). Clemens claimed that he and his comrades were too intimidated by the poor fare and its unsanitary preparation to partake, but Captain Duncan remarked, apparently of a visit to a similar establishment: "We . . . ransacked the kitchen and found half a Chicken–Some Stewed beef–ditto Mutton and Some eggs ordered the Whole Stock and Sat down–Made a comfortable lunch" (CCD, 17 August 1867).

[35] On 23 August Clemens wrote to the *Alta* from Constantinople: "If you want dwarfs–I mean just a few dwarfs for a curiosity–go to Genoa. If you want to buy them by the gross, for retail, go to Milan. There are plenty of dwarfs all over Italy, but it did seem to me that in Milan the crop was luxuriant. If you would see a fair average style of assorted cripples, go to Naples, or travel through the Roman States. But if you would see the very heart and home of cripples and human monsters, both, go straight to Constantinople" (*TIA*, p. 115).

[36] This sentence was added at a later but undetermined time. Finding no room after the preceding entry (to which it is obviously related) Clemens entered it in the left margin of the preceding notebook page beside "Porters . . Costumes."

[37] Following the establishment of the Church Missionary Society of Great Britain in Smyrna (1832), Turkish law had assigned the death penalty to any Moslem converting to another religion.

Sultan goes to Mosque on Fridays.

All Greeks & Armenians Christians.—thieves.

Pera is Christian.

Population of Constantinople 1,000,000—⅓ Christians.

On account of sympathy with Crete, Americans in bad odor here.[38]

All foreign consulates fine but American—bad—people in Europe & Asia respect style.[39]

Sailed for Crimea 20th.

New Palace[40] on the Asiatic side of the beatiful Bosphorus (3 m. wide,) is built on spot where Constantine erected gold cross to commemorate his conversion. When Turks took the place & began to build, many thought he would declare himself Christian when finished, & waited to baptise their Children then. They are waiting yet.

Dan & Jack Van Nostrand have remained behind in Constantinople.[41]

Got letter in Constantinople in mourning envelop—bad custom.

Beardless Jack has heard of a fearful Turkish custom & is scared.[42] [#]

---

[38] The principal cause for American unpopularity in Turkey is discussed in note 61.

[39] As late as 1895 an American authority on Constantinople regretted that "the United States possess no fixed habitation for their representative to the Sublime Porte. . . . Now the American Legation is so subject to spring and autumn removal from place to place that its appropriate emblem is a carpet-bag rather than an eagle" (Edwin A. Grosvenor, *Constantinople*, 2 vols. [Boston: Roberts Brothers, 1895], 1:106–107).

[40] The Beylerbey Serai was built by Sultan Abdul-Aziz in 1865. In 1895 Grosvenor wrote, "this remains, the fairest architectural achievement of his reign and the most beautiful structure on the Bosphorus. It is a pile of the purest, snowiest marble. No other Ottoman edifice so combines what is most exquisite in Eastern and Western architecture and art" (Grosvenor, *Constantinople*, 1:234–236).

[41] In addition to Dan Slote and Jack Van Nostrand, six other passengers remained in Constantinople: J. Heron Foster, Jacob S. Haldeman, Moses S. Beach, Emeline Beach, Solon Severance, and the Reverend Henry Bullard.

[42] Richard F. Burton noted in his translation of "The Arabian Nights" that an

Smoking Narghilis.[43]

Turkish Bath.[44]

"Makaloff & Seralgio"

Russia

Spent a day at Sebastopol.[45]

Melancholy place—wilderness of battered-down houses—look like forest of broken chimneys.

Not 3 dozen habitable dwellings—*they* all new.

Visited Redan, Malakoff &c. & picked up cannon balls & other light relics.

They say that during the 3-days assault of the Malakoff by the French it changed hands 3 times.

The English took the Redan & then turned their guns upon the Malakoff.

It is several miles out to Balaklava, & only a mile or two to Inkermann down by the sea.

Russia claimed the *exclusive right* to put a new dome on the

---

Arabic word for "beardless and handsome" was often "used in a bad sense, to denote an effeminate, a catamite." And in his concluding essay he alluded to "the 'unspeakable Turk,' a race of born pederasts" (*The Book of the Thousand Nights and a Night*, 10 vols. [Benares: Kamashastra Society, 1885], 1:327; 10:232).

[43] Clemens informed his *Alta* readers that when first trying a water pipe the neophyte "smokes at every pore, like a frame house that is on fire on the inside, and after that he lays down his hose and goes home sicker than ever he was before in all his life" (*TIA*, p. 123).

[44] Clemens wrote the New York *Tribune* on 31 August that "the books of travel have shamefully deceived me all these years" about "the narghili, the dervishes, the aromatic coffee, the Turkish bath—these are the things I have accepted and believed in, with simple, unquestioning faith, from boyhood; and, behold, they are the poorest, sickest, wretchedest humbugs the world can furnish. Wonders, forsooth!" (*TIA*, p. 132).

[45] The passengers spent August 21 touring the ruins of the siege and bombardment of 1854–1855 and sailed at nine o'clock that evening for Odessa. Daniel Leary explained to his brother on August 29 that "our time at Sevastopol was two days, but we saw everything in one, and the other day was given over to going to Odessa" (Lewis Leary, "More Letters from the *Quaker City*," *American Literature* 42 [May 1970]: 201).

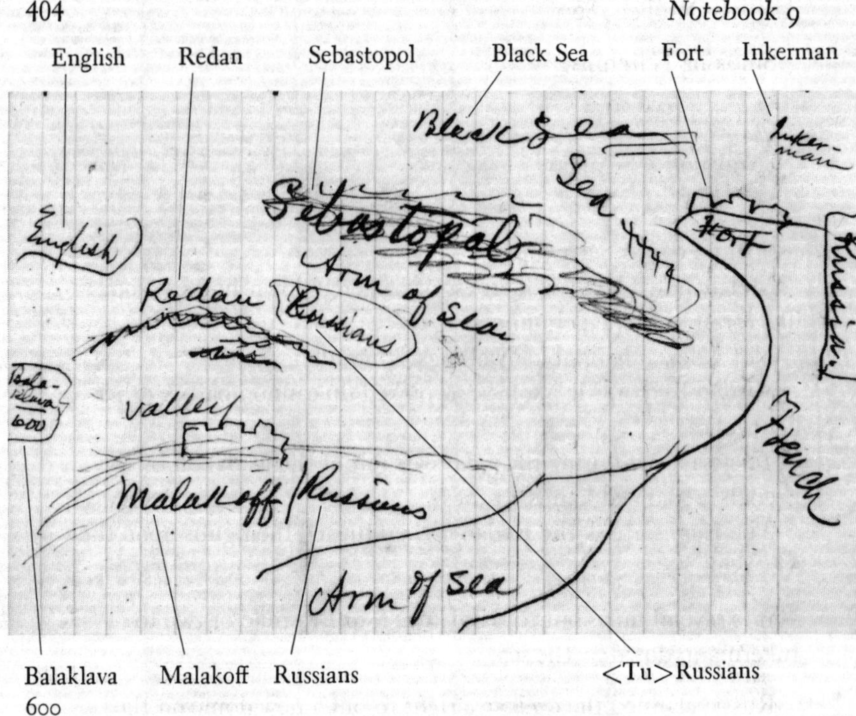

Church of the Holy Sepulchre at Jerusalem, & France claimed the same—England wanted a chance at Russia—hence the war. Sounds as absurd as the Crusades. Within the year, treaty, so the <4>3 build it in partnership

By the treaty of Paris Russia cannot rebuild her great docks & naval works here—she infringes a little on the law, though.

Stories of the havoc of the bombardment.

A large number of handsome young English & Russian ladies visited the ship & spent the afternoon. They were delighted at her fine appointments & great size. If we could have brought them back we might have taken them to Odessa. It was pleasant to hear <the> <them> our own language again. [#]

Several <officers> gentlemen insisted on our visiting the Emperor of Russia with the ship,—said they would ensure us a superb reception by him, & would not only telegraph but send a courier to notify him we were coming. He is spending the heated months at a little watering-place 30 miles from here.

For certain reasons we declined, & everybody was sorry enough, very naturally.[46]

This has been the pleasantest afternoon we have had for <m>a good while.

Everywhere the prints of cannon-balls are in these stone-walls—some as neat as if cut. Some balls still stick in the walls & from them iron stains run.

It is a *completely* destroyed town—*not one* of its old houses was left standing in that fearful 18 months siege.

They sell Circassian girls yet in Constantinople, but the markets are private.

Left Sebastopol at 8 P.M.

Aug. <25>23—Anchored before Odessa at 3 PM. Devil of a time getting the officials to let us go ashore. They have got all our passports.

Fine town—broad, well <pap>paved streets—fine large houses, substantial, & good architecture—stone—fine stores—gas—pretty women, fashionably dressed—100,000 inhabitants.

I guess <a>Dan is well tired of Constantinople by this time.

Aug. 25—On our way back to <Jolte>Yolta to call on the Emperor of Russia, who has telegraphed the Governor General of Odessa concerning the matter & the thing is all right.[47] [#]

---

[46] The passengers' "certain reasons" for declining a visit to the emperor, as well as Daniel Leary's personal motives in seeking an audience, are discussed in the headnote.

[47] Clemens' entry does not square precisely with Captain Duncan's account. Ev-

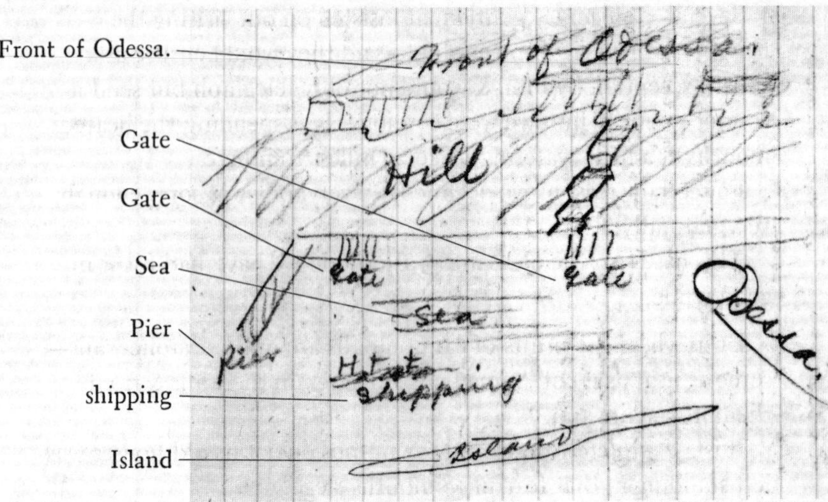

Oh, <h—! wh> Geeminy, what a stir there is!—what a calling of meetings!—what an appointing of committees!—<whi>what a furbishing-up of swallow-tail coats!

Your Imperial Majesty:
We are a handful of private citizens of America, traveling simply for recreation, & unostentatiously, as becomes our unofficial <condition> state, & therefore we have no excuse to tender for presenting ourselves before your Majesty, save the desire of offering our grateful acknowledgments to the lord of a realm which, through good & through evil report, has been the steadfast friend of the land we love so well.

---

idently, the *Quaker City* set sail for Yalta on August 24 at 11:00 A.M. without any positive assurance that the emperor would receive them and "trusting to luck for permission to enter" the harbor (CCD, 24 August 1867). By August 25 they were at Yalta, but it was not until Daniel Leary, Captain Duncan, and United States consul Smith (from Odessa) approached the governor-general of Yalta that plans for the audience with the czar were established firmly. "At 5 we were . . . informed that the Emperor would receive us all in the Palace Grounds the next day at Noon" (CCD, 25 August 1867).

We could not presume to take a step like this, did we not know well that the words we speak here, & the sentiments wherewith they are freighted, are but the reflex of the thoughts & the feelings of all our countrymen, from the green hills of New England to the <snowy peaks> shores of the far Pacific. We are few in number, but we utter the voice of a nation!

One of the brightest pages that <have>has graced the world's history since written history had birth, was recorded by your Majesty's hand when it loosed the bonds of twenty million serfs; and Americans can but esteem it a privilege to do honor to a ruler who has wrought so great a deed. The lesson that was taught us then, we have profited by, & are free in truth, to-day, <as we> even as we were before in name. America owes much to Russia—is indebted to her in many ways—and chiefly for her unwavering friendship in seasons of our greatest need. That that friendship may still be hers in times to come, we confidently pray; that she is & will be grateful to Russia & to her sovereign for it, we know full well; that she will ever forfeit it by any premeditated, unjust act, or unfair course, it were treason to believe.

(Signed)

Sam. L. Clemens, Ch'n

TD. Crocker
AN. Sandford, } Committee
Col. Kinney
Wm Gibson

On behalf of the passengers of the U.S. Steamer Quaker City, C. C. Duncan Commanding.

Yalte, Russia, Aug. 25, 1867.

That job is over.—Writing addresses to Emperors is not my strong suit.[48] However, if it is not as good as it might be, it don't signify—the other committeemen ought to have helped write it—they had

---

48 Clemens grew increasingly self-conscious about his address to the czar. At first he felt sufficiently pleased with it to send his family "the original draught . . .

nothing else to do, & I had my hands full.—But for <h[ol]ding [most]> bothering with this matter, I would have caught up entirely with my N.Y. Tribune correspondence, & nearly up with the San Francisco cor^{r}.[49]

The reception of our party by the Emperor is to come off at the summer palace at noon to-morrow.—

Aug 26.—The imperial carriages were in waiting at 11, & at 12 we were at the palace.

<At> In 5 minutes the Emperor & Empress, the Grand Duchess Marie & the <2> little <g>Grand Duke appeared & welcomed the party pleasantly.[50]

The Consul for Odessa read the address, & the Czar said frequently "Good—very good indeed"—and at the close: "I am very, very grateful."

---

to be put into alcohol and preserved forever like a curious reptile" (SLC to "Dear Folks," 25 August 1867, *MTL*, p. 133). The version in the notebook is obviously a fair copy of that draft. The text of the address, as it was read by Consul Smith to the czar, is substantially this one—which was also printed in the *Alta*, the *Sun*, the *Tribune*, and copied by the London *Times* (12 September 1867), *Littell's Living Age* (5 October 1867), and many other periodicals. Before the address was to be printed as a broadside on the *Quaker City* press, however, Clemens further revised and simplified the language: "the words we speak here, & the sentiments wherewith they are freighted" became "the words we speak and the sentiments we utter," for example. Further doubts about the speech led him to omit the text from *The Innocents Abroad*. There he merely imagined the emperor ordering the speech "filed away among the archives of Russia—in the stove," and he represented the crew of the *Quaker City* mocking "the phraseology of that tiresome address. . . . I never was so tired of any one phrase as the sailors made me of the opening sentence of the Address to the Emperor of Russia" (chapters 37 and 38).

49 As of August 25 Clemens had written only two letters to the New York *Tribune*, even though he had agreed to write that paper at least "two letters a month" (*MTLBowen*, pp. 15–16). On September 1 he wrote his family that he thought he had completed thirty-seven letters to the *Alta*, but, unknown to him, a number of these would never reach the paper (see *MTL*, pp. 134–136).

50 The Grand Duchess Marie, later duchess of Edinburgh, was the only daughter of Alexander and his wife, Maria Alexandrovna. She was thirteen at this time, and, as Clemens observed in chapter 37 of *The Innocents Abroad*, a favorite with her father. The "Grand Duke" was the emperor's fourth surviving son, Sergius Alexandrovitch, who was ten.

After talking half an hour the imperial party conducted us all through the palace & then all through the young Crown Prince's[51] beautiful palace.

By this time it was after 1, & an invitation came from the Grand Duke Michael[52] to visit his gardens, park & palace, and breakfast with him, which we did.

Prince Dalgorouki, went along, & so did that jolly Count Festetics, who is to marry the Governor General's daughter. So also, the Lord High Admiral of Russia & a number of the nobility of both sexes, connected with the Emperor's household.[53]

But the Grand Duke Michael is a rare brick!—and his wife is one of the very pleasantest of all these pleasant people—& both are <exceedingly> sociable.

What happened in the park—& again in the court of the palace where the fountain was & the flowers—& above all the occurence under the porch which has the caryatides in imitation of the Temple of Erecthus at Athens—these were RICH—they must <be> never be trusted to treacherous paper—memory will do—I guess no one in the world who could appreciate a joke would be likely to forget them.[54]

---

[51] The emperor's oldest living son was Alexander Alexandrovitch (1845–1894), who would become Czar Alexander III in 1881. His "palace" was immediately adjacent to the emperor's.

[52] Michael Nicholaevitch (1832–1909) was the youngest brother of the emperor and, since 1862, governor-general of the Caucasus.

[53] The individuals mentioned in this paragraph remain obscure, but were probably: Prince Nicholas Dolgorouki, aide-de-camp to the emperor; Count Festetics, a Polish officer on the staff of the governor-general; Governor Kotzebue, aide-de-camp to the emperor and governor of New Russia, whom Julius Moulton described as "a noble specimen of the Russian military class" (Saint Louis *Missouri Republican,* 22 October 1867); and Admiral Glasenapp, commander of the Russian Black Sea fleet.

[54] An officer from the U.S.S. *Swatara* wrote the Brooklyn *Eagle* (11 October 1867) that "some of the performances of these people are worthy of repetition. During the presentation to the Arch Duke Michael, of Russia, one man, immediately after his introduction, stepped up to the Duke, said, Where is your cabinet? The Duke showed not surprise but said, Follow me! showed him his cabinet, and then returned to finish the presentation." Paine presented this anecdote in his selection from the notebooks, identifying the passenger's remark as "Say, Dook, where's

We had not been at the Grand Duke's long when the Empress & the Grand Duchess Marie came, & shortly afterward the Emperor himself. He looks much nobler than the Emperor Napoleon, & a hundred times more so than the Sultan of Turkey. Remained half a day, nearly.

Aug. 27[55]—Carpets were spread on the pier & the Governor General & family came on board the ship (we saluted with 9 guns,) & afterward:

Prince Dalgorouki, the Grand Chamberlain.

<G>Baron Wrangel, former Ambassador.[56]

Baron Ungern-Sternberg,[57] the Director in Chief of the imperial railways.

Count Festetics of the household.

General Todtleben,[58] the <idoli> honored defender of Sebastopol all during the siege.

---

the water-closet?" (*MTN*, p. 80). And in *Mark Twain: A Biography* Paine quoted an unidentified memorandum by Clemens which was ostensibly written "seventeen years" after the event. "I observed that the most of [the Russian dignitaries] wore a very small piece of ribbon in the lapels of their coats. That little touch of color struck my fancy, and it seemed to me a good idea to add it to my own attractions; not imagining that it had any special significance." Clemens said he was embarrassed when Count Festetics inquired "what order of nobility I belonged to" (*MTB*, pp. 334–335).

[55] Here and in each entry through that for "*Aug 29*" Clemens has inadvertently fallen behind one day in his dating. The entry under "Aug. 27" actually conflates the events of that and the next day. The *Quaker City* sailed from Yalta on the evening of August 28, arriving back in Constantinople on August 30, according to Captain Duncan's log.

[56] Julius Moulton identified Wrangel as "the Ambassador to Washington, about six years ago" (Saint Louis *Missouri Republican*, 22 October 1867).

[57] "Baron Ungern-Sternberg, a boisterous, whole-souled, jolly old brick of a nobleman, came with the rest. He is a man of progress and enterprise—and representative man of the age—what is called a 'rustler,' in California. He is the Chief Director of the railway system of Russia—a sort of railroad king. In his line he is making things move right along in this country" (*TIA*, p. 162).

[58] General Franz Eduard Ivanovitch Todleben, an aide-de-camp-general to the emperor and director-general of engineers, had planned and overseen the land defenses of Sebastopol.

And a large number of army & navy officrs & titled & untitled ladies & gentlemen.

Shampagne blow-out.

Black Sea.

Aug. 28.—Sailed for Constantinople last night, saluting as we left —& fireworks. That beautiful little devil I danced with at the ball in that impossible Russian dance, still runs in my head. Ah me!—if I had only known how to talk Russian! However, she must have known I was saying *some*thing with all that absurd English which she couldn't understand.[59]

All day the ladies bathed naked in full view of the ship. They don't consider it any harm, I suppose. At Odessa all ages & sexes bathed together.

Constantinople.

Aug 29—Passed through the beautiful Bosphorus just after daylight & anchored away up in the Golden Horn nearly to the lower bridge. Been on shore & found Dan, & Foster, Jack Van Nostrand & Col. Haldeman.

The American Minister *Resident* (Mr. Morris,) is to drink wine on board to-night.[60] [#]

---

[59] According to "Esculapius" in the London *Times* for 12 September 1867, "the banquet on board the Quaker City on the eve of departure was a pleasant episode of the occasion. Among the numerous guests aboard were Governor-General Dr. Kotzebue, Prince Dolgozowsy, Baron Sternberg, Admiral Glassenapp, &c. During the occasion one of the officers remarked, 'that a delegation from any of the Powers or Courts of Europe would not have been entertained by the Emperor at his palace in so courteous and hospitable a manner as he extended to you Americans on Monday.'" In his *Alta* letter from Smyrna Mark Twain was still musing on the "beautiful little devil": "In that Russian town of Yalta I danced an astonishing sort of dance an hour long, and one I had never heard of before, with the most beautiful girl that ever lived, and we talked incessantly, and laughed exhaustingly, and neither one ever knew what the other was driving at" (*TIA*, pp. 166–167).

[60] Edward Joy Morris, United States minister resident to Turkey (1861–1869) and his wife spent the night of August 30 on board the *Quaker City*, according to Captain Duncan's log (2 September 1867).

Our imperial visit has had a good effect. It worries the Sublime Porte a good deal. It is well, for the offensive resolutions of Congress concerning the Cretan insurrection have just been received, & <they> it may prevent an offensive reply—may even avert war—who knows?[61]

Aug. 30.—Here yet.

Aug. 31—Ditto.

Sept. 1—Ditto.[62]

<Sea of> Scutari.

Sept. 2.—Went over to Scutari—took horse & went on top of mountain back of city—beautiful view of Con—Bosphorus—islands in Sea of Marmora—saw almost to Black Sea & &c &c &c.

Grapes, coffee & green English walnuts & the house below.

Found a gold mine—good live quartz—the gold in snuff-colored sulphurrets—ought to be very valuable here where labor is so cheap. Its presence is unsuspected. [#]

---

[61] A resolution endorsing the Cretan rebellion against the Turks was passed by the United States House of Representatives on 18 July 1867. On July 22 Secretary of State William Seward conveyed the resolution "declaring sympathy with the suffering people of Crete" to Minister Resident Morris, who in turn relayed it to the Turkish government. "His Highness, while apparently surprised at the character of the resolution and the order of Congress for its communication . . . made no comments whatever on its subject matter" (U.S. Department of State, *Papers Relating to Foreign Affairs* [Washington, 1868], pt. 2, pp. 14–15). Since they had already spent $15,000,000 by the end of 1867 in attempting to quash the rebellion, the Turks undoubtedly were offended by the American resolution. "Knowledge of the affair has at once become public throughout Europe" the New York *Times* reported on August 24.

[62] The delay was caused by difficulty in taking on needed coal. Captain Duncan recorded on August 31: "Coal Brig alongside and after an argument among the workmen lasting the whole forenoon work was begun in the afternoon but at a pace that bred utter despair among all our passengers. When shall we get our coal in is the question–some time next week–perhaps." Despite the absence of detail, Clemens had nevertheless been busy, for on September 1 he wrote his family: "I am staying in the ship, tonight. I generally stay on shore when we are in port. But yesterday I just ran myself down. Dan Slote, my room-mate, is on shore. He remained here while we went up the Black Sea, but it seems he has not got enough of it yet" (*MTL*, p. 136).

Dr Mattheosian[63]

Loitered on the bridge with Davis & watched the porters rest their prodigious loads.

Sept. 3.—Here 17 days.

The Sultan not pleased about our visit to the Czar.—says Americans show no disposition to visit him.

He is an ignorant, unrefined Turk, & his mother is chief over him.[64]

He was "kept back" because it was not supposed that he would <be> ever reach the throne.

His nephews will succeed him—not his son.[65]

Sea of Marmora.

Sept. 3—Tried to leave Constantinople at 7 PM, but, in dodging a schooner, whose mainsail we tore with our bowsprit, we fouled a buoy, just abreast the Grand Seraglio (but within the Golden Horn,) & drifted down on to the bowsprit of a Beuctra boat[66]—which cut our starboard quarter-boat clear in two. Maybe it is well we bought so many caiques. We got clear at 11 o'clock (of course we had to let go the anchor at first & it fouled the buoy) & in a few moments we nothing but five miles of lights elevated in pyramids lines & semi-circles—arches—the last of Constantinople [#]

---

63 On 3 September 1867 Dr. Benjamin Nesbit and several other passengers (probably including Clemens) visited an Armenian charity hospital and insane asylum in Scutari and were guided there by "Mr. H Bavonig [?] Matteosian M.D." (Benjamin Nesbit journal, 2 September 1867; PH in MTP).

64 "The chief female personage of the Empire, however, greater than any wife, is the mother of the Sultan, the *Valideh Sultan*. The Valideh Sultan of the day has frequently exercised a direct and important influence on home and foreign politics, and assiduous court was paid to her by ministers of state and political intriguers" (Murray's *Constantinople*, p. 19).

65 According to Turkish law the eldest surviving male in the sultan's family succeeded him. Abdul-Aziz attempted unsuccessfully to change the law for the benefit of his son.

66 Probably Clemens' phonetic rendering of the name *Buyukdereh*, a village several miles up the Bosporus. "Many of the rich merchants of Constantinople reside there, and go down to their business every morning by steamer" (Murray's *Constantinople*, p. 96).

Biography
of
Samson
for N. Y. Tribune[67]

This Sultan confiscated the house of his shoddy minister of public buildings[68]

Smyrna.

8 bells—AM—Sept. 5—Curious multitude of salt hills on Syrian shore above Smyrna.

Fields—villages of scattering houses or tents that look like <l>sugar loaves through the glasses.

Smyrna bay is very deep—shoal, too.

Country, low hills—rolling.

Afternoon—officers of gun-boat Swatara came aboard.[69]

Ascended Citadel Hill (Mt Pagus of Scripture)

Went to Caravan bridge to see the camel trains come in.

Oyster-veins in the hill-side.[70] [#]

---

67 Although no account of Samson figures in his dispatches to the New York *Tribune*, Mark Twain probably did complete something on the subject for *The Innocents Abroad* manuscript. On 29 April 1869, however, Clemens wrote Elisha Bliss, who had suggested several cuts in the manuscript then being set in type: "Certainly—snatch out *Sampson*—it isn't even necessary to mention him" (*MTLP*, p. 21).

68 In a lecture based on the *Quaker City* materials and written in January 1868, Clemens said: "One of [the sultan's] great officers came into office without a cent, & went out in a few years & built himself a palace worth 3 million. It brought tears to my eyes in that far foreign land—It was so like home. The Sultan confiscated it. He said he liked to see a man prosper, but he didn't like to see him get wealthy on 2,000 a year & no perquisites" (TS in MTP).

69 Captain Duncan recorded in his log for 5 September 1867 that the small gunboat *Swatara* "was at anchor before the town, we passed along close by her and exchanged friendly nods with her officers. Scarcely was our anchor down when a boat was sent bearing an officer with offers of assistance should we be in need of any."

70 From Smyrna Clemens wrote the *Alta* on September 6 that he had seen "three veins of oyster shells, just as you have seen quartz veins exposed in the cutting of a road in California" on a cliff "five hundred feet above the sea" (*TIA*, p. 169). In

Tomb of Polycarp, the marty of the 2d century (or the first.)[71]
Ran till pretty late, with the off'rs.
"7" churches (apocalyptic) here[72]

Ephesus.

Sept. 6—All hands took cars & went to ruins of ancient Ephesus 45 miles hence.

Another of the 7 churches of Asia was here.

Apollo & Diana were born here; here the God Pan lurked in the Corassus & the Pion hills; here Bacchus & Hercules fought against the Amazons; here Hannibal, Scipio, Lysander, Sylla, Cicero, Alexander the Great, Antiochus, & many another man great in ancient history tarried; here (& at Smyrna,) Homer was born; here Brutus & Cassius lay in refuge in the temple, & Antony & Cleopatra held their gorgeous revels.

Here stood the splendid Temple of Diana of Ephesus, <the Seven> one of the Seven Wonders of the World.

Here Paul & John preached; here the Virgin Mary lived with John & here both died & were buried.

Here is the tomb of St Luke the disciple.

Here Mary Magdalene lies buried.

Here John the Baptist labored & his font is shown.

From these noble ruins many a church in Christendom & many a mosque has been supplied with its grandest, its costliest, its most enduring columns. [#]

1869 Clemens would write to Elisha Bliss, who was supervising the setting of *The Innocents Abroad*, that the "'suppositions' I dealt in about the oyster shells were not funny, but foolish—and so, being disgusted I marked them out [of the proof] and was sorry I had ever printed them—so I think it much better to let them stay out" (*MTLP*, p. 21). Nevertheless, Clemens acquiesced in Bliss's decision to include them, and they appear in chapter 39 of the book.

[71] Saint Polycarp was burned at the stake in 155. His supposed tomb is among the ruins of a stadium in Ephesus.

[72] Clemens wrote the *Alta* on September 5 that "Smyrna is a very old city. . . . and here was located one of the old original seven apocalyptic churches spoken of in Revelations" (*TIA*, p. 164).

<Aug> Sept. 8.—

Isle of Samos[73] St. Paul.

Isle of Patmos St John's Revelations

Isle of Rhodes, where the Colossus stood. St. Paul

Isle of Cyprus—

Be at Beirut Sept. <11>10[74]

Syria.

Sept. 11.—Left Beirut for Jerusalem at 3 PM.
Our company is composed of 8 persons:[75]
Church, of Ohio,
WR Denny, Va,
Jack Van Nostrand, N.J.
Davis, Staten Island,
Dan. Slote, New York,
Moulton, Missouri,
Dr Birch, do.
Sam Clemens, Cal.
All mounted on horses.

---

[73] According to the log of Captain Duncan, Samos was passed on the morning of September 7.

[74] When the *Quaker City* arrived in Beirut on 10 September, those pilgrims who expected to visit Damascus discovered their plans had been disrupted: the stage-coach made only one daily trip, could carry only twelve passengers, and had already left for that day. Since the ship was to stop in Beirut for only about five days, the passengers decided among themselves who should have the privilege of a carriage ride to Damascus. While most of the remaining passengers toured Beirut and its environs, some went in small groups to visit Baalbek and Damascus by horseback, all except Clemens' party returning to the *Quaker City* afterwards.

[75] Clemens wrote to his family on September 11: "We are here, eight of us, making a contract with a dragoman to take us to Baalbek, then to Damascus, Nazareth, &c. then to Lake Genassareth (Sea of Tiberias,) then South through all the celebrated Scriptural localities to Jerusalem—then to the Dead Sea, the Cave of Macpelah and up to Joppa where the ship will be. We shall be in the saddle three weeks—we have horses, tents, provisions, arms, a dragoman and two other servants, and we pay five dollars a day apiece, in gold" (*MTL*, p. 136).

Abraham, of Malta, is Chief Dragoman, & Mohamed ——— of Alexandria, Egypt is 1st Assistant.

Camp Equipage: 3 sleeping tents; 1 kitchen tent, & 1 eating tent—all large, finely furnished & handsome.

Our caravan numbers 24 mules & horses, & 14 serving men—28 men all told.

Camped <fi> that night on high ground of the Lebanon foothills, 10 or 12 miles out of Beirut.

Noah's Tomb.

Sept. 12—Broke camp at 7 A.M. just as Col. Foster & Col. Hyde went by in the diligence bound for Damascus. We passed the Leary party & the Bond party during the day.

Came down into the great Lebanon Valley or Coelo-Syria at noon & rested & lunched at an old Khan. Far away on the right, the snow-spotted peak of Mount Hermon.

Passed up the Valley & camped on l. side under the dews of Hermon.—first passing through a dirty Arab village & visiting the tomb of Noah, of Deluge notoriety.

<Pilgrimage[76]

Sept 11—Camped at 6 PM.—10 or 12 miles out of Beirut on the Mountains of Lebanon—splendid supper & tents.

26 pack mules

Dragoman & 19 servingmen.

8 of ourselves—

Col. Denny, Church, & D[r] Birch, in one large tent.

Jack Van Nostrand, Davis & Moulton in the other.

Dan Slote & I in the small one.

5 tents in all—3 for us—one for kitchen & one for eating saloon.>

Sep. 13.

Ruins of Baalbec. [#]

---

[76] Clemens made the following entry on a full blank page of the notebook, probably on the day the pilgrimage began. He later completed the entry above, dated "Sept. 11" (p. 416), and canceled this parallel passage.

Broke camp at 6.30 AM, crossed the valley, & at 11 reached the magnificent ruins of Baalbec, marched about the ruined temples & the quarries 3 or 4 hours <(the> (found Bullard, Mrs. Fairbanks, James, & Beach & daughter there, <&c>met Jackson & party[77] Beirut bound<)>, & the Leary & Bond parties arrived afterwards fagged out.)—then departed.

Rode 7 hours, <&>partly through wild, rocky scenery, & camped at 10.30 on the banks of a pretty stream near a Syrian village—2 horses lame & the others worn out.[78]

Sept. 14—Broke camp at 7 A.M. & make a fearful trip through the <——>Zeb Dana valley & the rough mountains (temples carved in them) & finally along a beautiful stream in a chasm, lined, thick with pomegranate, fig, olive & quince orchards, & nooned an hour at 1 PM at the celebrated fountain of Figia, second in size in Syria, & the coldest water in the world.—Bathed in it. It is the principal source of the Abana river, & is only ½ mile long to where it joins.

Beautiful place—<gi> giant trees all around,—vast stream gushes from under the mountain in a torrent. Over it is a very ancient ruin, with no known history—supposed to have been for the worship of the fountain.

Where Baalam's ass lived—holy ground. [#]

---

[77] That is, Dr. Abraham Reeves Jackson, Julia Newell, and Dr. and Mrs. James H. Payne. Jackson's letter to the Monroe County (Pa.) *Democrat* characterized all the pilgrims' response to Baalbek: "One is naturally inclined to wonder how these huge blocks were transported such long distances, and placed in their present elevated positions. Certainly we have no means in the present day by which it could be effected. . . . Of course among so many Yankees as compose our company, there was much 'guessing' as to how the thing was done, some thinking the stones had been rolled; others, that they had been moved by immense derricks, &c." (14 September 1867). Clemens devoted half of his *Alta* letter of September 17 to the "noble ruin" of Baalbek: "I cannot conceive how those immense blocks of stone were ever hauled from the quarries, or how they were ever raised to the dizzy heights they occupy in the temples" (*TIA*, p. 191).

[78] In chapters 43 and 44 of *The Innocents Abroad* Clemens represented this and the following paragraph as "quoted" from his notebook. Although quoted in part, each has been elaborately paraphrased and expanded.

Damascus.

Left the fountain at 1 P.M. (that infernal fountain took us at least 2 hours out of our way<.>,)[79] & reached Mahomet's look-out place over the wonderful garden & plain of Damascus & the beautiful city, in time to get a good long look & descend into the city before the gates were closed.

Population 200,000.

Sept. 15.—Taken very sick at 4 AM.[80]

Sept. 16—Abed all day yesterday—got enough of Damascus. Don't want to see any more of it. Took a jackass & <a b>an Arab to drive it, & visited "the street called Straight"—<A>Judas' house<[-]>, where St. Paul lay blind after his adventure—house & well of Ananias (these are genuine, at any rate,) the <gentleman> disciple who <when> went & <invited>invested Paul with the sacred office <&>as commanded by the Savior—the house of Naaman the leper, whom the prophet Elijah (or Elisha) ordered to wash 7 times in Jordan & so cured him<.>[81]—the place in the city wall (evidently old Roman wall,) where Paul was let down in the basket & made his escape toward Jerusalem when the Jews

---

[79] Clemens' impatience was explained in chapter 43 of *The Innocents Abroad:* "Not content with doubling the legitimate stages [to avoid traveling on Sunday], they switched off the main road and went away out of the way to visit an absurd fountain called Figia, because Baalam's ass had drank there once. So we journeyed on, through the terrible hills and deserts and the roasting sun, and then far into the night, seeking the honored pool of Baalam's ass, the patron saint of all pilgrims like us." The party was indeed traveling rapidly; Murray's guidebook indicates that the distance between Baalbek and Damascus could not be covered "profitably and pleasantly in less than 3 days" (*A Handbook for Travellers in Syria and Palestine*, 2 vols. [London: John Murray, 1858], 2:554).

[80] In chapter 45 of *The Innocents Abroad* Clemens explained that he "lay prostrate with a violent attack of cholera, or cholera morbus."

[81] When Clemens gave the story of Naaman in his *Alta* letter, he had obviously consulted his Murray handbook as well as the Bible and could state that the servant of "Naaman's wife remarked one day that if the Prophet Elisha, who was living down in Samaria somewhere, would only take hold of Naaman's case, he could cure him" (*TIA*, p. 196).

sought his life—outside the wall, the tomb (red chicken-coop) of St George, a <person> gate-keeper beheaded for conniving at Paul's escape[82]—further out, the hole (genuine & ancient) where Paul lay hid till he got a chance to shove,)—& the great tomb of the 5,000 Christians massacred in Damascus 7 years ago.

Enough of Damascus.

Sept. 16—Left Damascus about <noon> 10 or 11—4 hours out, saw the spot where Paul was miraculously converted.

Nimrod's Tomb. 4,000 years old. The first King.

Camped at an Arab village (Kafir Something),[83] where Nimrod the Mighty Hunter, the builder of Babylon & the Tower of Babel lies buried. He was a fine old Sport & a great linguist.

Holy Land.

Sept. 17.—Edged in to the Holy Land proper, to-day.

After noonday lunch, climbed <the> a great cone 1,000 feet high, which overlooks the ancient ruined city of Cesarea Phillippi, Dan, & the great plain wherein are visible some little streams—sources of the Jordan. The mountain is in Bashan & is covered with olive groves & the oaks of Bashan. It is crowned with the grandest old ruined castle in the world[84]—1,000 feet long by 200 wide, & its walls & turrets have been from 30 to 60 feet high<.>—all of massive dressed stone masonry with beveled edges—very well preserved—some of the stones 12 ft long & 3 thick—

---

[82] "In front of the gate, shaded by walnut-trees, is a small cupola, covering a tomb said to be that of St. George, the porter who aided St. Paul in his escape and became a martyr to his benevolence" (Murray's 1858 *Syria,* 2:478).

[83] "*Kefr Hauwar,* a large prosperous village surrounded by gardens, orchards, and fruitful fields. . . . Tradition or fate has placed here one of the numerous tombs of Nimrod; but the spot is now unhonoured, if not altogether unknown" (Murray's 1858 *Syria,* 2:450). In his September 17 *Alta* letter Clemens approximated the name as "Kaf'r Houer" but would not vouch for his spelling. In chapter 45 of *The Innocents Abroad* the village became simply "Jonesborough."

[84] The Castle of Subeibeh was "one of the finest ruins in Syria; and one of the most perfect and imposing specimens of the military architecture of the Phœnicians, or possibly of the Syro-Grecians, extant. No traveller should fail to visit it" (Murray's 1858 *Syria,* 2:447–448).

Grand portcullis—old inscriptions—ruined vaults, arches, dungeons, tunnels, reservoir—goatherd lives there now.

No history supposd Phenician—castle first spoken of in the Crusades, but was very old then—Nureddin took it in 1135—it was abandoned in <17> 17th cent.

Banias.

This place—where we are encamped, is beautiful with olive groves, & the fountain which is the main source of the Jordan—we washed in it & drank of its waters. The fountain comes from a great grotto where the Greeks <or> (& the Romans after them), worshiped the god Pan (hence the name, Panias) & the niches are carved in the rock still, & Greek inscriptions.) At the same place Herod the Great erected a marble temple to commemorate the visit of Caesar Augustus to the city, & changed the city's name to Cesarea Phillippi, also.

Jordan hard road to travel.[85]

Cesarea Phillippi

This & Banias are one. A great, massive, ruined citadel of 4 acres. Ruined arches, waterways, bridges, columns, capitals, &c, everywhere.

Hoof-prints deep in old rocks.

This is the first place we have ever seen, whose pavements were trodden by Jesus Christ. Here he asked the disciples who the people took him to be, & asked Peter who *he* took him to be—& Peter's confident answer elicited that famous sentence upon which all the vast power & importance the Church of Rome arrogates to itself is founded: "Thou art Peter & upon this Rock &c—& what thou shalt bind upon the earth shall be bound in heaven" &c Here Christ cured a woman who had had an issue of blood for <3>7 years (now-a-days there would have been an affidavit published) and near here—possibly on the Castle hill, some claim that the Savior's Ascension/Transfig(?)_took place.[86] [#]

---

85 "Jordan Am a Hard Road to Trabbel" by T. F. Briggs was a popular, mildly comic plantation song.

86 Murray's 1858 *Syria*, citing the Book of Matthew, reminded its readers that

<E> Lake Hula—or the Waters of Meron.[87]

Sept. 18.—Broke Camp (at Cesarea Phillippi) at 7.15 AM & an hour afterward came to the Hill (½ m diam) ruins & fountain of Tel' el Kadi (Dan.) It is in the great valley which is the northern extremity of Palestine.

Dan.

It was first, ages ago, the Phoenician Laish—a lot of Danites from Sodom, 600, came over, like a pack of adventurers as they were, captured the place & lived <their>there as sort of luxurious agriculturists, till Abraham hazed them in after times.

The fountain is the largest in Syria<.>—forms a large pool then rushes off a chief source of Jordan. <[¶]J> The banks of the stream are bordered thick with oleanders & several other shrubs.

We traveled a long stretch (4 miles) of miserable rocky road overrun by water, & finally turned & followed down the other side of the valley over a half-green half-rusty country full of fine sheep, bulls of Bashan & Bedouin Shepherds. The Bed's are descended from <A>Esau, & scorn to live in houses. Saw their tents. Then through several large Arab villages made of coarse matting houses shaped like an omnibus, & finally after nooning <2 hours, reached a fountain & mill <abr> well up a> & riding 2 hours along a vast green swamp that occupies the whole width of the Valley, we camped at last at a fountain & mill well down abreast of Lake Hula, or the Waters of <Meron>Merom of Bible fame

30–31–2

Sept. 19—Left our camp by the Waters of Merom at 7 AM.

The Arabs threw stones into the camp last night & tried to stampede the horses.

"on one or other of [Mount Hermon's] wooded peaks" the Transfiguration took place. Murray's also corrected the "curious tradition" that it was at Banias that Christ healed the woman afflicted with an issue of blood (2:447).

[87] That is, Lake Huleh, mentioned in the Old Testament as the Waters of Merom.

Rode 2 hours over tolerably arable land (fast) & came in sight of the

Sea of Galilee
Lake Genessareth,
Sea of Tiberias.

Shortly came to an old Khan & in it examined the arched pit called

Joseph's Well,

where his brethren threw him.

Then over a horrible rocky, barren desert (like Nevada,) skulls with scattering goats & shepherds (with pipes,) & past

Safed,

and close to that

Bethsaida

from which Christ sent his disciples in a boat, after the miracle of 5 loaves

& 2 fishes,

performed at the other

Bethsaida,

which is above the mouth of Jordan 2 miles & a little to the eastward, & where Andrew & several other disciples hailed from.

1 mile from Bethsaida, we descended to the sea at

Capernaum,

Christ's dwelling-place, where he performed a great many miracles, (Jairus' daughter, I think<,>.) Some old <b>crumbling ruins, there, a ruined Khan & a fig tree & fountain. Arabs & camels.

Near here was the miraculous draught of fishes.

Tried to get a boat & didn't.[88]

Took a bath.

Crossed a long, rich, oleander plain along the sea to

---

[88] By late September, when Clemens wrote to the *Alta* from Tiberias (*TIA*, p. 231), he had already found this incident more significant than his brief entry might suggest. There, and again in chapter 47 of *The Innocents Abroad*, he developed at length his satiric rendering of the parsimonious pilgrims who lost their chance to sail on Galilee because they hesitated to pay the boatman's price.

Magdala,

the birth-place of Mary Magdalene—the rattiest, rustiest dirtest little collection of mud hovels, *tattooed women* & sore-eyed children in Palestine. One ruin in Magdala, (with an old pipe,) was good.[89]

Tiberias

Thence along the edge of a mountain to Tiberias, another nasty mud hovel village full of Arabs, Jews & negroes.

It was built by Herod Antipas, the murderer of John the Baptist, & named after his friend the Emperor Tiberias—so it is only mentioned in the *New* Testament.

The Sanhedrim met here last, & for 300 years it was the metropolis of the Jews in Palestine. It has been the abiding place of many famous & learned Jewish rabbins. They are here buried. The

Warm Baths

2 miles below are mentioned by Pliny.

Opposite Tiberias on the E side of the lake, the swine ran down into the sea.

Lake is surrounded by steep, barren, light brown hills 1500 ft high.

Splendid stars—when blue wave rolls nightly on Galilee.[90]

We have seen no country between here & Damascus capable of supporting any such populations as one gathers from the Bible.

The people of this region in the Bible were just as they are now—

---

[89] In the October 1870 issue of the *Galaxy* Mark Twain published "Curious Relic for Sale," which seems to be based on a recollection of an encounter with the person identified as a "ruin" here. Harassed by Arabs seeking "bucksheesh," Clemens said he was pursued in particular by one young Arab who was willing to exchange all his possessions for such contributions. "He was smoking the 'humbliest' pipe I ever saw—a dingy, funnel-shaped, red-clay thing, streaked and grimed with oil and tears of tobacco, and with all the different kinds of dirt there are, and thirty per cent. of them peculiar and indigenous to Endor and perdition. And rank? I never smelt anything like it. It withered a cactus that stood lifting its prickly hands aloft beside the trail" (*CG*, p. 82). Clemens explained that he bought the pipe and was given a "pouch of most unspeakably villainous tobacco" and proceeded to smoke them on the horseback trip through the Holy Land.

[90] The sentence was added in the margin of the manuscript page that faces the page containing the three preceding paragraphs about Galilee. The line is loosely quoted from Byron's "Destruction of Sennacherib," which Mark Twain identified in his *Alta* letter as the only poem he had ever learned by heart (see *TIA*, p. 235).

ignorant, depraved, superstitious, dirty, lousy, thieving *vagabonds*.[91]

Sept. 20.—Bathed in Galilee before breakfast. Passed through the strange old town (beautiful porphyry columns with flutings almost worn away). Had a wretched looking scalliwag imposed upon us for a *guard* by the shiek—a beat with a long, harmless silver-mounted gun & 2 pistols.

Saw from the top of the hill, Tiberias; Sea of Galilee; <Magda> Capernaum; Bethsaida; Magdala, <Hermon,> place where swine ran down; mouth of Jordan; exit of ditto; Mount Hermon; Safed; Mount Tabor; part of battle of Hattin; place where:

"The Ephraimites not being called upon to share in the spoils of the Ammonitish war, assembled a mighty host to fight against Jeptha, Judge of Israel; who, being apprised of their approach, gathered together the men of Israel & gave them battle & put them to flight. To make his victory the more secure, he stationed guards at the different fords and passages of the Jordan, with instructions to let none pass who could not say Shibboleth; the Ephraimites being of a different tribe, could not frame to pronounce the word, but called it Sibboleth, & so betrayed themselves. So forty-&-four thousand fell at the different fords & passages of the Jordan that day."[92] [#]

---

[91] Clemens elaborated this notion in a passage that was evidently written for (but omitted from) *The Innocents Abroad*: "Seen afar off,—as far as from America to the Holy Land—the ancient children of Israel seem almost too lovely & too holy for this coarse earth; but seen face to face, in their legitimate descendants, with no hope of distance to soften their harsh features & no glamor of Sabbath-school glory to beautify them, they are like any other savages. . . . Many of them were superior to the Digger Indians of California, but not all of them could rank the Sioux of the Great Plains. If this be doubted, read the Old Testament & then go among the Arabs of to-day in Palestine. . . . That six millions of *such* people should be selected & remain the chosen, of God, out of the untold millions & billions of far more promising subjects who were born & died in other lands during those long ages, is a mystery we may not solve—is simply a curious unexplained fact" (TS in MTP, DV 134).

[92] Mark Twain used this quotation, "imperfectly remembered, no doubt," in the *Alta* letter published on 2 February 1868 (*TIA*, pp. 240–241) and incorporated it into chapter 49 of *The Innocents Abroad*. Alexander E. Jones has pointed out that the " 'quotation' is in fact a fairly accurate rendition of a portion of the

Mount Tabor.

Transfiguration.

It is mentioned all through the Bible. New Convent & ruins of an old one built by the Crusaders. Saw XX[93] in it. Also ruins of Joshua's time.

Saw from its summit, Galilee, Hermon, Little Hermon, Gilboa, where Saul & Jonathan fell; Nain, Endor, <—>the fountain of Jezreel, the Plain of Ezdraelon, where, Napoleon, the Crusaders, the ancient Jews & all the nations of the earth have fought at different times.

Then came to NAZARETH, where Christ lived & carpentered till 30 of age (not allowed by Jewish law to teach sooner.

Glass windows,—some 2-story—many shops—many cone-shaped mud hovels;—camels & fantastic Arabs & dirty children—all around, the hills that were familiar to the eyes of Jesus—

Imagine Christ's 30 years of life in the slow village of Nazareth[94]

Saw the grotto of the Annunciation—the pillar miraculously sustained[95]—old columns by Saint Helena, mother of Constantine—

Grotto where lived Joseph Mary & infant Christ—

Workshop of Joseph & Jesus.

Great Stone on which Jesus & disciples rested after return from Sea of Galilee.[96]

Masonic ritual for the Fellow Craft degree" ("Mark Twain and Freemasonry," *American Literature* 26 [November 1954]: 368, n. 27).

[93] This is Mark Twain's usual symbol for crosses.

[94] "Whoever shall write the Boyhood of Jesus ingeniously," Clemens noted in chapter 51 of *The Innocents Abroad*, "will make a book which will possess a vivid interest for young and old alike. I judge so from the greater interest we found in Nazareth than any of our speculations upon Capernaum and the Sea of Galilee gave rise to." Clemens' interest in the life of Christ had been prompted by reading the *Apocryphal New Testament* in New York (see Notebook 8, note 34). The entry has been written across and perpendicular to the two previous paragraphs.

[95] Murray's 1858 *Syria* described "a fragment of a large granite column suspended from the roof, and another fragment of a marble one below it: this column, the monks inform us, was hacked through by the infidels in the vain attempt to pull down the roof, but was miraculously sustained in its place without visible support, and has since remained, and probably will remain for many a day to come, 'a suspended miracle' " (2:361).

[96] According to Murray's skeptical account, " 'The Table of Christ'—a small

Synagogue where Jesus taught & from which Jews took him to throw him down the mountain, when he "passed from their presence".

Fountain of the Virgin.

Sept. 21—Left Nazareth & its chalk hills at 7.30, came down a high, steep mountain & galloped across the Plain of Esdraelon. to

Endor,

the rustiest of all, almost—a few nasty mud cabins,—many caves & holes in the hill from which the fierce, ragged, dirty inhabitants swarmed. Pop. 250.

The Witch's Cave

has a fig tree before it & a spring within. Endor is a fit place for a witch.[97]

Camel dung on the roofs & caked against the houses to dry. Like to got yanked here I suspect.[98] Next, to

Nain,

an hour further—still smaller town. Little Mosque over spot once occupied by widow's house. Graveyard—*very* old & ratty—exists yet, & place shown where corpse was passing through city wall when Christ resurrected it.[99] Next around end of

Little Hermon to

---

vaulted chamber with a large table-shaped fragment of solid rock projecting about 3 ft. from the floor. This, according to tradition . . . is the very table at which our Lord and his disciples frequently ate both before and after His resurrection" (1858 *Syria,* 2:362).

97 "The only remarkable things here are the caverns hewn in the cliffs above the houses. They are rude irregular excavations, the object of which it is difficult to determine; but they strike one forcibly as fit habitations for a *witch*" (Murray's 1858 *Syria,* 2:358).

98 Clemens has added this sentence in the margin of the page beside the two preceding paragraphs. In chapter 51 of *The Innocents Abroad* Mark Twain explained his meaning: the inhabitants of Endor were "the wildest horde of half-naked savages we have found thus far. They swarmed out of mud bee-hives; out of hovels of the dry-goods box pattern; out of gaping caves under shelving rocks; out of crevices in the earth. In five minutes the dead solitude and silence of the place were no more, and a begging, screeching, shouting mob were struggling about the horses' feet and blocking the way."

99 See Luke 7:11–18.

El Fulah *Castle*[100] *Shunem,*
(cruse of oil—Elisha.—same widow (lemon orchards & dung), where woman built shanty on wall for Elisha & he raised her dead son. Think Samuel lived or was born here—doubtful. Next to

Ancient Ruined Castle

celebrated in the Crusades (this should have come *before* Shunem) & place where Napoleon won a splendid victory over the Syrians (Turks).[101] Next, crossed the *Valley of Jezreel* (which is an arm of Esdraelon) to

City of Jezreel,

on the hill, where Ahab King of Judah lived in splendor with his awful heifer Jezebel, who swore away a fellow's life who would not sell his valley vineyard to her & then took possession—on account of which <a>she fell under a curse.

Jehu the mighty rider, "rode furiously" (couldn't done it anywhere but in this plain), captured the city, threw Jez over the walls & she was eaten by dogs. Went next to the

Fountain of Jezreel,

Where Gideon slipped up on the Midianites & Amalekites with his 300 who lapped like dogs, & with candles, pitchers & trumpets, & made 15,000 (30,?) slay themselves.

Here Saul camped, while the Philistines lay at Shunem (big advantage of slope all the way.) In the night he passed over left shoulder of Little Hermon & to Endor, where witch called up Samuel, who proph. his defeat. Next day he & Jonathan & 2 other sons fled over Mt. Gilboa (over our heads), & the 3 were killed & Saul fell on his sword, thus making the throne to David.

<Around corner of this Gilboa> Esdraelon is what stands for the Armageddon of Scripture. Megiddo Here Neco-Pharaoh of Egypt gained splendid victory over Josiah, Israelitish King.

---

[100] Clemens probably added "El Fulah *Castle*" when he wrote "(this should have come *before* Shunem)" in the paragraph headed "Ancient Ruined Castle." He inserted "(cruse . . . widow" without a caret above this paragraph, which originally began "(lemon orchards & dung)." The events at Shunem are told in 2 Kings 4:1–37.

[101] The battle of Mount Tabor, fought in April 1799.

This Esdraelon is called the battle-field of the nations. 11 separate & distinct nations have fought in it. Here Deborah & Barak beat Sisera (nail in head by Jael) Jud 4–12, 24 Gideon Jud. 6–7. Saul (last battle with Philistines) 1 Sam. 31. Benhadad, Syrian King, defeated here by Ahab 1 K, 22. Josiah K of Juda, routed & put to death by Egyp. King 2 K 23–29. 2 Chron. 35–22. Bonaparte. Think of *all* these marshaled at once in this great level plain 25 m long & 8 broad!—the Assyrians & Persians, the Jews & Gentiles, Crusaders & Saracens, Egyptians, Turks, Arabs, and Franks—in divers costumes, a splendid array! Call up the shadowy warriors & deploy them again on the great plain under the moon! 5,000,000.

From uplands can see without a glass, El Fuleh, Tabor, Nazareth, Carmel, Great & Little Hermon, depression of Jordan, Jezreel, Shunem,

Next to
El Genin, where

<wh> we are camped. (Dr. Jackson & Payne are here, & the Pacha of Akka with a great retinue & many camels. Crocker party have gone on to Shechem.

The guard's empty pistol.

Armed gallants at Jezreel fountain

Women tattooed on arms, hands, chin, lips, & sometimes on cheeks.

Sept. 22—

Left Genin at 1 AM. Some time before daylight, passed near *another* place where Joseph's brethren pitted him.

Samaria.

About noon <as> after passing over a succession of mountain tops (saw the Mediterranean Sea 40 miles distant) & many Biblical cities (in which the inhabitants looked savage & would have liked to throw stones (women <w> & babies with elaborate coin headdresses,) we came to the singularly terraced hills which shewed that we were out of Galilee & into

Samaria.

Climbed a hill to visit the ruins of the city where the woman of Samaria conversed with Christ & gave him to drink—where the good Samaritan (the only one that ever lived there) dwelt,) & where Elisha was when Naaman came to be cured of his leprosy.

It is rough stone mud hovels & caml dung, as usual—& 100 limestone colums 2 ft diam., 20 ft high & no capitals or bases perceptible—lowest grade of architecture—& I suppose that *this* is all that remains of Herod's boasted beautifying of the city.

Ruins of a Christian church of the Crusades & the

Tomb of St John

the Evangelist—remains transferred to cch of the Annunciation, Genoa.

The Arabs stoned James here, & 2 stones hit Miss Brown—our party was not molested,[102] except that a small boy threw a stone at the Dr.

Nabulous.

Or Shechem. Lunched there at 2 P.M. The Crocker & Beach party on the hill.

Ebal on the left (hill of cursing) & Gherison on the right (hill of blessing)—6 tribes on one & 6 on the other side when the law was read & said So mote it be.

Ebal is cultivated with grapes—scattering olives on the other—disproves the enthusiasts who say the accursed mountain is barren & the other blooming.

On the hill is the oldest MSS in existence.—Jewish law. <Here>

Here Jacob (& I believe Abraham Isaac, Joseph &c) lived, & here Joshua gave the people his dying injunctions.

Very fertile narrow valley—rich soil.

<Camp>

---

102 "The inhabitants of this camp are particularly vicious, and stoned two parties of our pilgrims a day or two ago who brought about the difficulty by showing their revolvers when they did not intend to use them—a thing which is deemed bad judgment in California" (*TIA*, p. 258).

Joseph's Tomb
and
Jacob's Well

Both well authenticate—in valley 1 mile away. Well 90 ft deep—solid rock.

Camped at 7 PM at an Arab Village—Lubia (Libonia of the Bible). Tents behind. Slept on the ground in front of an Arab house. Lice, fleas, horses, jackasses, chickens, & worse than all, Arabs, for company all night.

Sept. 22.

Broke camp at 2.30 AM & passed the Severance party in the foot of the valley—lights burning in their tents.[103]

After daylight passed somewhere in the neighborhood of

Shiloh,

where the ark of the Covenant rested 300 years, &c. Ark taken to battle & it & Eli's 2 wicked sons lost—Eli fell & broke his neck. I-chabod—the glory of Israel is departed.[104]

<J>Beth-el

(House of God) Scene of Jacob's Ladder Dream—nothing left now but a shapeless mass of ruins.

Villages of
Ramah,
Beroth & Mount Nebo-Samuel

where Prophet Samuel is buried—in full sight from Jerusalem. [#]

---

[103] Mrs. Severance noted that on "Monday morning we arose *very* early, about two o'clock, but the moon was shining quite brightly. We waited a little longer than was necessary, but were in the saddle at four. The road was very bad, mostly over steep and rocky hills. While we were breakfasting another party had passed us, but we thought it could hardly be any one from the 'Quaker City.' However, it was not long before we came up to them, and it proved to be the eight gentlemen who had started from Beirut and gone via Baalbec and Damascus. They had left their tents behind for a single night, and were pressing on for Jerusalem" (*JLS*, p. 172). "Monday morning" was September 23, so Clemens' date is in error (see p. 429.23). Clemens' dates for entries through September 28 remained one day behind.

[104] See 1 Samuel 4:12–21.

Fountain of Beirah.

—very ancient—out in a plain white & thick with stones.

All the way to Jerusalem, rocks—rocks—rocks. Roads infernal. Thought we never *would* get there.

Arrived at last on a hill north of the city & overlooking Jerusalem.

<Loaf> Bits of ruin scattered everywhere, & the ground thick with Mosaics.

Could recognize the <Tower>

Tower of Hippicus
" " Antonio
Mosque of Omar
Damascus Gate
Mount Olivet
Valley of Jehoshaphat
Garden of Gethsemane
Mount Moriah

& could see where many other localities belonged.

Loafed all the afternoon in the Mediterranean Hotel.

We entered by the <Jaff> Damascus Gate, part of which is very old & part was repaired by the Crusaders.

Sept. 23.—Visited the Mosque of Omar—immense area—that part of it occupied by Omar is paved with flags & has pillared gates (4.)

Little Temple where David & some other party (*Goliah*) used to sit & judge the people.

Mosaic windows (ancient)

<Place where>

Footprint of (Abrahaim, I suppose, when he was going to sacrifice Isaac.

Great Rock of Abraham's Sacrifice (authentic)

Cords of pillars & sculptures from Solomon's Temple (authentic)

—peculiar forms.

Grip of the Angel Gabriel on the big rock.

Got some pieces of the old Temple.[105]

<Down>

Buckler of Mahomet's uncle

Place where they tie rags to let Mahomet know they have been there.

Down below is place where Mahomet shoved Rock up with his head.

The Rock is suspended between Heaven & Earth.

Hole in middle which leads down to Mahommedan Hell—<Men> Souls stand there & Mahomet lifts them up by hair of head—so they leave a scalp-lock—lose it, go to hell sure.

Legend of the old tale-bearing woman.

Mosque El Aksa.

Tombs Aaron's 2 sons. Formerly Crusader Church (they took city <1099>1199, & held it 300 yrs)

Stairways cedar Leb.

Pillars (squeeze.)

Walls full of relics of Solomon's Temple plastered in for preservation—Christians would steal & take home. Thank the Mohammedans.

Beautiful old inverted pillars.

---

[105] Clemens was evidently not innocent of the "vandalism" for which he attacked his companions in chapter 45 of *The Innocents Abroad*:

> The incorrigible pilgrims have come in with their pockets full of specimens broken from the ruins. I wish this vandalism could be stopped. They broke off fragments from Noah's tomb; from the exquisite sculptures of the temples of Baalbec; from the houses of Judas and Ananias, in Damascus; from the tomb of Nimrod the Mighty Hunter in Jonesborough; from the worn Greek and Roman inscriptions set in the hoary walls of the Castle of Banias; and now they have been hacking and chipping these old arches here that Jesus looked upon in the flesh. Heaven protect the Sepulchre when this tribe invades Jerusalem!

Underneath are the old monstrous arched pillars & foundations of Solomon's Temple, preserved excellently by the ruins that lay upon them so long.

Also the double gate where the first fruits came in for the priests.

And the subterranean way to the Pool of Siloam discovered by Dr Robinson.[106]

Crypts under temple 40 ft high arches—olive trees & pavements of great age above

No hogs in Palestine

Palace of Caiaphas

Pool of Bethesda.

The Gate Beautiful

and

Seat of Judgment

(pillar sticking out) where Mahomet will judge the world. Both overlook valley of Jehoshaphat, Tomb of St James, (apostle,) tomb of Absalom & that of a High Priest.

Doorway of Pilate's House.[107]

Place where Christ sat when people said His blood be upon us & upon our children.

Place near Tower Antonio where he took up his cross.

Via <Sacra.> Dolorosa.

3^d place where he fell with X <cr>& broke a great pillar.

4th place—where he left mark of elbow in wall.

Dives house

Lazarus House

Hous of Dog Moreover[108] [#]

---

106 Edward Robinson described his visit to the Pool of Siloam and his explorations of this underground passage in *Biblical Researches in Palestine, Mount Sinai, and Arabia Petraea* (Boston: Crocker & Brewster, 1841).

107 Clemens names several of the traditional stations along the Via Dolorosa.

108 Mark Twain remarked to his *Alta* readers that there was "nothing more at

Tombs of the Kings.

Quarries under the City.

CALVARY.

Church of the Holy Sepulchre.[109]
Organ & chanting of the Monks.
Repairing of the Dome.
Dim cathedral light of many smoking tapers.
Maximilians gift.
Place where Helena found the Cross—& her chapel & where she sat.
Pillar of Flagellation.
Stocks.
Place where soldier was beheaded who said Truly this was the Son of God.
Place where John & Mary stood looking at Christ on the X when he said Woman, behold thy Son—Behold thy Mother.
Place where Jesus appeared to Mary in the Garden.
Place where the women came at early dawn & saw the angels at the Sepulchre.
The rent rock & the holes where the 3 crosses stood.
Navel of the world in the Greek Chapel, where Adam's dust came from.
Russian gift to the Cross.
Sword & spurs of Godfrey of Bulloigne, first King of Jerusalem (genuine) worn by Patriarch of Greek Church at Installation.
Crown of thorns. [#]

Jerusalem to be seen, except the houses of Dives and Lazarus of the parable, and 'Moreover the dog' " (*TIA*, p. 291). He dropped this minimal joke, adapted from Luke 16:21, when he revised the Jerusalem passage for chapter 55 of *The Innocents Abroad.*

109 In chapter 54 of *The Innocents Abroad,* Mark Twain claimed: "Nothing has any fascination for us, now, but the Church of the Holy Sepulchre. We have been there every day, and have not grown tired of it; but we are weary of everything else." In fact all the notes made on this church (up to "Sept. 24") apparently date from the single day Mark Twain spent in Jerusalem before striking out for Bethlehem on a three-day excursion.

Sept. 24—Left Jerusalem at 8 AM.[110] Passed out at St Stephen's Gate along base of Olivet in Jehoshaphat by Jew Graveyard & tomb of Absalom—Jews throw stones at it to this day.

Hill of Offense over beyond village <o>& Pool of Siloam.

Job's well.

Brook & Valley of Kedron.

Village of Bethany.

It is fearfully ratty—some houses—mud—6 feet square & others holes in the ground—all windowless.

House & tomb of Lazarus & his 2 sisters.

Lunched.

Over mountain & saw Jordan Valley, Mountains of Moab & Dead Sea

<Modern> 2ᵈ Jericho.

8 Arched aqueduct—old walls, & river bed full of verdure.

Fountain of Elisha where ravens fed <him> Elijah & where he ascended in fiery chariot & his robe fell upon Elisha, who healed these waters. Where Gilgal stood—where the 12 stones taken from Jordan were placed—where Christ was baptised (?) where Desert wandres first touched Caanan—where they set up the ark & ate of the old corn & ceased from manna & quails—where they long remained.

Ancient Jericho.

Where Joshua marched around 7 times & blew down the walls.

---

[110] In chapter 55 of *The Innocents Abroad* Clemens suggested that the trip to the Jordan, Jericho, and the Dead Sea was planned as a diversion, although it is apparent that it always was part of their itinerary. Murray's 1858 *Syria* instructed the traveler that the excursion "will occupy 3 days, and the best way of arranging it, both for convenience and profit, is to encamp the first night at Jericho, taking care to visit the objects of interest near it in the evening; start the second morning *very early* for the Jordan and Dead Sea, and spend the second night at Mar Sâba. An early ride the third morning brings us to Bethlehem" (1:190). Clemens' party seems to have followed this schedule, leaving Jerusalem on Wednesday morning, September 25, and returning on Friday, September 27.

Many ruins still there (arches, *of course*), & mosaics in the brook. Precipice perforated with holes.

<Cam> This is the Plain of Jericho, noted as the most fertile spot in Palestine—they used to <I>irrigate it.

Apples of Sodom.

Campd near the old Square Tower (Middle Ages no doubt)—<garris> & Modern (mud) Jericho.—garrisoned by 15 men—Bedouin war.

<Sc>Priest only entered Holy of Holies once a year & then sent scape goat through Golden Gate to wilderness (some beat gobbled him up, sins & all, before he got 100 yds.[111]

Prodigal Son bet on King & Jack & coppered the ace & busted This man is a beat.

Father killed fatted calf—equivalent to champagne blow out.

Lazarus had a good deal of property.[112]

Lizards all emigrating.

Waltz back in the wilderness.

Jordan's a hard road to travel.

Gitting a King (& *bones*) from Tomb of the Kings.

Modern Jerusalem compared with the New Jerusalem of Revelations—<last> first.

Our shiek guards.

Scared parties to Jordan.[113] [#]

---

[111] Clemens' impatience with the Holy Land was expressed as he wrote of this custom for his *Alta* correspondence: "If they were to turn one loose now, he would not get as far [as] the Garden of Gethsemane till these miserable vagabonds here would gobble him up, sins and all. *They* wouldn't care. Mutton-chops and sin is good enough living for them" (*TIA*, p. 290).

[112] "They showed us the tomb of Lazarus. . . . And they showed us also a large 'Fountain of Lazarus,' and in the centre of the village the ancient dwelling of Lazarus. Lazarus appears to have been a man of property. The legends of the Sunday Schools do him great injustice; they give one the impression that he was poor" (*TIA*, p. 293).

[113] Clemens reported that some "lawless Bedouins" had "marched upon a camp

God protect the relics of Jerusalem when our tribe get there.

Burial of Moses.

Destruction of Sennacherib

Tried to take part of the hole.

Jack at Dead Sea wanted to know if *that* was why they called it asphaltum?

No Second Advent—Christ been here once—will never come again.[114]

I have only one pleasant reminiscence of this Palestine excursion —time I <was sick> had the cholera in Damascus.

Astonishing honesty of Europe—old drovers chasing me over Switzerland—Jack's watch & opera glass—Mrs Larrowe's sack—Leary letter of credit.

Dead Sea.

Sept. 25—Visited *ancient Jericho* & the *Fountain of* <Jer> *Elisha*. Found mosaics in the pool.

Abraham had a row with the Arabs about pitching the tents in a hot valley among the fig trees.

As usual, got up 2 hours too soon (at 2 AM) & at 4 had traversed the plain of Jericho & arrived at the

River Jordan,

—the ford, where the 12 stones were taken out.

Lay down in the bushes & slept 2 hours & caught cold. Got up & crossed the Jordan.

Then rode 2 hours to the <d>Dead Sea, & took a long bath. Face blistered & hair filled with crystalized salt.—Took a horse in & he upset.

---

of our pilgrims by the Jordan, and they only saved their lives by stealing away and flying to Jerusalem under whip and spur in the darkness of the night. Another of our parties had been fired on from an ambush and then attacked in the open day" (*TIA*, p. 292).

114 Mark Twain developed this punch line in an *Alta* passage ostensibly reporting a conversation in Jerusalem (see *TIA*, pp. 302–303).

After providing so many shieks & guides, never saw a Bedouin—one guard wanted to smouch me.

Rode 5½ hours through frightful heat, over the roughest mountain scenery, and arrived at last, brimming with gratitude, at the prodigious Convent of Mar Saber, in a wild glen on the brook Kedron.

Staid all night. *That bombardment.*

Bethlehem.

Sept. 26—Got up at 3 AM & traveled 2½ hours over mountains at got to the enclosure of olive trees in a plain where the angels announced the birth of the Saviour to the Shepherds.

Then ¼ hour to Bethlehem & to the

Milk Grotto.

Then to the convent of the Nativity—built by St Helena in 326.

The birth-place.

The Manger.

Prophet Zechariah.

St Jerome.

Joseph's retiring-grotto during the confinement.

Place where 20,000 children beheaded by Herod were buried.

St Eusebius.

Lunched there & left.—2 hours to Jerusalem. On the way, visited Rachel's Tomb (authentic.)

In Jerusalem breakfasted at noon at the Mediterranean Hotel, & then went to the Hill of Offense, where Solomon built a temple for his Egyptian wife. Tree there that Judas Iscariot hanged himself on.

Went to the Jews' wailing place alongside the old wall of Solomon's Temple—cyclopian masonry. Many Pharisees, with a curl forward of ear.

Another part of Temple wall, where Dr Robinson discovered the spring of the arch which Solomon built to connect Zion Hill with the Temple. The prophecy that 2 stones should not remain upon each other not strictly fulfilled. 3 or 4 of these stones are 20 feet long & 5 or 6 thick. How did they haul them with camels & jacks.

Retired to our tents outside the Damascus Gate.

Rough on the
RAVENS—

could hardly make their own living, let alone board Elijah.

Jerusalem.

Sept 27.—Left camp, outside the city walls, between the Damascus & Jaffa gates (in head of Hinnom Valley, which carries the waters of Gihon)—& passed Jaffa gate (on west of the city) & crossed Hinnom Valley between upper & Lower Gihon Pools, where an aqueduct built by Solomon crosses. Then went South & climbed the Hill of Evil Council & stood on the house of Caiaphas, where <Judas> the priests conspired against Christ & where Judas went to receive his 30 pieces of silver—& sat under the tree whereon he hanged himself. To the South was the Plain of Epraim & the Hill. In front was Zion Hill, Zion Gate, the Dung Gate, Davids Tower, David's Tomb, & the Tower of Hippicus by the Jaffa Gate<,>. On the left (west, were the Mountains of Judah & on the right, beyond the Valley of Jehoshaphat were the Hills of Benjamin. Over the Mosque of Omar was the Hill where Titus camped, & furthermost to the left was Scopus. Where Hinnom joins Jehoshaphat was the Village of Siloam at the foot of the Hill of Offense.

Went down into Hinnom & all along its high ledge rocks, saw gouged altars of Moloch, some with inscriptions. Much of the foot is the Field of Blood, Potter's Field, or Aceldama, purchased by the Priests with Judas's money. More altars <[---]> & some tombs, all the way down opposite Zion.

Saw where the altar of Moloch stood (& his image,) where they used to sacrifice the children.

Debouched into the Valley of Jehoshaphat (brook Kedron,) & drank at Job's well (near Sultana's) which is 8 × 15 × 100—men in water with feet, loading mules. It is older than Joshua—say nearly

4,000 years—is simply called En Rogel or Job's because he had a garden there.

Turned up to the left into Tyrophean or Cheese-monger's Valley, which used to run up <th> to the Damascus gate & divide the city, leaving Ophel & Mount Moriah in Benjamin, & Zion in Judah.

In foot of Tyrophean saw large tree under which Zecharias was killed. 50 <yards> feet above, it, Lower Pool of Siloam—right above it the *Main* Pool of Siloam, trench 30 ft, & little spring[115] woman drawing water—dug down into the solid rock. Robinson traced its tunnel to that of the Virgin. <Out>

Out <&>to left & turned up Jehosh, along under lee of Ophel, (seeing point of Moriah, with Temple wall high up above & before us, St Stephen's gate, the Golden Gate outside & the Gate Beautiful as a vestibule within, & the pillar projecting which Mahomet is to straddle & judge the world.

The King's Gardens all along—& the King's well. Passed by the curious old Village of Siloam, with some of its dens carved out of the rock, & came first to the Tomb of Zecharias, <(car> then to St James & then to Absalom & Jehoshaphats Tombs—all in a row & all cut out of the solid rock—Jews <through> throw stones at Ab's yet because he drove out his father—pile there. Passed Jew cemetery.—

Virgin Mary's Fountain.

<Turn> <Tur>

Proceeded to the Garden of Gethsemane, with its Garden <&>of Flowers & 8 hoary Olive trees.

Outside saw little lane where Judas betrayed, & just above, the rock on which disciples slept.

Turned up to left, past St Agnes & Virgin Mary's Tombs, & ascended to top of Mount of Olives. By<Convent> road which <Jose> David ascended when Absalom drove him out & member of hous of Saul threw stones after him. By Convent where Catholics say Jesus ascended to Heaven.

---

115 The following three words and dash were interlined without a caret above "spring dug down."

To the southeast saw another hill between Olivet & Bethany where Bible says he ascended—To the east & southeast saw plainly the Jordan, its valley, the Dead Sea & the Mountains of Moab. To the south saw the Frank Mountain & near it the desert where Christ was tempted of the devil—& <the> rather toward the S.W. the Plain of Ephraim, the Hill of Offense & toward Bethlehem. On the west, Jerusalem & beyond, the Mountains of Judah. On the north the hill where Titus pitched his camp, & beyond, Scopus. In the distance, Nebo-Samuel.

Crossed the Valley of Jehoshaphat, & whn abreast of the Damascus gate (north), came to the <noblest> stateliest tree in Palestine—Godfrey de Bulloigne's tree where he camped.

Mahomedan's believe that when the Golden gate is unwalled & opened, they pass out of power forever—both themselves, the Jews & Christians are expecting it now.

Went through the Via Dolorosa.

Sept. 28—Went all through the Holy Sepulchre again.

Saw the rock faces in a wall on Via Dolorosa that cried Hosanna! when Jesus passed.

Visited the Fountain of Hezekiah, where <S>David saw the mother of Solomon bathing.

Went to the Pool of Bethesda again for water.

Got a branch from the Cedar of Lebanon planted by Godfrey de Bouillon, first King of Jerusalem about 1085 to 1099.[116]

---

[116] Alexander E. Jones reports that the interest which Clemens felt in King Solomon's Temple and Godfrey de Bouillon stemmed from his interest in Masonic lore. "To a Master Mason this was an awesome spot" and Mark Twain "who elsewhere viewed sacred shrines with a jaundiced eye, behaved like a true Brother. Securing a piece of this special cedar wood, he had it fashioned into a gavel, which he sent to the Worshipful Master of his mother lodge." The gavel was inscribed as follows: "This Mallet is of Cedar cut in the Forest of Lebanon, whence Solomon obtained the Timbers for the Temple. The handle was cut by Bro. Clemens himself from a cedar planted just outside the walls of Jerusalem by Bro. Godfrey De Bouillon, the first Christian Conqueror of that City, 19th of July 1099. The gavel in its present form was made at Alexandria, Egypt, by order of Bro. Clemens" ("Mark Twain and Freemasonry," *American Literature* 26 [November 1954]: 365, n. 8). The gavel was presented in March 1868.

28 or 29

Went out by the Damascus Gate 3 PM & left for Ramleh—reached there at 8 PM. or 9. Tall, handsome Crusader's tower. This is the valley of Ajalon, where the moon stood still.

Next morning—Sep. 30—rode 3 hours in a gallop to Joppa—where timber for Solomon's temple was landed

Jonah sailed from here on his mission.

Visited house of Simon the Tanner where <the> Peter had the vision of unclean beasts.

Napoleon took this place once.[117]

Oct. 1.—Sailed for Egypt.

Oct 3—Landed at Alexandria.[118]

Cafe d'Europe

Hotel d'Europe—Ptr-per-Pce Wales.[119]

Catacombs—pass along another King.[120]

Pompey's pillar.

Cleopatra's Needles.

Great Cemetery.

Mahmoudeea Canal[121]

Nile boats.

Fine streets & dwellings.

Fine shade-tree avenues.

Luxurious bowers

---

[117] In March 1799 Napoleon refused to accept the surrender of the Muslim defenders, slaughtering four thousand captives.

[118] The *Quaker City* arrived at Alexandria on October 2, although most passengers did not visit the city until the following morning.

[119] Clemens reported that he and Jack Van Nostrand "found the hotel and secured rooms, and were happy to know that the Prince of Wales had stopped there once" (*The Innocents Abroad*, chapter 57).

[120] Clemens explained in *The Innocents Abroad*, chapter 58, that the Egyptian locomotives burned "mummies three thousand years old, purchased by the ton or by the graveyard for that purpose" and that "sometimes one hears the profane engineer call out pettishly, 'D—n these plebians, they don't burn worth a cent—pass out a King.' "

[121] The canal connects Alexandria with the Nile.

Great fountain in main street.
<Heliopolis.>

Oct. 4—To Cairo by rail—7 hours,—arrived after night.

Oct. 5—Donkeys to Pyramids of Ghizeh—past old Cairo, island of Rhodah.
Nilometer
Moses in Bulrushes.
Crossed the Nile from Old Cairo to Ghizeh
Splendid atmosphere
Beautiful Oriental scenery.
Naked girls in the streets.—finely built.
Noble shaded avenue leading to Old Cairo.

Ascent of Pyramid of Cheops
The Sphynx
Went *into* the Pyramid
The Shiek
Newly opened tomb behind the Sphynx.
Theatre of red granite opened near it.
The whole place round about is rich in art—under the sand.
Dr. Gibson at the Sphynx.[122]
Return to Cairo.

Mosque of Mehemet Ali—Oriental alabaster
Joseph's Well.
Citadel, & lofty wall, where the last Mameluke Bey jumped down.[123]

---

[122] "A nephew of the late Dr. Gibson, of Jamestown, speaking to a Pittsburg reporter, said that when his uncle and aunt were having their pictures taken in front of the Pyramids, Mark Twain who afterwards made the Doctor famous in his 'Innocents Abroad,' hired a band of dirty Bedouin Arabs to file in behind the group, where they were taken in various artistic and picturesque attitudes. The feelings of the Doctor when he received the picture can better be imagined than described" (quoted from the Greenville [Pa.] *Advance Argus*, 21 July 1887, by Henry F. Pommer in "Mark Twain's 'Commissioner of the United States,'" *American Literature* 34 [November 1962]: 390).

[123] In 1811 Mohammed Ali ordered the massacre of all the Memlooks. After

The birds in the Mosque.

View of Cairo & Memphis.

Heliopolis & the Petrified forest.

The City of the Caliphs.

300,000 pop.

Projecting lattices

Runners before carriages.[124]

Shepheard's infamous hotel

Buckshеesh.

The Museum.[125]

Said Pasha's Palace—shabby furniture

Splendid avenue of sycamores & acacias 3 or 4 miles, to The Pasha's great garden.[126]

Passed Red Sea Ship canal.

Expedition to Suez & the Red Sea. [#]

---

being trapped in the Citadel of Cairo, "all were shot except one, Emin Bey, who escaped by leaping his horse over a gap in the then dilapidated wall" (*A Handbook for Travellers in Egypt*, 4th ed., rev. [London: John Murray, 1873], p. 128).

[124] Dr. Jackson reported from Alexandria in his eighteenth letter to the Monroe County (Pa.) *Democrat:* "Here is the Arab or Turkish grandee, mounted on a gaily caparisoned Dongola horse, preceded by his groom bearing a long staff, and running ahead to clear the way before him."

[125] The Museum of Egyptian Antiquities in Cairo had the most important collection of Egyptian artifacts outside the British Museum. But Mrs. Severance reported that "the best of the collection is in Paris now, at the Exposition" (*JLS*, p. 187).

[126] "The road [from Cairo] to Shoobra lies along a beautiful avenue composed of the sycamore fig, and the acacia known in Egypt as the 'lebbekh,' a tree of most rapid growth, and of great beauty when in blossom. . . . The palace and garden of Shoobra were the work of Mohammed Ali, whose favourite residence it was. . . . The palace itself has nothing to recommend it but the view from the windows" (Murray's *Egypt*, p. 156).

Abasynnian expedition getting ready for the rescue of the prisoners.[127]

Shiek on a <ca>dromedary.

O

Oct. 7—Returnd to Alexandria—
Pyramids in the distance.
Cultivation—vast oceans of corn, &c

Queer villages.

Soft scenery.

Oct. 7—Left Dan & Vail & sailed for Africa.[128]

Oct. 11—At sea, somewhere in the neighborhood of Malta. Very stormy.[129]

Terrible death—to be talked to death. [#]

---

127 The British government had been trying since 1864 to negotiate the release of British diplomats and missionaries held prisoner by King Theodore of Abyssinia. After an ultimatum demanding their release on 17 August 1867 went unanswered, an expeditionary force set out from Bombay under command of General Robert Napier. On October 6 Napier published a proclamation directed at the rebellious Abyssinians, which said in part: "Now, all friendly measures tried to free them having proved useless, I am coming, commanded by the Queen, with an army to liberate them" (*The American Annual Cyclopaedia and Register of Important Events of the year* 1867 [New York: D. Appleton and Co., 1870], p. 6).

128 On 5 October Mrs. Fairbanks had written the Cleveland *Herald* that "our Purser [Robert Vail] . . . has made himself the hero of a pretty romance" and would "marry the handsome Turkish sister of the Vice Consul. An alarming case of 'love at first sight' " (published 11 December 1867). Dan Slote left the ship in Egypt for several more months of touring Europe. On 20 November Clemens would write from New York that Slote's mother "sent her carriage this morning, & I went up & kissed the whole family for Dan from his mother straight through aunts, cousins, sisters-in-law & everything, down to his youngest sister" (*MTBus*, p. 95).

129 Captain Duncan recorded the results of "rolling and tumbling about in Old Atlantic Style. Most of the passengers sea sick—a large sea rolling in from the westward . . . Dishes smash Organ top thrown off, Flower basket thrown down, While on deck salt water bathing is done on a large scale at short notice. If a luckless passenger ventures forward he is sure of a drenching" (CCD, 11 October 1867).

The storm has blown two small land birds & a hawk to sea & they came on board.

Sea full of flying fish.

Stromboli—Sicily—Sylla—Charybdis—Greece—the Hellespont—Constantinople—Black Sea—Sebastopol & Odessa,—Smyrna—Beirut—Holy Land—back to Jaffa—thence to Egypt.[130]

[260][131] Purser Wedding.[132]

Far-away Moses.[133]

Moonlight heal the scars

Dr. Gibson[134]

Capt Duncan

Mr. Crocker

---

[130] This entry is in blue ink on the back cover of the notebook and summarizes the itinerary which comprises the contents of the notebook.

[131] This line and the two following are on a slip of paper pasted to the back cover of the notebook; the first and third are in ink, the second in pencil. The writing has been so obscured by time that the text here depends on transcriptions made by Bernard DeVoto.

[132] The first entry in the following fragment in the private collection of Roger Barrett of Chicago is clearly related to the wedding of Robert Vail, the ship's purser. Although it was probably not torn from this notebook, it is given here as supplementary information:

> Vail's courtship.
>
> Down in tar-<schooner>sloop & back in kivered wagon.
>
> Wm Mason—What matter wh yr leg?—Me—<W>Hear you are writing book?
>
> Salting bird's tail.
>
> Nautical Yarn full of technicalities
>
> Some N.Y. Clerks.

[133] Murray's *Constantinople* noted that among the "best shops in the Stambûl Bazâr" was "*Sadoullah & Co.*, 'Faraway Moses,' whose shop is decorated in Turkish style, and who do a large business especially with Americans. Their carpets, which are made for them in Smyrna and in the interior, are beautiful, and their modern embroideries and woven stuffs are very good. They deliver goods free to England, and make arrangements with Americans" (p. 156). See also chapter 35 of *The Innocents Abroad*.

[134] This and all subsequent entries except those at p. 448.20 and p. 449.5 were written with the notebook inverted.

Mrs. ditto
Harry & George[135]
Mo. S. Beach.
Chas Dimon
Lockwood.
Dr Crane & son
″ Andrews
Greer
Cutter Bloodgood H.
Dr Brown
Foster
Hice
Dan Slote
Haldeman,
Jack Van N.
Moulton
Church,
Denny,
Birch

Lizards emigrating—ants.[136]

5 canes
1 portfolio
1 toothbrush &c.
2 boxes.

Maybe ve coom Moonday.[137]

---

[135] Henry and George Duncan, sons of the captain.

[136] In chapter 47 of *The Innocents Abroad* Clemens noted that the lizards were moving in to take over the desert through which he was passing and that there were also "a few ants . . . in this desert place, but merely to spend the summer. They brought their provisions from Ain Mellahah—eleven miles."

[137] "One of our passengers said to a shopkeeper, in reference to a proposed return to buy a pair of gloves, '*Allong—re tay trankeel*—maybe ve coom Moonday,' and would you believe it, that shopkeeper, a born Frenchman, had to ask what it was that had been said" (*TIA*, p. 316). Julia Newell sent the same anecdote to the Janesville (Wis.) *Gazette* on 29 July: "This lady would seriously say to the shop

45 at Goodenough's before breakfast./was up.[138]
Hospital ship—cripples.
"Examining committee."[139]
"No use my eating—go out & puke it overboard."—J. W.[140]

Christ been once—never come again.

X Simon the tinner[141]
X Mephistophiles—Themistocles
X Sylla & Carybdis.
X Woollen shirt
X Latrina.
X <M>G—tried borrow shirt of Goodenough to get likeness taken in.
Dr. B's manner of eating.
F<os> going round table talking loudly.

---

girls in Paris 'No buy now—we coom gain Moonday' " (published 12 September 1867).

[138] This cryptic entry seems to suggest that the *Quaker City* excursionists descended upon Consul General J. H. Goodenow in Constantinople before he had eaten breakfast.

[139] Possibly a reference to the "Committee on Applications," ostensibly designated to screen prospective passengers for their social and moral acceptability. As Dr. Jackson explained in a vituperative letter written after the voyage, "All applicants . . . were required to submit their requests in writing, accompanied by their vouchers of respectability" to this committee. But, Jackson claimed, it was eventually discovered that "the committee was only a myth, and that behind the curtain which veiled the imaginary faces of its members beamed only the bland countenance of the manager himself, and that all the essentials of a good character were covered by the 'twelve hundred and fifty dollars, currency' " required for passage (New York *Herald*, 21 November 1867).

[140] Apparently the words of Joshua William Davis.

[141] The items marked by a marginal X here and below seem to be reminders for some of the "Oracle's" malapropisms or for jibes at other passengers. Clemens used "Sylla and Carybdis" in chapter 32 of *The Innocents Abroad* where he described an encounter between the "Oracle" and "one of the boys":

> "It ain't mentioned in the Bible!—*this* place ain't—well now, what place *is* this, since you know so much about it?"
> "Why it's Scylla and Charybdis."
> "Scylla and Cha—confound it, I thought it was Sodom and Gomorrah!"

Hats on in palace.[142]
No buckshecsh at pal.[143]
D. & L.'s water skins.
"Synagogue."[144]
If a lunatic want to be a dangerous one.[145]
X Vermilion—chameleon.
The poet—[146]
Oracle's spy-glass[147]
Iconoclast[148]—Gib^{n}

---

142 Clemens is recalling the visit with the Russian Grand Duke Michael. Mrs. Severance noted: "The Duke insisted on the gentlemen wearing their hats, and preceded us around to the other side of the house" (*JLS*, p. 144).

143 "As a general thing, we have been shown through palaces by some plush-legged filagreed flunkey or other, who charged a franc for it; but after talking with the company half an hour, the Emperor of Russia and his family conducted us all through their mansion themselves. They made no charge. They seemed to take a real pleasure in it" (*The Innocents Abroad*, chapter 37).

144 According to chapter 4 of *The Innocents Abroad*, the upper after cabin of the *Quaker City*, "a handsome saloon fifty or sixty feet long," which "the unregenerated called . . . the 'Synagogue,'" was used for prayer meetings.

145 In an August letter from Naples Clemens had fumed, in a frank parenthesis: "(I am not aware that I know what I am trying to write about; this is the first time I have been on board the ship for six weeks, and this morning I was pluming myself upon the quiet day I was going to have, but now I have only written a dozen lines here in the cabin and already all those anticipations of quiet are blighted; there is one party of Italian thieves fiddling and singing for pennies on one side of the ship, and a bagpiper, who only knows one tune, on the other; I am expecting to go crazy every minute, and if I do, I hope I will be driven to massacre those parties before I come to my senses again)" (*TIA*, pp. 83–84).

146 Bloodgood Haviland Cutter, "Poet-Lariat."

147 Dr. Edward Andrews ("The Oracle") is characterized in *The Innocents Abroad* by his "eternal spy-glass" (chapter 32).

148 In chapter 2 of *The Innocents Abroad* Mark Twain noted that Dr. William Gibson, the commissioner of the United States of America to Europe, Asia, and Africa, undertook to collect "seeds, and uncommon yams and extraordinary cabbages and peculiar bullfrogs for that poor, useless, innocent, mildewed old fossil, the Smithsonian Institute." Gibson's penchant for artifacts may have extended to quite literal image-breaking. In chapter 58 of *The Innocents Abroad* an illustration depicts a "relic-hunter" perched on a ladder propped against the Sphinx: "While we stood looking, a wart, or an excrescence of some kind, appeared on the jaw of the Sphynx. We heard the familiar clink of a hammer, and understood the case at once. One of our well-meaning reptiles—I mean relic-hunters—had crawled up

Old Roman ruins cropping out there.

Egypt & Palestine.

<Bre>Coffee at 7 AM—breakfast at 12—dinner at 6. Bad arrangement.

The idea of the Children of Israel leaving Egypt to hunt up a better thing in Palestine is rich.[149]

Hotel d'Europe—"P. Wales."

Ants carry grub 11 miles.

Bible topography

Shabby Shepherd's Hotel.

Rice, corn, <&>cotton, &c

Date palms—fine.

River ¼ to ⅓ m wide.

Cemetery—forest dates.

Grand avenue of syc. & acacia

250,000 inhab.

Mosque Mehemet Ali

Mud Villages

Sunset

European look of Alex^{n}

Lanterns

Howling dervishes

Mountebank—juggler.

Millions for defense, but not a cent for bucksheesh.[150]

---

there and was trying to break a 'specimen' from the face of this the most majestic creation the hand of man has wrought. . . . Egyptian granite that has defied the storms and earthquakes of all time has nothing to fear from the tack-hammers of ignorant excursionists—highwaymen like this specimen. He failed in his enterprise."

[149] Mrs. Fairbanks also viewed the ancient migration ironically: "Perhaps the principle of contrast enhanced the charm of Attic's shores, for we had come hither [Alexandria] from Palestine—a land that is beautiful only in books. Certain it is, that the 'Promised Land' could scarcely have brightened the eyes of the Children of Israel with a more glad surprise, than that with which we looked upon the waving fields, the towering palm groves, and the fertile banks of the coquettish Nile" (Cleveland *Herald*, 11 December 1867).

[150] In chapter 58 of *The Innocents Abroad* Clemens reported being assaulted for "bucksheesh" by a "howling swarm of beggars" near the pyramids. "A sheik . . .

Pass along another King—these plebs won't burn.
Sell all ancestors £300[151]

Tomb of the Virgin would draw in New York.

---

was with them. He wanted more bucksheesh. But we had adopted a new code—it was millions for defense, but not a cent for bucksheesh. I asked him if he could persuade the others to depart if we paid him. He said yes—for ten francs. We accepted the contract."

[151] In a letter published in the 7 December Janesville (Wis.) *Gazette* Julia Newell reported that "one of our party [John Greenwood], an agent for Barnum, negotiated in Alexandria for two genuine mummies for the new museum. He could obtain them at a cost of fifteen thousand dollars each, which caused Mark Twain to wish that all his dead ancestors were mummies, and he would sell them all at that price, up to the last one that died, and I think he would."

X

"The Camping Grounds of the Patriarchs"

(August–December 1867)

NOTEBOOK 10 was used by Clemens intermittently and somewhat erratically between mid-August 1867 and the end of that year. It contains entries related to the *Quaker City* trip and entries made during Clemens' subsequent brief stint in Washington as a newspaper correspondent.

It is clear that Clemens originally intended to use Notebook 10 as a portable reference guide during his travels in the Holy Land. Some time before he reached Beirut, he compiled the two extensive lists in this notebook: one, a skeleton list of biblical references, providing chapter and verse information for a number of Holy Land localities which Clemens supposed he might be visiting (pp. 458.6–469.15); the second, a day by day itinerary for his Holy Land travels, including detailed historical and geographical notes (pp. 469.16–485.11). The background notes in the projected itinerary are extracted from the second volume of the Reverend David A. Randall's *The Handwriting of God in Egypt, Sinai, and the Holy Land*

(Philadelphia: John E. Potter and Co., 1862). Some of the notes are paraphrased from Randall's work, but the majority of them are quoted exactly, with a few irreverent parenthetical intrusions by Clemens. He had apparently read widely, if somewhat skeptically, among the books in the ship's library as the *Quaker City* approached Beirut. He mentions his researches in his letter of 5 September 1867 to the *Alta California* from Smyrna: "The ship is full of books concerning the Holy Land, and holy places . . . and you cannot be surprised to know that I have read whole volumes of the far-fetched conclusions of these curious prophecy-fulfillers" (*TIA*, p. 166). In one of his final letters to the *Alta* (*TIA*, p. 303), Clemens names the books in the *Quaker City's* library. Curiously, Randall's *Handwriting of God*, from which he drew so extensively, is not mentioned —unless it is the mythical " 'Dusenberry's Researches' " of Clemens' letter.

Upon arriving in Beirut, Clemens decided to make a longer, more difficult overland trip to Jerusalem than originally planned. This change in itinerary forced him to bypass several intended stops and to hurry through many others, so that most of the information in Notebook 10 became useless to him. There is little specific historical or biblical information in the *Alta* letters that Clemens wrote while actually traveling through the Holy Land (*TIA*, pp. 178–193)—rather, they contain a lively personal narrative drawn from the daily account of the trip in Notebook 9. It is only in the additional Holy Land letters which he composed some time after leaving Alexandria (*TIA*, pp. 193–306), when his recollections were no longer fresh, that Clemens' reliance on his background notes becomes apparent. In particular, his letters on Nazareth, Jacob's Well, and Joseph's Tomb (*TIA*, pp. 248–253, 260–266) draw upon the information, and even the language, of the notes in this notebook.

Notebook 10 contains two other sets of entries relating to the *Quaker City* excursion. The notes labeled "Holy Land." (pp. 485.12–486.19), apparently written when Clemens was in Jerusalem at the end of September, are a very brief continuation of the daily account of the trip in Notebook 9. In the middle of the notebook, preceded and followed by several blank pages, there is a page and a half of notes, apparently a fragment of a comic situation intended for a play about the *Quaker City* voyage. The fragment (p. 487.1–14) cannot be dated precisely in relation to the other entries in this notebook; however, Clemens probably sketched the comic scene shortly after the return of the *Quaker City* to America. Clemens did not incorporate the notebook fragment into the manuscript of his unfinished play, *The Quaker City Holy Land Excursion.*

The *Quaker City* docked in New York on 19 November 1867. By 22 November Clemens was in Washington ready to assume his post as secretary to Senator William M. Stewart of Nevada. Clemens had written to his family from Naples on 9 August 1867 that he had just accepted Stewart's "private secretaryship in Washington next winter." Clemens expected that this job, while providing him only a modest salary, would allow him time for literary work. He wrote to his friend Frank Fuller on 24 November 1867: "There is no question about that I have solemly yielded up my liberty for a whole session of Congress.—enrolled my name on the regular Tribune staff, made the Tribune bureau here my headquarters, taken correspondences for two other papers and one magazine" (Collection of Mrs. Robin Craven, New York City). In addition to his New York *Tribune* letters, Clemens would be writing "special correspondence" for the *Alta* and the *Territorial Enterprise,* as well as occasional pieces for several other journals.

Clemens felt that this newspaper work would put his reputation on a firm footing. "If I lecture *now,*" he wrote Fuller, "I shall have to do it solely on the Quaker City's fame, and take many, *very many* chances—chances that might utterly dam me. If I stay here all winter and keep on hanging out my sign in the *Tribune* and getting well acquainted with great dignitaries to introduce me . . . I can lecture next season on my *own* reputation, to 100 houses, and houses that will be readier to accept me without a criticism than they are now. . . . Here in the next six months I will make . . . a *reputation* that will not be as precarious a capital as it is now, See it?"

When Clemens arrived in Washington, the Fortieth Congress was in the final days of its first session. Clemens was a frequent visitor to the Congress, gathering impressions of congressmen and congressional language and manners and making friends among the correspondents of Washington's newspaper row. Clemens' capsule impressions of various congressmen occupy several pages in the notebook. He wrote to his family on 25 November, shortly after his arrival in Washington: "Tired and sleepy—been in Congress all day and making newspaper acquaintances. . . . Am pretty well known now—intend to be better known. Am hobnobbing with these old Generals and Senators and other humbugs for no good purpose" (*MTB,* pp. 346–347). The few pages of Washington notes in this notebook, written in November and December 1867, are all the notebook material that survives for the period. Many of these notes were incorporated within a few weeks into Clemens' newspaper correspondence for the *Alta* and the *Territorial Enterprise*.

Clemens grew progressively restless and discontented with Washington—with its weather, its hotels, its congressional "humbugs," and the legion of political scramblers in Washington society, whom he would later satirize in *The Gilded Age*. He gladly resigned from his position with Stewart and burlesqued this short-lived career in "My Late Senatorial Secretaryship" (*Galaxy* 5 [May 1868]: 633–636) and "The Facts Concerning the Recent Important Resignation" (New York *Tribune*, 13 February 1868). Senator Stewart presented his own rancorous recollections of his association with Clemens in his *Reminiscences* (New York: Neale Publishing Co., 1908, pp. 219–220):

> I was seated at my window one morning when a very disreputable-looking person slouched into the room. He was arrayed in a seedy suit, which hung upon his lean frame in bunches with no style worth mentioning. A sheaf of scraggy black hair leaked out of a battered old slouch hat, like stuffing from an ancient Colonial sofa, and an evil-smelling cigar butt, very much frazzled, protruded from the corner of his mouth. He had a very sinister appearance. . . . When I first knew him he was a reporter on the *Territorial Enterprise*, which was otherwise a very reputable paper. . . . He went around putting things in the paper about people, stirring up trouble. He did not care whether the things he wrote were true or not, just so he could write something, and naturally he was not popular. I did not associate with him.

Stewart describes Clemens' night-long, cigar-smoking vigils and recalls having threatened his ungentlemanly clerk with a "thrashing." Despite this uneasy relationship, Clemens remained for some time: "He wrote his book in my room, and named it 'The Innocents Abroad.' I was confident that he would come to no good end, but I have heard of him from time to time since then, and I understand that he has settled down and become respectable" (p. 224).

By 13 December 1867, with the regular session of the Fortieth Congress hardly begun, Clemens was reconsidering his position. He wrote Fuller: "I believe I have made a mistake in not lecturing this winter. I did not suppose I was any better known when I got back than I was before I started—but every day I find additional reasons for thinking I was mistaken about that. . . . When are you coming down? I might take a 'disgust' any moment & sail for Cal" (Collection of Mrs. Robin Craven, New York City).

Clemens had just received an offer which made him even more impatient with his safe berth in Washington. On 1 December 1867 a letter arrived from Elisha Bliss, Jr., of the American Publishing Company in Hartford, Connecticut, proposing a venture in subscription publishing: "We are desirous of obtaining from you a work of some kind, perhaps compiled from your letters from the East, &c., with such interesting additions as may be proper. . . . If you have any thought of writing a book, or could be induced to do so, we should be pleased to see you" (*MTL*, p. 140). Clemens' reply was predictably prompt and enthusiastic. With the prospect of preparing a book, his restlessness in Washington grew. He wrote his family on 21 February 1868: "I was at 224 first [Clemens had been rooming with Senator Stewart at 224 F Street]—Stewart is there yet—I have moved five times since—shall move again, shortly. Shabby furniture & shabby food—*that* is Wash^{n}—I mean to keep moving" (*MTBus*, p. 98). Hearing that the *Alta* was planning book publication of the *Quaker City* letters, Clemens left Washington in March without regrets and sailed for California to forestall those plans.

Notebook 10 now contains 184 pages, 92 of them blank. They measure 6½ by 4 inches (16.5 by 10.2 centimeters) and are ruled with twenty-four blue horizontal lines. The edges of the pages are marbled in red, black, and gold. The endpapers and flyleaves are white. The notebook is bound in stiff tan calf. There are single computations in pencil on each of the endpapers, entries in pencil on the front flyleaf, and a computation in ink on the front cover. Someone has dated the front cover "1867" in ink. The binding is worn and loose, and a few leaves are no longer bound in. Four and one-half leaves have been torn out and are missing. With the exception of one page inscribed in orange pencil, all the entries are in black pencil. There are use marks throughout, in black pencil, blue pencil, and black ink—all of them probably by Paine.

Because Clemens did not use the pages consecutively from first to last but several times turned the notebook end-for-end and wrote from the back toward the front, the left-to-right sequence of pages does not necessarily correspond to the chronological sequence of entries. When it can be determined, chronological sequence has been preferred to physical sequence.

Thus, the *Quaker City* entries have been grouped in the first portion of the printed text, although they actually are inscribed in various places throughout the notebook, and the several groups of *Quaker City* entries are themselves printed here in chronological rather than physical order. Likewise, the notes on Congress written on the front flyleaf are printed here immediately before the other Washington entries that Clemens made near the center of the notebook. All deviations from physical sequence are reported in Details of Inscription and the chronology of entries is discussed in the notes.

Clemens entered running heads throughout his notes on the Holy Land excursion. When they interrupt continuing entries, these headings are omitted from the text and are recorded as emendations.

1739
1867

3606

6) 100.50
16.75[1]

Smyrna.[2]

Rev. 1-11; 2-8; [#]

---

[1] These two computations appear on the front cover of the notebook and on the front endpaper, respectively.

[2] Clemens' extensive list of biblical places and citations concerning them was probably assembled on board the *Quaker City* before the steamer reached Smyrna. The list is much too extensive to have been a projected itinerary for Clemens' overland excursion through the Holy Land; it is likely that Clemens merely took advantage of the ship's library to prepare a scriptural reference guide to places he might be visiting in the succeeding weeks. At some point before reaching Smyrna, the original *Quaker City* itinerary had been modified to include a stop at Haifa, in order to allow the travelers to make the inland journey to Nazareth more easily. Since Clemens' list includes references to the Nazareth trip, the list must have been drawn up after this change in itinerary. The list is written from the back of the notebook toward the front with the notebook inverted, but it appears at the beginning of this text in accordance with its chronological inscription.

<Epessus>Ephssus—Ephesus.

Acts 18-21 and 24. Paul. also 19 & 21st verses. 19-1. 20-17;
1 Corinthians 15-32; 16-8;
1 Timothy 1-3;
2 " 1-18; 4-12;
Rev. 1-11; 2-1.

Beirut—Beroth.

2 Sam. 8-8. Eze. 47-15; 16.

Damascus.

Gen. 14-15; 15-2.—
2 Sam. 8-5.
1 K. 11-24; 15-18;
" 19-15; 20-<2>34; <20>
2 K 5-12; 8-7; 14-28;
" 16-9;
1 Chron. 18-5;
2 " 16-2; 24-23; 28-5.
Songs Sol. 7-4; <Isa 7-8>
Isa 7-8; 8-4; 10-9; 17-1;
Jer. 49-23;
Eze. 27-18; 47-16;
Amos 1-3;
Zech. 9-1;
Acts 9-2 &c. 22-6;
2 Corin 11-32;
Gala 1-17.

Phenicia
Sidon.—Zidon.

Gen. 49-13;
Ezra 3-7;
Zech. 9-2;
Matt. 11-21; 15-21.

Mark 3-8; 7-24.
Luke 4-26; 6-17; 10-13.
Acts 12-19; 27-3.

Zidon—Zidonians.

Gen. 10-15 & 19.
Deut. 3-9;
Josh 11-8; 19-28;
Judge 1-31; 3-3; 18-28;
2 Sam. 24-6.
1 K 5-6; 11-1; 16-31; 17-19.
2 K 23-13;
1 Chron. 22-4;
Isa. 23-<6>2.
Jer. 25-22; 27-3; 47-4.
Ezek. 27-8; 28-22.
Joel 3-8;

Zor—Tyre (Phenicia.)

Josh. 19-29
2 Sam 5-11; 24-7.
1 K 5-1; 7-13; 9-11.
1 Chron. 14-1; 22-4.
2 〃 2-3;
Ezra 3-7;
Nehemiah 13-16;
Psalm 45-12; 83-7; 87-4;
Isa 23-1;
Jer. 25-22; 27-3; 47-4;
Ezek 26-3 &c.
Joel 3-8;
Amos 1-9;
Zechariah 9-2
Matt 11-21; 15-21;
Mark 3-8; 7-24;
Luke 6-17; 10-13.

Acts 12-20; 21-3;

Mount Carmel.

Josh 19-26;
1 K 18-19;
2 ″ 2-25; 4-25; 19-23
1 Chron 11-37;
Songs 7-5;
Isa 33-9; 35-2;
Jer 4-26; 50-19;
Amos 1-2; 9-3;
Nahum 1-4;

<Nazareth.>

Japhia.

Josh. 9-12.

Nazareth.

Matt 2-23; 4-13; 21-11;
Mark 1-9; 6-1;
Luke 2-4<->, 39, 51; 4-16;

Sea of Tiberias & town of
(Lake Genessareth—Sea of Galilee)
Sea of Cinneroth.

John 6-1, 23;
Matt 4-13, & 18; 8-18; 13-1; 14-25 15-19
Mark—1-16; 2-13; 3-7; 4-1; 5-21; 7-21.
Luke 8-23;
Josh 6-1; <2->21-1;

MAGDALA. (near Tiberias.

Matt 15-39;

CAPERNAUM (on Sea)

Matt 4-13; 8-5; 11-23; 16-24.
Mark—1-21; 2-1; 9-33;

Luke 4-23; & 31; 7-1; 10-15;
John 4-47; 6-17; & 24.

Bethsaida. (Julius near Sea of Gal.

Matt 11-21;
Mark 6-45; 8-22;
Luke 9-10; 10-13;
John 1-44; 12-21;

Chorazin (on S. Gal.

Matt 11-21;
Luke 10-13.

Hamath <[city in]>—*Hamath-Dor.*

Josh 19-35.

Mount Tabor.

Josh. 19-22;
Judg 4-6; 8-18;
Ps. 89-13;
Jer. 46-18;
Hosea 5-1;
Matt 17-1;
Mark 9-1<;>
Luke 9-38.

Jezreel (*Esdraelon*)

Josh 17-16; 19-18;
Judg 6.-33;
1 Sam 27-3; 29-11;
2 " 2-9; 4-4;
1 K 4-12; 18-45; 21-1;
(?) 2 K—8-29; 9-15 & 30.
2 Chron. 22-6;
Hosea 1-5.

Samaria.

1 K 13-32; 16-24 & 29; 18-2; 1-34 22-37;

2 K—1-2; 2-25; 16-19 & 24. <10-1 & 17.> 10-1 & 17; 13-1; 14-15; 17-9;
2 Chron. 18-2; <&> 25-13; 28-15.
Ezra 4-10;
Isa. 7-9; 10-9;
Jer. 23-13; 41-5;
Ezek. 16-53; 23-4;
Hosea 7-1; 10-5;
Amos 3-9;
Obadiah 19.
Micah 1-6.
Luke 7-11.
John 4-4.
<[-]> Acts 1-8; 8-1; 15-3.

Mount Ebal

Deut. 11-29; 27-4 & 13.
Josh 8-30;

Mount Gerizin

Deut. 11-29; 27-12;
Josh 8-33;
Judge 9-7.

Shiloh.=

Josh. 18-1; 21-2; 22-12;
Judge 18-31; 21-12 & 19.
1 Sam. 1-3 & 34; 3-21; 4-12; 14-3.
1 K 2-27; 11-29; 14-2;
Ps. 78-60;
Jer. 7-12; 26-9; 41-5;

<Bethel.>Beth-El. Luz. <Bethel.>

Gen. 11-8; 13-3; 28-19; 31-13; 35-1.
Josh. 7-2; 8-9; 12-9 & 16; 28-22.
Judge 1-22; 4-5; 20-31; 21-19.
1 Sam. 7-16; 10-3; 30-27.
1 K 12-29; 13-1; 16-34;

2 K 2-2; 10-29; 17-28; 23-15;
1 Chron. 7-28;
2 Chron. 13-19.
Ezra 2-28;
Nehemiah 7-32; 11-31;
Hosea 12-5;
Amos 3-14; 5-5; 7-10.

Beeroth.

Josh. 18-25;
2 Sam. 4-2; 23-37;
1 Chron 11-39;
Ezra 2-25;
Nehemiah 7-29;

(?) Deut. 10-6;
Josh 9-17. ?

Ramah. (*Saul*).

Josh. 18-25;
Judges 4-5; 19-13;
1 Sam. 1-19; 2-11; 7-17; 15-34; 16-13; 22-6; 25-1; 28-3;
1 K 15-17; and 21.
2 " 23-26;
2 Chron 16-1;
Ezra 2-26;
Nehemiah 7-30; 11-33;
Isa 10-29;
Jer. 31-15; 40-1;
Hosea 5-8.

Gibeah.—Gibeah Benjamin

<In Judah)—Josh. 15-57.>
Josh. 18-28;
Judge 19-12; 20-4;
1 Sam 7-1; 10-26; 11-4; 13-2; and 15. 14-16; 15-34; 22-6; 26-1;

2 Sam. 6-3; 21-6; 33-29;
1 Chron. 11-31; 12-3;
2 " 13-2;
Nehe. 12-29.
Isa. 10-29.
Hosea 5-8; 9-9; 10-9;

Jerusalem.
(Jebus—Salem—Benjamin.)

Joshua. 10-1; 12-10; 15-63; 18-28;
Judge 1-7;
2 Sam 5-6; 9-13; 11-12; 14-23; 16-16; 20-3; 24-8;
1 K. 2-11; 3-1; 8-11; 11-29; 12-18; 14-21; and 25;
2 K—8-17; 12-1; and 17; 16-5; 18-2; 21-13; 22-14; 23-30; 24-10; 25-1;
1 Chron. 3-5; 8-28; 11-4; 29-7;
2 " 12-2; 26-9; 33-13; 36-19;
Ezra—1-2; 3-1; 8-2;
Nehe—1-2; 2-11; 11-1;
Ps. 51-18; 79-1; <1-22> 122-3.
Songs 6-3;
Isa—1-1; 7-1; 10-12; 22-10; 36-2; 37-10; 64-10;
Jere. 1-15; 4-5; 11-2; 34-7; 52-4;
Lamentations 1-7;
Ezek—4-1; 8-3; 21-10;
Danl 1-1; 9-2<;>and 25;
Joel 3-6 and 22;
Amos 1-2; 2-5;
Obad. 20
Micah 1-9; 3-12;
Zecha^{r} 1-12; 8-3;
Matt 2-1; 3-5; 4-25; 5-35; 16-21; 20-17; 21-1 and 10;
Mark 1-5; 3-7 and 22; 10-32; 11-11 and 15.
Luke 1-22 and 42; 4-9; 9-51; 13-22. 23-7; 24-33;
John 2-13; 5-1;

Acts 1-4; 8-1; 9-26; 11-2; 15-2; 19-21; 21-15; 22-17; 25-1;
Romans 15-19 and 25;
1 Corin 16-3;
Gal 1-17; <and> 2-1.

<*Jericho*>Jericho
City-of-Palm-Trees—Ir-hatēmarin.

Numb 22-1; 33-48;
Deut 34-1;
Josh 2-1; 4-13; 5-10; 6-1; 12-9; 16-1 and 7; 18-12 and 21; 20-<2[-].>8
Judge 1-16; 3-13;
2 Sam. 10-5;
1 K 16-34;
2 " 2-4; and 18; 25-5;
1 Chron 19-5;
2 " 27-15;
Nehemia—3-2;
Jere <59-3> 39-5; 52-8;
Matt. 20-29;
Mark 10-46;
Luke 10-30; 18-35;
Hebrews 11-30.

The River Jordan

Gen. 13-10; 32-11; 50-10.
Numb 13-30; 22-1; 34-12;
Josh 16-7;
Judge 7-24; 8-4; 10-9;
1 Sam 13-7; 31-7;
2 " 2-29; 10-17; 17-22; 19-15; 24-5;
1 <Corin> Kings 2-8; 17-3;
2 K 2-6; 5-10; 6-2; 7-15; 10-33;
Jere 49-19;
Eze 47-18;
Zech 11-4;
Matt 3-5 and 13; 19-1;

Mark 1-5; 10-1;
Luke 3-3;
John 3-26; 10-40.

The Dead Sea. (Salt Sea.)

Gen. 14-3;
Deut 4-40;
Numb 32-12;
Josh 15-2 and 5; 18-19;
Zech 14-8;

Bethlehem of Judah—(Ephratah).

Gen 39-19; 48-7;
Judge 12-10; 17-7; 19-1;
Ruth 1-1; and 19;
1 Sam 16-4; 17-14; 20-6;
2 " <2-33;> 2-32; 23-14;
1 Chron 11-16;
2 " 11-6;
Nehem 7-26;
Jere 1-17;
Micah 5-1;
Matt 2-1, 5, 8 and 16;
Luke 2-4;
John 7-42;

Bethany or Bethabara.

John 1-28;
Matt. 26-6;
Mark 11-11; 14-3;
Luke 19-29; 24-50;
John 11-1; <an> 12-1.

Hebron (South of Jerusalem—Cave of Macpelah)—
<Kirgath>Kirjath-arba.

Gen. 13-18; 23-2 and 19; 35-<26>27; <a> 37-14.
Numb 13-23;

Josh 10-3; 11-21; 12-10; 14-14; 20-7;
Judge—1-10 and 20; 16-3;
1 Sam 30-31;
2 " 2-1 and 11, and 33; 3-20; 4-1 and 12; 5-1; 15-7;
1 K 2-11
<2 Sam>
1 Chron. 3-1; 6-57; 11-1; 29-7;
2 " 11-10.

Mizpeh (north of Jeru).

In Benjamin
Josh 18-26.
Judges 20-1; 21-1;
1 Sam 7-5;
1 K 15-22;
2 Chron 26-6;
Nehem 3-7 and 19;
Jere. 40-6.

(To Joppa)
Kirjath-<[-]>Je-arim—Ba-alah and Kirjath-Baal.

Josh 9-17; 18-15;
Judge 18-12;
1 Sam 6-21; 7-1;
1 Chron. 13-5;
2 " 1-4;
Nehem 7-29;
Jere 26-20.

Ajalon. Levit. city.

Josh 10-12;
Judge 1-35;
1 Sam 14-31;
1 Chron 6-69; 8-13;
2 " 11-10; 28-18; [#]

Emmaus.

Luke 24-13.

Gimzo.

Chron. 28-18.

<Ram> *Lydia.*

Acts 9-32.

Ramleh.

<J>Beth Dagon (Juda)

Josh 15-31.

Joppa. Japho. Jaffa.

Josh 19-46;
2 Chron 2-16;
Ezra 3-7;
<Joh> Jonah 1-3;
Acts 9-36.

Beirut.[3]

Baalbec.

<1st Day>

Damascus.

The oldest city in the world. No time for 4,000 years that there has not been a city here. Never has changed its name.

Tangier next. Cadiz or Athens next. [#]

[3] Clemens' projected Holy Land itinerary, which begins here, is separated from the preceding list of biblical citations by the entire breadth of the notebook, being written from what is correctly the front of the notebook toward the back. The itinerary is the longest block of entries in the notebook. Place names and running heads are used to identify the projected stages of Clemens' trip, and it seems probable that the headings were mapped out on successive pages of the notebook and the detailed notes added later. The headings "Beirut." and "Baalbec." are written at the tops of two successive leaves; Clemens clearly intended to provide historical and descriptive notes under each heading, as he did for subsequent headings.

An altar seen here by Ahaz & one like it set up in the Temple—2 Kings 16-10.

Its conquest threatened Jer. 49-23.

Destroyed, Isaiah 17-1.

Saul proceeded to it on his persecuting errand—Acts 9-2.

<1st D.>

Kishon*

<1st D>

Cana.

Matthew 10-4.
Mark 3-18
John 2-1, 4, 46

1st D[4]

Mount Carmel.

1 Kings, 18-21, 38—here 450 prophets of Baal were slain—40.

A sacred Mt. of Schr. Its top projects & overhangs the Mediterranean—2,000 high. Its name The Park of the Fruitful Field. One side the rich plains of Okka, the other the vale of Pharon. The excellence of Carmel is put by the side of Lebanon.—Elijah here brought Israel back to God.—The place, of of sacrifice of wh there is no doubt, is called El Murah-Kah.[5] The condition of the

---

[4] Clemens' planned itinerary centers on a five-day trip inland from Mount Carmel to Nazareth and south to Jerusalem. The *Quaker City*, originally scheduled to make two stops along the coast of Palestine, at Beirut and at Joppa, had added an intermediate stop at Haifa close by Mount Carmel in order to facilitate inland excursions to Nazareth. When he drew up this itinerary, Clemens clearly meant to take advantage of the stop at Mount Carmel; however, he discarded this plan almost immediately after the *Quaker City* docked at Beirut on 10 September. Clemens wrote to his family from Beirut on 11 September that he and seven of his *Quaker City* companions had decided instead to make the long inland trip from Beirut to Jerusalem on horseback (*MTL*, p. 136). Thus, Clemens completely bypassed Cana, the river Kishon, and Mount Carmel and rejoined the *Quaker City* finally at Joppa just before the ship left the Holy Land. The itinerary is accompanied by copious notes, most of which proved useless once Clemens' real itinerary was established. The notes were condensed from the Reverend D. A. Randall's *The Handwriting of God in Egypt, Sinai, and the Holy Land*, vol. 2.

[5] Clemens interlined the words "of sacrifice of" in an attempt to clarify his rather

mountain—the Kishon—the place where Deborah & Barak ruled over Sisera 3000 ago—their blood ran in this stream. Terrace of natural rock overhanging the plain—here are ruins w^h mark the spot of the sacrifice close by a fountain w^h supplied Elijah w^h water. Baal's altar was here—God's altar had been thrown down, his <people> prophets slain—3 yrs & 6 mos no rain. Ahab said art thou he that troubled Israel—No, but thou & thy father's house in that ye have forsaken the commandments of the Lord. [*blank*] Now gather Israel unto Carmel & the prophets of Baal 450 & the prophets of the grove 400, which eat at Jezebel's table. Face to face they contend, & Elijah's God answers by fire—altar of 12 stones —one for each tribe—the wood—the sacrifice in order—the water— answer by fire—what results—the prayer, the sacrifice & all concerned. The prophets of Baal brought to the river Kishon & slain & the name of God vindicated—then the prayer for rain—the rain came. The apostle 1000 yrs afterward, refering to this, said, The effectual, fervent prayer of the righteous man availeth much.

End 1st Day

Nazareth.

Mark 1-9.
Luke 4-29
John 1-46
Luke 2-51; 4-16

Here Christ preached, & an attempt was made to put him to death.

1 day

Can there any good thing come out of Nazareth?[6] The *home*

---

obscure sentence, but the resulting construction is hardly more understandable. Clemens was drawing on Randall's remarks about Mount Carmel: "Tradition points out the very spot where the altar was erected and the strange events transpired, and the tradition seems to be well sustained. It is called El Mura-kah, *'the Sacrifice'* " (*Handwriting of God*, 2:322).

[6] Clemens' notes on Nazareth, condensed from Randall's remarks, are here and there interrupted by Clemens' own ideas for developing an *Alta* letter about Nazareth. The completed *Alta* letter (*TIA*, pp. 248–253) makes use of much of the information in these notes and expands considerably Clemens' satirical interjection about grottoes. Clemens did not incorporate the sketch of Christ's childhood into

of Joseph & Mary, where Jesus spent his early life,—walked & talked & taught. The *fountain of the* Virgin. Church of the Annunciation. Naz is built of stone—upon a hill,—substantial. English Mission school in wh are children whose parents were murdered recently by the Druses.

Latin Convent & Church—the church covers the ancient home of Jos & Mary—down 15 steps into a grotto in the hill-side—(they run a good many grottoes—well, grottos are durable—but an infernal piece of cheek to &c) in it is a beautiful altar—<[----]>Mary said to have stood there & received the <a>Annunciation. Staircase to *Mary's kitchen*—the *workshop of Joseph* transformed into a chapel —here Christ worked at his trade.

"J. Christ & <Co.> Son, Carpenters & Builders."

Recall infant Christ's pranks on his school-mates—striking boys dead—withering their hands—burning the dyer's cloth &c.

"Joseph of Arimathea, Carpenter."

"Orders executed with promptness & dispatch.—Particular attention given to thrones &c."

The Synagogue where Christ read the Schriptures now a Christian cch! (Withered teacher's hand & wouldn't say his letters.) The hill where the multitude intended to cut him down.

The hill in the rear of the town where an extensive view can be had—Tabor—Hermon—Carmel—Esdraelon—one's thoughts run on the boyhood of Christ so connected with these scenes. Here his mother marked the sayings of the Christ (Harper 4-yr old)[7] & pondered them in her heart.

2d Day **TRANSFIGURATION.**

Mt. Tabor.

Here <Bark>Barak assembled his army.

Judges 5 4-6, 14, 15.—[#]

---

the published piece, though the idea of writing such a sketch evidently interested him (see Notebook 9, p. 426).

[7] One of the most popular departments of the monthly *Harper's Magazine* was the humorous "Editor's Drawer," which frequently printed examples of the precocious utterances of four- and five-year-old children.

Supposed to be that on which Christ was transfigured.
Matt. 17-1.
Mark 9-2.
Luke 9-28
Therefore called by Peter the Holy Mount—2 Pet. 1-18.

Tabor in the distance—an isolated town in the plain of Esdraelon—on top, ruins since Joshua & Crusades. Here Deborah, by direction of God gathered 10,000 men under command of Barak—Judges<.>5. Bonapart, Kleber, with 3000 men engaged 27,000. Napoleon from Tabor, drove them back upon Murat's cavalry. Jesus took Peter, James, & John—while praying, his garment became white & shining—& there appeared Moses & Elijah from heaven talking with him—The <la>great lawgiver Elijah, the chief of the prophets—the cloud &c.

End of 2^{d} Day

Tiberias. (Sea of.)

John 6-23-1.
Matt. 8, 18–27.
Mark 4, 35–41.
Luke 8. 22–25. & 9th, 57–62.

3^{d} Day.

Endor.

1st Saul[8] 28.-7.—The Witch.

Nain.

Where Christ restored to life the widow's son.
Luke 7-8. 11.

3^{d} Day

<Jer>Jezreel (now Zerin)

South border of <Isachar>Issachar.
Josh 19-18.—Abner made Ishbosheth King over it. 2 Saul 2-9.

---

[8] Clemens is referring to the Book of Samuel. He corrects his citation finally on page 479.14.

Ahab had his palace in it—1 Kings 21-1.
The dogs ate Jezebel by the wall 23.
2 Kings 9-30–37.
Threatening Jehu Hos. 1-4.

3^{d} D.

Ain Jelude or Fountain of Jefrell ½ hour's ride from Jezreel Judges—8.

Shunem (now called Salem)—near Little Hermann.—2 K. 14.

3^{d} D

Mount Gilboa

Slaughter of Saul & Jonathan—1st Saul <3->31-1–6. 2 Saul 1-21.

Jenin.

End of 3^{d}.

4th D

Dothan.

Where Joseph's brethren sold him—
Gen. 37-17.
2 K 6-13.
The Syrians came to take Elijah the prophet.

4th D

Samaria.

1 K 16-24
2 " 6-24
Released by the flight of the Enemy. 7-6.
Taken by the Assyrians 18-9.
A mixture of different nations settle in it—17-24.
The country of the Ephraimites—1 K—13-32.
Luke 17-11
John—4-4.
Acts 8-1, 5, 14.
Luke—9-52, 53.
John 4-9.—8-48. [#]

4th D. End of 4th

Shechem.

Gen. 34-2; 4-12, 25; 33-19 50 13—C 24, 1 &c
John 4-5.

End of 4th

D 5th

Joseph's Tomb.

Joseph came came to this field, where is his tomb, in search of his brother.

Josh 24-32.

Joseph, when closing his eyes in death, said, "God will assuredly visit you & bring you out of this land, unto the land which he sware to Abraham, Isaac & to Jacob. There & then he exacted of them an oath that they would carry up his bones with them when they went out of Egypt.

"And the bones of Joseph, which the children of Israel brought up out of Egpt, buried they in Shechem, in a parcel of ground which Jacob bought of the sons of Hamor the father of Shechem, for a hundred pieces of silver—Josh 24-32.

At the base of Ebal is a little square area inclosed by a <hight> [li]ght[9] stone wall, neatly whitewashed—across one end of this enclosure is a Moslem tomb—the tomb of Joseph.

Samaritan & Jew, Moslem & Christian alike revere it, & honor it with their visits. The tomb of Joseph *the dutiful son., the affnate, forgiving brother, the virtuous man, the wise prince & ruler*. Egpt felt his <his> influence—the world knows his history.

5th D.

Jacob's Well

How many historic assons cluster around it! Here patriarchs

[9] The manuscript reading is unclear; however, the corresponding passage in Randall's *Handwriting of God* supplies the correct meaning: "toward the base of Ebal . . . a little square area, inclosed by a high stone wall, neatly whitewashed" (2:286).

watered their flocks—here Jesus rested & refreshed himself. It is just at the opening of the valley, between Gerezim & Ebal—it is 9 × 90 feet—an excavation into the solid limestone rock—it is hewn smooth & regular. An excavation 10 □ & 10 deep has been made about the mouth, walled up & arched over, making a vault or chamber over the mouth of the well. Here Christ talked with the woman (John 4-10.) This renowned parcel of ground was bought by Jacob of the children of Hamor <for> near 800 years before Christ for 100 pieces of money. It has lately been bought by the Greeks (had its value increased?—had real estate advanced?) & they have begun to make improvements around it.

This is an interesting spot. Here Jesus rested on his journey from Jerusalem to Galilee, while his disciples went to the city to buy meat. <(Try some of that meat.)> 2,000 years have not changed the scenery, & the customs of the inhabitants remain the same.—women with water pots on their heads. This well, these mountains, yonder city were looked upon by the Savior.

The old MSS of the Samaritans in the synagogue here done up in the form of a scroll, kept in an elegant silver case rolled in cloth of blue, purple & scarlet interwoven with threads of gold,—the transcriber's imprint is <interwoven> wrought in one portion of the scroll into the text in<to> the form of an acrostic & reads: "Written by Abishua, son of Phineas, son of Eleazar, son of Aaron."

5th Day

Old Shiloh (or Seilum)

Gen. <4->49-10
Josh—18-1, 8, 10[—18,-1], 19, 51.
Judges

One half hour from the main road the place is an utter desolation—it was once the centre of worship & the great rallying place of the tribes of Israel. A valley, perhaps a quarter of a mile broad, with sloping sides, forms the main feature. Projecting from the ridge, on one side of this, is a round-topped hillock presenting from one point of view the appearance of a small hill standing in the centre of the valley. 2 On this great natural mound was no doubt the sanctuary of God. The ark was brought from Gilgal to this place, & here it stood during all the time of the Judges, until the days of Eli the High Priest. Upon this site are the ruins of an old stone building. A Moslem tomb of a shiek is in the midst of the ruins.

The ark remained here for 300 years. This, therefore, cannot be common ground. That wonderful tabernacle, that holy ark built at the base of Sinai & carried with such devoted reverence was here permanently located in the very heart of the country. 3 Here the tribes gathered under Joshua when the land was divided among them.

4. Here Hannah dedicated Samuel her son to God. "For this child I prayed, & the Lord hath given me my petition,. Therefore, also, I have lent him to the Lord as long as he liveth." Here Samuel grew up amid the scenes of the Sanctuary, to honor his parents & bless his country.

5—Here Eli for a long time was high priest,—though an amiable man & well disposed, he was negligent & inefficient in the discharge of many of his duties. His 2 sons grew up in iniquity unrestrained by parental authority (like the sons of preachers generally).

The Lord signally rebuked his neglect (but which the text signally fails to show it—the armies didn't fight well, & now they want to blame it all on old Eli—the ark <catch> come-off wouldn't wash.) The armies of Israel were smitten by the Philistines (the Shepherd Kings) & they said—"It is because we have not the ark of God with us." They sent to Shiloh, & contrary to all precedent, took the ark from its place (they were playing their last trump,) in the tabernacle, placed it at the head of the army & again went out to battle. But Israel had sinned & god was not with them (or maybe they hadn't a good general).

6. And now by the gate of this city Eli, still anxious for the honor of Israel, & the safety of the ark, sat waiting & watching for tidings from the field. A runner comes: "Israel is smitten before the Philistines!" (Heavy news) "There hath been a great slaughter & 30,000 of our men have perished, & lo there is no San. Com." (Worse

& worse) "Thy two sons are slain!" Still the old man stood his hand. "Now, holy priest, call all thy courage up & summon all <the>thy fortitude: The Ark of God is taken Captive!"[10]

The old man passed. This was the beloved ark before which he had sprinkled the sacrificial blood for a generation—it was the glory of Israel—it was her citadel, her tower of strength. When he heard this he fell from his seat & brake his neck. The ark never returned to this place. Israel ceased to gather here. Here in this beautiful valley & along these sloping hill-sides thousands could have been congregated & all have been in the immediate vicinity & within sight of the Tabernacle of God.

7. Rape of the Sabines—(the Original.) This valley, in the days of the Judges, was made the scene of a singular adventure by the remnant of the Benjaminites who escaped from the frightful massacre with w[h] their brethren had been visited by the other tribes for e horrid crime perpetrated at Gibeal. Their women had all been slain & the other tribes had all bound themselves by an oath that they would not give them daughters for wives. Knowing that <e> the daughters of Shiloh had an annual festival in honor of the ark, by the connivance of e elders, 200 young B's hid themselves in the vineyards on these hillsides & while the Shiloh wenches were engaged in their open festivities, they suddenly sprang upon them & each man siezed a damsel & bore her away as his wife. [#]

---

10 Clemens' notes follow Randall's spritely remarks very closely—there are only rare interjections from Clemens himself. Randall's version of the episode above reads:

> And now by the gate of this city, Eli, still anxious for the honor of Israel and the safety of the ark, sat waiting for tidings from the battle-field. A runner approaches, and cautiously announces the result: "Israel is smitten before the Philistines." Heavy news for the man of God. "There has been a great slaughter, and thirty thousand of our men have perished." Worse and worse. "Thy two sons, Hophni and Phineas, are slain." Alas, those wicked sons; what a blow to an aged parent's heart; but still the old man could bear up under it. "And the Ark of God is taken captive." (*Handwriting of God,* 2:273)

Clemens' only contribution to the account was the runner's speech " '& lo there is no San. Com.' " In 1863 and 1864, writing for the *Territorial Enterprise* and the San Francisco *Call,* Clemens had reported on the efforts of the United States Sanitary Commission to raise funds for the relief of wounded soldiers.

5th D.

Gilgal.

Where the Israelites were circumcised. Josh. 5-2—

A place of idolatrous worship. Amos 4-4—5-5.

The Israelites passed miraculously over Jordan in the month of April, when the river is supposed to have been 1200 feet wide & 14 deep, & encamped at Gilgal, on the opposite plain of Jericho, to renew the ancient rite of circumcision. Here they ate of the old corn of the land, & here the manna ceased. Josh V.

5th D.

Bethel.

House of God—so called by Jacob—Gen. 28-19.—built an altar many years after—35-1, 6, 7—

Visited yearly by Saul—<1 Saul> 1 Saml 7-16.

Here Jeroboam set up his idol calf—1 K. 12-28, 29.

It is a long, low ridge, covered with great piles of stones—about 3 or 4 acres of ground are covered with <[vines.]> ruins. A few miserable huts—20 in all—constructed from fragments of the ruins, constitute the village.

In the valley, a little west, is a huge cistern, built of massive stone—one side is in good preservation, the other much dilapidated by the ravages of time. Its bottom is now a beautiful grass plat. Near by are two small fountains of pure clear water, from which this great tank was originally supplied.

Originally it was called Luz. Abraham, in his first journey through the land, & built an altar & worshiped God. On <th> his return from Egp he could not forget the rich pastures & their refreshing springs of water<,>. <rich>Rich in cattle, in silver & in gold, he returned to this altar & again called upon the name of the Lord. Here his flocks roamed—here the Maidens of Sarah came to fill their pitchers.

Here in these pasture grounds began the strife between Abraham & Lot's herdsmen, & here the old patriarch made that munificent offer to Lot:

"Let there be no strife, I pray thee, between thee & me, & between my herdsmen & thy herdsmen, for we be brethren. Is not the whole land before thee? Separate thyself, I pray thee, from me. If thou wilt take to the left hand, I will take to the right—or if thou depart to the right hand, I will go to the left." Lot looked down upon the beautiful plain of the Jordan & chose himself a residence among those cities which now lie buried the bitter waters of the Dead Sea.

Here the Lord promised Abraham this land: <(pre> "Lift up now thine eyes & look from the place where thou art, northward, & southward & eastward & westward,—for all the land which thou seest to thee will I give it, & to thy seed forever. Gen. XIII. So the old man went in & pre-empted <it> a county or two.

Time passed on—Abe rested in the Cave of Macpelah, & Isaac saw his sons growing up around him. A lone traveler is seen passing along this valley, his staff in his hand. (There was no style about Jacob.) He has made a long journey from Beersheba, 40 miles, & was necessarily pretty well fagged out. Night gathers around him—he takes a stone for a pillow—(Jacob was not particular) the hard earth for his bed (hard, but roomy) & the broad canopy of the heavens for his covering (he had enough, anyway, though there was too much wind under it for comfort on a cold night.) <He> Why was he traveling <so,> in that sort of style & his grandfather so rich? He had a long journey of near 500 miles before him. He was in the vigor of life, & though his fare was scanty & his pillow hard, he had a stout heart & was favored with pleasant dreams. He saw a ladder set upon the earth, & the top of it reached to Heaven!—& behold the angels of God ascending & descending upon it! Above that ladder he saw the vision of the Holy One, & heard a voice: "I am the Lord God of Abraham thy father & the God of Isaac; the land whereon thou liest, to thee will I give it & to thy seed. And here the promise was made him that he should be kept in all his ways, & brought again in safety to this land. He awoke from this strange vision. "Surely," said he, "the Lord <in>is in this place & I knew it not—How dreadful is this place!—this is none other but the house of God & the Gate of Heaven!"

Early in the morning Jacob rose up took the stone he had used for a pillow, set it up for a memorial & dedicated it to the Lord—& he called the name of that place Bethel—<house of the>House God.

Time passed on—J returned with wife children servants flocks & herds,. Again the Lord appeared unto him: "Arise, go up to Bethel, & make there an altar unto God. Again J & all his houshold dwelt upon this ground—again he built an altar & worshiped God

And he called the place El Bethel—God the house of God.

So, when Jacob wanted a farm, he only had to dream.

Here Deborah, Rebecca's nurse, died & they buried her beneath Bethel under an oak. What a history this place has! How strange to stand here on the camping grounds of the patriarchs!—

Bethel, in Josh's time was a royal city & governed by a King.

Here Samuel held one of his circuit courts (was *he* a circuit Judge?) when he traveled the circuit & judged Israel

The Ark (of the Covenant (not Noah's) seems to have been kept here at one time.

In the separation of the kingdom after the death of Solomon, Jeroboam fearing to have his people go up to Jerusalem to worship lest they should go back to their old allegiance, established idolatrous worship, <[no]> made 2 golden calves, set one up in Dan the other in Bethel. Here he built a MAGNIFICENT TEMPLE after an Egp model, intending to RIVAL THE ONE AT JERUSALEM. Such was the idolatrous worship that the name was changed to Beth-avan, House of Idols.

It was at one of those idolatrous festivals that Jeroboam attempted to lay hold of prophet of God who rebuked his abominable worship & his arm was paralyzed & withered. These iniquities drew down the wrath of God upon the place, & 2500 yrs ago the prophet Amos was inspired to say: "Seek not Bethel, nor enter into Gilgal—for Gilgal shall surely go into captivity, & Bethel shall come to nought."

Look upon these heaps of ruins, these broken <ciscerns>cisterns, these neglected vallys—has the prophecy been fulfilled whose handwriting is here! [11]

---

[11] The preceding comments on Bethel derive from Randall's *Handwriting of God* (2:265–269). The following notes on Bethel are Clemens' own. Credulous accounts like Randall's contributed greatly to Clemens' disillusionment with the

And with the same propriety you might point to the site of *any* city of that day & say the very same—only Jerusalem & Damascus have survived—& even the Jerusalem & Damascus of that day are desolate enough, goodness knows, for they lie 30 feet under ground! All the other cities are gone! There is a good deal of humbug about proving prophecies by this sort of evidence.

It is easy to prove a prophecy that promised destruction to a city—& it is impossible to prove one that promised *any* thing else—more particularly <long> life & property.

It seems to me that the prophets fooled away their time when they prophecied the desolation of cities.—old Time <w[il]>would have fixed that, easy enough.

—Solomon's Temple was not to have one stone resting upon another—but <Mr. Prime> infatuated travelers of the present day are determined to believe, in spite of prophets, Holy Writ & everything else, that they have found the foundations of Solomon's doomed temple! Possibly they can reconcile this with prophecy by saying it is only the ground layer they have found!

I can go as far as the next man, in genuine reverence of holy things—but this thing of stretching the narrow garment of belief till it fits the broad shoulders of a wish, is too much for my stomach. Especially do I copper those flimsy proofs of prophecy like the desolation of Bethel.

5 D

Beroth or Bireh

One of the 4 cities of the crafty Gibeonites. It is at present a considerable village. Piles of old ruins attract the attention—among them a fine old Gothic church, large portion of the walls of which are standing, another hoary monument of the days of Crusaders & Knights Templars.

5 D—

Gibeon or El Gib.

This place is spoken of in the O T. as "a great city—one of the

---

Holy Land. His own letters dwell on the shabby reality of the place and on the paltry proofs of sanctity offered to the traveler.

royal cities." Here lived the people when the Israelites invaded the land, gathered their old tattered garments, & worn-out shoes, packed their sacks with musty bread & came with their hungry, jaded animals & beguiled Joshua & the elders into a treaty of peace. It was a clever trick & evinced great shrewdness.

It is a small village, now, but great in historic interest. In the plain below, the five kings of the Amorites assembled together to punish Gibeon. Toward Gilgal, eastward, Joshua & his host encamped. The Amorites are defeated, the day is not long enough for Israel to continue the conquest, & Joshua gives that ever-memorable command: "Sun stand thou still on Gibeon, & thou moon in the valley of Ajalon." And the sun stood still, & the moon also, until Israel was avenged.

On the East side of the hill is the pool or spring. There is first, a natural cavity or grotto in the rock,—then an inner chamber has been excavated, which is entered by a low, narrow opening down several <sto>steps of stone. Here a copious fountain gushes apparently from the rock—a little below it on the hill-side are the ruins of a large reservoir. It was here that a remarkable meeting took place between Abner & Joab—they were <both> generals of the <army>armies of Israel & Judah.—12 men of Judah were challenged to fight 12 men of Israel. The whole 24 were slain. "For they caught every one his fellow by the head (got him in chancery,) & thrust his sword in his fellow's side, so that they fell down together." And on that plain the subsequent battle took place. Abner was defeated & the swift footed Asahel slain.

At this city also, David's nephew, Amasa, was slain, by his cousin Joab.

Here, too, on Gibeon, Solomon offered up his 1000 burnt offerings, & here the Lord appeared to him in a dream & gave him the desire of his heart—"Wisdom & Understanding."

5 D.

Ajalon

Is west of Gibeon & commences at the base of Gibeon & Beroth & runs west from that point. [#]

Mizpeh.

Signifies "a place of look-out." It is the Ramathaim-zaphim, the place of birth, residence <& death of> & burial of Samuel.

Israel made a solemn vow here never to return to their homes until they punished Gibea for the crime committed in <their>that city.

Here the prophet called them on another occasion. (the Philistines which they done)

And "Samuel took a stone & set it between Mizpeh & Shem, calling it "Ebenezer" saying "Hitherto hath the Lord <[-]>helped us."

Here Israel elected their King, Saul. Here the first shout went up, "God save the King!"

The Crusaders built a church here & its ruins are yet visible.

The Chaldean Governor lived here during the Babylonian captivity & was assassinated by the Jews.

Here Richard I looked upon Jerusalem & buried his face in his armor, saying, "Ah Lord God, I pray that I may never see the Holy City if I may not rescue it from thine enemies."

The antiquity of this place, &c make it one of the most interesting points around Jerusalem. It at present a poor little village with an old ruined Mosque. Ascend Minaret.

5

Gibeah—now called Suliel El Ful.

"The Hill of Bans." It is a round-topped hill about 3 miles north of Jerusalem.

This city gave the Israelites their first king.

It was the home of Saul & the seat of his government during a great part of his reign. It is now a heap of ruins.

On this little hill the Amorites of Gibeon hanged the 7 descendants of Saul in revenge for the massacre of their brethren.

Here the tragedy of the destruction of the concubines occurred, which was avenged by the other tribes & which almost destroyed the tribe of Benjamin—Judge 20 & 21[c.]

Here occurred one of the most touching instances of maternal tenderness on record. <B>Rizpah, the mother of 2 of the descendants of Saul, that were hanged here & left to rot upon the gallows, mourned her loss, "& took sackcloth & spread it upon the rock for herself, from the beginning of harvest until water dropped from the heavens upon them, & suffered neither the birds of the air to rest upon them by day nor the beasts of the field by night." "It must have been a mournful spectacle to see this <beautiful> bereaved mother sitting by the *wasting skeletons* of her sons, through the long days of a whole Assyrian summer, from the beginning of harvest in April till the first rains in autumn."[12]

Holy Land.—[13]

It is <h>so long ago, now, that I do not remember what we did <in Jerusalem> after the morning that Dr Birch & I went to the Pool of Bethesda to get a flask of the water. We visited the Baths of Hezekiah, where <Solomon> David saw & fell in love with Uriah's wife while she was bathing—also occasionally to the Church of the Holy Sepulchre—and around about the traditional houses of Pilate, Caiaphas, Dives & Lazarus.—& poked through the Via Dolorosa & so forth & so on—& got a most infernal Turkish bath one night—nothing to the baths of Damascus & Constantinople. These thieves don't like to wash Christians, I think.

* took his wife to <th>dinner at the Mediterranean Hotel one

---

[12] Clemens' notes are quoted from Randall's description of Gibeah (*Handwriting of God*, 2:185–186). The quotation about Rizpah's mourning for her slain sons is from 2 Samuel 21:10. The remainder of this entry, which Clemens evidently copied from Randall's book where it appears without a source, is from another popular Holy Land guidebook, *A Handbook for Travellers in Syria and Palestine*, 2 vols. (London: John Murray, 1858), 2:326.

[13] These Holy Land notes were evidently written during Clemens' second visit to Jerusalem, around 27 September, and they are the only personal notes about the trip which appear in this notebook. Clemens and four of his companions, Dan Slote, Jack Van Nostrand, Julius Moulton, and Dr. Birch, had hurried ahead of the rest of the overland party. They first reached Jerusalem on 23 September and, after a rather hectic day of sight-seeing, had set off on a three-day excursion to the sacred places surrounding the city. They returned to Jerusalem on the afternoon of 27 September and stayed two days before rejoining the *Quaker City* at Joppa.

night when we were there (they still <lef> live in their tents outside the Damascus Gate), & <af> came in himself after all the courses were served but dessert & coffee, & tried to get off from paying because he had not eaten a full meal. The old Dutchman made him pay, though, & served him right.[14]

Major Barry, Griswold, & party have been down to Jericho, the ford of the Jordan & the Dead Sea, & were attacked by a gang of Bedouins—a shot or two was fired—nobody hurt, but Griswold scared a good deal.

Leary's party[15] was threatened with a raid, one night, somewhere down there by the Fountain where the ravens fed Elisha, & had to decamp.

We are the crowd so far, that have gone to these localities unmolested<.>—weren't worth robbing, maybe.

The officers of the gunboat Swatara, who went from Smyrna to Ephesus with us, are here in Jerusalem. That is as much as to say that we are having a rather high time here in the hotel for such a slow old camp as the Holy City.

Left Jerusalem at 3½ in the afternoon and got away[16]

Curse their cursed carelessness to leave that dead-light open. Spoiled the cushions & everything—all the cigars in the locker & tobacco. It never seems to occur to them that ours is the weather side of the ship *sometimes*.[17] [#]

---

[14] The Mediterranean Hotel was described by Murray's guidebook: "*The Mediterranean*, kept by Hornstein, . . . is a large and commodious house, well situated near the British Consulate, and not far from the Damascus gate. The reports are favourable of the landlord's civility and attention to the comforts of his guests" (*A Handbook for Travellers in Syria and Palestine*, rev. ed., 2 vols. [London: John Murray, 1868], 1:73).

[15] The *Quaker City* passengers had split into several parties, some traveling the inland route from Haifa to Jerusalem and others steaming down the coast to Joppa aboard the *Quaker City* and then making an inland excursion to Jerusalem; only Clemens' party attempted the long overland route from Beirut to Jerusalem. The various parties occasionally crossed each other in their journeys.

[16] The Clemens party left Jerusalem for the coast on 29 September in order to board the *Quaker City* at Joppa.

[17] Clemens had written a similar note on 14 June (Notebook 8, p. 335), al-

<8>7—Bells—All hands on deck to pump ship!
Buttrw—You'll excuse *me*—(goes below.)

Gent & 1st Maid—Oh, how lovely, how serene the night is!—the sea is like a mirror it is <to> so smooth!

Enter Buttrw—(Drunk—Hic! Heavy sea again!—Plymouth Collection—*ain't* they never going to let up!

Gent & 1 Maid converse & he comments.

<8>6—Bells—Buttr—By geminy it ain't been forty minutes since that blame clock struck 5—I never

Butrw—How does she head, ship met
E.N.E & by Nothe ¾ nothe—
Well she's <[-]>crooked I should think—

Humph! ain't trying to get the ship along at all—no sails up.
Wh—Sails, you d'd fool & the wind dead ahead.[18]

House of Rep's—reading the Message—undignified resolution offered by Gen Logan [19] [#]

---

though the tone of this entry, probably written after boarding the *Quaker City* at Joppa, is considerably more exasperated. Fourteen blank pages intervene between this entry and the preceding one.

[18] These entries (p. 487.1–14) are evidently part of an unfinished play about the excursion. Clemens sent another attempt to Charles Henry Webb from Washington on 25 November 1867: "I send the inclosed to show you that I had the *will* to do that thing—but I haven't the time. . . . If you were *here* to stir me up, we could do the play, sure" (Henry W. and Albert A. Berg Collection, New York Public Library). Webb probably received the two acts of the play that are now in the J. K. Lilly Collection, Indiana University Library. This material appears in Dewey Ganzel's *Mark Twain Abroad* on pages 310–317. The burlesque character "Buttrw" in the notebook fragment does not appear in the incomplete manuscript, nor is there any indication Clemens planned to incorporate the notebook fragment into the play.

[19] This entry and the following ones through "Beautiful sky, view—& Indian summer." were written on the front flyleaf of the notebook but have been moved to their present position because of their obvious association with the notes on Congress which follow them here.

When Clemens arrived in Washington on 21 or 22 November 1867, the first session of the Fortieth Congress was in its final days. The second, or regular, session of the Fortieth Congress opened 2 December 1867. The following day, when President Andrew Johnson's annual message to the Congress was read in the House,

Westward the *Course* of Empire takes its way—on Cal picture with Diablio on r. h. because intervening hills on l. h.[20]

Whisky taken into Com rooms <by> in demijohns & carried out in demagogues.

Beautiful sky, view—& Indian summer.

Jennie German—Brumidi—passes as his wif.[21]

Horace Greeley
crowded around him

Reverdy Jonson[22] [#]

Representative John A. Logan of Illinois facetiously offered a resolution to the House concerning President Johnson's remarks about the possibility of a "violent collision" between the executive and legislative branches of the government. Logan's resolution suggested that the "corps of pages that now constitute the 'military force' of this House be . . . abolished, to the end that the civil conflict so vividly described in [President Johnson's message] may be avoided" (*The Congressional Globe for the Second Session Fortieth Congress*, pt. 1 [Washington, D.C.: Office of the Congressional Globe, 1868], p. 12).

[20] One of the most admired paintings in the Capitol was Leutze's immense canvas depicting in heroic terms the advance of the wagon trains across the Rockies. Over the painting were inscribed the words, "Westward the course of empire takes its way," the opening line of the final stanza of Bishop Berkeley's "Verses on the Prospect of Planting Arts and Learning in America." Clemens' emphasis of the word *course* was probably due to the fact that the line was frequently misquoted as "Westward the star of empire takes its way," a misreading popularized by its appearance as an epigraph on the early editions of George Bancroft's *History of the United States*.

[21] Italian painter Constantino Brumidi executed the fresco in the dome of the Capitol, a work which Mark Twain would describe in chapter 24 of *The Gilded Age* as the "delirium tremens of art." Washington journalist Frank G. Carpenter commented on the fresco: "in the dome is Brumidi's famous fresco, with Washington on the right and Victory on the left, and with thirteen female figures representing the thirteen original states. . . . The artists [*sic*] is said to have been a free liver, and the story is told that the thirteen fair faces which look down into the Rotunda include those of certain ladies of questionable reputation with whom he was acquainted" (*Carp's Washington* [New York: McGraw-Hill Book Co., 1960], p. 143). Jennie German has not been identified, although she may have been among the "thirteen fair faces" mentioned.

[22] Democratic senator from Maryland and constitutional lawyer Reverdy John-

Fame is a vapor—popularity an accident—the only earthly certainty oblivion.[23]

Sherman—
Hunt Indians—hadn't lost any.

A J. Moulder[24] married—in Ph. Head Ass Press S F Herald.—[Head]

Ill . . . . 450[25]
Benn 400
Ind
Ohio Clerks
Mass
N.Y.

Pac. Coast 12 in all the Depts—& polie

R I [#]

---

son was one of the influential figures in Congress who worked effectively against the impeachment of President Andrew Johnson.

[23] This entry was written very lightly in pencil; it was then traced over, probably by Albert Bigelow Paine, for legibility. The entry was among those gleaned from the notebook for chapters 9 and 10 of Paine's selections published as *Mark Twain's Notebook*.

[24] Andrew Jackson Moulder was on the staff of the San Francisco *Herald* and was promoted to associate editor of that paper in 1853. He was subsequently elected comptroller of San Francisco and served for a number of years as state superintendent of public instruction. Moulder accepted a position with the New York Associated Press in 1865. In his letter from Washington of 10 December 1867 (*Alta*, 15 January 1868) Clemens noted that Moulder "formerly of the San Francisco *Herald*, was married the other day in Philadelphia, and will shortly arrive here to be chief of the Associated Press for Washington."

[25] Clemens probably made these notes on 26 November 1867, when Representative Carman A. Newcomb of Missouri offered a resolution to the House. Clemens' letter from Washington of 14 December 1867 (*Alta*, 21 January 1868) concerning government salaries and clerkships demonstrates his use of these notes:

> These Departments are crowded with clerks and other small Government fish. Illinois heads the list. She furnishes four hundred and fifty of them! Whenever an official tooth needs filling, Mr. Washburne always stands ready with an

Washburn of Ill—[26]

Newcomb Res^{n}—Had many clerks—s[alry]—how long—What State—what Congrs Dist recommended.

1 P.M.
Reverdy Jonson

—Drakes Resn <of> condemning tone & lang of Mess[27] [#]

Illinois plug. . . . Pennsylvania comes next. She furnishes four hundred. Indiana comes next; then Ohio, then Massachusetts, and then the great State of New York! Rhode Island, which is so small that the inhabitants have to trespass on other States when they want to take a walk, furnishes more than the whole Pacific Coast put together. Oregon, California, Nevada, Utah, Arizona, and Washington Territory furnish *twelve*, all told. . . . But Mr. Newcomb, of Missouri, has just introduced a resolution into Congress, inquiring how many clerks are employed in the various Departments, how long they have held their offices, what salaries they get, and what Congressional Districts they were recommended from. This will make a stir; and if there were an inquiry added of how much these clerks do, and how much they don't do, the stir would become an absolute flutter. As it was, Mr. Washburne jumped to his feet and objected to the measure, and so it had to lie over under the rule.

26 Clemens' circled direction "over" appears above this entry, apparently indicating that material related to this or nearby entries was intended for the back of the notebook leaf. The entries "A J. Moulder . . . lang of Mess" (pp. 489.5–490.6) are on the front and "Jim Farley . . . sanguine expc—" (pp. 491.1–6) on the back of the notebook leaf.

27 President Johnson's annual message created a furor in Congress. The message had been secretly sold to the press before its official reading in Congress; the president's detractors claimed that the press release had the president's sanction and that an insult had thereby been offered to Congress. In the Senate, on 4 December 1867, Charles Drake of Missouri offered a resolution condemning the language of the message, language which was "calculated to derogate from the rightful authority of the law-making power of the nation and to incite insubordination, if not violent resistance, to laws which it is his duty as President to 'take care shall be faithfully executed.' " The message, Drake stated, constituted "a departure from official propriety, and a breach of official obligation" (*The Congressional Globe for the Second Session Fortieth Congress*, pt. 1, p. 19). Clemens' 4 December 1867 letter to the *Territorial Enterprise* (22 December 1867) mentioned the possible effects of the message: "The President's Message is making a howl among the Republicans—serenity sits upon the brow of Democracy. The Republican Congressmen say it is insolent to Congress; the Democrats say it is a mild, sweet document, free from guile. But one thing is very sure: the message has weakened the President. Impeachment was dead, day before yesterday. It would rise up and make a strong fight to-day if it were pushed with energy and tact."

Jim Farley Speaker of Lower House[28]

Maj. Bicknell, of Tenn—Chn of Com on Wines at Co Fair—

Farley said twas ridiculous apponting *him*—a man brought in East Tenn wher administer Sacrament with whiskey.

Hydraulic Ram

Expenses exceeded sanguine expc—

Didnt drink much in that ship—was like Congress—prohibit it save in Committee Rooms—<ta>carry it in in demijohns & carry it out in demagogues.

Acquainted with Gen Grant—said I was glad to see him—he said I had the advantage of him.[29]

J <[-]>. M. Harris of N.C.—<n>black—will be a next US Senator from N.C.—small

AH. Galloway—little heavier—mulatton will be Rep from Wilmington Dist N.C.—natural demagogue

both fat

Slave-drivers whip

There goes ½ sister

Convention at Raleigh just after close of war—the first.[30]

Taylor was writing in Nash [--] League Council—got so interested stopped writing—looked up—negro. Took ground agst univer suff & favor educational. [#]

---

[28] James Thompson Farley represented Calaveras County in the California legislature during two terms and during 1855/1856 was Speaker of the House. The "Maj. Bicknell" of the anecdote has not been identified.

[29] There are a number of apocryphal accounts of Clemens' first meeting with General Grant, including Clemens' own misdated recollections in Paine's edition of the *Autobiography* (1:13). It is probable that Clemens first met General Grant at this time through the offices of Senator William Stewart.

[30] A. H. Galloway and J. H. Harris, two of the influential Negro leaders of the Reconstruction era, were both present at the Convention of North Carolina Negroes held in Raleigh in September and October 1865, where a number of resolutions concerning wages, education, security, and discrimination were adopted by the delegates. Neither Harris nor Galloway was a member of Congress when Clemens was in Washington, although they may have been present in the gallery.

Washburne of Ill—gray, unshaved—fleshy a little[31]

Fer. Wood—iron gray hair—white moust good behaved

Jas. Brooks—gray & specs

Woodward (Dem) of Pa—bald, specs, unshaved—Ch. Jus—handsome old gent^{n} O.S.

Eldridge of Wis—leading & malig. copperhead.

Alison of Iowa sack coat, light blue pants—looks like village law student—plays for handsome—looks—30 <or 28>—hand s in pocket large flat foot—light, handsome brown hair—youngest looking member Excessively ordinary looking man Essentially ornamental Stands around where women can see him.

Jno Buckland[32] (O.) large, bald, never says anything—clothes ungainly on his shapeless body.

(Blue-gray hair predominates)

Thad. Steavens—*very* deep eyes, sunken unshaven cheeks, thin lips, long mouth, & strong, long, large, sharp nose—whole face sunken & sharp—full of inequalites—dark wavy hair Indian—club-footed.—ablest man.

Logan—black eyebrows long black implacable straight hair <without> hair without a merciful curve in it.—big black mous. pleasant look in eye, often & even makes bad jokes sometimes—but tigers play in a<n> ponderous sort of way.—splendid war record—15th army corps & Army of Tenn—one of Sherman's generals.—Better suited to war than making jokes. [#]

---

31 Clemens' observation of the scene in Congress—with his careful attention to physical characterization of both the venerable congressmen of the "Old Style" and the younger, more aggressive members—was clearly an invaluable source for the chapters on Washington in *The Gilded Age*. Since biographical information is readily available on all of the congressmen whom Clemens comments on here, annotation has been provided only when Clemens' entry may appear cryptic.

32 Clemens is referring to Representative Ralph P. Buckland of Ohio.

Thomas of Md.—belongs to another age—Whig—O.S. strong, unshaven face hermit—woman-hater—lives up in queer way in ε mountains alone in N.W. Maryland—one of oldest Reps—is a rad—<very> white hair laid in folds—hair comes washing forward over his forehead in two white converging waves over a bare-worn rock

converging

Judge Shellabarger—able

Bingham, Ohio, nervous, severe <de> & ready debater—

C

Garfield, young, able & scholarly—was chief of Rosecranz staff—preacher.

Carey of O—(8 hour) (witty speech— —large face—a little full—unshaven—Indian—long, iron gray hair turned back & not parted—heavy, large, portly man<—unshaven>—shaven—long, thin, strong mouth—slow of movement—ponderous every way—his strong suit is persistence, no doubt.—*Calhoun*

Bingham (continued) eloquent—commands attention of House, silky <li> very light hair just touched with gray—kinky—or rather, curvy—turned back so as to suggest loosely (apparently with a harrow)—large, high, broad forehead, slightly wrinkled—little gray side whiskers—eyes that have a drawn appearance of being drawn to the focus of glasses—a <b>sharp beak of a nose—chews nervously & when gets fagged out poking around, sits down—is generally around elsewhere than in his seat.

Covode the ungrammatical—of Honest John[33]—of Com. fame.

Horace Maynard Tenn—one of purest men in Congress—Union from 1st—very gentlemanly talented & fine speaker. Remarkable looking man—very tall & very slim—long black hair

---

33 Representative John Covode of Pennsylvania supported causes he believed to be worthwhile whether or not they were politically expedient and as a result was often referred to as "honest John Covode."

<comped>combed flat & behind ears, gives him a trim, shrewd, "cleared for action" O.S. look. *Indian*. Pleasant look in face. Very little black mous &

Jno D. Baldwin (of Mass.)—prop. Wooster Spy[34]—unblemished character—one of best read men—very large—specs gold—light gray hair—dark goatee & moustache—some patriarchal look.

Oakes Ames of Mass—Car'd Pac RR as much or more than any

Ben Butler—forward part of his bald skull looks raised, like a water blister—its boundaries, at the sides & at its base in front is marked by deep creases—fat face—small, dark moustache—considerable hair behind & the sides—one reliable eye. Is short & pursy—fond of standing up with hands in <poc>pants' in pockets & looking around to each speaker with the air of a man who has half a mind to crush them & yet is rather too indifferent. Butler is dismally & drearily homely, & when he smiles it is like the breaking up of a hard winter.

Ashley of O about stateliest looking.

Robinson, Brooklyn—hair kinky, thick, pretty long,—& in odd stripes of rich brown & silver—glossy

Paris Saloon—Stone fence.[35] [#]

---

[34] Journalist and congressman John Denison Baldwin of Massachusetts was for twenty years the proprietor of the Worcester *Spy*.

[35] The last few entries in the notebook are evidently notes about the manuscript of *The Innocents Abroad*. It is difficult to determine when Clemens started work in earnest, although it is clear that he had been thinking about the project since he first received Elisha Bliss's offer of 21 November 1867. On 27 January 1868 he formally agreed to supply the American Publishing Company with a book based on his *Quaker City* letters. Clemens wrote to his brother from Washington on 21 February 1868 that he had only retained "correspondence enough, now, to make a living for myself, and have discarded all else, so that I may have time to spare for the book. Drat the thing, I wish it were done, or that I had no other writing to do" (*MTL*, pp. 150–151). Thus it appears that Clemens was already in the midst of the work of revising and supplementing his *Quaker City* letters shortly after he signed the contract. Clemens' letter to the *Alta* describing his stay in Marseilles, his rail trip to Paris, and his first days of sight-seeing in the French capital, had mis-

Superstition

Relics

Guides.

23
5
115[36]

---

carried, and he was forced to expand the one existing *Alta* letter about Paris (*TIA*, pp. 36–41) with several imaginary episodes. One of these anecdotes (in chapter 15 of *The Innocents Abroad*) concerned Clemens' adventure in a French bar that advertised "ALL MANNER OF AMERICAN DRINKS ARTISTICALLY PREPARED." Clemens found that the "uneducated" French barman "could not even furnish a Santa Cruz Punch, an Eye-Opener, a Stone-Fence, or an Earthquake."

[36] This computation appears on the back endpaper of the notebook.

XI

"Left San Francisco for New York ...July 6, 1868"

(July 1868)

CLEMENS RECORDED most of the entries in Notebook 11 while traveling from San Francisco to New York, by way of the Isthmus of Panama, in the summer of 1868. This notebook is largely made up of the two literary sketches, one completed and the second abandoned, that Clemens probably worked on during the Pacific and Atlantic stretches of the journey. In addition, the notebook includes observations, anecdotes, names, and topics intended for development in Clemens' newspaper correspondence.

Unfortunately no notebook survives from Clemens' immensely productive stay in California during the spring of 1868. He had left Washington in March and sailed for California in haste, explaining in a letter to Mrs. Fairbanks on the eve of his sailing: "If the *Alta*'s book were to come out with those wretched, slangy letters unrevised, I should be utterly ruined" (*MTMF*, p. 24). When he arrived in San Francisco on 2 April, Clemens applied himself to the task of dissuading the owners of the *Alta California* from publishing a collection of his *Quaker City* letters, but it was over a month before he could send word of success to the publisher, Elisha Bliss, who was planning to issue Mark Twain's own revision of the *Alta* letters.

While waiting for the *Alta* to relent, Clemens kept busy by lecturing on the *Quaker City* pilgrimage. He filled a hall in San Francisco—"a little over sixteen hundred dollars in the house—gold & silver," he reported to Mrs. Fairbanks (*MTMF*, p. 26)—and then set off on a triumphant two-week lecture tour that retraced the circuit through the California Mother Lode country into Nevada which he made in 1866 with his Sandwich Islands lecture. Upon his return to San Francisco, Clemens learned that the *Alta* had finally accepted his terms. "I am steadily at work," he wrote to Bliss on 5 May, "and shall start East with the completed Manuscript, about the middle of June" (*MTL*, p. 153).

During the next two months, in all-night sessions, Clemens completed the *Innocents Abroad* manuscript. On 23 June he could write to Bliss, "The book is finished, & I think it will do" (University of Pittsburgh). With this prodigious labor accomplished, he could not resist postponing his departure, as he told Bliss on 5 July, "in order to lecture & so persecute the public for their lasting benefit & my profit" (TS in MTP). This was Clemens' 2 July farewell lecture to San Francisco on Venice. On 6 July he boarded the steamship *Montana* and sailed through the Golden Gate for the last time.

The midsummer voyage down to Panama was pleasant—"we had smooth water and cool breezes all the time"—according to his account published in the *Alta California* on 6 September. Clemens evidently took the opportunity to recuperate from his two months' burst of labor, for Notebook 11 is unusually spare in observation. The voyage passed largely without incident, and the most noteworthy event turned out to be an evening of amateur theatricals presented on July 10 by the shipboard stag party which Clemens helped organize.

After a stop at Acapulco on 13 July, the *Montana* continued on to Panama. It was probably during this leg of the voyage that Clemens turned his attention to the drafting of "The Story of Mamie Grant, the Child-Missionary." A burlesque of unctuous Sunday school literature (see *S&B*, pp. 31–32, for a fuller discussion), this heavily ironic sketch is a continuation in spirit of Clemens' attacks on the self-conscious piety of the *Quaker City* pilgrims.

The *Montana* docked at Panama on 20 July. While pausing at the bar of the Grand Hotel, Clemens unexpectedly met Captain Edgar Wakeman but the encounter is not recorded in this notebook. He did, however, make notes on the Panama Railroad Company, which carried him across the isthmus in three hours, in contrast to his two-day journey by river steamer across Nicaragua in 1866. At the end of the line in Aspinwall, Clemens was greeted by sights he had seen in March while hurrying to California—"the same combination of negroes, natives, sows, monkeys, parroquets, dirt, jiggers, and groceries in the small shops far up town; the same clusters of steamships in the harbor; the same business stir about the steamship office" (*Alta*, 6 September 1868). Here Clemens boarded the *Henry Chauncey* and on 21 July sailed for New York.

The idea for the story about a Frenchman's balloon voyage to a prairie in Illinois, which appears as the first entry following "Mamie Grant," had occurred to Clemens while en route to Panama, and he may well have taken the opportunity during the Atlantic voyage to begin work on the narrative. The date of composition, however, cannot be determined precisely. Clemens' note on the sketch, attributing its unfinished state to the publication of Jules Verne's *Five Weeks in a Balloon,* could not have been made before the spring of 1869, when the novel was first published in the United States. Yet the sketch itself appears to have been written on shipboard.

Although the similarity to Verne's novel was close enough to persuade Clemens to abandon his narrative, he would return to the idea at least twice. In April 1876 he incorporated a journey from France to the Midwest in a balloon into a manuscript titled "A Murder, a Mystery, and a Marriage," but it wasn't until 1894, in *Tom Sawyer Abroad,* that Mark Twain was able to exploit fully the idea of structuring a narrative around a balloon voyage.

The *Henry Chauncey* arrived in New York on 29 July. Five days later Clemens was still in New York, where he wrote to Mrs. Fairbanks: "I have met many friends, & have been very, very busy" (*MTMF*, pp. 34–35). On 4 August he took the train to Hartford and delivered the manuscript to Bliss. "Of all the beautiful towns it has been my fortune to see this is the chief," wrote Mark Twain in his 6 September letter to the *Alta,* "I never saw any place before where morality and huckleberries flourished as they do here." Clemens remained in Hartford for two weeks, working on the manuscript with Bliss and catching up on his newspaper correspondence, and in the last week of August, following several days in New York, he was at last ready to go to Elmira for the visit with the Langdons which was to begin his courtship of Olivia.

Notebook 11 now contains 108 pages, 57 of them blank. The pages measure 7⅜ by 4⁹⁄₁₆ inches (18.7 by 11.6 centimeters), and their edges are marbled in red, black, and gold. The pages are ruled with twenty-three blue horizontal lines and are divided by red vertical lines into four unequal columns in account book fashion. The endpapers and flyleaves are white. The cover is stiff natural calf; the binding has recently been repaired. There is an inscription in ink on the front cover, probably written by Paine:

July 1868
SF. to N.Y
2 Stories in here.

All entries are in pencil. Most, including all of the Mamie Grant and balloon voyage narratives, are on right-hand pages only. The notebook's first twenty-five right-hand pages, which contain the Mamie Grant sketch, are numbered consecutively. Paine entered occasional use marks in black pencil, though there are none in the two extended sketches.

<L>
Left San Francisco for New York in P.M. SS Co's Steamer Montana, July 6, 1868.<—J>
July <14,> 13, arrived at Acapulco.
Only 150 passengers on board.[1]

The Story of Mamie Grant, the Child-Missionary.

"Will you have <milk> cream & sugar in your coffee?"

<"I wish nothing but>

"Yes, if you please, dear auntie,—would that you could experience a change of heart."

The latter remark came from the sweet young lips of Mamie Grant. She had early <ex> come to know the comfort & joy of true religion. She attended church <rel>regularly, & looked upon it as a happy privilege, instead of an irksome penance, as is too often the case with children. She was always the first at Sunday School & the last to leave it. To her the Sunday School library was a

[1] These entries are written on the back of the front flyleaf.

treasure-house of precious learning. From its volumes she drew those stores of wisdom which made her the wonder of the young & the admiration of the aged. She blessed the gifted theological students who had written those fascinating books, & early resolved to make their heroines her models & turn her whole attention to saving the lost. Thus we find her at breakfast, at nine years of age, siezing upon even so barren an opportunity as a question of milk & sugar in her coffee, to express a prayerful wish in behalf of her aged, <godless> unregenerated aunt.

"Batter-cakes?"

"No, auntie, I cannot, I dare not eat batter-cakes while your precious soul is in peril."

"Oh, stuff! eat your breakfast, child, & don't bother.<"> Here is your bowl of milk—break your bread in it & go on with your breakfast."

Pausing, with the uplifted spoonful of milk almost at her lips, Mamie Grant said:

"Auntie, bread & milk are but a vanity of this sinful world; let us take no thought of bread & milk; let us seek first the milk of righteousness, & all these things will be added unto us."

"Oh, don't bother, don't bother, child. There is the door-bell. Run & see who <is there."> it is."

"Knock & it shall be opened unto you. Oh, auntie, if you would <be>but treasure those words."

Mamie then moved pensively down stairs to open the door. This was her first morning at her aunt's, where she had come to make a week's visit. She opened the door. A quick-stepping, quick-speaking man entered.

"Hurry, my little Miss. Sharp's the word. I'm the census-taker. Trot out the old gentleman."

"The census taker? What is that?"

"I gather all the people together in a book & number them."

"Ah, what a precious opportunity is offered you, for the gathering of souls. If you would but—"

"Oh, blazes! Don't palaver. I'm about my employer's work.

Let's have the old man out, quick."

"Mortal, forsake these vanities. Do rather the work of Him who is able to reward you beyond the richest of the <lord's>lords of earth. Take these tracts. Distribute them far & wide. Wrestle night & day with the lost. It was thus that young Edward Baker became a shining light & a lamp to the feet of the sinner, and acquired <[--]> deathless fame in the Sunday School books of the whole world. <This> Take these tracts. This one, entitled, "The <d>Doomed Drunkard, or the Wages of Sin," teaches how the insidious monster that lurks in the wine-cup, <[-]> drags souls to perdition. This one, entitled, "Deuces *and*, or the Gamester's Last Throw," tells how the almost ruined gambler, <a>playing at the dreadful game of poker, made a ten strike & a spare, & thus encouraged, drew two cards & pocketed the deep red; urged on by the demon of destruction, he <took> ordered it up & went alone on a double run of eight, with two for his heels, & then, just as fortune seemed at last to have turned in his favor his opponent coppered the ace & won. The fated gamester blew his brains out & perished. Ah, poker is a dreadful, dreadful game. You will see in this book how well our theological students are qualified to teach understandingly all classes that come within their reach. Gamblers' souls are worthy to be saved, & so the<y> holy students even acquaint themselves with the science & technicalities of their horrid games, in order to be able to talk to them <in>for the saving of their souls in language which they are accustomed to. This tract, entitled—<">—<[¶]"> Why, he is gone! I wonder if my words have sunk into his heart. I wonder if the seeds thus sown will bear fruit. I cannot but believe that he will quit his sinful census-gathering & go to gathering souls. Oh, I *know* he will. It was just in this way that young James Wilson converted the Jew peddlar, & sent him away from his father's house with his boxes full of Bibles and hymn-books—a peddlar no longer,<—>but a blessed colporteur.<"> It is so related in the beautiful Sunday School book entitiled "James Wilson, the Boy Missionary."

At this moment the door-bell rang again. She opened it.

"Morning Gazette, <m>Miss—<eighty> forty cents due, <or>on two weeks."

"Do you carry these papers all about town?"

"To mighty near every house in it—largest daily circulation of any daily paper published in the city—best advertising medium—"

"Oh, to think of your opportunities! This is not a Baptist paper, is it?"

"Well I should think not. She's a Democrat.—"

"Could not you get the editor of it to drop the follies of this world & make the Gazette a messenger of light & hope, a Baptist benediction at every fireside?"

"Oh, I haven't got time to bother about such things. Saving your presence, Miss, Democrats don't care a damn about light & hope—they wouldn't take the paper if she was a Baptist. But hurry, won't you, please—forty cents for two weeks back."

"Ah, well, if they would stop the paper, that would not do. But Oh, you can still labor in the vineyard. When you leave a paper at a house, call all the people of that house together & urge them to turn from the evil of their ways & be saved. Tell them that the meanest & the laziest & the vilest of His creatures is still within the reach of salvation. Fold these tracts inside your papers every day—& when you get out, come for more. This one, entitled "The Pains of hell, or the Politician's Fate," is a beautiful tract, & draws such a frightful picture of perdition, its fires, its monsters, its awful & endless sufferings, that it can<n> never fail to touch even the most hardened sinner, & make him seek the tranquil haven of religion. It would surely have brought Roger Lyman the shoemaker of our village to the fold if he had not become a raving maniac just before he got through. It is an awakening pamphlet for those Democrats who are wasting their time in the vain pursuit of political aggrandizement. Fold in this tract also, entitled—"

"Oh, this won't do. This is all Miss Nancy stuff, you know. Fold them in the papers! I'd like to see myself.<—> Fold tracts in a daily newspa— why <you're blamed if I> I never heard of such a thing. Democrats don't go a cent on tracts. Why, they'd raise more <c>Cain around that office—<geeminy,> they'd mob us. Come, miss—forty cents, you know."

"You are glib with the foolish words of the worldly. Take the tracts<.>, & enter upon the good work. And neglect not your own eternal welfare. Have you ever experienced grace?<">

"Why *he* is gone, too. But he is gone on a blessed mission. Even this poor creature will be the means of inaugurating a revival in this wicked city that shall sweep far & wide over the domains of sin. I know it, because it was just in this way that young George Berkley converted the itinerant tinker & sent him forth to solder the souls of the ungodly, as is set forth in the Sunday School books, though, still struggling with the <gall> thrall of unrighteousness that had so lately bound him, he stole two coffee-pots before he started on his errand of mercy. The door-bell again."

"Good morning, Miss, is Mr. Wagner in? I have come to pay him a thousand dollars which I borrowed last month."

"Alas, all seem<ed> busied with the paltry concerns of this world. Oh, beware how you trifle. Think not of the treasures of this perishable sphere. Lay up treasures in that realm where moths <corr> do not corrupt nor thieves break through & steal. Have you ever read "Fire & Brimstone or the Sinner's Last Gasp?"

"Well this beats anything I ever heard of—a child preaching before she is weaned. But I am in something of a hurry, Miss. I must pay this money & get about my business. Hurry, please."

"Ah, Sir, it is you<,> that should hurry—hurry to examine into <the> your prospects in the hereafter. In this tract, entitled "The Slave of Gain or the Dirge of the Damned," you will learn (pray Heaven it be not too late!) how a thirst for lucre sears the soul & bars it forever from the gentle influences of religion; <how it tortures it for a little> how it makes of life a cruel curse & in death opens the gates of everlasting woe. It is a precious book.—No sinner can read it & sleep afterward."

"You must excuse me, Miss, but—"

"Turn/Flee from the wrath to come! Flee while it is yet time. Your account with sin grows apace. Cash it & open the books anew.

Take this tract & read it—"The Blasphemous Sailor <[-]>Awfully Rebuked." It tells how, on a stormy night, a wicked sailor was ordered to ascend to the main hatch & reef a gasket in the sheet anchor; from his dizzy height he saw the main-tops'l jib-boom fetch away from the clew-garnets of the booby-hatch; next the lee scuppers of the mizzen-to'-gallant's'l fouled with the peak-halliards of the cat-heads, yet in his uncurbed iniquity, at such a time as this he raised his blasphemous voice & shouted an oath in the teeth of the raging winds. Mark the quick retribution. The weather-brace parted amidships, the mizzen-shrouds fouled the starboard gang-way, & the dog-watch whipped clean out of the bolt-ropes quicker than the lightning's flash! Imagine, Oh, imagine that wicked sailor's position! I cannot do it, because I do not know what those dreadful nautical terms mean, for I am not educated & <ex> deeply learned in the matters of practical every-day life like the gifted theological students, who have learned all about practical life from the writings of other theological students who went before them, but O, it must have been frightful, *so* frightful. Pilgrim, let this be a warning to you—let this—

"*He* is gone. Well, to the longest day he lives he cannot forget that it was *I* that brought peace to his troubled spirit, it was *I* that poured balm upon his bruised heart, it was *I* that pointed him the way to happiness. Ah, the good I am doing fills me with bliss. I am but an humble instrument, <but> yet I feel that I am like, very like, some of the infant prodigies in the Sunday School books. I know that I use as fine language as they do. Oh that *I* might be an example to the young—a beacon light flashing its cheering rays far over the tossing waves of iniquity from the watch-tower of a Sunday-school book with a marbled back. Door-bell again. Truly my ways are ways of pleasantness this day. Good morning, Sir. Come in, please."

"Miss, will you tell Mr. Wagner that I am come to foreclose the mortgage unless he pays the thousand dollars he owes me at once—will you tell him that, please?"

Mamie Grant's sweet face grew troubled. It was easy to see that a painful thought was in her mind.—She looked earnestly into the face of the stranger, & said with emotion:

"Have you<—have you> ever experienced a change of heart?"

"Heavens, what a question!"

"You know not what you do. You stand upon a volcano. You may perish at any moment. Mortal, beware. Leave worldly concerns, & go to doing good. Give your property to the poor & go off somewhere for a missionary. You are not lost, if you will but move quickly. Shun the intoxicating bowl. Oh, take this tract, & read it night & morning & treasure up its lessons. Read it—"William Baxter, the Reformed Inebriate, or, Saved as by fire." This poor sinner, in a fit of drunken madness, slew his entire family with a junk bottle—see the picture of it. Remorse brought its tortures & he signed the temperance pledge. <The tempter led> He married again & raised a pious, interesting family. The tempter led him astray again, & when wild with liquor <he> again he brained his family with the fell junk bottle. He heard Gough[2] lecture, and reformed once more. Once more he reared a family of bright & beautiful children. But alas, in an an evil hour his wicked companions placed the intoxicating bowl to his lips & that very day his babes fell victims to the junk bottle & he threw the wife of his bosom from the third story window. He woke from his drunken stupor to find himself alone in the world, a homeless, friendless outcast. <Let him be a warning to you.> Be warned, be warned by his experience. But see what perseverance may accomplish. Thoroughly reformed at last, he now traverses the land a brand plucked from the burning, & delivers temperance lectures & organizes Sunday Schools. Go thou & do likewise. It is never too late. Hasten, while yet the spirit is upon you.<—>

"But *he* is gone, too, & took his mortgage with him. He will

---

[2] After rescuing himself from alcoholism at the age of twenty-five, John Bartholomew Gough achieved wide renown and a sizable income as a temperance lecturer. Gough was noted for a particularly energetic platform style that often sent him staggering and falling across the stage in a portrayal of the terrors of alcoholism. When he was twenty-eight, he published his *Autobiography* (1845).

reform, I know he will. And then the good he will do can never be estimated. Truly this has been to me a blessed day."

So saying, Mamie Grant put on her little bonnet & went forth into the city to carry tracts to the naked & hungry poor, to the <r>banker in his busy office, to the rumseller dealing out his soul-destroying abominations.

That night when she returned, her uncle Wagner was in deep distress. He said:

"Alas, we are ruined. My newspaper is stopped, & I am posted on its bulletin board as a delinquent. The tax-collecting census-taker has set his black mark opposite my name. Martin, who should have returned the thousand dollars he borrowed has not come, & Phillips, in consequence, has foreclosed the mortgage, & we are homeless!"

"Be not cast down, dear uncle," Mamie said, "for I have sent all these men into the vineyard. They shall sow the fields far & wide & reap a rich harvest. Cease to repine at worldly ills, & attend only to the behests of the great hereafter."

Mr. Wagner only groaned, for he was an unregenerated man.

Mamie placed a happy head upon her pillow that night<,>. <for she>She said:

"I have saved a paper carrier, a census bureau, a creditor & a debtor, & they will bless me forever. I have done a noble work to-day. I may yet see my poor little name in a beautiful Sunday School book, & maybe T. S. Arthur[3] may write it. Oh, joy!"

Such is the history of "Mamie Grant, the Child Missionary."

Trip of a man in a balloon from Paris over India, China, Pacific Ocean, the Plains, to a prairie in Illinois, in a balloon.

Write of Herald office & Tribune Weekly to Alta.

Something of Detective Baker.[4] [#]

---

[3] Timothy Shay Arthur was the editor and author of numerous moral stories and pamphlets. His most popular work, the novel *Ten Nights in a Bar-Room and What I Saw There* (1854), was in 1855 the best-selling book in the United States.

[4] Stephen Baker, one of the four captains of the San Francisco Police, had already been the victim of Mark Twain's satire in an article written for the *Territorial Enterprise* in 1866 (*MTSF*, p. 220).

Lc on California

Boy on way to Texas—wagon broke down.

C[t] the colts.

Eat personal property &—real estate.

If you know the way, I guess I can follow that.

Some says it's an abscess—only common bile.

Don't like sis's—

Darned old house ain't plumb.

Montana fine ship—state rooms ought to have draught over berths.

Superb China ships—Japan.[5]

Kohler & Frohling—wines.

California Labor Exchange.[6]

Maximilian dollars.[7]

Peddlars & chocolate at Acapulco. [#]

---

[5] The Pacific Mail Steamship Company's new steamship *Japan* had arrived in San Francisco on 3 July. Two days later Clemens wrote to his fellow passenger on the *Quaker City*, Mrs. Fairbanks: "Saw [y]our engineer, Harris, last night. He is just in, from around the Horn–is 1st assistant in the Japan–new steamer, & Oh, such a perfect palace of a ship. I do want to sail in her so badly. She leaves for China shortly" (*MTMF*, p. 34).

[6] In a letter published by the Chicago *Republican* (23 August 1868), Mark Twain reported: "The business men of San Francisco invented the California Labor Exchange. . . . For the past six or seven months it has found labor and the customary wages for from fifteen hundred to two thousand immigrants a month–her full share of the immigration. . . . Every 'steamer day' (incoming) its offices were crowded with immigrants. They were sent to work in mines, mills, factories, on railroads, and in shops" (*Republican Letters*, ed. Cyril Clemens [Webster Groves, Missouri: International Mark Twain Society, 1941], pp. 30–31).

[7] The silver peso bearing the portrait head of Emperor Maximilian was discredited following the restoration of the Republic of Mexico in 1867.

Programme.[8]

Oration—You'd scarce Expect one of my age.
Recitation—Boy stood on Burning Deck.
1st Class in spelling—k-a-w, cow.
Duett—
Composition—The cow
Recitan—Twinkle, twinkle
Instrumental—Jewsharp.

Heretofore built PMS for passengers—now build for frt.

$25 (Eastern in greenbks) 10 cts a pound for baggage for each & every passenger crossing RR—Opposition took 1st cabin at $45 the day we sailed, paying RR $25 in gold. RR pays 24 per cent *per* annum, & is the best RR stock in world—is 45 miles long, cost 11,000,000 & several thousand lives—ties & sleepers are laid on dead men. RR owned chiefly in <New York and> England, I think.[9]

---

[8] This is a partial list of the attractions that made up "the thrilling tragedy of the Country School Exhibition," an evening of amateur theatricals presented on July 10 by the Port Guard Theatre of the *Montana*. Other acts included a "Declamation–Patrick Henry on War," the "*Poem*–Mary had a little Lamb," and a choral rendition of "Old John Brown had One little Injun." Mark Twain was featured in the delivery of a "*Composition*–The Cow," and in his letter to the *Alta* of 6 September 1868, he commented: "I have seen many theatrical exhibitions, but none that equalled the above."

[9] The Panama Railroad was begun in May 1850 and completed in January 1855 at a cost of about $8,000,000 and an undertermined number of lives. Although workers sometimes died faster than they could be replaced, reliable accounts agree in refuting the persistent legend that every tie cost the life of a laborer. The railroad's rates for passengers were set at an intentionally prohibitive twenty-five dollars in gold for first class and ten dollars in gold for steerage in order to limit its use until facilities were adequate for the anticipated heavy traffic. Acceptance of this convenient new mode of isthmus transit was so great that by 1868 a planned reduction of these inflated rates had still not been necessary. Passengers traveling, as Mark Twain was, on vessels of the Pacific Mail Steamship Company, whose directors had a controlling interest in the railroad, could pay the railroad tariff in greenbacks, in effect a discount on the fare that passengers on the North American Steamship Company's "opposition" steamers continued to pay in gold. The Panama Railroad did not consistently return as high a dividend as the one Mark Twain correctly noted for 1868, but it was at this time the most profitable of United States-owned

Tradition[10]—The lease of the Right-of-way being about to expire, they began to send delegations of wise men from Washington—men of weight, reputation & influence—to talk with Mosquera, Prest of Panama English Co doing same & <urge> the Govt, & urge the extension of the franchise—<but [u]> to 99 yrs (offering $3,000,000 & stock) but unfortunately the Prest's proclivities & predilections were all in favor of the English—& so dark did the one party's prospects seem, & so bright the other's, that the latter had made valuable presents to the gov^{t}, had already begun to talk ? to contractors about building steamships for their new mail line, & it was said that the patent of the Gov't. to the Eng Co <only> was ready to be signed. At this critical time two Americans, large owners in the Amer. Co, & thoroughly well known to the natives of the Isthmus & the mexicans through to everywhere in Mex., hurried down to Panama with a cargo of wines & liquors, & at the end of 3 days had everybody drunk, a <promi> riot under way, the seeds of a promising revolution planted, & the Pres in prison. Result, the renewal of the lease to the Amer Co for 99 years, for $1,000,000. There is nothing like knowing your men.

---

lines. Mark Twain's suggestion of British ownership had some basis in fact, for in the 1860s English bankers were represented on the railroad's board of directors.

[10] Mark Twain's source for the following information considerably elaborated on fact. In 1867 the directors of the Panama Railroad Company became afraid that Colombia, of which Panama was then a province, would exercise its option of assuming control of the lucrative railroad at the expiration of the original concession in 1875. They had also received reports of other influences at work to acquire the railroad, perhaps the British investors who had displayed interest in building a canal through Panama. They therefore dispatched Colonel George M. Totten, the engineer chiefly responsible for building the railroad, and William Nelson, the company's commercial agent at Panama, to negotiate a new lease for ninety-nine years. The price Colombia extracted from them for this lease was $1,000,000 in gold, an annual subsidy of $250,000, a commitment to make a costly extension of the railroad, and a pledge not to oppose the building of a canal. The agreement was signed by Colombian president Santos Acosta, successor to Tomás Cipriano de Mosquera, who in 1867 was exiled after a revolution in Bogotá. There is no indication that the American negotiators played a part in the deposition of Mosquera. These notes concerning the railroad across the Isthmus of Panama became the substance of a letter from Mark Twain published on 23 August 1868 by the Chicago *Republican* (*Republican Letters*, pp. 34–37).

In Aspinwall,[11] all it is necessary to do is to cry Viva Revolucion! at head of street, & instantly is commotion. Doors slammed to, 50 soldiers march forth & cripple half dozen niggers in their shirt tails, a new Presi. is elevated, & then for 6 mos (till next Rev) the proud & happy survivors inquire eagerly of new comers what was said about it in <New York> Amer & Europe.

Good table & cook mighty well on Montana.
Alligator pear salad.
Tropic-bird busted.
Thunders-storms.
Fine sunset.
Huff (Mme.)
Dorcas Soc. in Soc[l] Hall.[12]
Mr. Hall, Minneapolis, Wis.
Uhlhorn
Boyd, Capt. Simmons }
Dolan } from China.[13]
Jno Orr,

---

[11] Now Colón. The town that grew at the Caribbean terminus of the railroad was named by the president of the Panama Railroad Company after the company's founder. The local government had no part in this decision, however, and it steadfastly refused to recognize the name Aspinwall, calling the town Colón, after Columbus. In time the American name fell into disuse.

[12] In his letter to the *Alta* published on 6 September 1868 Mark Twain reported: "There were a hundred and eighty-five quiet, orderly passengers, and ten or fifteen who were willing to be cheerful. These latter were equally divided into a stag party and a Dorcas Society. The stag party held its court on the after guard, and the Dorcas Society, presided over by a gentleman, amused itself in the little social hall amidships."

[13] "On this side we came up with Captain Gray, and had fine weather all the voyage except the first two days out. Very singularly, all those people who did not get sick in the smooth Pacific, and who had ventured to say, toward the last, that they never *did* get sea-sick, got a very great deal in that condition during the first two days on this side. Some how, the best of people will lie about sea-sickness when they get a chance. Even our three gentlemen from China—Boyd, Dolan & Captain Simmons—after crossing the entire Pacific, got dreadfully sick on the Atlantic, while God permitted mean men to escape entirely" (*Alta*, 6 September 1868).

Bevell, purser[14]
Zwell, <D>Surgeon
Coy, 1st officer
Caverly, Capt.
Brierly, Ch. Engineer

(*Mem.*—While this was being written, Jules Verne's "Five <weeks>Weeks in a Balloon" came out,[15] & consequently this sketch wasn't finished.

John L. Morgan,[16] of Illinois, a farmer & a man of good reputation, told me the following a few weeks ago, while I was visiting at his house. I give it <simply> as he gave it to me. He said:

In January, three winters ago, we had a heavy snow-storm. It lasted the best part of three days, & at the end of that time it lay on the ground fifteen inches deep. The prairie in front of my house, as far as the eye could reach, was a level plain of snow. The roads were covered up. There was no sign of hoof or track, or road. About noon, two days after the snow had ceased falling, I walked out, intending to go to a grove of large timber which stood, a solitary landmark in the prairie, some four or five hundred yards from my house. When I had proceeded half way, I suddenly came upon a man lying on the snow. He was insensible. The snow was broken, as if he had fallen <there> <thre> there & then rolled <of> over once. He had on heavy brogan shoes, somewhat worn, a sort of grey striped knit night-cap on his head, & wore a shirt & pantaloons of grayish striped stuff. He did not look like an American. He seemed to be an invalid, for he was very much emaciated. This is a runaway scrape, I thought. He was too weak to hold his horse, & has been thrown from a wagon or from the saddle. <I look> I knelt down

---

[14] Clemens' list of the officers of the *Montana* was apparently made shortly after boarding the *Henry Chauncey* to sail for New York.

[15] This memorandum must have been added in the spring of 1869, when *Five Weeks in a Balloon* was published by Appleton and Company in New York.

[16] Mark Twain may have appropriated the name of a fellow passenger on the *Henry Chauncey*, J. M. Morgan, for the narrator of his story.

<to> & placed my hand on his heart to see if it were still beating, & very naturally glanced around <to see> half expecting my eye to fall upon the horse or the wagon but neither were in sight. His body was warm, & his heart still throbbed faintly. I rose up to run for assistance, when an odd circumstance attracted my attention: He could not have lain there the two last cold days & nights, <without> in his feeble condition, without <day> dying—no snow had fallen during that time to obliterate tracks, & yet there was no sign of wheel, hoof or boot anywhere around, except my own clearly-marked footprints winding away toward my house! Here was a living man lying on the snow in the open prairie, with the smoothness of the snow around him totally unmarred except where he had turned over in it. How did he get there without making a track? That was the question. It was as startling as it was unaccountable.

I saw one of my hired men at a distance & shouted to him. While he was coming I stooped down & felt the stranger's pulse, & then I <won> found another curious thing. His hand, which was half buried in the snow, appeared to have something in it. I lifted the hand & from the nerveless grasp a sextant fell! I never have been at sea, but I knew the instrument with which mariners take the altitude of the sun, because a gentleman who had been a chaplain in the navy had recently lectured in our neighborhood upon "Life on board a Man-of-war," & had exhibited a sextant & other nautical instruments in illustration of a part of his discourse. As my hired man approached, he stooped, within thirty steps of us, & picked up something from the snow. It was a square box. I unfastened the lid, & disclosed a mariner's compass! More mystery. Here was a starving foreigner, traveling by land, with compass & sextant, & leaving no <[*one word*]> track or wake behind him.

We carried the stranger to the house, & my wife & daughters set instantly to work, with simples, & bathings & chafings, to turn the ebbing tide of his life & restore his failing vitality. In the meantime we sent for the country doctor, who was also the postmaster & the store-keeper, & by the middle of the afternoon our strange discovery had got abroad among the neighboring farmers, & they began to arrive at my house by couples & by dozens to wonder, ask questions & theorize. They visited the spot where we found the man, & the wisdom they delivered there & then in elucidation of the mystery of a man traveling in snow without leaving a track, would fill a book. None of the theories were entirely satisfactory, however. The spiritualists came to the conclusion that the spirits brought the man there, & this seeming to be the most reasonable idea yet advanced, spiritualism rose perceptibly in the favor of unbelievers.

By & bye all returned to the house, anxious to hear the man's story from his own lips as soon as he should return to consciousness. <Sev> He moaned occasionally, & partly turned in his bed. Once or twice he seemed making an effort to speak, but his voice died away in inarticulate murmurs. After a while the doctor gave him an opiate & he sank quietly to sleep. Everybody sat up late that night & theorized. Everybody got up early in the morning & eagerly inquired of the watchers if the patient had spoken. No, he had not. But at nine of the clock, he raised his head, looked around, rubbed his eyes—looked around again, rubbed his eyes again, clutched at the sides of the bed, suddenly, as a man might who was expecting to be dashed from a buggy,—then felt of the bed clothes critically with his fingers, & the wildness & the anxiety passed from his face & he smiled. Everybody drew nearer & bent forward in listening attitude. His lips parted<.>, & <He>he spoke. Alas! it was a bitter disappointment; he spoke in an unknown tongue.

The schoolmaster was sent for. He lived in the village, ten miles distant. He could not arrive until the next day. In the meantime the patient grew rapidly stronger & better. He had a ravenous appetite, & it was soon apparent that his emaciation was the result of a lack of food, & not of sickness. He would have killed himself eating if we had given him half the food his beseeching eyes & expressive gestures <beg> begged us for. He had found his tongue, & he talked now, nearly all the time. He could not help knowing that none of us understood him, yet it seemed an entirely sufficient gratification to him simply to hear himself talk. He seemed glad &

happy to have somebody to listen—whether they could comprehend or not appeared to be a matter of small consequence to him.

In due time the schoolmaster arrived. He said at once the man was French.

"Can you understand him?"

"Perfectly," said the schoolmaster, who was now lion No. 2.

"Then ask him how in the mischief he got there where he was in the snow."

The Frenchman said he would explain that, cheerfully. But he said that that explanation would necessitate another, & maybe he had better begin at the beginning & tell the whole story, & let the schoolmaster translate as he went along. Everybody said that would answer, & the stranger began:

I am Jean Pierre Marteau. Age, 34. I was born in the little village of Sous-Saone, in the South of France. My parents cultivated a little patch of ground on the estates of the Marquis Labordonnais. Our good priest taught me to read & write, & my parents looked upon me with much pride, for they thought was going to amount to something some day. They could not understand how it could be otherwise with one so highly educated as I. I read a good deal, especially books of travel & adventure. It is a thing which other boys have done. I grew restless & discontented. I longed to go to sea—to visit strange lands—to have adventures of my own. At the age of 16 I ran away from home. I found myself in Marseilles. It was a beautiful city & its wonders so filled me with pleasure <that I banished all anxiety from my> until something occurred. It was this. My money was exhausted. I was hungry. I shipped as a <cabin> ship's boy on a coasting vessel. I soon came to like my occupation. We saw no strange lands—nothing but ports & shores of France—but it was an idle, happy life. In two years I became a full seaman. In three I rose to second mate. In <four> five I saw myself first officer. I remained <s>first officer for six years. I read a good deal on shipboard, & behaved myself dutifully; but I generally went on a spree at the end of the voyage, & spent all my money. All except a little which I was careful to mail first to my mother. In these sprees I had never been guilty of any ill-conduct more serious than giving & acquiring a bloody nose occasionally, but even these little episodes had recommended me somewhat to the notice of the police. At last, in one of our rows, a sailor was shot & killed. There were several circumstances which cast strong suspicion upon me, & I was arrested. I was tried & condemned to the galleys for twelve years. These letters "P. A. L." which you see branded upon my body, will remain to remind me of it if I should chance to forget it.

I served nearly seven years in the galleys. During all that time I never once lost heart or hope, I think. I schemed always; I planned methods of escape, <whether> & tried to put them in execution. Once in my second year<s>, once in my fourth & twice in my fifth year I got away from my guards & my prison—once with a good-bye <shot> bullet through my left arm—but each time I was captured again within a fortnight. At last, one day when I was at work—in Paris, a week ago—a week before you found me—

"How? In *Paris* a week ago!"

"Yes, it is as I said—in Paris."

"It is incredible—it is impossible."

"Let me tell my story, Messieurs. I shall not falsify. We were in Paris—I & <my>many of my fellow galley-slaves. We had been taken there to <work> labor on some government works. It was ten in the morning. An officer was sent for some tools of various kinds—<a> some chisels, <a>files, augurs, & a hatchet. I was sent with the officer, to bring the things. I had them all in my arms, except the hatchet. The officer had that. In a great open space we saw a crowd of people gathered together. The officer locked his arm in mine & pressed through the crowd to see what the matter was. We could see an immense balloon swaying about, above the people's heads. We elbowed our way through, & stood beside the car. It was made fast to the ground by a rope. A man was making a little speech. He begged the multitude to be patient. He said he was only waiting a minute or two for his assistant to come and make a line fast to something—a valve, I think he said—& then he would be off. The balloon was distended with gas, & struggling to get away. An idea flashed like lightning through my brain. I tore loose from the guard, snatched the hatchet from his hand, threw my tools into the car, jumped in & cut the anchoring rope with a single stroke!

Whiz! I was a thousand feet in the air in an instant.

2 Indians at dinner with whites—one ate spoonful mustard—other said "What crying about?"

"Thinking about the good old Chief that died."

No. 2 took mustard—"What *you* crying about?"

"Thinking what a pity you didn't die when the old Chief did!"

Political parties who accuse the one in power of gobbling the spoils &c, are like the wolf who looked in at the door & saw the shepherds eating mutton & said—

"Oh certainly—it's all right as long as it's *you*—but there'd be hell to pay if I was to do that!"

Bad Boy—Mother had *two* good sons—didn't see why she couldn't be satisfied.

XII

"My First Experience in Dictating"

(June–July 1873)

THE ONLY surviving notebook between 1868 and 1877 is the fragmentary stenographic notebook kept by a young theological student named S. C. Thompson, whom Clemens hired as his secretary just before his trip to England in May 1873. Thompson was employed by Clemens for only a few weeks—during the Atlantic crossing and for a short time thereafter in London—before Clemens dismissed him. It is clear that, apart from the personal antipathy he developed toward Thompson, Clemens found dictation impracticable at the time. He advanced Thompson enough money for his return passage to America and promptly forgot his existence. Thirty-six years later the man was recalled to Clemens' mind when Thompson, by then the pastor of a poverty-stricken parish in upstate New York, sent the author a check in partial payment for the advanced money (S. C. Thompson to SLC, 20 April 1909, DV 268). Thompson's 1909 letter and Clemens' note about that letter provide the only available biographical information about Thompson and his short-lived association with Clemens. Clemens wrote:

> I can see him now. It was on the deck of the *Batavia,* in the dock. . . . Mrs. Clemens & little Susy & the nursemaid were leaving for England—& properly

> garbed for the occasion, in accordance with the custom of the time. . . . Every individual was in storm-rig—heavy clothes of sombre hue & melancholy to look upon, but new, & designed & constructed for the occasion, & strictly in accordance with sea-going etiquette. . . . Very well. On that deck, & gliding placidly among those honorably & properly upholstered groups, appeared Thompson, young, grave, long, slim, with an aged & fuzzy plug hat towering high on the upper end of him & followed by a gray linen duster which flowed down without break or wrinkle to his ancle-bones!
>
> He came straight to us & shook hands, & compromised us. Everybody could see that we knew him. To see those passengers stare! A nigger in heaven could not have created a profounder astonishment. . . . I can still see him as he looked when we passed Sandy Hook & the winds of the big ocean smote us. He had not seen the big ocean for a good while, & he stood apart absorbed in it. Erect, & lofty, & grand he stood, facing the blast, holding his plug on with both hands, & his generous duster blowing out behind level with his neck & flapping & flopping like a loosed maintogallant royal in a gale. There were scoffers observing, but he didn't know it, & wasn't disturbed. He was dreaming: dreaming of the stately spectacle before him, & of ways to earn the money & pay his debts & be a free man again—a dream destined to last thirty-six years, & be only a dream after all!

Clemens had returned to Hartford from his first trip to England in November 1872 so enthusiastic about the country and its people that he proposed to take Livy and Susy, with the nursemaid, his secretary Thompson, and Livy's Elmira friend, Clara Spaulding, for a stay of several months in Great Britain. The idea of employing a shorthand secretary had occurred to Clemens during the 1872 trip: "If I could take notes of all I hear *said*, I should make a most interesting book—but of course these things are interminable—only a shorthand reporter could sieze them" (SLC to OLC, 25 October 1872, TS in MTP). The experiment was hardly successful, however, since Thompson was clearly not proficient enough in transcription to reproduce any extended conversation.

Clemens was taking the manuscript of *The Gilded Age* to his English publishers, George Routledge and Sons. The British edition of the book was to be published in England simultaneously with the American edition, and it was necessary, in order to assure clear British copyright for the novel, for the author to be a resident on the date of publication. Clemens expected to confer with his publishers throughout the summer and to correct proofs in London in time for an early fall publishing date.

The party sailed from New York aboard the S.S. *Batavia* on 17 May

1873 and reached London at the end of May. They established themselves at Edwards's Hotel in Hanover Square for a few weeks. However, Clemens soon announced: "We go to the Langham Hotel next Wednesday to live. My wife likes this awfully quiet place but I don't. I prefer a little more excitement" (SLC to FitzGibbon, 19 June 1873, Henry W. and Albert A. Berg Collection, New York Public Library). On 29 June Clemens wrote to Twichell that they were installed in "a luxuriously ample suite of apartments" at the Langham Hotel in Portland Place (*MTL*, p. 207 [misdated]).

London was busy throughout the summer months. The trial for perjury of the claimant to the Tichborne title and estates, under way since April, was attended by crowds of Londoners; banquets, exhibitions, and military reviews were prepared for the state visit of the shah of Persia in mid-June; the tragedienne Madame Ristori and opera stars Christine Nilsson and Adelina Patti were popular public attractions; and the Derby, the Oaks, and Ascot races occupied the last days of May and the first two weeks of June.

Mark Twain's entrance into London society was easily accomplished—he already had a large circle of acquaintances made during his visit in 1872. The current object of literary London's attention was another American—Joaquin Miller, "the Poet of the Sierras"—whom Clemens had first known in San Francisco in the early sixties, when both were contributing to the *Golden Era*. Miller's *Life Amongst the Modocs: Unwritten History* and his *Songs of the Sun-Lands* had just been published with great success, and the author could be found in the most fashionable houses in town, strutting about in his flamboyant Western costume.

It was undoubtedly Miller who introduced Clemens to Lord Houghton (Richard Monckton Milnes), the poet and statesman, and to Lord and Lady Thomas Duffus Hardy, whose daughter, Iza, Miller was engaged to marry. Sir Thomas, the archivist, and Lady Hardy, who was a popular novelist, entertained a "host of bright people" at their Saturday evening parties. Clemens evidently made other friendships in England's literary and political society through George and Edmund Routledge, his English publishers, and through Sir Charles Wentworth Dilke, whom he had apparently met on his first trip to England. Clemens also visited the Savage Club, the Whitefriars Club, and the Athenaeum. He attended the races on Ascot Cup Day (12 June) and the Lord Mayor's ball on 11 July and visited Stratford-on-Avon in early July. Joaquin Miller recalled that Clemens was "shy as a girl . . . and could hardly be coaxed to meet the learned and great who wanted to take him by the hand" (M. M. Marberry, *Splendid Poseur: Joaquin Miller–American Poet* [New York: Thomas Y. Crowell, 1953], p. 116). Clemens himself admitted his occasional timidity: "the *really* great ones are very easy to get along with, even when hampered with titles. But I will confess that mediocrity with a title is (to me) a formidable thing to encounter–*it* don't talk, & I'm afraid to" (SLC to Mrs. Fairbanks, 6 July 1873, *MTMF*, p. 174).

Thompson's notes cover the period from 10 June through 16 or 17 July 1873. The first dated entry (10 June) is preceded by about 3½ notebook pages of shorthand notes, of which 2½ pages are a very rough transcript of the testimony given at the Tichborne trial on 10 June 1873. The full transcript of the trial can be found in the London *Standard.* Thompson's notes about the trial and the unrecovered shorthand on the page following these notes–neither apparently written at Clemens' dictation–are not included in this text.

Early entries in the notebook concern Ascot and were dictated at various times between 12 and 15 June. The notes dated "Westminster Abbey, June 15" (which are too chaotic to decipher) and other occasional short entries about sermons, scripture, and church services were probably initiated by Thompson himself.

The Ascot notes are followed by several pages about the arrival in London of Nasr-Ed-Din, shah of Persia, and his attendance at the review of troops at Windsor on 24 June. Mark Twain had contracted with Dr. G. W. Hosmer of the New York *Herald's* London office to report the shah's visit for American readers, and on 18 June he and Thompson crossed over to Ostend in order to describe the shah's gaudy progress across the Channel. Mark Twain's letters appeared in the *Herald* in July 1873 but were not collected for book publication until *Europe and Elsewhere* appeared in 1923.

The rest of the entries in the notebook, except for the incomplete "Story of a casual acquaintance," are brief. All of the entries suffer noticeably from the inadequacies and hesitancy of Thompson's shorthand transcription and from Mark Twain's difficulties with dictation. Despite these defects and the lack of distinctive personal comment from Clemens, the notebook entries provide a number of insights into Clemens' recurring interests. Clemens is present in two of his characteristic roles–as reporter (in the "O'Shah" notes) and tourist. His interest in Shakespeare, in the Delawarr case, and in the Tichborne Claimant are evidence of his fascination with impostors, claimants, and double identities; there are several entries dealing with the curiosities of English history and custom, which he would explore later in *The Prince and the Pauper* and *A Connecticut Yankee.*

It seems likely that shortly after the last dated entry in the notebook (the letter of 16 or 17 July to Bliss) Clemens dismissed Thompson. Thompson decided to stay on in Europe for a time to economize his slender resources and did not return to the United States until the fall (Thompson to SLC, 20 April 1909, DV 268). The Clemens party spent the end of July and August in Scotland and Ireland. They returned to London in early September. After Mark Twain's successful one-week engagement lecturing on "Our Fellow Savages of the Sandwich Islands" at the Queen's Concert Rooms in London (13–18 October), the Clemenses left for Liverpool, where Mark Twain lectured again before they sailed for home on 25 October 1873.

Clemens returned to England alone just two weeks later. And by mid-November, with Charles Warren Stoddard as his secretary-companion, he was again installed at the Langham Hotel, awaiting the delayed publication of *The Gilded Age* and preparing a new lecture, "Roughing It on the Silver Frontier," for an early December presentation before an enthusiastic British public.

Notebook 12 is a stenographic notebook, hinged at the top, rather than at the side. It now contains 192 pages, 73 of them blank. An undetermined number of leaves are missing. The pages measure 7⅝16 by 4⅝16 inches (18.6 by 11 centimeters) and are lightly ruled with thirty-four blue horizontal lines arranged in pairs as an aid in writing stenographic symbols. The cover is stiff calf, dyed maroon, with blind stamped borders on the front and back and figured endpapers. There is a leather pocket attached to one side of the cover for carrying a pencil. The notebook is worn and tattered: the covers and several leaves are loose, the pages are yellowed, and the pencil entries are now faint. Except for a very few brief entries in ink, Thompson used pencil throughout.

Notebook 12 is written primarily in shorthand, with interspersed words and passages in longhand. The shorthand is based on the phonetic system in James E. Munson's *The Complete Phonographer,* of which a number of editions were published in the late 1860s and early 1870s, with Munson's system freely modified by Thompson's own shortened forms and by more or less standard abbreviations.

The transliteration of shorthand notes depends quite heavily on context. The shorthand secretary himself would ordinarily rely on his recollection of the context as an aid in deciphering his symbols; thus, shorthand words which he had rendered incorrectly would still be decipherable to him.

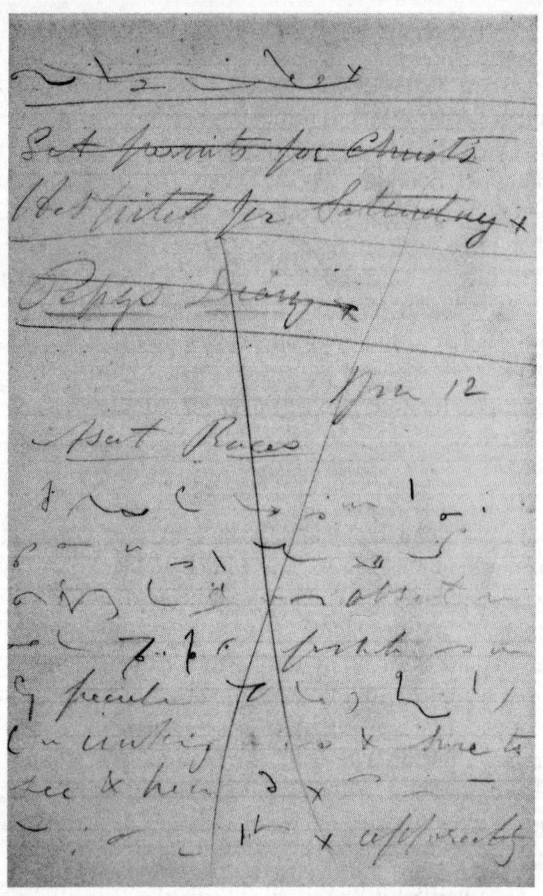

[*A sample of Thompson's longhand and shorthand notes. These notes are transcribed on pages* 527.13 *through* 528.9 *of the present text.*]

Critics of phonographic stenography have pointed out the inefficiency of a system in which the attention is on recording the sounds of speech, rather than the sense, using a number of "strokes and dots and dashes which you cannot read afterwards, except with a staggering amount of disquietude and uncertainty, or with careless inaccuracy, while all the while you have been unable to give any intelligent heed to the 'words spoken' " (Thomas Anderson, *History of Shorthand* [London: W. H. Allen & Co., 1882], p. 220).

The task of the textual editor, coming to the shorthand text at a later date without independent knowledge of the content to aid him, is one of re-creating the original context. The difficulties are multiplied—and the incidence of error is inevitably increased—when problematical shorthand symbols have to be resolved within a context which is itself largely conjectural. Since Mark Twain's dictation comes to the reader through the double mediation of Thompson and the present editor, no claim can be made to a full recovery of the author's words, much less his intentions. The accuracy of the text depends upon the accuracy of the transcriber, and the text has therefore been presented without textual apparatus.

To avoid distracting the reader with Thompson's inaccuracies and idiosyncracies, his longhand abbreviations, capitalization, spelling, and punctuation have been consistently emended.

Thompson used his longhand abbreviations as an adjunct to his shorthand symbols. His abbreviations are only occasionally standard forms; most often they consist of the first few letters of a word, hastily scrawled. Thus, the letters *luxu* would be enough to recall *luxurious* to his mind; *ad* serves for *admirals, contri* for *contrivance, fashb* for *fashionable*. Moreover, Thompson's abbreviation of individual words varies from line to line, so that both *ad* and *admr* represent *admirals* in one entry; *Duke* appears as *D, Duk,* and *Dk*; and *Shakespeare* is abbreviated variously as *Shak, Shk, S,* and *Sh*. Odd abbreviations that incorporate misspellings such as *Charring* X for *Charing Cross* and W *Abby* for *Westminster Abbey* occur frequently. In order to avoid such confusing and arbitrary usages in this text, abbreviations which are inconsistent or ambiguous have been expanded to the full words.

Thompson's numerical short forms and his erratic shilling and pence signs have been normalized—thus, 3^{d} and 3rd have been normalized to *third* in prose passages; $^{2}/_{3}{}^{d}$ has been normalized to *two-thirds* in prose passages; 3^{d} and 3 *d* have been normalized to 3*d*.; *d* and *S* have been normalized to *1d.* or *a penny* and *1s.* or *a shilling* to fit the context. Thompson's *M*[r]., *M*[r], *D*[r]., and *D*[r] have been normalized to *Mr.* and *Dr.*

Thompson's usual style of capitalizing titles of nobility, which was also Mark Twain's practice, has been retained. Thompson, however, was by no means consistent in this practice, and it has been necessary occasionally to supply capitals. Since, according to standard shorthand practice, the initial words of sentences written in shorthand are not marked for capitalization, these initial capitals have been provided throughout the text. Longhand words which Thompson capitalized in an apparently random or accidental fashion appear in lower case here. In no instance has a substantive change in the text occurred because of the normalization of capitals.

Spelling has been normalized.

The erratic and unconventional punctuation throughout the notebook has been normalized when the existing punctuation creates ambiguity. The stenographic punctuation mark *x*, signaling a stop, is used with great flexibility in Thompson's notes and has no set punctuation value; therefore the *x*, and Thompson's *x*–, –*x*, *x*[c], and *x*[c]*xx*, have been rendered variously, in accordance with the sense of each passage. Quotation marks and other necessary punctuation related to quoted passages have been normalized, since Thompson often neglected to supply adequate punctuation at the beginnings or ends of quotations. In short entries referring to church services, the name of the presiding minister, the name and address of the church, and the date and time of the service have been separated by commas for the sake of clarity.

In addition, punctuation has been provided in place of four kinds of natural breaks in the manuscript that Thompson used as a form of silent punctuation. Punctuation appropriate to the context has been supplied when necessary at the end of a notebook line, at the end of a notebook page, at points where Thompson switched from shorthand to longhand, and at points where Thompson left extra space on the line between words –in all four cases, Thompson used the natural break in his writing as a form of silent punctuation. Paragraphing, about which Thompson was equally casual, has been supplied when clearly necessary.

Certain stenographic errors which Thompson consistently made (confusing the stenographic symbols for *pl* and *pr*, for *bl* and *br*, and for *and* and *the*) have been silently corrected wherever context makes a choice possible.

There are very few cancellations in the notebook. Those cancellations which represent a substantive change in the text are printed within angle brackets. Fragmentary stenographic symbols which have been incompletely or incorrectly formed, then canceled and rewritten, have not been noted.

Doubtful words and phrases appear in square brackets.

The notebook presents a number of other problems: it is in poor condition, with many words partially obliterated; Thompson's stenographic symbols are poorly formed, irregular, and often incorrect; some words are written in Thompson's nearly illegible longhand (letters are fused with each other, and word endings are characteristically omitted). Clemens himself found Thompson's illegible hand exasperating. He wrote to Richard Bentley of London's *Temple Bar* on 13 October 1873: "Did my <late [turnip-headed]> clerk take that French Jumping Frog Sketch to you some time ago? And could you read his writing?"

Moreover, Thompson occasionally seems to have fallen behind the speaker and lost some part of the passage, characteristically indicating his lapse by a series of dots, a dash, or a blank space. This is clearly the case in the "O'Shah" transcription (and in the notes taken at the Tichborne trial, which have not been included here). The draft of "O'Shah" in the notebook has a number of such lapses. At such points Thompson's stenographic symbols become even more irregular and hurried, and the punctuation is chaotic. For example, Thompson's notes read, "If Ostend could impress him England could [head] clear off his headx—that not even—x." The published version of "O'Shah" supplies the missing readings: "If Ostend could impress him, England could amaze the head clear off his shoulders and have marvels left that not even the trunk could be indifferent to" ("O'Shah," *Europe and Elsewhere*, 1923). The missing words may have been added by Thompson from memory when he transcribed a longhand version of the piece or, more probably, by Clemens himself when he revised the longhand version.

Thompson has lined through almost every entry in the notebook, probably to indicate that he had completed such a longhand transcription for Clemens' perusal. None of Thompson's transcriptions are known to have survived except those for letters of 16 July 1873 to Elisha Bliss and Charles Dudley Warner. Thompson's longhand copies of these two letters, made from the shorthand drafts near the end of the stenographic notebook, are in the American Literature Collections, Beinecke Library at Yale University (PH in MTP).

Throughout the notebook there are occasional interlineations in red and blue pencil in an unidentified hand. These are evidently the traces of an attempt to translate the shorthand symbols at some later period in the notebook's history. The interlineations seem to be random, often only a word or two on the notebook page, and they are often inaccurate. They have not been included in this version of the notebook.

Undoubtedly, some notebook pages have been lost. The pages were originally bound into two gatherings, and there are loose pages at the front of the notebook and in the middle of the notebook at the juncture of these two gatherings. The "Story of a casual acquaintance," at the close of the first gathering, ends abruptly in midsentence. The fact that the notebook commences almost two weeks after Clemens reached England seems to indicate that some initial pages have been lost.

The last entry in the notebook is a list of subjects covered in the shorthand notes; the final pages of the notebook are blank. The items on the list which are identifiable occur only in the second gathering of pages. The items on the list which cannot be found in the notebook, such as notes taken on board the *Batavia* on the way to England, are presumably missing from the front of the notebook or from the midpoint juncture of the two gatherings.

The entries in this notebook are longer and more detailed than most of Mark Twain's notebook entries, but they are also more stilted. Clemens later recalled: "Doubtless it was my first experience in dictating, for I remember that my sentences came slow & painfully, & were clumsily phrased, & had no life in them—certainly no humor" (DV 268).

Notebook 12 was transliterated at the Mark Twain Papers by Lin Salamo.

S. C. Thompson[1]

Dictations of Sam'l Clemens (Mark Twain) taken down 1873. [#]

---

[1] Apart from the information disclosed in the Reverend S. C. Thompson's letter of 20 April 1909 and Clemens' notes about that letter (DV 268), no biographical information has been found concerning Clemens' shorthand secretary. The name and address of the Reverend Wallace Fawcett Thompson are in an unknown hand; the relationship of the two Thompsons is unknown.

Rev Wallace Fawcett Thompson
St. John's Rectory
Mt. Morris, New York

[3½ *notebook pages occurring at this point have not been included*][2]

June 10th 73.

Dined at Mr. Routledge's in the evening with Mrs. Clemens, Miss Spaulding, and others. Notes—use of *j* for *di.* Have noticed the affecting of it in Americans who have traveled abroad.

Is he the Q[ueen's] C[ounsel]? [Buying of high posts] in America —man murdered his father and mother—and [plea] is being orphan. At first the [practice of boring stories] was disagreeable; but when we got a little accustomed to them we agreed to like them. There's something picturesque [in their persons].

Get permits for Christ's Hospital for Saturday.[3] [#]

---

[2] The first 2½ pages of the notebook contain a partial and very rough transcription of the testimony given by Colonel George Greenwood at the Tichborne trial on 10 June 1873. The trial for perjury of Arthur Orton, a cockney butcher who claimed to be Roger Charles Tichborne, heir to the Tichborne estate, had begun in April 1873 and would last 188 days. Evidently Thompson, and perhaps Clemens as well, attended the public trial on 10 June 1873, when these notes were made. A full report of the progress of the trial can be found in the London *Standard's* daily transcriptions of the testimony. The *Standard's* accounts from 23 April 1873 to 13 October 1873 were later collected for Clemens by his secretary Charles Warren Stoddard in 1873–1874 (scrapbooks 13–18 in MTP). Clemens' later recollections of the Tichborne case can be found in *Following the Equator* (chapter 15) and in Paine's edition of the *Autobiography* (1:139). Thompson's notes about the trial are followed by a page of shorthand material which has not been recovered. The undeciphered page is faded and illegible. Isolated shorthand phrases and words which are decipherable seem to indicate that the page may have been the text of a personal letter Thompson was drafting.

[3] Christ's Hospital, the school founded by Edward VI, provided an education for indigent children and included among its alumni Samuel Coleridge and Charles Lamb. Clemens would recall the history of Christ's Hospital in *The Prince and the Pauper* when young King Edward VI declares that thenceforth the children of Christ's Hospital would have "their minds and hearts fed, as well as their baser parts" and gives Tom Canty the "chief place in its honorable body of governors" (chapter 33).

Pepys Diary.[4]

June 12

Ascot Races[5]

Trains leaving every few minutes—had secured the saloon car—couldn't be [enough] unless more [*three words*]—[*one word*] [absent] —scores of gorgeously-dressed ladies, fashionable men—[*one word*] peculiar English [*one word*] sit staring at each other—[walking—comments] & sure to see & hear [words]. Man may [go along and] stare in the daytime. Apparently gentleman. May be <looking> walking with her grandfather. Look over shoulder 10 steps.

Perfectly bewitching country. Beyond Richmond & Bushy Park. Grass lands dotted with colossal oaks. Over dozen [dollar-new] houses. Usually a rich cream-color. ½ dozen colors. Never see red brick unless [*one word*]. Could be no more<.> fascinating than on the [T---].

Bushy Park is a royal park. Has a sailing vessel of 500 tons, completely rigged—came tearing down [*two words*]<.>, just missing the houses tree etc. Thought she would just get to the rail[-way] in time to [get herself] in trouble [*three words*]. I thought she was doing some marvelous [demonstration]. [Carry her] through gratings etc. [without picking up] something. But I thought I should die with anxiety. [But by] that time we got even with the vessel and I saw it [a school-ship]<—>[for the reformatory].[6]

---

[4] Clemens would write to Twichell on 29 June 1873 from the Langham Hotel that he was "luxuriating in glorious old Pepys' Diary" (American Literature Collections, Beinecke Library, Yale University).

[5] The highlight of Ascot Race Week was the Ascot Cup Day on 13 June 1873, when the royal party attended. The London *Times* estimated that 13,000 persons were present (14 June 1873).

[6] The route of Clemens' excursion to Ascot is obscure. The most direct route was via the South Western Railway from Waterloo Station, skirting Richmond Park on the way to Ascot. The notes here, however, indicate that the Clemens party may have made a short side trip on the branch line to Bushy Park. The large reformatory in the area, one of the oldest institutions of its sort in England, was the London County Council Industrial School for boys at Feltham, a short distance beyond Richmond Park on the direct rail route to Ascot. No evidence has been found of any training ship having been in use at Bushy Park.

It was a remarkable thing as [first day] boys went to [work] in that vessel—were never [awkward]. Talk language of the sea in that ship. Swagger around. Go out on the yards—*imagining* sea conversations of sailors.

Miss Bowles [*two words*] 3859

Sir Chas Wentworth <B>Dilke's Greater Britain.[7]

Drury Lane theatre 3 tickets for Wednesday evening.[8] <Ne>Perfect near stage; if not R

At Ascot [followed] long line about 3 or 400 yards. Climbed [moderately] higher—all gentlemen ladies didn't see a rough all day long.

Usual price 10s. got at the grandstand. When one leaves cane or an umbrella in London it is customary to give check keeper from 2 to 6d. when you take it again. Here they charge a shilling in advance which was the first outrage complained of by the Englishman. Next [bar] they charge 18d. for a drink of some kind, which would ordinarily be 9d.—that was the second outrage. We necessarily went to a luncheon, for none of us had had anything to eat for 1½ hours. Charged 6s. for a luncheon which should be nothing more than 3d. —another outrage.

Presently <Gypsy woman> an old woman came along begging and asked for a penny—[Rob] said, "Didn't I see you at the Oaks'[9] back gate<.>?" Yes she said he did. "Well," he said, "you were

[7] Clemens was among the political and literary people who attended the dinner parties of statesman Sir Charles Wentworth Dilke. Dilke's *Greater Britain: A Record of Travel in English-Speaking Countries During 1866 and 1867* was published in 1868.

[8] During Clemens' stay in London Madame Adelaide Ristori, the renowned Italian tragedienne, was appearing at the Theatre Royal in Drury Lane. The performance on Wednesday, 18 June 1873, was the historical drama *Elizabeth*. Clemens had been unflattering in his comments on Madame Ristori during her triumphant tour of the United States several years earlier, marveling that the "wretched foreign woman" and her "foreign jabbering" could so impress his countrymen (*MTTB*, pp. 168, 173).

[9] The Oaks, one of the events during Epsom Race Week, was run on 30 May 1873 at Epsom Downs.

only asking a penny there, everything is double here—you should put up your price." He gave her 2d.

But after complaining awhile of the exorbitant prices, they decided that it was the very feature that made the place delightful —[all the dirty ragged] hardly ever had to be [present]—couldn't stand the prices. But the roughest of the rough element was so unspeakably superior to the rough element in America<.> [*six words*].

No serving drinks [*two words*] & no noise but the customary Greys. Only one set of [able] singers on the grounds. Except everlasting [niggers].[10]

Long row of double-tiers private boxes, 3 long tiers of theatrical boxes. Every woman seemed to have trained her hair [so well indeed]. Without regard to prices or [wicked] eyes. Never seen anywhere except in a house of prostitution. No [straight backs]. Some were just as tasteful as [*three words*]; but it was the exception. Ladies' dresses which combined every imaginable material—daintiest silks—heaviest richest satins—velvet trimmings. There was no material, <no> which was not represented there. There seemed to be hardly ugly woman on the grounds—nearly all [comely, handsome]. I saw 4 or 5 exceedingly beautiful.

Perhaps 50,000 [persons present]. Climb on top of the grandstand to see the [royal party] come along. [Right over] their heads in the air. Came in 4 horse car from some private country estate[11] in the [neighborhood]. Lord Cork,[12] master of the Queen's hounds—noble

---

[10] The note may refer to the Moore and Burgess Minstrels, London's popular "burnt cork" entertainers, who had one of the longest consecutive runs in English theatrical history. Minstrels and gypsies were common sights at outdoor entertainments in England, especially at the fashionable races and at seaside resorts.

[11] During the race week, the Prince and Princess of Wales and their party were staying at Cowarth Park, Virginia Water, the estate of Mr. J. Arbuthnot, high sheriff of Berkshire.

[12] Clemens was evidently slightly acquainted with Lord Cork. Years later he recalled a brief, embarrassing encounter during a fox hunt with the excitable "Master of the Buckhounds." The anecdote probably dates from the 1872 trip to England (*Following the Equator*, chapter 20).

custom—great-[titled] people—long [*one word*] preceded the carriage —it was a fine spectacle—[*four words*].

Then came Prince of Wales' carriage, with postilion mounted on each of the 4 horses in fiery liveries—open car—Prince of Wales, Duke of Edinburgh on front seat—didn't know who was on the other seat—crowd cheered extensively—they bowed continually. Got good view of the <P.>Duke's face but not of the Prince's. But when took his hat off got good top of his head. No hair—otherwise I had that climb for nothing.

Prince Arthur & some more people. And in the next, Duke of Teck & some more people.

Prince of Wales dressed in ordinary everyday costume. Gray coat & stovepipe hat.

Between the races [went up] sat with about 10,000 [people]. Stared at the royal [party] except Prince. Sat in the royal [*one word*], [neat open shed].

Princess of Wales very trim graceful figure and a winning face, dressed with exceeding neatness—simplicity. [Bright pretty dress with rows of bows] down front. She sat there a long time with 2 ladies, Duchess of Teck & some other lady looking out at the crowd with perfect ease, though [need opera glass at the racing]. Prince Arthur sat talking with another lady, at ease—like any other man. Duke of Edinburgh talks with Duke of Teck.

Between every 2 races, crowds would flock to the front of royal box to stare—occasionally cheer a little. First nobody was cheered at except those with the Prince of Wales. Everybody was being lady. Gentlemen & all.

Gentlemen [of our party] won several pounds<—>except me. Came very near winning several pairs of gloves,[13] would have but

---

13 Clemens is referring to the English betting practice of "going for the gloves," which, according to J. C. Hotten's *Slang Dictionary* (London: Chatto & Windus, 1874), derives from the "custom of ladies who bet GLOVES, and expect . . . to be paid if they win, but not to pay if they lose." Clemens remarked on the custom of betting gloves at the Melbourne Cup races as late as 1897 (*Following the Equator*, chapter 16).

other horse came in ahead. One lady won 23 pairs of gloves [another]. In all £9. There were [about] 20,000 ladies present, and so far [perhaps half of them] won £9 of gloves; and near ½ million $ worth of gloves [brought] changed hands—[*four sentences*].

[Red water mugs]; and the waiters presented <silver> [pewter] mugs with silver bottoms. More people—that mug was passed from hand to hand in the [box], like offering gift. As there was only 2 ladies in the [box] and 5 gentlemen, the [*three words*] was next.

When we got to the station, trains were leaving every <5>4 or 5 minutes—on train. Gave station master half crown, gave compartment [at wish]. But we [*five words*]. [All the way home] we played game of cards whose name I have forgotten. Very simple game. Everybody bet on the [*two words*]. Each one deals in turn 3 cards to each player but none to himself. He turns card, and the first player on his left without looking at his card bets 6d. if it is King or Queen, bets that he has high score. If it is low card like <7>9 or <8>10 he bets a shilling, if 7 or 8 bets 2. If 5 or 5 bets [other] limit, 3s. If he wins dealer [pays] 3s. Next player on the left bets his could show higher score<.>; then shows his hand. Sometimes nearly everybody would lose. Then again nearly everybody would win, and the dealer would find himself out of pocket 12 or 15s. We hadn't much silver, we would just remember our indebtedness to people—up to 10 or 12s. then odd or even [and when that player], in the course of 2 [*two words*] [unselfishly] managed to lose a shilling or 2 and the other win a shilling or 2. The whole day was exceedingly enjoyable one.

The Claimant: Lord Houghton[14] said that for a long time he fully believed in the Claimant. Doesn't suggest the butcher at all. Quiet patient gentleman. Ways suggest the gentleman. Language <was not> not perfect but neither was Roger Tichborne's. Curious he can recollect no French but occasionally he [*one word*]

[14] Richard Monckton Milnes, Lord Houghton, the poet and statesman, is most often remembered for the brilliant company which he collected for his famous breakfast parties. Clemens was evidently introduced to the ebullient Houghton and his circle by Joaquin Miller.

kind of French accent. Until the fatal tattoo marks[15] were related, he didn't have [them].

Lord Houghton [pointed out the stately mansion of the Mayor of London].

25 or 6 years of age. [*four words*]. Great position for a young man just starting in life. Said <was> didn't [not] have to start in life, already started.

Went to see Athenaeum Club,[16] very dignified, composed place with a dim religious light. All manner of books—tables full of them. Luxurious chairs. Huge reading room. Very few people there<.>; those sitting reading with their hats mashed down over their eyes English fashion.

Introduced to Lord Monk[17]—very pleasant gentleman.

Close by is the monument to the Duke of York—once commander in chief of the Royal Army whose course was just a monotonous repetition of defeats. When died swallowed up in debt. Was a member of the royal family. And out of gratitude for [unselfish] service to his country, nation built this monument with his statue [upon] its top with lightning rod sticking out of his head.[18]

I thought they ought to build monument to Shakespeare—but they said that that would be out of character. [Their] idea of a monument

[15] One of the revelations of the Tichborne trial which proved most damaging to the Claimant's case was testimony concerning the existence of a distinctive tattoo on the arm of Roger Tichborne. The prosecution was able to show that an inept attempt had been made to reproduce a similar tattoo on the arm of the Claimant.

[16] Clemens was made a visiting member of the distinguished literary club in Pall Mall a few months later.

[17] Possibly Sir Charles Stanley Monck (1819–1894), the former governor-general of Canada and since 1871, a commissioner of education in Ireland.

[18] The York Column was the object of considerable derision. The statue of the chronically debt-ridden duke, "cresting his column, draped in inky swathings, and with a lightning conductor rising from his head," was said to have been put atop the lofty column "in order to place him beyond the reach of his creditors" (Charles G. Harper, *More Queer Things About London* [Philadelphia: J. B. Lippincott Co., 1924], pp. 106–107). Another popular theory was that the lightning rod was for the purpose of filing the duke's bills.

was to keep in memory the man that might otherwise be forgotten.[19]

Saw [table] with a [*two words*] stating that Napoleon III left <it> in 1848.

Came up Pall Mall which said to have gotten its name from Pallo & Mallo, [persons in] some book. Like croquet or old croquet, pallo bat & mallo ball. Greensward then.[20]

June 14

Work upon Persia by a representative of Great Britain at the court of Teheran. Title something like *Ali Baba* in Arabian Nights.[21]

Lord Houghton says that cab drivers are a [part of every world] for men take them all around; and that they are made up from all circles of social life. Butcher, brusher & [*three words*]. Quiet refuge of broken-down talent and broken-down wealth. The printing-office

---

[19] Clemens had voiced a similar sarcasm about London's monuments in his speech at the Savage Club on 28 September 1872. Moncure Conway recalled the reaction of Clemens' auditors to his remarks about the Albert Memorial: "He got off a satire so bold that it quite escaped the Englishmen. 'I admired that magnificent monument which will stand in all its beauty when the name it bears has crumbled into dust.' The impression was that this was a tribute to Albert the Good, and I had my laugh arrested by the solemnity of those around me. Indeed, one or two Americans present with whom I spoke considered it a mere slip, and that Mark meant to say that the Prince's fame would last after the monument had crumbled" (Moncure Conway, *Autobiography: Memories and Experiences*, 2 vols. [Boston: Houghton, Mifflin and Co., 1904], 2:143). The speech is included in *Mark Twain's Speeches*, and, although the line Conway quotes is rendered somewhat differently there, the editor also found it necessary to clarify Clemens' rather elusive remark in a parenthetical explanation: "Sarcasm. The Albert memorial is the finest monument in the world, and celebrates the existence of as commonplace a person as good luck ever lifted out of obscurity" (*MTS* [1910], p. 420).

[20] The name of Pall Mall derived from the game *pail mail* (from the Italian *palla* [a ball] and *maglio* [a mallet]), an early form of croquet popular in the sixteenth and seventeenth centuries.

[21] The note undoubtedly refers to *The Adventures of Hajji Baba of Ispahan*, a satire upon Persian manners and thought written by James Morier, secretary of the embassy at Teheran from 1810 to 1814. Clemens' library included an 1824 edition of the work, possibly purchased at this time in preparation for Clemens' projected series of letters for the New York *Herald* covering the arrival of the shah of Persia in London ("The Library and Manuscripts of Samuel L. Clemens," Anderson Auction Company catalogue no. 892—1911, 7–8 February 1911, item 340).

and the butcher's-stall seems <to be> [no better]. [*four words*]. Lord Houghton never had words [with] cabman but once and Houghton said in sudden indignation "damned rascal" or something like that, and the cabman touched his hat and said, "Please remember that though I am cabman I am man"—he replied, "I beg your pardon."

300,000 people have witnessed the Derby at one time <and the> and 100,000 were at Ascot the other day. That was the biggest day Ascot has seen yet. There was no mob. Especially because properly speaking there is no mob in the country, compared to ours.

Betting at an English race covers all [ground]; they bet 2 to 1, 3 to 1, 4 to 1 & 40 to 1 etc. If you keep on raising your terms you would get [bet] by and by. I believe if they enter cow on an English track, [against Gladiateur],[22] somebody come along singing out 400 to 1 [*two words*] cow can get all the bets wanted. [*one word*] no bet 100 to 1. Those people would argue that if [*two words*] [took ¾ hour to go] around <100 to 1> 1 to 100 chances that the [horse that does] breaks his neck.

In Westminster Abbey [*one word*] [of] Richard II [tomb]. [Curious tomb] of De Courcy, Lords of Kinsale,[23] who to this day [share] the singular privilege of standing in the presence of royalty with hats on and it is said that they of course make no further use of it than to simply keep the privilege intact by putting hat on in presence of

[22] Count Lagrange's Gladiateur won both the Derby and the St. Leger races in 1865; the Derby victory marked the first time that race had ever been won by a foreign horse.

[23] In Westminster Abbey the tomb of Richard II and his queen is not very distant from that of Almericus de Courcy of Kinsale, whose family was granted by King John II the privilege of remaining covered in the king's presence. Miles Hendon would retell the story of de Courcy's privilege and win for himself and his heirs the privilege of remaining seated in the king's presence in *The Prince and the Pauper* (chapter 12). The other curious tradition mentioned here is the ancient ceremony in which "certain gigantic horse-shoes, suitable for the fore-feet of a great Flemish mare, and sixty-one nails, to be used in fastening them on . . . are solemnly handed to the King's Remembrancer by the City Solicitor, and the nails are counted out" as a token rent paid by the Corporation of London to the king (George C. Williamson, *Curious Survivals* [London: Herbert Jenkins, 1925], p. 15).

royalty and immediately put it off again; just as the Lord Mayor of London's first duty is to [go in state to] the Lord High Chancellor of England and count 36 hobnails just as a proof that he is right man in the right place. Simple to [*one word*] old customs for their own sake—a living record of [old things] providing [*four words*]. And the historic privilege of remaining covered in the presence of royalty and the counting of hobnails is in the same spirit of some of the old land tenures, though in the latter case to take the custom might break the laws.

2 books in the British Museum—Burke's Criminal Trials, Curious Land Tenures[24]

Charterhouse.[25] Magnificent old governors' room just to think of [being a home]. I liked the fireplaces so much. The old men sitting around in the large court, reading. And the old man going by in such style. You ask if he were not <a> some nobleman.

[*one word*] P—thinks that the crypt at St. Paul's very impressive sight [*one word*]—Duke of Wellington's tomb with lights burning.

Ivory store on south side of Oxford, east of Arthur.

[*1½ notebook pages dated* 'Westminster Abbey, June 15' *occurring at this point have not been included*][26]

Dr. Hosmer[27]
47 Fleet St. [#]

---

[24] The exact titles of the books referred to here have not been determined. "Burke's Criminal Trials" could be any of a number of accounts of "celebrated trials" collected by Peter Burke.

[25] London's Charterhouse, originally a Carthusian monastery and later the private residence of Thomas Howard, the fourth duke of Norfolk, was bought in 1611 by a wealthy merchant, Thomas Sutton. A charity school and a home for poor men were established there.

[26] These entries, evidently made at Westminster Abbey on Hospital Sunday, a day dedicated to the collection of charitable contributions for the poor of London, were probably Thompson's own notes about a sermon. The entries are scrawled and chaotic and, unlike most of the other entries in the notebook, have not been crossed through to indicate some later use of them. Because of the difficulty of rendering a coherent text of these notes, they have been omitted.

[27] Dr. George Hosmer was a member of both the medical profession and the

June <1> <19> 18th

We idled about this curious Ostend[28] the remainder of the afternoon and far into long-lived twilight—apparently to amuse ourselves but secretly I had deeper motive—I wanted to see if there was anything there which might impress the Shah. In the end I was reassured and content. If Ostend could impress him, England could [head] clear off his head, that not even—

These citizens, Flanders or Flounders I think call them, I think I have I seen. Thrifty industrious—as Chas'. Prolific. One could hardly get along for children. All the women hard at work. In nearly every door women at needlework or knitting. Many women sat in—making point lace. Hold on her knee. Punctures—like spokes of a wheel. <Ma> Throws these spools, so <hard fas> fast—hardly follow. <How> Wonder how she can go on talking without missing a stroke. Very tasteful<.> and [delicate] in design.

Sea shells—men & women of shells. Lobster claws. [Some] of frogs. Some fighting etc. Some without description. In the windows where they could be seen by young girls and children could see. Hairy lipped woman waiting to sell them.

There was a contrivance attached to the better sort of houses, had heard of but never seen. Set of looking glasses outside of the door. Fine thing for seeing welcome or unwelcome visitors or seeing weather—without twisting head off. People in the upper stories had another contrivance which showed who was passing underneath.

---

bar; however, his interest in journalism led him to work for many years in various capacities on the New York *Herald;* in later years he was physician and companion to Joseph Pulitzer.

[28] In his notes on Thompson, written in 1909, Clemens recalled: "The Shah of Persia had come to England, & Dr. Hosmer had sent me to Ostend to view his majesty's progress across the Channel & write an account of it for the *Herald*. He was in charge of the London office of the paper at the time" (DV 268). Clemens wrote five letters for the New York *Herald* which appeared on 1, 4, 9, 11, and 19 July 1873. They were later collected as "O'Shah" in *Europe and Elsewhere*. Clemens and Thompson, who figures as "Mr. Blank" in the account, evidently crossed over to Ostend on 17 June and came back to Dover aboard the *Lively*, in the shah's wake, on 18 June. Thompson's shorthand notes cover the major portion of the first "O'Shah" letter of 1 July 1873. There are no drafts in the notebook for any of the subsequent *Herald* letters.

The dining room of our hotel was very spacious, very elegant—one whole plate glass. If [one entered]—might think open. [*four words*]. Completely covered in oil paintings.

Went to bed at 10 but [said] that I was not one. Next & so. Reverberatings down the hall & died away. Again. Again at 12. Told no—not me, [call] next but didn't [care]. Didn't understand my English. Told them at 2. Told him I'd call myself. <But> Didn't mean it. Mistrusted me. When came at 3 felt rather bad. Woke me up, gave me cup of coffee & kept me awake until I drank it. Just then in came <S> Mr. Blank. Said was a very good hotel but they took too much pains.

We wandered around about the town until 6 and then drifted aboard the Lively. She was trim<.> and bright<.> and clean and white.

Cock hats lined with silk. Judged all were admirals—got [afraid], went ashore.

Shah's brother & some uncles etc.

Vessel just ahead <was to>, Vigilant, was <Shah> only Shah, Queen's <Em>, Persians. Very glad I was not to go in the vessel with Shah for several reasons: first with him not immediately under my eye not feel responsibility. Second, because I wanted to impress him wanted practice on his brother first.

Now the after part of the vessel was specially for Shah himself. Decorated within & without. Among was the charming color of green which I will speak of in tomorrow's letter.

It was getting along toward time for Shah to arrive from Brussels. Didn't know when I was ever so troubled. I saw a sealed letter. After I saw all those splendid officers I gave that idea up.

Presently long line of Belgian troops. Carpets<.> and flags. The sailor met me with mop to <[wip]>—pointed at some officers asked what the law would do [with] man for speaking [with] one of those admirals. One knew me <I> if he was not mistaken. Furthermore still, all London correspondents would go in the same ship<.> and if it was not lively etc. etc. I could have jumped for joy if not afraid of breaking some naval law and being hanged for it.

Belgians straightened up. Fl[ounders] [trumpets]. Train of 13 cars. [*one word*]. Music. Guns. English officers filed down carpet, uncovered their heads, [unbolted] door.

He was handsome strong-featured man, rather European lightness of complexion, 5 feet high, simply dressed, wore glasses, about 40—<P> not wholly without ornament. Persian behind covered with quilt. Stepped out and down to the ship to slow music. Not Flounder cheered. Attendants crowded. Shah walked aft look at his quarters. London telegraph. Bowed to the King of Kings etc. <Blaze of> [Shah's brother, Shah] perfect blazes of Persian [uniform].

Don't know that I ever looked so simply ostentatious and [imposing] before in my life.

Baggage—

Last got out—long slip—never a cheer. 3 batteries, royal salute. Vigilant ahead, ours next, rest third. Jollification set in. I was thoroughly glad I was got over to fetch the Shah.

Oxford v Cambridge
23 & 24 at *Lord's Grounds*[29]

£1 1s. from S'l Clemens
19th & 20th.
[*two words*] 22d

Wilberforce, bishop of Winchester, 11:30 A.M., Grosvenor Ct., S. Audley St.

N. Hall, 3 <A>P.M., St. James Hall

Mackarness, bishop of Oxford, St. Paul's, Covent Garden.

11 A.M., St. James Chap., York St., Master of Balliol. [#]

---

[29] Oxford was victorious at the annual cricket match, played on 23 and 24 June 1873.

In Sloane St. London they have 19 deliveries of the mail, and on Sunday 23.

£2, June 21.

View of the Castle[30]—light granite, above tops of trees,—stopped a short time at Datchet (Royal St., Datchet) then the train passed on, crossed the river and circling around the "Home Park" (Eton on the right) and ran in to the station right under the Great Tower at the southwest angle of the Castle. Park with rows of immense oak and birch trees, around high hedges of <ivy,> holly etc. Drays, stages, four-in-hands & passing over drive. Flags flying. 130 steps up. Light colored blocks of stone alternating with 4 inch flint layer. Corners of light brown stone. Other parts all light <granite> brown. Others dark granite.

Weather very cloudy—with occasional shower. Flags innumerable —every window church etc.

Passed up with continual stream of people, the Long Walk— immense double rows of trees—very quiet

All kinds of flags except American—did not see an American flag.

It is generally "off the grass and on the walk," but here in central road it was "off the road and onto the grass."

You might suppose you were going through the Great Park, but only the neck connecting Home <Walk>Park (500 acres), where the Castle is, with the Great Park (1800)

---

[30] Thompson's predominantly longhand notes on the review of troops at Windsor Park on 24 June 1873 have no use marks and were not incorporated into "O'Shah." Evidently Clemens' enthusiasm for his "O'Shah" correspondence had diminished considerably by the time he wrote his fifth letter. He finally decided against following the shah to Paris as the *Herald's* correspondent. Despite the availability of Thompson's copious notes, Clemens made only a brief, rather offhand, mention of the Windsor review in his fifth and last letter: "It has been estimated that there were 300,000 people assembled at Windsor—some say 500,000. That was a show in itself. The Queen of England was there; so was Windsor Castle; also an imposing array of cavalry, artillery, and infantry" (*Europe and Elsewhere*, p. 79). A full account of the review, amplifying much of the information in Thompson's notes, is in the London *Times* (25 June 1873).

Side avenues <30> about 30 feet wide & the central drives between 4 or 5 [*two words*].

Very lofty & large green trees. Sky hardly visible between in large spaces.

No vehicle [*one word*] ever allowed in this drive except royal. (?) Small <limb> branches <make the trees> down to your head—higher large branches.

Royal vegetable garden off to the east.

Everything filling to overflow, the wood grand—on large scale.

Length of walk 3½ miles. 20 miles around <W> park. Up the walk came flocking people, all quiet.

South end colossal statue of Geo III.

<Turne> Avenue 3⅓ miles. Turned to right about mile to Queen's Walk.

Stand facing east.

Stand next to great stopping <of> point of Queen. Front of foreign ministers. House of Commons to left, Queen to right & House of Lords.

<Fr[-]> Next neighbor said his friend undertook history of park <neve>—could find no time when there was not a Windsor Park. <Every> No park in the world surpassing it in the matter of nature being kept up and the avoidance of anything that betrays artificiality. Many trees 700 years old—oaks mostly—some elms.

Long Walk planted in times of Chas II.

Several [carriageloads] of Queen's servants (about 100) arrived back of Queen's position [back]. Next <t> on left elegant little covered stand for Persian spectators.

Large open space. Just at the first trees ran line of troops at rest. Other side stretched army <flag> poles <with> white poles with flags. White with gold lion [rayed] with gilt. (*Chas* [*first*]) alternating white. At royal stand two: one red silk-gilt lion, [rayed]<; other> with silver sword; the Prussian, other <ro> British royal standard.

Refreshments furnished for press, foreign ministers etc. (?)

4 Queen, although always very prompt, not on hand. One

remarked that not her fault, <for>. She <always> frequently torments her servants by rising at 6 o'clock. Another remarks <—tha> how she must [*one word*] punctuality itself.

<4> Was to leave at 3. 3:35 at Windsor, 4 at [ground]; arrived at Windsor at <3>4:35

(Interpreter at Guildhall like in synagogue.) Very comprehensive language if reply contained all <the> repeated [for him] (Sir H. Rawlinson).[31] Everybody began to [fear] it would rain before he got there.

Stands <covered> red painted and seats & writing-desks covered with red cloth. Festoons and gilt. (Daily Telegraph [contains 24 positions])

Line presented [line] of to the left colored horses. Then next black horses mounted by Horse Guards, <glittering> red <white> and shining gilt. And next the biggest row of red coat infantry, black <ru>Russian hats & black [pants]. Then some all in black. Then more cavalry—then white [horse] cavalry <the> and on extreme left artillery

4:25 Just as advance body guard came in view, and some dependents, sun burst forth.

Left <[town]> Castle 4:40 <just as they>

<The salute>

(Clouds as heavy as possible not to pour.)

Long distance ahead came 3 Persians & 3 Englishmen—hurried them out with articles in hand, one like [censer] and cleared field of the carriage. Next carriage <3 off> English officers. Next <3

---

[31] Noted Assyriologist, Sir Henry Rawlinson, was the queen's special ambassador to the shah during the visit and occasionally acted as the shah's translator. Clemens had met Rawlinson during his 1872 stay in London at a dinner of the Royal Geographical Society for Henry Stanley, at which the explorer's achievements were belatedly recognized. In a letter to Livy, Clemens described the occasion and the speech of Sir Henry Rawlinson, then president of the society: "And when Sir Henry R. stood up & made the most manly & magnificent apology to Stanley for himself & for the Society that ever I listened to, I thought the man rose to the very pinnacle of human nobility" (25 October 1872, TS in MTP).

Persians & 1 English> [closed carriage] <4 Persians> 3 or 4 Persians. Next 3 Persians & 1 English. Disposed of in same way.

(Pasha, really of more use than any other, not treated well. Pity he and Sultan were not so well treated<.)>—remarks)

Persians dressed like knee short dresses like ladies, some broadcloth, some like gilded dressing gowns. A boy among them.

At about 5 <ab> a body of dragoons galloped off, wheeled down Long Walk to meet the royal party.

4:06 Cannons <fired> commenced firing every few seconds for over a dozen times.

As they circled around by the people and row of troops <doing gu> guard duty. People cheering all along—

Dog little black one heading procession—(look at dog! Isn't he most remarkable beast?) On 3 legs [walking] back-

48 Scotch Greys.

Shah on white horse. Duke of Cambridge on right, dressing gown style, blue sash—Queen 4 white horses, open carriage with 3 ladies.

(Officer thrown & horse ran far off into park)

Black dog, [Shah's] carriage & 4 went out after him in a hurry

Queen in black—looked very happy. With Princess of Wales and Princess Dagmar.

Thrown Persian got another horse and galloped off amid cheers.

<Persians had>

Shah looked quite animated when came up and <looked> spoke to the Queen. Riding proudly. Nearly spilled. The Burgomaster of Berlin. That Shah's horse white tail bound with gold band or brass about middle, rest dyed red.

Eton boys cheer lustily with beavers on.

Shah, blue over left shoulder—

<June 18>

Prince of Wales & Czar[32] with blue sashes over right [shoulder].

---

[32] The heir apparent to the Russian throne and his wife, Princess Dagmar of Denmark, were visiting London and attended most of the festivities arranged for the shah's visit.

Next to Shah, [brother] with green sash broad over right shoulder. Then Band of Guards <&> played in front on horseback. Other music to right while troops marched by

Behind Queen, John Brown Scotchman[33]

Cavalry stacked behind right wing

(Music "Man of Airlie")

Shah's brother covered with gilt.

While cavalry passes, sun comes out. (Was told by man coming in in the train, Queen always brings fair weather)

One host of musicians after another came up to the right & left and played away

Cheered the beautiful lines as they marched by—man said that thought [troops] must get this idea from [*two or three words*] etc.

Prince of Wales went to join his regiment. Prince Arthur, captain in this same regiment. Blackest plainest looking body of troops there.

Band played quick music while cavalry & artillery cantered briskly by.

Prince of Wales in uniform of his regiment.

Then galloped <cavalry> the infantry in—

Then skirmishers

Then general firing

Artillery run forward on the right & fire awhile, limber up & fly away on right & left, exposing infantry who fire by brigade. Continually! Then down centre—the artillery—then left & all—continuous roar

Two princes with Shah's picture on.

Then cavalry and charged—trumpeters giving the orders. Then halfway [troops]—then several brigades down from left, followed

---

33 John Brown, once a stable boy at Balmoral Castle, was Queen Victoria's personal attendant from 1865 until his death in 1883. Brown had come into the public eye in February 1872 when he saved the queen from a would-be assassin who thrust himself into her carriage. The queen's attachment to Brown was a subject of some scandalous speculation. An artist's rendering of the scene at the Windsor review in the *Illustrated London News* shows Brown, in Highland costume, sitting behind the queen in her carriage (5 July 1873).

by others<.> and others <weaving> cutting their way through while

Shah presented sword to Duke of Cambridge, showed it to Queen. Curving with purple scabbard. Left in Queen's carriage to carry home for him.

Then all took up line. 3 cheers. Sunshine.

Prince Leopold—

Persian with dressing gown off horse.

Then the whole creation of people poured over the field—

Fishing Cottage in place of old temple at Virginia Waters. Shah said better pleased with it than with anything during tours.

Postal Telegraph, "Come to have my photograph took"

R.W. Johnston one of "Goodwood Races,"

7 short of 1,000

[Showing] to be more effective than field military.

Scudamore head of <Telegraph> Postal Telegraph system in England.[34]

10 minutes of 8. <Will> This establishment be removed from here in ¼ hour and early tomorrow will be [working] at [*blank space*] on the Th[---] for the races.

Police officer explained. Two Persian officers on the horse road

35,000 people 8,000 troops.

<L June>
Langham hotel
June 25th

Dear sir;

I thank you very much for your kind offers, but I fear that I shall not have an opportunity of visiting Manchester. I shall probably have no time to travel about any while I am here. I am dear sir yours faithfully.

R. Cowley—Esq.[35] [#]

[34] As second secretary of the General Post Office, Frank Ives Scudamore initiated many reforms in England's postal system before he resigned in 1875. He was later hired by the Ottoman government to organize the Turkish post office.

[35] Although they appear in the usual position for signatures, the names at the

<Langham hotel>
June 25th

<Dear sir,>
<Dear Watterson,>[36]
Dear sir,

You are under a misapprehension, I have not called at the Examiner office; but [all that have] said in your note<—>should go very well. Very dearly,

R. Cowley—Esquire

L. L. Sergeant
The Langham hotel
June 25

My dear sir,

I shall be very glad indeed to renew the acquaintance. I am usually at home about noon, but after that, like everybody else in London I am uncertain. With many thanks for your former kindnesses to me, I am yours very sincerely.

Lewis Sergeant Esq.
Chas E. [Soth] Smith Esq. [#]

---

ends of this and the following two letters are evidently those of the persons to whom the letters are addressed. R. Cowley and Charles Smith have not been identified. Lewis Sergeant was a journalist and author, for several years a writer for the London *Daily Chronicle*.

36 Colonel Henry Watterson, editor of the Louisville *Courier-Journal* and a distant relative of Clemens, had sailed for England a week before Clemens and was in London throughout the summer. Watterson and Clemens met frequently during that time (Joseph Frazier Wall, *Henry Watterson* [New York: Oxford University Press, 1956], pp. 116–117). One of the objects of their mutual interest was the case of the Tichborne Claimant and the parallel claim of their Kentucky kinsman, Jesse Leathers, who claimed to be the earl of Durham. Watterson later recalled Clemens' interest in the two cases: "During the Tichborne trial Mark and I were in London, and one day he said to me: 'I have investigated this Durham business down at the Herald's office. There is nothing to it. The Lamptons passed out of the earldom of Durham a hundred years ago. There were never any estates; the title lapsed; the present earldom is a new creation, not in the same family at all. But I'll tell you what: if you'll put up $500, I'll put up $500 more; we'll bring our chap over here and set him in as claimant, and, my word for it, Kenealy's fat boy [the counsel for the obese Tichborne Claimant was Dr. Edward Kenealy] won't be a marker to him'" (*MTB*, p. 497).

Left Waterloo Station about 1. Rather slow trains £30,000. Rained occasionally. "Queen always brings fair weather." (Old fellow & Queen)

Same road. Ship.

Poppy flowers. & trees.

Staines

Just before getting to Datchet Station first sight of Windsor Castle.[37]

Points of description:

<Rising> Whitish grey mass rising out of green old trees—no ground visible around.

Begun by Wm Conqueror, added to different [sums], last amount expended by Geo IV, $3,855,000.

Present reign $350,000 on stables.

Round tower in all 150 ft above Quadrangle.

Datchet where <Q> royalty.

Pontoons.

N. W., Crossed over down S. W.

View across park.

Crowds & flags everywhere. No American flags.

Long Walk.

Flocked very quietly

(?) People chime in with police. Public sense of decency

What Shah thought of <P> Virginia Waters etc.

Troops

4 P.M. <Impatient Q> Nobody came

Previous arrangement 3—3:35—4. Remarks about promptness of Queen.

Next to me Telegraphman Scudamore, head of Postal Telegraph System in England.

Looking very like rain—wished for Queen to bring clear weather if nothing more.

Shah arrived at Windsor 4:35. ½ million patient people quietly

---

[37] The route to Windsor via South Western Railway from Waterloo Station ran past the towns of Staines and Datchet.

waiting. Only 4 police for nearly 1,000 Eton boys who are considered very unruly, on public occasions—<beav>. These [latter] distinguished themselves by cheering—beaver hats. In America college boys & beavers.

Carriages began to arrive. Watching for Queen in distance. People all along line. Some never got to see all day<—saw>—heard them say so afterwards.

At last at about 5 Queen came. Incident on the way. Good manners of the people. Come in with salute. Description of all. Cheering. Dog—notice—headed procession in spite of arrangement. Take position—salute. Start round

Persian thrown.
Persian March
Cheering coming back—especially Eton boys
Positions, and appearance.
Music moves up and marches around.
Scotch.

In England they use very much coarser needlework than in America.

Block on Portland Place has 6 lamps.

St. James'(?), Duncan Terrace, Islington.

Archbishop Manning, St. Peter's, Italian Church, Hatton Gardens, 7 P.M.

2 Book of Chron., 7 verse

Mrs. Susanna Carrington who died 18th April 1719
Mary Bowles first daughter of Carrington and Anne Bowles

The within are gone to rest. "This tomb was discovered in its present position in 186[9] and [bricked] around by the Corporation of London."

Sacred to the memory of David Nasmith founder of city

missions, born at Glasgow died at Guilford Nov. 17th 1839, 41st year[38]

Archdeacon Claughton, St. Luke 14th v, 18 ch

4th July (Friday) 8 P.M., Hanover Sq. Rooms.

King's College, July 9th, apply to J. W. Cunningham Esq. K.C.

Floral Hall, July 5 (Saturday), commence at 2 P.M.[39]

Saw a white nurse taking [care of] colored baby—today in Regent's Park saw a pretty, modest [lady] looking English girl, hanging on the arm of a darkey, conversing. Both quiet, honest looking air. Never taking any notice. Never seeming to see anything improper or unusual about it.

Attended church. The centre equipped by benches, more benches full length of the church; plenty [that come up] to sit on. Great [part] of the church on the other hand was boxed up in pews. When one got in the pew, <he> there was only room for his knees; and the seats so high from the floor that he must have footstool. Room enough for his knees—[but very close time otherwise]. 12 inches wide. And the back of the pew was shut up and down. And it reached up just to a person's ears. And of all the infernal contrivances for making men sin right in church, that's the most ingenious.

There were some old women pew-openers; one with a very sweet face. And they showed nice discrimination in the matter of clothes. They spot a nice [dress] in moment. Put that person in purgatory. Good cloth in central aisle, good [easy seats]. Other [*one word*] for confessions. Take turns. People had to listen to you. 1.20 for Litany.

---

[38] A list at the end of the notebook indicates that Clemens and Thompson visited Saint Saviour's Church and Saint Helen's Church in London. The tomb inscription to David Nasmith, however, is in the Bunhill Fields burying ground on the outskirts of London. This and the other tomb inscriptions which Thompson entered in his notebook may not have been copied at Clemens' direction.

[39] The last Floral Hall concert of the season took place on 5 July 1873 with Adelina Patti and the band and chorus of the Royal Italian Opera performing.

Lord's Prayer <3>4 times. 35 for sermon etc. and then 3 prayers.

There was one old lady evidently regular attendant there who knew all the ropes; and it delighted her to say [*one word*] to resp., sing hymn while [performing] [*two words*] looking at her book. Happier there than ever be in heaven. Cock her head—

There was beadle in front of the church, but didn't see him doing anything. For style, I suppose.

There is to be service here at 8 next Sunday morning. So will try to get up early [enough and go]. Have to get secured seats, else break neck looking up at him.

300 witnesses swear positively that Claimant is Roger Tichborne. And about as many more swear positively that he is not. That he should have attempted this imposture seems incredible when one remembers the number of persons he must at least know by name and have some general idea of anyhow. And of localities also [however] vague. And an infinitude of trifling circumstances stretching over two thirds of generation that he must have some little acquaintance with<.>; even relationships he ought to know. It would be easy for his lawyer to say to him, one of your cousin's named Mary Ann Smith & is married. Another, Mary Jane Jones & is not married. Wm Johnson. Some other relatives are [W^{m}, Bill, Geo., Bill, Willi, Jim, W^{m} being] married. Easy enough for a lawyer to say that to [*one word*] client but how is he going to keep it in his head. <Stra> Wonder that should ever have undertaken it. Evidence did show that he had a lot of names at his tongue's end. But he didn't [*three words*]. He should give details all along in Roger Tichborne's life. Couple of dates confused. But wonderful in <that he kept> the odds and ends he was able to [deliver] in his evidence.

To show the value of evidence [anyway] I talked with a gentleman who is very cultivated man, with an acknowledged place in science. Man who has mixed in the world [a bit]. Had a conversation with Claimant. Says that he is low, vulgar, cockney-speaking butcher. Then I talked with member of aristocracy who is known all over the world<,> as a very able man, and he said that <the Claimant had> there is nothing vulgar or low about the Claimant. Refined —every inch a gentleman. No cockney in his speech. Had touch of accent in his speech common to Roger Tichborne and that he never for a moment doubted that he was Roger Tichborne until the fatal tattoo mark. If that Tichborne property belonged to me so great is my curiosity in this business and so great is my [*one word*] I give ¾ to know. If he is the man this is the most pathetic case in history. Poor devil could have gentle tender heart. Overturned by his matrimonial project. He shall go wandering [away life time], finally he [*three words*] to savage lands by the sea. And then taking [ship] again to be cast away at sea. Suffer 3 days and nights. Insensible <3> of his rescue. Then life [nobody] knows out in the wilds of Australia, 14 years. Then coming back [healed, wealthy] easy for life. Finds the whole world arrayed against him. Finally after having seen his estates torn away from him and given to another, had been brought up on a charge of perjury, 3 months. Result probably 20 years in penal colony. And if he is an impostor, [the bravest, the brightest] that ever lived. Had got to go and personate [foreigner]. For he only learned the English language after he was 18 or 19 or 20 years old. And he went away from here 22. Knew he'd have to describe things that he never had seen, and people—another man's handwriting—copy another man's inaccuracies. New inaccuracies would not do, must be those of the person he impersonated.

July 2.

Didn't introduce anybody to anybody else except that they introduce person to one other person, and that was sufficient. I saw that in 2 or 3 other cases<.> and my own case. Sat around among fine people ½ hour. Took pity on our lonely condition. Came and introduced lady near—<and introduced lady nearest to me, whose name I didn't [understand]. There were dozen around about of ladies, but> it just so happened that I was introduced to this one. And she couldn't speak any English except very few struggling words. She brightened up and said she could speak French. Then I said I couldn't. Then she brightened up and said she could speak German. Conversation flags. Spanish. Looking in opposite direction. With blood in [her eye]. Italian <5> was spoken 5 minutes. Finally, this time without much confidence, hopeless [kind of way]<.>—Greek. So I passed. [Through] all the [*one word*] in the world with this little polyglot. Between us we spoke all the languages there are; I one and she all the rest. [*three words*].

Melancholy spectacle of the son of Douglas Jerrold[40] sitting around in the hall of magnificent house. His turn to come out and speak or recite or imitate something, then be up and go about his business. 45 years old. (Icebergs), from all I can see. Young [*one word*], yes, yes awful jolly. You don't tell me so.

Talk ten minutes with 6 chowder heads. Looking round at people, & down the table. This sort of conversational ability among the ladies of Great Britain is [probably to be accounted for from the fact] that all men belong to a dozen clubs<.>; and are never at home except when the justices are after them.

Horse Guards (Black G'ds)

Servant to Sir Fred. Pollard,[41] at luncheon said, "Will you 'ave some hice in your 'ock Sir."

The man who attempts to wield a dialect which he has not been actually bred to is a muggins. Neither Bret Harte nor Dickens nor anybody else can write a dialect not acquainted with. I never undertook to produce an [early] cockney [lest] I should not succeed. Unless I had heard him say it. But when Mr. Dickens tries to

---

[40] Clemens mentioned having met journalist and author "Douglas Jerrold, Jr" (William Blanchard Jerrold, son of the English humorist) at a dinner party in his letter to Mrs. Fairbanks of 6 July 1873 (*MTMF*, p. 173). Clemens made a note in Notebook 23 (1884–1885) to describe the "polyglot woman" in the preceding entry and "poor Douglas Jerrold jr & his dirty shirt standing in hall with footmen."

[41] Sir Frederick Pollock (1815–1888) of the Court of Exchequer made a brief note of the occasion in his diary: "*28th June.*—Luncheon at home. Lady Castletown, Madame Mohl, Clemens (Mark Twain) and his wife, Joaquin Miller, G. S. Venables, George Cayley" (*Personal Remembrances of Sir Frederick Pollock*, 2 vols. [London: Macmillan and Co., 1887], 2:252–253).

produce Yankee dialect, he [showed for once mistake]. He made his Yankee talk as no Yankee.

Bret Harte <was the> is not acquainted with Pike County dialect. And been called the great master of dialect. Defy him to write 3 sentences. [*one word*] Christmas ([one of] his sketches)[42] he mixes about 7 dialects, put them all in the one unhappy Missouri mouth. [*four words*] [showed] to me that what was always apparent in the novels as the grossest burlesque and nonsense <is the> is actually underwrought.

As usual didn't hear his name. Don't suppose he heard mine. Bowed stiffly. I went one better, looked off. Then out of his left eye and coughed. I went one better & cleared my throat. "Do you know who it is that's singing?" "Ah yes charming," etc. Didn't understand<.>—I could gather that from the nature of the reply. Turned to him, said, "Do you know who it is?" "Yes charming," etc. Going to ask him to dinner, but turned away [*one word*] [club]. One of pleasantest briefest acquaintances. Person of brains never delivers the commonplace. But [first] Jerrold said the <commonplace.> good thing. Told me didn't look like man. No. Didn't think [*two words*]. No not altogether. <I said> 2 or 3 distinguished singers.

"I suppose you know Madame Christine's[43] going to sing here tonight."

"Who is Miss Christine?"

"One of the distinguished singers of London."

"I will listen to her."

He said, "I will see how she looks."

Craned his neck. Disenchanted. Just so in this case. Old, and brown and wrinkled. Splendidly attired. In diamonds. Red satin dress

---

[42] Clemens may be referring to Bret Harte's Christmas story "How Santa Claus Came to Simpson's Bar," which appeared first in the *Atlantic Monthly* (29 [March 1872]: 349–357).

[43] Swedish soprano Christine Nilsson was appearing with Her Majesty's Opera, Drury Lane, performing several times in May, June, and July 1873 in her most famous roles, Marguerite and Mignon.

quilted. Slippers—feet crossed. [Cloud] about the neck. Court train on behind. (Perfectly queenly-looking large woman)

Some of the [others] were very best in England, descended from the Duchess of Cle[veland] and several other particular friends of Chas II.

Museum Sheriff, Hutton Park, Yorkshire

Mr. Benj. Bowles, Pinchbeck Road, Spalding, Lincolnshire.

Curious books in "Old Catalogue of London."
"*Glasses for weak eyed citizens*"[44]
"Pair of spectacles for the Citye."
—A Case for the City Spectacles.
—A Looking-glass for the Well affected in London.
—A Candle for the Blind citizens of London to see by.
—An eye salve for the City of London
—A speedy cure to open the eyes of the blind, and the ears of the deaf citizens of London

Cases of Personal Identity
6485.d

An Exercitation Concerning the frequent use of Our Lord's Prayer in the Publick Worship of God and a view of what hath been said by Dr. Owen concerning the subject—by Thomas Long, Preacher of the Gospel 1658.

In London women vote in municipal elections.

Call a woman a female
Druggists are called chemists [#]

---

[44] The political broadsides noted here were among those distributed daily in London in 1647 and 1648 by both Royalists and Roundheads shortly before the execution of Charles I. These notes may have been made at the British Museum, where the broadsides are part of the extensive Thomason Tracts collection.

"[Enr]aged that she should enquire for whiting rag at oil store."

Get pen-maker and lot of quill pens.
Blotting paper.

Plenty of people of more or less distinction bang away and write you a note, without signing it at; and you hardly know sometimes who it does come from.[45]

THESE
ALMS-HOUSES
Were Founded by
ANDRE JUDD
Citizen & Skinner
And Lord Mayor of London[46]

"Out of the Windmill" 1632

Here Lockyer lies interr'd enough his name
Speakes one who hath feu competitors in fame:
A name, soe Great, soe Generall may scorne
Inscriptions w^c^h doe vulgar tombs adorne:
A diminution tis, to write in verse
His eulogies, w^c^h most mens mouths reherse,
His virtues & his PILLS are soe well known,
That envy cant confine them under stone,
But they'l survive his dust, and not expire,
Till all things else at th'universall fire,
This verse is lost his PILL Embalmes him Safe
To futures times without an Epitaph:

---

[45] Livy commented on this custom in a letter to Jane Clemens and Pamela Moffett: "Some Great people here do not sign their letter[s] [f]or fear their names will be removed for autographs or the entire letter taken as an autograph letter—I think I must adopt that habit—" (TS in MTP, [July] 1873).

[46] The monument and inscription to Sir Andrew Judd are in Saint Helen's Church, Bishopsgate, London.

Repaired Octo^{br} 1741.
Deceast Aprill ye 26th
Anno D: 1672.
Aged 72.[47]

<In> To the memory of Mr. Richard Bliss, of this parish, A Faithful Friend and most affectionate Husband his wife.

Crying baby—deathhead with wings

"To encourage the Minister"

Behests similar to tenures.

Spurgeon's sermon "Race between old, & novelty."
<Westminster>
Sing-song, giving out notice

Something better than <gold and silver> gold and [*one word*].
Lord Chesterfield.
Inglorious liberty of the pen.
Shah
"Once a child of God always the child of God."
Jehovah. End.

One of the gentlemen present at the dinner given to me here by B was a high [Ch— tenor] from D—; Christ Church, Dublin; (?) Sunday night, he sang love songs, sentimental songs, pleasantly too. And was an exceedingly pleasant & sociable man.

Said in England the [*three words*]<.> that great [*blank space*] [*one word*] lake in Regent's Park, 6 feet deep. [Somebody broke through ice]. Nearly drowned. Authorities reduced & artificially supplied [to] 3 or 4;[48] so Mr. Hardy[49] tells me. [#]

---

47 The tomb and the curious epitaph of Lockyer, a notorious London quack, is in Saint Saviour's Church near London Bridge.

48 This partially deciphered entry may refer to a disastrous accident in the winter of 1866/1867 in which nearly forty skaters died when the ice of the artificial lake in Regent's Park broke.

49 Sir Thomas Duffus Hardy was for many years deputy keeper of the Public Record Office in London. Clemens remembered him as "loving, cordial, simple-hearted as a girl; fond of people of all ranks, if they are only good & have brains;

Story of a casual acquaintance.[50]

Re Mr. Stevenson, [*one word*] friend of [Lady] Hardy. To Nor[mandy] for his health. Very feeble indeed. Stopped awhile in Rouen. One day strolled out to outskirts of the city<.>; found himself on the top of St. Michel's Mont [each sunny] day. Very [gentlemanly modest] well-dressed French [gentleman] addressed him in English with French accent; said that he had worked hard to learn English language and had learned it after fashion, but he seldom had opportunity to talk with Englishman. Very fond of the English. [Wished he could come cross]. Hope not intruding. Not at all, [bear] company. So they sat on the grass some time. Very pleasant time. Finally Frenchman said, "You are traveling for pleasure?"

"No, anything but that; health very precarious."

"Indeed," said man, "let me feel pulse," which he did. Man said, "What are you taking?" Told him. "That's very good very good: but if you will allow me I'll suggest something better than that. Surer than that. Have this medicine immediately, see it right away." So he gave Stevenson a prescription, told him get filled at Cher[bourg]. And have [care about] his own name which is necessary thing in country. Dr. La Balle. Gave Stevenson card.

---

devoting his house, his heart & his hospitalities four hours every Saturday night to a host of bright people . . . & he is heartily aided & abetted in all this by his wife & daughter" (*MTMF*, p. 175).

[50] Clemens attended one of the Hardys' Saturday evenings on 5 July 1873, probably the occasion upon which Lady Mary McDowell Duffus Hardy, a well-known novelist in England, told him "the *facts* upon which her 'Casual Acquaintance' was founded—a thrilling recital & admirably done" (*MTMF*, p. 176). Lady Hardy's *A Casual Acquaintance: A Novel Founded on Fact* was published in 1866 (London: Low & Co.) and received very favorable reviews. The novel concerns a Frenchman, Raoul St. Pierre, who frees himself to marry an English heiress by murdering his first wife "in a railway carriage, and sending her corpse on to Paris in a first-class *coupé*" (review in the *Athenaeum* 2005 [March 1866]: 426). One of St. Pierre's aliases in the book is "De la Belle." The Mr. Stevenson in Thompson's stenographic account of the story has not been conclusively identified—possibly the innocent traveler was the Reverend Joseph Stevenson, historian and archivist in the Public Record Office. Thompson's stenographic account breaks off abruptly in the midst of the story; the account stops at the end of a gathering of pages in the stenographic notebook, and the worn binding and loose leaves at this point indicate that pages have been lost.

Stevenson so fascinated [by the] man<:> never supposed go right off and have it filled. But when he thought, ashamed of his doubts. Said, "What [motive]? None at all. Crazy man might. This [only] pleasant, good man." Got it filled. Went Cher[bourg] asking [unquiet]. Was reassured. Hotel—took medicine, felt immediately better. Next day felt better. To Mt. St. Michel. Find. Thank. Ingracious, no fee. Wandered some time. By and by [sure enough, found Doctor]. Said that he had come up there in hope that he might come back there<.>, so could learn what effect it had. So Stevenson thanked him very cordially and faithfully. Said wanted to pay. But Doctor refused, and said he had offered advice without being asked, reward [unnecessary]. "Well," Doctor said by and by after some talk<.>, "you said you'd like to testify little service I been able to afford. You say going to Paris direct and in that case you can do me quite a service. If any inconvenience<.> [*one word*]. I have in the house last 3 weeks [*blank space*] very wealthy, can't cure. Have relieved her all I can. Very nervous, excitable—perhaps mind's little touched. She is perfectly harmless. And as I have done all I can for her, it's just as well she should return to her friends. They are aware. Been waiting opportunity to send. Alone won't do that. I have patients can't leave for day. Won't do for me to go. Now if you be kind enough to take this lady in charge, and just sit with her till you get Paris."

Awkward kind of business, take flighty woman to Paris. Train at one o'clock in the morning: and he supposed it would hardly do to send sick person in the night. Doctor said that was little uncomfortable but only chance; entirely healthy, night air not hurt. If no inconvenience would send her. Stevenson said not at all [*one word*] to him. Doctor said, "Very well I'll reach station at about 15 to one." "All right." So they parted.

This disturbed Stevenson great deal. W[alked] about Rouen bothering about it. Inquired of someone in casual way if <nothing> nobody knew Dr. La Balle. Head of that stair. Getting twilight. Went by the name on the plate. Wanted to go in, but some instinct. No reason. Put in restless time till 15. Doctor [on station from] 5 minutes, hoped he would rest [*one word*]. Touched him presently.

Said, "She is slightly paralyzed in lower limbs. If you will walk along platform I'll help her in the coupé. Have taken coupé for you 2. She's elderly lady. Needn't expect be [full of any] remarks." In 2 minutes was time for train to start. Took in the coupé; says, "Now there she is." Woman sitting up in the corner, heavily veiled. Said, "She's not talkative person. Not talkative. All you have to do step out on the platform, and ask for Madame —'s carriage . . . there are purse, tickets, chest. There is vial containing medicine to keep her quiet & soothe her, and relieve her pain. If she complains in the night [why] just a drop on sugar."

Corner seat, middle seat basket of flowers, other for Stevenson. Odor of flowers mixed up with stench of cologne and some other villainous smell. Doctor said, "Sorry for this. Guess some [German] smoking. Oh no, leave window if . . . ! Oh no, wind a lot better for her."

[La Balle got off, cleared out]. Woman sat there; by and by Stevenson spoke to her pleasantly. But no reply. And

Negro minstrel statue near Trafalgar Sq.

Statuette [pike].

Ugly faces—in Westminster

Old custom—blue coat boys without any caps.

Chancels long, and inclined to one or the other side a little.

Quarreling in public. "Bear"

Send you to the Zoological Society. That's where you came from.

History of 2 Queens by Hepworth Dixon—Cath. of Aragon & Ann Boleyn.

Recollections of Page to Court of Louis XVI. From the French by Charlotte M. Yonge

Hurst & Blackett, Great Marlborough[51] [#]

---

[51] Hurst & Blackett, a publishing company at 13 Great Marlborough Street, had issued the first two volumes of William Hepworth Dixon's blank verse history and Charlotte Yonge's translation of the Comte d'Hézecques' French work shortly before Clemens' arrival in London.

5 Guinea Atlas, 6 & 7 Charing Cross

[Sleadman] & Co., 134 Upper Thames St.

There was formerly an earldom of Delawarr[52] and in the same family another peerage which belonged to the second son; he would be Lord Buckhurst. And that Buckhurst peerage became extinct. Finally in Lord Palmerston's time this family asked him to revive that old Buckhurst peerage. Said he was not in favor of poor peers. If they would [put] property enough to support that peerage he would. Which was done. By and by there was time when there was but one son. He inherited both the Delawarr & Buckhurst property and titles. He died leaving 3 sons. The eldest claimed now to hold the whole concern just as the [father] had done. And it was contested in the courts by the second son who was a master of the [G-s]. He held that now etc. Quite a knotty question with lawyers. "[Was a] peer always Lord Buckhurst?" Before it was decided, this last committed suicide. Third son came forward and claimed his. This [*one word*] changed his mind [naturally]. Claimed that this property got mixed up in his father's time, and descended to the eldest son etc., and now this Buckhurst property is not inhabited during the lawsuit; and the case goes on.

Conversation of 2 American women.

First said they couldn't go Kew Gardens without a carriage. Didn't believe it<.>: who told you so? First, said—man. Second doesn't believe it. Third said didn't believe they could go without car. Asked her if she had been there <so>. No. Second said abominable that they couldn't go without car. Couldn't turn around in England without paying something. Greatest place to spend money she ever saw. <Told> Information without paying. Third asked <if> second if she had been to Crystal Palace. No. . .

---

52 The conflicting claims on the Delawarr and Buckhurst titles, which had arisen during the lifetime of the fifth earl of Delawarr, had been precipitated by the suicide of Charles, sixth earl of Delawarr in April 1873. Having left no issue, the sixth earl was succeeded by his brother Reginald Windsor, Baron Buckhurst.

Third said couldn't go in anywhere there without paying penny. First second seemed so indignant that they were not going.

kr kr kr[53]

Richmond Park July Wed—

Lines on James Th—[54] the poet of Nature.

Ye who from London's smoke & turmoil fly,
To seek the purer air and drier sky,
Think of the bard who dwelt in yonder dell,
Who sang so sweetly what he loved so well.
Think as ye gaze on these luxuriant bowers
How T— loved the sunshine and the flowers.
He who could paint in all their varied forms
April's [laughing] bloom, December's dreary storms
By yon [very] stream which [calmly] glides along
Pure as his life and lovely as his song,
There oft he roved; in yonder churchyard lies,
All of the deathless bard that ever dies;
For there his gentle spirit lingers still,
In yon sweet vale,—on this unchanged hill;
Flinging the [*two words*] o'er the grove,
Stirring the heart to poetry and love;
[Few so] prize the favored scenes he trod,
And view in nature's beauty, nature's god.

July 11th

Last month Shakespeare[55] took in $300. And his yearly income now

---

[53] Throughout the preceding anecdote, Thompson systematically confused the shorthand symbols for *kr* and *kl* (writing *cal* and *calage* for *car* and *carriage*). He evidently realized his mistake after finishing the entry and wrote this line of practice symbols.

[54] Numerous memorial verses dedicated to the eighteenth-century pastoral poet James Thomson are quoted in Douglas Grant's *James Thomson* (London: Cresset Press, 1951, pp. 271–282); however, no mention is made of the verse entered here.

[55] During his 1872 English visit Clemens had received an invitation from Mr. Flower, mayor of Stratford-on-Avon, to visit Shakespeare's birthplace as his guest

is $2500 just from [completing] his house; and the income of Anne Hathaway, his wife, is just about as great. So that they both prosper more now than they ever did in life.

Halliwell[56] has placed 2 or 3 doz. volumes of manuscript [*one word*], neatly bound in the Shakespeare house [to be read] when he is dead. [Evidently there] no man in Shakespeare's day able to appreciate him. Ben Jonson said Bacon was not a great man because he couldn't comprehend or appreciate him. It is curious there is not scrap of manuscript in the shape of a letter or note of Shakespeare in the present day except the letter of somebody trying to [borrow] £30 from him.[57] It is <a> most remarkable destr. annihilation of manuscripts. [Proof that] Shakespeare existed; man would not go around trying to b[--] from shadow. <There is a [doubt] that> It

---

(*MTMF*, p. 168). Clemens finally took advantage of the invitation in the second week of July 1873, when these notes were made. The trip to Stratford involved an amiable deception by Clemens and Moncure Conway on the unsuspecting Livy. Conway retold the episode in his autobiography: "Mrs. Clemens was an ardent Shakespearian, and Mark Twain determined to give her a surprise. He told her that we were going on a journey to Epworth, and persuaded me to connive with the joke by writing to Charles Flower not to meet us himself but send his carriage. On arrival at the station we directed the driver to take us straight to the church. When we entered and Mrs. Clemens read on Shakespeare's grave 'Good frend for Jesus sake forbeare,' she started back exclaiming, 'Heavens, where am I!' Mark received her reproaches with an affluence of guilt, but never did lady enjoy a visit more than that to Avonbank" (2:145). A conspiratorial letter from Conway to Clemens written on 7 July, "the eve of the glorious and never-to-be-disremembered-or-underestimated day when we are to visit Hepworth, the birthplace of a great man" confirms the story in Conway's published memoir. On 14 July 1873 Clemens wrote to Mr. Flower from the Langham Hotel in London, thanking him for the pleasant visit and adding that "no episode in our two months' sojourn in England has been . . . so altogether rounded & complete" (Folger Shakespeare Library, Washington, D.C.).

[56] James Orchard Halliwell-Phillipps, English antiquarian and Shakespeare scholar, arranged and catalogued the archives of Stratford-on-Avon and in 1848 published an extensive biographical and bibliographical work, *The Life of William Shakespeare*.

[57] The letter, preserved at Stratford, is the appeal of Richard Quiney for the loan of £30 from his "loveinge contreyman" William Shakespeare and "enjoys the distinction of being the only surviving letter which was delivered into Shakespeare's hand" (Sidney Lee, *A Life of William Shakespeare*, 4th ed. [New York: Macmillan Co., 1925], pp. 294, 295).

is an amazing thing that Pe[pys] or Bos[well] [*six words*] Shakespeare in the diary. Yet certainly very celebrated man. [When without doubt] he had been publishing and writing as many as 5 or 6 books at least bearing his name. And when his big book came, <1883>1683, then they put up that painted horror which passes for his bust. They say reason why [long] lips[58] etc.<.>, man who was making it chipped [amiss] and had to chisel it up in order to cover the imperfections.

In the garden back of Shakespeare's garden they grow no flowers except those mentioned in his books. But still it makes a pretty good-sized garden—pretty [variegated]. It is more respected than any other [man's]. [For] certainly [without travelers he would have] stately sepulcher. But [even] they had too much respect to <whittle> chip. But they have [wasted] a lot of time. Have only caught 2 or 3 persons trying to chip off little pieces of the wood.

Shakespeare's mulberry tree[59] has been cut [down] by that thieving monster.[60] Yet plenty of the wood left. Man in Warwick furnishes

---

58 The bust of Shakespeare in the Stratford church is believed to have been executed shortly before the publication of the First Folio in 1623 by Garret Johnson the younger. Sir Sidney Lee describes the bust as "a clumsy piece of work. The bald domed forehead, the broad and long face, the plump and rounded chin, the long upper lip, the full cheeks, the massed hair about the ears, combine to give the burly countenance a mechanical and unintellectual expression" (Lee, *A Life of William Shakespeare,* p. 524).

59 Some years later (probably between 1880 and 1882), Clemens wrote a humorous twelve-page letter to the New York *Evening Post* about a cutting from the Shakespeare mulberry tree which he had been given while a guest "in the hospitable home of the Mayor of Stratford-on-Avon" (Mark Twain Memorial, Hartford). The manuscript was never sent to the *Evening Post* and never published, although Clemens evidently later suggested the piece for inclusion in *The Stolen White Elephant* volume of sketches. William Dean Howells, in his 7 April 1882 letter to J. R. Osgood, selected the sketches for the book and suggested that "The Shakespeare Mulberry" be dropped.

60 The "thieving monster" was the Reverend Francis Gastrell, one of the subsequent owners of Shakespeare's New Place, who had the mulberry tree cut down in 1756. A Stratford artisan, Thomas Sharp, secured most of the wood from the felled mulberry tree and "by converting it into goblets, cassolettes, tooth-pick cases, boxes, inkstands, and other ornamental objects, drove a thriving trade for many years" (Henry G. Bohn, *The Biography and Bibliography of Shakespeare* [London: Privately printed, 1863], p. 253). Clemens' "man in Warwick" appears to be the successor to Sharp.

any amount of these trinkets. If you wanted a bootjack <if you> you could get it. And this man I called on him and he showed me through his [various] departments. 33 sets of [*one word*]. 3[00] bedsteads. Same tree. Third floor sofas & such things. And they were building a [*one word*] in the 5th floor out of the mulberry tree.

The man's lumberyard covers 13 acres of this mulberry tree.

July 11th

Dear Mr. Smith,

[*one sentence*]. We should be at Mr. MacDonald's on the 16th. And then, as you say, we can arrange the date.

Sincerely yours.[61]

July 11th

Dear Sir,

Will Tuesday evening 15th do? And if so, at what hour should we be at the <W> Victoria Station? We were out of town, and didn't get your note until last night.

<My dear Sir John,>[62]

July 11th

"[*four words*] a man whose wife's a widow?"

2 young men wanted to see Sir W. Scott's name<.> scratched on Shakespeare's window. Wanted to find it themselves. Did find it. Hunted it out of the spider webs & [*blank space*]. Reason, because 20 years ago their father [*blank space*]. Spoken so often about it, described place; that they knew they could find the place.

Stratford is full of Shakespeare stories. Falstaff inn etc. But there is a singular absence of [kingly] titles. In any other place there would

---

61 The Clemenses attended the garden party at the home of preacher and novelist George MacDonald on 16 July 1873. The writer's wife, Louise MacDonald, described the party in her letter of 10 July 1873 to Livy: "The 16th—Wednesday aft—is the day on wh. we are going to act our play we call it our *July Jumble*—our programme includes the inhabitants from some of the courts of Mary-le-bone—some of the élite of St James' doctors lawyers clergymen artists and this year those Jubilee singers from Nashville College are coming."

62 The salutation to an undictated letter was probably intended for Sir John Bennett, sheriff of London and Middlesex, whom Clemens had met in 1872.

be a lot of [*four words*]. Then there would be Wellington, Nelson etc. [*four words*] lordly & aristocratic. But in Stratford the greatest king England ever sat upon the throne. They have fought shy of the glory of such men. Didn't notice the name of anybody except Shakespeare.

The great granddaughter of A. Hathaway, descendant of the Hathaways, runs the H— mansion yet at Shottery which is 2 or 3 miles from Stratford.

137 Regent St. glasses, before 1 o'clock on Thursday next—12th July

Calculating machines
one in 1664 by Sir Sam'l Morland
" " 1775 by Viscount Mahon, physicist, 3d earl of Stanhope[63]
4 of them

"If you want anything done in math., just write it on a piece of paper, put it in that hole and it will <all> come out all worked."

Archbishop of Canterbury, 11 A.M. at Christ Church, Lancaster Gate.

Kensington Chapel, Allen St., Dr. Schaff of N.Y., 6½ P.M.

3 *P.M. Dean* Stanley, Westminster

Reunion of [Christendom] Monday evening at St. George's Hall, 8 P.M. [*one word*] 6. [#]

---

[63] Sir Samuel Morland, at one time Pepys' tutor at Magdalen College, Cambridge, experimented with mechanical devices and steam engines. Pepys mentions, in his diary entry of 14 March 1668, having seen Morland's "late invention for casting up of sums of £.*s.d.*; which is very pretty, but not very useful" (*The Diary of Samuel Pepys*, ed. Henry B. Wheatley [London: George Bell & Sons, 1900], 7:363). Viscount Charles Mahon, third earl of Stanhope, an eighteenth-century statesman and scientist, invented the Stanhope printing press and lens and experimented in steam navigation. Clemens' interest in inventions was already well-established. In 1870 he had written to his sister Pamela: "An inventor is a poet—a true poet . . littler minds being able to get no higher than a comprehension of a vulgar moneyed success" (*MTBus*, p. 114). A month before leaving for England, in April 1873, he had taken out a patent on his "Self-Pasting Scrap Book," and a few years later he would be investing disastrously in various other inventions.

July 13th

I just instituted a memorial [to get by] subscription only [by] Americans—$1000

St. Philip's, Granville Sq., 7 P.M., Mitchinson, the bishop of Barbados.

July 14.

To show the little [knowledge the English] have of each others' titles, the lady of the house proposed to introduce Lord Somebody, to Lady Cl[----] so and so; and he says, "Why that's my wife." Next day gentleman was telling incident to a young lady whose title was such and such a one and she says, "Why that's my father."

The Marchioness of We[stminster] is a very large lady, handsome & rather ornate in her [get up]. S— introduced said he heard of [often]. She turned to someone said, "Why, he takes me for Westminster Abbey."

Attended the assizes at Warwick and saw a woman convicted of passing 2-shilling pieces. Second offense. Been in prison 6 months before. But first conviction was not made known to the grand jury until sentence was passed. She was sentenced to prison for 5 years which was very kind. The prosecution's witnesses had been [*one word*] enough to mark the coins; so that they could be identified without any trouble.

S. E. R. W. & Steam Packet, 31s.6d. 3d class, 14 return. Brig Cunard 15 to 26s.

	£ s d
Fare to America	16/.0/0
To Paris & back	1.11.6
back	
Board & lodging to Tuesday	2. 0.0
Few days in Paris[64]	0.10.0 [#]

[64] Clemens had considered going to Paris in the first week of July in order to continue his account of the shah's tour; however, he decided against the trip. Thomp-

Mrs. Lipscomb—

Langham hotel
London July 16th
17?

Friend Bliss,

We should issue copyright edition of novel[65] here in fine style, 3 volumes, and in order that there should be no mistakes I wish you would be particular to send duplicate sheets and duplicate casts of pictures by successive steamers always. And send these casts and proofs along as fast as you get the signature done. Be sure to write now to Routledge and state as nearly as you can the exact day at which you can publish. Routledge will publish on that day or the day before. If you change the date <of> publication telegraph Routledge. I told <W> Miller to write you proposing 7½ percent for his book.[66]

Yours Truly.

My dear Warner,

I have just written Bliss asking him to send 2 sets of sheets always and 2 sets of casts for pictures by successive steamers so that if one set is ever lost it need not stop the book. I wish you would see that this is done<.> and don't let <them miss> <fire or>

---

son's notes about third-class fare, written in mid-July shortly before he left Clemens' employment, were more likely for his own use.

[65] This letter, to Elisha Bliss of the American Publishing Company, and the following one, to Charles Dudley Warner, Clemens' collaborator on *The Gilded Age*, show Clemens' concern that the English edition of the novel should be issued before the American, a precaution required by British copyright law. Clemens' residence in London at the time of English publication was also necessary to establish British copyright. The final versions of the two letters are in Thompson's hand and vary only slightly from the shorthand texts here (*MTLP*, pp. 77–78).

[66] Clemens wrote to Mrs. Fairbanks on 6 July 1873: "We see Miller every day or two, & like him better & better all the time. He is just getting out his Modoc book here & I have made him go to my publishers in America with it (by letter) & they will make some money for him" (*MTMF*, p. 174). Joaquin Miller's *Unwritten History: Life Amongst the Modocs,* a fictionalized version of the author's Indian adventures, appeared in England in the summer of 1873 and was published by Bliss's American Publishing Company in 1874.

<fire.> a sheet <just as soon as> <[and see f -]> <fire> be carelessly kept back for a week or 2 scaring a body to death with the idea that it is lost, but have the sheets sent in their regular order faithfully. Don't wait for a quantity but send it right along signature by signature. And I have told Bliss to name the date of publication, and to write Routledge about it, and that if he should change that date to telegraph Routledge, because if Routledge makes a mistake of publishing date of Bliss it may cost us our copyright. Now you know what I have written Bliss, and you will know how to proceed.

Yours Truly.

LETTER NOTES and others

Pa's love for oak trees.

Twilight.

Mother at the Kew Gardens

Mr. Burdett<—>: If my gospel be hid, it is hid to those that are <de> lost. <a>At home & in Maine

Fragrance of flowers in this world; the fruit hereafter. Bearing fruit unto eternal life

The head of a family being cut down, some other branch rises up. Other branches need to be surrounded and helped up by example.

Resurrection. beech-nuts in Maine.

Richard II, in prison listening to a poor minstrel outside

Note of MT's—umbrellas back of coaches. People particular about soiling liveries of servants, costly. Lord Mayor's & Sheriffs.

Adventure with French Dr. La Balle.[67]

Peer Delawarr. lawsuit.

Buckhurst peerage lawsuit

Close American ladies

Shakespeare. Income. No mention of by Pepys etc.—No manuscripts left, but one. His bust, his garden—mulberry tree

---

67 Thompson's list is the last entry in the notebook and recapitulates various previous entries. A number of the items on the list are not in the shorthand notebook—presumably because of missing pages.

Walter Scott's name on the window
Stratford—absence of aristocratic titles. No monument to him.
Titles of nobility. Their ignorance of
Warwick Court of Assizes
Batavia—notes aboard
Celebrities—[trips of]
English peculiarities of intonation.
Objects. <[tri]> of passengers
Knowing man
Another type.
Another still
Englishmen that have traveled in America
Dress & jewelry
Seasick—[*one word*].
Judgment of [age].
P
Capt. Mouland's passengers criticize Capt. Mouland's partiality.[68]
Roommates.
Clumsy passenger
Foliage—luxuriant
Hedges & fences
Cottages brick & [stone—no] wooden.

---

[68] Clemens' friendship with Captain John E. Mouland of the S.S. *Batavia* dated from his 1872 return trip from England to America, when the ship's passengers, with Clemens foremost among them, had warmly commended the captain, his officers, and crew for the daring midsea rescue of some shipwrecked sailors. The reference here to the captain's partiality is not explained elsewhere in the shorthand notebook. Livy's letter to her mother from the *Batavia* indicates that the Clemens party were recipients of the captain's attentions: "Capt. Mouland is just about perfection, he has done every thing that he possibly could to make us comfortable and to make things pleasant for us, he and Clara take long walks on the deck together—I do not know hardly what we should do if it was not for his chart room, the baby goes there early in the forenoon & stays until her bed time. It crowds Capt. Mouland very much but he insists that it does not—He grows more & more delightful the better one knows him—We would not come back with any one else on any account if it is possible to come with him" ([23?] May 1873, Mark Twain Memorial, Hartford).

Jubilee Singers[69]
Dolby Mr.[70]
American corruption
Cricket Oxford *vs* Cambridge
Expressions curious
Quarreling in public
Rubbish
English emigrants replaced by Ger
Punches jokes
Crowd waiting to see royal party at [Windsor].
Negro minstrel statue
Ch. Chancel in [de--] to suit theology
Queer expressions
Calculating machines.
Liveries
Mail deliveries frequent
St. Saviour's Ch.
Epitaph.
Curious titles to political [pro---ts]

---

[69] The Jubilee Singers, a group of former slaves sponsored by Fisk University in Nashville, Tennessee, gave a series of concerts at the Hanover Square Rooms in London in May 1873 before starting a concert tour in England. On 16 July they entertained at the garden party of George and Louise MacDonald, which the Clemenses attended.

[70] During his previous trip to England in 1872 Clemens had written to Livy of an impending meeting with George Dolby, an English lecture agent: "Livy, darling, everybody says lecture—lecture—lecture—but I have not the least idea of doing it—certainly not at present. Mr. Dolby, who took Dickens to America, is coming to talk business to me tomorrow, though I have sent him word once before, that I can't be hired to talk here, because I have no time to spare" (*MTL*, p. 199). Clemens did eventually come to an agreement with Dolby during the 1873 trip to England, and six lectures, from 13 to 18 October at the Queen's Concert Rooms in Hanover Square, were announced. Dolby and Clemens renewed their friendship when Clemens returned in November for an extended lecture engagement that would keep him in England until January 1874. Clemens later recalled Dolby as "large and ruddy, full of life and strength and spirits, a tireless and energetic talker, and always overflowing with good nature and bursting with jollity . . . [a] gladsome gorilla" (*MTA*, 1:140).

St. Helen's.
Almshouses—old
Behests.
Everybody going abroad
Such facilities.

TEXTUAL APPARATUS

Textual Introduction

FOR ALL but one of the twelve notebooks in this volume the manuscript is the only authoritative version known to exist and is therefore the copy-text. For a single exception, Notebook 1, a photocopy of the manuscript serves as copy-text, because the original is not now accessible. Eleven of the notebooks are in Clemens' own hand, while Notebook 12 is an amanuensis notebook in shorthand, consisting almost entirely of remarks Clemens dictated to a secretary.

Except for Notebooks 2 and 3, which are represented by excerpts, the texts of the holographic notebooks are presented exactly as Clemens wrote them, so far as educated eyes can recover the material and the limitations of print can render the idiosyncrasies of inscription in informal private documents. As far as possible, the entries in these notebooks appear in their original, often unfinished, form, with Clemens' irregularities, inconsistencies, errors, and cancellations unemended. However, a wider editorial discretion has been exercised in the presentation of the amanuensis notebook. Errors and inconsistencies which are obviously scribal in origin and hence do not reflect Clemens' usage or intentions have been silently purged from this text. Uncertainties about the secretary's accuracy in transcribing Clemens' remarks and difficulties caused by the conventions of shorthand have prompted other departures from the editorial procedures outlined here. The headnote to Notebook 12 describes the measures adopted for presentation of its text.

Information about the nine notebooks in Clemens' hand presented in full in this volume is provided in two sections. The text of each notebook is accompanied by a headnote and footnotes, which supply the historical, biographical, and textual information needed to read and understand the notebook as Clemens left it. The Textual Apparatus contains two lists for each notebook: Emendations and Doubtful Readings, and Details of Inscription. These lists report all recoverable significant facts about the manuscript not fully represented in the text itself and enable the reader to trace the course of a notebook's composition. While this arrangement does not produce a "clear text," which in any case would require a degree of editorial reworking incompatible with such unfinished private documents, it does allow for the presentation of a text relatively uncluttered by minor details and at the same time offers the fullest possible account of the notebooks.

The headnote to each notebook includes a physical description of the manuscript and a discussion of textual characteristics or problems peculiar to that notebook. Although the footnotes do not often contain textual information, they do discuss textual matters that significantly affect the meaning of the text. All textual details brought to the reader's attention in footnotes are repeated in the fuller listings in the Textual Apparatus. Emendations and Doubtful Readings reports all departures from the language of the manuscript, except for the points of holographic or typographic style described below, and records editorial conjectures about ambiguous and unrecovered passages. Details of Inscription records readings such as interlineations that apparently were added by Clemens after the initial inscription of a passage, describes the details of complex revisions, and reports other aspects of the manuscript that may bear on the evolution of the text.

The list of emendations includes editorial corrections of obvious author's errors in the few cases when there is no doubt about the intended reading, when the error is of an excessively disconcerting or distracting nature and when the emendation makes no appreciable change in the meaning of the text. For example, "soild" has been emended to "solid" at 431.5, "Mr.s" has been emended to "Mrs." at 154.29, and "thesese" has been emended to "these" at 141.18. (Line numbers in cues and citations refer to Clemens' text only and do not count editorial language on the same page.)

Sometimes letters are missing because Clemens inadvertently wrote off the edge of a page or because part of a page has been torn away. When such a gap is very short and there can be little doubt what letters are missing, the probable reading is supplied in the text in square brackets and is reported as an emendation, as in the word "Americ[an]" at 18.25.

A few emendations report the substitution of words for ditto marks. The printed text follows Clemens' use of ditto marks, *ditto*, and *do*, except when the vertical alignment of words is not naturally the same in print as in the manuscript notebooks. In such cases, to avoid awkward spacing of words or lines, the appropriate word is supplied in place of the abbreviation, and the substitution is reported as an emendation.

The list of emendations also reports the omission from the text of two special kinds of headings that are clear enough in their original contexts but that would be pointlessly obscure, or even misleading, if transferred without modification into print. Sometimes Clemens prepared a notebook for use by distributing among its pages a series of headings for the subjects he intended to write about later, but occasionally when he had done so the entries he subsequently wrote did not fit into the allotted spaces. When this happened, the pre-inscribed headings were surrounded by unrelated matter and were effectively superseded, although not always canceled. At other times, after using a notebook Clemens occasionally jotted words at the tops of successive pages as a kind of index to what he had written, usually without trying to fit the headings grammatically or logically into the passages around them. When the presence in the printed text of a heading of either kind would interrupt an entry or sequence of entries to no purpose, the heading is omitted and reported in the list of emendations. For example, the headings "5th Day" and "5th D," which occur many times between pages 475.6 and 484.14, are dropped from the text by emendation wherever their presence would disrupt a passage but are retained where they cause no confusion. In other cases, headings that would interrupt the text if left in place but that cannot be omitted without a significant loss of meaning are moved instead of being dropped from the text, and their manuscript position is described in Details of Inscription. Such a heading is "Tiberias" (424.5). Clemens' use of outline and index headings is discussed in the headnotes to the notebooks where the headings occur.

The doubtful readings reported in the list include possible alternative versions of words which are partly or completely illegible in the manuscript or whose form is unclear. For example, Clemens' habit of running words together when writing hastily and his inconsistent use of hyphens in compound words (usually *to-day* and *good-bye*, but occasionally *today* and *good bye*) sometimes make it difficult to say whether the author intended to write two separate words, a hyphenated compound, or one solid word.

Similarly, possible compounds hyphenated at the ends of lines in the manuscript could be transcribed either as hyphenated words or as solid words. Whenever the intended form of a compound word is in doubt, the form Clemens used most frequently at the time is printed in the text. If no authorial preference can be established, the conventional form according to dictionaries of the period appears in the text. In either case, the editorial decision is reported in Emendations and Doubtful Readings.

Clemens' grasp of the use of accents in foreign languages, especially French, was never firm: he omitted them, placed them over the wrong letter, used the wrong accent mark, and occasionally resorted to the schoolboy trick of using a flat mark that can be read as either an acute or a grave accent. All Clemens' accent marks are retained in the text, whether they are right or wrong. His ambiguous mark is rendered in the text as the accent it most resembles, and the alternative possibilities are noted in Emendations and Doubtful Readings.

Certain characteristics of the manuscript which do not normally affect meaning are discussed in footnotes or apparatus when some special significance attaches to them. Thus, when Clemens changed writing materials, the fact is reported in Details of Inscription as possible evidence of a lapse of time between inscriptions, but minor peculiarities of ink and paper, vagaries of handwriting, and the points in the text where manuscript pages begin and end are mentioned only when they cast light on the meaning of an entry or the sequence of composition. The lengths of lines and the positions of words or lines on the manuscript pages are not reproduced in the text, except for headings, verse, addresses, tables, lists, and similar formal elements. Clemens' regular division of the text into entries has been followed, but no attempt has been made to reproduce the inconsistent means by which he separated entries. In particular, the horizontal lines or flourishes following many, but not all, entries have been omitted; the separation of entries is indicated here by extra space between lines or, when the end of a manuscript entry coincides with the end of a page of the printed text, by the symbol [#].

Uniform paragraph indentation has been imposed on the first lines of all entries except those that require special alignment, such as the formal elements mentioned above. Clemens indented most entries, but neither this fact nor his occasional failure to indent affects the meaning of the text. Moreover, the depth of indentation (which has been standardized in this text) varies so widely throughout the notebooks that in places it is difficult to tell which lines are indented and which are not. Indeed, occasionally when Clemens neglected to indent the first line, he indicated paragraphs by indenting the second and succeeding lines instead. Since in such cases the author's intention the form paragraphs is clear, these are also presented in the conventional manner. When the separation of entries is in doubt or an ambiguity in paragraphing affects the meaning of the text, the problem is reported in the apparatus and if it is crucial is discussed in a footnote.

The occasional dots and lines under superscript letters, which Clemens tended to write indistinctly when he used them at all, have been silently omitted. Thus, words which might at different times be interpreted as $M^{\underset{.}{r}}$, $M^{\underset{.}{r}}.$, $M^{\underline{r}}$, or $M^{\underline{\underline{r}}}$ are all rendered as M^r. However, a period following a superscript letter appears on or above the line as Clemens wrote it, thus: M^r. or $M^{r\cdot}$.

Although Clemens' cancellations are generally retained, purely mechanical problems which he repaired himself, such as corrected misspellings and words or word fragments so miswritten that he canceled them and rewrote them for clarity, are omitted. However, every authorial change which might possibly provide a clue to anything more significant than a moment's inadvertence is included in the text. Thus, words originally written clearly and spelled correctly but which nevertheless were canceled and then rewritten are retained in the text as evidence of possible authorial indecision. While most spelling errors corrected by Clemens are omitted, when he misspelled and then corrected a proper name, both the error and the correction are included in the text as evidence that Clemens may have been unfamiliar with the subject.

Drawings related to the text or having some other intrinsic significance are reproduced in positions which reflect as clearly as possible their relationship to the text. Scrawls and random marks are reproduced or described only if they may bear on the meaning of the text. When Clemens, and later Paine, copied or adapted a passage for use in a work intended for publication, they frequently indicated the fact by marking the section with a simple stroke or two of pencil or pen. Most such "use marks" reveal nothing about the meaning of a passage or the use made of it, if any, and are omitted. However, when on a few occasions Clemens organized entries into recognizable and meaningful categories by marking them with sets of special symbols, the symbols are represented in the text and their implications discussed. Occasionally when revising a passage Clemens used proofreader's marks such as *stet* and ¶, or he indicated the placement of passages with lines, arrows, or written instructions. His intention is followed in each case, and the mechanism is described in Details of Inscription.

Clemens underlined words in the notebooks so unsystematically that it is often impossible to say whether he intended to convey different degrees of emphasis by single, double, and triple underlining. While no attempt has been made to impose a system where Clemens apparently intended none, differences in the manuscript are reported by means of the normal typographic conventions: letters underlined once have been set in italic type, letters underlined twice in small capitals, and letters underlined three times in full capitals. Triple underlining is recorded in Details of Inscription, to preserve the distinction between words underlined and words actually written in capital letters.

Most entries are presented in the physical order they follow in the manuscript notebooks, although that order is not necessarily the order in which they were written. Endpapers and flyleaves, in particular, usually contain notes jotted at various times during a notebook's use. Since such short notes cannot usually be precisely dated and since their aggregation at either end of a notebook is typical of Clemens' practice, these groups of entries have been presented intact. Elsewhere in the notebooks, however, occasional entries or blocks of entries have been moved into chronological order when a reconstruction of the order of their inscription can be defended and the rearrangement does not separate passages deliberately juxtaposed by the author. Entries are moved most often when Clemens turned a notebook and began writing from the opposite end. Sometimes he turned a notebook more than once, as with Notebook 9, so that three or more sequences of use can be identified. When the order of entries has been changed, the list of details of inscription describes the original manuscript sequence and any textual peculiarities bearing on the rearrangement. When the order of entries has been left unchanged because the chronology of their inscription cannot be firmly established, the list nevertheless reports aspects of the manuscript that suggest a chronological sequence different from the physical sequence, such as the fact that an entry was written with the notebook inverted. Footnotes explain the external evidence for moving or dating a passage.

Passages whose intended position Clemens did not clearly indicate and pages which have come loose from the notebooks are placed in the text where the available evidence suggests they belong. Words written at an angle across other entries or in the margin are usually placed following the entry with which they are associated. A special problem arises in parts of some notebooks where Clemens used only the right-hand pages for the main sequence of his remarks but wrote a few scattered entries on the otherwise blank left-hand pages. In such cases the context sometimes suggests that Clemens deliberately placed the isolated entry opposite a particular passage on the facing manuscript page, while at other times it seems more probable that he simply picked a convenient blank space to write in. In the present text an isolated entry of this kind normally is placed in a position which reflects as nearly as possible its manuscript location and its logical relationship to other entries, but it may be moved, to avoid interrupting a continuing sequence of entries. Problems of the appropriate sequence or placement of entries vary so widely from case to case that no general statement of editorial principles can cover them all. In each instance the situation in the manuscript is described in Details of Inscription and is discussed if necessary in a footnote. Clippings and notes not in Clemens' hand which are interleaved in the notebooks or attached to them are described or printed in full, according to their importance and length, in the footnotes.

Clemens occasionally wrote in his notebooks while on horseback or aboard ship, in a carriage or a crowd, or in very bad light. Such passages may be chaotic scrawls. Even in passages written under more favorable conditions, minor lapses and inaccuracies sometimes produce puzzling ambiguities. These characteristics cannot be rendered in type, and some of them defy verbal description. But, except under unusual circumstances, Clemens' handwriting is clear, and a description of the occasional problems makes it appear more challenging than it is in fact. The sometimes confusing resemblance of *a* and *o*, *n* and *u*, and *w* and *m*, and Clemens' occasional crossing of an *l* mistaken for a *t* or dotting of part of an *n* or *u*, misread as an *i*, are characteristic of hasty and informal notes. Finally, a terminal *s* may be no more than a hook on the penultimate letter. Context easily resolves most of these problems. When a word is so badly written that it is impossible to tell whether it is spelled correctly or incorrectly but there is no question what word was intended, it is assumed that Clemens spelled the word correctly. When an obscurity cannot be resolved, the alternatives are registered in Emendations and Doubtful Readings and, if crucial to the understanding of an entry, are discussed in a footnote as well.

Clemens' punctuation has not been changed even when it is clearly wrong. Except for simple errors like double commas and missing halves of pairs of parentheses or quotation marks, which sometimes result from careless revision, his punctuation is precise, if occasionally eccentric. According to his own statement in Notebook 4, Clemens believed that "while most men have a manner of speaking peculiar to themselves, no arbitrary system of punctuation can apply. Every man should know best how to punctuate his own MS." He used both the exclamation point and the question mark as internal punctuation, and he frequently followed a terminal period with a dash. He also sometimes used a terminal dash in place of a period or extended a period so that it looks like a dash or a comma. Colons, semicolons, and commas sometimes resemble each other. These difficulties are often compounded by the similarity between the capital and lower-case forms of some of Clemens' letters such as *t*, *s*, *c*, and *m*. Problems caused by these characteristics of the author's handwriting and punctuation are resolved silently here on the basis of familiarity with Clemens' hand and of any other information available. Ambiguities are reported in the list of emendations when doubt persists.

To keep the text as uncluttered as the demands of completeness and clarity will allow, the number of special symbols used has been held to a minimum. Readings canceled by Clemens have been enclosed in angle brackets, and the spacing following the closing angle bracket indicates how a cancellation was made. When Clemens canceled a word or word-ending simply by striking it out, a normal space follows the closing angle bracket, thus: "<American> passengers" and "bell<s> rang." When he canceled a word or word fragment by writing something else over it, the original reading is enclosed in angle brackets and the new reading follows the closing angle bracket without the customary intervening space. Thus, when Clemens wrote "organ" over "part" the text reads "<part>organ," and when he wrote "take" to cover and cancel the false start "s" the text reads "<s>take."

On the rare occasions when Clemens revised a word by writing over a part of it or by striking out one or more letters within it (other than the terminal letters), the entire original reading is given within angle brackets, the entire revised reading follows the closing angle bracket without an intervening space, and an entry in Details of Inscription explains exactly how the change was made. Thus, when Clemens wrote "sen" (possibly intending originally to write "sent") and then changed it to "stayed" by writing "tayed" over "en," the text reads "<sen>stayed" and the revision is explained in Details of Inscription. Similarly, if he had written "t" over the "s" of "sake" the text would read "<sake>take," and if he had canceled the "t" of "stake" the text would read "<stake>sake."

The process of revision in such cases is described in Details of Inscription. The same procedure applies to revised numerals: when the text reads "<10>30-ton rocks" Details of Inscription records that "3" was written over "1" (that is, "30" was not written over "10"). For ease of reading, punctuation marks have been spaced normally even when they fall within or immediately follow a cancellation. Therefore, the lack of an extra space after the closing angle bracket in readings like "<">How" and "I will <not>!" does not necessarily mean that the canceled material was overwritten by what follows it. When a mark of punctuation is written over a word or letter, or when something is written over a mark of punctuation, Clemens' revision is explained in Details of Inscription.

Interlineations and other readings apparently added by Clemens after completion of the initial inscription appear in the text unaccompanied by special symbols except for one limited category. When Clemens interlined a word or phrase as an alternative to a previously inscribed reading but canceled neither version, both readings are printed in the text, separated by a slash mark and with the earlier reading first, thus: "Turn/Flee."

Although they are not generally set off by symbols in the text, all Clemens' identifiable additions are recorded in Details of Inscription, where they are enclosed within vertical arrows, thus: "↑innocently↓." To help the reader find the additions in the text, a word or two of context may be included in an entry in Details of Inscription, thus: "↑the↓ noted occasions." Similarly, for the reader's convenience, extra words, often including cancellations associated with additions, may be presented in an entry if doing so provides enough context to clarify the revision, thus: "<mighty> ↑very↓" or "Hotel↑s↓ gouge<s>." (All cancellations, whether or not they are repeated in Details of Inscription, are enclosed in angle brackets in the text.)

Conjectural reconstructions of illegible readings and of letters missing where the manuscript page is torn are enclosed in square brackets in the text. Within square brackets hyphens stand for unreadable letters and italics are used for editorial explanations. Thus "[------]" stands for an illegible word of about six letters and "[*three words*]" stands for three unrecovered words. (To preserve square brackets for editorial insertions, Clemens' square brackets, which he used interchangeably with parentheses, are rendered as parentheses.) In the apparatus a vertical rule has been used when necessary to indicate a line-ending, thus: "to-|day." An asterisk in Emendations and Doubtful Readings refers the reader to the corresponding entry in Details of Inscription.

In descriptions of Clemens' revisions, words identified as written "above" other words are interlined, while words written "over" other words are written in the same space, covering the reading they supplant. The word *follow* indicates a spatial but not necessarily a temporal relation. The word *endpaper* designates the pasted-down page inside either cover of a notebook and the word *flyleaf* refers to the leaf next to an endpaper.

Key To Symbols

<word>	Clemens' cancellation
↑word↓	written later than the surrounding passage
[word]	doubtful reading, marginally legible
w[- -]d	illegible letters
[*page torn*]	editorial remarks
word/word	alternative readings proposed but never resolved by Clemens
word | word	end of a line
[#]	last line of text on the printed page is the end of an entry in the manuscript
*	cross-reference in Emendations and Doubtful Readings to Details of Inscription

Notebook 1

Emendations and Doubtful Readings

	MTP Reading	MS Reading
18.25	Americ[an]	[*written off the edge of the page*]
21.9	glanced	glanced [*centered*] <Leçon 8.>
22.20	intensity, but	intensity, but [*centered*] <Leçon 9.>
*23.14	another.	another. [*centered*] Leçon 10.
23.15	Bilious.	<Leçon 11.> Bilious.
*30.11	2 maps Mo & U.S. | 2 spittoons	2 maps | 2 spittoons Mo & U.S.
31.1	[Boy]	[*very doubtful*]
31.1	15,	[*possibly* '13, –']
31.2	married	[*ditto marks below preceding* 'married']
31.4	[*three? words*]	[*possibly* 'Die by g– ' *or* 'Dirty xg– –'; *nearly illegible*]

Details of Inscription

17.1	Samuel L. Clemens [*written on the front cover*]
17.2–4	10 . . . *words*] [*written on the front endpaper*]
18.11–12	[.]25 . . . 2[.]00 [*Clemens used a vertical ledger line on the page to indicate the decimal places*]
18.21	<mamma> ↑mamam↓
19.13	<seasons> ↑months↓

19.34 L'<Asiè>Asié, [*the acute accent written over the grave accent*]

21.5–9 Uncle . . . glanced [*written at the bottom of two facing pages in the space below French lessons 6 and 7*]

22.2 ↑or gray↓

23.14 another. [*followed by* 'Leçon 10.' *on an otherwise blank page; emended*]

24.26 skin. [*followed by a blank right-hand page*]

25.1–27.6 Hopson's . . . me– [*upside-down in relation to the surrounding entries*]

26.13–27.6 Orion . . . me– [*not in Clemens' hand*]

28.8 4. The [*follows a blank left-hand page*]

30.8 1856. [*followed by a blank right-hand page*]

30.11 ↑Mo & U.S.↓ [*misplaced beside* '2 spittoons' *on the line below* '2 maps'; *emended*]

32.1–2 ↑$502.50 . . . killed.↓ [*written alongside the previous entry and separated from it by a vertical line*]

32.8 <Benevolent>Benevolence ['ce' *written over* 't']

33.5 Love. [*followed by a blank right-hand page*]

34.3–35.12 Tall . . . broadcloth.> [*apparently written later than the laundry list (35.13–36.6) in whatever space was available;* 'Tall . . . hide.' *(34.3–13) written on a right-hand page numbered* '1' *and with the instruction at the bottom* '(Continued 2 pages back)' ; 'But . . . of the' *(34.13–35.1) written on the preceding right-hand page numbered* '2' *and with the instruction at the bottom* '(Turn back a page)'; 'parlor. . . . forever.' *(35.1–10) written on the facing left-hand page numbered* '3'; '<True . . . broadcloth.>' *(35.11–12) numbered* '4' *is between the entries at 33.16–18 and 34.1–2 on the left-hand page facing page* '1']

34.3 ↑rather regular features↓

34.4	↑dark hair,↓
35.7	<pines> ↑sighs↓
35.9	quick ↑as↓
39.2–10	John . . . shirt [*written on the back endpaper*]

Notebooks 2 and 3 have no textual apparatus

Notebook 4

Emendations and Doubtful Readings

<table>
<tr><th></th><th>MTP Reading</th><th>MS Reading</th></tr>
<tr><td>68.2</td><td>watch-<y>key</td><td>watch-|<y>key</td></tr>
<tr><td>69.8</td><td>à vient</td><td>[possibly ‘á vient’]</td></tr>
<tr><td>69.10</td><td>&c</td><td>[possibly ‘& c’]</td></tr>
<tr><td>69.12</td><td>vieu</td><td>[possibly ‘vien’]</td></tr>
<tr><td>72.16</td><td>Loud</td><td>[possibly ‘Land’]</td></tr>
<tr><td>73.19</td><td>some</td><td>[possibly ‘same’]</td></tr>
<tr><td>74.23</td><td>whih</td><td>[possibly ‘while’]</td></tr>
<tr><td>76.20</td><td>dishwater</td><td>dish-|water</td></tr>
<tr><td>77.1</td><td>to-day</td><td>[possibly ‘today’]</td></tr>
<tr><td>79.6</td><td>landslide</td><td>[possibly ‘land-slide’]</td></tr>
<tr><td>81.10</td><td>snow storm</td><td>[possibly ‘snow-storm’ or ‘snowstorm’]</td></tr>
<tr><td>81.17</td><td>cast-iron</td><td>[possibly ‘cast iron’]</td></tr>
<tr><td>81.20–21</td><td>snow storm</td><td>[possibly ‘snow-storm’ or ‘snowstorm’]</td></tr>
<tr><td>82.3</td><td>to-morrow</td><td>[possibly ‘tomorrow’]</td></tr>
<tr><td>82.4</td><td>hellfired</td><td>hell-|fired</td></tr>
<tr><td>82.14</td><td>to-morrow</td><td>[possibly ‘tomorrow’]</td></tr>
<tr><td>83.17</td><td>halfbreed</td><td>[possibly ‘half-breed’ or ‘half breed’]</td></tr>
<tr><td>84.1</td><td>Sallow faced</td><td>[possibly ‘Sallow-faced’]</td></tr>
</table>

Details of Inscription

68.1 Use . . . trip. [*written lengthwise along the left edge of the front cover*]

68.2–3 (New . . . date. [*written on the front endpaper; four blank pages—the recto and verso of the flyleaf and the first ruled leaf—follow*]

69.7 Daniel ['aniel' *written over what may be shorthand for same*]

69.9 B Gls [*written over what may be shorthand for same*]

73.4 <–>she ['she' *written over a dash*]

74.1 <18[0]5>1865 ['6' *written in blue ink over what may be* 'o']

74.21 ↑Reads . . . French.↓

77.7 <2,000>4,000['4' *written over* '2']

78.8 <J[im]>J & me ['& me' *written over what may be* 'im']

78.16 parce <queil>qu'il [*the apostrophe written over* 'e']

79.6 <ge>great ['r' *written over* 'e']

80.4–5 ↑Wrote . . . Press.↓ [*written in blue ink lengthwise on the page across the preceding entry*]

82.21 ↑Refer back.↓ [*written in blue ink lengthwise on the page across the preceding entry*]

85.16 ↑apparently↓

85.18 <ap>absolutely ['b' *written over* 'p']

86–87 *illustration* [*the Vide Poche Mine illustration is preceded by 40 blank pages and followed by* 'Report' (84.6)]

88.25 <placed>places ['s' *written over* 'd']

88.27 <in>is ['s' *written over* 'n']

88.29 ↑he wears.↓

88.33 <some even> even some [*originally* 'some even'; 'even' *canceled following* 'some', *then interlined before* 'some']

89.4 <present.>presented. ['ed.' *written over the period*]

89.15 ↑seeming↓

89.23 eternity. [22 *blank pages follow; then a leaf has been torn out, leaving a remnant with* '5.' *still visible on its verso; then three blank pages–the recto and verso of the last ruled leaf and the recto of the back flyleaf–follow*]

89.24–90.1 W Bilgewater . . . hands. [*written on the verso of the back flyleaf; three lines of wavy marks which cannot be identified as words, shorthand, or a diagram appear on the back endpaper*]

89.26 <Wrigh>Write ['te' *written over* 'gh']

90.2 [*shorthand*] [*written on the back endpaper*]

Notebook 5

Emendations and Doubtful Readings

	MTP Reading	MS Reading
112.15	Excelsior, instead	[*possibly* 'Excelsior instead']
113.15	far	[*possibly* 'for']
114.5	set	[*possibly* 'get']
122.20	flag-ship	flag-|ship
126.10	good paying	[*possibly* 'good-paying']
128.1	235	[*possibly* '255']
130.6	watermelons	[*possibly* 'water melons']
130.15	outspoken	[*possibly* 'out-spoken']
130.23	half hours	[*possibly* 'half-hours']
131.9	*Aolé*	[*possibly* '*Aolē*']
131.18	attention,	[*possibly* 'attention!']
131.21	bootjack	[*possibly* 'boot-jack']
132.3	[kiki]	[*possibly* 'wiki']
132.23	ask<e>	[*possibly* 'ask<i>']
137.4	to-morrows	[*possibly* 'tomorrows']
139.9	awhile	a awhile ['on awhile' *possible but doubtful*]
141.18	these	thesese
142.3	Henry's <showed>	Henry's never <showed>
145.9	abroad at large	['at large' *possibly intended as an alternative to* 'abroad']

145.10	grand (tremendous)	['(tremendous)' *possibly intended as an alternative to* 'grand']
147.15	wheelbarrow	wheel-|barrow
150.12	gimcrack	gim-|crack [*possibly* 'jim-crack']
152.2	men-o-wars-men	men-o-wars-|men
153.18	topsail	top-|sail
153.19	staysails	stay-|sails
154.29	Mrs.	Mr.s
157.11	snowwhite	[*possibly* 'snow-white']
158.6	mainmast	main-|mast
158.11	main-brace	main-|brace
*159.20	painkiller. 78	painkiller.
160.3	cow dung	[*possibly* 'cow-dung']
162.19	astern	a-|stern
163.1	forecastle	fore-|castle
*163.3–5	[¶]Further along: She is . . . [¶]Aug 13	[*possibly* '[¶]She is . . . [¶] Further along: [¶]Aug 13']
163.20	126.33	[*possibly* '126.32']
169.28	broomstick	broom-|stick
170.13	she's	[*possibly* 'sh is']
170.28	table-cloth	table-|cloth
172.1	low-neck	low-|neck

Details of Inscription

109.1–6	Ch 19 . . . 452 [*written in what appears to be black ink on the front cover*]

110.1–5 “Wife . . . creeping [*written on the front endpaper*]

110.2–3 Rev. . . . N.Y. [*written with the notebook inverted*]

110.4 Mark Twain. [*written diagonally across the front endpaper*]

110.5 Ferns . . . creeping [*written with the notebook inverted*]

110.6–111.15 <March . . . New York. [*written on the recto of the front flyleaf; the verso is blank*]

110.8–111.4 ↑A. Gamble . . . Q Pac↓ [*written across the two preceding entries*]

111.3 ↑Barney Rice↓

111.8–15 Prov . . . New York. [*written with the notebook inverted, with lines drawn enclosing each of these three entries in a separate box*]

111.13 <Mrs>Messrs. [‘essrs.’ *written over* ‘rs’]

112.3 shipp<ed> [‘ed’ *canceled in brown ink*]

112.9 told. [*followed by a blank left-hand page*]

112.13 <worthless> <↑worthless↓> brother [*the first* ‘worthless’ *is canceled in blue ink; the second was interlined in pencil, then erased*]

113.2 ↑Sea-gulls . . . catch.↓.

113.8 acquaintance. [*the bottom half of the page is blank below this entry*]

113.9 ↑smooth as↓

114.5 Sunday– [*a flourish originally ending the entry here was overwritten and the entry was continued*]

119.3 <deal>dead [‘d’ *written over* ‘l’]

120.10 ↑innocently↓

125.1–2 White . . . each. [*written in brown ink*]

125.14 <did>died ['ed' *written over* 'd']

126.1 <it>is ['s' *written over* 't']

128.21 ↑& mats↓

128.23 dirt on. [*a flourish originally ending the entry here was overwritten and the entry was continued*]

129.3–4 Pr. V. . . . abortions. [*circled*]

130.11 <28>25 ['5' *written over* '8']

131.12–19 ↑When . . . I'll brain you!↓ ['When . . . (impressively' *interlined above canceled* ' "Mr. Brown . . . *pilikia* now!" ' (131.10–11); 'Well . . . I'll brain you!' *crowded diagonally into the right margin of the page*]

131.15–16 <Out with it, then.> ↑What's up now?↓

131.18 ↑([------])↓

131.20–21 <comb . . . bootjack!> ↑brain you↓

131.23 <native> ↑Kanaka↓

131.23 week↑,↓

131.23 after↑ward he↓

131.25 <mighty> ↑very↓

131.29 ↑else↓

131.30 you ↑say you↓

132.2–3 ↑–if you would . . . oni"↓

132.4–5 <presumption &>presumptuous ['uous' *written over* 'ion &']

132.10 <man> ↑puppy↓

132.13 ↑every day↓

132.17 ↑Howries . . . so–↓ [*written lengthwise in the left margin of the page beside* '<Mr. Brown . . . afterward' (131.10–23)]

133.7 <spirit> ↑feature↓

134.10 longitude? [*a flourish originally ending the entry here was overwritten and the entry was continued; the uncanceled flourish serves as the dash that follows* 'weakening' *in the manuscript line below* 'longitude?']

137.25 <you> ↑boy↓

141.15 <over 1200>1,270 ['7' *written over* '0'; *the comma added*]

141.18 ↑of↓ these ['ese' *written over final* 'e' *of* 'these'; *emended*]

142.3 Henry↑'s↓ <showed> [*originally* 'Henry never showed'; 'never' *inadvertently left standing when* ''s' *added,* 'showed' *canceled, and the entry continued; emended*]

142.6 never ↑to↓

142.23 <co>came ['a' *written over* 'o']

143.6 <or> ↑and↓

143.7 <Effie> ↑Jeanie↓

143.8 ↑Simplicity↓

143.13 ↑just↓

144.6 cucumber. [*the bottom half of the page is blank below this entry*]

144.9 Dont . . . Pali. [*boxed*]

145.9–10 ↑drifting <about>abroad ↑at large↓ in that grand ↑(tremendous)↓ solitude &↓ ['at large' *interlined above* 'abroad'; 'abroad' *mended from the original* 'about' *by interlining* 'road' *above* 'out'; '(tremendous)' *interlined below* 'grand']

146.7 ↑They . . . music↓

146.8 <awakened> ↑creating in imagination↓

147.19–148.1 <Wthr . . . Sea-currents. [*flourishes originally ending the entry successively at* 'Wthr Cck', 'Bill of Fare–', *and* 'Weather Cock' *were overwritten and the entry was continued each time*]

148.9 ↑with a negro steward↓

148.11–13 ↑Romantic . . . boy↓ [*scrawled lengthwise on the page across the preceding entry*]

149.6 <their>there ['re' *written over* 'ir']

149.8 ↑a point or two↓

149.13 The Larboard Ahoy! [*boxed*]

149.14 THE KING [*written with initial capitals; then underlined three times*]

150.3 ↑official↓ <↑great↓>

150.5 ↑his↓ whole country

150.6 ↑the↓ noted occasions

150.6–7 <not . . . past,> ↑to w^{h} I have referred,↓

150.9–10 <↑& irresponsible↓>

150.11 <but,><yet> ↑and↓ ↑who↓

150.13 ↑a↓ soul

150.14 <woul>wound ['n' *written over* 'l']

150.15 ↑of↓ forgetting

150.19 ↑loved and↓ cherished

150.19 English <↑Court↓>

150.22 <is possessed of> ↑possesses↓

150.24 <↑American↓> hands

150.25 lifted <it> ↑her↓

150.26 Dam! [*a flourish originally ending the entry here was overwritten and the entry was continued*]

151.14 ↑in 43↓

152.11 ↑atrocious↓

153.8 <a> joke↑s↓

153.30 women. [*followed by a blank right-hand page*]

154.5 daughter.) [*the bottom half of the page is blank below this entry*]

154.29 Mrs. [*originally* 'Mr.'; *the* 's' *added following the period but not canceling it; emended*]

155.3–5 ↑—but *she* . . . nails.↓[*inserted after the dialogue had been written as far as* 'smart?' (155.8); '—but *she* had stretched' *written on the line following* 'Yes.'; 'till . . . nails.' *written following* 'smart?' *in what was then the next available space. A line drawn from* 'stretched' *to* 'till' *indicates the intended sequence*]

155.6 ↑But↓ She

155.6 <warn't>wasn't ['s' *written over* 'r']

155.12 <Shon>Shoshone ['sh' *written over* 'n']

155.16 California, ↑then,↓

155.31 anyhow." [*followed by two blank pages*]

156.10–166.6 "This . . . Perls [*18 leaves are inscribed on right-hand pages only, except for entries at 158.11–15, 162.1–2, 163.6–23, 166.7–8, and 166.9–10 written on left-hand pages*]

157.27 <smell> ↑live↓

158.1 ↑Little . . . too↓ [*crowded lengthwise into the margin beside the preceding line*]

158.11–15 main-brace . . . eye. ['brace . . . eye.' *written on an otherwise blank left-hand page; since surrounding leaves (beginning at 156.10) are inscribed on right-hand pages only, it is likely that Clemens added these entries, probably beginning on the preceding manu-*

script page at 'Tie' (158.11), *after writing at least some of the entries which follow* 'eye.']

158.12–13 string. Tying . . . knots. ↑Go aloft.↓ [*a flourish on the line below* 'string.' *originally ended the entry either there or possibly at* 'knots.' *which precedes the flourish on the same line;* 'Go aloft.' *follows the flourish and clearly was added as an afterthought*]

158.16 ↑Lie.↓ [*crowded into the top margin of the page and boxed*]

159.12 <one s>these ['t' *written over* 's']

159.14 expression. [*a flourish originally ending the entry here was overwritten and the entry was continued*]

159.16 <Danl.>Daniel. ['iel.' *written over superscript* 'l' *and the period*]

159.19–20 Joe . . . coffee. 78 | Cat & painkiller. 78 [*a single* '78' *is written across both entries; emended*]

160.1 ↑Superstition.↓

160.11 <threat>thread ['d' *written over* 't']

160.17 ↑only↓ because

160.19 <It was>They were ['They' *written over* 'It'; 'ere' *written over* 'as']

160.21 ↑The End.↓

160.22 <& p> ↑& preserved↓

160.23 <storm> ↑the dangers of the sea↓

160.23–24 by that <Power> ↑him↓ <which>who ['o' *written over* 'i' *of* 'which'; 'ch' *canceled*]

160.27 <like unto the> [*follows a caret; there is no interlineation*]

161.1 ↑& was as bitter↓

161.10 ↑with amazing gravity↓

162.1–2 Harris . . . Speaker. [*written on an otherwise blank left-hand page; since most surrounding leaves (beginning at 156.10) are inscribed on right-hand pages only, it is likely that Clemens wrote these lines later than at least some of the entries which follow* 'Speaker.'; 'The . . . Speaker.' *written lengthwise on the page in faded brown ink*]

162.7 <east> ↑west↓

162.16 <cheering> ↑sociable↓

163.3–4 Further along: ↑She is . . . blood.↓ [*the intended position of* 'She is . . . blood.' *is uncertain; it is written lengthwise in the left margin of the page beside* 'In my journal . . . freedom' (*162.14–163.6*); 'Further along:' *is written on the line immediately preceding the paragraph beginning* 'Aug 13' (*163.5*); *see Doubtful Readings and note 146*]

163.6–23 gone. . . . out. [*written on a left-hand page, filling it; since most surrounding leaves (beginning at 156.10) are inscribed on right-hand pages only, it is likely that Clemens added these entries, probably beginning on the preceding page at* 'Aug 13' (*163.5*), *after writing at least some of the entries which follow* 'out.']

163.7–8 ↑God help me,↓

164.7–8 ↑Dogs so no account↓ ↑Nothing . . . tails–↓Cut . . . ↑balance of the↓ . . . –Brown [*originally* 'Cut off dog's tail & throw the dog away. –Brown'; 'Nothing . . . tails–' *and* 'balance of the' *interlined; then* 'Dogs so no account' *interlined above* 'Nothing about']

165.14–15 ↑Don't believe w^{d} welcome *any*body.↓ [*interlined without a caret above* 'cased . . . shell' (*165.15*)]

166.3 ↑*women*↓ They think

166.6 Perls [*written in the left margin and boxed; two lines,* 'has . . . indifferent' (*166.4–5*), *indented to fit around the box*]

166.7–10 Had . . . Ewa [*written on two consecutive left-hand pages which are otherwise blank; since these entries interrupt the long entry which precedes them here (165.7–166.6), and since most surrounding leaves (beginning at 156.10) are inscribed on right-hand pages only, these entries were probably added later.* 'Had . . . it.' *is at the top of an otherwise blank page, opposite* 'time . . . possessed *(165.11–13) on the facing right-hand page.* 'Wyllie . . . Angel.' *is at the top of the following left-hand page, opposite* 'from the rest . . . happy.' *(165.23–25) on the facing page.* 'Pearls at Ewa' *is scrawled at an angle below* 'Wyllie . . . Angel.' *and opposite* 'Perls' *and* 'not dead . . . no doubt.' *(166.2–5) on the facing page*]

166.17 Brown . . . Family. [*written in brown ink*]

167.3 ↑dinner↓ bell<s>

167.4–5 ↑Never . . . hurry.↓

167.26 <They>Then ['n' *written over* 'y']

168.4 <his>her ['er' *written over* 'is']

168.7 <Excellent>Exceedingly ['edingly' *written over* 'llent']

169.8 ↑hungry↓ ghosts

169.20 ↑–of course . . . women–↓

170.20 <considered> <put> ↑set↓

170.28 ↑(he leaves)↓

171.3 <woul>wound ['nd' *written over* 'l']

171.22 her<.>– [*the dash written over the period*]

171.26 <th><slam> threw ['slam' *written over* 'th', *then canceled*]

172.9 End. [*the bottom quarter of the leaf has been torn out following this word on the recto and* 'day.' (172.16) *on the verso*]

172.10 (Letter Kanaka [*written at the bottom of a page, following* 'herself–' (170.29)]

172.20 <bur>bird ['ird' *written over* 'ur']

172.21 <yersif>yersilf ['lf' *written over* 'f']

172.24 ass. [*followed by a blank left-hand page*]

172.26 Ram. [*three quarters of the page is blank below this entry*]

173.2 at the min [*three quarters of the page is blank below this entry; followed by nine blank pages and the end of the sequence of entries at 173.3–175.9*]

173.3–175.9 These boys . . . Both Races. [*written from the back of the notebook toward the front, with the notebook inverted, beginning on the manuscript page preceding the compass diagram reproduced here on page 175*]

173.6–13 Henry . . . language. [*written in brown ink*]

175.8–9 ↑Recapitulation . . . Races.↓

175 *illustration* –176.26 [*diagram*] . . . ded. [*written on the last three ruled pages and the recto of the back flyleaf, with the notebook held right side up*]

175.10 <NE×N>NNE ['NE' *written over* 'E×'; *original terminal* 'N' *canceled*]

175.11–13 Lawrence Giles . . . New York [*possibly not in Clemens' hand*]

176.4 ↑sired↓

176.17–18 ↑always been gifted with↓

176.19–20 <solid> ↑practical↓

176.22 ↑or contain a worthy moral,↓

176.23 ↑most <charmingly> ↑elaborately↓ humorous passages↓ jokes

176.25 ↑not↓ discover

177.1–7 XYZS . . . faint-hearted." [*written on the verso of the back flyleaf*]

177.3–5 ↑Republic . . . inhab–↓ [*written over the preceding entry*]

177.8–178.31 600<[o]> . . . 1730 [*written on the back endpaper;* 'Smyrniote . . . 1730' *(178.1–31) written over* '600<[o]> . . . U.S.>' *(177.8–19) which is extremely faint*]

178.8 ↑DEAD CALM↓ [*these words and the wavy lines beside them were added to the list*]

178.17 ↑3 . . . 130.↓

178.32–33 Sale . . . 1854 [*written in what appears to be brown ink on the back cover*]

Notebook 6

Emendations and Doubtful Readings

	MTP Reading	MS Reading
*193.9	Cross	* 3 Cross
194.4	noon	noo
*194.10	pilot<.>–	[*possibly* 'pilot–']
194.16	horseback	horse-|back
195.16	demijohns	demi-|johns
195.19	bedclothes	bed-|clothes
206.7	<in w>	[*possibly* '<in m>']
215.7	came	[*possibly* 'come']
215.23	hala-nut–necklaces	hala-|nut [*possibly* 'hala-nut-necklaces']
218.13	<M>Rode	[*possibly* '<U>Rode']
222.2	hand-cart	hand-|cart
222.3	smallpox	[*possibly* 'small-pox']
222.16	to-day	[*possibly* 'today']
224.8	silk worm	[*possibly* 'silk-worm' *or* 'silkworm']
224.22	Good-bye	[*possibly* 'Good bye']
227.5	first rate	[*possibly* 'first-rate']
228.11	Bob-tail	Bob-|tail
229.6	sea-sickness	sea-|sickness
230.6	Silver sheer	['Silver' *possibly* 'Silver-' *or* 'Silvy'; 'sheer' *possibly* 'sheen' *or* 'shiny']

231.16	half-witted	half-|witted
234.5	jackass	jack-|ass

Details of Inscription

180.1–7	Steamer . . . fire - - - - !" [*written on the front endpaper*]
180.7	"Sleep . . . fire - - - - !" [*written with the notebook inverted*]
180.8	"I feeds . . . out" [*written on the recto of the front flyleaf; the verso is blank*]
181.16	Hawaii. [*at the bottom of the page below this word Clemens wrote the instruction* '(over)']
182.1	↑gets $3,000 a year.↓
184.2	↑& a newspaper↓ ↑H Gazettee↓ ['H Gazettee' *interlined without a caret above* 'Fancy' *in what was the only available space in the top margin of the page*]
185.3	↑Hotels . . . passengers.↓
185.3	<add>and ['nd' *written over* 'dd']
185.13	fees<.>, [*the comma written over the period*]
186.14	↑Dougherty . . . 4 yrs.↓
186.25	↑gauges of oil,↓
187.20–188.3	↑Young . . . Board.↓ [*written on a page originally left blank; follows three blank pages*]
187.21	Sunday ↑eveing↓
188.4	<Sunday.> ↑Monday↓
189.7	<10>30-ton rocks ['3' *written over* '1']
189.9	Moral Phenomenon. [*circled*]
190.4	↑& Captain, Godfrey.↓
190.6	watches, ↑repeated↓

190.7 ↑<mo> evening–↓

190.9 <Kananka>Kanaka [*the second* 'n' *of* 'Kananka' *canceled*]

190.29 gens d'armes./↑servants.↓ ['servants.' *interlined below* 'gens d'armes.']

191.9 ↑on there↓?"

191.11 <about>↑'↓bout ['a' *canceled and the apostrophe added*]

192.19 ↑on left↓

193.4 grandfather." [*a flourish originally ending the entry here was overwritten and the entry was continued*]

193.5–6 <father> ↑big brother↓ . . . <father> ↑big brother↓

193.9–20 St George's Cross . . . 22½ feet p[--] [*the paragraph about the Hawaiian flag (193.8–13) is interrupted in the manuscript by the entries describing the* Ajax *(193.14–20) which probably were written earlier. At the bottom of manuscript page* 39 'St George's' *is followed by the instruction* 'see page after next.'; *at the top of manuscript page* 41 *the entry continues with* 'Cross' *preceded by the instruction* '(go back 2 pages.)' *and by an asterisk and the figure* '3'; *the* Ajax *entries* ('*2 Harp Engine . . . p[--]') *occupy the intervening manuscript page* 40. *The asterisk and the* '3', *apparently a repetition of those at the head of the flag entry (193.8), have been deleted by emendation.*]

194.10 McIntyre . . . Scot. [*a flourish below the manuscript line* 'McIntyre, pilot<.>–old' *originally ended the entry within that line, probably at* 'pilot.'; *it was overwritten and the entry was continued; the dash preceding* 'old' *appears to cover a period*]

194.12 ↑old↓ leather complexion

195.3 <American hotel>Hotel↑s↓ gouge<s> ['H' *written over* 'h']

195.3 charges ['s' *possibly added as an afterthought*]

195.18 <on>in ['i' *written over* 'o']

195.24 <choos>chose ['se' *written over* 'os']

197.9–11 Cigar . . . yet. [*written in brown ink except for the asterisk and* '2' *in pencil*]

197.10 Whistler ↑left . . . arrived↓

197.15 <Ka-*meaa-meeah*><Ka-*meea-meeah*> ['*e*' *written over first* '*a*' *of* '*meaa*']

201.4–5 for him. [*a flourish originally ending the entry here was overwritten and the entry was continued*]

201.6 ↑See Friend↓

201.8 <First> ↑Second,↓

202.1 400,000 [*a flourish originally ending the entry here was overwritten and the entry was continued*]

204.2–3 ↑born . . . produced↓

205.6 Union Question. [*a flourish originally ending the entry here was overwritten and the entry was continued*]

206.1 <Anderson's> ↑Andrews'↓

206.5 <su>dusk ['du' *written over* 'su']

207.5 Missions [*circled at the top of a page above* 'night by no other' (206.16); *apparently written as a heading and subsequently engulfed by the passage describing the volcano*]

207.6 ↑* the "Legend"↓

208.13 <ded>dead ['ad' *written over* 'd']

212.5 year<.>— [*the dash written over the period*]

212.20 ↑on Koloa.↓

214.7 tobacco<.>, [*a flourish originally ending the entry at* 'tobacco.' *was overwritten and the entry was continued; the period was mended to a comma*]

217.7 ↑but↓ few

217.9 ↑–they . . . daylight↓

218.20 yet. [*a flourish originally ending the entry here was overwritten and the entry was continued*]

219.1 Gas . . . night [*circled*]

220.5 <Queen> ↑La Reine↓

220.9–10 ↑Lord opens for him.↓

222.11 <Waikkiki>Waikiki [*the second* 'k' *canceled*]

225.9 ↑with . . . Corunna.↓

229.22 ↑Sickness China↓

231.3 $<100,000>150,000 ['150' *written over* '100']

231.5 ↑could . . . years↓

232.1–4 The rose . . . so–↑are↓ *you*. [*originally* 'The rose . . . so–you.' *not in Clemens' hand; Clemens added* 'are' *and italicized* 'you']

233.4 Capt. <Hammond> ↑Hannam↓

234.3 ↑English↓ Women

234.9–12 July 4 . . . 5th.– [*written in black ink; followed by 18 blank pages*]

234.13–235.17 Kanaka . . . mahea [*written on the last ruled page*]

234.13–235.7 Kanaka . . . kakunani [*written with the notebook inverted*]

235.8 ↑Thy–kou↓

235.10 ↑name inoa↓

235.18–236.3 What is this? . . . don't know [*written on the recto of the back flyleaf*]

235.28–236.3 How much . . . don't know [*written lengthwise on the page*]

236.4–11 1 –page <4> . . . foliage [*written on the verso of the back flyleaf; the numbers in each group are written in a single line so that the first group (the* '8' *of* '28' *and* '32 . . . 72') *and the third* ('51, 52, 84,') *carry over onto the endpaper*]

237.1–5 25 . . . again [*written on the back endpaper*]

237.4–5 Boy . . . again [*written with the notebook inverted*]

237.6 J.Q.A. . . . here. [*written in black ink on the back cover*]

Notebook 7

Emendations and Doubtful Readings

	MTP Reading	MS Reading
245.17	midnight	mid-|night
245.20	state room	[*possibly* 'stateroom']
246.2	They	The
246.20	everywhere	every-|where
247.13	clipper-built	clipper-|built
247.20	figure-head	figure-|head
247.29	under way	[*possibly* 'underway']
248.12	bulkhead	bulk-|head
248.29	runaway	run-|away
249.7	whale ships	[*possibly* 'whaleships']
249.28	blow out	[*possibly* 'blow-out']
*250.16	booming	booming [*miswritten*] booming
252.6	Midnight	Mid-|night
254.5	headline	[*possibly* 'head line']
254.14	woodpile	[*possibly* 'wood pile' *or* 'wood-pile']
254.15	endways	[*possibly* 'end ways' *or* 'end-ways']
255.34	moonlight	moon-|light
256.11	up town	[*possibly* 'uptown' *or* 'up-town']
256.26	Store-keeper	Store-|keeper

256.30	have made	[*possibly* 'need made']
256.30	Departure	[*possibly* 'Deposition']
258.20	bannaner	[*possibly* 'bannanner']
258.33	barefooted	bare-|footed
259.14	bouquets	[*possibly* 'banquets']
262.23	they sang	the sang
264.2	state room	[*possibly* 'stateroom']
267.23	woodyard	[*possibly* 'wood yard' *or* 'wood-yard']
267.29	<soo>	[*possibly* '<wo>']
268.8	under way	[*possibly* 'underway']
268.11	shipboard	[*possibly* 'ship board']
268.21	Lander	[*possibly* 'Lauder']
269.2	yard-arm	yard-|arm
269.17	yellow fever	[*possibly* 'yellow-fever']
272.18	baldheaded	[*possibly* 'bald-headed' *or* 'bald headed']
273.5	to-night	[*possibly* 'tonight']
273.12	sea-sick	sea-|sick
273.25	shipboard	[*possibly* 'ship board']
280.4	roadstead	road-|stead
281.33	boarding	[*possibly* 'hoarding']
282.17	blessed	[*possibly* 'kissed']
282.22	window sill	[*possibly* 'window-sill']
285.1	chicken-hawk	chicken-|hawk
285.21	cocoa-nut	cocoa-|nut

286.1–2	foot back	[*possibly* ‘footback’ *or* ‘foot-back’]
286.6	greenbacks	green-|backs
287.4	sandstone	sand-|stone
287.9	cocoa-nuts	cocoa-|nuts
*287.15	shrivels	shrivels [*miswritten*] shrivels
*291.8	8m	[*possibly* ‘8th’ *or* ‘8 hr’]
292.26	sea-sick	sea-|sick
294.11	overcoats	over-|coats
295.7	stateroom	state-|room

Details of Inscription

244.1–5 San Francisco . . . Isthmus. [*written on the front cover*]

244.6–8 *Chinese . . . China [*written on the front endpaper*]

244.9–15 Kind . . . drink? [*written on the recto of the front flyleaf with the notebook inverted; followed by four blank leaves*]

245.20 <&> | a case [‘&’ *canceled by a paragraph sign*]

245.21 cabin<.[¶]S>—then [*originally* ‘cabin.’ *followed by* ‘S’ *beginning a new paragraph on the next line; the dash was written over the period and the entry was continued, overwriting the* ‘S’]

246.18 coast. ↑in 3 years.↓

247.14 <says,>said [‘id’ *written over* ‘ys,’]

247.22 <thought> ↑judged↓

247.26 up <on> ↑with↓

247.29 cast <loose> ↑off↓ [*altered in blue ink*]

247.29 got under way/↑stood out to wind'ard↓ ['stood out to wind'ard' *interlined in blue ink without a caret above* 'under way']

248.17–18 on!<"> ↑shaking . . . back-stay.↓

249.1 <Saturday–> ↑Thursday–↓

249.30 <sea-turtles>sea-turkles ['k' *written over* 't']

250.13–19 <Genius is . . . <howling> ↑booming↓ . . . <lie> ↑sleep↓ . . . gutter. ['is a' *canceled and the paragraph completed; then* 'consists . . . man to' *canceled,* 'es' *added to* 'Genius', 'are people who' *interlined with a caret, and* 'prompts him to' *canceled; there is no indication of when* 'booming' *and* 'sleep' *were interlined;* 'booming' *miswritten and then rewritten for clarity; emended*]

250.20 <its possessor> ↑a man↓

250.21 <earth> ↑world↓

250.25 <Genius is>Geniuses are ['es' *added and* 'are' *written over* 'is']

250.26 <a> ↑frowsy hair & a↓

251.1–2 <as lordly an>a lordly air ['s' *canceled and* 'air' *mended from* 'an']

251.5–6 ↑If he hangs . . . true genius.↓ [*written on the facing page opposite* 'to save . . . genius.' *(251.3–4) and* 'If he . . . wears out' *(251.7–8) with an arrow indicating placement*]

251.7–8 <crushes> ↑wears out↓

251.10 ↑sound↓

251.12 <infamous> [*canceled in black ink*]

251.16 surest ↑of all the different↓ sign↑s↓

252.11 23^{d} ↑Sunday↓

253.4 with ↑that↓ old

253.5 good-natured ↑old sailor,↓

253.9 ↑awe &↓ <the liveliest> admiration ['the liveliest' *canceled in pencil;* 'awe &' *added in brown ink*]

253.14 <rig> ↑build↓

253.15 <athward>athwart ['t' *written over* 'd']

254.1 ↑passengers↓

254.16 ↑to them rats?↓

255.8 <wicker> [*canceled in black ink*]

255.10 <slee>slept ['p' *written over the second* 'e']

255.11 <run> ↑scampered↓

255.13 <precious> ↑monstrous↓ [*altered in brown ink*]

255.17 to cat [*follows a caret; there is no interlineation*]

255.18–19 <blatting>blattin' ['g' *canceled and the apostrophe added*]

255.21–22 <hog> ↑sow↓–had to <pull> ↑haul↓

255.28 <ly>laying ['a' *written over* 'y']

255.30 provisions ↑&↓

255.30–31 ↑that a rat might prefer,↓ [*written in brown ink*]

255.31 <to-morrow–> ↑next day↓

255.33 <devilish> ↑cussed↓ [*altered in brown ink*]

256.9–10 ↑who . . . see↓

257.8–10 ↑Met . . . Brown.↓

257.16 <perhaps>phaps ['er' *canceled*]

258.27 <ac/>ac. ['c' *written over* 'c/']

260.26 <San Carlos> ↑Castillo↓ [*altered in brown ink*]

261.27 of . . . shapes [*a small penciled* 'x' *appears before and after the phrase*]

262.3 <Nun> ↑Hamlet's ghost.↓

262.22 a mother– [*followed by four blank lines, probably to allow the list to be extended*]

262.27 ↑(& so . . . ahoy!)↓

262.32 <they>that ['at' *written over* 'ey']

263.2 D–n Dog Tray. [*a line drawn from here to* ' "Homeward' *(262.25)*]

263.22 ↑Doking the Jew.↓ [*written in brown ink*]

263.23 on <myself> ↑a white passenger↓

265.17 all. [*followed by a blank left-hand page*]

266.18 faro. [*followed by a blank left-hand page*]

270.3 <Gross yield> <↑Dividends↓> ↑Yield↓ of ten <↑other↓> mines

271.3 <two hours> ↑an↓ hour ['two' *and* 's' *canceled*]

271.7 ↑For Mayor &↓ Custom House

271.16 ↑*Brown*↓

272.1 ↑2d Jan.↓ Midnight

272.24 passengers. [*a flourish originally ending the entry here was overwritten and the entry was continued*]

273.15 ↑He said↓

274.1–275.6 Miss . . . tongue! [*written on two right-hand pages whose versos are blank*]

274.2 ↑*Air*–Auld Lang Syne.↓

274.3 ↑1↓ [*written in the left margin*]

274.4 <sweet> ↑trim↓

274.7 behind [*a flourish originally ending the entry here was overwritten and the entry was continued*]

274.8 ↑2↓

274.13 ↑3↓

274.18 ↑4↓

274.23 ↑5↓ [*follows a blank left-hand page*]

274.28 ↑6↓

274.29–275.1 ↑She crowded . . . destroyed.↓ [*these two stanzas follow stanza 8 on the manuscript page, overwriting a flourish that originally ended the entry; the order of the stanzas was established by the interlined numbers*]

274.33 ↑7↓

275.1 might be <cussed.> ↑destroyed.↓ [*altered in brown ink*]

275.2 ↑8.↓

275.6 Trice/↑Dry↓

275.7 Jan. 5 [*follows a blank left-hand page*]

276.22 dead↑–5th death.–↓ [*a flourish originally ending the entry after* 'dead' *was overwritten and the entry was continued*]

278.1 <Mason> ↑XXX↓

278.18 <boat>bolt ['l' *written over* 'a']

278.25 Indian Summer ↑there↓

278.28 ↑MEM↓ [*boxed*]

279.8 worms [*a flourish originally ending the entry here was overwritten and the entry was continued*]

279.11–12 ↑1 Harlan . . . died.↓↑–died . . . 25th↓

279.13 ↑2↓ Jerome . . . ↑Jan. 2.↓

279.19 ↑3↓ Martin

279.25 ↑4↓ Capt

279.28 ↑5↓ Andrew

279.30 ↑6↓ At

280.8 pleasant. [*a flourish originally ending the entry here was overwritten and the entry was continued*]

280.14 ↑7↓ Jan.

280.15 ↑8↓ ↑Jan 11.↓

280.16 A Novel [*follows a blank left-hand page*]

281.11 ↑The . . . Bite.↓

281.18 <on>in ['i' *written over* 'o']

282.30 ↑Everything goes.↓ [*probably added after the following paragraph was canceled*]

283.2–3 <fear> ↑joy↓

283.24 <last> ↑uppermost↓

283.25 <latt>ladder ['dd' *written over* 'tt']

283.25–26 ladder, <when–> <[¶]You . . . thi> ['You . . . thi' *indented to begin a new paragraph following the paragraph originally ending at* 'ladder, when–'; 'when–' *canceled*, 'You . . . thi' *canceled, and the earlier paragraph continued following* 'ladder,']

284.1 fluctuate<.> ↑in the smoke.↓

284.6–7 <came> ↑arrived↓

284.12 <left.> ↑went to sea.↓

284.17 ↑V alone remained–↓

284.24 ↑4 days without food.↓

285.1 <4 days without food.> [*replaced by the interlineation at* 284.24]

285.16 <most of> ↑half↓

287.6 sea level. [*one leaf has been torn out following this entry*]

287.15 <dries> ↑shrivels↓ ['shrivels' *miswritten and then rewritten for clarity; emended*]

287.24 ↑Key West, <6>7th↓

287.27–28 <to fr> ↑tickets to↓ remaining friends

287.30 ↑Jan. 7.↓

288.11–12 ↑1st Cal steamer in 2 yrs↓ ↑Brown↓ [*written in brown ink across the preceding entry*]

289.16 ↑Jan. 7.↓ 18

289.23 <coat> ↑roundabout↓

290.11–12 ↑abreast of Florida.↓

291.8 ↑8m↓ ↑8↓ ↑Usual . . . 24^{h}↓ [*what appears to be* '8m' *is written in the margin in pencil, and* '8' *is written in the margin in brown ink; see Doubtful Readings*]

291.22 <hell> [*canceled in purple ink*]

292.8 ↑Key West.↓

292.9 ↑$1250↓

292.21 13. ↑ft.↓

293.4 half↑'s↓

294.10 <6>72 ['7' *written over* '6']

295.1 ↑Mean W.↓

295.9 ↑On↓

296.4 ↑P.↓ Peterson . . . died ↑dropsy↓—

296.7 <7th or 8th> ↑8↓ death

296.7–8 ↑Bury . . . soundings.↓

296.14 N.Y. [*follows a blank left-hand page*]

296.18–19 ↑(300 of them soldiers↓

297.5 <200>250 ['5' *written over* 'o']

298.2 San Juan. <[¶]Lef>—Buried ['Lef' *indented to begin a new paragraph; it was overwritten by the continuation of the paragraph originally ending at* 'San Juan.']

298.5 <currently reported> ↑believed by passengers↓

298.13–14 Man . . . stranger. [*written in brown ink*]

298.18 glass. [*followed by 24 blank pages*]

299.1–16 Notice . . . coin. [*written on the verso of the back flyleaf with the notebook inverted*]

299.14 *free.* ↑as usual.↓

299.17 Regulations. [*written on the last ruled page with the notebook inverted*]

299.18–20 Song . . . cases 2ᵈ— [*written on the back endpaper*]

Notebook 8

Emendations and Doubtful Readings

	MTP Reading	MS Reading
318.7	loveliness	[*possibly* 'loneliness']
322.2–3	Captured [by] Indians	Captured [by] | Indians [*possibly* 'Captured Indians' *with a brace to the right of both words connecting them*]
323.8	midnight	mid-|night
326.3	pop-eyed	pop-|eyed
326.6	[work]	[*very doubtful*]
332.11	sea-sick	sea-|sick
332.18	sea-sickness	sea-|sickness
332.22	bly-ak	bly-|ak
333.10	seasick	[*possibly* 'sea-sick']
333.16	sea-sick	sea-|sick
335.1	let up	[*possibly* 'let-up']
336.3	overcoat	over-|coat
336.7	Jurymen	[*possibly* 'Jury men']
337.1	woodcut	[*possibly* 'wood-cut']
337.15	blackfish	black-|fish
340.14	overboard	[*possibly* 'over board']
341.11	snow-white	[*possibly* 'snow white']
342.6	checker-boarded	checker-|boarded
342.12	barefooted	bare-|footed
343.2	checker-boards	[*possibly* 'checker boards']

344.5	best dressed	[*possibly* 'best-dressed']
344.6	Port^{e}	[*possibly* 'Port'']
348.8	<little>	[*possibly* '<like>']
349.6	bold	[*possibly* 'bald']
349.17	lighthouses	[*possibly* 'light-houses']
350.13	<sen>	[*possibly* '<sin>' *or* '<sw>']
*352.10	Gen–something/ Genesta	Gen–something/esta
354.6	one	[*possibly* 'our']
*362.12–13	ago, [*blank*] [¶]& when	[*possibly* 'ago, [*blank*] & when']
364.5	contact	[*possibly* 'contract']
367.21	star-lit	star-|lit
368.2	to-night	to-|night

Details of Inscription

314.1–5	LK . . . Tangier 3 [*written on the front endpaper*]
314.3–5	Brown . . . Tangier 3 [*written in brown ink*]
314.5	Tangier 3 [*written lengthwise in the right margin of the front endpaper*]
314.6–315.4	Mark Twain . . . No. 12. ['Mark Twain . . . N.Y.' *written diagonally across the recto of the front flyleaf;* 'Edwin . . . Chicago.' *written above* 'Mark Twain . . . N.Y.' *at a later time;* 'Upton . . . No. 12.' *written at the foot of the flyleaf with the notebook inverted, also at a later time*]
315.5	Billy Fall– [*follows the blank verso of the front flyleaf and four leaves originally left blank; the first leaf was later inscribed with the entries at 368.26–369.10*]

316.6 <$3^{d.}$><34> [*originally* '$3^{d.}$'; *then* '4' *written over superscript* 'd.'; *then* '34' *canceled*]

316.6 9th Ave. [*the bottom quarter of the page is blank below this entry*]

316.7 ↑X↓ [*use mark added here and at 317.1, 317.4, 317.5, 317.6, 317.8, 317.9, and 318.1*]

316.7–317.4 <Gathers>Gathering . . . window [*struck through in brown ink*]

316.7 <Gathers>Gathering ['ing' *written over* 's']

317.1 ↑X↓ <192> ['X' *written over previously canceled* '192']

317.2–3 Libertines . . . spree [*boxed*]

317.10 <all short> ↑out↓ of shirts

318.2–7 That . . . loveliness [*struck through in brown ink*]

318.8 Architecture of Academy [*written in brown ink*]

319.1 Greeley Bail for Max. [*followed by four blank pages*]

319.8–9 ↑Bead | Knitting↓

319.14 <are al>all are ['all' *written over* 'are' *and* 'are' *written over* 'al']

320.5 French . . . landlord. [*written in brown ink*]

321.2 Racing– [*the bottom quarter of the page is blank below this entry*]

321.11 Johnston . . . grandmother! [*struck through in brown ink*]

322.6 Must . . . languages. [*struck through in brown ink*]

322.9–14 Return-ball . . . now [*struck through in brown ink*]

323.2 Artemus Ward's body– [*struck through in brown ink*]

324.1–3 union . . . grog. [*struck through in brown ink*]

324.1 ↑union down↓

324.2 interrupted/↑interfered↓

324.2 perform^{s}/↑exercises↓

324.4–8 The Cooper . . . Ass^{n} [*written in brown ink*]

325.5–6 Dr. . . . Olive [*written in brown ink in the top margin of the page*]

325.9 ↑Bro of Senator Cole.↓

325.13–14 ↑Would . . . anyway.↓ [*written lengthwise in the left margin of the page beside the six preceding entries* (325.5–12)]

326.2 ↑708.↓ [*written above the first line of the following paragraph*]

326.3 ↑August↓ Brentano ['August' *interlined without a caret*]

326.13–14 Orpheus | Divorced [*the bottom half of the page below this entry and the following page are blank; two subsequent leaves have been torn out; followed by* 'What . . . genuine' (368.20–25)]

327.1–3 ↑*Paris Exposition.*↓ . . . request. [*written at the top of the back endpaper*]

327.4–6 3800 . . . Gibraltar. [*written at the bottom of the back endpaper with the notebook inverted*]

328.1–27 *I spoke* . . . Tangier . . . 2 . . . 0 [*written on the verso of the back flyleaf*]

328.22–27 Irving's . . . Tangier . . . 2 . . . 0 [*written in brown ink*]

329.1–10 Regulations . . . allowed. [*followed by one blank leaf and the blank recto of the back flyleaf; follows a blank page and the beginning of the sequence of entries at* 329.11–368.19]

329.11–368.19 Holy Land Pleasure Excursion . . . chosen people. [*written, except for the entries at* 340.16–341.7, *from the back of the notebook toward the front, with the notebook inverted, beginning on the fifth page from the back flyleaf*]

330.12 ↑general↓ disposition <& general style.>

330.14 <too> ↑so↓

332.3 <main> ↑upper↓

332.9 breeze, ↑&↓

333.31 schemes, Miss? [*followed by two blank leaves*]

334.13 work. [*half of the page is blank below this entry*]

335.16 that?" [*followed by one blank page*]

336.11 soul. [*the bottom quarter of the page is blank below this entry*]

336.17 forncation [*the bottom quarter of the page is blank below this entry*]

337.5 ship,.– [*a flourish originally ending the entry at* 'ship.' *was overwritten and the entry was continued; the comma and the dash were probably added*]

337.6 burn,– [*a flourish originally ending the entry at* 'burn,' *was overwritten and the entry was continued; the dash was probably added*]

337.9–10 ↑These . . . nautilli.↓ [*written in the top margin of the page above* 'hanging down–saw' (337.7)]

337.15 blackfish<.>– [*a flourish originally ending the entry at* 'blackfish.' *was overwritten and the entry was continued; the period mended to a dash*]

338.1 <Mr>Moses ['o' *written over* 'r']

339.10 ↑(Constantinople)↓

340.12 ↑Brown↓

340.16–341.7 Questions . . . state? [*written with the notebook held right side up on two right-hand pages apparently se-*

lected at random in the middle of the notebook; subsequently engulfed by the unrelated entries from 365.12 through 365.19; see 329.11]

342.1 ↑Full chaffinch & canaries.↓ [*written lengthwise in the left margin of the page beside the preceding entry*]

342.6 <hav>half ['lf' *written over* 'v']

342.8 <Portugu>Portugese ['ese' *written over* 'u']

342.14 ↑*sekki-yo!*↓ [*written lengthwise in the left margin of the page beside the preceding entry*]

342.17 <Two hundred> ↑A thousand↓

343.6 mostly. [*a quarter of the page is blank below this entry*]

343.7 (Jesuit↑)↓<Colle>

344.9 ↑Place . . . barefoot.↓ [*written diagonally across the preceding paragraph*]

344.15 ↑Have . . . head wind.↓ [*written diagonally across the first sentence of the preceding paragraph*]

344.16–17 ↑Woman waiting . . . texture.↓ [*written lengthwise along the left margin of the page across portions of the preceding entries,* 'common . . . perhaps' (344.5–11)]

345.15 <this>their ['eir' *written over* 'is']

346.1 <wagon> ↑cart↓

346.6 The party [*follows three blank lines at the top of the page*]

348.2 Daughters . . . Alva. [*written in brown ink*]

348.5 Eyes as [*follows two pages with drawings (reproduced here on page 347) and one blank page*]

348.9 canvas. [*the bottom quarter of the page is blank below this entry*]

348.14 port. [*the bottom quarter of the page is blank below this entry*]

349.11 <Spain> ↑Africa↓

350.4–5 ↑"clouds . . . locality.↓ [*interlined without a caret below* 'robed in misty gloom' *and above* 'a more magnifi-|' *and continued into the right margin*]

350.9 <wa>were ['ere' *written over* 'a']

350.18 ↑It stood . . . siege.↓

351.1 hours<?>. [*the question mark mended to a period*]

352.5 <Brown> ↑Dan↓

352.10 Gen–something/Gen↑esta↓ [*originally* 'Gen–something'; 'esta' *interlined above the dash;* 'something' *uncanceled*]

353.1 ↑between↓

353.4 ↑Tangier, Morocco.↓ [*written in brown ink*]

353.5 ↑Oran↓

353.6 <Algiers>Algria ['ria' *written over* 'iers']

353.10–11 ↑Only . . . allowed↓

353.13–15 Cape Spartel . . . same [*boxed*]

353.16–17 ↑from Mediteranean↓

353.22–23 ↑flood tide goes . . . out.↓ [*written lengthwise along the left margin of the page across part of the preceding paragraph*]

354.3 <Morr>Morocco ['o' *written over* 'r']

354.10 ↑of cattle↓

357.1–4 Man . . . with stones. [*struck through in brown ink*]

357.7–9 Koran . . . & Morocco. [*struck through in brown ink*]

359.15 <Tabebe> ↑El↓ Tabeeb

360.14–15 ↑talked . . . month↓ [*interlined without a caret above* 'the Moors with great']

360.15 <sen>stayed ['ta' *written over* 'en']

361.12 ↑Meyers↓

362.12–13 ago, [*blank*] [¶]& when [*it is unclear whether Clemens intended to start a new paragraph with* '& when'; *he left blank space at the end of one line and the opening of the next, between* 'ago,' *and* '& when'; *see Doubtful Readings*]

362.23 500. [*a flourish originally ending the entry here was overwritten and the entry was continued*]

364.4 ↑there yet.↓

364.18–20 Moorish . . . she him. [*struck through in brown ink*]

366.6 <Sahib> ↑Sadi↓

367.5–6 ↑Got . . . ↑at Gibraltar,↓ . . . 1867.↓

367.6 <June>July ['ly' *written over* 'ne']

368.9 <8>10.50 ['0' of '10' *written over* '8']

368.14 <[1877]>1867 ['6' *written over what appears to be* '7']

368.19 Curious . . . people. [*written in brown ink; followed by 51 blank pages and the page of entries at 368.20–25*]

368.20–25 What . . . genuine. [*written with the notebook held right side up on the recto of the leaf following* 'Orpheus | Divorced' *(326.13–14); two intervening leaves have been torn out; followed by 51 blank pages and the end of the sequence of entries at 329.11–368.19*]

368.26–369.10 Gave . . . room. [*written on the first ruled leaf of the notebook (see 315.5)*]

368.26–27 ↑*Promised* . . . room↓

369.11–13 679 . . . Africa. [*written in ink on the back cover*]

Notebook 9

Emendations and Doubtful Readings

	MTP Reading	MS Reading
384.9	endways	end-|ways
385.6	sea-walls	sea-|walls
387.18	Athens.	Athens. Greece
390.23	our	[*possibly* 'on']
391.3	gas-lights	gas-|lights
391.6	moonlight	moon-|light
392.5	overlooking	over-|looking
398.1	Visited	Turkey | Visited
398.18	barefoot	bare-|foot
398.19	the abominations	Turkey | the abominations
399.5	Fire tower	Turkey | Fire tower
399.7	gateway	gate-|way
400.9	Some people	Turkey | Some people
402.1	Sultan goes	Turkey | Sultan goes
405.1	& spent	Russia | & spent
405.14	cannon-balls	cannon-|balls
405.15	as neat	Russia | as neat
405.22	Aug. <25>23	Russia | Aug. <25>23
406.5	swallow-tail	swallow-|tail
411.6	fireworks	fire-|works
412.1	Our imperial	Constantinople | Our imperial

413.2	Loitered	Constantinople | Loitered
415.11	man great	Ephesus–Syria. | man great
415.21	labored	Syria. Ephesus. | labored
417.5	Our caravan	Syria. | Our caravan
417.8	foothills	foot-|hills
417.9	Noah's Tomb.	Noah's Tomb. | Syria.
417.23	servingmen	[*possibly* 'serving men']
417.29	Sep. 13.	Syria–Sep. 13.
418.10	Sept. 14	Syria | Sept. 14
418.21	Where Baalam's	Syria Sep. 14. | Where Baalam's
419.7	Population	Sep. 15. Syria–Damascus Sep. 16. | Population
419.16	the prophet	Sep. 16 Syria–Damascus | the prophet
420.1	outside	out-|side
420.5	5,000	Syria–Sep. 16 | 5,000
420.16	overlooks	[*possibly* 'over looks']
421.19	Ruined	Cesarea Philippi | Ruined
421.19	waterways	water-|ways
421.22	Here	Holy Land. Sep. 18. | Here
422.26	Sept. 19	Holy Land | Sept. 19
425.2	*Sept*. 20.	Holy Land. | *Sept*. 20.
425.13	Jeptha, Judge	[*possibly* 'Jeptha Judge']
427.5	Sept. 21	Holy Land. | Sept. 21
427.18	Graveyard	Grave-|yard
429.24	daylight	day-|light

429.31	headdresses	[*possibly* 'head dresses' *or* 'head-dresses']
431.5	solid	soild
431.6	Camped	Holy Land.– | Camped
433.13	scalp-lock	scalp-|lock
434.16	overlook	over-|look
437.14	blow out	[*possibly* 'blowout' *or* 'blow-out']
439.10	the enclosure	Annunciation | the enclosure
*439.10	of olive trees in a plain	of olive in a plain trees
439.28	alongside	along-|side
440.1	them	[*possibly* 'then']
441.3	Cheese-monger's	Cheese-|monger's

Details of Inscription

380.1	↑Sam . . . Sept.↓ [*written lengthwise on the front end-paper*]
380.26	great/↑vast/grand↓
382.23	↑Italy.↓ [*written in the upper right corner of the page and boxed*]
383.13	↑(In Rome.↓[*boxed*]
384.2	<$30,000>$50,000 ['5' *written over* '3']
384.5	↑–wipe . . . necklace↓
384.8	↑Sicily–Straits Messina.↓
384.17	↑Greece.↓ [*written diagonally in the upper left corner of the page*]
385.13	↑The Piraeus.–↓ ↑Greece.↓ ['The Piraeus.–' *written diagonally in the upper left corner and* 'Greece.' *in the upper right corner of the page*]

386.6–387.17 On Board . . . Respectfully [*written from the back of the notebook toward the front, with the notebook inverted, on two pages apparently chosen at random near the back of the notebook; see 447.3 and note 11*]

387.3 <have>having ['ing' *written over* 'e']

388 *illustrations* [*the first picture is drawn on the page opposite* 'Athens. . . laws in' (*387.18–27*); *the second picture is drawn with the notebook inverted on a page apparently chosen at random near the back of the notebook, following the petition to Captain Duncan (386.6–387.17); see 447.3 and note 12*]

389.3 ↑Themistocles' Tomb.↓ [*written in the top margin of the page above* 'these countries' (*387.27*)]

389.11 <stran>straggled ['g' *written over* 'n']

390.12 <[well r]>fluted ['f' *written over what appears to be* 'r']

390.16 <looking> ↑glancing↓

390.22 <cha>chimney ['i' *written over* 'a']

391.5 <old> ↑white↓

392.8 ↑*TROY*.↓

392.9 <of ancient> ↑the Plains of↓

392.32 <on>in ['i' *written over* 'o']

393 *illustration* [*the map is drawn across and extends below the inscription* 'hills. . . . two.' (*392.14–17*)]

393.2–3 ↑Phocion . . . Euclid.↓

394.3 ↑–about 10 ft thick↓

394.5 ↑Pericles . . . built.↓

394.5 <Propylieia>Propylaea ['aea' *written over* 'ieia']

394.16 <2,500,000>2,600,000 ['6' *written over* '5']

394.26–27 <↑–all . . . worth of gold.↓>

396 *illustrations* [*the maps are drawn on two facing pages between* 'come aboard.'(395.9) *and* 'Aug. 16.' (395.10)]

397.3 ↑Turkey↓ [*written diagonally in the upper left corner of the page*]

401.3 ↑The Bosphorus↓ [*boxed*]

401.6–7 ↑The lovely . . . ARE palaces.↓ [*written lengthwise in the margin beside* 'Porters. . . . Costumes.' *(400.13–401.2), on the page which faces the page beginning at* 'The Bosphorus' *(401.3)*]

401.10 ↑(suspected)↓

402.8 ↑Sailed . . . 20th.↓

403.4 ↑Russia↓ [*boxed*]

404 *illustration* [*the map is drawn on the right-hand page opposite* 'Beardless . . . Seralgio" ' *(402.18–403.3)*]

404.3–4 ↑Within . . . partnership↓ [*written in the top margin of the page above* 'chance at' *(404.2)*]

405.5 <officers> ↑gentlemen↓

405.22 Aug. <25>23 ['3' *written over* '5']

405.25 <pap>paved ['ved' *written over* 'p']

405.29 <Jolte>Yolta ['Y' *written over* 'J'; 'a' *written over* 'e']

406 *illustration* [*the map is drawn below* 'Left . . . 8 P.M.'*(405.21)*]

406.4 <whi>what ['at' *written over* 'i']

407.7 <snowy peaks> ↑shores↓

407.9 <have>has ['s' *written over* 'v' *and* 'e' *canceled*]

407.11 ↑Majesty's↓

407.24 ↑TD.↓

407.25 ↑AN.↓

407.28 ↑W^{m}↓

410.4–5 ↑Remained . . . nearly.↓

411.4 ↑Black Sea.↓

411.14 ↑Constantinople.↓ [*written in the top margin of the page above* 'view of the ship' (*411.11*)]

412.4 <they> ↑it↓

412.9 ↑<Sea of> Scutari.↓

413.11 ↑Sea of Marmora.↓

414.7 ↑Smyrna.↓

415.3 ↑"7" . . . here↓

415.4 ↑Ephesus.↓ [*written diagonally in the upper left corner of the page above* 'Tomb of' (*415.1*)]

416.1 <Aug> ↑Sept.↓

416.2 ↑St. Paul.↓

416.3 ↑St John's Revelations↓

416.4 ↑St. Paul↓ [*interlined without a caret above* 'Colossus']

416.6 Sept. <11>10 ['0' *written over* '1']

417.8 Beirut. [*half of the page is blank below this entry*]

417.9 ↑Noah's Tomb.↓ [*written diagonally in the upper left corner of the page*]

417.29 ↑Sep. 13.↓

418.11 <——>Zeb ['Zeb' *written over a line indicating a blank to be filled*]

418.21 ↑Where . . . ground.↓ [*written in the top margin of the page above* '<gi> giant trees' (*418.17*)]

419.10 <a b>an Arab ['n' *added to* 'a' *and* 'Arab' *written over* 'b']

419.13–14 <gentleman> ↑disciple↓

419.14 <invited>invested ['es' *written over* 'i']

420.7 <noon> ↑10 or 11↓

420.9 ↑4,000 . . . King.↓

421.3 ↑supposd Phenician↓

421.16 ↑Jordan . . . travel.↓ [*written in the top margin of the page above* 'we washed'(421.9)]

421.31 Ascension/↑Transfig(?)↓

422.1 ↑Waters of Meron.↓

422.9 <their>there ['re' *written over* 'ir']

422.12 Jordan. <[¶]J>The banks ['J' *indented to begin a new paragraph; it was overwritten by the continuation of the paragraph originally ending at* 'Jordan.']

422.24 <Meron>Merom ['m' *written over* 'n']

422.25 ↑30–31–2↓ [*written in the upper right corner of the page beginning* 'Sodom, 600, came over, like' *(422.8)*]

423.9 ↑skulls↓

424.5 ↑Tiberias↓ [*written in the top margin of the page above* 'One ruin' *(424.4) and boxed*]

424.19 ↑Splendid . . . Galilee.↓ [*written lengthwise in the right margin of a left-hand page beside* 'learned Jewish . . . between here' *(424.13–20) on the facing right-hand page*]

425.8 ↑Magdala, <Hermon,>↓

425.10 ↑part of↓

426.2 ↑*Transfiguration.*↓

426.16 ↑Imagine . . . Nazareth↓ [*written lengthwise on the page across* 'Crusaders . . . columns' *(426.8–18)*]

427.5 ↑& its chalk hills↓

427.15 ↑Like . . . suspect.↓ [*written lengthwise in the left margin of the page with a caret indicating placement*]

428.1 ↑El Fulah *Castle*↓ [*interlined before* 'Shunem', *probably when Clemens wrote in the following paragraph* '(this should have come *before* Shunem)' *(428.6)*]

428.2 ↑(cruse . . . widow↓ [*the intended position of this phrase is uncertain; interlined without a caret above* '& dung' *(428.2)*]

428.28 <Around . . . Gilboa> ↑Esdraelon↓

428.29 ↑Megiddo↓

429.12 ↑without a glass,↓

431.15–17 ↑Ark . . . departed.↓

433.12 <Men> ↑Souls↓

433.17 <1099>1199 ['1' *written over* 'o']

434.10 ↑Palace of Caiaphas↓ [*written lengthwise in the left margin of the page beside* 'Pool . . . Judgment' *(434.11–14)*]

434.22 *<Sacra.>* ↑*Dolorosa.*↓

436.14 <Modern> ↑2^{d}↓

437.13 beat. [*a flourish originally ending the entry here was overwritten and the entry was continued*]

438.10 <was sick> ↑had the cholera↓

439.7 ↑*That bombardment.*↓

439.10 olive trees ↑in a plain↓ ['in a plain' *interlined with a caret inadvertently placed between* 'olive' *and* 'trees'; *emended*]

441.9 ↑woman drawing water–↓ [*interlined without a caret above* 'spring dug down' *(441.8–9)*]

441.22 ↑Virgin Mary's Fountain.↓

442.11 <noblest> ↑stateliest↓

443.2 ↑3 PM↓

447.3	fish. [*followed by 13 blank pages, a drawing of Athens (the second illustration on page 388), the petition to Captain Duncan (386.6–387.17), another eight blank pages, and the end of the sequence of entries at 451.2–452.3*]
447.4–6	Stromboli . . . Egypt. [*written in ink on the back cover*]
447.7–9	[260] . . . scars [*written on a paper strip pasted to the back cover;* 'Far-away Moses.' *written in pencil, the other inscriptions in ink*]
447.10–448.20	Dr. Gibson . . . ants. [*written on the back endpaper*]
447.10–448.19	Dr. Gibson . . . Birch [*written with the notebook inverted*]
448.21–449.5	5 canes . . . again. [*written on the verso of the back flyleaf*]
448.21–449.4	5 canes . . . J. W. [*written with the notebook inverted*]
448.21–24	5 canes . . . boxes. [*written in the lower left corner of the page and boxed; two lines,* 'Maybe . . . breakfast.' *(448.25–449.1), indented to fit around the box*]
449.1	breakfast./↑was up.↓
449.6–451.1	X Simon . . . there. [*written on the recto of the back flyleaf with the notebook inverted*]
451.2–452.3	Egypt . . . York. [*written from the back of the notebook toward the front on both sides of the last ruled leaf with the notebook inverted*]

Notebook 10

Emendations and Doubtful Readings

	MTP Reading	MS Reading
464.1	2 K	['K' *replaces ditto marks below preceding* 'K']
465.26	Amos 1-2	Jeru | Amos 1-2
466.17	<59-3>	[*possibly* '<39-5>']
467.14	17-14	[*possibly* '17-15']
471.3	overhanging	over-|hanging
472.7–8	they run	the run
472.14	school-mates	school-|mates
475.18	father of Shechem	5th D. | <Jacob's Well.> | father of Shechem
475.21	whitewashed	white-|washed
476.27	[–18,-1]	[*punctuation doubtful*]
477.1	valley.	5th Day | valley.
477.12	Samuel	5th D | Samuel
478.7	neck	5th D | neck
478.16	e horrid	['e' *possibly a symbol for* 'the']
478.18–19	<e> the daughters	['e' *possibly a symbol for* 'the']
478.19	ark	5th D | ark
478.20	e elders	['e' *possibly a symbol for* 'the']

479.25	Originally	5 D | Originally
480.20	for his covering	5 D | for his covering
480.33	Lord	5 D | Lord
481.8	So, when Jacob	5 D | So, when Jacob
481.23	Beth-avan	Beth-|avan
481.29	nor enter	5 D | nor enter
481.33	handwriting	hand-|writing
482.15	determined	5 D | determined
483.26	swift footed	[*possibly* 'swift-footed']
484.14	a church	5 D. | a church
485.19–20	& so forth	Holy Land. | & so forth
486.3	tried to get	Holy Land. | tried to get
486.19	Left Jerusalem	Holy Land. | Left Jerusalem
488.3	demijohns	demi-|johns
*489.1	accident–	[*possibly* 'accident<–>;']
489.13	polie	[*possibly* 'polic']
490.2	Had	[*possibly* 'How']
491.8	demijohns	demi-|johns
491.12	<n>black	[*possibly* '<w>black']
491.20	Nash	[*possibly* 'Wash']
*492.7–8	Alison of Iowa sack coat . . . student	Alison of sack coat . . . student Iowa
493.2	ε mountains	['ε' *possibly a symbol for* 'the']
*493.17	(continued) eloquent . . . House,	eloquent . . . House, (continued)

Details of Inscription

458.1–3 1739 . . . 3606 [*written on the front cover*]

458.4–5 6 . . . 16.75 [*written on the front endpaper; followed by the sequence of entries beginning at* 487.15]

458.6–469.15 Smyrna. . . . Acts 9-36. [*written from the back of the notebook toward the front, with the notebook inverted, beginning on the last ruled page; followed by the sequence of entries beginning at* 485.12]

459.1 <*Epessus*>*Ephssus* ['*h*' *written over* '*e*']

459.6 2-1. [*followed by one blank page*]

459.27 ↑Phenicia↓ [*squeezed in above* 'Sidon.–Zidon.' *and boxed*]

460.17 Zor [*boxed*]

461.21 ↑Sea of Cinneroth.↓

461.26 <2->21-1 ['1' *written over the hyphen;* '-1' *added*]

462.3 ↑near Sea of Gal.↓

462.11 <[city in]>*–Hamath-Dor* ['*–Hamath*' *written over what appears to be* 'city in']

463.28 <*Bethel.*>*Beth-El.* ['*-El.*' *written over* '*el.*']

464.14–15 (?) Deut. 10-6; | ? | Josh 9-17. ['?' *written beside both lines and enclosed in a jagged square*]

464.28 ↑–Gibeah Benjamin↓

464.32 ↑and↓ 15

465.24 9-2<;>and ['and' *written over the semicolon*]

466.5 <*Jericho*>Jericho ['Jericho' *originally underlined; then the underline was canceled*]

466.9 20-<2[-].>8 ['8' *written over* '2'; *the unrecovered numeral and the period were canceled*]

466.29 <Corin> ↑Kings↓

467.4 ↑(Salt Sea.)↓

467.13 ↑and↓ 19

467.31 <Kirgath>Kirjath-arba ['j' *written over* 'g']

467.32 35-<26>27 ['7' *written over* '6']

469.16–485.11 Beirut. . . . autumn." [*written from the front of the notebook toward the back, with the notebook held right side up, beginning on the third ruled page; follows the sequence of entries at 487.15–488.5; followed by four blank pages and the sequence of entries beginning at 487.1*]

469.16 Beirut. [*written at the top of an otherwise blank page, preceded by two blank pages, and followed by another blank page*]

469.17 Baalbec. [*written at the top of an otherwise blank page and followed by another three blank pages*]

470.3 Its conquest [*marked to begin a paragraph with a paragraph sign and a dash*]

470.5 Acts 9-2. [*followed by one blank page*]

470.6–7 <1st D.> . . . Kishon* [*written at the top of an otherwise blank page; the purpose of the asterisk beside* 'Kishon' *is unknown*]

470.20 place, of ↑of sacrifice of↓

471.6 <people> ↑prophets↓

472.13 <Co.> ↑Son,↓

472.29 <Bark>Barak ['ak' *written over* 'k']

472.30 Judges ↑5↓ 4-6 ['5' *written as an afterthought above and to the right of* '4']

473.8 Judges<.>5. ['5' *written over the period*]

473.20 57-62. [*followed by one blank page*]

473.26 7-8. 11. [*followed by one blank page*]

473.28 <Jer>Jezreel ['z' *written over* 'r']

473.29 <Isachar>Issachar ['ss' *written over* 's']

474.4 Hos. 1-4. [*followed by one blank page*]

474.11 <3->31-1–6 ['1' *written over the hyphen*]

474.19 the prophet. [*followed by one blank page*]

475.5 4th [*followed by two blank pages*]

475.12 ↑unto the land↓

475.21 <hight>[li]ght [*what appears to be* 'li' *written over* 'hi']

476.26 <4->49-10 ['9' *written over the hyphen*]

477.1 ↑2↓ On this great ['2' *boxed*]

477.9 ↑3↓ Here ['3' *added in the margin and boxed*]

478.2 <the>thy ['y' *written over* 'e']

478.13 ↑made↓

479.28 water<,>. <rich>Rich [*originally one sentence; the period written over the comma and* 'R' *written over* 'r' *to create two sentences*]

480.33 <in>is ['s' *written over* 'n']

481.2 <house of the>House God. ['H' *written over* 'h' *and* 'God.' *written over* 'of the']

481.11 ↑the↓ patriarchs

481.15 Ark ↑(↓of the Covenant (not Noah's)

481.21 MAGNIFICENT TEMPLE [*originally* 'magnificent Temple'; *underlined three times*]

481.31 <ciscerns>cisterns ['t' *written over* 'c']

482.11 <w[il]>would ['o' *written over what appears to be* 'il']

482.12–13 enough.–Solomon's [*the dash may originally have been a flourish ending the entry with* 'enough.']

482.30	Templars. [*followed by one blank page*]
483.17	<sto>steps ['e' *written over* 'o']
483.21	<army>armies ['ies' *written over* 'y']
483.35	point. [*followed by one blank page*]
484.5	<their>that ['at' *written over* 'eir']
484.22	Minaret. [*followed by two blank pages*]
485.5	↑for↓ herself
485.11	autumn." [*followed by four blank pages which precede the entries at 487.1–14*]
485.12–486.23	Holy Land . . . *sometimes.* [*written from the back of the notebook toward the front, with the notebook inverted, beginning on the page following the sequence of entries at 458.6–469.15; followed by 42 blank pages and the end of the sequence of entries at 488.6–495.3*]
485.16	<Solomon> ↑David↓
486.14	unmolested<.>— [*the dash written over the period*]
486.19	and got away [*followed by 14 blank pages*]
486.23	*sometimes.* [*there are 42 blank pages between the sequence of entries ending here, which is written from the back of the notebook toward the front, and the final entry in the sequence ending at* 'Guides.' *(495.3), which is written from the front of the notebook toward the back*]
487.1–14	<8>7—Bells . . . ahead. [*written from the front of the notebook toward the back, with the notebook held right side up, on two pages apparently chosen at random, beginning on the fifth page following the sequence of entries at 469.16–485.11; followed by 14 blank pages and the sequence of entries beginning at 488.6*]
487.4	↑it↓ is <to>
487.8	↑ain't↓

487.15–488.5 House . . . summer. [*written on the recto of the front flyleaf; the verso and the first two ruled pages are blank; followed by the sequence of entries beginning at 469.16*]

488.6–495.3 Jennie . . . Guide. [*written from the front of the notebook toward the back, with the notebook held right side up, beginning on the fifteenth page following the sequence of entries at 487.1–14; followed by 42 blank pages and the end of the sequence of entries at 485.12–486.23*]

488.8 ↑crowded around him↓

489.1–2 Fame . . . oblivion. [*written lightly by Clemens, then traced over, probably by Paine; a semicolon written over the dash following* 'accident' *is probably Paine's*]

489.5–6 ↑A J. Moulder . . . [Head]↓

489.7–490.6 Ill . . . Mess [*written in orange pencil*]

489.14 R I [*to the right of* 'R I' *Clemens wrote and circled the instruction* 'over' *in black pencil; the entries at 489.5–490.6 are on the recto of the leaf, and the entries at 491.1–6 are on the verso; see note 26*]

490.6 –Drakes . . . Mess [*written lengthwise in the right margin of the page*]

491.12–22 J<[-]> . . . educational. [*a wavy vertical line is drawn through these entries in dark brown ink*]

491.13 ↑–small↓

491.14 ↑–little heavier↓

491.16 ↑both fat↓ [*written between the two preceding entries*]

492.2 ↑good behaved↓

492.4–5 ↑, unshaved . . . O.S.↓

492.7–8 Alison of Iowa ↑sack coat . . . student↓ ['sack coat . . . student' *interlined with a caret inadvertently placed before* 'Iowa'; *emended*]

492.9 pocket [*the bottom half of the leaf has been torn out following this word on the recto and* 'ablest man' *(492.18) on the verso, apparently before these entries were written*]

492.9–11 large . . . hair–↑youngest . . . him.↓ ['youngest . . . member' *added following* 'hair–'; 'Excessively . . . man' *squeezed in above* 'large . . . light'; 'Essentially ornamental' *below* 'foot . . . handsome'; *and* 'Stands . . . him.' *below* 'brown . . . looking']

492.16 mouth, ↑& strong,↓ [*the caret interlining* '& strong,' *is below* 'mouth']

492.18 ablest man. [*one leaf has been torn out following this entry*]

492.19 ↑black eyebrows↓ [*interlined without a caret above* 'Logan–long black']

493.1–2 Thomas . . . Md.–↑belongs . . . face↓ ['belongs . . . O.S.' *squeezed in above* 'Thomas . . . hermit'; 'strong . . . face' *squeezed in below* 'Thomas']

493.2 ↑in queer way↓

493.4–5 ↑–hair comes . . . rock↓

493.5–6 converging . . ↑converging↓ ['converging' *rewritten, probably for clarity*]

493.16 ↑–*Calhoun*↓

493.17 (continued) ↑eloquent . . . House,↓ ['eloquent . . . House,' *interlined with a caret inadvertently placed before* '(continued)'; *emended*]

493.18 ↑just↓

493.19 ↑so as to suggest↓

493.26 ↑Tenn↓

494.1 <comped>combed ['b' *written over* 'p']

494.12 <poc>pants' ['an' *written over* 'oc']

494.17 stateliest looking. [*three leaves have been torn out following this entry*]

494.18 –↑&↓ in

494.20 Paris . . . fence. [*enclosed in a jagged square*]

495.4–6 23 . . . 115 [*written on the back endpaper; both sides of the back flyleaf are blank*]

Notebook 11

Emendations and Doubtful Readings

	MTP Reading	MS Reading
501.35	door-bell	door-|bell
504.7	cat-heads	cat-|heads
509.15	Mex.,	[*possibly* 'Mex<.>,']
510.5	new comers	[*possibly* 'newcomers' *or* 'new-comers']
511.2	Zwell	[*possibly* 'Zevell']
512.10	footprints	[*possibly* 'foot-prints' *or* 'foot prints']
512.34	postmaster	[*possibly* 'post-master']
512.35	store-keeper	store-|keeper
514.3	schoolmaster	school-|master
514.12	schoolmaster	school-|master

Details of Inscription

499.1–5	<L> . . . board. [*written on the verso of the front flyleaf*]
499.6–506.25	The Story . . . Missionary." [*written on right-hand pages only and followed by one blank left-hand page*]
499.13	<rel>regularly ['g' *written over* 'l']
500.9	↑unregenerated↓
500.22	see who <is there."> it is." ['there." ' *canceled;* 'it' *and punctuation following* 'is' *added*]
500.24	<be>but ['ut' *written over* 'e']

501.3 <lord's>lords [*the apostrophe canceled*]

501.15 ↑ordered↓

501.22 the<y> ↑holy students↓

501.23 ↑science &↓

501.26 entitled—<">↑—↓<[¶]">Why [*a paragraph break after* 'entitled—"' *was canceled by removing the closing and opening quotation marks and adding a dash*]

502.2 <or>on ['n' *written over* 'r']

502.33 myself↑.↓<—>

502.34 ↑I never↓

502.35 ↑go↓

503.30 ↑how↓ it makes

503.34 Turn/↑Flee↓

504.22 ↑heart,↓

505.24–25 ↑<Let . . . you.> Be . . . experience.↓

505.29 you.<—> [*the dash canceled by a paragraph sign*]

506.19–20 night<,>. <for she>She [*originally one sentence; the period written over the comma,* 'for' *canceled, and* 'S' *written over* 's' *to create two sentences*]

508.10 ↑10 . . . baggage↓ [*the intended position of this phrase is uncertain; interlined without a caret above* '(Eastern in greenb^{ks})']

509.1–516.10 Tradition . . . what a pity [*written on right-hand pages only*]

509.1 ↑Tradition . . . of the↓

509.4 ↑English . . . same↓ [*the intended position of this phrase is uncertain; interlined without a caret above* 'Mosquera, Prest of']

509.5 ↑to 99 yrs↓

509.6 ↑& stock↓

509.9–10 presents . . . talk↑?↓ [*the question mark was added in the margin and boxed, beside the manuscript lines ending* 'gov^{t},' (509.9) *and* 'talk' (509.10)]

510.17 ↑from China.↓ [*written lengthwise in the right margin of the page*]

511.3–5 ↑Coy . . . Engineer↓ [*written lengthwise in the left margin of the page*]

511.6–8 ↑(*Mem.* . . . finished.)↓

511.7 <weeks>Weeks ['W' *written over* 'w']

511.11 ↑to↓

513.24 parted<.>, ↑&↓ <He>he [*originally two sentences; the comma written over the period, the ampersand added, and* 'h' *written over* 'H' *to create one sentence*]

514.28 ↑ship's↓

514.31 ↑five↓

515.13 year<s>↑,↓

515.16 ↑one . . . work–↓

515.22 <my>many ['any' *written over* 'y']

516.6 ↑2↓

516.17 satisfied. [*followed by 12 blank pages*]

Notebook 12 has no textual apparatus

Index

Webster's Biographical Dictionary is normally the authority for accepted forms and spellings of names of people of public record. People of little historical note or those whose identification is uncertain or incomplete have been included selectively. Newspapers, periodicals, and scholarly publications which appear merely as citations are not listed. Mark Twain's writings are indexed by title.

The text of this book is set in Electra, a type face designed by W. A. Dwiggins (1880–1956) for the Mergenthaler Linotype Company and first made available in 1935. Electra avoids the extreme contrast between "thick" and "thin" elements that marks most modern faces, and is without eccentricities which catch the eye and interfere with reading. It is a simple, readable type face which immediately conveys a feeling of ease, vigor, and speed, characteristics that were much prized by Dwiggins. Headings are set in Michelangelo and Palatino, two display faces designed by Hermann Zapf for Stempel Type Founders in 1950. These graceful types blend admirably with the text face.

The book was composed by Heritage Printers, Inc., Charlotte, North Carolina, printed by Publisher's Press, Salt Lake City, Utah, and bound by Mountain States Bindery, Salt Lake City, Utah. Paper was manufactured by P. H. Glatfelter Company, Spring Grove, Pennsylvania.